OXFORD MONOGRAPHS IN
INTERNATIONAL LAW

General Editor: PROFESSOR VAUGHAN LOWE,
Chichele Professor of Public International Law in the University of Oxford and Fellow of All Souls College, Oxford

The Interpretation of Acts and Rules in Public International Law

OXFORD MONOGRAPHS IN INTERNATIONAL LAW

The aim of this series is to publish important and original pieces of research on all aspects of international law. Topics that are given particular prominence are those which, while of interest to the academic lawyer, also have important bearing on issues which touch upon the actual conduct of international relations. Nonetheless, the series is wide in scope and includes monographs on the history and philosophical foundations of international law.

Jurisdiction in International Law
Cedric Ryngaert

The Fair and Equitable Treatment Standard in International Foreign Investment Law
Ioana Tudor

Targeted Killing in International Law
Nils Melzer

Defining Terrorism in International Law
Ben Saul

The Immunity of States and Their Officials in International Criminal Law and International Human Rights Law
Rosanne Van Alebeek

Diplomatic Protection
Chittharanjan F. Amerasinghe

Human Rights and Non-Discrimination in the 'War on Terror'
Daniel Moeckli

The Decolonization of International Law
Matthew Craven

Investment Treaty Arbitration and Public Law
Gus van Harten

International Organizations and their Exercise of Sovereign Powers
Dan Sarooshi

Peremptory Norms in International Law
Alexander Orakhelashvili

The Interpretation of Acts and Rules in Public International Law

ALEXANDER ORAKHELASHVILI
Fellow, Jesus College, Oxford

OXFORD
UNIVERSITY PRESS

OXFORD
UNIVERSITY PRESS

Great Clarendon Street, Oxford OX2 6DP
United Kingdom

Oxford University Press is a department of the University of Oxford.
It furthers the University's objective of excellence in research, scholarship,
and education by publishing worldwide.
Oxford is a registered trade mark of Oxford University Press in the UK
and in certain other countries

Reprinted 2013

British Library Cataloguing in Publication Data
Data available

Library of Congress Cataloging in Publication Data
Data available

ISBN 978-0-19-954622-0

General Editor's Preface

It is a sign of truly original scholarship when a monograph provides insights and answers into problems of whose existence one was at best dimly aware. All international lawyers know that a rule is nothing until it is interpreted and applied, but few venture beyond the Vienna Convention on the Law of Treaties in the quest to understand what the process of interpretation and application is and what it does. This powerful analysis, drawing upon a vast range of legal materials, aims to illuminate this critical area of the law. Whether or not one shares the author's view on a particular point, none can read the book without being impressed by the perceptiveness with which he identifies the critical issues and by the weight of learning that he brings to bear upon them.

AVL

Oxford
May 2008

Acknowledgments

First and foremost I would like to express my gratitude to Jesus College, Oxford, for electing me to a Junior Research Fellowship, without which this study would never have been produced and completed. For useful discussions and insights I am grateful to several individuals, above all Sir Elihu Lauterpacht and Professor Vaughan Lowe. The anonymous referees at Oxford University Press, especially the first referee who repeatedly read the pertinent parts of this monograph in the process of peer review, have made an important contribution to the process of writing and completing this study, by drawing my attention to a number of issues and factors the consideration of which has substantially benefited this final product. I am equally grateful to Mr John Louth, Miss Rebecca Smith and Miss Lucy Stevenson of the Oxford University Press for their helpful approach throughout the process of completion and production of this monograph.

Parts of the argument developed in this study have been taken up and pursued in my earlier contributions published in *European Journal of International Law, International and Comparative Law Quarterly, German Yearbook of International Law, Leiden Journal of International Law, Law and Practice of International Courts and Tribunals, Nordic Journal of International Law*, and *Max-Planck Yearbook of United Nations Law*. Thanks are due to the editorial staff of those periodicals as well.

Oxford
October 2007

Foreword

As hardly needs saying, interpretation is perhaps the central process in the application of international law. As such, it is not limited to the interpretation of treaties by judicial bodies. It extends, as regards actors, to States in the determination of their individual positions and to organs of international organisations; it extends, as regards subject matter, to resolutions adopted in international organisations and unilateral declarations by States. It embraces also the attribution of specific content in particular situations to such general concepts as equity, fairness, proportionality and so on.

The present work is a far-reaching attempt to encompass within a single study a consideration of all aspects of interpretation, both doctrinal and practical, and the many problems that arise in connection with them. The coverage of academic writing, of judicial decisions and State practice is extensive and impressive. The study is one to which anyone working in the field will need to refer for its coverage of the many issues that arise in connection with problems of interpretation and the varying solutions that they require.

E. Lauterpacht CBE, QC

January 2008

Contents—Summary

PART V—TREATY INTERPRETATION AND INDETERMINATE PROVISIONS OF NON-LAW

Contents

PART IV—THE REGIME AND METHODS OF INTERPRETATION IN INTERNATIONAL LAW

PART V—TREATY INTERPRETATION AND INDETERMINATE PROVISIONS OF NON-LAW

Table of Reports and Decisions

UN REPORTS AND DOCUMENTS

(a) International Law Commission

(b) Other UN Documents

JUDICIAL DECISIONS

(a) Permanent Court of International Justice

(b) International Court of Justice

(c) **Arbitral Tribunals (General)**

(d) Investment Arbitration

(e) UN Human Rights Committee

(f) European Court of Human Rights

(g) International Tribunal for the Law of the Sea

(h) International Criminal Tribunal for the Former Yugoslavia

(i) World Trade Organisation Dispute Settlement Bodies

(j) **National Courts**

Introduction

This study constitutes the first ever comprehensive monograph on interpretation of acts and rules in public international law. Interpretation has always been an indispensable topic for international law because it forms an integral part of its daily operation. At the same time, the diverse nature of different international acts, instruments and rules raise the question of the regime of interpretation that has to govern the process of clarification of their scope and meaning.

The classical concept of interpretation relates to the clarification of meaning of legal rules and instruments. In order to understand interpretation, it is first and foremost necessary to identify the proper conceptual basis for the binding force of international law and the essence of international obligation. Then it is necessary to identify the field to which legal interpretation applies. This latter task involves distinguishing law from non-law. Non-law refers to the factors and concepts that neither directly derive from the established sources of law nor have determined content and scope, but are still present within the international legal system with the potential to affect the rights and obligations of international legal persons. Non-law creates the possibility for the indeterminacy of legal regulation.

The process of interpretation has to confront not only those acts and rules that are clear and determinate, but also those which are ambiguous and indeterminate. This raises the question of what the impact of such ambiguity and indeterminacy is on the process of construction of international legal rules and obligations. The process of interpretation derives its conceptual and normative foundations from the basic fact of international law being agreement between States, and serves the preservation of the content and parameters of that agreement. This takes place as those stronger and more powerful states attempt to manipulate the content of agreed rules so as to make them appear to conform to their interests.

Despite the fact that law is not all-embracing, the principal point in having a legal regulation on the relevant subject-matter is to enable this regulation to apply to the facts and conduct it covers. If the decentralised legal system is not overseen by the overarching government it is mostly up to the relevant international legal actors whether they will invoke their legal rights, whether they will choose to pursue the legal means for vindicating those rights, and whether they will instead prefer to resort to extra-legal outcomes to settle their differences. But the crucial point is that the relevant international legal actors have the right to insist on those rights, prerogatives or powers that belong to them in the face of existing legal regulation. And as soon as they choose to insist on those, the principal task is to ascertain what the relevant legal regulation is. In order to do that, the means and methods of interpretation, focusing on the effectiveness of legal regulation (as distinct from the views of law) as being all-embracing, emphasises the necessity of viewing existing legal regulation as independent from and unaffected by the extra-legal factors that may be involved in the relevant situation. Without adopting this perspective, the consistency, transparency and predictability of the legal regulation in guaranteeing the rights and expectations it is designed to protect appears impossible.

Consequently, a proper assessment of the relevance of interpretation in international law requires us to consider the implications of the basic character of international law as the body of the rules agreed between States. Does the consensual nature of international law require us to think of individual legal persons as being as omnipotent as possible in dealing with their legal obligations, particularly those that are allegedly ambiguous or indeterminate? Or does this consensual nature of international law require us to adopt an approach based on the effectiveness of legal regulation, according to which, once the relevant regulation is agreed, it acquires objectively identifiable content that has to be construed and applied effectively in order to give proper effect to the original consensual intendment?

The emphasis on the effectiveness of legal regulation has not always been among the doctrinal priorities of international lawyers. For most of the nineteenth century and the second half of the twentieth century international legal doctrine failed to elaborate upon the conceptual approach that demonstrated the necessity and implications of the effectiveness of legal regulation.

This study aims to fill an important doctrinal gap that has persisted in the doctrine of international law for the past 50 years, that is since the pertinent questions were dealt with in the writings of James Brierly and Sir Hersch Lauterpacht. These writers examined some aspects of the relationship between law and non-law, and the consequent implications for the interpretation of rules, with a view to ensuring their integrity and effectiveness. Both authors examined the relationship between legal and political disputes. Lauterpacht's analysis of non-law (although he never mentioned this term) was broader as he covered issues of interest and equity as well. This was done in his work on *The Function of Law in the International Community* (OUP, 1933). In his later work on *The Development of International Law by the International Court* (1958), Lauterpacht examined the issues of the relationship between law and freedom of action of States, auto-interpretation, legal and non-legal disputes, and effective interpretation of rules. These encompass the basic issues relating to the effectiveness of rules in the face of non-legal considerations. In this sense, Lauterpacht developed the first doctrinal approach on the effectiveness of legal regulation properly so-called. Unfortunately, despite its inherent merit and its consistent reflection in international judicial practice, this central approach developed by Brierly and Lauterpacht does not receive the degree of doctrinal recognition nor the use it deserves.

Even though law is not all-embracing and omnipresent (a point as we shall see, shared by Lauterpacht), the principal task of the interpretation of legal rules and regimes is to provide for transparency, predictability and consistency of international legal regulation, which is the only way of motivating States, and other international legal actors, to be interested in observing international law. The predictability of the exchange of burdens and benefits is an inevitable precondition of the viability of the international legal system.

The issues dealt with by Brierly and Lauterpacht are at the heart of the present study, which addresses the issues and fields that have emerged since the last major works were written. The aim is twofold: to consolidate the doctrine of the integrity of legal obligations; and to apply this doctrine to fields not known to its original authors. Although some individual, or particular, aspects of the approach of these two great writers can and will be the subject of discussion and debate, their above works are essential for the proper understanding of fundamental issues of international legal regulation and the interpretation of legal rules. Consequently, the approach developed by Brierly and Lauterpacht will be taken as the starting point for the present study.

The current state of international legal doctrine often sees the inflation of its conceptual basis, developing diverse theories questioning the real foundations of international law. In our time, when many international lawyers have opted for a narrow field of specialisation, the risk of general structural factors being misunderstood and underestimated is greater than ever. The generalist perspective of international legal scholarship is necessary for understanding those structural and systemic aspects of international law that come into play in the individual fields of this legal system. Yet, these structural and systemic factors do not arise and operate in those individual fields specifically. They are due to the general legal framework to which each individual field of international law belongs. None of the specific fields of international law on their own can provide the room for self-sustained legal analysis. Consequently, the relevance and implications of these structural and systemic factors inevitably have to be explained from the generalist perspective. Likewise, the relevance of interpretation is above all a warning against adopting preconceived attitudes to the relevant legal position in the relevant field. Whatever the specificity of the relevant field of international law, legal positions under it arise, continue and change not because they belong to that particular field, but because of the general legal framework that makes this process possible. Consequently, the use of methods of interpretation can prove that the legal position is not necessarily what would be expected in terms of the specificity of the relevant field of international law, but what follows from the agreement of States as embodied in the relevant legal instrument. Interpretation is meant to ensure that international law is never seen as what one perceives it to be, but only as what can be deduced from the agreement between States.

Seen from this perspective, this monograph goes back to basics, and at the same time undertakes a comprehensive analysis of different fields. It is a study of substantive legal regulation, as opposed to the enforcement of international law.

It is obvious that the international legal system is decentralised but, as is clear from the writings of Brierly and Lauterpacht, the inherent ability of international law to provide determinate and effective legal regulation is not affected by its structural or procedural shortcomings. This book is primarily about the means to clarify the content and scope of substantive rules of international law.

Part I of this study examines the thesis of effectiveness of legal regulation, its essence and implications. It deals with questions of interaction between legal obligation and residual sovereignty, the relevance of political factors, and judicial approaches to confronting and eliminating the ambiguity or indeterminacy of international legal regulation. Part II examines the threshold of legal regulation, in order to both determine the conceptual and normative basis of the legal regulation in relation to which the principles of interpretation operate, and to delimit the field of law from that of non-law. Part III deals with various categories of non-law, examining their essence, normative standing and relationship with established rules of law. The interaction of law and non-law must be examined by reference to the fact that, as Professor Lowe observes, 'Legal categories are not the categories of ordinary perception; they are superimposed upon the categories of ordinary perception.' Furthermore, 'legal argument narrows down the issue, and excludes as irrelevant a host of surrounding circumstances' (12 *AYIL* (1992), 57, 72).

Part IV deals with interpretation 'proper', that is the application of the principles of interpretation to different categories of acts and rules. It takes on the theoretical approaches that express doubts as to the consistency of the regime of interpretation in international law. The analysis then proceeds to examine the types and nature of acts that are interpreted. After that the methods of interpretation are examined in every single category of acts and norms covered by this study. The issue of interpretation methods is relevant in all cases of interpretation, whether or not the interpreter expressly acknowledges that it engages in interpretation of the relevant text. Even where the decision-maker evaluates the ambit of textual provision without expressly mentioning interpretative principles, his decision can still be evaluated by reference to those principles. In this analysis, it is opportune to develop first the reasoning in relation to treaty interpretation, as the only field governed by codified rules of interpretation. After this, it becomes more convenient to assess the relevance of interpretation regimes and presumptions in other fields in which codified rules of interpretation are lacking. Finally, and after identifying the methods, the question of the agency of interpretation is examined.

Part V combines the outcome of the analysis performed in Part III with that performed in Part IV. It deals with the interpretation of those treaty provisions which are indeterminate or ambiguous because of their reference to the elements of non-law. To clarify this problem, Part V analyses the application of the principles of interpretation to these indeterminate and ambiguous clauses in treaties. Part V thus fulfils one of the ultimate goals of this study, namely to illustrate the feasibility of applying the principles of interpretation in dealing with textual ambiguity and indeterminacy.

Although dealing with several problems, the argument of the monograph is single, complex as it may be. The argument and reasoning in the different parts of this study are interconnected, and the conclusions in the relevant parts either depend on, or prepare the ground for, the outcomes reached elsewhere. It has to be emphasised that Chapters 1 to 10 constitute the exercise of building up to the principal argument of the study, which is presented in Chapters 11 to 18. This should not be misunderstood as Chapters 1 to 10 being of relatively minor importance, because without them the argument embodied in the subsequent chapters would have been impossible to develop or perceive from the reader's perspective.

As is obvious, this study elaborates upon a vast amount of material, and some selection criteria had to be applied from the outset in terms of what should be covered. Thus, this study focuses mainly on such material in relation to which judicial pronouncement has been made with the effect of clarifying the merit of the conflicting assertions of the States concerned. There are obviously other interesting issues, such as the impact and possibility of effective construction of Article VI of the 1968 Non-Proliferation Treaty for the purposes of clarifying its possible impact on the decision of the British Government to renew the Trident nuclear deterrent. Any legal analysis on this issue, which would of necessity pronounce on similar decisions of other nuclear powers, can only be based on the present stage of the exchange and the correlation of different views, as Article VI of the NPT has not received any judicial clarification. However, authoritative interpretation is useful, though not a necessary precondition for valid and consistent interpretation to be made, as is illustrated in various parts of this study. Hence it is hoped that the reasoning and evidence provided in this study will prove useful for working out the parameters of the interpretative approach for the relevant, still unresolved, questions of which Article VI NPT may be only one.

PART I

THE EFFECTIVENESS OF INTERNATIONAL LEGAL REGULATION

1

Doctrinal Treatment of the Effectiveness of Legal Regulation

International legal doctrine has, at various stages of its development, viewed the nature and designation of international law in different ways. The classic scholars of international law such as Grotius, Wolff and Vattel aimed at locating the idea of law in the context of the international State system. The emphasis of this school of natural law was meant to conceive sovereign States, above which there is no sovereign government, as bound by law in relation to each other. In other words, Law among nations was considered by this school as inherent to inter-State relations. This contrasts with the contemporary realist approach, notably represented by Hobbes, and later reinforced in the writings of Austin,[1] that denies the existence of international law because of the absence of centralised legislative and coercive machinery in the State system.

From the late eighteenth century onwards the doctrine of international law is no longer centred on asserting or denying the existence of international law. Another trend—to an important extent, but not exclusively, positivist—enters the scene. It is characterised, on the one hand, by empiricism and the prevailing emphasis on State practice and, on the other hand, by treating international law not as a free-standing discipline or system of rules guided by its own imperatives as a legal system, but as a side aspect of international politics. This trend included those jurists who accepted and studied international law as a legal system. The principal problem faced in their writings is not the existence of international law, but the recognition of its independent relevance and profile. For instance, Westlake had submitted that although international law is not necessarily the same as politics, 'an adequate notion of law' could not be gained without understanding the surrounding society and the power position of States.[2] This approach observes what is happening in State practice and politics, and constructs the nature and content of international law by reference to that. At the same time, the doctrine of international law between the eighteenth century and World War I is pervaded by the perception of eurocentrism and 'European international law', associating this legal system with the will and attitude of one of several parts of the world. This

[1] See below Chapter 3.
[2] J Westlake, *Collected Papers* (1914), 92–93.

prevented the doctrine of that period from fully acknowledging the nature and implications of the thesis that international law is a body of rules agreed on and binding on sovereign States.[3]

In short, reference to the inter-State character of international law in this case caused the imperatives of the idea of law to be neglected. This trend persisted and dominated the science of international law until the inter-war period. According to WE Hall, 'the proper scope of the term law transcends the limits of the most perfect examples of law', but 'to what extent it transcends them is not fully certain'.[4] At a later stage, Kelsen portrayed the primitive nature of international law as the factor figuring among its principal and central features, mainly emphasising the technical and structural insufficiency of this legal system.[5]

It was in this doctrinal context that the other approach emphasising the nature of international law as law developed. This approach does not contradict the consensual and inter-State basis of this legal system. It merely emphasises that international law also embodies and reflects the idea of law. In other words, international law is not less law just because it is not produced by the centralised sovereign authority. It still operates as the legal process, in a way meeting the legitimate expectations of international persons in the observance of legal rules. Thus, rules that are consensually accepted and agreed by States have to be seen as operating effectively: applying to the acts and conduct they cover and achieving their goals and intendment, that is making the difference on the ground they are intended to make.

One may venture to formulate tentatively the basic parameters of this approach as working assumptions:

(1) international law as a body of rules agreed between States must be viewed as independent of the State action which it regulates, unless State action validly forms part of the law-making process;
(2) international legal rules apply to State conduct to the full extent of their content and scope; neither the fact that these rules are not established by the central sovereign nor the sovereign status of legal persons affects this outcome;
(3) international law is separate from international politics; political reasons do not translate into legal obligations; political reasons and factors change more frequently than legal rules do;
(4) in order to ensure the systemic coherence of international law, tie up loose ends and fill gaps, certain allowance has to be made for the existence and operation of rules and principles that do not strictly derive from the consus of States.

[3] For detail see A Orakhelashvili, The Idea of European International Law, 17 *EJIL* (2006), 315–345.

[4] WE Hall, *International Law* (8th edn, 1924), 14.

[5] H Kelsen, *Law and Peace in International Relations* (1947), 48–49.

The emphasis on the nature of international law as a legal system embodying the idea of law finds its expression in the writings of JL Brierly and Hersch Lauterpacht which diverge from contemporary 'mainstream' thinking on international law in several important aspects. Their writings constitute an opposition to viewing international law as a 'specific' legal system in the sense of overstating its inter-State character. In essence, Lauterpacht and Brierly stand out among their contemporaries and predecessors by their emphasis on the rule of law, legal certainty, legal stability, and separation of law and politics. Under their approach, international law is no longer conceived of as an incidence of international power and political relations, or a mere generalisation of practice. The nature of international law must be identified not merely by reference to the absence of international government, but to the basic parameters due to which law operates as law.

There may be different doctrinal options as to how to explain the legal character of international law in the absence of central government. Brierly's remedy for the absence of centralised law-making and law-enforcement machinery is to appeal to extra-consensual factors, to some extent natural law, for addressing the issue of the imperfection and incompleteness of international law.[6] According to Brierly, 'law cannot and does not refuse to solve a problem because it is new and unprovided for'. Such situations can be resolved on the basis of principles of reason and natural justice.[7] Lauterpacht did not expressly adhere to natural law and whether he implicitly accepted naturalism can only be a matter for speculation. What is certain, however, is that neither Brierly nor Lauterpacht adopted a natural law or related approach to counter the positivist perspective of international law. The doctrinal efforts of both authors are directed to situations where the positive law is arguably silent on the relevant material point. Both authors aim at securing the completeness and effectiveness of positive legal regulation in international law.

Lauterpacht searches and finds an alternative for the 'primitivist' approach by putting the emphasis on the substance of international law as opposed to its structure. However, it is the substance of legal relations that is predominantly important: 'There is no good reason why primitive law, if law it be, should drive out developed law as the decisive factor in determining the conception of law.'[8] Lauterpacht puts forward several principal theses illustrating this approach, focusing on the completeness of international legal regulation and examining the problem of gaps in law. He also assesses the thesis of the freedom of action of States under international law. Finally, he addresses the situations where legal regulation could possibly be seen as unsatisfactory, and examines alternatives. In general terms, a principal feature of Lauterpacht's approach in *Function of Law* is

[6] JL Brierly, *The Basis of Obligation in International Law* (1958), 10–14.
[7] JL Brierly, *The Law of Nations* (4th edn, 1949), 24–25.
[8] *The Function of Law in the International Community* (1933), 433.

its focus on the nature of judicial process, judicial function, judicial application of law and judicial reaction to the 'inadequacy' of the existing legal position. But this procedural focus notwithstanding, this analysis is essentially an analysis of the determinacy of legal rules and their reflection of, or interaction with, non-legal factors.

Lauterpacht does not advance the idea that international law is all-embracing and accepts the relevance of sovereign freedom of States in fields not regulated, or not susceptible of regulation, by international law. Consequently, legal regulation is limited in nature, and international law:

> cannot regulate the matters which, having regard to the nature and the function of the law, are beyond the sphere of legal regulation. And it must stop short of relations which, although in principle amenable to regulation by law, cannot become so having regard to the state of the political and social development within the particular society.[9]

There are a number of subject-matters in international law 'although obviously falling within the domain of matters subject to regulation by international law, cannot be said to be actually so regulated, because the practice of States shows, in respect of them, conflicting legal views based in part in conflicting interests'. In other fields the lack of agreement is due less to the divergence of interests and more to historical peculiarities or accidental reasons.[10]

Thus, Lauterpacht does not suggest pre-empting the will of States in terms of legal regulation of fields in which there is currently none. Obviously, most of international law derives from the consensus of States and there is no legal regulation unless States are agreed on it. However, disagreement on details of applicable rules should not be allowed to undermine legal regulation of the relevant subject-matter in general. This problem is located in the context of the thesis of the completeness of law:

> The fundamental principle of the completeness of the international legal system cannot be affected by the mere fact of a number of States disagreeing on a particular subject.... There is no reason why an international tribunal, confronted with a dispute involving a controversial subject of this nature, should not disregard altogether the conflicting views and proceed to give judgement by reference to a more general principle of international law, on which there exists a substantial measure of agreement.[11]

This approach is further reinforced by the fact that '... starting from the proposition that the law is complete and that there is therefore no room for looking behind the few specific rules and prohibitions...we come dangerously near to lending ourselves to the use of a narrow and unscientific method which will defeat the very end of law'.[12] International law 'is complete from the point of view of its adequacy to deal with any dispute brought before an international

[9] Lautespacht (1933), 251, 387.
[10] *Id*, 76.
[11] *Id*, 77.
[12] *Id*, 87.

judicial tribunal'.[13] Thus, Lauterpacht emphasises the ability of international law to effectively apply to inter-State legal disputes. His thesis may thus be denoted as the thesis of effectiveness of legal regulation, which is secured by the emphasis on the substantive as opposed to the mechanical completeness of law.

Gaps do exist in law, but these are 'material gaps in the teleological sense as judged from the point of view of the general purpose of the law, and as distinguished from formal gaps identical with a break in the continuity of the legal order'.[14] Presenting gaps in this way will allow the decision-maker to ensure the completeness of the legal system by resorting to more general standards in the absence of more specific ones. The rigid theory of formal completeness assumes that there are specific rules on anything that falls within the ambit of international law and that if such specific rules are absent there is no legal regulation on the relevant subject. Lauterpacht suggests that there are gaps in international law in the sense that not every specific situation is addressed by a specific rule. However, such 'gaps' do not militate against the existence of legal regulation as soon as a more general principle can be found within which the relevant situation would be subsumable. This is, in essence, the thesis of the effectiveness of legal regulation.

This goes hand in hand with the observation that law is not all-embracing. The point is, however, that once law in principle extends to the relevant field, it does regulate it meaningfully and effectively, and the absence of more specific rules on that subject cannot change this.

The thesis of completeness of law leads Lauterpacht to address the issue of the threshold of legal regulation. It is pointed out that 'when we accept the principle that every claim must be rejected unless there are agreed rules of law in support of it, all depends on what we understand agreed rules of law to mean'.[15] A combination of a rigid theory of the formal completeness of international law with an emphasis on the sovereignty of States as a law-creating principle may easily produce results inimical to the purposes of law.[16]

It is not a secret that Lauterpacht was never a follower of orthodox positivism. Nevertheless, the cardinal point of his approach, material for the entire present study, is to emphasise the compatibility of the inter-State consensual character of international law with the idea of law on which it is based:

> The view that States are bound only by rules expressly accepted is obviously the assertion of the extreme positivist view. However, it is not necessary here to refute that opinion which has no reference to the question of subjection to *existing* law. It is not inconsistent with the assumption of the existence of a legal command, in the form of a basic legal hypothesis—to abide by obligations expressly or tacitly undertaken. So long as the binding force of this basic postulate is assumed, the view that international law is a 'system of promises' is only of secondary importance.[17]

[13] *Id*, 134.
[14] *Id*, 86–87.
[15] *Id*, 87.
[16] *Id*, 96.
[17] *Id*, 419.

Furthermore, it is observed that:

From the rule that obligations of international law owe their origin to the will of States, it follows that new obligations cannot be imposed upon an unwilling State by an international legislature. But from the principle that a State is objectively bound by an obligation once undertaken there follows, with inescapable logic, the juridical postulate of the obligatory rule of law.[18]

This thesis, as can be seen, does not deny the consensual, decentralised, inter-State character of international law. It only suggests that this character does not militate against the ability of States to place reliance on international rules and obligations, and to expect their reasonable certainty and determinacy, with a view to providing the stability and predictability of legal regulation. As a broad thesis, international law is not only inter-State; it is also law. Even as it applies to sovereign States it is still based on the idea of law.

The next relevant issue directly following from the legal character of international law is the determinacy of legal regulation, that is the susceptibility of the relevant matter to resolution through the application of law. One problem that has been raised in this context with some vigour, and which was addressed in detail both by Brierly and Lauterpacht, is the problem of so-called 'political disputes'. Lauterpacht points to the understanding, in doctrine and practice, of 'vital interests' and other 'important' matters that are arguably so dependent on subjective valuation that it is hardly possible to expect an international organ to deal with them.[19]

Lauterpacht's conception of political disputes must be located in the context of his thesis of the effectiveness of legal regulation. The essence of legal obligation necessarily means its determinacy, and the line of progress lies 'in abandoning conceptions which are incapable of forming part of a legal obligation'.[20] More specifically: 'There may or may not be justification for the unreality of language attempting to elevate the generalisations and technicalities of mere evasion to the dignity of a legal obligation, but the lawyer can be no party to any such attempt.' Consequently, 'A tribunal must either base its decision on law or disregard the law. *Tertium non datur.*' In a community accepting the rule of law disputes can be settled in only one way: on the basis of the existing law.[21] From the modern perspective, this approach is further relevant to the doctrinal argument that some rules are indeterminate and no straightforward legal judgment can be formed in relation to them *a priori*. This approach is further relevant for demonstrating the importance of interpretation for clarifying the content and scope of these rules.

Lauterpacht's preference for the determinacy of legal regulation goes hand in hand with his argument on the primacy of law within the field of international

18 *Id*, 420.
19 *Id*, 190.
20 *Id*, 188–189.
21 *Id*, 193, 326, 373.

legal regulation. Legal disputes must be resolved on the basis of the existing law only, and he is opposed to the approach that the application of legal rules may be avoided because they may entail an unjust result, or because a party to the dispute argues that the dispute is not legal.[22]

Lauterpacht is not an idealist prioritising the importance of abstract justice or equity at the expense of the law currently in force, and does not call for over-ruling or neglecting existing legal regulation just because it may appear unjust or unfair. As he states, 'It is not the function of the law to prevent individual hardship following upon the operation of rules of law. On the contrary, its task is to give effect to legal rights, notwithstanding the inconvenience of those subjected to a legal duty. Law is more than loose conceptions of justice and equity. . . . A State "sitting on its rights" is not necessarily in the wrong.'[23]

The plea for completeness and effectiveness of legal regulations leads both Brierly and Lauterpacht to disapprove of the notion of 'political disputes' in international law. In general, the notion of political disputes must be conceived of in terms of what a dispute generally is. This has been defined by the Permanent Court in the *Mavrommatis* case as a disagreement as to the point of fact or law, a positive opposition between claims of two legal persons.[24] One way of perceiving the nature of political disputes is to view international law as a body of rules covering the less important matters of inter-State relations.[25] Political disputes would thus be those covering the most important matters. The weakness of this point of view is that there is no established way of distinguishing between more and less important matters.

According to Brierly, practically every dispute contains a legal and a political element. The fact that States are parties to a dispute makes it political, but does not prevent it from being legal.[26] Brierly identifies the purported original basis for denoting certain disputes as political as being that some rules are allegedly imprecise and international law is consequently an immature system. This thesis implies, 'a contrast between municipal and international law which is at least very much exaggerated'.[27] Brierly opposes the thesis that from the juridical perspective relations between States are something crucially different from relations and disputes between individuals within the State.[28] Brierly emphasises that many major interests of States are outside law not because they are political but because there is no legal regulation on them.[29] In other words, the existence of legal regulation,

[22] *Id*, 373, 378.

[23] *Id*, 252.

[24] *Mavrommatis Palestine Concessions*, *PCIJ Series* A, No 2, 1924, 11.

[25] Lauterpacht (1933), 403.

[26] JL Brierly, The Judicial Settlement of International Disputes, in *The Basis of Obligation* (1958), 93 at 96.

[27] *Id*, 97.

[28] *Id*, 99.

[29] *Id*, 103; in illustrating the argument on the political character of certain disputes, Lauterpacht refers to Anzilotti's view that international legal regulation does not cover the most important

which relates to voluntary law-making by States as opposed to the inherent political nature of the relevant dispute, is the key to the problem.

The general gist of Brierly's argument is that there are no genuinely political disputes. There are merely some disputes in relation to which States are not willing to be subjected to the rule of law.[30] In response to that, Brierly suggests that the test of distinguishing between legal and political disputes is found not in the attitude of States but in the character of disputes. There have been cases where allegedly political disputes were settled by legal means which proves that there are no inherently political, that is non-legal, disputes.[31] If States do not submit 'important' issues to the rule of law, the importance of international law itself will be minor. One attribute of a civilised legal system is that a legal person cannot withdraw a matter from being subjected to the rule of law.[32] Thus, it can be seen that Brierly's entire argument perceives the deficiency of the notion of political disputes as being closely connected to the completeness and determinacy of international law, and to its basic legal character.

If there is no legal regulation on the relevant subject-matter because States do not want it, that is the end of the matter. But if the solution falls within the legal rule, then the political character of the relevant problems is no longer relevant. There is no inherent contradiction between the notion of political disputes and international law. As Lauterpacht observes, 'The interpretation of a controversial treaty of alliance is a political dispute which affects the vital interests of a nation. But the dispute is at the same time a legal dispute *par excellence* involving a judicial interpretation of the terms of the treaty.'[33] In other words, within the realm of law the political elements of the relevant dispute have no significance.

Lauterpacht also exposes the fact that the notion of political disputes is merely a term of art related to a problem that surfaces in the international legal system with the same essence but with different names. He addresses the question whether 'conflicts of interests' as opposed to 'disputes as to rights' can be adjudicated by an impartial organ, and states that in this way the distinction between legal and political disputes appears in one of its many traditional forms.[34]

interests of States and these are left to political and economic processes, cited in *The Function of Law in the International Community* (1933), 169. This description is in fact twofold. It emphasises not only that certain interests are important, but also, and most importantly, that these interests are not legally regulated, that is there are no legal rules in relation to them accepted by States. Arguing that a certain dispute is political because it covers very important interests and it is political because there is no legal regulation on its subject-matter are two substantially different things.

[30] JL Brierly, Law, Justice and War, in *The Basis of Obligation* (1958), 265 at 266–267.

[31] JL Brierly, The Judicial Settlement of International Disputes, *id*, 106.

[32] *Id*, 265 at 267.

[33] Lauterpacht (1933), 159.

[34] *Id*, 337; along similar lines, Lauterpacht suggests that the question whether the dispute is one of domestic jurisdiction is in substance the same question as whether the dispute is legal or not, *id*, 199. A dispute falling within domestic jurisdiction is one not regulated by international law and it may hence be denoted as 'political'. But the key aspect of this problem is the lack of legal regulation on the subject-matter of dispute, as opposed to its 'political' character.

Most importantly, Lauterpacht emphasises the highly subjective nature of the notion of political disputes, stating that 'It is not the nature of an individual dispute which makes it unfit for judicial settlement, but the unwillingness of a State to have it settled by the application of law.'[35] The notion of political disputes, inasmuch as it tries to prevent the judicial determination of important issues, is not in accordance with existing international law and is contrary to the purposes of law.[36] No juridical test has ever been suggested as to how the exclusion of important issues from judicial process might be determined. There could in reality be no such criterion. 'A juridical criterion, like any other test, can be formed only on the basis of data capable of objective ascertainment.'[37] On the other hand, any attempt to determine the importance of the matter is necessarily subjective. 'The interests involved are so subjective as to exclude the possibility of applying an objective standard' in regard to each individual dispute.[38]

These statements emphasise the need for an objective approach to and analysis of the nature of the dispute, as opposed to its characterisation by the State. This objective analysis implies deciding whether there is a legal rule applicable to the dispute. The political character cannot be an inherent element of any dispute. Empirically, the thesis that international law may not extend to some matters of great importance to States may be right. But the issue of principle is that these issues are outside the law not because of their inherent nature but because States have not been willing to lay down legal regulation regarding them. For instance, there is no straightforward and determinate legal regulation on naval exercises by one State in the Exclusive Economic Zone of another State. This is so not because this issue is political or important, but because States have not agreed to introduce such limitations. In addition, it has to be emphasised that international legal scholarship since Brierly and Lauterpacht has not come up with a consistent and coherent explanation of the thesis rejecting or downplaying the applicability of international law to the conduct of States in the same way as national law applies to the conduct of individuals.

Lauterpacht emphasises that subjectivism has no place in international law, and 'although the will of the State is essential for the creation of the common will, it is the latter, and not the will of the individual State, which is the source of international obligations'. The binding force of international obligations definitionally excludes subjectivism in the sense of allowing States to subjectively determine, that is auto-interpret, the content of their obligations.[39] Consistently with this approach, the elimination of the objective legal authority endowed with the competence to ascertain whether international obligations are observed in good faith would be destructive of the legal obligations under treaties if so interpreted.[40]

[35] *Id*, 369.
[36] *Id*, 183.
[37] *Id*, 183.
[38] *Id*, 187–188.
[39] *Id*, 415, 423.
[40] *Id*, 181.

The next cardinally important question is how the factor of sovereignty influences the legal character of disputes and the determinacy or effectiveness of legal rules that apply to those disputes. Lauterpacht perceives sovereign freedom of action not as a regulatory principle but as the residual factor that is relevant only after it is ascertained that there is no specific obligation operating on the relevant matter. Law consists in the regulation of human conduct and hence in the limitation of the freedom of action. Sovereignty is thus a quality conferred by international law. It cannot be the basis or source of international law.[41] In other words, sovereign freedom of action is relevant only in the absence of a legal obligation. In international jurisprudence the thesis that the limitation on sovereign freedom of action follows only from an express stipulation is rejected.[42] This argument seems to be more about interpreting the will and consent of States rather than projecting the limitation of sovereignty in the absence of such will and consent.

The issues raised by Brierly and Lauterpacht about the fundamental character of international law persist in their relevance, and pervade the entire system of the international legal system. To sum up, these issues relate to: (1) the completeness of law, that is the existence of legal regulation; (2) the determinacy of rules, that is the content of legal regulation; (3) the effectiveness of legal regulation, that is its ability effectively to apply to facts and conduct that fall within the scope of that regulation; (4) the freedom of action of States and its relationship to the effectiveness of legal regulation, which in fact is the other side of the coin of the effectiveness problem; (5) subjectivism and discretion in the application of legal rules.

These conceptual issues are faced in the multiple frameworks of international jurisdiction, encompassing a vast amount of material. All these issues are in the final analysis crucially interrelated. Determinacy of rules is crucial in terms of how the relationship between obligation and sovereign freedom must be construed, because indeterminacy of rules may create the impression that a presumption in favour of sovereign freedom of action exists. Both the issues of indeterminacy and presumption in favour of sovereign freedom can support the position that relevant rules and obligations can be determined by reference to the subjective attitude of and assessment by the relevant State.

[41] *Id*, 95–96.

[42] H Lauterpacht, *Development* (1958), 359; as will further be seen, Lauterpacht argues, in support of this thesis, for the non-consensual character of customary law, see among others *id*, 360, and below Chapter 4.

2

Characteristics and Implications of the Effectiveness of Legal Regulation

1. The Essence of the Effectiveness of Legal Regulation

As pointed out at the outset, the traditional debate on the legal character of international law focuses on structural factors, such as the existence of centralised legislature, executive and judiciary. But this issue has another dimension too, which is more important in terms of the current state of international legal doctrine, given that the above-mentioned structural objection no longer carries any serious weight. The essence of this question today focuses on more complex issues such as the interaction of international law with non-law, with the residual sovereign freedom of action, and consequently the determinacy and effectiveness of legal regulation. This analysis reveals international law as an independent system of rules—independent from other factors that may be relevant for the conduct of States in the international legal society. For, if international law binds States in the same way that national law binds individuals, then non-legal factors should not possess crucial relevance in determining the applicability of international legal rules to the conduct and position of States.

Thus, this study proceeds from asking the fundamental question of whether international law is law. But it poses this question from the dynamic, as opposed to structural, perspective. This current perspective focuses on the question of whether, apart from the dimension of law-making and law enforcement, international law can *operate* and *apply* as law. Following from the thesis that international law is based on State consent and agreement, this study examines whether and to what extent the product of that consent and agreement has a determinable content.

The principal thesis advanced here is that if international law is law, then the content of the rule agreed upon by States must be viewed as capable of offering the required outcome that applies to facts, gives them legal characterisation, and extends to the field that is covered by this content. If, despite the fact that the rule is agreed by States as having the relevant content, it still does not, due to the factors external to this agreement, suggest the objectively observable outcome and extend to the field covered by its content, then international law is purely and simply not law.

It is intended to clarify this basic question by addressing the current merit of the basic questions raised and considered by Brierly and Lauterpacht. It is not the purpose of this study to elaborate upon each and every question that both writers examined in their major studies. The aim instead is to identify the basic concepts and factors that inevitably characterise the international legal system, as discernible from their thoughts. These are effectiveness and completeness of legal regulation, separation between law and politics, and consequently determinacy of international legal regulation. These basic categories will be taken further, expanded upon, consolidated, and their implications will be located in multiple areas of international law.

Effectiveness of legal regulation is a phenomenon in which effectiveness is adjectival to legal regulation. It is the existing legal regulation on the relevant matter that should operate effectively, rather than the alternative option of construing the existing legal regulation in a way to make it more effective than it is or promoting the general effectiveness of the international legal system. This latter version of effectiveness would almost inevitably generate diverse views as to what should be seen as effective, and open the door for subjectivism in decision-making. It also would undermine by the back door the basic systemic precondition of international law being created by agreement between States. Effectiveness of law is served by such interpretation of rules and instruments as renders them effective.

Completeness of international legal regulation is a necessary requirement for the operation of the international legal system. Completeness, as follows from the teachings of Lauterpacht, does not imply that the legal regulation must be all-embracing in the sense that it should cover those areas and matters that are not regulated under the recognised sources of international law. But the completeness of international legal regulation does imply that the established rules and principles cover the subject-matter of their regulation in its entirety. This understanding is required by those expectations that States and other actors have in relation to the established rules of international law. If international law does not regulate the relevant subject-matter, the relevant actors cannot have legally valid expectations in relation to that subject-matter. Thus, it may be a deficiency of international law that it does not proclaim the universal and enforceable right to food, or the 'responsibility to protect' the victims of humanitarian catastrophe. But from the legal perspective these matters are simply outside the field of regulation of general international law, because States have not agreed to establish the relevant rules regulating those subjects. If, however, the matter relates to a field that is included within international law, the relevant legal regulation, that is the relevant rules, principles and sources of law, must be presumed to apply to the complete field covered by that regulation.

International law is a complete legal system. It does not admit gaps. In the *Nuclear Weapons* Advisory Opinion, the International Court refused to pass straightforward judgment on the legality of nuclear weapons in the extreme circumstances of self-defence where the survival of the State is at stake.[1] This has been seen as the Court's affirmation of *non liquet*.[2] One cannot, however, lose sight of the fact that the Court was pronouncing not in terms of the existence of legal regulation in general, but in terms of the entitlement that possibly exists under existing conventional and customary law regulation on the inherent right to self-defence. This disqualifies the *Nuclear Weapons* Opinion from counting as an example of judicial reference to *non liquet*. This is even clearer from the Court's earlier statement in the Operative Part of the Opinion that use of nuclear weapons that fails to meet the requirements of Article 51 of the UN Charter is contrary to international law. The gist of the Court's argument seems to be that use of nuclear weapons can be justified in very limited circumstances of self-defence, but only if the relevant situation can be characterised as self-defence in the first place.

As Weil observed in the aftermath of the *Nuclear Weapons* Opinion, the statement of the absence of legal regulation is inadmissible. Whenever States decide, by way of a special agreement, compromissory clause or otherwise, to ask for judicial settlement of a dispute, they impose on the judge or arbitrator an obligation to settle the dispute and find the applicable law for this purpose.[3] This process does not involve legislating, which tribunals are precluded from doing due to the basic nature of the international legal system. This task involves finding the applicable rules and principles in the existing law.

The issue of completeness of legal regulation is also affected by the possible silence of the relevant legal rules and how to understand that silence. As Visscher observes, silence engenders uncertainty and equivocation in inter-State relations.[4] This problem has to be clarified and resolved through the process of interpretation.

Usually the notion of silence is used in different contexts of international law. Silence in terms of State practice and *effectivités* can be constitutive of consent to the relevant legal change. It may imply acceptance of a claim, unless the general context of the pertinent State practice points to the opposite conclusion.[5] The silence of legal rules, including those embodied in a treaty or other written instruments, in relation to the pertinent subject-matter is a more complex problem. The silence of language does not necessarily suggest a lack of legal regulation under the relevant treaty or other instrument, if that regulation can be deduced from the general scope, or the object and purpose, of the treaty.[6] But this cannot

[1] *ICJ Reports*, 1996, 266.

[2] P Weil, 'The Court Cannot Conclude Definitively …' *Non Liquet* Revisited, 38 *Columbia JTL* (1998), 109 at 117.

[3] Weil (1998), 115. See further Chapter 12 below.

[4] Visscher (1963), 164.

[5] See below Chapter 5, and see further Chapter 13.

[6] As in the case of effective interpretation, for instance with regard to positive obligations under the European Convention on Human Rights, when such positive obligations must necessarily be implied if the relevant Convention right is to operate effectively, *cf*, below Part IV.

always be implied without more. The silence of the language in a treaty or another pertinent instrument may well be indicative of a lack of intention to regulate the relevant subject if, for instance, the purposes of the treaty or other legal instrument demonstrate that it is limited functionally or by space.[7] In such a case, general international law could acquire relevance.

Thus, in some cases the silence of the relevant instrument could mean that the relevant matter is simply beyond its intendment of regulation. In this case it should be presumed that the parties did not decide to regulate the relevant issue in the relevant instrument. In other cases, however, the silence of the instrument does not necessarily place the relevant matter outside its ambit. The problem of silence has to be dealt with through the use of the principles of interpretation.

2. Determinacy of International Legal Regulation

A principal problem pertaining to the legal character of international law is the determinacy of its rules. What is determinacy from the substantive legal regulation point of view can be denoted as judicial manageability from the procedural, or adjudicative, perspective.[8] The whole concept refers to the existence of such legal regulation as can be intelligibly identified and applied to the underlying facts. This problem did not directly feature in the works of Brierly and Lauterpacht. Yet, determinacy of legal regulation inherently pertains to the theses of effectiveness and completeness of legal regulation. The determinacy of legal regulation is indispensable when assessing whether the relevant legal regulation is complete and effective; especially in terms of the development of a number of legal frameworks as a consequence of the expansion of international law subsequent to the writings of Brierly and Lauterpacht.

[7] In *Jan Mayen*, the International Court faced the plea that the 1965 Agreement between Norway and Denmark delimited all maritime frontiers between the two States, with the outcome of a median line as the basis for delimitation. The Court found it 'clear that Agreement contains no provision for the definition of the position of a median line specifically between Greenland and Jan Mayen'. After interpreting the Agreement, the Court concluded that it delimited only the specified parts of the maritime boundary between the two States, and did not include Jan Mayen. While not addressing the boundaries in the Jan Mayen area, the 1965 Agreement could not be seen as waiving the 'special circumstances' criteria under the 1958 Convention on Continental Shelf in relation to the very same area. *ICJ Reports*, 1993, 49, 51–52; the 1958 Convention applied as between the Parties. In *Ligitan/Sipadan*, the International Court was unable to consider that the 1891 Anglo-Dutch Convention established the maritime boundary in relation to islands in question. The Convention was a boundary treaty, but had no intendment to apply to that particular sector of maritime boundary. *ICJ Reports*, 2002, 625. See further Part II below.

[8] The notion of judicial manageability has been used both in national and international jurisprudence. Lord Wilberforce in the *Buttes Gas* case applied the Act of State doctrine to the issues that were not, according to his judgment, covered by the judicially manageable legal standards, [1982] AC 938.

In general, the determinacy of legal regulation is required so that States know what rights and obligations they have, and are able to rely on not being subjected to a legal regime different from that to which they have consented. The question is whether international law can offer such transparent and determinate legal regulation applicable to the conduct of States that will respond to the basic requirements of the rule of law. This relates above all to the uniform and indiscriminate applicability of legal prescriptions.

The problem of determinacy is inherently linked to some other conceptual issues pervading the entire international legal system. One such conceptual issue is that of the interaction between legal regulation and sovereign freedom of action, which focuses on whether and to what extent sovereign freedom of action can override the expectations States have in relation to the relevant legal rule. The issue of whether legal regulation is determinate is inherently cognate to the issue of whether and to what extent State consent and agreement exist in relation to that regulation; that is to what extent sovereign freedom of action is preserved. Another conceptual issue relates to the notion of political disputes. The principal question in this field is whether the political, or important, nature of the issue can preclude the application of international legal rules to that issue, or its judicial determination. Finally, all these categories relate to the effectiveness of legal regulation. For the effectiveness of legal regulation is directly impacted upon by whether it can be set aside by reference to residual sovereign freedom, political factors involved, or lack of determinacy.

Determinacy of legal regulation is a complex problem. Some legal rules are straightforward and determinate, for instance, the rule that the breadth of territorial sea may not exceed 12 nautical miles, or the rules specifying the type of majority of votes required for adopting decisions in the organs of international organisations. The determinacy of a rule means that it applies to facts immediately and without reference to any other factor. But not all other rules are so specific and determinate. Some rules may be too general; others may refer to non-legal factors which are not defined on their face. The crucial question raised by these types of rules is whether, how and to what extent they are capable of offering the specific legal outcome that can be applied to facts and specify the rights and obligations of States. This is just another way of asking whether and to what extent these rules are legal rules at all.

The question of determinacy eventually raises the issue of subjectivism and discretionary interpretation of rights and obligations. In this aspect it is an issue conceptually, and in some cases practically, cognate to that of freedom of action in the alleged absence of legal regulation. Arguing that there is no determinate regulation on the relevant matter and that the State is itself the judge of its legal obligations is essentially the same as arguing that the State is not bound by international law on the relevant matter. The legal rule, though indeterminate, is meant to have an intendment and rationale behind it. Rules are meant to apply to State conduct. Hence, the problem of indeterminacy must be dealt with keeping this priority in mind.

There may be different types of indeterminacy. The lack of determinacy may relate to the ambiguity of terms included in the written instrument. Certain notions or words included in the treaty may be uncertain or require some degree of appreciation for capturing their meaning. Sometimes definitions of terms are employed in the relevant texts of agreements. If not, they could cause disputes because of their alleged uncertainty. One such instance is the definition of torture under Article 1 of the 1984 Convention against Torture, which is effectively incorporated into the understanding of torture under some other human rights treaties such as the European Convention on Human Rights,[9] and refers to the element of severe treatment. While severity is difficult to define *a priori* and some appreciation may be needed, it is still possible to apply this notion to individual cases. The European Court of Human Rights repeatedly had to tackle the threshold of severity for the conduct of the State to amount to torture or inhuman treatment under Article 3 of the European Convention on Human Rights. In *Poltoratskiy v Ukraine*, the European Court specified that:

The assessment of this minimum level of severity is relative; it depends on all the circumstances of the case, such as the duration of the treatment, its physical and mental effects and, in some cases, the sex, age and state of health of the victim. Furthermore, in considering whether treatment is 'degrading' within the meaning of Article 3, the Court will have regard to whether its object is to humiliate and debase the person concerned and whether, as far as the consequences are concerned, it adversely affected his or her personality in a manner incompatible with Article 3. However, the absence of such a purpose cannot conclusively rule out a finding of a violation of this provision.[10]

Further to that, the European Court emphasised that:

the suffering and humiliation involved must in any event go beyond that inevitable element of suffering or humiliation connected with a given form of legitimate treatment or punishment. Measures depriving a person of his liberty may often involve such an element. In accordance with Article 3 of the Convention the State must ensure that a person is detained under conditions which are compatible with respect for his human dignity, that the manner and method of the execution of the measure do not subject him to distress or hardship exceeding the unavoidable level of suffering inherent in detention, and that, given the practical demands of imprisonment, his health and well-being are adequately secured.[11]

[9] *Selmouni v France*, Application No 25803/94, Judgment of 28 July 1999, paras 79ff, where the European Court of Human Rights uses the 1984 Convention as interpretative guidance for locating the scope of Article 3 of the European Convention.

[10] *Poltoratskiy v Ukraine*, Application No 38812/97, Judgment 29 April 2003, para 131.

[11] *Poltoratskiy*, para 132; the same approach is visible in the observation of Judge Fitzmaurice in the *Tyrer* case: 'To amount to an infringement of Article 3 (art. 3) therefore, the punishment in question must entail a degree of degradation recognisably greater than that inherently bound-up with any normal punishment that takes the form of coercion or deprivation of liberty,—or else it must be accompanied by circumstances of degradation greater than what are necessary for the carrying-out of the punishment according to its due and intended effect', *Tyrer v UK*, Application No 5856/72, Judgment of 25 April 1978, Separate Opinion of Judge Fitzmaurice, para 6.

This is a reference by the European Court to the requirement that the treatment of the detained persons must be commensurate with the necessary aims of detention and shall not go beyond that. After this, the European Court proceeds to specify the parameters of the threshold of severity in the specific cases of detention on death row:

> Where the death penalty is imposed, the personal circumstances of the condemned person, the conditions of detention while awaiting execution and the length of detention prior to execution are examples of factors capable of bringing the treatment or punishment received by the condemned person within the proscription under Article 3. When assessing conditions of detention, account has to be taken of the cumulative effects of those conditions, as well as the specific allegations made by the applicant.[12]

Given all these specifications, the lack of definition of 'severity' in general terms is not a factor preventing the application of legal rules to facts. In the relevant context of adjudication the identification of severe treatment to qualify it as torture or inhuman treatment is regularly practised.

In general, the presence in treaty provisions of terms and notions that are vague or subject to appreciation is not the most problematic case of indeterminacy as the meaning and definition of relevant terms can be clarified by the process of examining the factual and real-world perspective of the subject-matter that is covered by those terms. What seems complicated in abstract terms can be quite straightforward in specific cases. This can be seen from the analysis of the WTO Appellate Body of the notion of 'exhaustible natural resource' in the *US-Shrimps* case. The meaning of 'exhaustible' was contested. Nevertheless, the Appellate Body referred to the data of biological sciences to confirm that living species along with non-living resources can fall within the notion of 'exhaustible resources'.[13] After that, the Appellate Body went on to examine whether the relevant species, sea turtles, were exhaustible, and after considering all available evidence, including treaties and reports, concluded that 'The exhaustibility of sea turtles would in fact have been very difficult to controvert.'[14]

These instances demonstrate that law is vague or relative in many cases but the vagueness is still placed within the process of application of legal rules to facts. The vague notions are part of legal rules and their appreciation is part of the application of law to facts. The principles of interpretation assist the identification of the meaning of uncertain terms and their incidence in the relevant case. The context, rationale and preparatory work of the relevant written instrument can provide the guidance as to what the more precise meaning of the relevant term is. In this case, the practice of interpretation adopts the same approach of completeness and determinacy of treaty regulation as was voiced by Lauterpacht in relation to the completeness of legal regulation in general.

[12] *Poltoratskiy*, para 133.
[13] *US–Shrimp*, Appellate Body Report, para 128.
[14] *Id*, para 133.

There is, however, another type of indeterminacy, which is essential to the methodological and structural aspects of the present study. This type of indeterminacy requires not assessing the meaning of the relevant terms of the instrument, but deals with rules that have an open-ended outer limit, which is impossible to define by reference to the factual context to which the rule is supposed to apply. Instead, this outer limit of the rule involves an element of appreciation of the relevant matters on which there is room for subjective judgement and disagreement. In these cases, the legal rule in question does not itself define the relevant term or formulate the legal limit on State action, but subjects the issue to other, initially undefined, non-legal criteria. This particular field of indeterminacy is the field of the relevance of non-law. Non-law refers to a set of factors that are not approved as law through the accepted modes of law-making, but impact on rights and duties in international law. Separating law from non-law is an essential prerequisite for viewing international law as a separate discipline.

3. Judicial Responses to the Alleged Lack or Incompleteness of Legal Regulation

After having clarified the doctrinal and conceptual side of the problem of indeterminacy, the judicial responses to situations in which the governing legal framework is alleged to be indeterminate or incomplete must be examined. The absence of a specific legal rule of positive law addressing a particular point arising in an international dispute can be addressed in different ways. The relevant outcome should obviously depend on all normative considerations involved in the relevant case. One option is to presume that States are free to act, provided that no legal limitation on their freedom can be identified.

Another option is to resort to the relevant rules and principles of domestic law, if the particular question relates to issues that normally arise in domestic law and if the relevant situation is covered by the domestic legal system of the relevant State. To illustrate, the decision of the International Court in *Barcelona Traction* was largely motivated by concepts and categories developed in municipal law, such as the position of private corporations. As the Court put it, 'If the Court were to decide the case in disregard of the relevant institutions of municipal law it would, without justification, invite serious legal difficulties. It would lose touch with reality, for there are no corresponding institutions of international law to which the Court could resort.'[15] Furthermore, according to the Court, 'It is to rules generally accepted by municipal legal systems which recognise the limited company whose capital is represented by shares, and not to the municipal law of a particular State, that international law refers. In referring to such rules, the Court

[15] *Barcelona Traction*, *ICJ Reports*, 1970, 37.

cannot modify, still less deform them.'[16] This approach is permissible only in the absence of international legal regulation on the subject. If such international regulation exists, domestic law cannot justify the violation of international rules.

Yet another option is to resort to inherent structural principles of international law, such as good faith, *pacta sunt servanda* or other general principles of law under Article 38(1)(c) of the International Court's Statute. The relevance of these principles is limited, because they relate to the structural operation of established rules rather than determining their existence or content.

A further way could be to enact recommendations if authorisation has been given to the decision-making organ through the consent of the parties, as was the case in the *Behring Sea* Arbitration. In this case, it seems that the parties, Britain and the United States, had acknowledged that the protection and preservation of the fur seal in that maritime region was a genuine problem needing a response. As the Tribunal would find that under international law there was no regulation conferring upon the State the entitlement to establish regulations for the protection of the fur seal, the parties authorised it to determine what concurrent regulations both parties should enact and comply with, with a view to securing that goal. The Tribunal issued a set of regulations on competence and procedure relating to the preservation of the fur seal species.[17] The enactment of these regulations took place in the absence of legal regulation on this subject, and followed a request by the parties.

Multiple international controversies have demonstrated that very often none of the above three strategies are able to address the problem of indeterminacy and incompleteness of legal regulation. The principal way of addressing the alleged indeterminacy or incompleteness of legal regulation, as developed in this study, relates to the effective construction of the general legal framework to which that legal regulation belongs. The approach of the International Court in the *Fisheries* case was to favour the presumption of determinacy and completeness of legal regulation, very much in line with Lauterpacht's thesis of the completeness of law, effectiveness of legal regulation, and limits on the freedom of action. The Court identified the legal regime governing the legality of the Norwegian method of delimitation of its territorial waters. According to the Court:

> It does not at all follow that, in the absence of rules having the technically precise character alleged by the United Kingdom Government, the delimitation undertaken by the Norwegian Government in 1935 is not subject to certain principles which make it possible to judge as to its validity under international law. The delimitation of sea areas has always an international aspect; it cannot be dependent merely upon the will of the coastal State as expressed in its municipal law. Although it is true that the act of delimitation is necessarily a unilateral act, because only the coastal State is competent to

[16] *Id*, 37.

[17] Award of the Tribunal of Arbitration constituted under the Treaty concluded at Washington, 29 February 1892, between US and UK, 15 August 1893, 6 *AJIL* (1912), 233 at 234, 237–240.

undertake it, the validity of the delimitation with regard to other States depends upon international law.[18]

Thus, by assuming that in the absence of specific and detailed rules the relevant subject-matter is governed by the more general rules, the Court presumes against the indeterminacy of those general rules. The essence of determinacy of legal rules is to ensure that there is always a legal regulation on the relevant subject-matter that falls within the ambit of international law. The generality of a rule does not prevent it from applying to the relevant situation. This aspect also links the issue of determinacy with that of effectiveness of legal regulation, requiring that general rules shall effectively regulate particular situations in principle falling within the scope of that general rule.

The *Fisheries Jurisdiction* (UK v Iceland) case is a notable example of a judicial attempt to tackle indeterminacy. The Court's entire analysis is opposed to the acceptance of the lack of legal regulation on the subject-matter of the litigation, which in this case was the preferential fishing rights of the State and the corollary obligation to have due regard to other States' interests under Article 2 of the 1958 High Seas Convention. However, the Court was unable to infer any determinate legal regulation on this subject, the consequence of which was that it ordered the parties to pursue negotiations with a view to achieving equitable settlement on the basis of due regard to each other's rights and interests. In terms of determinate outcome, the Court could not go beyond specifying that the Icelandic fishery zone was not opposable to the United Kingdom.[19] At the same time, the Court could not have left the matter without directing the parties to ensure the compliance with the requirements of the 1958 Convention.

In *Gulf of Maine* the International Court emphasised that international law provides only basic legal principles of maritime delimitation. It does not provide the practical or technical methods for attaining that objective.[20] It was unrewarding

> in a new and still unconsolidated field like that involving the quite recent extension of the claims of States to areas which were until yesterday zones of the high seas, to look to general international law to provide a readymade set of rules that can be used for solving any delimitation problems that arise. A more useful course is to seek a better formulation of the fundamental rule, on which the Parties were fortunate enough to be agreed, and whose existence in the legal convictions not only of the Parties to the present dispute, but of all States, is apparent from an examination of the realities of international legal relations.[21]

Thus the Court concluded that the existence of legal regulation should be presumed. In this case the product of legal regulation was the fundamental rule

[18] *ICJ Reports*, 1951, 132.
[19] *ICJ Reports*, 1974, 4 at 34–35 (operative paragraphs).
[20] *ICJ Reports*, 1984, 290.
[21] *Id*, 299.

on maritime delimitation which required the application of equity to individual exercises of delimitation.

In principle, it is part of judicial function and a duty of international tribunals to arrive at results that do not affirm the absence of legal regulation on matters that fall within the ambit of international law. As Judge Valticos specified in the *Libya–Malta* case, the judicial task is 'to elicit, state and exemplify the relevant rule of international law'. Furthermore:

> where the legal rule (the equitable solution) is a guideline framed in deliberately broad terms, it is by means of a gradual refinement of its scope, through the resolution of particular questions, that the Court will eventually be able to elicit objective principles capable of guiding States which encounter similar problems (and there are many such States, apparently). In so doing, it will also be able to contribute to that clarity, certainty, predictability and stability which are so essential in international law.[22]

This observation is made by reference to the role of equity in the absence of specific rules of continental shelf delimitation. A necessary caveat is that this process is not the same as judicial law-making. The clarification and application of existing legal regulation is different from introducing a new rule. In fact, as the further analysis of equity demonstrates, this process is in its entirety part of the process of application of existing rules of international law.

4. Separation of International Law from Politics

The determinacy of international legal prescriptions necessarily requires the strict separation of politics and law in the international system. For political considerations are inherently subjective and can be subjectively manipulated, unlike agreed and accepted rules of law, but which not only determine the rights and obligations of States, but derive from the mutual consent and agreement of the very same States. States have rights and obligations not for political reasons, but on the basis of legal rules. In order to be applied to facts independently and consistently, law must be seen as independent of politics in terms of its creation, content and operation.

Still, there has continuously been a doctrinal trend that emphasises the relevance of political factors for the creation, operation and implementation of international law. For several decades, the policy-oriented school has been disputing the identity of international law as the body of agreed rules and promoting it as a set of authoritative policy decisions.[23] As a consequence, the view has

[22] Separate Opinion, *ICJ Reports*, 1985, 108.

[23] M McDougal, International Law, Power and Policy: A Contemporary Conception, 82 *Recueil des cours* (I-1953), 133.

been promoted that 'law and politics are not necessarily inimical'.[24] A century later than Westlake's thesis of the interconnectedness of international law and politics, the view has been expressed that 'International law and international politics cohabit the same conceptual space. Together they comprise the rules and the reality of "the international system", an intellectual construct that lawyers, political scientists, and policymakers use to describe the world they study and seek to manipulate.' In line with this, the formulation of 'an integrated theory of international law and international relations' is attempted.[25]

Such an 'integral' approach to the variety of phenomena that are displayed in the realm of the international State system cannot be accommodated within the discipline of international law. For international law is not what 'lawyers, political scientists, and policymakers use to describe the world they study and *seek to manipulate*,' but what States agree about. Legal decision-making is inherently about identifying the basis for decision in agreed and accepted rules and sources of law, as opposed to political perceptions. There is arguably room in the international legal system for decision-making on political grounds, notably in the context of international organisations. But even where the relevant forum deals with political decision-making, such discretionary competence is conferred on the relevant bodies subject to their obligation to respect the legal limitations applicable to their powers.[26]

The definition of dispute as political or legal is the issue in the analysis of applicable law. The definition of dispute implies that if the State cloaks the 'political' dispute in legal terms, it will become a justiciable dispute. Thus, the concept of political disputes does not even have initial relevance in international law. Disputes of any kind would be admissible before an international tribunal as soon as they involved the positive opposition of the parties' claims. The allegedly political character of the dispute can only impact its substantive consideration if the tribunal in question were to discover no applicable legal rule. Even then, the outcome would not be due to political factors, but to the absence of legal regulation.

In judicial practice, the issue of the political character of dispute is raised once it is established that there is a legal dispute in the first place; or, alternatively, where the displacement of the applicable legal regime is being sought. The jurisprudence of international tribunals consistently rejects the relevance of the political character of the relevant issue as immaterial, in clear and intelligible terms. The International Court has observed that:

> It has been argued that the question put to the Court is intertwined with political questions, and that for this reason the Court should refuse to give an opinion. It is true that

[24] R Higgins, *The Development of International Law through the Political Organs of the United Nations* (1963), 9.

[25] A-M Slaughter, International Law in a World of Liberal States, 6 *EJIL* (1995), 503.

[26] *Admission to the United Nations*, *ICJ Reports*, 1947–48, 64; *Tadic*, IT-94-1 (Appeal Chamber), 2 October 1995, paras 28–29.

most interpretations of the Charter of the United Nations will have political significance, great or small. In the nature of things it could not be otherwise. The Court, however, cannot attribute a political character to a request which invites it to undertake an essentially judicial task, namely, the interpretation of a treaty provision.[27]

In the *WHO/Egypt* Advisory Opinion, the Court likewise dealt with the allegations that political elements of the case impacted on the process of the request and grant of the Court's advisory opinion. The Court dealt with the allegation that the request for an advisory opinion was motivated by political purposes. The Court responded that 'if, as in the present case, a question submitted in a request is one that otherwise falls within the normal exercise of its judicial process, the Court has not to deal with the motives which may have inspired the request'. The Court's next observation is particularly pertinent, because it emphasises that it is both feasible and necessary that the law-based judicial process clarifies questions that may also have a political connotation:

Indeed, in situations in which political considerations are prominent it may be particularly necessary for an international organization to obtain an advisory opinion from the Court as to the legal principles applicable with respect to the matter under debate, especially when these may include the interpretation of its constitution.[28]

In the *Tehran Hostages* case, it was Iran's attitude that the problem before the Court related to the overall situation in Iran and the overall problem of Iran–US relations. The Court was not convinced that the specific dispute under the 1961 Vienna Convention on Diplomatic Relations could not be resolved on the basis of adjudication independently of that 'overall problem'. As the Court put it, Iran had not made any attempt:

to explain, still less define, what connection, legal or factual, there may be between the 'overall problem' of its general grievances against the United States and the particular events that gave rise to the United States' claims in the present case which, in its view, precludes the separate examination of those claims by the Court. This was the more necessary because legal disputes between sovereign States by their very nature are likely to occur in political contexts, and often form only one element in a wider and longstanding political dispute between the States concerned. Yet never has the view been put forward before that, because a legal dispute submitted to the Court is only one aspect of a political dispute, the Court should decline to resolve for the parties the legal questions at issue between them. Nor can any basis for such a view of the Court's functions or jurisdiction be found in the Charter or the Statute of the Court; if the Court were, contrary to its settled jurisprudence, to adopt such a view, it would impose a far-reaching

[27] *Certain Expenses of the United Nations*, Advisory Opinion of 20 July 1962, *ICJ Reports*, 1962, 151 at 155.

[28] *Interpretation of the Agreement of 25 March 1951 between the WHO and Egypt* (Advisory Opinion of 20 December 1980), *ICJ Reports*, 1980, 73 at 87.

and unwarranted restriction upon the role of the Court in the peaceful solution of international disputes.[29]

Thus, even as legal disputes occur in political contexts, the law that governs these disputes is separate from that political context.

At the jurisdictional stage of the *Nicaragua* case, the International Court observed, by reference to its previous jurisprudence, that it 'has never shied away from a case brought before it merely because it had political implications or because it involved serious elements of the use of force'. The allegations of use of force and intervention in domestic affairs could have political connotations, yet these would not suffice to exclude these issues from adjudication.[30] The Court in *Nicaragua* also dismissed a related objection by the United States to the admissibility of the Nicaraguan application that:

> The resort to force during ongoing armed conflict lacks the attributes necessary for the application of the judicial process, namely a pattern of legally relevant facts discernible by the means available to the adjudicating tribunal, establishable in conformity with applicable rules of evidence and proof, and not subject to further material evolution during the course of, or subsequent to, the judicial proceedings. It is for reasons of this nature that ongoing armed conflict must be entrusted to resolution by political processes.[31]

This has effectively been the contention as to the non-justiciability of 'political' issues involving the use of armed force. This can be further seen from the following claim of the United States:

> The situation alleged in the Nicaraguan Application, in particular, cannot be judicially managed or resolved; continuing practical guidance to the Parties in respect of the measures required of them is critical to the effective control of situations of armed conflict such as is there alleged to exist. But the Court has, it is said, recognized that giving such practical guidance to the Parties lies outside the scope of the judicial function.[32]

The Court dismissed this objection to admissibility as well, which means that judicial function is meant to specify the applicable law and its implications for facts. Judicial function would not encompass giving to the parties directions as to how the situation in question must be resolved, if it is not regulated under the law or does not fall within the relevant tribunal's jurisdiction. The Court's approach mirrors that of Brierly that judicial function is aimed at resolving the relevant dispute. It is not aimed at sorting out the general situation of which the particular legal dispute is part.[33]

[29] *United States Diplomatic and Consular Staff in Tehran* (US v Iran), Judgment of 24 May 1980, *ICJ Reports*, 1980, 3 at 20.

[30] *Military and Paramilitary Activities In and Against Nicaragua* (Nicaragua v US), Jurisdiction and Admissibility, *ICJ Reports*, 1984, 392 at 435.

[31] *Id*, 436.

[32] *Id*.

[33] Brierly, The Essential Nature of International Disputes, in *Basis of Obligations* (1958), 187.

In *Armed Actions*, Honduras submitted that Nicaragua's application, which alleged a number of violations of the prohibition on the use of force and intervention in domestic affairs, was a politically inspired, artificial request which the Court should not entertain. According to Honduras, this was an attempt by Nicaragua to exert political pressure on other States. The Court responded that:

political aspects may be present in any legal dispute brought before it. The Court, as a judicial organ, is however only concerned to establish, first, that the dispute before it is a legal dispute, in the sense of a dispute capable of being settled by the application of principles and rules of international law, and secondly, that the Court has jurisdiction to deal with it, and that that jurisdiction is not fettered by any circumstance rendering the application inadmissible. The purpose of recourse to the Court is the peaceful settlement of such disputes; the Court's judgment is a legal pronouncement, and it cannot concern itself with the political motivation which may lead a State at a particular time, or in particular circumstances, to choose judicial settlement. So far as the objection of Honduras is based on an alleged political inspiration of the proceedings, it therefore cannot be upheld.[34]

The separation between legal rights and political context can be seen in the *Congo-Uganda Armed Activities* case where the Court refused to accept that the state of political relations between States can affect their legal rights:

A period of good or friendly relations between two States should not, without more, be deemed to prevent one of the States from raising a pre-existing claim against the other, either when relations between the two States have again deteriorated or even while the good relations continue. The political climate between States does not alter their legal rights.[35]

The *Nuclear Weapons* Advisory Opinion provided at the request of the World Health Organisation extends the treatment of 'political' questions to the broader area of international law, as opposed to the narrower area of interpreting international instruments. As the Court emphasised:

The fact that this question also has political aspects, as, in the nature of things, is the case with so many questions which arise in international life, does not suffice to deprive it of its character as a 'legal question' and to 'deprive the Court of a competence expressly conferred on it by its Statute'. Whatever its political aspects, the Court cannot refuse to admit the legal character of a question which invites it to discharge an essentially judicial task, namely, an assessment of the legality of the possible conduct of States with regard to the obligations imposed upon them by international law.[36]

[34] *Border and Transborder Armed Actions* (Nicaragua v Honduras), Jurisdiction of the Court and Admissibility of the Application, Judgment of 20 December 1988, *ICJ Reports*, 1988, 69 at 91.

[35] *Case Concerning the Armed Activities on the Territory of the Congo* (Democratic Republic of the Congo v Uganda), Judgment of 19 December 2005, General List No 116, para 294.

[36] *Legality of the Use by a State of Nuclear Weapons in Armed Conflict*, Advisory Opinion, *ICJ Reports*, 1996, 66 at 73–74.

In the Appellate Decision on Jurisdiction in the *Tadic* case, the International Criminal Tribunal for the Former Yugoslavia likewise addressed the political question, considering this notion as archaic and unfounded in law. As the Tribunal put it, as long as the case turns on a legal question capable of a legal answer, courts are duty-bound to take jurisdiction over it, regardless of the political background or the other political facets of the issue, and decide it by reference to the relevant legal principles. Consequently, 'The Appeals Chamber [did] not consider that the International Tribunal is barred from examination of the Defence jurisdictional plea by the so-called "political" or "non-justiciable" nature of the issue it raises.'[37] That 'political' issue was the scope of powers of the UN Security Council, in relation to which the Tribunal thoroughly exercised judicial review.

Another relevant point is that of the political implications of decisions of international tribunals. As Judge Onyeama emphasised in the clearest possible terms in the *Namibia* case:

> In exercising its functions the Court is wholly independent of the other organs of the United Nations and is in no way obliged or concerned to render a judgment or opinion which would be 'politically acceptable'. Its function is, in the words of Article 38 of the Statute, 'to decide in accordance with international law'.[38]

Thus, the independence of the Court goes hand in hand with the separation of international law from politics.

As we can see, the international tribunals strictly separate the political and legal factors present in the particular controversy and focus only on the latter. As soon as the rules of international law can be applied to the relevant dispute, its arguably political character is no longer relevant. This indicates that the value of doctrinal attempts to present international law as influenced by political interests or notions must be assessed accordingly. The international community of States places its reliance on the determinacy of legal regulation through which States, together with other subjects and beneficiaries of international law, know what their rights and obligations are and what the implication of the application of these rights and obligations to their conduct is. The system of legal decision-making does not admit of introducing into it the extra elements of political or policy factors as this would undermine the determinacy and stability of legal regulation.

One significant problem with the entire concept of 'political' disputes or questions is that there is no established criterion for distinguishing them from legal ones. Adherence to such doctrine will necessarily involve subjectivism and arbitrariness in decision-making which would in such cases deprive States of the minimum degree of predictability and fail to protect their expectations in the process of international dispute settlement.

[37] *Tadic*, IT-94–1 (Appeal Chamber), 2 October 1995, para 24.
[38] *ICJ Reports*, 1971, 143.

The consistent treatment in practice of the notion of political questions and disputes makes it abundantly clear that this notion has no independent standing in the international legal system and cannot be taken seriously in determining the meaning of international legal rules or rights and obligations of international legal actors. If a tribunal confronts what is a legal dispute in the first place, it both can and is obliged to settle it through the application of law. The political side of the dispute cannot prevent the tribunal from performing its principal task. This procedural or institutional phenomenon of the judicial function to settle legal disputes has a substantive law corollary, which is the effective applicability of the pertinent legal rules in such a way that the non-legal elements of the dispute do not undermine the resolution of its legal aspect.

The issue of political disputes is by now arguably a resolved question. The implications of this question, however, pervade the multiplicity of questions of interpretation of acts and rules, of the adoption of certain presumptions in the interpretative process, and of the agency in charge of interpretation. Thus it is clear that the judicial function can deal with issues that allegedly (also) appear as political. While it is indisputable that political factors cannot obstruct the application of law to legal disputes, ascertaining the separation between law and politics in the international legal system leads to a related issue of how far legal decision-making can go in assessing the policy issues that may form part of international legal regulation.

In principle, international courts cannot pronounce on issues that are political in the sense that they are outside international legal regulation. As Judge Kellogg emphasised in the *River Meuse* case, if the parties to the Statute of the Permanent Court (and *a fortiori* International Court) had intended to enable the Court to decide the disputes of a purely political nature, in accordance with political and economic expediency, they would have used appropriate language in the text.[39] But the assessment of policy questions could arise in the context where the relevant policy element is part of the relevant legal regulation. As Higgins observes, 'policy considerations,' even though they differ from legal rules, can be an integral element of the legal decision-making process of international tribunals. The assessment of 'extra-legal' considerations is part of the legal process.[40]

Higgins rejects 'the doctrine that decisions made on the narrowest possible basis, avoiding reference to the complex of relationships in the world community, are "legal", whereas a more flexible approach is "political", and therefore not open to the [International] Court'.[41] Higgins further clarifies that 'a dispute is a "legal" dispute if it is to be resolved by authoritative legal decision, no matter what the component elements of that dispute. In other words, there is little reality

[39] Observations by Mr Kellogg, *The Diversion of Water from the Meuse*, Series A/B No 70, Judgment of 28 June 1937, 4 at 34, 40.

[40] R Higgins, Policy Considerations and the International Judicial Process, 17 *ICLQ* (1968), 58 at 61–62.

[41] Higgins (1968), 70.

in any definition of a political, or legal, question; what is relevant is the distinction between a political *method* and a legal *method* of solving disputes.'[42]

If a legal dispute can be resolved by application of international law 'no matter what the component elements of that dispute,' then it follows that international adjudication can resolve the issues of non-law that appear as component elements of governing legal rules involved in the legal dispute. This would be a corollary of the requirement of determinacy of legal regulation, in the sense of obtaining a straightforward and determinate outcome in legal disputes. In international jurisprudence, as the subsequent parts of this study will demonstrate, this process works not in terms of equating or subordinating legal rules to policy factors, but in terms of locating the meaning of policy concepts that constitute part of established legal standards.[43]

5. The Interaction between Legal Regulation and the Sovereign Freedom of Action

The problem of sovereignty has long since been a central issue both in international legal science and in general legal theory. International law is the product of the exercise of sovereignty by States. As the Sole Arbitrator Huber specified in the *Island of Palmas* Award, 'Sovereignty in the relation between States signifies independence. Independence in regard to a portion of the globe is the right to exercise therein, to the exclusion of any other State, the functions of a State.'[44] In this sense, sovereignty implies the supremacy of territorial jurisdiction in relation to persons and events within the territory of the State. At the same time, sovereignty also has an external dimension to it, which is the independence of States in relation to other States. The concept of sovereignty may or may not have undergone some evolution or transformation. A number of factors that were not recognised by international law a hundred years ago, such as individual and group rights, or environmental protection, are currently systemic elements of the international legal system. They do not fall within the sovereignty of the State even if the relevant processes involve the activities of the State within its sovereign territory. But such 'evolution' of State sovereignty does not really concern the structural characteristics of the concept of sovereignty itself, but the agreement and consensus between States to consider or not to consider the relevant matter as being part of the State's sovereign competence. Examples of such agreement and consensus are the expression of the community attitude in multilateral treaties such as the United Nations Charter, or non-binding declarations embodying customary law,

[42] Higgins (1968), 74.

[43] See below Part V.

[44] *Island of Palmas case*, Netherlands v USA, The Hague, 4 April 1928, 2 *RIAA* 829.

such as certain resolutions of the United Nations General Assembly.[45] Thus, the doctrinal views that emphasise 'the impossibility of reconciling the notions of sovereignty which prevailed even as recently as fifty or sixty years ago with the contemporary state of global interdependence'[46] has to be seen as referring to the evolution of the attitude of the international community in relation to legal aspects of certain subject-matters possessing global importance, and not as referring to the inherent and structural elements of State sovereignty.

The present study does not address the broader merits of doctrinal and conceptual aspects of sovereignty. Focusing on sovereignty here is rather intended to examine sovereignty in action, in its relation to established legal obligations and rules. While the existence and fundamental importance of State sovereignty in international relations cannot be sensibly disputed, the present study addresses the dynamics of interaction between sovereignty and obligation, which consists in the question whether the sovereignty of States can affect the content of established international law, and thus of the obligations assumed in the exercise of that very sovereignty.

It is conceptually possible to view the State and its sovereignty as the starting point of the international legal system and to maintain that these come before international law, which is merely the product of State consent to accepting the limitation of its sovereignty. However, this idea would be misguided as it neglects the premise of reciprocal respect for sovereignty as the cardinal principle of international law. The thesis of the primacy of sovereignty only explains the existence of sovereignty; it does not explain why one State is bound to respect the sovereignty of another. The legal concept of sovereignty is possible only if it is seen as the quality if not conferred by, then at least integrated within, the system of international law. The refusal to see sovereignty as such a phenomenon is a denial of the very idea of international law.

It is certainly not the position of this author to subscribe to certain views about the erosion of sovereignty and its replacement by some versions of global governance or global covenant, still less by patterns of hegemony. The international legal system has always been and remains a decentralised legal society in which rules, and hence the limitations on sovereignty, are produced by the consent and agreement of sovereign States. This position has always been among the structural underpinnings of international law, as confirmed at all relevant stages of jurisprudence. In the *Behring Sea* Arbitration, the Arbitral Tribunal made an Award which confirms that sovereign freedom of action can be limited only through consent and agreement. Extra-legal concerns and considerations, even if based on higher goals and values, can have no such effect. The United States claimed the competence to unilaterally exercise jurisdiction in the Behring Sea with a

[45] On UNGA resolutions embodying customary international law see the *Nicaragua* case, *ICJ Reports*, 1986, 100–101.

[46] T Franck, *Fairness in International Law and Institutions* (1995), 4.

view to fur seal preservation. Russia as the Predecessor State had renounced its earlier similar claims and had admitted that its jurisdiction was limited to within cannon shot reach. In any case, Great Britain had not recognised Russian jurisdiction outside its territorial waters that would in any way restrict high seas freedoms. Russia therefore had no such exclusive rights and this legal position passed to the United States with the 1867 Treaty. Therefore, the US had no rights of protection in relation to fur seals.[47]

As the Permanent Court of International Justice observed in the classical case of *Lotus*, no limitation on sovereignty can be presumed to exist. Such limitations can instead only be identified on the basis of specific rules of international law. As the Court put it in the much-quoted passage:

> International law governs relations between independent States. The rules of law binding upon States therefore emanate from their own free will as expressed in conventions or by usages generally accepted as expressing principles of law and established in order to regulate the relations between these co-existing independent communities or with a view to the achievement of common aims. Restrictions upon the independence of States cannot therefore be presumed.[48]

The Court further specified that 'all that can be required of a State is that it should not overstep the limits which international law places upon its jurisdiction; within these limits, its title to exercise jurisdiction rests in its sovereignty'.[49] Even though opposed in some doctrinal quarters, this principle of *Lotus* remains a predominant underlying principle of international law. No viable alternative or replacement of it has so far been developed.

At the same time, the *Lotus* principle is relevant only in terms of clarifying whether there is legal regulation on the relevant subject-matter. But sovereign freedom of action is no longer a relevant principle once it is demonstrated that the pertinent subject-matter in relation to which such freedom is claimed is already regulated by international law. Once this is established, the presumption in favour of sovereignty is no longer relevant. As, for instance, the Permanent Court emphasised in *Wimbledon*, the conclusion of treaties is the exercise of State sovereignty. The Court specified that 'Germany ha[d] to submit to an important limitation of the exercise of the sovereign rights which no one dispute[d] that she possesse[d] over the Kiel Canal.'[50] This perspective accords, among others, with Lauterpacht's approach that sovereign freedom of action is not a regulatory principle.

[47] Award of the Tribunal of Arbitration constituted under the Treaty concluded at Washington, 29 February 1892, between US and UK, 15 August 1893, 6 *AJIL* (1912), 233 at 235–236. The case of *Fisheries Jurisdiction* (Spain v Canada) before the International Court, had it reached the merits stage, would certainly have provided a useful conceptual insight into this problem. See, in general, *Fisheries Jurisdiction* (Spain v Canada), *ICJ Reports*, 1998, 432.

[48] *Lotus*, 1927 *PCIJ Series* A, No 10, 18.

[49] *Id*, 19.

[50] *SS Wimbledon*, Judgment of 17 August 1923, *PCIJ Series* A, No 1, 15 at 24–25.

In the *Lake Lanoux* case, the Arbitral Tribunal dealt with the issue of whether the French diversion of water in the Lake Lanoux area required a prior agreement between France and Spain. This was arguably an area of common interest between the two States, which must have implications for understanding the relevance of freedom of sovereign action in this case. More specifically, according to the Tribunal, 'it must be admitted that the State which is normally competent has lost its right to act alone as a result of the unconditional and arbitrary opposition of another State'. The Tribunal observed that withholding the agreement by the other State could result in 'admitting a "right of assent", a "right of veto", which at the discretion of one State paralyses the exercise of the territorial jurisdiction of another'. The less extreme outcome, according to the Tribunal, was that the parties had an obligation to seek to reach the agreement. However, the Tribunal was explicit in emphasising that:

> the rule that States may utilize the hydraulic power of international watercourses only on condition of a *prior* agreement between the interested States cannot be established as a custom, even less as a general principle of law.[51]

The implication of this approach is that sovereign freedom of action in an area of territorial sovereignty continues unabated. It is noteworthy that even in the area of community of interest, the Tribunal could not go so far as to suggest that, in the absence of specific commitment, the territorial State is under an obligation to accept the limitation of its territorial jurisdiction.

Thus, the *Lake Lanoux* Award follows the previous jurisprudence that sovereign freedom of action of States can only be qualified through the properly established rule of international law. Non-legal considerations are not sufficient to restrict the sovereignty of the State or affect the established legal position.

The *Lotus* framework of interaction between sovereignty and obligation was further refined in the *Barcelona Traction* case which dealt with the exercise of diplomatic protection in relation to the individual shareholders of the company. It was contended that international law allowed such diplomatic protection. As the Court specified:

> the Belgian Government has repeatedly stressed that there exists no rule of international law which would deny the national State of the shareholders the right of diplomatic protection for the purpose of seeking redress pursuant to unlawful acts committed by another State against the company in which they hold shares. This, by emphasizing the absence of any express denial of the right, conversely implies the admission that there is no rule of international law which expressly confers such a right on the shareholders' national State.[52]

[51] 12 *RIAA* 306, 318.
[52] *ICJ Reports*, 1970, 37.

The Court's response was that:

> International law may not, in some fields, provide specific rules in particular cases. In the concrete situation, the company against which allegedly unlawful acts were directed is expressly vested with a right, whereas no such right is specifically provided for the shareholder in respect of those acts. Thus the position of the company rests on a positive rule of both municipal and international law. As to the shareholder, while he has certain rights expressly provided for him by municipal law as referred to in paragraph 42 above [dealing with the relationship between the shareholders and the company], appeal can, in the circumstances of the present case, only be made to the silence of international law. Such silence scarcely admits of interpretation in favour of the shareholder.[53]

Thus, in order to admit diplomatic protection in favour of the shareholder as opposed to the corporation, the Court required the existence of a specific rule to that effect. There was no general principle of international law regulating the protection of shareholding individuals specifically. The protection of the corporation as such could be accommodated within the concept of the nationality link. But the existence of corporations as separate entities linked to their States of nationality made it impossible to conclude that individual shareholders injured in consequence of injury caused to the corporation should enjoy protection through States of their own nationality. The respondent State could not be held judicially answerable. The silence of international law in relation to the position of shareholders specifically favoured presuming against the existence of a rule enabling diplomatic intervention on behalf of shareholders, and the burdening of the host State with having to accept the standing of a State of nationality of shareholders.

Furthermore, the pronouncement in *Barcelona Traction* on the existence of legal regulation and the silence of international law on the particular issue of standing to protect shareholders, as elaborated upon, simultaneously constitutes pronouncement on the completeness and effectiveness of existing general legal regulation on diplomatic protection of shareholders. That rule of international law which links the protection of the company with the State of its nationality is by implication construed effectively so that it is considered as covering both the field of treatment of companies and that of treatment of shareholders. In relation to the former field this rule applies expressly, while in relation to the latter field it applies by implication as the position of shareholders is connected with that of the company. If the rule emphasising the link between State and company is construed effectively, it has to be presumed to apply to the position of shareholders as well. This ensures the *effectiveness of existing legal regulation*. On the other hand, the lack of a specific rule regarding shareholders militates in favour of the residual sovereign freedom of action of States in this field.

Another pertinent question of sovereign freedom of action rarely confronted in doctrine relates to the context in which this sovereign freedom is claimed. Some

[53] *Id*, 38.

fields of international law conceptually based on sovereign freedom of action also operate on a condition of concurrent and competing freedom of action, as opposed to the freedom of one State exclusive of that of another State. The scope of the freedom of action of States depends on *where*, that is in which sphere and area, States act, and on *what is meant by* the freedom of action. The first aspect of the question queries whether the relevant action is performed within the sovereign realm of the State, within its territory, or in the area beyond sovereign powers where the rights of other States also come into play. The second aspect of the question queries whether the freedom of action is *absolute*, that is solely reserved as a matter of right to the State that acts, or *concurrent*, and can also be enjoyed by other States in similar circumstances if such arise.

States are arranged as territorial entities independent of each other and the question of where they act is often material in clarifying whether they are free to act. Thus, in *Lotus*, the Permanent Court emphasised that while the exercise of jurisdiction over the foreign sea vessel through investigation and evidence-gathering would be illegal on the high seas, the very same action would lawfully fall within the jurisdiction of the same State if that jurisdiction were exercised on the national territory of that State.[54]

Similarly, the perception of the freedom of action in certain cases as *concurrent* is necessary for accommodating the basic requirement that in exercising its freedom of action, a State shall not be justified in encroaching upon similar freedom of action that other States in principle possess. As the Arbitral Tribunal emphasised in the *Casablanca* Award, 'The conflict of jurisdictions cannot be decided by an absolute rule which would in a general manner accord the preference to either of the two concurrent jurisdictions.'[55] The Permanent Court in *Lotus* similarly approved the objective territorial jurisdiction of Turkey on the condition that this jurisdiction was concurrent with the nationality jurisdiction France could potentially exercise in relation to the same situation. The Court denied that there was a customary rule upholding the exclusive jurisdiction of the State of nationality of the perpetrator.[56] As the Permanent Court further specified:

> Neither the exclusive jurisdiction of either State, nor the limitations of the jurisdiction of each to the occurrences which took place on the respective ships would appear calculated to satisfy the requirements of justice and effectively to protect the interests of the two States. It is only natural that each should be able to exercise jurisdiction and to do so in respect of the incident as a whole. It is therefore a case of concurrent jurisdiction.[57]

Thus, freedom of action is not always conceived of as absolute in jurisprudence but refers to the rights of other States as well. In this particular context of jurisdiction

[54] *Lotus*, 25.
[55] JB Scott, *Hague Court Reports* (1916), 114.
[56] *Lotus*, 25–26.
[57] *Id*, 30–31.

of States, freedom of action means mandating the exercise of jurisdiction on a first come, first served basis. In other fields, for instance those relating to the exercise of territorial sovereignty, the *Lotus* principle may signify the absolute freedom of action by the State.

The exercise by the State of its sovereign freedom could affect the fields that may overlap with the comparable jurisdiction and competence of other States. Consequently, some graduation of the freedom of action can be seen in jurisprudence. In the cases of *Anglo-Norwegian Fisheries* and *Nottebohm* the International Court addressed the rights of States that were originally based on their freedom of action, and moreover form part of normal sovereignty prerogatives. In *Fisheries* this was the right to adopt the method of delimiting the territorial sea; in *Nottebohm*, this was the right to confer nationality on individuals. In both cases, however, the Court emphasised the international aspect of the exercise of the right, as complementing and constraining the initial sovereign freedom of action.[58] In *Fisheries*, the national regulation of the territorial sea delimitation method affected what otherwise would have been the high seas, which justified viewing the problem as having an international aspect. In *Nottebohm*, the unfettered freedom of States to confer nationality on anyone they please would impose too much of a burden on other States by making them accountable, in terms of the rights of foreigners, to the States that have a nominal nationality link to the relevant person, but no effective connection.

Another perspective on the freedom of action of States is given by the International Court in the *Fisheries Jurisdiction* case, in the context of interaction between the freedom of action and concurrent rights of other States. The Court focused on the notion of preferential rights to fishing, and pronounced that:

> The concept of preferential rights is not compatible with the exclusion of all fishing activities of other States. A coastal State entitled to preferential rights is not free, unilaterally and according to its own uncontrolled discretion, to determine the extent of those rights. The characterization of the coastal State's rights as preferential implies a certain freedom but cannot imply the extinction of the concurrent rights of other priority States, and particularly of a State which, like the Applicant, has for many years been engaged in fishing in the waters in question, such fishing activity being important to the economy of the country concerned. The coastal State has to take into account and pay regard to the position of such other States, particularly when they have established an economic dependence on the same fishing grounds. Accordingly, the fact that Iceland is entitled to claim preferential rights does not suffice to justify its claim unilaterally to exclude the Applicant's fishing vessels from all fishing activity in the waters beyond the limits agreed to in the 1961 Exchange of Notes.[59]

[58] On the *Fisheries* case see above note 18; on *Nottebohm* see below Chapter 5.

[59] *Fisheries Jurisdiction*, *ICJ Reports*, 1974, 27–28.

The Court further emphasised that 'preferential rights of the coastal State and the established rights of other States were considered as, in principle, continuing to co-exist'.[60] The Court also stated the conceptual underpinnings of this position:

> It is one of the advances in maritime international law resulting from the intensification of fishing, that the former laissez-faire treatment of the living resources of the sea in the high seas has been replaced by a recognition of a duty to have due regard to the rights of other States and the needs of conservation for the benefit of all.[61]

This legal position of balancing the rights and obligations of different States results from the exercise of sovereign freedom of action in an area which is not under the sovereignty of any State.

The pattern of *Behring Sea* and *Lotus* is a dominant pattern of relationship between sovereign freedom and legal obligation in the international legal system. On the other hand, the pattern of *Fisheries* and *Nottebohm* emphasises the limitations that follow where the exercise of sovereign freedom intersects international legal regulation or sovereign freedom of another State. As we can see, Britain could in principle freely perform the relevant activities in the Behring Sea, because these activities burdened the rights, jurisdiction and sovereignty of no other State. On the other hand, in the similar context of maritime spaces Norway could not establish its maritime boundary without respecting the relevant requirements of international law, however general. Doing so would cause Norway to intersect the high seas freedom of other States. In this latter case, sovereign freedom continues but becomes qualified by the respective outer limit imposed by international law.

6. Standards of Reviewability and Excusability under International Law

The dichotomy between sovereign freedom and legal obligation is a starting point in understanding the graduated field of conflicting claims, one of which is based on freedom of action and the other on the rule restricting that freedom. The above analysis has demonstrated that such conflicting claims can be advanced not only in the blanket field of sovereign action, but also in that of conflict between preferential and concurrent rights.

Before moving on to the more detailed analysis developed in subsequent chapters, it is necessary to examine the normative framework in which the dynamics of sovereign freedom and its relationship to legal obligation can develop. In general freedom of sovereign action and legal obligation appear as two mutually coexistent precepts, and their fields of operation are separated from each other.

[60] *Id*, 30.
[61] *Id*, 31.

However, current international law has a more complex and multi-level background against which State action can be reviewed, excused or presumed to be left to the field of sovereign freedom of action. Apart from the straightforward understanding of residual sovereign freedom of action that comes into play in the absence of a specific rule limiting it, there may be some grounds for attempting to reserve that sovereign freedom in defiance of existing legal obligations, but seemingly with due normative basis and justification. The determinacy of legal regulation necessarily implies that claims that there are multiple grounds of reviewability and excusability of State action in respect of the same subject-matter have to be resolved by identifying the single legal outcome that applies to the relevant facts. However, just like the relatively simple dichotomy of sovereign freedom and legal obligation, these more complex frameworks offer, as it were, the 'initial' dichotomy between the two normative standards, one of which is seen by the relevant State as appropriate to rely on for the same purposes as it would rely on sovereign freedom of action resulting from the absence of a relevant legal obligation.

These frameworks, allegedly preserving freedom of action, do not strictly derive from the *Lotus* principle, which points to a residual freedom of action in the absence of legal regulation. These are instead grounds that are integrated within the structure of international legal regulation, provided for under general international law, or under specific treaty frameworks. Without prejudice to the actual outcomes, claims of such excusability may be found in the following related examples:

(1) It may be claimed that an obligation under a treaty rule does not prejudice the operation of the pertinent general international law rule.[62]

(2) It may also be asserted that an obligation under a substantive rule of conduct is overtaken by the freedom to act under a defence rule, such as circumstances precluding wrongfulness, or reciprocity rules under the law of treaties.[63]

(3) It may be claimed that a reservation entered to a specific provision of a treaty precludes the invocation of that provision in relation to the reserving State.[64] Reservation does not inherently qualify as law, because it expresses merely the will of the State that authors it. Whether it will ultimately end up as expressing the consent of the relevant States depends on the acceptance of

[62] See Article 31(3)(c) of the 1969 Vienna Convention on the Law of Treaties. See Chapter 10 below.

[63] On circumstances precluding wrongfulness see Chapter V of Part I of the ILC's Articles on State Responsibility, Articles 20–27 and their commentary, in Report of the International Law Commission on the work of its Fifty-third session (2001), *Official Records of the General Assembly, Fifty-sixth session, Supplement No. 10* (A/56/10). See also Article 60 of the 1969 Vienna Convention on the Law of Treaties.

[64] See Articles 2.1(d) and 19 to 23 of the 1969 Vienna Convention, on the legal regime governing reservations to treaties. The legal regime of reservations to treaties is beyond the scope of this study.

this reservation and its general permissibility, including its compatibility with the object and purpose of the treaty. However, the fact of making a reservation could provide at least a *prima facie* basis for making a claim that competes with the existing legal regulation.

(4) It may be claimed that the obligation stipulated in a mainline treaty obligation is restricted by the more specific exception to that obligation, which results in reserving the sovereign freedom of action of the relevant contracting State. Such claims arise and are often upheld in relation to the margin of appreciation arrangements in the relevant treaties, or clauses relating to emergency derogations from treaty obligations. Such treaty-based exceptions are normally justified by reference to public interest and policy factors such as the prevention of disorder or crime; protection of health or morals, or natural resources; the interests of national security, territorial integrity or public safety; or war or other public emergency threatening the life of the nation. For instance, applying the margin of appreciation under Article 8 of the European Convention on Human Rights, relating to the protection of private and family life, proceeds from the assumption that while the privacy rights are guaranteed as a whole, the State-party is entitled, under the specified circumstances, to act in a way that adversely affects those guaranteed rights. Likewise, while Article 1 of Protocol I to the European Convention protects property rights, States-parties are permitted to adversely affect those protected rights if the public interest so requires. The philosophy of this phenomenon is well illustrated in the judgment of the European Court of Human Rights in *Sporrong & Lönnorth*, where the Court stated that Article 1 of Protocol I:

> comprises three distinct rules. The first rule, which is of a general nature, enounces the principle of peaceful enjoyment of property; it is set out in the first sentence of the first paragraph. The second rule covers deprivation of possessions and subjects it to certain conditions; it appears in the second sentence of the same paragraph. The third rule recognises that the States are entitled, amongst other things, to control the use of property in accordance with the general interest, by enforcing such laws as they deem necessary for the purpose; it is contained in the second paragraph.
>
> The Court must determine, before considering whether the first rule was complied with, whether the last two are applicable.[65]

In the case of the European Convention on Human Rights, there is no express determination or allocation of priorities as between the mainline obligations defining human rights and specific exceptions that define their limitations and consequently vest States with a certain degree of freedom of action. Nevertheless, the European Court of Human Rights uses the test of compatibility of the

[65] *Sporrong & Lönnorth v Sweden*, Application Nos 7151/75, 7152/75, Judgment of 23 September 1982, para 61; see further Chapter 11 below.

exception with the mainline obligation. As the Court emphasised in the *Vogt* case, it had to determine whether the 'restriction' on the freedom of speech under Article 10(2) was compatible with that very freedom under Article 10(1). Even if the exceptions of 'legitimate aim' under Article 10(2) of the Convention form part of the freedom of expression under the entire Article 10, the Court's approach was to verify whether the restriction was reconcilable with freedom of expression. Such hierarchical relationship between the mainline obligation and exceptions went hand in hand with the narrow construction of the exception.[66]

All this illustrates the interaction between different rules addressing the same subject-matter. It is certainly true that the relevant rules operate with those built-in limitations, which distinguish the margin of appreciation phenomenon from other collisions between reviewability and excusability standards. But what matters at the present stage is that the legal framework admits of the *prima facie* validity of conflicting claims regarding conduct and legal regulation on the same subject-matter. This phenomenon is the same in substance, though not in form, as in other contexts of normative conflict or defence.

These fields are regulated by their individual frameworks in the law of treaties, the law of State responsibility or the general framework of the sources of law. But they are conceptually united by their potential basis for conflicting assertions as to the existence and scope of sovereign freedom of State action. In way that all these correlations relate to the modification of the qualification of State action, they constitute the ramifications of one single phenomenon.

In practice, the commonality in essence of these different categories is confirmed in the field of treaty interpretation. For instance, the *Wimbledon* case before the Permanent Court of International Justice simultaneously related, as a matter of single issue and context, to the operation of the letter of the treaty in contrast to the residual sovereign freedom of action, and to a general international law regulation, namely the regime of neutrality in time of war, which arguably prescribed a result different from that required under the treaty.

The inherent commonality in substance between these formally diverse fields can also be seen from the observation of Judges Matscher *et al* in the *Brannigan* case before the European Court of Human Rights, which concerned the application of Article 5 of the European Convention. As the Judges observed:

> a derogation pursuant to Article 15 [of the European Convention on Human Rights] may be classified as a temporary 'reservation' (within the meaning of Article 64) as regards its 'substantive' effects. The difference between the two devices—reservation and derogation—lies in the fact that, in respect of the former, the Court's power of review is confined to the formal aspects of the validity—within the meaning of Article 64—of the declaration relating thereto, whereas for the latter the Court must also satisfy itself that

[66] *Vogt v Germany*, Application No 17851/91, 26 September 1995, para 52; see further Chapter 11 below.

> the substantive conditions for its validity have been met (not only when the derogation is notified, but also subsequently whenever the Government relies on such a derogation). However... the 'substantive' effects of a reservation and a declaration of derogation, provided that they are validly made, are exactly the same, in other words quite simply the inapplicability of a specific provision of the Convention.[67]

This statement is particularly noteworthy because it emphasises the substantive impact of certain transactions on the existing legal position, and this substantive impact is not exclusively due to the form of those transactions.

All these correlations may require, in a general sense, some sort of balancing values behind each relevant conflicting claim, which in a juridical sense relates to the assessment of the legal framework they are part of. Thus, the ultimate outcome depends on the requirements of the relevant treaty regime, including its object and purpose, or the relevant aspects of the general nature of international law, of which the *lex specialis* principle is the most prominent. Guidance in resolving such controversies is an indispensable precondition and an inevitable task before any meaningful doctrine of effectiveness of international legal regulation, notably treaty obligations, can be formulated. The conclusive clarification of those controversies involves the examination of the principles of interpretation, and of the relevance of various headings of non-law.

7. Evaluation

This chapter has dealt with a number of fundamental questions related to the problem of integrity of international legal regulation, and these constitute the starting point for analysis of the problems dealt with in the subsequent parts of this study, such as the issues of the interaction of law with non-law and interpretation of rules and instruments. This chapter has demonstrated that the relationship between law and non-law is in essence a problem of determinacy of legal regulation. It also has demonstrated that identification of the scope of non-law elements in a legal rule, as well as interpretation of legal standards in general, serves the goal of securing the determinate outcome produced by legal regulation to apply to facts and conduct of States. It has also demonstrated that the interpretation of legal standards, including their non-law elements, may crucially depend on the understanding of interaction between legal obligation and sovereign freedom, which ultimately translates into the problem of effectiveness of legal regulation.

[67] *Brannigan v UK*, Application Nos 14553/89, 14554/89, 25 May 1993, Concurring Opinion by Judge Matscher Joined by Judge Morenilla.

Having established the criteria of completeness, effectiveness and determinacy of legal regulation in international law, these criteria must be applied to specific areas involving the elements of non-law that can contest this effectiveness. In order to identify the relevant headings of non-law, it is first necessary to elaborate upon the characteristics of legal rules that distinguish them from the categories of non-law. In other words, the threshold of legal regulation must be identified.

PART II

THRESHOLD OF LEGAL REGULATION

3

The Essence of the Threshold of Legal Regulation

1. Consensual Basis of International Law and the Threshold of Legal Regulation

This part of the study deals with identifying the threshold of legal regulation in international law. The threshold of international law is defined as 'a point where non-law ends and where law begins'. This is different from viewing law not as an independent system but as part of social development, there being no clear-cut threshold between what is legal and what is not in the international legal society. If there is no legal formalism, what differentiates law from other social sciences disappears.[1] For the purposes of this study, the identification of the threshold of legal regulation will delimit the field in which categories of non-law will be identified, as distinct from the field in which principles of interpretation secure the effectiveness of legal regulation.

More specifically, this analysis focuses on the factors responsible for the crossing of the threshold of law-making. For a start, the conceptual and systemic aspects of the threshold of legal regulation have to be examined, which requires establishing the scope of positive law and the relevance of natural law, including its modern versions. In terms of specific sources of positive law, this analysis will examine the factors responsible for the crossing of the threshold of legal regulation in the process of custom-generation. With the other principal source of positive international law—treaties—the crossing of the threshold of legal regulation is a very straightforward matter unlikely to give rise to any doctrinal controversies.[2] The main issue arising from the threshold of legal regulation in terms of customary law is the relevance of the consensual element, especially the essence of the psychological element of custom-generation, because this is the principal factor when assessing the relevance of customary law as source of positive law. Finally, the link between customary law and natural law, for example,

[1] A Pellet, The Normative Dilemma: Will and Consent in International Law-making, 12 *Australian YIL* (1988–89), 22 at 22, 25.

[2] See, in particular, Articles 6 to 17 of the 1969 Vienna Convention on the Law of Treaties, regarding the expression of consent to be bound by the treaty.

the issue of inherent rules, is examined in order to demonstrate the parameters of the limits on positivism.

The scholarship of international law has for centuries elaborated upon diverse doctrinal explanations of international law. Given the range of the sources of international law in terms of Article 38 of the International Court's Statute, above all treaty and custom, it seems that the most plausible explanation of the basis and character of international law is positivism. This does not mean, as the following analysis will demonstrate, that there are no limits on positivism. There are indeed certain fields in relation to which positive law reasoning may prove insufficient to provide effective legal regulation. In such cases appeal can and should be made to certain extra-positivist factors which complement, rather than contradict, positive legal regulation. But in terms of background reasoning, the search for the relevant international legal position must always take account of the sources of positive law. At different historical stages of the development of international legal reasoning, positivism had different degrees of acceptance and doctrinal implications. In some instances positivism coexisted with other theories, such as that of natural law, while in other cases it aspired to exclude the relevance of rules and principles not properly derived from externally ascertainable sources of law.

Positive law generally refers to law that is positively laid down. As Ago defines it, positive law is 'law which is laid down (*gesetzt*), and the character of positivity is always conferred on the legal rule by its being derived from some creative act which actually came into being, thus being historically perceptible'.[3] The essence of positivism does not refer to the form or procedure in which the legal rules are produced. It merely requires that the law be laid down in an externally ascertainable way. Given that, not all 'positivist' approaches can explain the essence of international law. In terms of early positivism, Austin identified positive law with law laid down by the supreme government to the subordinated persons and entities, and on that basis denied the legal character of international law. As Austin put it, 'if the government receiving the command were in a state of subjection to the other, the command, though fashioned on the law of nations, would amount to a positive law'.[4] Consequently, international law as law formed between independent political societies is not considered to be positive law.[5]

Identifying positivism with Austin's version results in the negation of international law. It does not seem that subordination and hierarchy between the law-giver and subjects of law is a necessary attribute of positive law-making. Nor does positivism restrict its focus to one specific type of positive rules, such as written law, to the exclusion of other categories of rules.[6] All positivism implies is that

[3] R Ago, Positive Law and International Law, 51 *AJIL* (1957), 691 at 697.

[4] J Austin, *The Province of Jurisprudence Determined* (1954), 141–142.

[5] *Id*, 200–201.

[6] As argued, among others, by Hans Morgenthau, Positivism, Functionalism, and International Law, 34 *AJIL* (1940), 260.

law must be laid down through the externally ascertainable process; it must be possible to refer to the externally identifiable source it derives from.

Positivism separates law from mere aspirations and subjective expressions of the exigencies of justice. Positive law is defined differently on different occasions. It is conceived as the law enacted by the competent authority; law that actually operates with efficacy; or law that is regarded as socially desirable in terms of social pattern and opinion.[7] In terms of positivist philosophy, all these approaches are acceptable as they refer to positively observable rules and data. But from the viewpoint of the character of international law, where State consent is the principal basis of legal obligations, positive law can only be described as the law laid down through consent and agreement of the actors that are entitled to create rules of international law. Positivism and consensualism are necessary in international law owing to the need for coherency and predictability of the legal system, the legitimacy of which rests on the expression of the will of States which know of no sovereign government over and above them. The main essence of international law is best explained by reference to consensual positivism as developed in the writings of Anzilotti.

Anzilotti develops the classic positivist vision of international law in which he tries to negate the relevance of extra-legal, or extra-consensual, factors in explaining the basis and binding force of international law. As a starting-point, Anzilotti accepts that the rules of State behaviour respond to specific needs and interests of these States, or to the exigencies of justice which penetrate the social consciousness of the time. However, these are only material factors behind the rules of international law. The rules themselves are established through the expression of will and through this the social consciousness is translated into legal rules. But law, as a system of rules, exists only because this process of translation of values through will into rules takes place and only to the extent that this process is accomplished.[8]

Positivism is the only possible way of explaining how the bulk of international law is created and operates. Unlike other schools of thought, such as policy-oriented, sociological, liberal, critical, feminist or others, positivism does not refer to values or perceptions. Positivism is unique in referring to structural foundations of international law. In this sense, positivism is not a doctrine; it is a reflection of the structure and system of international law. In other words, positivism is the basis of international legal reasoning. It follows from the fact that States are both principal producers and principal consumers of international law. In this sense, positivism can explain the legitimacy of international rights and obligations that bind States in a way that no other approach can explain it. Likewise, positivism is the only framework that can provide for uniform understanding of the international legal position on a particular matter, by referring to what

[7] For discussion of all these options see Ago (1957), 712–717.
[8] D Anzilotti, *Cours de droit international* (1929), 44–45, 67.

has actually been agreed as between international legal persons. In this respect positivism differs from theories that are subjectively manipulable.

While there can be meaningful discourse on individual aspects and implications of positivism, there can be no sound basis for challenging the thesis of positivism itself because it constitutes the main explanation for the creation and operation of international law.

There have been several attacks on the relevance of legal positivism in explaining the essence of international law. The most persistent doctrinal attack is undertaken in support of the theory that emphasises socio-political factors in understanding international law. Even before the formation of the New Haven policy-oriented school, Hans Morgenthau argued that positivism fails to consider the socio-political realities underlying the process of international law and to pass judgement upon the ethical value or practical appropriateness of legal rules.[9] Morgenthau develops a functional theory under which 'any fundamental change of social forces underlying the system of international law of necessity induces the prospective beneficiaries of the change to bring about a corresponding change of the legal rules'. Thus, the validity of international legal rules has to be derived not from their enactment, but from the will and interest in complying with them, and from actual compliance. Morgenthau thus suggests 'the functional condition of validity' under which only those rules are valid that can be enforced at a particular moment.[10] As can be seen, Morgenthau does not deny that international law is a body of rules. In this sense his approach differs from the New Haven policy-oriented school which prefers to view international law as a set of policy-oriented decisions. What unites these different trends is the emphasis on the fluidity and flexibility of international law as they perceive it, which, if implemented in practice, would deprive much of international law of its dependable and intelligible meaning.

Morgenthau's functional theory contradicts the fundamental thesis of continuous validity and binding force of international legal rules that are properly enacted according to law-making techniques. To say the least, there has never been suggested a method which would help in determining how and to what extent non-compliance with legal rules undermines their validity. The evaluation of existing legal rules by reference to their ethical value or practical appropriateness necessarily involves pre-empting the will and judgement of States in adopting the relevant legal regulation. Such evaluation also opens the door for perpetuating the diversity of mutually exclusive appreciations of ethical value and appropriateness, and effectively approves the auto-interpretation by States of their rights and obligations. In practical terms, this position amounts to justifying non-compliance with, and violation of international law by another name. A further shortcoming of this attack on positivism is that, by contradicting

[9] Morgenthau (1940), 260 at 261, 267–268.
[10] *Id*, 275.

the consensual premise of positivism, this approach justifies attempts by States and groups of States to impose legal regulation on others. Given that positivism expresses the reality of international legal regulation, this approach is not sustainable.

The two principal implications of the positivist profile of international law relate to the threshold of legal regulation. The first impact is that this threshold is crossed only by those rules that are established as rules following from the accepted sources of law. The establishment of rules in this way contrasts with the assessment of their inherent or social value and utility. The second impact is that the threshold of legal regulation is crossed by the relevant rule or standard only *after* it crystallises through the relevant source of law, as opposed to consideration of the likelihood that the relevant legal change may occur in the future.

The first of the above implications is easily observable in jurisprudence. No international case has ever been decided on the basis of desirability or utility of the projected legal regulation. The International Court's positivist approach is observable in the *Gulf of Maine* case. The Chamber of the Court emphasised that legal regulation is produced not by 'preconceived assertions' of the parties, but by 'any convincing demonstration of the existence of the rules that each had hoped to find established by international law'.[11]

If the positive law is silent on the relevant subject, the desirability or utility of the relevant rule cannot be a replacement. In some cases, the matter is simply not subjected to a determinate legal regulation. This was emphasised in the *North Sea* case where the Court had concluded that the equidistance method of continental shelf delimitation could not be applied to the case. The 1958 Geneva Convention stipulated that that method was not applicable to Germany which was not party to it. According to Judge Tanaka, equidistance was the most practical and appropriate method, and he found it necessary for the delimitation method to be objective and clear.[12] As the Court itself emphasised, the equidistance method was a useful and practicable method, but it did not consider this method to be based on the accepted legal rule. As the Court further emphasised, 'it is not the case that if the equidistance principle is not a rule of law, there has to be as an alternative some other single equivalent rule'. In the same context, the Court maintained that 'there are still rules and principles of law to be applied; and in the present case it is not the fact either that rules are lacking, or that the situation is one for the unfettered appreciation of the Parties'.[13] The solution in this case was to be sought by reference to equity, which possessed normative value not on its own, but due to the reference to it in the fundamental rule of international law regarding the delimitation of maritime boundaries.

[11] *ICJ Reports*, 1984, 298.
[12] *ICJ Reports*, 1969, 182.
[13] *Id*, 46.

In *Gulf of Maine*, the Chamber of the Court likewise denoted equidistance as a practical method. It had rendered undeniable service in a number of cases. But it was not a legal rule.[14] The Chamber dealt with the long arguments of the US and Canada regarding methods of maritime delimitation, including the factors of adjacency and proximity. The Chamber stated that each party's reasoning was based on a false premise. Their 'error lie[s] precisely in searching general international law for, as it were, a set of rules which are not there'.[15] The Chamber thought it 'unrewarding, especially in a new and still unconsolidated field like that involving the quite recent extension of the claims of States to areas which were until yesterday zones of the high seas, to look to general international law to provide a readymade set of rules that can be used for solving any delimitation problems that arise'.[16] In other words, the relevant legal regulation would exist only if it could be proved with adequate evidence. The Court's approach largely reflects Anzilotti's approach to correlation between social utility of the projected rule and the actual legal regulation.

The second of the above implications is also well received in jurisprudence. An important aspect of identifying the threshold of law is to distinguish between the accepted legal rule and the possibility of the emergence of a new legal regime. According to Lauterpacht, the application of law means application of the existing law. Law may be changed by the appropriate means of particular or collective legislation. But this is not a task to be performed by tribunals.[17] This problem has been judicially discussed in relation to the law of the sea. The International Court in the *Fisheries Jurisdiction* case faced the question of relevance of codification efforts that were in progress at that stage:

In recent years the question of extending the coastal State's fisheries jurisdiction has come increasingly to the forefront. The Court is aware that a number of States has asserted an extension of fishery limits. The Court is also aware of present endeavours, pursued under the auspices of the United Nations, to achieve in a third Conference on the Law of the Sea the further codification and progressive development of this branch of the law, as it is of various proposals and preparatory documents produced in this framework, which must be regarded as manifestations of the views and opinions of individual States and as vehicles of their aspirations, rather than as expressing principles of existing law. The very fact of convening the third Conference on the Law of the Sea evidences a manifest desire on the part of all States to proceed to the codification of that law on a universal basis, including the question of fisheries and conservation of the living resources of the sea. Such a general desire is understandable since the rules of international maritime law have been the product of mutual accommodation, reasonableness and co-operation. So it was in the past, and so it necessarily is today. In the circumstances, the Court, as a court

[14] *Gulf of Maine*, 1984, 297.
[15] *Id*, 298.
[16] *Id*, 299.
[17] H Lauterpacht, *The Function of Law in the International Community* (1933), 373–374.

of law, cannot render judgment *sub specie legis ferendae*, or anticipate the law before the legislator has laid it down.[18]

Thus, the Court adopts a cautious view on legal proposals that do not clearly express the agreement of and between States. The Court further notes that its judgment 'cannot preclude the Parties from benefiting from any subsequent developments in the pertinent rules of international law'.[19]

In the *Tunisia–Libya* case the International Court was asked in the Special Agreement to decide not only on the basis of international law but also taking account of 'accepted trends' of the law of the sea developed at the Third Law of the Sea Conference. These 'trends' are not precisely the same as the accepted legal rules. The Court's approach views such trends as relevant only so far as they reflect the evolution of the legal position. The Court was ready to consider such a 'trend' if 'it embodies or crystallizes a pre-existing or emergent rule of customary law'.[20] According to Judge Arechaga, such a trend 'still may have a bearing on the decision of the Court, not as part of applicable law, but as an element in the interpretation of existing rules or as an indication of the direction in which such rules should be interpreted'.[21]

A further indication of the limitation of legal standards to those accepted and agreed by States can be found in the *Mox Plant* case. In this case the Arbitral Tribunal faced the interpretation of Article 9(3) of the OSPAR Convention which provided for the right to refuse a request for information which, under 'applicable international regulations', qualifies as information affecting commercial and industrial confidentiality. According to Ireland, these applicable regulations meant 'international law and practice' regarding access to environmental information. That allegedly included the 1992 Rio Declaration on Environment and Development. Such instruments were to be interpreted in the light of evolving international law. According to Britain, 'applicable international regulations' meant only properly enacted and legally binding regulations.[22]

The Tribunal distinguished this case from *Libya–Malta*, where the law *in statu nascendi* was made relevant by express designation in the Special Agreement. In that case the International Court applied these standards because the parties instructed it, not because they were 'almost law'. The Parties could in principle instruct the Tribunal to apply standards that were not part of general international law, but without such authorisation the Tribunal could not go beyond the existing law. As the Tribunal eloquently put it, 'This is not to say that a tribunal cannot apply customary international law of a recent vintage, but that it must in fact be

18 *Fisheries Jurisdiction*, UK v Iceland, Merits, *ICJ Reports*, 1974, 23–24.
19 *Id*, 33.
20 *ICJ Reports*, 1982, 38.
21 Separate Opinion, *ICJ Reports*, 1982, 108.
22 *Mox Plant*, Ireland v UK, Final Award of 2 July 2003, paras 93–98.

customary international law.'[23] Evolving international law could not impact the rights and obligations of States, either directly or as an interpretative factor. This was so, because 'States Parties are entitled to have applied to them and their peoples that to which they have agreed and not things to which they have not agreed.'[24]

In *EC–Hormones*, the WTO Appellate Body similarly rejected the relevance of non-binding normative standards. In interpreting Article 3.2 of the Agreement on Sanitary and Phytosanitary Measures (SPS Agreement), the Appellate Body observed that the measures that must, according to that clause, be 'based on' certain international standards, are not the same as those which must 'conform to' those standards. The reference to these standards was meant as a goal to be achieved, while equating 'based on' with 'conform to' would mean that States-parties had accepted these standards as binding. This was not the case.[25]

While the threshold of legal regulation is strict and has to be cleared with evidence, the requirement of the effectiveness of existing legal regulation can justify implying the consequential legal regulation in the existing (expressly stipulated) regulation. The clarification of this latter question depends not on the consensual evidence as such, but on interpretation of the relevant rules and instruments. For instance, in the *Polish War Vessels* case, the Permanent Court of International Justice addressed the issue of whether the treaty-stipulated rights to station commercial vessels implied the right to station war vessels. As the Court put it:

The fact that Poland claims special rights and privileges for her war vessels in the port of Danzig, renders it necessary to find some juridical basis for the claim. The port of Danzig is not Polish territory, and therefore the rights claimed by Poland would be exercised in derogation of the rights of the Free City. Such rights must therefore be established on a clear basis.

The Court acknowledged that the treaty was silent on the issue of war vessels, yet went on to observe that:

the Treaty of Versailles makes no mention of Polish war vessels in connection with Danzig. It contains no stipulations specifically conferring any rights upon them. That

[23] *Id*, paras 99–100; this is in accordance with the affirmation in the *Nicaragua* case that the resolutions of international organisations can be applicable law only if they embody customary rules, *ICJ Reports*, 1986, 14 at 99 ff.

[24] *Mox Plant*, paras 101–102.

[25] *EC Measures concerning Meat and Meat Products (Hormones)*, WT/D526/AB/R, AB-1997–4, Report of the Appellate Body, 16 February 1998 paras 164–165; the improper appreciation of evidence in support of the relevant claimed rule of conventional or customary law can cause in some cases the undue encroachment on the ambit of the pertinent treaty provisions. For instance, the reference to the allegedly existing general international law on State immunity caused the European Court of Human Rights in *Al-Adsani* and the UK House of Lords to justify according the immunity to relevant States in defiance of the absence of any corresponding limitation in Article 6 of the European Convention on Human Rights. While general international law is anyway subordinated to *lex specialis* under treaties (see below Chapter 10), the European Court and the House of Lords defied the *lex specialis* principle on the basis of customary rules whose existence they had not established. For detail see the references in Chapter 6 below (note 21).

fact alone, however, is not sufficient to dispose of the question. It is necessary to examine these provisions in order to see whether their natural interpretation would cover such rights as are now claimed by Poland, even though they make no specific mention of war vessels.[26]

The Court then went on to interpret the relevant provisions of the Versailles Treaty to clarify the effect of the silence of the Treaty. The conclusion was that Polish war vessels had none of the rights that Poland claimed for them. The Court was 'not satisfied that the principles which are said to be inherent in the establishment of Danzig as a Free City afford any basis for a claim of right on the part of Poland for access to and anchorage for war vessels in the port of Danzig'.[27] But in terms of approach the Court affirmed that crossing of the legal threshold is to be proved with clear and specific evidence. In particular, establishing the rights of the State outside its territory is subject to strict proof. The Court simultaneously affirmed that crossing of the legal threshold, in this case the bare claim or interest being translated into a legal rule, is a matter of interpretation of the relevant legal instrument, a complex analysis requiring the consideration of all available and admissible evidence. The silence of the text is material, but not absolutely crucial.

A similar approach is observable in the decision of the UN Human Rights Committee in *JB v Canada*. The question was whether Article 22 of the International Covenant on Civil and Political Rights, which guarantees freedom of association, also implies the right to strike. The Committee emphasised that 'Since the right to strike is not *expressis verbis* included in Article 22, the Committee must interpret whether the right to freedom of association necessarily implies the right to strike, as contended by the authors of the communication.'[28] The Committee examined the ordinary meaning, object and purpose, and preparatory work of the Covenant, and found out that the right to strike was not included or implied in Article 22.[29] This is yet another confirmation that the silence of the text did not dispose of the issue and the outcome depended on interpretation as opposed to consensual evidence.[30]

All these instances confirm that the threshold of international legal regulation is based on the precepts of consensual positivism, which emphasises the consent and agreement between States as opposed to other considerations such as utility, social desirability, or prospective change of the relevant legal position. At the same time, positivism leads to the requirement of effectiveness of legal regulation to enable the outcome of state consent and agreement to operate meaningfully.

[26] *Access to, or Anchorage in, the port of Danzig, of Polish War Vessels*, Advisory Opinion No 22 of 12 November 1931, *PCIJ Series* A/B, No 43, 142.

[27] *Id*, 143–144.

[28] *J. B. et al. v. Canada*, Communication No 118/1982, UN Doc CCPR/C/OP/1 at 34 (1984), paras 6.1–6.2.

[29] *Id*, para 6.3.

[30] See also above Chapter 2, and below Chapter 4, Section 6, and Chapter 11.

If the proper role of positivism is considered, it relates to the emergence of legal rules. Once we deal with legal rules already in existence, it is unsound to rigidly apply consensual positivism to every single element of the relevant rule, its normative implications, or the outcome of its interpretation. Positivism only warns against adopting legal regulation contrary to the will and consent of the State. It does not put constraints on the operation of existing legal regulation that serves the final and effective solution of the relevant legal controversies and situations.

None of the above is to say that there are no limits on positivism. But the existence of such limits cannot be assumed without more. Where a positive legal regulation affirmatively governs the relevant situation, it can only be set aside if it contradicts a rule of public policy (peremptory norm). Such considerations absent, there can be no qualification to the scope and operation of positive legal rules in the international legal system. There are, however, cases where positivism cannot explain the outcome because there is no positive law regulation on the specific matter in question. In such cases, recourse can be had to other factors, such as the nature of legal institutions and systemic patterns of international law which may require the use of inherent rules or general principles of law, to ensure completeness of legal regulation.

Given that the doctrinal discourse on this subject occasionally appeals to categories not subsumable within consensual positivism, it is necessary to examine the normative and conceptual setting in which such categories can be perceived, above all natural law. It is intended to focus on natural law in clarifying where the dividing line between positivist and extra-positivist argument lies.

Bearing in mind that international law is an inter-State legal system in which there is no central government, only those rules that are accepted by States can be part of international law. The same can, to a certain extent, hold true for certain rules that are not strictly, or originally, based on State consent, but which are inherent in the very nature of international law as a legal system. Such a factor of inherency is essentially different from the desirability or social acceptability of the relevant rule. It is one thing to say that the rule must be seen as part of international law because it is indispensable to its structural underpinnings. It is another thing to argue that a certain substantive legal regulation is part of international law because it is a desirable or sound regulation, even though State consent does not support it.

2. The Relevance of Natural Law

(a) Doctrinal Aspects

Natural law (*jus naturale*) has during the entire history of legal science occupied a central place in terms of understanding the nature of law in general and international law in particular. The issues of its essence, origin, scope and interaction with positive law are essential in considering whether it has its place in the international legal system and can be the legitimate object of the study of international law. The concept of natural law refers to rules and principles deducible from nature, reason, or the idea of justice. In addition, the concept of natural law also relates to phenomena that are not expressly denoted as natural law, but cannot be explained by reference to positivist criteria.

In line with these broad characteristics, the precise definition and parameters of conceiving of natural law have evolved and altered over different periods of history. This has demonstrated the different logical possibilities of viewing natural law, which is caused not least by legal, social, religious or political sentiment at the relevant time.

In terms of its origin, natural law is perceived as law that is not laid down by the human authority generally competent to create law in the relevant legal system, that is the legislature in national legal systems and State consent in international law. In terms of its essence, natural law is often perceived as the law of natural state, that is the law applicable to societies that have not yet established an organised legal community. It may or may not survive after such organised community is established. Another way of perceiving the essence of natural law is as the law applicable to nature, that is the law regulating the most natural elements of the life of human beings as well as other biological creatures. Yet another possibility is to conceive of natural law as the law expressing the essence and idea of law, the basic values law is supposed to serve and embody, that is rules expressive of the ideal of justice, or the principles concerning the inherent nature of the relevant legal institutions. Viewed from different angles, natural law may be conceived as paramount and immutable, or as subject to changes whenever the need for them arises in the relevant legal community. It is, on occasion, conceived of either as divine law derived from the will of God or secular law reflective of the nature of law or of legal community.

The essence of natural law calls for understanding its interaction with positive law. Depending on doctrinal orientation, natural law is perceived as law from which the validity of positive law derives, or the law which sets limits to the validity and operation of positive law, or again the law which provides a fallback source of applicable rules and principles should positive law have no answer as to how the relevant situation is governed. Given these different logical possibilities, natural law has been accorded different levels of relevance in different historical contexts. In one way or another, the relevance of natural law is acknowledged not only by naturalists but also within those doctrinal trends that do not expressly state their adherence to the natural law doctrine, and even those that on the face of it are generally opposed to the natural law doctrine.

Among the Roman jurists, natural law was viewed as law derived from the nature of human beings, and as law expressive of the basic ideas of justice. According to Cicero, natural law is immutable. In the Middle Ages, the divine concept of God-given natural law acquired increasing relevance, especially in the writings of Thomas Aquinas who at the same time did not view it as immutable. In this period natural law is sometimes made subservient to the reason of State, for instance in terms of the concept of 'just war' which, while claiming to restrain States in their recourse to force, effectively leaves them as sole arbiters in determining the justness of war.[31]

The link between natural law and international law figures in the writings of Vitoria, where international law is perceived as universal law which restrains the freedom of action of nations in relations with one another. For instance, the European powers are limited in the means they can legally apply to the Indian tribes in the Western hemisphere who are protected by natural law. Vitoria's writings also show that natural law can be manipulated. This is witnessed by the thesis of Vitoria that natural law not only protects native Indian tribes but also can justify coercing them.[32] On the other hand, and again in the context of the international legal system, Grotius conceives of natural law as purely secular law, which would be there even if God did not exist.

In the classical scholarship of international law, from Grotius onwards, natural law is perceived as one of the basic elements and sources of international law. This is due partly to the influence of the Hobbesian approach that asserts that States live in a natural state without any form of government and hence there can be no international law. On the other hand, this is also due to the well-perceived need to elaborate upon some principles of law, justice or equity that should guide States in their relations with each other and, above all, to locate the growing legally relevant practice of States within that framework of law, justice and equity. In some instances this practice is perceived as merely expressive of the dictates of natural law, and in other instances it is perceived as an element of positive law.

With Wolff and Vattel, natural law exists parallel to, and above, the positive law. According to Wolff, the voluntary law of nations is not created through general consent of nations whose existence is assumed, but due to the purpose of the supreme State which nature itself established. So nations are bound to agree to that law.[33] Wolff suggests the notion of 'the necessary law of nations which consists in the law of nature applied to nations'. This law of nature is immutable and hence 'the necessary law of nations also is absolutely immutable'. Consequently, 'neither can any nation free itself nor can any nation free another from it'.[34]

For Vattel, 'the law of nations is originally no other than the law of nature applied to nations'. But there is also a voluntary law of nations, which follows

[31] For an overview see G Schwarzenberger, Jus Pacis ac Belli? Prolegomena to a Sociology of International Law, 37 *AJIL* (1943), 460; Ago (1957), 691.

[32] F Vitoria, *De Indis*, in Vitoria, *Political Writings* (1991), 233; A Nussbaum, *A Concise History of the Law of Nations* (1954), 80–81.

[33] C Wolff, *The Law of Nations Treated According to a Scientific Method* (1934), 6.

[34] *Id*, 10.

from the system of the law of nations as a system based on perfect equality of nations; and the law which States can establish through their agreement, through entering engagements with each other, and this includes stipulative law and customary law based on tacit consent. This natural law of nations is, according to Vattel, 'necessary, because Nations are absolutely bound to observe it'. The necessary law of nations 'is not subject to change'.[35]

The nineteenth-century scholar Georg Friedrich von Martens perceives the law regulating the relations between the government and citizens as internal public law. In relation to foreigners and foreign States, States and governments are conserved in a state of natural relations. Therefore, natural law applies to a State's external relations and forms external public law (*droit public exterieur*). Such external public law is a branch of the law of nations. At the same time, a simple natural law does not suffice to govern the relations between nations. Positive law of nations (*droit des gens positif*) operates to mitigate the rigours of natural law, determining doubtful points, regulating where natural law is silent, or altering on a reciprocal basis the universal laws established by natural law for all nations. Such positive law of nations rests on conventions, whether express or tacit, or on a simple usage; it is divisible into conventional and customary law.[36] Under this approach, natural law and positive law can coexist and complement each other.

In the twentieth century, the relevance of natural law in international law is the subject of deep doctrinal controversy and debate. Morgenthau conceives natural law as metaphysical non-legal principles, referring, among other things, to ethics. In so doing, he opposes the positivist view that the study of legal science is limited to law and nothing but the law.[37] The most prominent representative of twentieth-century naturalism is Alfred Verdross. Although Verdross avoids giving naturalist orientation to his magisterial treatise on international law due to the perception that the audience would reject the reasoning based on natural law,[38] he observes in other places that natural law as based on universal reason is essential to ensure the stability and fairness of the international legal system.[39] Apart from the straightforward naturalism of Verdross, twentieth-century scholarship witnesses the adherence to the natural law doctrine within the framework of the sociological conception of international law in the writings of Georges Scelle. This social solidarity doctrine conceives of law as existing in terms of legal necessity to enable legal persons to achieve security and satisfaction of their basic needs. Scelle rejects the relevance of static and immutable natural law which applies to any society at any time. Societies

[35] E Vattel, The Law of Nations or the Principles of Natural Law applied to the Conduct and to the Affairs of Nations and of Sovereigns in Scott (ed), *Classics of International Law* (1916), 4–5.

[36] G-F Martens, *Précis du droit des gens moderne de l'Europe* (1831), 42–43.

[37] Morgenthau (1940), 262, 268.

[38] *Cf* B Simma, The Contribution of Alfred Verdross to the Theory of International Law, 6 *EJIL* (1995), 1.

[39] A Verdross & H Köck, Natural Law: The Tradition of Universal Reason and Authority, in R MacDonald & D Johnson (eds), *The Structure and Process of International Law* (1983), 42.

differ from each other and the natural law of social development is dynamic because it is biological law. Law, including natural law, develops following the dictates of social necessity. At the same time Scelle accepts that social and material factors are not the only ones that determine the development of law. Considerations of justice and morality also contribute to this process by influencing the content and direction of legal rules.[40]

Still, Scelle argues that the conception of morality and justice varies from society to society. Justice, in particular, is perceived in terms of individual utility and the consequent understanding of interests. Legal order ends up expressing interests of legal persons. For Scelle, positive laws are the expression of basic social laws in the development of society. If positive law were to conflict with what Scelle denotes as objective natural law, rupture of social solidarity possibly leading to revolution would ensue. Effectively, Scelle advocates the idea of judging positive law in the light of natural law reflecting the dynamics of society.[41] This approach is in fundamental contradiction to classic positivism as formulated by Anzilotti.

Natural law, in whichever version or fashion it is presented, can in some circumstances undermine legal stability by providing justification for not complying with the written word. While natural law expresses the idea of law and justice that should apply to States in international society, positivism also expresses an idea that is most inherent in the international legal system, namely that States shall only be bound with their consent and shall be able to rely on the commitments thus assumed. Therefore, for international law not all ways in which natural law can be generally perceived in a theoretical perspective are relevant. The natural law views that deny the positivist element of international law can certainly not be taken as the starting point in explaining where natural law stands in international law—the relevance of natural law in international law can never be perceived as compromising the relevance of legal positivism.

On the other hand, the relevance of natural law means that the relevance of positivism is not unlimited. In principle, the dominance of the positivist sources of law in international law can logically entail two different results: the denial of natural law or viewing natural law as the fall-back source that provides solutions where positive law provides none. The nature of the international legal system requires giving preference to the second option. Positivism cannot escape the recognition that certain rules, which are indeed of fundamental character, are not based on consensual sources. Even in that part of the doctrine which states its obvious semi-absolute preference for positivism, its incompleteness is recognised. Anzilotti accepts the limits on positivism by admitting that the fundamental rule of international law—*pacta sunt servanda*—from which all other rules derive their validity through the expression of State will and which

[40] G Scelle, *Précis de droit des gens* (1923), 1–5.
[41] *Id.*

indeed operates as the criterion for determining the legal basis of positive rules and thus as the criterion for distinguishing binding rules of law from other rules, is not a demonstrable rule in the sense of positivist requirements of rule-identification.[42] This fundamental rule operates as a matter of legal necessity.

Kelsen also acknowledges that while law is generally what has been postulated as law by the competent authority, the basis on which that postulated law—in this case law agreed upon by States—shall be binding cannot be provided by the positivist approach because there is no data confirming the existence of such agreement in terms that would satisfy the positivist requirements. Therefore, they assume the existence of the basic rule (*Grundnorm*) which requires that States have to keep promises they give, or that they have to behave as they have customarily behaved. Although Kelsen claims that the basic rule (*pacta sunt servanda*) is part of customary law, he asserts this without adducing evidence.[43] More specifically, and while accepting the consensual character of stipulative obligations, Brierly points out that the obligation upon which the binding nature of the consensually assumed obligations rests is not by itself consensual, and some extra-consensual basis must be sought to identify the legal basis of such obligation.[44] Likewise, Ago refers to the doctrinal recognition of the 'extremely small' nucleus of primary and fundamental rules conferring value to legal sources of law-making process.[45]

Such relevance of extra-positivist or extra-consensual factors in international law, and moreover the link between those factors and the very foundation of this legal system, requires identifying the character of that natural law which can be relevant and applicable in the international legal system in a way that conforms to the nature of that system. If, for instance, Justinian's version of natural law referring to human nature is applied to the society of nations, then the relevance of natural law in international law would have to be totally excluded, because States are not the same as individuals. The Hobbesian perception of the state of nature is also unsuitable because of its antagonism with legal positivism. The most plausible explanation of natural law in international law is that which draws on the legal institutions recognised under positive international law, explains their inherent character and makes them operate justly and fairly. In other words, international law can accommodate that natural law which suits the nature of the society of nations and at the same time expresses the ideal of law and justice in relation to positive legal institutions to ensure a meaningful degree of justice, and states where justice can reasonably be found and be functioning, so that this goal is not compromised by the absence of specific positive rules that would require such an outcome. This approach is furthermore consistent with the thesis that the natural law argument is not limited solely to speaking expressly in terms of

[42] Anzilotti (1929), 43–44.
[43] H Kelsen, *General Theory of Law and State* (1961), 369ff.
[44] JL Brierly, *The Basis of Obligation in International Law* (1958), 11–13.
[45] Ago (1957), 724.

natural law, but also covers the argument focusing on the inherent nature of legal institutions and the consequent limits on positivism.

This leads to dualistic composition of international law in which naturalist and positivist elements coexist. The necessity of the positivist approach is justified by the stability and coherence of the system: promises and consent must be demonstrated through observable evidence and once they are so demonstrated, be regarded as binding. If international law is in the first place positive law, natural law cannot be its substitute, and its relevance must be judged by asking in which cases is it justified to look for and accept solutions not based on positive law. The relevance of natural law today is determined not by asking whether, or asserting that, international law is based on natural law, but by asking whether natural law can be relevant in situations where positivism cannot, owing to its limits, explain legal outcomes, either through filling gaps or providing guidance in choosing the interpretation of legal rules and institutions conducive to justice, reason, logic and fairness, to the exclusion of interpretation which evidently contradicts the postulates of justice. Given that the principles of natural law are independent of positivist constructs of law-making, the positivist argument cannot be successfully used against the relevance of natural law.

(b) Practical Aspects

International law accepts the relevance of natural law in several ways. The primary and most frequently used sources of international law—treaty and custom—are sources of positive law. They furnish the objectively observable data evidencing consent. Another source mentioned under Article 38 of the International Court's Statute—general principles of law—can have some positive aspect if understood, as it often is, as the body of principles accepted in national legal systems.[46] While this refers to positive data, it falls short of demonstrating such positive data as would qualify for the positivist test in terms of international law. On the other hand, no positive data can be found in those general principles of law that are regarded as expressions of the general character of international law and its basic ideas. The reference to such principles in the International Court's Statute is, among other things, a recognition of such principles as the principles of natural law. As Schachter points out, the idea behind the 'general principles of law' does not depart too far from the classic concept of natural law.[47]

In examining which principles can belong to the category of natural law, the starting point is not to look for rules expressly designated as natural law rules—which would be meaningless as natural law rules cannot be expressly and externally designated—but for rules that have the essence of natural law. These are

[46] For analysis see W Friedmann, The Uses of 'General Principles of Law' in the Development of International Law, 57 *AJIL* (1963), 279.

[47] O Schachter, *International Law in Theory and Practice* (1991), 75ff.

rules that are indispensable for the functioning of international law in general or its specific institutions. The most obvious examples are the principle of legal equality of States, *pacta sunt servanda*, good faith, and the rule against the abuse of rights. The natural law element is presumably present in fundamental human rights, in accordance with the stance taken in the 1948 Universal Declaration on Human Rights that the basic rights of an individual are inherent and inalienable. The right to self-defence is also denoted as an inherent right in the English text of Article 51 of the UN Charter and as a natural right in the French text. These characteristics notwithstanding, the parameters of the exercise of this inherent right are determined in positive law. The law of the use of force is codified in the United Nations Charter, which includes all conditions on which the exercise of the right to self-defence can be claimed. Justness of war in this case is not relevant in modern international law. Another obvious principle inherently existing in international law is that of reparation for violations of international law. As the Permanent Court of International Justice confirmed in the *Chorzow Factory* case, the duty to make reparation for an international wrong is an inherent consequence of that wrong and does not need to be stipulated in the treaty the violation of which the court is dealing with.[48]

A further category of natural law includes those inherent rules that are meant to enable the relevant legal institution justly and meaningfully. Thus in the *North Sea Continental Shelf* case, the International Court addressed the issue of the natural law of the continental shelf. The Court faced the submission that the equidistance method of delimitation of the continental shelf was based on a source of law other than sources that operate on the basis of State consent. Denmark and the Netherlands submitted among other things that such a delimitation method was based on the source of law that operated unless the States involved otherwise agreed. The Court characterised this claim as expressive of the 'natural law of continental shelf, in the sense that the equidistance principle is seen as a necessary expression in the field of delimitation of the accepted doctrine of the exclusive appurtenance of the continental shelf to the nearby coastal State, and therefore, having an *a priori* character of so to speak juristic inevitability'.[49] In addition, the Court accepted that the outcome under this natural law argument would predetermine the answer under positive law as well: if the equidistance principle was based on the rule of inherency, then positive law would be applied as responsive to that; if not, this would not bar a similar result under the sources of positive law.

Thus, the Court did accept that natural law can have play in such fields. The Court then identified what it called 'real issue'—whether the basic concept of the continental shelf required that equidistance should operate in all circumstances and prohibited the allocation of the shelf areas to the relevant State unless they were closer to it. The Court found that the inherent necessity of equidistance did not

[48] *Factory at Chorzów*, Merits, Judgment No 13, 1928, *PCIJ Series* A, No 17, 29.
[49] *ICJ Reports*, 1969, 28–29.

follow from the basic concept of the continental shelf.[50] On the basis of the nature of the continental shelf, the Court concluded that only proximity in a general sense was required, not equidistance in strict terms. The Court also referred to an alternative fundamental consideration—that of natural prolongation. It treated at length and interpreted both parties' submissions as to the applicable fundamental rules not based on the sources of positive law and concluded that the notion of equidistance was not logically necessary. Even if the relevant State had the inherent right to certain shelf areas, this did not impose any method of delimitation. Thus, the Court examined the natural law argument on its merits and rejected the method of equidistance while in principle approving that the argument based on notions such as inherent or natural right can potentially succeed if consistent with the nature of relevant legal relations. Whatever the merits of the Court's argument under the law of the sea, it must be acknowledged that it engaged with the natural law argument and examined it on its merits. In so doing the Court admitted that in principle, cases in international law can be decided on the basis of natural law should the nature of relevant legal institutions require this.

Inherent rules related to the competence of international tribunals, and inherent judicial powers derived from those rules have never been expressly denoted as an aspect of natural law but they are not fully explainable from the positivist perspective either.[51] The normative basis for inherent powers can be the concept of inherent rules in the same way that this concept operates in other fields of international law. For instance, tribunals possess the power to determine their own jurisdiction because there is an inherent rule requiring that tribunals must be able to judge on their own jurisdiction. Tribunals possess inherent power to indicate provisional measures because there is an inherent rule requiring that States cannot frustrate by their action the subject-matter of litigation. The Permanent Court identified in the *Electricity Company of Sofia and Bulgaria* case the rule prohibiting the parties to the litigation from acting in a way to frustrate the object of litigation as a universally recognised inherent rule. As the Court states, Article 41 of its Statute regulating the indication of provisional measures 'applies the principle universally accepted by international tribunals and likewise laid down in many conventions to which Bulgaria has been a party—to the effect that the parties to a case must abstain from any measure capable of exercising a prejudicial effect in regard to the execution of the decision to be given'.[52] Speaking broadly, such rule can be denoted as the natural law of international adjudication, that is the law specifying the natural requirements of such adjudication. On the other hand, they are in some instances positively embodied in the statutes of international tribunals and in relevant cases this dispenses with, or softens, the requirement to elaborate on the inherency of the relevant rules.

50 *Id*, 35.

51 On this see A Orakhelashvili, The Concept of International Judicial Jurisdiction: A Reappraisal, 3 *LPICT* (2003), 501–550.

52 1939, *PCIJ Series* A/B, No 79, 199.

(c) Evaluation

In the international legal system which is for the most part composed of consensually produced rules, natural law is not what governs the relations between States in the first place. Much of what can qualify as natural law principles is received in positive—conventional and customary—law as well. Yet, the rejection of the relevance of natural law is unsound. It has a valid, sometimes indispensable, role to play in ensuring that fairness and the ideal of justice are not compromised by the strict adherence to the positivist approach, and that the inherent nature of specific legal institutions is not perverted and disregarded. Natural law as accepted in the contemporary international legal system is not antithetical to the sources and rules of law based on consent, nor does it aspire to make them irrelevant or undermine them. What it does is to complement them and step in in situations where the consensual sources of law are insufficient for providing a legal solution. In this sense natural law is neither very transcendent nor exclusively theoretical. It refers to the inherent nature of the existing legal institutions. Consequently, the natural law argument is a valid and received part of the international legal argument with utility in a number of fields of international law.

Natural law does not itself provide for substantive legal regulation in international law. Its role consists either in reinforcing the structural foundations of international law, or in contributing to the interpretation of legal institutions that exist and operate under positive law. At the same time, the modern natural law argument is in a position to reinforce the theses of Brierly and Lauterpacht on completeness and effectiveness of legal regulation.

4

Customary Law and Inherent Rules

Having identified the merits of positivism and the natural law approach in the context of the threshold of legal regulation, the issue that now comes to the fore is that of customary law. It is the intention to deal with the relevant doctrinal approaches, assess them against developments in practice, and thus identify where the process of custom-generation stands in relation to the threshold of legal regulation in international law. The aim of this analysis is not to provide yet another comprehensive discussion of the elements of customary law but to address the issues that have not so far received adequate attention, are left open or are subject to disagreement, and so to take a further doctrinal step. The principal issues are the relevance of the consensual element, especially the meaning of the psychological element of custom-generation, the link between customary law and natural law, and the issue of inherent rules. The relevance of the other element of customary law—State practice—is hardly ever disputed. Despite occasional objections,[1] it is firmly recognised that customary law develops on the basis of State practice.

A variety of writings advance different theories that must be confronted and examined. It is particularly important to bring all the relevant approaches together and assess them in terms of the governing systemic framework of international law, which has not been done for a long period of time. The lack of doctrinal consensus on the emergence of customary law[2] is as observable today as it was at earlier stages. In terms of evidence, there are few pronouncements on customary law made by international tribunals. The gist of the doctrinal debate relates to the understanding of these pronouncements and this analysis will be no exception to this pattern.

[1] There are occasional objections to the role of State practice in custom-generation. Judge De Castro, following the approach of the German historical school, asserted that 'practice (usages) is not the foundation of customary law, but that it is the sign by which the existence of a custom may be known. The custom is produced by the community of conviction, not by the will of men, whose acts only manifest this community of ideas'. Separate Opinion, *Fisheries Jurisdiction* (UK v Ireland), *ICJ Reports* 1974, 100.

[2] For the latest such attempt see A Verdross, Entstehungsweisen und Geltungsgrund des universellen völkerrechtlichen Gewohnheitsrechts, *ZaöRV* (1969), 635.

1. Consent as Basis of Customary Law

International law is generally said to be based on State consent. This is most obvious in the example of treaties. Whether such a consensual pattern also extends to customary law is the subject of intense doctrinal debate and disagreement. There are obvious structural differences between the two sources of law. Treaties are formally concluded and drawn in writing; customary rules are less formal and drawn from State practice.

The real issue, however, is whether the difference in form is crucial in terms of the legal nature of the two sources. More specifically, the question is whether the process of agreeing in writing is substantially different, in terms of legal effect and implications, from agreeing informally and through State practice.

Apart from the difference in terms of their form, the two sources are similar as the consensual and reciprocity elements are present in both. In terms of both these sources, States are able to avoid the binding force of a rule by refusing to accept it—which in the case of custom is manifested by the ability of persistent objection[3]—and after the rule has already emerged such avoidance is not possible in the case of either source. This is reflected in Wolff's observation that treaties and custom are similar in character, only different in form, one being expressly consented to and the other based on tacit consent; customary law is not universal but binds, like treaties, only the States that accept it.[4]

Furthermore, the compliance structure and pattern of allocation of rights and obligations under both sources, as well as the regime governing the measures in response to non-compliance are in principle similar. As specified in Articles 34 to 36 of the 1969 Vienna Convention on the Law of Treaties, a treaty cannot bind third States unless they manifest their consent through one of the ways provided for under these provisions. In relation to customary law, there is an intensive ongoing debate as to whether (reciprocally established) customary rules can bind third States, which is an issue at the heart of the consensual dimension of custom-generation. If customary rules bind third States only if they properly and knowingly acquiesce and do not object to them, then custom-generation is a matter of consensual law-making, and thus the emergence of customary law is as much a process of agreement as the emergence of treaty law. In this case, however, it is not possible to strictly separate the case of States becoming bound by customary law from that of custom arguably binding third States.[5]

[3] See below Section 5(d).

[4] C Wolff, *The Law of Nations Treated According to a Scientific Method* (1934), 6, 18–19.

[5] K Skubiszewski, Elements of Custom and the Hague Court, *ZaöRV* (1971), 810 at 846, emphasises that the binding force of customary rules is governed by principles other than those of treaties, but does not specify such difference any further. It is this author's opinion that such difference may indeed be possible. But for identifying such, an express provision confirming it must be referred to. Skubiszewski (at 847) may be right that the process of custom-formation is different

An additional problem is posed by the apparent fluidity of law-making in the area of customary law, in comparison with conventional law. Nevertheless, the real question is whether the relevant binding rule exists. The alleged fluidity of the law-making process in this area cannot be taken as an all-disposing factor because it cannot obstruct the basic task of identifying the existence of the relevant rule.

There have been several doctrinal attempts to formulate the difference between custom and treaty in terms of their nature or structure. Grotius understood custom as an informal analogy of treaties or tacit agreement. Wolff similarly regarded customary rules as tacit agreements.[6] But in the twentieth century this approach has been subjected to some objections.

According to Visscher, the special value of custom, and its superiority over conventional instruments, consists in its reflection of the 'deeply felt community of law', through developing of spontaneous practice. The contractual origin of treaties remains a cause of weakness, manifested through the difficulties of interpretation and risks of nullity attached to manifestation of will.[7]

Kelsen contends that the understanding of custom as tacit treaty is a fiction motivated by the desire to trace international law back to the 'free will' of States and thereby to maintain the idea that the State is 'sovereign', in the sense that it is not subject to a superior legal order restricting its liberty. Kelsen contradicts this analogy between treaty and custom by arguing that treaties can bind non-parties, as in the case of treaties establishing 'objective' regimes, and so can custom. A State cannot, according to Kelsen, 'escape from the validity of the rule of general international law by proving that it did not participate in the creation of this rule'.[8]

Kelsen's assumption that certain treaties can bind States on their own and without the additional consensual process is an exaggeration, and contradicts the *pacta tertiis* rule. While it is generally true that the State cannot escape the validity of a rule in the creation of which it has not affirmatively participated, it may well escape the operation of the rule by proving that it did not give its consent to it. The formation of a general rule of customary law cannot proceed without the general knowledge of all States, and the inaction of States in this process can only signify their expression of will and an attitude that they are not opposed.

Ago's characterisation of custom as spontaneous law is based on his perceived distinction between treaty and custom. Ago explains the binding character of customary rules as a consequence not of law being laid down by a competent body, but by its 'sociality'. Ago considers that law is there not because the members of a society want to consider it as binding but because it is so considered

from the expression of consent to treaties. This is obvious. But the real point is the *essence* of the process and its relation to consent, as opposed to formal details of this process. In the former case, the alleged difference has to be shown with evidence.

[6] Wolff (1934), 7.

[7] C de Visscher *Theory and Reality in Public International Law*, (1968) 161.

[8] Kelsen, *General Theory of Law and State* (1961), 351–352.

'by human thought which reflects on social phenomena'.[9] Therefore, law is not laid down, it is spontaneously formed, 'following various causes and motives which have nothing to do with a formal process of production'. Thus, Ago sees no need for constructing the 'imaginary productive facts' which are supposed to have laid down law, and sees this as an arbitrary restriction of positivism imposed in the sphere of law.[10] However, Ago still recognises that what he calls the 'imaginary legal law-creating process', contained in the elements of custom, is the only way in which customary rules can be manifested.[11] As Kunz correctly commented, Ago's 'theory of ill-defined "spontaneous" law', which is formulated by the science of law, leads 'to the danger... of blurring the dividing line between law and non-law, to identify law with the *fait accompli*'.[12]

In the end, Ago's thesis is not free of contradictions, because even as it rejects the relevance of law-producing facts and bodies, it still accepts that the legal character of rules is to some extent a matter of conscious evaluation and decision. What really distinguishes Ago's thesis from consensual positivism is its reference to the 'sociality' of law—a notion that, as will be seen below, is on occasion seen as the factor that explains *opinio juris*. In this respect, Ago's thesis does not clarify how these spontaneous rules should be identified and distinguished from those spontaneous practices that do not become law. Instead, Ago effectively accepts that the manifestation of customary rules takes place through externally cognisable data.

The issue of consent in the context of creation of customary rules raises several problems. It is emphasised that the voluntarist approach has been brought to the fore by the rejection of natural law and the rise of positivism.[13] This is certainly true in terms of explaining the *dominance* of the voluntarist approach. However, already the classical writers of international law, many of them adherents of naturalism, have emphasised the relevance of consensual and voluntary law. Naturalism has rarely been absolutist in the sense of excluding the relevance of what is not natural law and of consent for the creation of international rules; while positivism is often presented in a near-absolutist way.

Brierly contradicts the view that consent is the basis of customary rules, suggesting that:

> *implied* consent is not a philosophically sound explanation of customary law, international or municipal; a customary rule is observed, not because it has been consented to, but because it is believed to be binding, and whatever may be the explanation or the

[9] R Ago, Positive Law and International Law, 51 *AJIL* (1957), 727–728.
[10] Ago (1957), 729–730.
[11] Ago (1957), 723.
[12] J Kunz, Roberto Ago's Theory of Spontaneous International Law, 52 *AJIL* (1958), 85 at 90–91.
[13] M Mendelson, The Subjective Element in Customary International Law, 76 *BYIL* (1995), 177 at 184.

justification of that belief, its binding force does not depend, and is not felt by those who follow to depend, on the approval of the individual or the State to which it is addressed.

States, according to Brierly, are bound by principles to which they cannot, except by the most strained construction of the facts, be said to have consented, and it is unreasonable to force facts into such preconceived theory. Furthermore, Brierly rejects the relevance of implied consent as an exclusively theoretical construct.[14] Similarly, Condorelli argues that the 'presumption of acceptance' through implied consent is artificial, as jurists have never sought to prove that the rule is accepted by each State individually.[15]

But there is no reason why implied consent should not operate in practice. Consent can be inferred from conduct and attitude as much as from an express statement, and will be brought to the attention of other States through inaction or conduct, and is as good as will expressly stated. Action can be conscious whether it manifests that consciousness expressly or by conduct.

The consensual nature of customary law has long been accepted in doctrine. Wolff has seen customary law as produced by practice which implies inter-State agreement. Wolff states that customary law 'is so called, because it has been brought in by long usage and observed as law'.[16] This statement could be understood as referring to both material and psychological elements of customary law. But the next statement specifies that custom is based on usage (*Herkommen*): 'since certain nations *use* it with the other, the customary law of nations rests upon the tacit consent of the nations or, if you prefer, upon a tacit stipulation'.[17]

This statement implies a causal connection between practice (usage) and the agreement that follows from it. Wolff at that stage did not expressly articulate the notion of *opinio juris*. Vattel likewise refers to customary law based on tacit consent. Customary law binds only those States who consent to it and in this respect it is similar to treaties.[18] In the later period, Phillimore emphasised that custom is one of the ways of expressing consent by States to legal rules. It is tacitly expressed by long usage, practice and custom.[19]

Anzilotti considers custom as a tacit agreement. The content of a customary rule is determined by its repetition (usage).[20] But custom, according to Anzilotti, is a rule observed with the same conviction as for a juridical rule. In international law there is not simply custom but legal custom, as States behave in a certain way being convinced that in doing so they comply with an obligation.[21] This

[14] JL Brierly, *The Law of Nations* (1949), 53.
[15] L Condorelli, Custom, in M Bedjaoui (Gen ed), *International Law: Achievements and Prospects* (1991), 179 at 203.
[16] Wolff (1934), 18.
[17] Wolff (1934), 18–19.
[18] E Vattel, *The Law of Nations or the Principles of Natural Law Applied to the Conduct and to the Affairs of Nations and of Sovereigns* in Scott (ed), Classics of International Law (1916) 4–5.
[19] Phillimore, *Commentaries on International Law* (1879), vol I, 38.
[20] Anzilotti (1929), 68.
[21] Anzilotti (1929), 73–74.

approach, besides being a landmark of positivism, also demonstrates the commonality between the consensual approach and the essence of *opinio juris* as later emphasised in international jurisprudence, notably in *Lotus* and *North Sea*.

Fitzmaurice offers a down-to-earth approach to the consensual element of general customary law, which sees the problems attendant to the consensual perspective yet emphasises its essential importance:

> Where a *general* rule of customary international law is built up by the common practice of States, although it may be a little unnecessary to have recourse to the notion of agreement (and a little difficult to detect it in what is often uncoordinated, independent, if similar, action of States), it is probably true to say that consent is latent in the mutual tolerations that allow the practice to be built up at all; and actually patent in the eventual acceptance (even if tacit) of the practice, as constituting a binding rule of law. It makes no substantial difference whether the new rule emerges in regard to (in effect) a new topic on which international law has hitherto been silent, or as change of existing law.[22]

This perspective allows for customary rules to emerge and consolidate in a context where practice is sufficiently public. The problems involved in this process will be seen as those of evidencing rules, and should not detract from the basic principle that if the State has not given consent to the rule, it cannot be seen as bound by it.

In fact, the relevance of tacit, or implied, consent is dictated by the need for systemic effectiveness of the international legal order. On the one hand, it leaves each State free to accept or reject the rule; on the other hand, it operates to deny the possibility of treating the sufficiently long and widespread silence of States as a tool for infinitely obstructing the establishment of rules through the practice and attitude of other States. The device of tacit or implied consent corresponds to the decentralised character of the international legal system more than any other perceived tools of law-making.

2. Consent and *Opinio Juris*

It may on occasion seem that the issue of consent as part of custom-generation has little practical significance. In jurisprudence, the real and immediate problem is to find whether there is sufficient State practice and *opinio juris* and tribunals simply look at this without burdening themselves with expressly addressing allegedly theoretical issues as to whether customary law is based on State consent or some other factor. In the *Lotus* case, the Permanent Court referred to the absence of legal conviction as the factor precluding the formation of a customary rule on the relevant aspect of State jurisdiction; in *Asylum*, the International Court was unable to see

[22] G Fitzmaurice, *The Law and Procedure of the International Court of Justice* (1986), 198 (emphasis in original).

the customary law developed because the relevant practice was conducted with political expediency in mind, as opposed to the sense of legal obligation; in *North Sea*, there was no practice involved that would 'show a general recognition that a rule of law or legal obligation is involved'.[23] In *Nicaragua*, the International Court inferred *opinio juris* from acceptance by States to the formulation of the rule in the General Assembly Resolution which was meant to codify the applicable law.[24]

Thus, judicial decisions refer to factors of an intellectual and mental dimension—acceptance, recognition and conviction of States—as factors that bring about the legal change of transforming non-law into law. The reference to these concepts presumably implies the existence of some element constitutive of legal obligation, for if some practice is accepted or recognised as law, it would not be law but for such acceptance and recognition, which constitutes the will of the States. If the expression of conviction of States that the relevant practice expresses law is indicative of the existence of custom, then without demonstrating such conviction, which is a conscious attitude of a State, such a customary rule would not exist. In particular, recognition is a device expressing the consent of the recognising State, as can be seen from the wording of Article 38(1) which denotes treaties, that is consensual instruments, as being expressly recognised by States-parties. This further confirms the thesis, developed above, that there is much room for regarding implied recognition too as an aspect of consensual law-making. Similarly, as Skubiszewski illustrates, acceptance of a rule is also an act of will, that is consent.[25]

Thus, the issue of consent is in the background and it must be addressed in view of a number of explanations of the nature of *opinio juris* advanced in doctrine, if only because the elements of acceptance, recognition and legal conviction, as elaborated upon in practice, need to be explained. At the same time, the legal conviction focused upon here is not that of the individual State, but the shared *opinio juris*, which definitionally implies an element of agreement in making a rule binding, and further reinforces the consensual understanding of customary law.

Individual judges have extensively affirmed the relevance and necessity of *opinio juris*. Judge Tanaka in *North Sea* emphasised the need to prove *opinio juris* for establishing the existence of customary rules and added that *opinio juris* is a 'qualitative factor of customary law', 'by which a simple usage can be transformed into a custom with binding power'.[26] A similar requirement was implied by Judge Ammoun in *Barcelona Traction*, where he explained that diplomatic protection of shareholders did not amount to customary rule, as it was not based on adequate State practice and was not accompanied by the psychological element of *opinio*

[23] *ICJ Reports*, 1969, para 74.
[24] *ICJ Reports*, 1986, 101ff.
[25] Skubiszewski (1971), 847.
[26] *ICJ Reports*, 1969, 175.

juris.[27] In the *Fisheries Jurisdiction* case, Judge De Castro made several significant observations on the relevance of *opinio juris* as an implication of the voluntary profile of customary law, which is based on:

General or universal acceptance. There should be no doubt as to the attitude of States. The rule in question must be generally known and accepted expressly or tacitly. What has led to the view that international custom is binding is that it expresses a *consensus tacitus generalis,* if not as a sort of tacit agreement, at least as the expression of a general conviction. For an international custom to come into existence, the fact that a rule may be adopted by several States in their municipal legislation, in treaties and conventions, or may be applied in arbitral decisions is not sufficient, if other States adopt a different rule, and it will not be opposable to a State which still opposes its application (ICJ *Reports 1951,* p. 131). The existence of a majority trend, and even its acceptance in an international convention, does not mean that the convention has caused the rule to be crystallized or canonized as a rule of customary law (*ICJ Reports 1969,* p. 41).[28]

Thus, despite his stated adherence to viewing customary law as reflecting and responding to the community of societal conviction, Judge De Castro still effectively requires the presence of *opinio juris* in terms of the individual State's agreement to the rule.

This psychological element of acceptance (*opinio juris*) is the key issue in determining the nature custom from naturalist and positivist perspectives. The approach that explains the nature of *opinio juris* must be such as accords with the basic structure and nature of the international legal system; and can be accommodated in terms of the requirements approved within the century-long *acquis* on custom-generation. This must be borne in mind when the specific approaches are examined.

Article 38 of the International Court's Statute describes customary law as the general practice accepted as law. This implies that practice is an element antecedent to its acceptance as law. As Verdross notes, having examined different modes of recognition and acceptance of customary rules, including those pursuant to a treaty rule or the decision of an international organisation, all these modes fall within the pattern covered by Article 38(1)(b) of the Statute, and they all imply the expression of attitudes of which all are aware.[29] The mere practice cannot amount to customary law. There can be practice that could be perfectly able to give rise to rights and duties and be applicable as law, but it happens not to do so because there is no supportive common belief.[30]

In *Fisheries*, the Court refuted the British contention that Norway's use of straight baselines was contrary to international law, by reference to the fact that

[27] Separate Opinion, *ICJ Reports*, 1970, 329.

[28] *ICJ Reports*, 1974, 89–90; see further *Ahmadou Sadio Diallo*, Preliminary Objections, General List No 103, Judgment of 24 May 2007 on the independence of the content of customary law from the development of treaty regimes.

[29] Verdross (1969), 649.

[30] Mendelson (1995), 177 at 198.

Britain acquiesced in this practice due to its knowledge and inaction in the face of it.[31] The *Fisheries Jurisdiction* decision of the International Court deals with the problem of customary law without expressly mentioning the concept of *opinio juris*. This case concerned the development of preferential fishing rights at and after the 1960 Second Conference on the Law of the Sea: 'the law evolved through the practice of States on the basis of the debates and near-agreements at the Conference'. The Court suggested that the concept of preferential rights had 'crystallized as customary law in recent years arising out of the general consensus revealed at that Conference'.[32] Furthermore, the Court emphasised that:

> State practice on the subject of fisheries reveals an increasing and widespread acceptance of the concept of preferential rights for coastal States, particularly in favour of countries or territories in a situation of special dependence on coastal fisheries. Both the 1958 Resolution and the 1960 joint amendment concerning preferential rights were approved by a large majority of the Conferences, thus showing overwhelming support for the idea that in certain special situations it was fair to recognize that the coastal State had preferential fishing rights.[33]

The Court refers to State practice, and the consensus reached at the Conference, without elaborating upon the legal nature of that consensus. The Court does not specifically search for *opinio juris*. This may create the impression that the customary rule is deemed to have emerged without its *opinio juris* being proved. However, the Court's judgment does not stop at that point, and to support the legitimacy of its findings, it refers to the repeated occasions on which both parties to the litigation have accepted and recognised each other's preferential rights in the relevant maritime areas. To specify further, the Court uses the State practice and consensus achieved at the Conference to demonstrate the existence on a general plane of the concept of preferential rights. It does not, however, regard this concept as self-operating in a way that enables it to allocate rights and obligations to States. Preferential rights belong to the State which is exceptionally dependent on the fisheries in the relevant area, and only if such exceptional dependence is recognised by other affected States.[34]

Thus, the legal position in any case depends on the agreement between the relevant States. The *Fisheries Jurisdiction* Judgment does not suggest any standard whereby the legal position established without *opinio juris* of States can bind them merely on the basis of State practice.

In *Libya–Malta*, the Court was requested to affirm the equidistance rule of delimiting the continental shelf, on the basis of extensive practice consisting of delimitation agreements. The Court found that this practice revealed the numerous deviations from the strict application of the equidistance rule, and fell

[31] M Akehurst, Custom as a Source of International Law, 47 *BYIL* (1975–76), 1 at 25.
[32] *ICJ Reports*, 1974, 23.
[33] *Id*, 26.
[34] *Id*, 24, 26–27.

short of proving the existence of the rule of equidistance, or any other method, as obligatory.[35] It seems that the analysis of practice was just the first step in what normally is the ascertainment of the law-making process. As practice provided no straightforward material for the rule, no examination of *opinio juris* was necessary. The question of whether, had the practice been straightforward and uniform enough, the Court would have found it sufficient even without *opinio juris*, is purely hypothetical.

The science of international law has witnessed proposals to abandon *opinio juris* as the requirement for custom-generation. This can be seen from doctrinal contributions in which *opinio juris* is described as the mirror-image of the consensual approach which does not explain the creation of customary rules, and how they bind non-participants. Thus, it is considered unnecessary to seek proof of *opinio juris*, any more than it is necessary to prove consent. One should not insist on the requirement of *opinio juris* where there is 'a constant, uniform and unambiguous practice of sufficient generality, clearly taking place in a legal context and unaccompanied by disclaimers, with no evidence of opposition at the time of the rule's formation by the State which it is sought to burden with the customary obligation'.[36]

Along the lines of opposition to the requirement of the psychological element, Judge Read in the *Fisheries* case argued that in terms of defining the relevant rights or titles, the starting point is the actual practice of physical action.[37] Another similar approach is to argue that the judge has an unfettered discretion to insist on, or dispense with, the requirement of *opinio juris*.[38]

There are significant problems with the feasibility of this thesis. One can rarely find practice which is constant, uniform and unambiguous, and at the same time of sufficient generality. This thesis cannot explain practice with deviations—that is most of the situations in which customary rules are created—unless additional resort is made to the attitudes and beliefs of States, their *opinio juris*. It is hardly possible to know that the relevant practice is taking place in a legal context unless we can identify the evidence of the conviction of States that this is indeed so, that is their *opinio juris*. In addition, the lack of opposition of the State which is burdened by the relevant customary rule expresses its attitude, belief and even consent, and thus emphasises the need to search for and identify the psychological element of custom along with State practice.

If the psychological element were to be dispensed with, the line separating relevant practice from irrelevant practice would disappear; and some alternative tool would be needed to clarify which practice is relevant and which is not. Such

[35] *Libya–Malta*, *ICJ Reports*, 1985, 38, 48.

[36] Mendelson (1995), 177 at 201–202, 204, 206–207.

[37] Judge Read in *Fisheries*. For similar, see Thirlway, The Law and Procedure of the International Court of Justice, *BYIL* (1990), 43.

[38] *Cf* Akehurst (1975–76), 1 at 33.

a criterion cannot be found at the present stage. Therefore, the requirement of a psychological element cannot be abandoned.

As Akehurst observes, the frequency or consistency of practice provides no answer as to the existence of legal obligation; *opinio juris* alone can provide the answer or distinguish legal obligations from non-legal obligations based on morality, courtesy or comity. 'If *opinio juris* is abandoned, some other criterion for making such distinctions will be needed to take its place. Most authors who seek to eliminate *opinio juris*, in whole or in part, do not face this problem.'[39]

Thirlway correctly observes that the acceptance of a claim in a bilateral dispute can be expressive, in terms of *North Sea*, of the 'belief that this practice is rendered obligatory by the existence of a rule of law requiring it'.[40] Verdross also emphasises that certain customary rules are created through the adjustment of competing State claims.[41] State practice, however, does not consist only of controversies. There can also be—and it is mostly so—constructive State practice that builds up the substratum of customary law and expresses the concordant effort of States towards effecting normative change.[42] This constructive practice does not often come up in judicial practice, because adjudication is about dealing with controversies.[43] Such constructive practice poses the question most acutely whether the customary rule emerges through the action of States in the belief of the existence of the obligatory rule, or in being conscious of their practice and action implying their attitude, agreement and consent as to the emergence of the customary rule.

3. The Process of Emergence of *Opinio Juris*

How and at what stage can practice be seen as expressive of or accompanied by legal conviction? Cassese considers that in the custom-generation process the element of *opinio juris* does not need to be present from the very outset of the development of the relevant practice. Practice is motivated initially by the impulse of economic, political or military demands and at this stage it may be regarded as 'being imposed by social or economic or political needs (*opinio necessitatis*)'.

[39] Akehurst, (1975–76), 1 at 33.

[40] Thirlway (1990), 41, 50; Thirlway also points to the requirement that the practice shall not be motivated by compliance with other rules, such as treaty rules, *id*, 44. This is still something different from positively addressing the issue of practice that affirmatively expresses the opinion of compliance with customary rules specifically. Thirlway explains away this latter issue too easily. Showing that practice in pursuance of the treaty does not build up customary *opinio juris* falls short of demonstrating *how* such *opinio juris* is built up whenever it is relevant.

[41] Verdross (1969), 646.

[42] As Mendelson points out, 'The rules relating to such matters as diplomatic immunity and the freedom of the high seas have evolved as the result of the *conduct* of States which was either parallel and uniform from the outset, or (more commonly) eventually fell into a common pattern.' Mendelson, The Formation of Customary International Law, 272 *RdC* (1998-II), 165 at 197.

[43] Skubiszewski (1971), 853.

If such practice encounters no significant opposition, it gradually crystallises into a customary rule through acceptance or acquiescence. At this stage, practice is already dictated by international law (*opinio juris*), and States comply out of their sense of legal duty as opposed to economic, political or social factors. This process of transformation cannot, according to Cassese, be pinpointed precisely, because it is a continuous process.[44] Cassese considers that telling examples of rules initially based on *opinio necessitatis* and subsequently endowed with *opinio juris* are the rules on the continental shelf, and outer space.[45] Along similar lines, Mendelson deals with *opinio juris* at the formative stage of custom and when the customary rule is mature, suggesting that at the former stage 'pioneers' believe that the rule is desirable; at the later stage the general belief is that the rule is law.[46] Mendelson also observes that 'The will or the belief of a State is more difficult to ascertain than its conduct, which is often, by its nature, public and objectively verifiable.'[47] While this problem cannot be denied, it is not insurmountable. The very public character of State practice, the consistency of it, other States' knowledge of it and their non-contradiction of it may be indication of consent, acquiescence through *opinio juris*.

Cassese's thesis as to the exact moment of transformation of *opinio necessitatis* into *opinio juris* is correct in many cases. At the same time, the criteria for telling one from the other are still necessary, because the ultimate task is always to ascertain whether there is *opinio juris*, that is whether the practice is complied with as a matter of legal obligation.

In this respect, there can be no detailed criteria with universal application. There can, however, still be some guidance related to the context in which the relevant practice develops. And in these terms several criteria can be identified:

- Practice consisting of mere action of the State will never be as good as the practice that expresses or implies the conscious correlation of attitudes.
- Practice taking place within *domaine reserve* may in some cases imply acceptance by the relevant State of the legal limitation of its sovereign freedom; and in other cases it may signify just a discretionary action. This would again depend on the correlation of attitudes between that State and other involved States.
- Practice in compliance with some other extra-customary rule will not be independent evidence of customary *opinio juris*, as was established in the *North Sea* case.
- Practice developing in a field in which there has hitherto been no certainty of legal regulation or no specific applicable rule, and in relation to which

[44] A Cassese, *International Law* (2005), 157–158; see also Skubiszewski (1971), 838.
[45] Cassese (2005), 158.
[46] Mendelson (1998-II), 281.
[47] Mendelson (1998-II), 197.

States are supposed to expect clarity of their rights and obligations because it involves the exercise of and correlation between their sovereign rights and obligations, provided that there is evidence of the correlation of State attitudes, can be particularly indicative of a rule endowed with *opinio juris* being formed.

- Most general customary rules are formed as bundles of bilateral normative relations. Thus—and in a way cognate to the phenomenon of persistent objection—if the relevant State accepts or rejects the rule in relation to itself, and depending on the context, the existence of the rule on a general plane can presumably be identified.

Therefore, the doctrinally postulated uncertainty notwithstanding, there can be criteria that help identify the existence of *opinio juris* in the relevant case, as distinct from other motivations of State practice. Not that these criteria are absolute, but they can provide guidance for distinguishing the relevant factors from irrelevant ones.

Once the indispensability of *opinio juris* is established, it must be ascertained whether State practice and *opinio juris* are always and necessarily separate, or whether *opinio juris* can be implied in practice. As Skubiszewski considers, the evidence of *opinio juris* is the weakest point of the study of customary law.[48] According to Akehurst, *opinio juris* can be inferred from the very acts that constitute State practice.[49] An important part of jurisprudence on this issue suggests that for a customary rule to exist, it must relate to the practice followed in belief of the existence of the rule of law requiring such conduct. For instance, in the *Lotus* case the Permanent Court held that the abstention of Turkey from exercising jurisdiction on the basis of an objective territorial principle was not accompanied by a belief that there was a legal obligation and hence it was merely bare practice. States had abstained from prosecuting individuals in similar circumstances, but they were not deemed to have been abstaining 'being conscious of having a duty to abstain', which would be a prerequisite for a customary rule to exist. In addition, it seemed hardly probable, according to the Court, that the French Government in certain incidents 'would have omitted to protest against the exercise of criminal jurisdiction by the Italian and Belgian courts, if they had really thought that this was a violation of international law'.[50] Practice can by itself signify the acceptance of customary rule as law. As Judge Lachs emphasised in *North Sea*, 'the general practice of States should be recognized as prima facie evidence that it is accepted as law. Such evidence may, of course, be controverted—even on the test of practice itself, if it shows "much uncertainty and contradiction"'.[51] Similarly, in the *North*

[48] Skubiszewski (1971), 854.

[49] Akehurst (1975–76), 39.

[50] 1927, *PCIJ Series* A, No 10 at 28–29.

[51] Dissenting Opinion, *ICJ Reports*, 1969, 231, further referring to the *Asylum* case. In this latter case, practice was not seen as sufficiently uniform to demonstrate acceptance of the rule and it

Sea Continental Shelf case, the International Court specified that practice must be such 'as to be the evidence of a belief that this practice is rendered obligatory by the existence of a rule of law requiring it. ... The States concerned must therefore feel that they are conforming to what amounts to a legal obligation.'[52]

This statement assumes the pre-existence of the legal rule that renders the practice as obligatory. Conceived in strict terms, this statement means that States do not create the rule through expressing *opinio juris,* but conform to the existing rule. As Akehurst observes in this spirit, '*opinio juris* is to be found in assertions that something is already law, not in statements that it ought to be law'.[53] Does acting in pursuance of a rule or in consciousness of a legal obligation create the rule or assume its existence? It seems that the field of *opinio juris* still leaves some room for the relevance of assertions or attitudes of States such that the relevant practice *thereby becomes* law. In fact, whether *opinio juris* is expressed at once, gradually or subsequently is a question of technique and form. It does not prejudice the basic conceptual question of whether *opinio juris* is an expression of consent.

However, it is arguable that the perspective of States acting in the belief that an obligation exists, potentially takes matters out of positivist reasoning and implies the emergence of customary rules on a basis other than consent and agreement. There are criticisms of that approach. According to Skubiszewski, to consider *opinio juris* as implying that the relevant practice is required by prevailing international law is wrong, because practice is creative, not corroborative, of customary rules. Moreover, the change of customary rules cannot be effected by belief that one acting in accordance with an existing rule.[54] This is arguably reflected in the fact that the *North Sea* Judgment, referring to the action in belief that there was a legal obligation, related to the creation of rules in a context where none existed on that specific subject-matter.

The limits on this approach and the necessity of alternatives can be seen from the analysis of Judge Lachs in *North Sea*. As Judge Lachs observes, 'In view of the complexity of this formative process and the differing motivations possible at its various stages, it is surely over-exacting to require proof that every State having applied a given rule did so because it was conscious of an *obligation* to do so.'[55] According to Judge Lachs, it is not necessary to have the straightforward *opinio juris* from the very beginning of the practice. It is a fiction to assume that all States believe themselves to be acting under a legal obligation. The process may begin from voluntary acts inspired by a calculation that acceptance from other States will follow.[56]

involved political expediency as motivation of State conduct, as opposed to conviction as to the legal obligation.

[52] *ICJ Reports*, 1969, 41.

[53] Akehurst (1975–76), 1 at 37.

[54] Skubiszewski (1971), 839.

[55] Dissenting Opinion, *ICJ Reports*, 1969, 231 (emphasis original).

[56] *ICJ Reports*, 1969, 230–231.

In some cases, the State which introduces new practice at variance with law has no belief in acting in conformity with the law. For instance, with the Truman proclamation, the United States first claimed *opinio necessitatis*, that the exercise of the relevant rights on the continental shelf was 'reasonable and just', which was an expression of legal necessity.[57] But this is more a question of *ratio legis*, than of the psychological element of customary rule. *Opinio juris* is implied in the response other States gave to this through claiming their own continental shelves, as opposed to the US claim *per se*.

Akehurst's final observation holds the real key to the solution of this problem: 'It is not necessary that the State making such statements [on the conduct being required or prohibited by international law] believes them to be true; what is necessary is that the statements are not challenged by other States.'[58] Beliefs are indeed subjective and difficult to verify. But the fact of acceptance of this stated belief by other States constructs *ex post facto* an agreement regarding the legality or illegality of certain action as between the relevant States, and further upholds the relevance of the consensual element in the creation of customary rules. The other State's acceptance of the stated belief makes the difference and effectively amounts to consent, and the legal rule emerges at that point. It is not whether the States making statements actually believe in whether the relevant conduct is obligatory, but whether the outcome regards the rule as legally obligatory; whether on balance there is agreed and objectively certifiable *opinio juris*, as opposed to the presumably subjective beliefs at the launching stage of the relevant practice. This implies concordance of attitudes and therefore confirms that the recognition of a rule through action pursuant to a legal obligation complies with the consensual framework of the creation of customary rules. However we describe it, recognition, consensus or shared conviction, the psychological element of custom is an expression of will that transforms the non-rule into the rule.

4. Doctrinal Criticisms of and Alternatives to the Consensual Explanation of Custom

The issue of theories alternative to consensual approach is at the heart of the issue of the threshold of law-making and the relevance of non-law in generating legal rules. The consensual approach is widely criticised in doctrine, and several alternatives are proposed to explain how customary rules acquire their binding character. According to Charney, 'most writers argue that States do not have the

[57] Mendelson (1995), 177 at 196–197, 201–202. See also Verdross (1969), 647. Legal necessity or utility shall not be confused with the inherency of the rules, unless one views this claim as made pursuant to the perceived natural law entitlement to the continental shelf. On which see above Chapter 3 and below Section 6.

[58] Akehurst (1975–76), 1 at 53.

free will to decide whether or not to be bound by rules of international law'.[59] The last two decades especially have witnessed an enthusiasm for replacing consensual understanding of custom with the sociological theory of custom, mirroring in some ways the sociological approach of Scelle.

The almost inherent and irreconcilable contradiction between the sociological approach and the consensual, or positivist, perspective can be seen from the Dissent of Judge Tanaka in the *North Sea* case in which he advocated the customary status of the equidistance rule of continental shelf delimitation rejected by the Court as a whole. Judge Tanaka suggested sociological factors contribute to the speedy formation of customary rules, and that elements of custom-generation, including those related to State practice and its duration, are relative. Judge Tanaka argued that 'We must not scrutinise formalistically the conditions required for customary law and forget the social necessity, namely the importance of the aims and purposes to be realised by the customary law in question.' In addition, Judge Tanaka suggests with approval that 'those who advocate the objective existence of law apart from the will of States, are inclined to take a more liberal and elastic attitude in recognizing the formation of a customary law attributing more importance to the evaluation of the content of law than to the process of its formation'.[60] The sociological approach was used against the Permanent Court's consensual approach in *Lotus*, as can be seen from Judge Nyholm's dissent, which bases custom on 'international legal ethics', on the basis of which the continual recurrence of events creates rules with 'an innate consciousness of their being necessary'.[61] Similarly, Judge De Castro came closer to the sociological approach, by advancing the thesis that, as customary law expresses the community conviction, 'In order to be binding as a legal rule, the general conviction (*opinio communis*) does not have to fulfil all the conditions necessary for the emergence of a custom.'[62]

These passages, and above all Judge Nyholm's approach, reflect the approach of the classical natural law school which has explained a certain part of customary law as reflective of some sort of natural necessity as opposed to consensual agreement; or viewing this consensual agreement as compliance with those natural necessities.

This argument also implies that the mere social interest behind the rule can justify its binding force at the expense of the formal elements of law-making which express the will and attitude of States. Furthermore, in broader perspective this approach advocates the independent influence of non-legal considerations on international law-making. Social necessity can be a motivation behind customary rule, causing States to accept a rule in the exercise of their sovereign freedom.

[59] J Charney, The Persistent Objector Rule and the Development of Customary International Law, 56 *BYIL* (1985), 1 at 16.

[60] Dissenting Opinion, *ICJ Reports*, 1969, 176, 178.

[61] Dissenting Opinion of Judge Nyholm, *PCIJ Series* A, No 10, 60.

[62] Separate Opinion, *Fisheries Jurisdiction*, *ICJ Reports*, 1974, 100.

But it cannot by itself make the rule binding. This can only happen through State consent, in some cases with motivation to respond to social necessity.

Visscher considers that the development of customary international law is the result of the repeated action of power. Some States have a larger footprint than others and therefore their practice and action are more influential in developing customary law.[63] This approach follows from Visscher's general approach to viewing international law as the product of power and reality.

It must be asked whether Visscher's approach to customary law inherently contradicts consensual approach. Even if some powerful States were to have predominant influence in developing customary law, customary rules would still owe their validity to consensual acceptance by the rest of the States. This would be so unless one were to specifically deny the relevance of the consent of those other States and assert that customary rules bind them against their will. Visscher does not advance this thesis expressly and his theory is therefore incomplete. Instead, although developing the view that customary law is the consequence of the repeated exercise of power, Visscher eventually accepts that 'a custom becomes compulsory only from the moment when the practice which is its material substratum is generally accepted "as law" '.[64]

From here Visscher proceeds to explain the acceptance of customary rules by States in moral and sociological terms, suggesting that 'This psychological judgment implies a moral judgment which, relying on the criteria of reason, justice and common utility, separates what in a given practice appears to be dictated by a certain conformity with the general interest and with principle from what appears to be due solely to accidental circumstances or individual motives.'[65] Therefore, Visscher suggests that practice can be transformed into custom if it corresponds to the perception of general interest. But Visscher does not specify whether the perception of general interest itself generates customary law, or whether it is merely a motivation inducing States to consent to an emerging customary rule.

Kelsen suggests that 'general international law is binding upon many States which never, expressly or tacitly, consented to it'.[66] Kelsen views customary law in terms of power of States, submitting that the consistent and effective violation of a customary rule cannot leave the old law unimpaired. If these States are sufficiently numerous and powerful, their action can deprive the existing customary law of 'that degree of effectiveness which forms an indispensable condition of its continued validity'.[67]

Another observation on Kelsen's approach relates to his above-mentioned thesis that the State cannot escape the operation of customary rules on the basis of its lack of consent to them. This thesis, coupled with Kelsen's reference to the role

[63] Visscher (1968), 153ff.
[64] Visscher (1968), 156.
[65] Visscher (1968), 156.
[66] Kelsen, (1967) 448.
[67] Kelsen (1967), 454.

of powerful States in modifying customary rules, effectively implies that some States can legislate for others, which is a view antithetical to the fundamental character of international law.

Kelsen's approach raises several other problems. In the first place, this approach falls short of explaining how many States there should be violating the 'old' law to deprive it of its legal effectiveness. Kelsen's approach also contradicts the principle of the independent operation of customary rules, asserting that the validity of customary rule can be undermined by group violation. The framework of international law-making does not sustain this view. The change of customary rules necessarily presupposes the coincidence of the attitudes of all affected States such that the old rule is replaced and the new rule is established. This fundamental question is also left unanswered by Kelsen, who does not examine what the legal position would be if the 'old' customary rule were indeed to be deprived of its validity; is the outcome the non-regulation, legal vacuum or some kind of *non liquet*? Is the mere violation enough unless it can bring with it new legal regulation of the field governed by the 'old' rule? The failure to address these issues confirms that Kelsen's theory fails to formulate a viable alternative to the consensual explanation of customary law.

In fact, in other places in his work, Kelsen points out that 'it is redundant to stress the importance of consent in the development of custom since it is obviously implicit in the constituent elements of custom. Without the general consent of States custom clearly cannot arise.'[68]

Mendelson likewise criticises the consensual approach, suggesting that 'Though the voluntarist approach is plausible and hard to disprove definitely, there are important respects in which it does not furnish a convincing answer. At the theoretical level, it is often based on a logical error concerning the level of analysis; and empirically it postulates a will which is often lacking in fact.'[69] Mendelson tries to narrow the gap in the dichotomy between the consent approach and belief approach, and states that 'consent plays a role in some conditions, but belief in others'. The difference between the two is that between necessary conditions and sufficient conditions. Consent may be a sufficient condition, but not a necessary one.[70]

Interestingly enough, Mendelson's objections to consensual explanation of custom run parallel to some objections to the relevance of *opinio juris*. According to Mendelson, in the process of general custom-generation, the relevance of consent is simply untrue in describing the general process of non-objection and acquiescence. *Opinio juris* relates to belief, not consent. The lack of objection may in formal terms be presented as giving consent, but 'it does not describe what actually happens'.[71]

[68] Kelsen (1967), 453–454.
[69] Mendelson (1995), 177 at 193–194.
[70] *Id*, 183, 188.
[71] *Id*, 185–186.

But what actually happens is that the consent is implied in inaction. Taken literally, *opinio juris* may relate to belief or view, but its manifestation for the attention of other States results in communicating a will to treat the relevant rule as legally binding, that is in giving consent. In fact, Mendelson accepts that acquiescence is equivalent to consent.[72] If so, then it is unclear why acquiescence to the rule of general customary law, itself a conscious decision, is not an incidence of consent.

Mendelson does not object to the thesis that customary rules are a product of the mind, and that some States indeed will their creation. But he characterises the voluntarist theory as going further and requiring the will and consent of each and every State.[73] Mendelson submits that 'Initiation, imitation and acquiescence may plausibly be described in terms of will. But others still, who were not directly affected, sat by and did nothing, and in due course found themselves bound by the emerging rule.' Mendelson further reinforces this view with a domestic law analogy, in which 'movers and shakers' create the rules which end up binding the entire society, without others consciously consenting to it.[74] In fact, those States are deemed to have acquiesced, that is consented, as well; if they did not know that the rule was being created, they would become entitled to persistent objection from the point of time from which they knew or ought to have known in good faith of the creation of the rule, and their failure to use this entitlement would also amount to acquiescence, that is consent. Domestic law analogy cannot be adopted either because the international legal system does not admit of any centralised law-making.

Another objection to the consensual explanation of customary law is developed by Thirlway by reference to certain passages in the *Nicaragua* case. In this case, the International Court pointed out that the 'shared views of the parties' as to what they regarded as a customary rule and their 'recognition' of it could not prejudice its opinion on this issue: it had to ascertain that the existence of *opinio juris* was confirmed in practice.[75] Thus, Thirlway suggests that the Court did not speak of consent, but of shared views and recognition of the rule, which arguably confirms that customary rules are not based on consent, and they can bind States that have not participated in their creation. 'Shared views' of the Parties can at most evidence a bilateral custom, but not general custom, and these views, or consent of the parties, are irrelevant in the case of general customary rules.[76]

It seems that this view is inconsistent. Binding States without their consent obscures the issue of acquiescence and lack of objection to which every State is entitled. But most importantly, the Court's mentioning of *opinio juris* did not touch upon the issue of whether this concept is consensual or sociological: it

[72] *Id*, 192.
[73] Mendelson (1998-II), 165 at 255.
[74] *Id*, 256.
[75] *ICJ Reports*, 1986, 97–98.
[76] Thirlway (1990), 51.

merely means that *opinio juris* has to be ascertained. Neither does the Court's proclamation of insufficiency of the parties' 'shared views' certify the irrelevance of consent. All this means is that 'shared views' can evidence the existence of a custom established on the basis of consent that has been given by States previously, but they cannot prejudge the question whether or not such consent to the customary rule has been properly given. Therefore, *Nicaragua* cannot be used as evidence against the consensual view. All *Nicaragua* says is that 'shared views' are not crucial by themselves, not that they determine what else may or may not be crucial, or that the irrelevance of 'shared views' of the parties means their subjection to general custom to which they do not consent.

Thirlway speaks not 'of consent but of conviction of the existence of the rule'.[77] Whatever the terminology, it is the attitude of States expressed for the attention of other States that brings about the rule and without it there will be no rule. This, now, is the very foundation of the consensual approach, emphasising the shared conviction as opposed to the conviction *per se*.

The issue of view as to the customary status of the relevant rule is normally treated as an issue of consent to that rule, as is clear from Judge Sorensen's approach to the reception of treaty rules into customary law. Judge Sorensen thus commented on the relevance of the attitude of Germany in relation to the 1958 Continental Shelf Convention:

> At a decisive stage of this formative process, an interested State, which was not a party to the Convention, formally recorded its view that the Convention was an expression of generally applicable international law. This view being perfectly well founded, that State is not now in a position to escape the authority of the Convention.[78]

Further, in opposing the consensual explanation of custom, Thirlway favours the 'sociological' concept of *opinio juris* that puts emphasis on the social desirability of the rule.[79] Thirlway repeatedly suggests in his writings an explanation of this process: at early stages States consider the rule either as 'potentially rule-creating' or 'useful and desirable'.[80] The concept of 'potentially rule-creating' can indeed express the view of States that the rule can potentially acquire legal character or is suitable to do so, but this does not by itself prove that the rule has actually acquired legal character. Viewing rules as 'useful and desirable' is not the same as their acceptance as legally binding rules. The criterion of 'useful and desirable' refers to the potentiality and likelihood but not to the actual process of law-making. Whether or not the problem is seen from a consensual perspective, the

[77] Thirlway (1990), 52.

[78] *North Sea*, Dissenting Opinion, *ICJ Reports*, 1969, 248.

[79] Thirlway (1990), 45.

[80] Thirlway (1990), 43, referring to his *International Customary Law and Codification* (1972), 53–54; and also acknowledging that the Court in *North Sea* refused to rely on the criterion of desirability (1990), 45.

establishment of customary rule through the expression of *opinio juris* necessarily requires ascertaining the *actual* conviction of States that the rule *is* a legal rule.

Further vigorous support for the sociological understanding of customary law is offered by Charney. According to Charney, 'the obligation to conform to rules of international law is not derived from the voluntary decision of a State to accept or reject the binding force of a rule of law. Rather, it is the societal context which motivates States to have an international law and obligates them to conform to its rules.'[81] Charney further argues pursuant to Visscher that 'If it is the societal context that is the source of the obligation to conform to specific rules of international law, then consent, either express or tacit, is irrelevant to the obligation.'[82]

This can be a plausible sociological explanation of why States ought to conform to international law in general and what the general motivation behind international law is. But this cannot be a proper explanation of why the State is to be considered as bound to comply with the individual and specific rules of international law. As Akehurst observes, 'practice accompanied by a sense of social or moral obligation does not always create the rule of customary law'.[83] The fact that something is required by morality, comity, courtesy or social needs does not support the existence of the legal rule.[84]

In fact, the thesis of rationality of customary rules as the factor of their validity, which is an issue very cognate to the 'social desirability' approach, has been rejected in jurisprudence. In *North Sea*, the International Court refused to infer the existence of a customary rule from the principle of equidistance in maritime delimitation, even though it acknowledged that the rule was reasonable, practicable and convenient. Instead, the Court required evidence in terms of State practice and *opinio juris*.[85]

Another rejection of the rationality argument can be seen in the *Ahmadou Sadio Diallo* case, in which the Court rejected the claim that international law admits of the diplomatic protection rule allowing protection of company rights 'by substitution', through vindicating the rights of individual shareholders. As the Court put it, 'The theory of protection by substitution seeks indeed to offer protection to the foreign shareholders of a company who could not rely on the benefit of an international treaty and to whom no other remedy is available, the allegedly unlawful acts having been committed against the company by the State of its nationality.' However, State practice could not support the view that any such rule, despite the stated rationale, achieved the status of a customary rule.[86]

[81] Charney (1985), 1 at 16.
[82] *Id*,18.
[83] Akehurst (1975–76), 35.
[84] *Id*, 1 at 37.
[85] *ICJ Reports*, 1969, para 23.
[86] *Ahmadou Sadio Diallo*, Preliminary Objections, General List No 103, Judgment of 24 May 2007, paras 88–90.

On the other hand, the rationality and usefulness of the *uti possidetis* rule was affirmed in *Burkina-Faso/Mali*, extending an originally Latin American rule to Africa as a general rule of international law.[87] This rule was also derived as an inherent element of the broader principle of self-determination, which also explains the reference to its usefulness. Thus, mere rationality did not matter. In fact, rationality and inherency of a rule are essentially different matters: one refers to the inherent merit of the projected rule, while the other links the rule that cannot, or not completely, be empirically proved, to the essence of another, broader, rule of undisputed status.

Thus, it must be admitted that none of the approaches that oppose the consensual nature of custom-generation advances a consistent alternative that would be consistent with the basic nature of the international legal system and would be capable of being accommodated within the requirements developed in jurisprudence.

In the end, the device of implied consent removes all potential problems in this area and spares international legal science from inventing alternatives to consent such as social necessity or moral desirability of rules. It is no less important that none of the relevant judicial pronouncements justify a customary rule by reference to its social, political and economic desirability, as opposed to a sense of legal obligation. In addition, the *Asylum* case even expressly excludes the relevance of practice pursued in terms of political expediency.[88]

5. Consensual Basis of Custom and the Side Aspects of Custom-Generation

(a) General Aspects

In doctrine, the problem of consensualism in custom-generation is often approached from the side, in terms of the contested and marginal aspects of custom-generation, rather than focusing on its principal nature. Ultimately, whether the process of custom-generation is consensual depends not on side issues such as regional custom-generation, persistent objection, protest, or the issue of new States—which are on their own quite useful in enabling us to discern the merits of the consensual approach—but on what the mainline process of custom-generation actually means. Judging the process of custom-generation relates to the positive process of custom-generation, while side issues involve additional considerations and this should not affect the understanding of the process of custom-generation where other things are equal. The analysis of the mainline process of custom-generation ultimately

[87] *Case Concerning Frontier Dispute* (Burkina Faso/Republic of Mali), Judgment of 22 December 1986, 554.

[88] *Asylum Case* (Colombia/Peru), Judgment of 20 November 1950, *ICJ Reports*, 1950, 266.

holds the key to explaining the essence of side elements as well as the mainline process itself. Nevertheless, these side aspects still need to be examined if only to demonstrate that they involve no inherent contradiction with the consensual essence of customary law.

(b) The Problem of Regional Customary Law

One of the objections against viewing custom-generation as a consensual phenomenon is based on the alleged difference in the process of creation of general and regional customary rules. The principal doctrinal emphasis is made on the alleged distinction that while the emergence of regional custom is more dependent on will and consent of individual States, the emergence of general or universal custom is less so. Mendelson regards the *Lotus* case as dispensing with the requirement for consent by each and every State, because it referred to 'usages generally accepted'. This is contrasted with the *Asylum* case on regional custom-generation where it was held that the party asserting that the customary rule exists must prove that it has become binding on the other party.[89] However, in *Lotus*, even in terms of general customary law, the attitudes of individual States have been treated as relevant.

The *Asylum* case is often portrayed as supportive of the thesis that the International Court emphasised the relevance of individual consent in the case of regional custom and thus implied the absence of a similar requirement in the case of general customary law. But even though the Court was addressing regional custom-generation, it said nothing to prejudice the consensual nature of general custom, which is clear from the relevant passages of the case. The Court emphasised that the Colombian Government in this case:

> has relied on an alleged regional or local custom peculiar to Latin-American States. The Party which relies on a custom of this kind must prove that this custom is established in such a manner that it has become binding on the other Party. The Colombian Government must prove that the rule invoked by it is in accordance with a constant and uniform usage practised by the States in question, and that this usage is the expression of a right appertaining to the State granting asylum and a duty incumbent on the territorial State. This follows from Article 38 of the Statute of the Court, which refers to international custom 'as evidence of a general practice accepted as law'.[90]

It is difficult to see from this passage that the Court meant formulating different standards for the emergence of different customary rules depending on their geographical scale. Although the Court addresses the regional custom and

[89] Mendelson (1995), 177 at 181; similarly, Judge De Castro in *Fisheries Jurisdiction* suggests that regional customary rules need to be proved, while general customary rules are based on general conviction as to their validity, *ICJ Reports*, 1974, 79.

[90] *ICJ Reports*, 1950, 276–277.

speaks of 'a custom of this kind', this is due to the context of the case rather than the Court's conception of the normative framework. This is clear also from the Court's reference to Article 38 of its Statute and the consequent placing of all customary rules on the same footing in terms of their psychological element. It should therefore be concluded that the formation of regional customary rules does not include any such binding element of rules on States that is absent in the process of formation of general customary law.

(c) The Problem of New States

According to Brierly, a new State joining the international society is not bound by international law on the basis of consent: 'it does not regard itself, and it is not regarded by others, as having any option in the matter'.[91] Along similar lines, Kelsen argues that if custom is based on consent, the thesis that new States are automatically bound by all rules of customary law in existence at the time of their becoming independent cannot stand. Whether or not the new State gives consent to these rules is therefore irrelevant. This allegedly explains that the consensual understanding of custom is only a fiction.[92] But Kelsen is quick enough to add that this does not affect the relevance of consent in the development of custom.[93]

It is a common and indisputable ground that new States are bound by the bulk of international law in force when they join the international society. However, the thesis that a new State is bound by the existing international law created before it joined the international society as the condition of joining is not conceptually the same as the thesis that the same new State can, after joining the international society, be subjected to the operation of subsequent customary rules against its will. Therefore, the issue of new States and customary law has little to do with the mainline issue of consensual character of customary international law.

At the same time, the relevance of the consent of new States, especially implied or tacit consent, cannot be disregarded altogether. A further explanation of their implied consent can be the absence of their reservation to one or another customary rule.[94] Even though the rules may well be consolidated upon their independence,[95] new States still may object to them within reasonable time and this will be seen as withholding their consent to the rule.

[91] Brierly (1949), 53.

[92] Kelsen, *Principles of International Law* (R Tucker ed, 1967), 445, 453; Mendelson (1995), 177 at 188–198.

[93] Kelsen (1967), 453.

[94] Akehurst (1975–76), 1 at 27.

[95] *Id*, 27–28.

(d) Protest and Persistent Objection

It is generally recognised that protest is a factor in the creation of customary rules, and timely protest can prevent the formation of custom.[96] Obviously, protests operate as withholding consent to the rules that would be established had protests not been made. Therefore, there is room for suggesting that the absence of protest implies giving consent. It is difficult to argue that States can preclude the emergence of custom by withholding consent, but they can actually be bound by customary rules to which they have not consented.

The Permanent Court's approach in *Lotus* is that if States do not protest against practice, they view this practice in conformity with international law. This view cannot be without limits, because in this case it would expect States to protest against anything and everything in order to avoid the adverse implications for law-making. Although the negative side of protest is quite clear in precluding agreement, the positive implication of the lack of protest is far from being clearly established. Mere toleration is not the same as acceptance of practice as law. This can be seen in the Permanent Court's Opinion in *Danube Commission*, where the Court faced the argument that the exercise of certain powers of the Commission commanded mere toleration of the territorial State, not its legal acceptance. The Court did not ascribe any legal effect to mere toleration. It instead identified the basis of the relevant powers in Article 6 of the Definitive Statute as opposed to customary practices.[97] There are implications for the doctrine of acquiescence, the burden of proof for which is very high, presupposing long and consistent inaction accompanied by consciousness of legal change.[98]

The essence of the persistent objection rule is that a State which objects to the evolving rule of customary law is exempted from its operation.[99] The International Court in *Fisheries* affirmed that the ten-mile rule related to maritime bays was not binding on Norway which had consistently opposed it.[100] In essence, the normative implications of persistent objection are practically indistinguishable from those of protest. The affirmation of the persistent objection rule in the *Fisheries* case must therefore be seen as its support for the consensual element present in the process of custom-generation. Similarly, Judge Lachs' reasoning in *North Sea* signifies acceptance of the persistent objection thesis as an example of the equidistance rule allegedly translated into customary law from Article 6 of the 1958

[96] For the criteria, see Akehurst (1975–76), 1 at 39–40.

[97] *Jurisdiction of the European Commission of the Danube between Galatz and Braila*, Series B, No 14, 8 December 1927, 36–37.

[98] On acquiescence and customary law, see I McGibbon, Customary International Law and Acquiescence, *BYIL* (1957), 115.

[99] Charney (1985), 1 at 2.

[100] *Fisheries* (UK v Norway), *ICJ Reports*, 1951, 116 at 131; see further Judge De Castro in *ICJ Reports*, 1974, 90; for doctrinal support and historical overview, see Verdross (1969), 650–652; Skubiszewski (1971), 848.

Geneva Convention on Continental Shelf. Judge Lachs admits that this rule could have been opposed by certain States from its inception.[101] This runs parallel to the rejection by the Court as a whole of the customary status of that rule, which presumably signifies that the withholding of consent to a rule through persistent objection is not essentially different from the rule's failure to secure the *opinio juris* necessary for it to be binding.

There are different doctrinal perspectives on persistent objection. Brownlie considers the persistent objector rule important in view of the increase of majoritarian tendencies in the law-making process.[102] This means effectively that the persistent objection rule protects individual States from being subjected to rules to which they do not consent. Charney follows Visscher in denying the relevance of consent in custom-generation in favour of the societal context and contends that:

> if the societal context is the source, then an objection at any time, persistent or not, is irrelevant to the binding effect of a rule of law. If this is true, there is no place in international law for the persistent objector rule. . . . Only if one actually believes in the reality of the tacit consent theory of international obligation might there be any room for the persistent objection rule.[103]

Charney argues that the persistent objector rule can only possess the temporary value of strategic bargain, but 'cannot serve a permanent role, unless, of course, one really does believe that States have the independence freely to grant or withhold their consent to rules of customary international law'.[104] In fact, persistent objection cannot even serve, in legal terms, that strategic temporary role Charney allocates to it unless it is viewed as a tool for withholding the consent of the objecting State. If consent is not being withheld, the objecting State cannot achieve its bargaining purposes in legal terms. Thus, whatever doctrinal perspective one adopts, one cannot avoid explaining the persistent objection rule by reference to the consensual nature of custom-generation.

In fact, the dimension of persistent objection in emerging customary law contributes to consolidating the consensual perspective of custom-generation. With persistent objection, States preclude something which is not yet law in relation to them from becoming such. With *opinio juris* they acknowledge something as being law. One process involves saying no to what is not yet law, while the other process involves saying yes to what arguably 'already' is law. One wonders how this can be so, for if *opinio juris* relates to what already is law, persistent objection is thus not possible, which cannot be true. Persistent objection is always possible provided that it is timely made. If States can prevent the emergence of a customary rule through expression of an attitude consisting in an

[101] Dissenting Opinion, *ICJ Reports*, 1969, 229.
[102] I Brownlie, *Principles of Public International Law* (2003), 11.
[103] Charney (1985), 1 at 18.
[104] *Id*, 23–24.

objection, then the relevance of such attitude relates also to the positive process of the emergence of a rule. *Opinio juris* is thus not just an acknowledgment of an already existing rule but can also involve the attitude relating to the very emergence of the rule. To put it in simpler terms, those who can say no to the emergence of the rule will, at some stage and in some form, be supposed to have said yes to this process. Whether such consent is inferable from long-time conscious silence and non-objection, or from other factors, is more a question of evidence than of principle.

The doctrinal opposition to persistent objection cannot prove that it is irrelevant. On the contrary, all such opposition does is emphasise the indispensable link between persistent objection and the consensual basis of customary law. Most importantly, the institution of persistent objection is not self-explanatory—it is there because it represents and explains the broader framework of custom-generation. Thus, given the ability of States to object through the expression of will before a rule becomes law and is so acknowledged, there must be some psychological element involved that expresses the will of States to make it part of law. It is simply inconsistent to suggest that the emergence of the rule can be precluded through withholding consent, yet the very emergence of the rule would not be based on consent. If persistent objection is possible, then the whole process of custom-generation is consensual.

6. The Issue of Inherent and Fundamental Rules

Bearing in mind that international law is an inter-State legal system in which there is no central government, only those rules can be part of international law which are accepted by States. The same can, to a certain extent, hold true for certain rules that are not strictly, or originally, based on State consent, but which are inherent in the very nature of international law as a legal system. Such inherency is essentially different from the desirability or social acceptability of the relevant rule. It is one thing to say that the rule must be seen as part of international law because it is indispensable to its structural underpinnings. It is another thing to argue that a certain substantive legal regulation is part of international law because it is a desirable or sound regulation, even if State consent does not support it.

In certain cases, the rules of customary law, designated as fundamental or inherent rules whose normative status derives from the structural necessity of the international legal system, are identified without much enquiry into the supportive State practice and *opinio juris*. Whether such fundamental or inherent rules can be seen as customary in the mainstream sense of this term can be the subject of debate. This is presumably a field in which incidences of customary law overlap with those of natural law. The consensual pattern of customary international law is therefore subject in certain cases to limitations defined by the need for systemic effectiveness.

Certain legal frameworks may show that if one were to require empirical evidence for each and every rule of fundamental evidence, there would practically be no legal regulation in the relevant field.

As Fitzmaurice emphasises in conceptual terms, 'If a rule is necessary, or if the existence of a system of rules is a necessary condition of a certain state of affairs, the rule or system must also necessarily be binding, or it would not fulfil, or be able to fulfil its function. . . . It is something that arises logically and inevitably out of the requirements of international intercourse, relations and transactions. It is an inherent necessity of the case, and no theory of consent need to be postulated in order to account for it.'[105]

In two of the very few contributions on this subject, Bleckmann develops the rationale behind the inherency of rules. There are fields in which the existence of certain legal rules is objectively necessary and independent of practice, such as the fields of territorial sea, nationality or outer space.[106] These can also be areas which relate to the structure of international law and the consequent allocation of territorial competence, or liability of the State organs for its actions.[107] There are further areas in which consequential rules (*Folgesätze*) can be derived from governing legal principles. These consequential rules can be confirmed through practice as well, but this is not necessary, because consequential rules can exist without being corroborated in practice.[108]

It must also be examined whether this approach to customary rules, that is the reliance on the inherency of rules, or on the practice only as the basis of general rules, implies the revival of the natural law argument. Classic writers and nineteenth-century writers refer on occasion to State practice while at the same time accepting the relevance of natural law. This can be seen in the example of Puffendorf's reasoning, according to which ambassadorial inviolability is based on 'tacit consent, as evidenced by the usage of nations', that is voluntary law, and also on natural law.[109] This may be seen as a reference to the inherency of the rule, arguably derived from natural law, its legal status also being based on usage (practice). The consensual and voluntary element is also underlined. Similarly, the *Fisheries Jurisdiction* Judgment demonstrates that a reference to practice-based consensus is not sufficient for the normative allocation of rights and obligations, and the Court had to base its reasoning on the recognition of this allocation by the affected States.[110]

[105] G Fitzmaurice, The General Principles of International Law Considered from the Standpoint of the Rule of Law, 92 *RdC* (II-1957), 39–40.

[106] A Bleckmann, Völkergewohnheitsrecht trotz widersprüchlicher Praxis? *ZaöRV* (1976), 374 at 389.

[107] A Bleckmann, Zur Feststellung und Auslegung von Völkergewohnheitsrecht, *ZaöRV* (1977), 505 at 508–509.

[108] *Id*, 390.

[109] *Cf* Wheaton, *Elements of International Law* (1866), 8.

[110] See above p. 78.

One field in which the existence of certain legal regulation can be seen as objectively necessary is that of the continental shelf delimitation. Presumably, the continental shelf is not by itself inherent in international law for it can exist and survive without it. But the inherency relates to the inherent nature of the continental shelf and the implications of such inherency.

In the *North Sea* case, the International Court identified:

> the most fundamental of all the rules of law relating to the continental shelf... namely that the rights of the coastal State in respect of the area of continental shelf that constitutes a natural prolongation of its land territory into and under the sea exist *ipso facto* and *ab initio,* by virtue of its sovereignty over the land, and as an extension of it in an exercise of sovereign rights for the purpose of exploring the seabed and exploiting its natural resources. In short, there is here an inherent right. In order to exercise it, no special legal process has to be gone through, nor have any special legal acts to be performed. Its existence can be declared (and many States have done this) but does not need to be constituted. Furthermore, the right does not depend on its being exercised.[111]

This is reasoning that does not share the positivist approach as to the evidence required for identifying a legal rule. This reasoning is transcendent and self-explanatory, and presumably implies a naturalist element. But this reasoning also relates to the well-recognised institution dealing with the structural aspects of territorial sovereignty. This perhaps evidences the link between the structural aspects of the international legal system and the inherency of rules.

The Court refused to identify a fundamental rule on the continental shelf requiring that the State should own the parts of shelf closer to its coast than to the coast of the other State. This followed from the absence of an inherent link between adjacency and proximity. As the Court put it, 'the notion of adjacency, so constantly employed in continental shelf doctrine from the start, only implies proximity in a general sense, and does not imply any fundamental or inherent rule the ultimate effect of which would be to prohibit any State (otherwise than by agreement) from exercising continental shelf rights in respect of areas closer to the coast of another State'.[112] The rule of equidistance was not a 'logical necessity deriving from the fundamental theory of the continental shelf'.[113]

Support for the thesis of inherent rules was also voiced by individual judges in the *North Sea* case regarding the principle of equidistance as the inherent normative consequence of the concept of the continental shelf. In advancing the argument of inherent rule, Judge Morelli in *North Sea* argued that:

> the equidistance criterion for the delimitation of the continental shelves of various States to be a necessary consequence of the apportionment effected by general international law on the basis of contiguity. I am therefore of the opinion that it is not necessary to ascertain if a specific custom has come into existence in this connection. State practice in this

[111] *ICJ Reports*, 1969, 22.
[112] *ICJ Reports*, 1969, 30–31.
[113] *Id*, 45–46.

field is relevant not as a constitutive element of a custom which creates a rule, but rather as a confirmation of such rule. Confirmation of the rule is also provided, within certain limits, by the provisions of the Geneva Convention.[114]

Thus, from this perspective, the inherency of a rule can provide for relevance of practice as explanatory of pre-existing rules, as opposed to constitutive of new rules. Practice seen in this light is arguably not part of the consensual law-making process. In other words, at the conceptual level, such practice presumably does not need to evidence the overlap of attitudes between the relevant States.

In *Tunisia–Libya* both parties accepted the relevance of the fundamental concept of the continental shelf as the natural prolongation of the coast, but differed on the principles and rules deriving from this concept.[115] In *Gulf of Maine*, both parties agreed that there was a fundamental rule that governs the delimitation of maritime boundaries in all cases, and it requires the delimitation on the basis of applicable law and equitable principles, either by agreement or by dispute settlement bodies. Apart from this fundamental rule, the parties were not in agreement on any specific rules that could mandatorily govern the delimitation of their maritime spaces.[116]

The Court referred to the fundamental rule on which the parties had agreed and which is present in the legal conviction not only of the Parties, but also of all States, and requires delimitation on the basis of applicable law and equitable principles, either by agreement or by dispute settlement bodies. The Court's judgment suggests that this fundamental rule is part of customary law. Customary law did not provide any more detailed rules determining the specific ways and criteria of delimitation.[117] In particular, there was no evidence that customary law accommodated the 'combined equidistance-special circumstances rule'.[118]

It is noteworthy that apart from the acknowledgment by the parties to the proceedings, the Court did not search for any specific evidence required to establish customary rules, and this is not *prima facie* compatible with its refusal to base itself on 'shared views' of parties in *Nicaragua*. But this field is presumably different as it relates to the inherency of the legal rule without which there could be no general international law on delimitation of maritime spaces.

All these passages from different cases convey the impression that the 'fundamental' character of the rule refers in this context to its subject-matter, not to its special status or origin. It is the rule defining the most fundamental aspects of delimitation. Fundamental rule is not discovered by consensual evidence or State practice *per se*; nevertheless, the Court still refers to the acceptance of this rule by States-parties to the proceedings, as was the case, for instance, in *Gulf of Maine*. In addition, the fundamental character of the relevant rule does not influence its

[114] Dissenting Opinion, *id*, 202.
[115] *Tunisia–Libya*, *ICJ Reports*, 1982, 43.
[116] *Gulf of Maine*, *ICJ Reports*, 1984, 295–296.
[117] *Id*, 299–300.
[118] *Id*, 302.

content and scope. The rule exists to the extent of its indispensability felt within the international legal community, but it cannot cover what States disagree on.

Thus, in the law of the sea, fundamental rule has not been viewed as a substitute for regulating where there is no agreed regulation. In addition, the existence of allegedly inherent and non-consensual fundamental rules does not prejudice specific legal outcomes. The rejection of the inherency of a specific rule does not prejudice the general merit of the inherency argument either.

In *Libya–Malta*, the Court rejected the relevance of the principle of sovereign equality as the principle requiring equidistance in delimiting the continental shelf area between the two States. It mattered whether the equidistance rule derived from the legal rule accepted by States, not whether sovereign equality had any implication.[119] In this case there was presumably no adequate structural connection between the two rules. However, the relevance of inherent corollaries to rules was affirmed in *Burkina-Faso/Mali*, where the Court saw the *uti possidetis* principle as logically connected with the attainment of independence,[120] that is the principle of self-determination of peoples. In the *Ottoman Debt* Arbitration, the Tribunal treated the payment of interest as part of compensation for internationally wrongful acts as an aspect of inherent rules. The Tribunal stated that 'the general principle of the responsibility of states implies a special responsibility in the matter of delay in the payment of a money debt'.[121]

The field of inherent or consequential rules is not detached from the positivist framework of analysis, but it may in some aspects imply a natural law element, for instance in terms of the necessity of legal regulation. In other cases, inherent or consequential rules can be explained through the positivist approach, that is by the need to ensure the operation of the original rule to which the consequential rule relates. In this way general rules can address specific situations, which ensures the completeness and effectiveness of legal regulation.

7. Conclusion

The above analysis demonstrates that the field of customary law does not tolerate any strict separation of naturalism and positivism, and the proper understanding of this field cannot be reached only on the basis of adherence to one of these doctrines to the exclusion of the other.

It is not possible to view the mainstream area of customary international law as independent of the consent of States and no alternative theory is in a position to replace it. Both the practice in this field and the conceptual framework of international law require accepting this outcome. On the whole, the consensual

119 *ICJ Reports*, 1985, 43.

120 *ICJ Reports*, 1986, 565.

121 *Ottoman Debt Arbitration* in G Wilson (ed), *The Hague Arbitration Cases* (1915) 305.

element confers on international law the distinct legitimacy that is not present in a national legal system, in the sense that the legal person is bound by rules it directly consents to, as opposed to the representative legislation. The consensual foundation of international law is not its weakness but its strength. The positive character of international law has to guide the study of the relationship between law and non-law in the international legal system, the interpretation of legal rules and the identification of the meaning of non-law when it constitutes part of a positively accepted legal rule.

At the same time, neither can the outcome that the natural law argument is necessary to explain some normative developments be escaped. While natural law does not contribute to the mainstream process of creation of customary rules, the natural law argument is necessary to ensure that the rules are applied in accordance with their rationale and the inherent nature of the relevant legal institutions is respected.

PART III

LAW AND NON-LAW IN THE INTERNATIONAL LEGAL SYSTEM

Introduction

The work of the international legal system often involves factors whose normative status, meaning or scope is not straightforwardly based on recognised sources of international law. They cannot, or not fully, be said to be accepted and recognised by States in the same way as of creation of international legal rules. Yet, these non-legal elements have an impact on rights and obligations of international legal persons. The problem of determinacy of legal regulation inherently relates to that of the relationship between law and non-law. It is crucial to ascertain to what extent international law allows factors that are not the product of State consent and agreement to affect the rights and obligations of States.

As the analysis of the threshold of legal regulation has demonstrated, the field of non-law is reserved for such factors, concepts, notions or principles as have not achieved legally binding status through the agreement of States, yet are relevant in terms of what the rights and obligations of international legal persons may be in specific situations. These factors of non-law may reflect considerations of fairness, expediency, social and political reasonableness, or economic soundness. But because the international society has not agreed about their legal status, they remain non-law. International law is a body of binding rules. Thus, anything that has no such status has arguably to be reduced to the category of non-law.

The key implication of the sovereign freedom of action being preserved unless it is limited by binding rules of law is arguably that factors that have not achieved the status of binding law should not restrict sovereign freedom of action. One reason for this is the very indeterminacy that characterises these factors of non-law: if their meaning is not determinate, it is then unclear how far they can bind States and how they can constitute an effective legal regulation.

In this respect, non-law may refer to free-standing factors or phenomena that have not (yet) become law. On the other hand, the categories of non-law may be embodied in binding legal prescriptions and form their element. Still, such 'legally based non-law' would be indeterminate and would command no consensus of States as to its meaning and ambit.

This analysis involves those categories of non-law that are treated as relevant in practice. If a theoretical approach were to be adopted, more categories could presumably follow. But the limit of this study dictates that it has to be restricted to what is or may be relevant from a practical perspective. This Part consists of four chapters each focusing on a different aspect of non-law: fact, interest, value and quasi-normative non-law. Since they often form part of a legal rule or interact with its operation in some way, each of these categories of non-legal consideration raises important problems relating to the determinacy of legal rules. For that reason, certainty regarding the status and relevance of non-law is crucial if international legal actors are to know what they can expect from the application of a legal rule, which in turn is crucial for legal certainty.

It is necessary to explain why these four categories are singled out as the subject of study. The simple answer is that these four categories are the only genuine and structurally perceptible categories of non-law in the international legal system. There is hardly anything, apart from the factors subsumable within these four categories, that has claimed legal significance. These four categories express all non-legal categories that appear in the international legal process: political, economic, humanitarian, security and other considerations. Fact, interest, value and quasi-normative non-law are the forms of expressing these various non-legal considerations. In order to examine all relevant non-legal categories, some way must be found to classify them and thus adopt the most consistent and suitable typology. At the same time, categorising non-law into fact, interest, value and quasi-normative non-law is the closest possible way to perceive them in terms of jurisprudential categories that facilitates their understanding in relation to emergence, interpretation and application of legally binding rules. The categories of fact, interest and value are received categories of legal science, each of them expressing a contrast with positive law. As for the category of quasi-normative non-law, it is arguably used here for the first time. Its purpose is to bring together what is already present in practice.

All these categories of non-legal considerations involve the actual or potential argument that the relevant legal position should be established or amended because this would be fair, reasonable, sensible, socially acceptable or conducive to peace and security. These categories do not analyse the merits of the relevant legal position as the position accepted as part of legal regulation. The likely, even if not inevitable, outcome of this approach is to try to impact on the rights and duties of States without their consent and agreement. What unites all categories of non-law is that their content is not defined straightforwardly. States do not know what they mean on their face. Yet they are invoked all the time in the international legal process.

Each of the following four chapters examines the essence of the relevant category of non-law, its legal basis and its scope. It is preferred to examine these categories by proceeding from the most simple and straightforward category towards more complex ones. Hence, fact is examined first, and then interest and value follow. Finally, quasi-normative law is given extensive treatment which it deserves due it its complexity and diversity.

The fundamental question the next four chapters address, though in different contexts, is whether international law, fundamentally a consensual system, can be influenced by factors and standards which are not agreed upon by States, and not produced by their consent. This is a fundamental aspect of the determinacy of rules. This is raised both by the phenomenon of non-law and the issue of determinacy of treaty provisions. Consequently, the analysis of this part is later complemented by the conclusive analysis of Part V. Part V is about the interpretation of treaty provisions embodying indeterminate clauses referring to non-law.

5

Fact as Non-Law and the Limits on its Relevance

1. Conceptual Aspects

The doctrine of international law has not yet elaborated upon the general and consolidated theory of the relevance of facts in international law. In general, facts are often perceived as impacting on the creation, content, interpretation, application and modification of legal rules. This is alleged to happen either by reference to the specific context of the particular international legal institution, or to the incidences of power politics in international relations. The aim here is to examine the relevance of fact in various fields of international law and evaluate how far it can go.

The conception of fact as non-law requires understanding how international law distinguishes between factual and legal questions. Fact is normally understood as something that actually exists, which is much broader than what can be subsumed by the rules and standards accepted as law. However, denoting something as 'fact' does not really clarify the kind and scale of the relevant fact, and emphasises the inherent indeterminacy of legal requirements that may be linked to a factual consideration. Action certainly is a fact, attitudes may be too; likewise, the adoption of a legal instrument, its implementation and its breach are all facts. This diversity of what can be encompassed by the broad notion of fact cannot but underline the need to avoid any clear-cut conclusion on the relevance of facts for the emergence, maintenance and modification of rights and obligations in the international legal system. There are no authoritatively laid criteria to distinguish between fact and law. Still, in practice such distinction is always drawn *in casu* or on a more general plane.

This is especially visible from the jurisprudence of the WTO Appellate Body, whose appellate jurisdiction is limited to the examination of legal questions related to the facts that are established in the preceding panel proceedings. This follows from Article 17.6 of the WTO Dispute Settlement Understanding, which stipulates that the analysis of the Appellate Body shall be confined to the issues of law and legal interpretation developed by the

Panel.[1] Thus, there seems to be a division of labour and competence in this aspect between the panels and the Appellate Body. As the Appellate Body itself specified in the *EC–Hormones* case:

Under Article 17.6 of the DSU, appellate review is limited to appeals on questions of law covered in a panel report and legal interpretations developed by the panel. Findings of fact, as distinguished from legal interpretations or legal conclusions, by a panel are, in principle, not subject to review by the Appellate Body.[2]

The Appellate Body further specifies what the facts are, by observing that 'The determination of whether or not a certain event did occur in time and space is typically a question of fact.' Establishing the existence of the fact through evidence is thus a question of fact and not of law: 'Determination of the credibility and weight properly to be ascribed to (that is, the appreciation of) a given piece of evidence is part and parcel of the fact finding process and is, in principle, left to the discretion of a panel as the trier of facts.' But the matter of fact may simultaneously constitute part of the legal framework. This may relate to the Panel's exercise of its statutory duty to objectively assess facts and duly consider all the relevant evidence:

The consistency or inconsistency of a given fact or set of facts with the requirements of a given treaty provision is, however, a legal characterization issue. It is a legal question. Whether or not a panel has made an objective assessment of the facts before it, as required by Article 11 of the DSU, is also a legal question which, if properly raised on appeal, would fall within the scope of appellate review.[3]

Thus, the Appellate Body effectively assumes the competence to review the Panel's determination of facts on certain grounds such as the deliberate disregard of, or refusal to consider, the evidence submitted to a panel, or the wilful distortion or misrepresentation of evidence which would qualify as 'an egregious error that calls into question the good faith of a panel'. The Appellate Body would of course not engage with each and every factual issue the panel has gone through, unless the above specified circumstances are claimed to exist.[4] But by raising the issue of error, disregard or distortion, in principle every factual matter can come before the Appellate Body and be subjected to its review, the outcome of which would depend on the truth of those allegations.

[1] As Article 11 of the DSU specifies the task of panels, 'a panel should make an objective assessment of the matter before it, including an objective assessment of the facts of the case and the applicability of and conformity with the relevant covered agreements, and make such other findings as will assist the DSB in making the recommendations or in giving the rulings provided for in the covered agreements'.

[2] *EC Measures concerning Meat and Meat Products (Hormones)*, WT/DS26/AB/R, AB-1997–4, Report of the Appellate Body, 16 February 1998, para 132.

[3] *Id.*

[4] *Id*, para 134.

The division between law and fact in international law is strict, there being no intermediate category. Judge Lauterpacht in the *Admissibility of Hearings* case developed the doctrine of approximate application of treaties to explain the reasons behind the International Court's Opinion that the refusal of South Africa to transmit to the UN General Assembly the petitions by the inhabitants of South West Africa prevented the Assembly from exercising effective supervision, and justified the arrangement of hearings of petitioners themselves.[5] This may convey the impression that the Court impliedly applied the remedy for a breach of the duty to submit to supervision. As Rosenne points out:

> The Court carefully avoided the pejorative language of 'breach' and preferred the circumlocutions of a 'refusal to assist' and a refusal 'to co-operate' with the United Nations—refined judicial and diplomatic formulations for what many... regarded not merely as breach but as 'material breach' within the meaning of what was later adopted as Article 60 of the Vienna Convention.[6]

But it seems that the Court could not have raised the issue of material breach on its own and without the invocation of this reciprocal termination rule by the General Assembly, as the Assembly itself did years later. In this specific case, the Court was merely expected to pronounce on the submission relating to the implications of the South African refusal to transmit the petitions to the United Nations.

In this respect, Judge Lauterpacht emphasised in the same case that:

> It is a sound principle of law that whenever a legal instrument of continuing validity cannot be applied literally owing to the conduct of one of the parties, it must, without allowing that party to take advantage of its own conduct, be applied in a way approximating most closely to its primary object. To do that is to interpret and to give effect to the instrument, not to change it.[7]

In terms of the implication of his approach, Judge Lauterpacht observed that:

> The treaty as a whole does not terminate as the result of a breach of an individual clause. Neither is it necessarily rendered impotent and inoperative as the result of the action or inaction of one of the parties. It continues in being subject to adaptation to circumstances which have arisen.[8]

Judge Lauterpacht's doctrine of approximate application is undoubtedly constructive. It has the potential to explain the pertinent legal relations. However, it was not followed up at subsequent stages, among other things, because it was seen, rightly or wrongly, as an attempt to blur the distinction between law and facts. The International Court in *Gabcikovo/Nagymaros* refused to engage with the approximate application argument. However, Judge Bedjaoui tackled this question in his Separate Opinion as part of the analysis of the applicable rules of

[5] *ICJ Reports*, 1956, 23 at 31.
[6] S Rosenne, *Breach of Treaty* (1985), 98.
[7] *ICJ Reports*, 1956, 35 at 46.
[8] *Id*, 49.

interpretation and offered a strong disapproval of the relevance of this phenomenon in international law.[9]

As recognised in doctrine, legal science is specific in its appreciation of the relationship between law and fact. As Kelsen observes, 'a sociologist or psychologist sees only the factual, not the normative aspect of law and morality. He conceives of law and morality as a complex of facts, not as a system of valid rules . . . that is to say, of propositions about what men ought to do, and not of statements about what men actually do.'[10] Thus, for most of the other social sciences law is also included in the category of facts, and is approached from various perspectives, presumably including the perspective of its psychological impact on its addressees, or the social impact of its enforcement. Law, however, perceives facts as what actually happens, and requires the separation of rules and facts in the sense that the former prescribe the regulation of the latter.

Speaking generally, facts are either nature-given, such as geographic factors and realities, or the product of human conduct. Facts and their properties, in order to have legal relevance, must be approached objectively. In *Gulf of Maine*, the International Court, while dealing with the delimitation of the single maritime boundary between Canada and the US, faced the submission of characterising certain coasts as 'primary' and 'secondary'. Thus, 'the former would be regarded as of greater importance than the latter for the purposes of delimitation to be carried out in the waters off these coasts'. The Court held that such reasoning was dubious. Geographical facts cannot be characterised as primary or secondary. Such characterisation was 'the expression, not of any inherent property of the facts of nature, but of a human value judgment, which will necessarily be subjective and which may vary on the basis of the same facts, depending on the perspectives and ends in view'.[11] In other words, subjective characterisation cannot replace the objective property of facts. It is the latter and not the former that may bring about legal consequences.

In certain cases facts may have differentiated relevance on the basis of their legal designation by States. This can be seen, for instance, from the jurisprudence of the International Court of Justice regarding the jurisdiction of the Court *ratione temporis* on the basis of Optional Clause declarations on the basis of Article 36 of its Statute. As the jurisprudence culminating with the case of *Certain Property* affirms, the declarant States can, in their declarations, classify the relevant facts as those relating to the legal dispute and those constituting the very cause of the legal dispute. The implication is that the Court's jurisprudence thus accepted will cover, in a temporal sense, only the latter and exclude the former.[12] But, apart

[9] *Cf* below Part IV.

[10] H Kelsen, *General Theory of Law and State* (1967), 376.

[11] *Gulf of Maine* (Canada v USA), *ICJ Reports*, 1984, 246 at 271; later in the judgment the Court rejected the specific outcomes it was asked to attach to these subjective characterisations.

[12] *Certain Property* (Liechtenstein v Germany), Preliminary Objections, Judgment of 10 February 2005, *ICJ Reports*, 2005, 6 at 22–26.

from such consensual designation of facts, there is no warrant in international law for assuming their specific standing, characteristics or legal implications due to their factual characteristics.

The perception of the relevance of fact essentially depends on the essence of positive law either as the body of rules agreed upon by States, or rules actually observed and enforced by States. It follows from the basic concept of the sources of international law, as specified in Article 38 of the International Court's Statute, that the validity of legal rules derives from the agreement and acceptance of States. The *Lotus* case classically and clearly describes the idea of international law-making. It suggests that actual conduct or abstention cannot give rise to legal rules unless it is accompanied by viewing the relevant standard as legally binding. Facts, then, are measured in terms of their legality and their conformity with the rules of positive law. It is the standard job of international adjudication to ascertain the facts, evaluate them in the light of legal rules, and determine the applicable legal consequences thus deriving from the facts. As the Permanent Court of International Justice has observed, 'municipal laws are merely facts which express the will and constitute the activities of States, in the same manner as do legal decisions or administrative measures'. Their legality must be assessed in terms of international law.[13] Similarly, the WTO Appellate Body in *India–Patent* emphasised that 'municipal law is a fact that must be established before an international tribunal'. In addition, municipal law may serve as evidence of facts. It may provide evidence of State practice. Its interpretation at the international level may thus be necessary from time to time.[14]

In the territorial dispute cases of *Burkina-Faso/Mali* and *Benin–Niger*, the International Court examined the relevance of domestic law, including colonial law, in the context of territorial sovereignty. The Court has continuously held that such domestic law has no legal quality in international legal relations, but merely constitutes 'one factual element among others', or evidence of the *effectivités*.[15] The Court further reiterated in *Benin–Niger* that 'in the application of the principle *uti possidetis juris*, French law does not play a role in itself but only as one

[13] *Certain German Interests in Polish Upper Silesia*, *PCIJ Series* A, No 7, 19; see also *US–Import Prohibition of Certain Shrimp and Shrimp Products*, AB-1998–4, Report of the WTO Appellate Body, WT/DS58/AB/R, 12 October 1998, para 138. According to Article 27 of the 1969 Vienna Convention on the Law of Treaties, a State 'may not invoke the provisions of its internal law as justification for its failure to perform a treaty'. As the ILC's Article 3 on State responsibility confirms, 'The characterization of an act of a State as internationally wrongful is governed by international law. Such characterization is not affected by the characterization of the same act as lawful by internal law.' For the text of ILC Articles and commentaries thereto, see the Report of the International Law Commission on the work of its Fifty-third session (2001), *Official Records of the General Assembly, Fifty-sixth session, Supplement No. 10* (A/56/10).

[14] *India–Patent Protection for Pharmaceutical and Agricultural Chemical Products*, AB-1997–5, Report of the Appellate Body, WT/DS50/AB/R, 19 December 1997, paras 64–66.

[15] *Case concerning the Frontier Dispute* (Benin–Niger), Chamber of the Court, Judgment of 12 July 2005, *ICJ Reports*, 2005, 90 at 110 (further referring to *Burkina-Faso/Mali*).

factual element among others, or as evidence indicative of what has been called the "colonial heritage" at the critical date'.[16]

The factual relevance of colonial law was ascertained by the Chamber in the fact that 'under French colonial law, the Lieutenant-Governor of the colony had no competence to unilaterally delimit the external boundaries of the colony'. Thus, the acts of such Governor could not serve as the basis of the title to territory or determine the boundaries.[17] The Chamber thus places national legal acts in the context of factual analysis by using them as evidence for ascertaining whether the relevant factual circumstances are present in the case.

In some cases, notably where international law has no regulation of its own on the relevant subject, municipal legal regulation can be taken as the starting-point in clarifying the international legal position in the relevant field. This happened, for instance, with regard to the concept and rights of corporations in national law in the *Barcelona Traction* case.[18] The Court pointed out that if it 'were to decide the case in disregard of the relevant institutions of municipal law it would, without justification, invite serious legal difficulties. It would lose touch with reality, for there are no corresponding institutions of international law to which the Court could resort.'[19] The matter related to the exercise of diplomatic protection in relation to the injury done to the company. The Court pointed out that:

> It is to rules generally accepted by municipal legal systems which recognise the limited company whose capital is represented by shares, and not to the municipal law of a particular State, that international law refers. In referring to such rules, the Court cannot modify, still less deform them.[20]

One could argue that even in *Barcelona Traction* the actual and ultimate relevance of Spanish law was little more than that of fact. But the Court proceeds to emphasise that 'thus the position of the company rests on a positive rule of both municipal and international law'.[21] The fact of the separate status of the company as a legal entity was used as point of reference to determine to which entity the nationality and diplomatic protection should relate.[22] It is thus arguable that municipal law can be more than fact from the viewpoint of international law,

[16] *Id*, 120.
[17] *Id*, 125.
[18] *Barcelona Traction*, Second Phase (Belgium v Spain), *ICJ Reports*, 1970, para 50; similarly, in *Benin–Niger* the Chamber of the Court studied French domestic law and French colonial law to ascertain the internal competences and regulation as to the establishment and abolition of colonial possessions; see also *Azurix Corp. and the Argentine Republic*, ICSID Case No ARB/01/12, Award of 14 July 2006, para 336, on the municipal law conception of property, suggesting that any acceptable concept of property incorporates as property rights the expectations based on the legal system that begets them.
[19] *Barcelona Traction*, *ICJ Reports*, 1970, 37.
[20] *Id*, 37.
[21] *Id*, 38.
[22] *Id*, 38–44.

but only if international law does not itself regulate the subject to which the relevant municipal law relates. On a general plane, if national law and legal decisions can constitute internationally wrongful acts, it is difficult to avoid the conclusion that if the division is made between factual and legal factors in the international legal system, national laws would belong to the former rather than to the latter category.

This being the general position strictly and inevitably following from the very essence and definition of positive law, facts can still be inherently linked to legal regulation. Bare facts obviously have no such effect. Facts expressive of the will of the State can have law-making potential if other prerequisites of this process will be satisfied. Facts violating a legal requirement can in principle be validated and accepted as legal, through the expression of the will of the affected legal person. In other situations, objective facts can merely represent subjective claims under international law, unable by themselves to achieve the desired legal effect. Then, there can be systemically relevant facts that support certain basic aspects of the operation of international law. Furthermore, there are facts that form the part of the rationale of the relevant legal rule in terms of determining its applicability. This makes rules workable in the sense that they do not lend themselves to abuse and do not unduly disadvantage some States by benefiting other States. Yet another question is whether facts that are external to a rule can impact on its content and applicability.

Positive law refers to abstract rules designed to regulate multiple situations. Thus, only those facts that either express the legally relevant attitude, or have attached to them some legal consequences by virtue of some legal principle can have legal impact. Although empirically it may look as if facts themselves produce legal effects, if viewed from a systemic perspective, in most if not all cases those legal effects are due to the legal principle that relates to those facts. Finding the balance between these basic factors is an inevitable requirement for any general and workable theory of fact in international law.

A great deal of doctrinal attention has gone to the issue of whether and how facts, by virtue of their effectiveness, are relevant in transforming illegality into legality. As Kelsen explains, the 'principle of effectiveness' attaches to effective factual situations, particularly to violations of law, the legal consequences of which they would otherwise not have.[23] At the same time, the essence of this 'principle of effectiveness' and its parameters has never been properly defined, and there would be some conceptual problems in effecting such definition. As Kelsen further observes, 'legal consequences cannot simply be deduced from facts, but only from legal rules which confer upon facts the effect of creating the new law'.[24] This can be understood as referring to a general principle of the international legal order that affirms the law-creating potential of facts. If there were such a general

[23] H Kelsen *Principles of International Law*, (R Tucker, ed, 1967) 422.
[24] Kelsen (1967), 421–422.

principle, it has to be asked how far it would go and, if taken to extremes, it would in essence contend that law should always follow facts On the other hand, this can mean that the international legal order includes some specific legal principles under which some specific kinds of facts, as taken in that specific context, impact the respective legal position.

As Kelsen accepts, 'facts are never a source of legal rights, let alone facts which are the result of conduct violative of international law. Not facts, but rules are the source of legal rights. It is only the validation of facts through a principle of law which in effect considers these facts as law-creating facts that can give rise to new legal rights and duties. It is precisely this latter function, the validation of facts, that forms an important part of the content of the rule of effectiveness.'[25] Thus, Kelsen in principle accepts that it is legal rules, not facts *per se*, that generate legal rights, and that the principle of effectiveness operates as part of the systemic arrangement of international law. But Kelsen's view of the relevance of the principle of effectiveness is rather circular and contradictory. Facts having no normative force would in practice be the same as facts having normative force by virtue of some general systemic principle. To argue that the principle of effectiveness, which refers to factual effectiveness, operates as validating facts that do not by themselves have the same effect is to restate the point that is being denied.

The normative relevance of facts is also focused upon in the writings of Visscher. Visscher portrays the relevance of factual effectiveness as an aspect of stability and security in the international legal system. As a starting-point, Visscher emphasises that effectivity 'has often a pre-eminent place in international law', even though 'it still lacks clear elucidation'. Effectivity denotes 'the degree of social reality that certain facts or situations must reach before they can be integrated in a legal order and there receive technical elaboration'. Visscher admits that 'the passage from fact to law takes place here only in so far as the human mind perceives conformity to fact as dictated by the social values that inspire it. The legal significance of effectivity may thus vary infinitely.'[26]

Thus, Visscher does not advance the law-creating influence of facts as a blanket thesis. However, Visscher still argues that 'sometimes effectivity appears as itself a constitutive element of law. This is so in territorial appropriations, where effectivity is the condition as well as the title of sovereignty.' This provides for territorial title *par excellence*, in the interests of stability and security in international relations.[27] The relevant practice demonstrates, however, that, as will be seen below, the mere factual effectiveness of territorial appropriation can never be constitutive of the legal position. In addition, Visscher makes another sweeping statement in terms of the existence and exercise of legal rights. Visscher claims that 'any long-neglected right weakens by non-use: the time elapsed casts doubt

[25] Kelsen, 422.
[26] Visscher, *Theory and Reality in Public International Law* (1968), 318.
[27] Visscher (1968), 318–319, 331.

upon its existence and reduces the belief in its foundation'.[28] This does not specify whether passage of time alone is sufficient or the change in belief must also be demonstrated by separate evidence. But the approach of Visscher demonstrates that there is no single homogenous concept of effectiveness and no consolidated doctrine on this issue.

The doctrinal debate confirms that the relevance of facts that express the effective exercise of State activity can be conceptually used as an argument for affirming the primacy of power and politics over law and the predominant importance of these factors for States' rights and obligation. This approach has to be located in the context of the profile of international law as the body of rules agreed and consented to between States. The outcome of the general doctrine of fact accounts for, indeed constitutes another side of, the doctrine explaining what international law really is.

2. Facts and the Creation of International Rights and Titles

The view of factual effectiveness in the field of international law-making is illustrated by the view that accepts the creation of customary rules through State practice only, without the respective legal conviction (*opinio juris*). A conceptually similar question is the acquisition of territorial title without consent. The doctrinal discourse notwithstanding, consistent judicial practice accepts that *opinio juris* is indispensable for customary law to emerge. This requirement emphasises the consensual nature of customary rules.[29]

This factor also contradicts Visscher's approach to the influence of power on custom. Visscher criticises as fictitious the voluntarist doctrine of customary law which sees custom as tacit agreement. According to Visscher, this doctrine misunderstands 'the action of power on the formation of customary law', in a way that 'instead of looking at a practice in the stages of the historical process of its development, this school reconstructs it ex post facto and projects it, completely formed, on the plane of contractual notions'.[30] Visscher further asserts that 'every international custom is the work of power'. Some States have a stronger footprint than others, because of their weight and this applies above all to Great Powers. Without their role customary rules would find no sufficient basis in social reality.[31]

Nevertheless, this so-called *ex post facto* view of custom is absolutely necessary and inevitable for any sensible criteria of custom-identification to exist. It is crucial to know the moment or stage from which the relevant customary rule is in force. There have to be criteria for defining this. If the reference is made

[28] Visscher (1968), 327.
[29] On this see above Chapter 4.
[30] Visscher (1968), 153.
[31] Visscher (1968), 154–155.

exclusively to the historical aspect of practice, this will inevitably fail to suggest any established criteria for rule-identification. Practice at any given stage would be as good or as bad as the practice at any other stage. As for Visscher's 'realist' approach, its point is not very clear. If the point is that the process of law-making and law-enforcement in the international legal system always involves the element of power, this is certain anyway. If, however, the point is that this power element crucially impacts the creation and validity of legal rules, this fails to be supported by the appropriate evidence. It is moreover antithetical to the basic nature of international law-making.

In the end Visscher acknowledges and emphasises the crucial relevance of the psychological factor in custom-formation.[32] This renders dubious the need for his reference to the relevance of the elements of power. Visscher indeed concludes that 'if, then, it is true that the fact precedes the qualification as law, the latter remains alone decisive and the mere uniformity or external regularity of certain attitudes never justifies a conclusion of normativity. . . . No custom is established until the moment when human thought comes to regard a way of social behaviour as an element of order important enough to be observed henceforth as legally binding.'[33] Therefore, Visscher fails to make a consistent case demonstrating the free-standing role of fact and power, independent of, or capable of displacing, the requirement of assent and agreement, in the creation of customary rules.

A cognate issue of factual effectiveness is considered doctrinally in relation to interaction between the effective action and the consent or attitude of the State affected by that action.[34] O'Connell emphasises the potential of facts to impact law by stressing that 'While it is true that States are obliged to respect the rights of other States, an effective interruption of those rights can result in a change in the legal situation to an extent not contemplated by municipal law.'[35] However, O'Connell is careful to add that 'it is, of course, not unilateral action alone that creates law or transforms an illegal situation into a legal one, but the whole context'.[36]

The question is twofold: how effective can practice and action be in the absence of protest that expresses the attitude of disapproval; and how far or effectively can that protest operate as preventing the relevant action or practice from being legitimised?

As Lauterpacht suggests, the absence of protest may constitute evidence that the relevant fact or practice is viewed to be in conformity with international law, that is 'accepted as law',[37] which further emphasises the similarity of this context

[32] Visscher (1968), 156ff.

[33] Visscher (1968), 156.

[34] As McGibbon illustrates, the phenomenon of acquiescence in the factual events is essentially the same in nature, though not necessarily in scale, as custom-generation, and is based on consent. Acquiescence results from inaction in the face of a situation that constitutes a threat to or infringement of the rights of the State, and is manifested through silence or absence of protest. See I McGibbon, The Scope of Acquiescence in International Law, 31 *BYIL* (1954), 143 at 143–144.

[35] DP O'Connell, *The International Law of the Sea* (1982), vol I, 41–42.

[36] *Id.*

[37] H Lauterpacht, Sovereignty Over Submarine Areas, 27 *BYIL* (1950), 375 at 395.

with that of custom-generation which depends on the psychological element and State consent. Fitzmaurice and O'Connell emphasise that protest by the affected State must be effective. O'Connell further points out that the efficiency of protests will be undermined by the retreat of the protesting State. If the claimant State refrains from protesting with a view to avoiding confrontation, the claim based on fact can be consolidated.[38] Fitzmaurice emphasises that protesting States should 'take equivalent action if they want to',[39] which admits of the lack of obligation to that effect. O'Connell discusses how far the protesting State should go in backing up its protest with effective action, but does not suggest a definitive solution and only observes that the protesting State should follow up by 'every available action'. Arguably the protesting State does not have to use force or sever diplomatic relations to retain the rights that constitute the subject-matter of the protest.[40] But this is not a very clear picture in terms of what sort of inaction is likely to impact the effectiveness of protest.

Fitzmaurice emphasises that 'Apart from the ordinary case of a diplomatic protest, or a proposal for reference to adjudication, the same effect could be achieved by a public statement denying the prescribing country's right, by resistance to the enforcement of the claim, or by counter-action of some kind.'[41] This basically implies that factual effectiveness can be prevented from producing a legal outcome if it is duly countered by the appropriate attitude. There is no absolutely straightforward criterion, but it would certainly matter where the relevant activities take place. If the State is opposed to the encroachment of its existing rights and titles, even mere verbal protests would carry more weight than they would carry in the context of competing claims to gain the relevant title or right. Another pertinent implication follows from the International Court's decision in the *Benin–Niger* case which demonstrates that physical actions are not the only part of *effectivités* as State practice, but so too are attitudes.

The concept of State practice cannot indeed be seen as according blanket and indiscriminate legal relevance to State action. As O'Connell puts it, 'State practice is not a matter of counting heads but of juristic evaluation of the factors that tend to legitimize the action by individual States.'[42] As can be seen from the analysis of Fitzmaurice and O'Connell, inaction as a factual process can obtain legal significance and have legal implications only if it carries with it

[38] O'Connell (1982), vol I, 42.

[39] G Fitzmaurice, *The Law and Procedure of the International Court of Justice*, 30 *BYIL* (1953), 1 at 42.

[40] O'Connell (1982), vol I, 43–44.

[41] Fitzmaurice (1953), 42; ILC Study on Juridical Bays also emphasises that 'These are some of the acts by which the opposition of foreign States could be expressed, and there are, no doubt, other means which could be used. More important than establishing a list of acts, is to emphasize that whatever the acts they must effectively express a sustained opposition to the exercise of sovereignty by the coastal State over the area in question.' *Juridical Regime of Historic Waters, including Historic Bays*, Study prepared by the Secretariat, II *YbILC* (1962), 1 at 17.

[42] O'Connell (1982), vol I, 39.

toleration of sufficient extent necessary to validate the factual situation.[43] That the change of legal position is due not to factual but consensual factors is further visible from the following statement of Fitzmaurice on protest:

> All that a protest can do in such circumstances is to preserve and keep alive the claim of the protesting Government, so that no inference of *abandonment* can be drawn from its silence, or of *recognition* of the other party's position.[44]

Confirmation of this approach can be seen in the ILC Study on Juridical Bays which emphasises that this concept originally relates to an illegal situation that is validated subsequently. However, the Study is careful to point out that this validation does not take place by the passage of time; it must be consummated by the acquiescence of rightful owners. This would be acquiescence that implies recognition of sovereignty of the relevant State, that is the expression of legally relevant attitude.[45]

The issue as to the degree of relevance and type of State practice as fact in terms of the emergence of legal rules, rights and titles has arisen in jurisprudence. The notion of *effectivités*—the effective exercise of State authority over the relevant territory—is widely resorted to in practice, but conceptually it is elusive and cannot be straightforwardly defined. Factual effectiveness is difficult to measure. It cannot provide the guidance as to how much and what kind of effectiveness is necessary for effecting the legally relevant change, that is a rule, title or status. In addition, the existence of competing *effectivités* does not allow the identification of the best option. Consensual elements are, however, more straightforward: consent either is or is not given, and this can be measured by the appropriate evidence.

The relativity and elusiveness of the concept of *effectivités* has been confirmed by the Eritrea–Ethiopia Boundary Commission in the following way:

> The actions of a State pursued *à titre de souverain* can play a role, either as assertive of that State's position or, expressly or impliedly, contradictory of the conduct of the opposing State. Such actions may comprise legislative, administrative or judicial assertions of authority over the disputed area. There is no set standard of duration and intensity of such activity. Its effect depends on the nature of the terrain and the extent of its population, the period during which it has been carried on and the extent of any contradictory conduct (including protests) of the opposing State. It is also important to bear in mind that conduct does not by itself produce an absolute and indefeasible title, but only a title relative to that of the competing State. The conduct of one Party must be measured against that of the other. Eventually, but not necessarily so, the legal result may be to vary a boundary established by a treaty.[46]

[43] Fitzmaurice (1953), 1 at 42; O'Connell (1982), vol I, 39–40.

[44] Fitzmaurice (1953), 44 (emphasis original).

[45] *Juridical Regime of Historic Waters, including Historic Bays*, Study prepared by the Secretariat, II *YbILC* (1962), 1 at 16.

[46] Decision Regarding Delimitation of the Border between the State of Eritrea and the Federal Democratic Republic of Ethiopia, Boundary Commission, Award of 13 April 2002, para 3.29.

In the *Grisbådarna* Award, the Arbitral Tribunal referred to *effectivités* to assign the ownership of the maritime area of Grisbådarna. The Tribunal determined that a demarcation which assigned the Grisbådarna to Sweden was supported by several circumstances of fact which were disclosed in the course of the argument. The principal circumstances were that:

> the fact that lobster fishing in the shoals of Grisbådarna has been carried on for a much longer time, to a much greater extent, and by a much greater number of fishermen on the part of the subjects of Sweden than on the part of those of Norway; [and] the fact that Sweden has performed in the Grisbådarna region, particularly in recent times, many acts based on the conviction that these regions were Swedish, as, for example, the placing of beacons, the survey of the sea and the installation of a lightship, which acts involved considerable expense and by which she not only thought she was exercising a right but even more that she was performing a duty; while Norway, by her own admission, showed much less concern in this region in these various regards.[47]

Relying on these factors, the Tribunal emphasised that 'it is a well established principle of the law of nations that the state of things that actually exists and has existed for a long time should be changed as little as possible'.[48] The Tribunal also emphasised that 'Swedes were the first to fish for lobsters by means of the tackle and craft that are necessary to fish as far out at sea as the banks in question are situated.' Furthermore, 'Sweden had no doubt as to her rights over Grisbådarna, and that she did not hesitate to incur the expenses incumbent on an owner or possessor of these banks even to a very considerable sum of money.' Further, in accordance with the *effectivités*, the Tribunal observed that 'Sweden took the first steps, about thirty years before the beginning of any dispute, toward making exact, laborious and expensive surveys of the regions of Grisbådarna, while the surveys made some years later by Norway did not even reach the limits of the Swedish survey.' Consequently, 'the assignment of the Grisbådarna banks to Sweden [was] in absolute accord with the most important circumstances of fact'.[49]

This determination took place in a context where the ownership of the relevant areas had not been adjusted by written agreement between the parties. In addition, the reliance on factual considerations was accompanied by reliance on the expression of will and agreement by Norway and the correlation of the Norwegian admission of what Sweden had regarded as its right. The actions of the parties assessed by the Tribunal referred not only to their factual side, but also to the attitudes that would inherently attend such actions.

The *Anglo-Norwegian Fisheries* case before the International Court touches upon the relevance of facts in creating the legal regime of territorial sea that is different from the otherwise applicable general international law. The case involved the

[47] *Grisbådarna* (Norway v Sweden), Award of 23 October 1909, G Wilson (ed), *The Hague Arbitration Cases* (1915), 111 at 127–128.

[48] *Id*, 128.

[49] *Id*, 129–131.

use of straight baselines as the inner limit of the territorial sea, instead of the low-water mark line. Although the distinctive characteristics of the Norwegian coast were among the material considerations, they did not by themselves predetermine the outcome of the case. This was rather due to the attitude, will and awareness of the parties, especially the United Kingdom. The Court began by observing that the relevant Norwegian coast 'does not constitute, as it does practically in all other countries, a clear dividing line between land and sea. What matters, what really constitutes the Norwegian coast line, is the outer line of "skjaergaard."' Such were the realities to be borne in mind when appraising the validity of the 1935 Norwegian decree. This was dictated by 'geographic realities'.[50]

Noting these factual realities, the Court observed that the baselines system consistently applied by Norway had not encountered opposition from other States. The general toleration of this system by other States was an unchallenged fact. This was further consolidated by 'Great Britain's position in the North Sea, her own interest in the question, and her prolonged abstention' from contesting the Norwegian method of delimitation.[51] The Court emphasised that 'the general toleration of foreign States with regard to the Norwegian practice is an unchallenged fact'. For 60 years the UK had not contested this practice. The Court dismissed the British argument of not knowing about this system, because of its notoriety. Therefore, the Norwegian straight baselines system was deemed to be enforceable against all States.[52] Thus, while factual realities were the first consideration, the case hinged on the factors of consent and law-making *inter se*. These proved that other States accepted the legality of the Norwegian delimitation system.[53]

Judge Read asserted that the validity of Norway's entitlement should be judged in terms of its practice in relation to foreign ships in the relevant maritime area. The only relevant and convincing practice was that consisting of physical actions, the actual assertion of sovereignty over the relevant ships and seizures.[54]

Judge Read's reasoning excludes the relevance of will and agreement in terms of the creation and consolidation of legal rules, titles and regimes and eventually reinforces the view of law-making as the incidence of bare factual power. Such an attitude, if developed on a general plane, can be acceptable from the position of political realism. But practice is not just facts, and facts are not just physical actions. State practice includes, along with actual physical actions and exercises of power, a variety of activities without immediate physical impact but expressive of the will and attitude of States.

[50] *ICJ Reports*, 1951, 127–128.

[51] *Id*, 129, 136–139.

[52] *ICJ Reports*, 1951, 116, 139.

[53] This can be contrasted to the reasoning of Judge Alvarez, who argued that the existence of the uniform rule on delimitation of territorial waters was impossible due to the diversity of geographic factors, *ICJ Reports*, 1951, 150. Thus, Judge Alvarez attempted to derive the rules from facts.

[54] *Id*, 191.

But even this would not be enough. The Court itself disposed of the case by reference to the correlation of attitudes. Judge Read also referred to lack of objection by the UK to the relevant seizures by Norway.[55] Thus, Judge Read effectively acknowledged that seizures as facts are not by themselves crucial and the absence of a coincidence of attitudes, will and consent decided the case. Similarly, Judge Read referred to the alleged lack of sufficient knowledge of the Norwegian baselines system by other States, and to this lack of constructive knowledge as the basis of dissent.[56]

The assertion of the law-creating force of facts is most extensively witnessed in the context of territorial acquisitions. As Kelsen suggests, 'when territorial change occurs which is not in itself a violation of international law, that change is a condition of new rights and obligations provided that it is effective'.[57] The real question, however, is whether the territorial change in legal terms is due to the factual effectiveness of the change as such, or whether it takes other factors to complete and confer legal relevance on such territorial changes.

Visscher stresses the crucial importance of the effective exercise of State functions in acquiring territorial sovereignty.[58] However, the acquisitive prescription can result in a territorial title if the continuous, uninterrupted and peaceful administration of the territory is followed by the acquiescence of all interested and affected States.[59] The title is acquired when the material element of factual effectiveness is complemented by the psychological elements of agreement and acceptance. This simple and straightforward perspective is repeatedly illustrated in jurisprudence.

Some starting criteria of factual effectiveness are provided in jurisprudence, even though the feasibility of its establishment cannot be taken for granted. The *El Salvador/Honduras* decision of the International Court emphasises that the *effectivités*, whatever they consist of, must be positively established. The fact that one State's *effectivités* cannot be proved in a specific area does not entail the presumption that the *effectivités* of another State have existed.[60] The *Ligitan/Sipadan* decision affirms that the relevant *effectivités* must relate to the specific area in dispute, and not just constitute aspects of the general exercise of authority by the State. The Court would 'only consider those acts as constituting a relevant display of authority which leave no doubt as to their specific reference to the islands in dispute as such. Regulations or administrative acts of a general nature can therefore be taken as *effectivités* with regard to Ligitan and Sipadan only if it is clear from their terms or their effects that they pertained to these two islands.'[61]

[55] *Id*, 191.
[56] *Id*, 205.
[57] Kelsen (1967), 422.
[58] Visscher (1968), 321.
[59] D Johnson, Acquisitive Prescription in International Law, 27 *BYIL* (1950), 353–354.
[60] *El Salvador/Honduras*, 436, para 125.
[61] *Ligitan/Sipadan*, para 136.

Generally, legislative regulations and administrative documents can be useful in confirming the facts of the effective exercise of State authority for the purpose of determining territorial title.[62] Track-working of the colonial authorities can prove their intentions as to the acquisition and exercise of territorial sovereignty.[63] Erecting lighthouses and navigational aids is generally not a sign of the exercise of State authority, but can be so in the case of small islands.[64] There is, however, not much else in terms of criteria of factual effectiveness. This difficulty of measuring inherently suggests the need for viewing the relevance of factual effectiveness as limited in terms of producing legal rights and titles, for the sake of legal security. This concern is adequately displayed and addressed in jurisprudence.

In *Land, Island and Maritime Frontier Dispute*,[65] the Chamber of the International Court examined the variety of situations in which the effective exercise of State authority was claimed, yet did not find it justified to dispose of the issues on the basis of *effectivités*. In a number of instances, the Chamber did not regard the *effectivités* as backed by sufficient evidence to dispose of the boundary question. The exercises of sovereign power included here civil registrations and criminal prosecutions.[66]

Therefore, it is fair to say that factual effectiveness can be relevant only if there is no ambiguity. It is critically contingent and consequent upon the clarity of data and the situation. The relevance of factual effectiveness is also qualified by the relevant legal factors. It can produce legal effect only if complemented by the will of the relevant States. To illustrate, in *Minquiers and Ecrehos*, the International Court dealt with the Anglo-French dispute regarding sovereignty over those two islands. The Court emphasised the evidence supporting the centuries-long administration and exercise of jurisdiction by Britain over these two islands. France could not prove a similar pattern of its own effective exercise of authority.[67] In addition to these effective governmental activities of Britain, the diplomatic correspondence proved France's acceptance that the islands were in British possession. France had in fact complied with British protests regarding actual or possible activities of France that would imply the existence of its sovereign powers over the islands. Therefore, Britain had sovereignty over the islands.[68] As for France's own practice, the Court held it that was 'sufficient

[62] *Case Concerning Frontier Dispute* (Burkina-Faso/Republic of Mali), Judgment of 22 December 1986, 554 at 588 (para 66).

[63] *Id*, 620 (para 124).

[64] *Sovereignty over Pulau Ligitan and Pulau Sipadan* (Indonesia/Malaysia), Judgment of 17 December 2002, General List No 102, para 147.

[65] *Land, Island and Maritime Frontier Dispute* (El Salvador/Honduras: Nicaragua Intervening), 11 September 1992, *ICJ Reports*, 1992, 351.

[66] *Id*, 471–472 (paras 180–181), 515–516 (paras 264–266), 542–543 (para 304), 551 (para 319) (regarding the land boundary).

[67] *The Minquiers and Echrehos Case* (France v United Kingdom), *ICJ Reports*, 1953, 47 at 67–70.

[68] *Id*, 71–72.

to show that France has a valid title to the Minquiers'. The Court stated that acts 'including the buoying outside the reefs of the group, ... can hardly be considered as sufficient evidence of the intention of that Government to act as sovereign over the islets; nor are those acts of such a character that they can be considered as involving a manifestation of State authority in respect of the islets'.[69]

In *Burkina-Faso v Mali*, the parties invoked the colonial *effectivités*, that is the conduct of administrative authorities, as proof of the effective exercise of territorial jurisdiction in the relevant region. Burkina Faso argued that the *effectivités* must be examined in the light of the title and cannot be substituted for it. Mali likewise argued that *effectivités* cannot displace a treaty-established boundary. But where there is no such boundary, it is necessary to ascertain the boundary by other methods. An investigation into *effectivités* then becomes essential.

The Chamber of the International Court observed that:

a distinction must be drawn among several eventualities. Where the act corresponds exactly to law, where effective administration is additional to the *uti possidetis juris*, the only role of *effectivités* is to confirm the exercise of the right derived from a legal title. Where the act does not correspond to the law, where the territory which is the subject of the dispute is effectively administered by a State other than the one possessing the legal title, preference should be given to the holder of the legal title. In the event that the *effectivités* do not co-exist with any legal title, it must invariably be taken into consideration. Finally, there are cases where the legal title is not capable of showing exactly the territorial expanse to which it relates. The *effectivités* can then play an essential role in showing how the title is interpreted in practice.[70]

In *Qatar–Bahrain*, the Court faced the claims of Qatar and Bahrain regarding their *effectivités* on the Hawar Islands. The parties extensively argued this point, as summarised in the Court's judgment in passage deserving quotation at length:

Qatar relies on the primacy of its title over the *effectivités* claimed by Bahrain. Recalling the schema set out in its Judgment of 22 December 1986 by the Chamber of the Court dealing with the case concerning *Frontier Dispute (Burkina-Faso/Republic of Mali)*, Qatar maintains that the significance of *effectivités* in relation to a territory depends upon the status of that territory and on any legal title that may be validly invoked over that territory by another State. Thus, if a territory is *res nullius*, effective occupation creates a title of sovereignty provided that it fulfils the necessary conditions. If, on the other hand, another State has sovereignty over the territory, it is a matter of illegal occupation or usurpation, which can have no legal effect; this, in Qatar's view, is the case of Bahrain's occupation of the Hawar Islands. Such a *de facto* occupation cannot metamorphose into a *de jure* situation, into territorial title, unless there is acquiescence by the territorial sovereign. Qatar maintains that the Court is not therefore required in this case to resolve a conflict between two claims based on *effectivités* whose respective merits have to be evaluated, and which has to be settled by granting the territory to the party with the

[69] *Id*, 71.

[70] *Case Concerning Frontier Dispute* (Burkina-Faso/Republic of Mali), Judgment of 22 December 1986, 554 at 586–587 (para 63).

better established *effectivités*. If one State occupies an uninhabited part of the territory of another State, there can be no question of invoking the occupying State's *effectivités* against the lack of *effectivités* of the holder of the territorial title. According to Qatar, the whole of Bahrain's argument as to the precedence of the *effectivités* of its occupation of the Hawar Islands is therefore irrelevant. Only acquiescence by Qatar, the territorial sovereign, could have created a title. Qatar further states that, assuming it possible to invoke the *effectivités* relied upon by Bahrain, these would remain ineffective because they do not meet the standards required to create a right. In any event, according to Qatar, all of Bahrain's acts subsequent to the claim to the Hawar Islands addressed by it to the British Government on 28 April 1936, without Qatar being informed thereof, are inopposable to the latter; these acts are simply evidence of Bahrain's desire to seize territory belonging to somebody else and cannot override Qatar's pre-existing sovereignty.[71]

Thus, Qatar's arguments effectively followed the Court's previous jurisprudence regarding the scope and relevance of factual effectiveness. The Court decided the issue on other grounds, namely the 1939 British decision, the binding character of which Qatar had accepted in advance.[72] The issue of the original title and the *effectivités* thus became irrelevant.[73] The case was decided on consensual grounds as opposed to factual grounds.

Effectivités were similarly involved in the *Ligitan/Sipadan* case, where examination of them became necessary after the Court found that none of the litigating States had treaty-based title to the relevant islands.[74] In the absence of conflicting adverse factors, the Court went on to examine the relative weight of the evidence advanced for proving each party's effective display of State authority on the islands. The activities of Indonesian fishermen were not sovereign activities and there were no other activities whereby Indonesia considered the islands as its own.[75] This was contrasted with the Malaysian island-specific regulation and control of turtle eggs and establishment of a bird sanctuary on the islands, as an example of effective administration of the islands, 'as regulatory and administrative assertions of authority over territory'.[76]

The Court noted that 'the activities relied upon by Malaysia, both in its own name and as successor State of Great Britain, are modest in number but that they are diverse in character and include legislative, administrative and quasi-judicial acts. They cover a considerable period of time and show a pattern revealing an intention to exercise State functions in respect of the two islands in the context of the administration of a wider range of islands.'[77] Moreover, the Court could not

[71] *Maritime Delimitation and Territorial Question between Qatar and Bahrain* (Qatar v Bahrain), Merits, 16 March 2001, General List No 87, paras 107ff.

[72] *Id*, paras 110ff.

[73] *Id*, para 148.

[74] *Sovereignty over Pulau Ligitan and Pulau Sipadan* (Indonesia/Malaysia), Judgment of 17 December 2002, General List No 102, paras 127ff.

[75] *Id*, paras 139–140.

[76] *Id*, paras 143–145.

[77] *Id*, para 148.

disregard 'the fact that at the time when these activities were carried out, neither Indonesia nor its predecessor, the Netherlands, ever expressed its disagreement or protest. In this regard, the Court notes that in 1962 and 1963 the Indonesian authorities did not even remind the authorities of the colony of North Borneo, or Malaysia after its independence, that the construction of the lighthouses at those times had taken place on territory which they considered Indonesian; even if they regarded these lighthouses as merely destined for safe navigation in an area which was of particular importance for navigation in the waters off North Borneo, such behaviour is unusual.'[78]

Thus, the case was disposed of by the relative preference for Malaysian *effectivités* as supplemented by the implicit consent of Indonesia which understood the sovereign nature of Malaysia's activities, yet did not object to them over a considerable period of time. In addition, the Court's reference to Malaysian activities that were diverse yet 'modest in number' confirms that the crucial factor is not the scope of the factual effectiveness of the administration of territory, but type of sovereign power exercised coupled with their acceptance.

In *Benin–Niger*, both parties invoked *effectivités* in relation to the relevant areas of territory and islands. The Chamber reiterated its finding in *Land, Island and Maritime Boundary Dispute* that post-independence *effectivités* can be used to confirm respect for the *uti possidetis juris* boundary.[79] Under this approach, *uti possidetis juris* as a legal principle forms the governing framework for the factual *effectivités*. At the same time, in applying the *uti possidetis juris* principle, the Court aims at finding evidence of the effective exercise of State authority over the relevant territory.[80] This would be the task where there is no conflicting treaty title. In the presence of such, the *effectivités* have to give way to it.

The Chamber examined, in the absence of any conflicting normative consideration or significant opposition by the opposing State, the consolidation of *effectivités* of France as the colonial power.[81] As can be seen from the above analysis, the Chamber's analysis of *effectivités* involved judging whether the French colonial legal instruments had validly established territorial boundary and possession in the period between 1914 and 1954. Niger's *effectivités* in terms of administration, such as the administrative activity and electoral registers, were also taken into account.[82]

Relatively minor contradictions will not normally affect the overall picture of consistency of practice or attitude related to practice. It will be recalled that in *Anglo-Norwegian Fisheries*, the International Court refused to treat as relevant the 'few inconsistencies or contradictions' involved in the Norwegian

[78] *Id*, para 149.

[79] *Case concerning the Frontier Dispute* (Benin/Niger), Chamber of the Court, Judgment of 12 July 2005, *ICJ Reports*, 2005, 90 at 109.

[80] *Id*, 133.

[81] *Id*, 112.

[82] *Id*, 130–131.

practice related to its straight baselines system.[83] A similar approach was upheld in *Benin–Niger*, in relation to the *effectivités* regarding the ownership of disputed territories between 1954 and 1960. Unlike the previous period from 1914 (when the *modus vivendi* was concluded through the Sadoux Letter) to 1954, the period after 1954 had witnessed a conflict of attitudes of the parties. Dahomey (subsequently Benin) asserted claims to administer the territory of Lété on which Niger had exercised effective authority before 1954. In a number of communications, Niger officials maintained that this was Niger's territory and Niger was consequently entitled to administer it. This met no visible contradiction from the officials of Dahomey. Lété continued to be subject to Niger's administration, for instance through being including in Niger's polling station lists.[84]

It is significant here that mere attitudes and statements are treated as illustrative of *effectivités* as practice. The very State practice is perceived as consisting of a psychological element. This is also clear from the Court's further expressions. The Court's principal conclusion was that 'The entitlement of Niger to administer the island of Lété was sporadically called into question for *practical* reasons but was neither *legally nor factually* contested.'[85] Thus, the Court not only points to the sporadic nature of objections to Niger's attitude but also emphasises that not every objection can be a legally relevant objection. In the end, what matters is not individual parts of State practice but the overall attitude characteristic of that practice.

The irrelevance of factual effectiveness in the absence of consent has been witnessed in the *Cameroon–Nigeria* case. This case dealt with claims of State practice shaping entitlement to a maritime area through establishing the maritime boundary by way of influencing the Court-determined line of provisional determination. Nigeria argued that 'State practice with regard to oil concessions is a decisive factor in the establishment of maritime boundaries.' Cameroon, for its part, argued that the existence of oil concessions was irrelevant for the delimitation of maritime boundaries.[86] The Court decided that 'oil concessions and oil wells are not in themselves to be considered as relevant circumstances justifying the adjustment or shifting of the provisional delimitation line. Only if they are based on express or tacit agreement between the parties may they be taken into account.'[87] In this case there was no such agreement made between the parties.

Another instance where the irrelevance of the factual situation to legal entitlement to maritime spaces was affirmed is the earlier decision in *Gulf of Maine*. In this case, the Chamber of the Court, while delimiting the maritime spaces

[83] *ICJ Reports*, 1951, 138.

[84] *ICJ Reports*, 2005, 130–131.

[85] *Id*, 132 (emphasis added).

[86] *Land and Maritime Boundary between Cameroon and Nigeria*, General List No 94, 10 October 2002, para 303.

[87] *Id*, para 304.

between Canada and the USA, emphasised that 'there is no reason to consider *de jure* that the delimitation which the Chamber has now to carry out within the areas of overlapping... must result in each party's enjoying an access to the regional fishing resources which will be equal to the access it previously enjoyed *de facto*'.[88]

Thus, practice demonstrates that the role of factual effectiveness in the resolution of territorial disputes is by no means crucial. In most cases territorial titles are decided by factors other than factual effectiveness, such as consensual factors. Wherever relevant, factual effectiveness can only operate if supplemented by simultaneous or subsequent expression of attitudes implying agreement.

Therefore, it is generally accepted that both the acquisition and loss of territorial title is due not to the factual effectiveness of possession as such. It is due to the action with the appropriate intention that is acknowledged and accepted by all interested States. Occupation of territory must be effective, but it will not by itself secure the title. Similar requirements are relevant for the loss of territorial sovereignty. In the process of acquiring territorial sovereignty *animus* signifies the statement of claim that in principle must be approved by other relevant States. In the process of loss of territorial sovereignty *animus* essentially signifies the consent of the State which already owns the territory that other States may be free to acquire the territory.

In the *Clipperton Islands* Award, the Arbitral Tribunal emphasised that, just as with the acquisition of territorial sovereignty, its loss by dereliction required the *animus* of the territorial State. The mere factual aspect of non-exercise of sovereignty was never sufficient.[89] In *Eastern Greenland*, the Permanent Court of International Justice rejected the argument that the disappearance of the two Nordic settlements in Greenland implied the relinquishment of Norwegian sovereignty. There was no basis for assuming that the renunciation of sovereignty through abandonment had taken place. There was no evidence that such intention had been expressed.[90] In doctrine it is also recognised that the abandonment of territory requires both the actual non-exercise of sovereignty and the demonstrable evidence of intention of abandonment.[91] Thus, the establishment of the abandonment of a right requires positively establishing the intention of the relevant State to this effect. It may also be of accessory relevance in this process that protests can prevent the inference that a State has abandoned its right or recognised that of another State.[92]

It has to be concluded that the *effectivités* do not constitute a smooth process conducive to viewing international law as a fluid system depending on factual realities.

[88] *ICJ Reports*, 1984, 342.

[89] *Clipperton Island* (France v Mexico), 26 *AJIL* (1930), 390.

[90] *Legal Status of Eastern Greenland*, 1934, *PCIJ Series* A, B, No 53, 46–47.

[91] F Pfluger, *Die Einseitigen Rechtsgeschäfte im Völkerrecht* (1936), 277–288; see further Johnson (1950).

[92] Fitzmaurice (1953), 43–44.

But it is a systemic tool whereby certain activities can be displayed for the attention and knowledge of all, making it reasonably probable for them to pass judgment on these activities and object to them in due course, in order to prevent the consolidation of the relevant rights and titles. What counts is not the activity or display of action, but consent and correlation of attitudes. Attitudes can be expressed, with consequent impact on the legal position, by all States, whatever their size or power.

3. Fact-based Claims to Affect Existing Legal Regulation

While facts by themselves do not lead to the creation, modification or abrogation of legal rules and rights, it is even clearer that they cannot prevail over established legal rules and titles. For instance, the principle of *uti possidetis juris*, though referring to factual situations, provides for juridically and formally established territorial titles. After these titles are established, they are unaffected by considerations of factual effectiveness and subsequent conduct (unless those were to imply contrary agreement to be identified through proof subject to a high standard). In *El Salvador/Honduras*, the Chamber of the Court recognised Honduran entitlement to the relevant territory on the basis of *uti possidetis juris*. Therefore it was no longer relevant whether there was sufficient 'effective practice' confirming the Honduran title.[93] No sufficient proof of factual effectiveness could have been adduced anyway in this case. In *Ligitan/Sipadan*, there was no conflicting consensual factor. However, there was such a factor in *Cameroon–Nigeria*, which involved the situation of the treaty displacing the factual effectiveness. While *Burkina-Faso/Mali* limits the role of effectiveness but still allows some interpretative role to it, *Cameroon–Nigeria* denies even such an interpretative role if there is an opposing regime established on the basis of the normative instrument. Both in *Burkina-Faso/Mali* and *Benin–Niger*, the International Court emphasised that 'pre-eminence is to be accorded to legal title over effective possession as a basis of sovereignty'.[94]

At the conceptual level, the preference of the treaty title, over the 'title' gained through practice and action, could potentially also give rise to an agreement between the relevant States and raises the question why the written and formal agreement should prevail over the unwritten and informal one. The explanation is that the written agreement as to the title is concluded with a view to final, conclusive and effective resolution of the relevant territorial issue. As treaties constitute solemn undertakings to be respected in good faith (*pacta sunt servanda*), any practice of States in defiance of the treaty title has to be disregarded, unless it offers conclusive evidence, subject to a high threshold of proof, that the parties intend replacing the old agreement with a new one.

[93] *El Salvador/Honduras*, *ICJ Reports*, 1992, 463, para 125.
[94] *ICJ Reports* 1986, 586–587; *ICJ Reports*, 2005, 120.

The *Namibia* case confirms that the traditional titles of territorial acquisition cannot operate in face of the conflicting treaty title. In *Namibia*, South Africa argued that it had the right to administer the Namibian territory because of the lapse of the League of Nations Mandate over Namibia, and due to its military conquest, together with its openly declared policy and consistent practice of administering this territory. As the Court put it, 'These claims of title, which apart from other considerations are inadmissible in regard to a mandated territory, led by South Africa's own admission to a situation which vitiates the object and purpose of the Mandate.' The annexation was precluded both by the Mandate and Article 22 of the League of Nations Covenant.[95]

In *Cameroon–Nigeria*, the Court addressed the relevance of the 1913 Anglo-French Treaty which allocated sovereignty over the Bakassi peninsula to Germany, and by succession to Cameroon. Nigeria asserted that this Treaty was never effectively put into practice and in the material period between 1913 and 1960, Bakassi was never administered as part of Cameroon. On the other hand, there were widespread sovereign activities whereby Nigeria administered this territory.[96]

The crucial question the Court had to address was whether the established treaty title can be displaced by the factual effectiveness of administration. The Court identified the basic question it had to address by observing that 'The legal question of whether *effectivités* suggest that title lies with one country rather than another is not the same legal question as whether such *effectivités* can serve to displace an established treaty title.' The Court noted the previous cases in which the effective exercise of State authority had eventually, albeit in conjunction with other factors, led to the establishment of the territorial title. But the Court observed that 'in none of these cases were the acts referred to acts *contra legem*; those precedents are therefore not relevant'.[97] Therefore, the Court has given firm preference to considerations of legality over considerations of fact. The Judgment clearly affirms that the territorial title that has been established on the basis of the Treaty could operate in spite of the contrary factual effectiveness and the latter would not affect it. The philosophy behind *Cameroon/Nigeria* and *a fortiori* the entire jurisprudence in this field is that the facts external to the legal instrument cannot affect the scope and effect of that instrument.

The *Gabcikovo/Nagymaros* Judgment of the International Court contains important pronouncements regarding the limits of relevance of factual considerations for determining the rights and obligations of States. In this case, the Court dealt with a situation in which both parties had undertaken steps diverging from the 1977 Treaty, and addressed the principal question of whether this combined non-compliance would affect the applicable legal regime. The conclusion was

95 Advisory Opinion, *ICJ Reports*, 1971, 43.
96 *Cameroon–Nigeria*, paras 201, 211–212.
97 *Id*, para 221.

that the original regime continued to govern the rights and obligations of the parties.[98]

The first relevant fact was the decision of Hungary to relinquish most of the construction of the System of Locks for which it was responsible by virtue of the 1977 Treaty. In response to this, Czechoslovakia, instead of terminating the Treaty in response to the material breach, chose to insist on the implementation of the Treaty by Hungary. It repeatedly called upon Hungary to resume performance of its obligations under the Treaty. After Hungary's refusal, Czechoslovakia decided to put the Gabcíkovo system into operation unilaterally.[99]

The Court focused on the legal and normative characterisation of the relevant facts. It pointed out that the Treaty provided for joint and co-ordinated activities and 'By definition all this could not be carried out by unilateral action.' Therefore, 'In spite of having a certain external physical similarity with the original Project, [Czechoslovakia's actions] thus differed sharply from it in its legal characteristics.' Therefore, this was not the application of the 1977 Treaty but its violation.[100]

Thus, the Court's decision demonstrates that legal regimes exist autonomously. Their meaning and operation is independent from the—even combined and complex—factual conduct of the parties to the relevant regime.

In addressing the legal consequences of this situation, the Court made another pronouncement regarding the relevance of fact for the operation of law:

> In this regard it is of cardinal importance that the Court has found that the 1977 Treaty is still in force and consequently governs the relationship between the Parties. That relationship is also determined by the rules of other relevant conventions to which the two States are party, by the rules of general international law and, in this particular case, by the rules of State responsibility; but it is governed, above all, by the applicable rules of the 1977 Treaty as a *lex specialis*.
>
> The Court, however, cannot disregard the fact that the Treaty has not been fully implemented by either party for years, and indeed that their acts of commission and omission have contributed to creating the factual situation that now exists. Nor can it overlook that factual situation—or the practical possibilities and impossibilities to which it gives rise—when deciding on the legal requirements for the future conduct of the Parties.
>
> This does not mean that facts—in this case facts which flow from wrongful conduct—determine the law. The principle *ex injuria jus non oritur* is sustained by the Court's finding that the legal relationship created by the 1977 Treaty is preserved and cannot in this case be treated as voided by unlawful conduct.[101]

Therefore, it was required that the:

> factual situation as it has developed since 1989 shall be placed within the context of the preserved and developing treaty relationship, in order to achieve its object and purpose

[98] *Gabcikovo/Nagymaros Project* (Hungary/Slovakia), Judgment of 25 September 1997, *ICJ Reports*, 1997.

[99] *Id*, paras 72–73.

[100] *Id*, paras 77–78.

[101] *Id*, paras 132–133.

in so far as that is feasible. For it is only then that the irregular state of affairs which exists as the result of the failure of both Parties to comply with their treaty obligations can be remedied.[102]

By this statement the Court arguably manifests its intention to accommodate the factual context within the legal framework of the 1977 Treaty. This can also be seen from the statement that 'that part of the obligations of performance which related to the construction of the System of Locks—in so far as they were not yet implemented before 1992—have been overtaken by events. It would be an administration of the law altogether out of touch with reality if the Court were to order those obligations to be fully reinstated and the works at Cunovo to be demolished when the objectives of the Treaty can be adequately served by the existing structures.' This was in line with, and followed from, the fact that 'The 1977 Treaty never laid down a rigid system.' What is most important is that to the Court's statements over the material period 'explicit terms of the Treaty itself were therefore in practice acknowledged by the parties to be negotiable'.[103] This situation was the basis of the Court's pronouncement that while existing structures could serve the objectives of the Treaty, there was no need to demolish them and replace them with originally perceived ones. Therefore, the Court gave the factual situation relevance only in so far as it was compatible with the legal regime established by the 1977 Treaty.

That said, the Court observes, in terms of the application of its stated approach, that the Treaty was still in force and that, under its terms, the joint regime was a basic element. Unless the Parties agreed otherwise, such a regime was to be restored. The restoration of the joint regime was required not by demolition of the constructed works, but by their transformation so as to reflect the Treaty regime. Therefore, the Court observed that 'Variant C, which it considers operates in a manner incompatible with the Treaty, should be made to conform to it. By associating Hungary, on an equal footing, in its operation, management and benefits, Variant C will be transformed from a *de facto* status into a treaty-based regime.'[104] This approach enabled the Court to accommodate the factual situation within the legal regime without upholding or implying the primacy of factual considerations.

Was the Court's approach in *Gabcikovo/Nagymaros* an implicit application of the doctrine of approximate application? Possibly it was, though the Court refused to engage with this doctrine.[105] The refusal to straightforwardly recognise this doctrine may be due to the difficulties its blanket statement and general applicability could cause in terms of understanding the interaction between fact and law. In *Gabcikovo/Nagymaros*, the key was the flexibility of the treaty regime, as opposed to the general principle that allows adapting law to subsequent facts.

[102] *Id*, para 133.
[103] *Id*, paras 136, 138.
[104] *Id*, paras 144–145.
[105] *Gabcikovo/Nagymaros*, para 76.

4. The Factual Element in the Justification of Legal Rules

As previous analysis demonstrates, the relevance of factual circumstances in terms of the operation of international law does not give them free-standing predominance. The legal conception of the relevant factual circumstance is superimposed on its purely factual, or common-sense, understanding. Yet another illustration of this phenomenon can be seen in the legal framework within which the factual element is incorporated in the legal rule or which constitutes its rationale and basis.

This can be seen in the first place in the example of the development of the law of maritime areas, especially the continental shelf.[106] The factual criterion of natural prolongation entitles the relevant coastal State to claim the area in question as an exercise of its 'inherent and primordial rights' which 'are not susceptible of being subverted by any of the recognised means, such as prescription'.[107] Thus, this inherent right produced by the systemic fact operates irrespective of the attitude of other States that may have interest in the matter. The factor of *effectivités*, protest and competing claims would not in principle have the same relevance in this field as they have in the standard context of State practice crystallising rights and entitlements.

As the International Court emphasised in *Anglo-Norwegian Fisheries*, 'it is the land which confers upon the coastal State a right to the waters off its coasts'.[108] In the *North Sea* case the International Court emphasised the law-creating relevance of the fact of the natural prolongation of the continental shelf. The Court pointed out that the legal institution of the continental shelf had arisen out of the recognition of the legal relevance of the physical fact of natural prolongation. 'The link between this fact and the law, without which that institution would never have existed, remains an important element for the application of its legal regime.'[109] The Court defined the concept and relevance of natural prolongation by observing that the proximity of submarine areas to the coast did not by itself bring the relevant area within the ownership of the State. This would not suffice to confer the title. What *ipso jure* conferred the title was 'the fact that the submarine areas concerned may be deemed to be actually part of the territory over which the

[106] Article 76 of the 1982 UN Convention on the Law of the Sea specifies that 'The continental shelf of a coastal State comprises the seabed and subsoil of the submarine areas that extend beyond its territorial sea throughout the natural prolongation of its land territory to the outer edge of the continental margin, or to a distance of 200 nautical miles from the baselines from which the breadth of the territorial sea is measured where the outer edge of the continental margin does not extend up to that distance.'

[107] O'Connell, (1982), vol I, 476.

[108] *ICJ Reports*, 1951, 133.

[109] *ICJ Reports*, 1969, 51; as Judge Tanaka further suggested in this case, the geographical factor was the only condition for sovereign rights to arise in relation to continental shelf. This was most reasonable from geographical and economic viewpoints, *ICJ Reports* 1969, 180. As Judge Shahabuddeen pointed out in *Jan Mayen*, *ICJ Reports* 1993, 162, this followed the ILC's identification of the geological concept of continental shelf.

coastal State already has dominion—in the sense that, although covered with water, they are a prolongation or continuation of that territory, an extension of it under the sea'.[110]

The Court's reasoning emphasises the systemic and title-creating (and thus law-creating) relevance of geographical or geological fact of natural prolongation. This fact consists in an extension of what the State 'already' has dominion over. It thus confers to it the dominion which it would not otherwise have. This approach is however not the predominant one anymore. In the *Anglo-French* case, the Arbitral Tribunal also addressed the question of 'what areas of continental shelf are to be considered as *legally* the natural prolongation of the Channel Islands rather than of the mainland France'. This was required as 'in international law the continental shelf is a juridical concept'. Hence, 'its scope and the conditions for its application are not determined exclusively by the physical facts of geography but also legal rules'.[111]

The International Court in the *Aegean Sea Continental Shelf* case offers a somewhat modified perception of the basis to the continental shelf entitlement. This can also be seen as a response to the approaches that achieved predominance later. As the Court observes, rights over the continental shelf derive from the sovereignty of a State and the fact of natural prolongation is merely a reference point in this respect.[112]

In *Tunisia–Libya*, the International Court noted that the concept of the continental shelf, linked to the physical fact of the natural prolongation of the State coast, is not to be identified with the phenomenon denoted by the same term in other disciplines. The legal concept of the continental shelf does not overlap with the geographer's assessment of the same concept. What matters is the conception of the continental shelf as accepted in State practice. The concept of natural prolongation as referring to the physical object or location of the rights of the coastal State was novel at the time of the *North Sea* judgment. But the contemporary law did not treat these factors as sufficient for determining the precise extent of States in relation to these areas. Although derived from the natural phenomenon, the continental shelf had become a legal institution and 'pursued its own development'.[113] In fact, as Sir Robert Jennings observes,

110 *ICJ Reports*, 1969, 31; the criterion of natural prolongation is also embodied in Article 76 of the 1982 Law of the Sea Convention. The parameters of this concept are clarified in the International Law Association 2006 Report in *Legal Issues of the Outer Continental Shelf* (Ong & Oude Elferink, Co-Rapporteurs), at 3–4, elaborating on factual geographical notions such as oceanic ridge, submarine ridge, continental margin etc.

111 *UK–French Continental Shelf* case (1977), 54 ILR 303, para 191 (emphasis added).

112 *Aegean Sea Continental Shelf* (Greece v Turkey), Judgment of 19 December 1978, *ICJ Reports*, 1978, 3 at 36.

113 *Tunisia–Libya*, *ICJ Reports*, 1982, 45–46. This was accompanied by a statement in the Separate Opinion of Judge Arechaga that the legal concept of continental shelf is not defined by natural prolongation, even though both parties had contended this. The decision of the case was to be based on legal principles, putting aside the expert evidence submitted by parties, *ICJ Reports*, 1982, 110. For a useful analysis of this process of evolution of concepts see LDM Nelson, The Roles of Equity in the Delimitation of Maritime Boundaries, 84 *AJIL* (1990), 837 at 846–848.

'natural prolongation appears not to be a term known to geology, geography or any other allied sciences. It is an invention of the legal mind'.[114]

In the same case, the Court received the geological advice that the continental shelf is 'an evident prolongation' of one or another State. The Court concluded that 'for legal purposes it is not possible to define the areas of continental shelf appertaining to Tunisia and to Libya by reference solely or mainly to geological considerations'. The Court's function was 'to make the use of geology only so far as required for the application of international law'. What mattered were physical circumstances contemporaneous to the case, not their long-standing evolution.[115] The mere concept of natural prolongation is determined as a matter of scientific fact by the application of geological criteria. This would not predetermine legal regulation on this subject nor prejudice the assessment of the continental shelf boundaries.[116] The natural prolongation defined the physical object and location of the rights of the State. It was not sufficient to determine the precise extent of the rights of one State in relation to the rights of another State.[117] Therefore, the Court rejected the Libyan suggestion that once the natural prolongation of the shelf is determined, the delimitation becomes a simple matter of complying with the dictates of nature.[118]

In *Gulf of Maine*, the Court dealt with the submission that the concept of geographic adjacency of maritime spaces constituted the basis of the title of the coastal State. The Court observed that the concept of adjacency expressed the link between sovereignty and sovereign rights to the adjacent submerged land and water over it. Still, the legal title 'is always and exclusively the effect of legal operation. The same is true of the boundary of the extent of the title. The boundary results from a rule of law, and not from any intrinsic merit in the purely physical fact.' Although States have titles in adjacent maritime spaces, 'it would not be correct to say that international law recognises the title *conferred in the State by the adjacency* of that shelf or that zone, as if the mere natural fact of adjacency produced legal consequences'.[119]

This is a clear enough explanation that the facts by themselves cannot provide legal title and regulation. The Court also rejected the existence of a rule determining that the fact that the maritime area is less distant from the coast of the State meant that the State 'would *ipso jure* be entitled to have the zones recognised as its own'.[120] Having rejected the law-making relevance of facts, the Court

[114] RY Jennings, The Principles Governing Maritime Boundaries, in K Hailbronner, G Ress & T Stein (eds), *Staat und Völkerrechtsordnung, Festschrift für Karl Doehring* (1989), 397 at 405.

[115] *Tunisia–Libya*, *ICJ Reports*, 1982, 53–54.

[116] *Id*, 1982, 44.

[117] *Id*, 46.

[118] *Id*, 47.

[119] *ICJ Reports*, 1984, 296 (emphasis original).

[120] *Id*, 296–297.

decided the case on the basis of 'fundamental rule' on maritime delimitation that it identified from the common attitude of the parties.[121]

In the same spirit, the Arbitral Tribunal in *St Pierre & Miquelon* emphasised that geographical facts cannot determine the limits of maritime areas. 'Rules of international law, as well as equitable principles, must be applied to determine the relevance and weight of the geographical features.'[122] As Judge Shahabuddeen observed in *Jan Mayen*, the concept of the continental shelf still has a physical aspect. But from the practical perspective and with the adoption of the 1982 Law of the Sea Convention, 'natural prolongation has now been replaced by the geometric and more neutral principle of adjacency measured by distance'.[123] While this is true, natural prolongation still retains some, though marginal, relevance in specific aspects, for instance in terms of the requirement that the continental shelf of one State shall not encroach upon the natural prolongation of the territory of another State.[124] But this is essentially different from natural prolongation as geographical fact independently providing the basis of the entitlement to the continental shelf.

The consideration of fact can possibly be incorporated within the legal rule or principle, as a determinant of its operation. In *Corfu Channel*, the standard of the attribution of conduct to the State was impacted on by reference to the exclusive territorial control of the area of Albanian territorial waters in which British vessels were struck by mines. How far such factual references can and should go is crucial. The *Corfu Channel* case remains of fundamental importance as no other case has addressed this problem since. A proper understanding of the case is vital.

The Court observed that knowledge of minelaying could not be imputed to the Albanian Government just because mines were laid in their territorial waters. This fact neither involved *prima facie* responsibility nor shifted the burden of proof. However, the Court observed that 'the fact of this exclusive territorial control exercised by a State within its frontiers has a bearing upon the methods of proof available to establish the knowledge of that State as to such events'. The victim State would not otherwise be able to furnish direct proof of the facts and therefore it 'should be allowed a more liberal recourse to inferences of fact and circumstantial evidence', provided that this left no room for reasonable doubt.[125]

As circumstantial evidence, the Court referred to some evidence confirming that Albania was actively watching its territorial waters over the relevant time period. In addition, the geographical configuration of the area made it easy to watch. Therefore, Albanian coastal defences could, according to the Court, hardly fail to observe the minelaying, the distance between the coast and the place of minelaying being not more than five hundred metres. The

[121] See above Chapter 4.

[122] *Delimitation of Maritime Areas between Canada and the French Republic*, 31 ILM (1992), 1149, para 24 at 1160.

[123] *ICJ Reports*, 1993, 166.

[124] *North Sea*, *ICJ Reports*, 1969, para 44; *Canada–France* Arbitration, para 58.

[125] *ICJ Reports*, 1949, 18.

Court concluded that the minelaying could not have occurred without the knowledge of the Albanian Government.[126] The grave failure to warn British ships was Albania's responsibility.

As Visscher comments on this case, 'the effectivity of the State's territorial control justifies imputing to it, up to a certain point, knowledge of enterprises organised on its soil against the security of foreign States. Without going so far as to found upon territorial control alone a general presumption of knowledge, the Court's judgment in the *Corfu Strait* case makes it clear on the one hand that a defendant State may not plead ignorance, and on the other hand that its exclusive territorial control affords it information facilities for prevention and repression which are not at the disposal of the plaintiff State—an equality which justifies the latter in making larger use of presumptions of fact and circumstantial evidence.'[127] However, Visscher observes that this presumption of the sufficiency of public powers would yield to proof of accidental paralysis owing to a state of belligerency or revolutionary events as factors that prevent the State from protecting the rights of foreigners.[128]

In general, it is interesting to consider whether the Court would have done better to refer to territorial sovereignty in a juridical sense as opposed to factual control and in line with, and as an emanation of, the *Island of Palmas* pronouncement that sovereignty entails responsibility for the observance of other States' rights as its corollary.[129]

The criticism of the Court's approach is included in the dissenting Opinion of Judge Krylov, who examined the possibility of clandestine operation in Albanian waters. In principle the area was visible in good weather, but the watch could not be exercised with the same efficiency in rainy weather or on dark nights.[130]

If Judge Krylov's approach is well founded, then it is unjustified to apply a too rigid and blanket rule of attribution of the wrongful act to the State in such a way as to hold it responsible for what cannot really be attributed to it. Therefore, the factual circumstances, such as geographic or meteorological factors impacting the extent of knowledge, should modify the rigidity of such a rule so that the State is held responsible for what it has actually contributed to. The Court did not positively address these issues and did not specify whether there was some legal requirement to consider or disregard them.

5. Effective Control of Territory or Conduct

Effective control, a notion frequently used in international legal practice and occasionally referred to as actual control or overall control, has never

126 *Id*, 18–22.
127 Visscher (1968), 332.
128 *Id.*
129 *Island of Palmas* (Netherlands v US), PCA 1928 (Sole Arbitrator Huber), 2 *RIAA* 829.
130 *ICJ Reports*, 1949, 70.

been defined, nor has its relationship with actual or overall control been conclusively or authoritatively clarified. The factual condition of effective control is a precondition of having the status of occupying power in the law of armed conflict and hence generates a set of rights and obligations in relation to the relevant State and non-State actors. Effective control may also be constitutive of State liability for actions performed in the relevant territory. This problem has been addressed judicially on many occasions, but there has been no elaboration upon a consistent principle that would dispel the uncertainties of its applicability.

The *Nicaragua* case involved a situation in which the facts of intervention and use of force by the United States in and against Nicaragua had to be proved to entail the respective legal consequences. The International Court's Judgment demonstrates that the standard of proof of intervention in the internal affairs of the other State is quite high.

In terms of the operations of the *contras* rebels, the Court found it established that the financial, logistical, intelligence and organisational support of the United States authorities for the activities of the *contras* had been important to enable them to conduct their armed struggle, and the military and paramilitary operations of this force were decided and planned by or in collaboration with United States advisers. In addition, the legislative and executive branches of the US Government had openly admitted the nature, volume and frequency of their support for the rebels. However, the Court did not consider it established that the *contras* were created by the United States.[131] Nor were the *contras* in a position of 'complete dependence' on United States aid, although this assistance had been crucial for their activities.[132] The high degree of dependence and general control would not by itself and without further evidence mean that the United States was responsible for every individual act performed by the *contras*. Therefore, the United States was responsible only for its own actions performed against Nicaragua by providing support for the *contras*.[133]

In the same case, the United States justified its attacks against Nicaragua by reference to collective self-defence in relation to the alleged armed attack by Nicaragua against El Salvador in the form of arms supply to the opponents of the Salvadorian Government.[134] From the presented reports and maps, the Court was unable to infer that in the material period the transboundary arms supply took place from Nicaragua into El Salvador.[135] Even though there had been ideological similarity between the Nicaraguan Government and Salvadorian rebels, and the political interest in Nicaragua to weaken the Salvadorian Government,

[131] *Military and Paramilitary Activities in and against Nicaragua*, Merits, *ICJ Reports* 1986, 14 at 61–62.

[132] *Id*, 62–63.

[133] *Id*, 64–65.

[134] *Id*, 72.

[135] *Id*, 78.

there was still no direct evidence of aid being given by Nicaragua to the armed opposition of El Salvador.[136] In addition, by reference to the *Corfu Channel* case, the Court noted that the mere control of the territory through which arms may have been transferred to El Salvador did not mean that Nicaragua knew of the transfer or of the perpetrators. This neither involved *prima facie* responsibility nor shifted the burden of proof.[137]

Thus, the *Nicaragua* case focuses on effective control of the State over certain conduct. It has to be specifically established that the State controls the relevant conduct, and the control of the territory over which the relevant conduct has arguably taken place is not crucial. The reference to effective control is, once again, a conceptual alternative to using the fact of territorial sovereignty to find the territorial State responsible for actions performed on its territory. Both the case of *Tellini*[138] and that of *Island of Palmas* support this latter approach.

In *Bosnian Genocide*, the Court again adhered to the test of dependence and control. In clarifying whether the perpetrators of genocide at Srebrenica were organs of the FRY, the Court had to examine whether they could be deemed completely dependent on it, which was the only precondition of equating them to the organs of the FRY for the purposes of attribution and responsibility.[139] Having found neither a structural connection of the perpetrators with, nor complete dependence of their action on, FRY,[140] the Court turned to the question of direction and control. The Court emphasised that the applicable test consisted in the control of the relevant conduct, requiring for it to be shown that 'this "effective control" was exercised, or that the State's instructions were given, in respect of each operation in which the alleged violations occurred, not generally in respect of the overall actions taken by the persons or groups of persons having committed the violations'.[141] The Court thus disapproved the applicability of the 'overall control' test suggested by the ICTY Appeal Chamber in *Tadic*, stressing that this test was unsuitable in a case which, unlike those dealt with by that Tribunal, was aimed at establishing the responsibility of the State. As the Court put it, 'the "overall control" test has the major drawback of broadening the scope of State responsibility well beyond the fundamental principle governing the law of international responsibility: a State is responsible only for its own conduct, that is to say the conduct of persons acting, on whatever basis, on its behalf'.[142] Given all that, the Court was unable to find Serbia responsible for the acts of genocide perpetrated on Bosnian territory.

[136] *Id*, 82–83, 86.
[137] *Id*, 84.
[138] Committee of Jurists established by the Council of the League of Nations, *LN Official Journal*, No 4, 1924, 524.
[139] *Application of the Genocide Convention* (Bosnia v Serbia), Judgment of 26 February 2007, General List No 91, para 393.
[140] *Id*, paras 394–395.
[141] *Id*, para 400.
[142] *Id*, para 406.

In the law of State responsibility, the International Law Commission has specified that in order for the State to be responsible for the conduct of other entities, it must be exercising effective control over the relevant conduct.[143] Yet effective control can become relevant in cases where the responsibility of the relevant State is determined in relation to the acts committed on territory over which it has no sovereignty. For much of the practice on this subject, effective control is purely a question of fact, to be identified as such.

In the *Namibia* case the International Court determined that South Africa was responsible for its dealings in the Namibian territory even if it had no legal title to it. The Court observed that:

> The fact that South Africa no longer has any title to administer the Territory does not release it from its obligations and responsibilities under international law towards other States in respect of the exercise of its powers in relation to this Territory. Physical control of a territory, and not sovereignty or legitimacy of title, is the basis of State liability for acts affecting other States.[144]

Effective control is, again, purely a question of fact and depends on the ascertainment of the fact as to who is in control, and correlation of different physical presences in the area. In *Congo–Uganda*, the International Court noted that 'although Uganda recognized that as of 1 September 1998 it exercised "administrative control" at Kisangani Airport, there is no evidence in the case file which could allow the Court to characterize the presence of Ugandan troops stationed at Kisangani Airport as occupation in the sense of Article 42 of the Hague Regulations of 1907'. The Court could not 'uphold the DRC's contention that Uganda was an occupying Power in areas outside Ituri controlled and administered by Congolese rebel movements'.[145]

The operation of the law of occupation depends on the occupant's effective control of the relevant territory, as specified in Article 42 of the 1907 Hague Regulations. As the International Court stated in *Congo–Uganda*, territory is considered to be occupied when it is actually placed under the authority of the hostile army, and the occupation extends only to the territory where such authority has been established and can be exercised.[146] Such control, according to the Court, places legal responsibility on the occupying power for its dealings in the occupied territory.

The Court observed 'that the DRC makes reference to "indirect administration" through various Congolese rebel factions and to the supervision by Ugandan officers over local elections in the territories under UPDF control.

[143] Article 8 on State Responsibility and its commentary, Report of the International Law Commission on the work of its Fifty-third session (2001), *Official Records of the General Assembly, Fifty-sixth session, Supplement No. 10* (A/56/10).

[144] *ICJ Reports*, 1971, 54.

[145] *Congo–Uganda*, para 177.

[146] *Id*, para 172.

However, the DRC does not provide any specific evidence to show that authority was exercised by Ugandan armed forces in any areas other than in Ituri district.'[147] Thus, Uganda was not an occupying power outside the Ituri area, was not in control there and could not be held responsible for the breach of its duty of vigilance regarding the exploitation of the Congo's natural resources.[148]

These decisions related to contexts where the relevant rules of conventional law, such as Article 42 of the Hague Regulations, and customary law, expressly require the existence of effective control for generating responsibility. Another significant factor is that in all the contexts examined so far effective control related to the issue of establishing whether or not the relevant illegalities were committed by the State in question.

The notion of effective control has, however, been applied in a context where it does not directly follow from the governing law, for instance in terms of the application of Article 1 of the European Convention on Human Rights which does not refer to the notion of effective control. In addition, the European Court of Human Rights has used this notion in some cases, such as *Bankovic*, in a context where it was established that the relevant conduct, namely the bombing of the Radio-Television Station in the territory of the Federal Republic of Yugoslavia, was performed by the respondent States. The reason for the Court's use of the notion of effective control in this case was its willingness to assess whether the actions actually performed and established contravened the European Convention. The Court's admissibility decision rejected the claim that the Convention was violated.[149]

The *Bankovic* case was decided against the background of the previous jurisprudence of the European Commission and European Court of Human Rights interpreting Article 1 of the Convention requiring that States-parties shall secure Convention rights to every person within their 'jurisdiction'. The Convention organs' practice has demonstrated, for instance in the *Drozd* case, that they view 'jurisdiction' under Article 1 not as jurisdiction in the ordinary sense of international law, but in the sense of what the respondent State has actually done.[150] Limiting Article 1 'jurisdiction' to ordinary State jurisdiction is bound to exclude nearly all extraterritorial conduct from the ambit of the European Convention. The *Loizidou* case follows this approach by stating that 'the responsibility of Contracting Parties can be involved because of acts of their authorities, whether performed within or outside national boundaries, which produce effects

[147] *Id*, para 177.

[148] *Id*, para 247.

[149] *Bankovic v Belgium et al.*, Admissibility Decision No 52207/99 of 12 December 2001; for an analysis see A Orakhelashvili, Restrictive Interpretation of Human Rights Treaties in the Recent Jurisprudence of the European Court of Human Rights, 14 *EJIL* (2003), 529.

[150] *Drozd and Janousek v France & Spain*, Application No 12747/87, Judgment of 26 June 1992, paras 91–96.

outside their own territory', and then citing *Drozd*. After this, the European Court proceeds to add that:

the responsibility of a Contracting Party may *also* arise when as a consequence of military action—whether lawful or unlawful—it exercises effective control of an area outside its national territory. The obligation to secure, in such an area, the rights and freedoms set out in the Convention derives from the fact of such control whether it be exercised directly, through its armed forces, or through a subordinate local administration.[151]

Consequently, *Loizidou* acknowledges that effective territorial or other control is not a necessary prerequisite for responsibility under Article 1 to arise. The European Convention applies to State action within and outside its boundaries. One of the modalities of this is the case where the relevant State exercises extraterritorial effective control over the territory. But such control is not a necessary requirement for Article 1 to be triggered nor does it exhaust the ambit of this provision.

In other words, the fact that the occupying power must allegedly have effective control over the relevant territory to be accountable under Article 1 of the European Convention does not mean that such effective control, undefinable as it is, constitutes the necessary condition for responsibility under Article 1 of any State-party to the European Convention, whether or not it is also the occupying power.

The European Court in *Bankovic* refers to *Loizidou* on this issue, yet misrepresents its findings. *Bankovic* asserts that Article 1 would extraterritorially apply only exceptionally where the respondent State exercises through military occupation all or some of the public powers normally to be exercised by the territorial sovereign.[152] This finding improperly narrows down the outcome of earlier jurisprudence, which factor enabled the Court to find that the bombings performed in the territory of Yugoslavia were beyond the reach of the Convention.

No decision before *Bankovic* laid down a requirement that Article 1 applies extraterritorially only to situations involving effective control of a territory. Furthermore, none of the earlier decisions elaborates upon the structural characteristics of such 'effective control' or sets any requirement as to its kind or duration. The jurisprudence suggests that extraterritorial applicability of Article 1 is its normal consequence and this takes place merely by virtue of the conduct of a State having consequences beyond the territory of that State. A logical assumption is therefore that any control of an area where alleged breaches are committed, if it would suffice to bring about such breaches, brings the matter within the 'jurisdiction' of a State under Article 1. But if the necessity of 'effective control' is still

[151] *Loizidou v Turkey*, Preliminary Objections, Application No 15318/89, Judgment of 23 March 1995, para 62 (emphasis added); nor does the case of *Cyprus v Turkey* contemplate the extraterritorial reach of Article 1 as limited to effective control, see *Cyprus v Turkey*, Merits, Application No 25781/94, Judgment of 10 May 2001.

[152] *Bankovic*, paras 70–71, 74, where the Court professes following *Loizidou*.

insisted upon, the fact of bombing the RTS in Belgrade may also be considered as an exercise of effective control by the respondent States. For if the capacity during a military operation—whether lawful or unlawful—to cause major damage to lives and property of the population, including acts likely to result in serious violations of the European Convention, is not effective control, then it really has to be asked what would constitute effective control at all.

But the danger of arbitrariness following from reading undefined factual conditions into treaty clauses does not end with *Bankovic*. The Court in the *Ilascu* case[153] found that breaches of the applicants' rights under Article 3 (freedom from torture and inhuman treatment) and Article 5 (freedom from arbitrary detention) of the European Convention of Human Rights were attributable to both defendant States—Moldova and Russia. According to the Court, the applicants came under the jurisdiction of both Moldova and Russia in terms of Article 1 of the Convention.

The relevant part of the Moldovan territory on which the 'Moldavian Republic of Transdniestria' is based comes, according to the Court, under Russia's 'jurisdiction' as the MRT exists because it is supported by Russia militarily, politically and economically.[154] As the violations of Articles 3 and 5 took place on that territory, they engaged Russia's responsibility. While the Court accepted that the Moldovan Government did not exercise authority over part of its territory which was under the effective control of the 'Moldavian Republic of Transdniestria', it still asserted that even in the absence of effective control over the Transdniestrian region, Moldova had a positive obligation under Article 1 of the Convention to take the diplomatic, economic, judicial or other measures that were in its power to take and were in accordance with international law to secure to the applicants the rights guaranteed by the Convention.[155] Given all that, the Court awarded just satisfaction under Article 41, ordering that both Moldova and Russia had to pay separately compensation to three victims, as well as their costs and expenses.

The reasoning that as Moldova had positive obligations to secure the relevant rights of the applicants and the situation came within its jurisdiction under Article 1 is rather strange. The Convention's proper interpretation allows determining State obligations, whether positive or negative, only after the situation otherwise comes within Article 1.

The Court's reasoning affirming the responsibility of Moldova even in the absence of its effective control on the relevant territory contradicts the Convention's previous jurisprudence, such as *Bankovic*, which requires that the State have effective control over the area where it conducts its military campaign. If *Bankovic* is right, then *Ilascu* had to be decided otherwise; if *Bankovic* is wrong, the Court

[153] *Ilascu v Moldova & Russia*, Application No 48787/99, Judgment of 8 July 2004.

[154] *Id*, para 392.

[155] *Id*, paras 330–331, 333–335; the Court added that Moldova had not been sufficiently attentive to this issue in its bilateral relations with the Russian Federation.

ought to have said so. In *An v Cyprus* the claims originated from Northern Cyprus were rejected because Cyprus had no effective control there.[156] In this case effective control had evidentiary significance: Cyprus did not commit the relevant wrongs as it had no effective control in Northern Cyprus. It simply had done nothing to violate the European Convention. The Court's reasoning in *Iliascu* involves a substantial degree of arbitrariness which also undermines the credibility of its finding that each of the defendants had to pay compensation individually.

In *Bankovic*, States which in the Court's view had no effective control over the territory of FRY were not obliged under Article 1 of the Convention to abstain from the forcible action that had directly caused deaths and injuries, while in *Ilascu*, Moldova, although having never actually done anything to violate the applicants' rights, nor having been in the factual position to do so as it lacked territorial control in the relevant territory, was considered bound to take positive measures, possibly diplomatic *démarches* and protests, to secure Convention rights to the applicants. While *Bankovic* was killed off at the jurisdictional stage, the case of *Ilascu* which had much less justification under Article 1 was taken to the merits stage and pursued until the end. Such divergent treatment of different States is possible if one adopts, as the European Court did, mutually exclusive interpretations of Article 1 on different occasions.

To sum up so far, while in most cases effective control is used as an evidentiary factor to establish whether wrongful conduct has been committed, in *Bankovic* effective control is asserted to mean that even as the conduct is committed, it cannot be judged under the European Convention. In *Ilascu*, the requirement of effective control mysteriously disappears and the respondent State is held responsible even if it did not actually affect the applicant's rights.

The European Court's jurisprudence contains the obvious evidence that 'effective control' is not a necessary precondition for finding responsibility of the State under Article 1 of the European Convention. In the *Issa* case, dealing with the Turkish operation in Northern Iraq—well beyond the Convention's claimed '*espace juridique*'—the European Court found that 'notwithstanding the large number of troops involved in the aforementioned military operations, it does not appear that Turkey exercised effective overall control of the entire area of northern Iraq'. Yet the Court proceeded to state that the crucial criterion was 'whether at the relevant time Turkish troops conducted operations in the area where the killings took place. The fate of the applicants' complaints in respect of the killing of their relatives depends on the prior establishment of that premise.' The Court concluded that it had 'not been established to the required standard of proof that the Turkish armed forces conducted operations in the area in question, and, more precisely, in the hills above the village of Azadi where, according to the applicants' statements, the victims were at that time'.[157] The rationale for the Court's approach was

[156] *An v Cyprus*, 13 *HRLJ*, at 44.
[157] *Issa v Turkey*, No 31821/96, 16 November 2004, paras 75–76, 81.

amazingly straightforward, stressing that 'Accountability in such situations stems from the fact that Article 1 of the Convention cannot be interpreted so as to allow a State party to perpetrate violations of the Convention on the territory of another State, which it could not perpetrate on its own territory.'[158]

Thus, the violations claimed were not established as a matter of fact. This straightforward approach applying the general principle of Article 1 to facts was the precondition of the finding that the relevant events were not under Turkey's Article 1 'jurisdiction'. This demonstrates that the legal principle embodied in Article 1 is perfectly capable of applying to fact without having the factual requirement of 'effective control' incorporated into itself. This demonstrates that the use of the 'effective control' test in *Bankovic* was superfluous and resulted in the improper limiting of the obvious scope of Article 1 of the European Convention. Seen from this perspective, *Issa* can be seen as a subsequent overruling of the restrictive reading of Article 1 in *Bankovic*.

In the *Al-Skeini* case, dealing with the applicability of the European Convention on Human Rights to the activities of British forces in Iraq, the House of Lords did not properly consider the impact of *Issa* and applied the restrictive approach of *Bankovic*, including its 'effective control' test.[159] This enabled the House of Lords to find that only the applicant captured by British forces was entitled to the protection under the Convention, while other victims who were killed were outside its scope. Given that the attribution of conduct to the State without finding its 'effective control' over the relevant situation is only one of the options developed by the European Court, and that responsibility is certainly possible, and practised, without it, the House of Lords was not justified in treating the *Bankovic* approach as central and indispensable.

The saga of effective control continues with the decision of the European Court in the *Behrami* case, in which it held that the acts committed by KFOR national contigents in Kosovo (FRY) were not attributable to the relevant States-parties to which the contingents belonged. This was explained by the fact that KFOR was under the UN Security Council mandate.[160] The Court originally referred to Article 5 of the ILC's Draft on Responsibility of International Organisations, the commentary of which specifies that 'The conduct of an organ of a State or an organ or agent of an international organisation that is placed at the disposal of another international organisation shall be considered under international law an act of the latter organisation if the organisation exercises effective control over that conduct.'[161] This is the perspective of the law of responsibility, and further

[158] *Id*, 71.

[159] *Al-Skeini and Others v Secretary of State for Defence* [2007] UKHL 26, Judgment of 13 June 2007.

[160] *Behrami & Saramati v France*, Application Nos 71412/01 & 78166/01, Admissibility Decision of 2 May 2007.

[161] Draft Articles adopted by the Commission on Responsibility of International Organisations, Article 5.

accords both with the International Court's jurisprudence and the ILC's own treatment of the law of State responsibility.

In the latter part of its judgment, the Court asserts that 'the key question is whether the UNSC retained ultimate authority and control so that operational command only was delegated'.[162] Furthermore, the Court specified that:

> The UNSC was to retain ultimate authority and control over the security mission and it delegated to NATO (in consultation with non-NATO member states) the power to establish, as well as the operational command of, the international presence, KFOR. NATO fulfilled its command mission *via* a chain of command (from the NAC, to SHAPE, to SACEUR, to CIC South) to COMKFOR, the commander of KFOR. While the MNBs were commanded by an officer from a lead TCN, the latter was under the direct command of COMKFOR. MNB action was to be taken according to an operational plan devised by NATO and operated by COMKFOR in the name of KFOR.[163]

But this refers to mandate, delegation and formal authority, as opposed to the actual commission of the wrongful act and the actual effective control over it. In order to find that the United Nations and not the individual States are responsible for the wrongful detention of the individual, it has to be established that the United Nations or another organisation has actually committed such conduct. Otherwise, the responsibility rests with individual States which have actually committed that conduct. The United Nations does not authorise KFOR to perform extrajudicial detentions either. The European Court's decision in *Behrami* avoids the real factual essence of 'effective control' as developed in earlier jurisprudence and instead equates it to legal notions of mandate, delegation and formal authority. The outcome is that States which actually violate the European Convention are effectively excused, with the possibility of speculation on whether the United Nations has to be held responsible even if it has neither performed nor authorised the relevant activities.

All this demonstrates that the reading into a treaty clause of factual conditions is ridden with the dangers of arbitrariness and the application of double standards. The normal approach to effective control in general international law relates to control over the wrongful conduct, or uses effective control as an evidentiary factor to prove that the relevant wrongful conduct has been performed. The use of 'effective control' by the European Court of Human Rights in relation to a treaty clause which does not on the face of it include this condition, and in a way requiring the control of territory as opposed to conduct, has only served to produce a state of profound uncertainty making it difficult if not impossible for potential applicants to figure out in which of the above several ways Article 1 will be applied to their cases.

Jurisprudence has also offered instances where, while otherwise accepting the 'effective control' test, the International Court has found a State responsible for

[162] *Behrami*, para 133.
[163] *Id*, paras 134–136.

a wrongful act that was committed outside its control. Having found that Serbia had not actually committed genocide, and in dealing with the issue of State responsibility for the failure to prevent genocide in the *Bosnia* case, the Court stated that it does not aim to develop the general jurisprudence on this point, and every point of its analysis on this point reveals the acknowledgment that the Yugoslav authorities had no effective authority and control over the events in Bosnia. As for factual points, the Court stressed that the Yugoslav federal authorities were aware of the likelihood of the commission of genocide in the relevant parts of Bosnia. The Court proceeded to find Serbia responsible for the failure to prevent genocide on the basis of its alleged 'influence' over the Bosnian Serbs, in the absence of effective control. The only evidence of this 'influence' the Court cited—the information that President Milosevic had claimed to have dissuaded Bosnian Serbs from killing male civilians in Srebrenica but did not succeed—actually negated the claim that the authorities in Belgrade had sufficient influence over Bosnian Serbs.[164] The Court does not support its line of reasoning with any other evidence to prove what it calls the 'undeniable influence' of Serbia over Bosnian Serbs.

Yet the Court proceeded to find Serbia responsible for not having prevented genocide. In terms of remedies, the Court refused to award financial compensation, considering it inappropriate, and limited itself to pronouncing the wrongfulness of this alleged conduct as part of just satisfaction.[165]

The Court's manipulation of the term 'influence', together with its emphasis that no attempt was made to lay down the general jurisprudence on the subject, confirmed both that the Court defied the normally applicable principle that responsibility should be generated by effective control, and that it took the path of administering justice on a case-by-case basis without basing its approach on the generally applicable legal principle. The shortcomings and deficiency of the Court's reasoning on this point is well illustrated in the Declaration of Judge Skotnikov, which emphasised that the Court's position resulted in 'a political statement which is clearly outside the specific scope of the Genocide Convention'. As Judge Skotnikov emphasised more specifically, 'What the Court should have said on the subject is, in my opinion, the following: a State fails its duty to prevent under the Genocide Convention if genocide is committed within the territory where it exercises its jurisdiction or which is under its control.' Instead of having resorted to the above-stated straightforward legal principle, the Court 'has introduced a politically appealing, but legally vague, indeed, hardly measurable at all in legal terms, concept of a duty to prevent with the essential element of control being replaced with a highly subjective notion of influence'.[166]

[164] *Application of the Genocide Convention* (Bosnia v Serbia), Judgment of 26 February 2007, General List No 91, paras 435–438.

[165] *Id*, paras 461–462, and operative para 5.

[166] Declaration of Judge Skotnikov.

This seems to be the correct assessment, for the Court's solution is unconnected with the generally applicable law, and is also open to subjective manipulation. On a more general plane, the Court's approach fails to consider the implications for similar situations in other parts of the world, and the problem of determining what legal standard should apply to those other situations. 'Influence' refers neither to the actual commission of the wrongful act, nor to any visible control over it, and effectively approves holding the State responsible for what it has not done.

6. The Factual Element and its Impact on the Scope of Legal Rules

Although factual considerations do not *per se* provide the basis for legal rights and titles nor create legal rules, the relevance of fact is recognised in a number of fields of international law as part of the relevant legal rules, determining the scope and conditions of their applicability. In these fields international law has to appeal to facts that provide the criteria for the application of rules, or define the degree of their determinacy.

The law of the nationality of claims largely operates by reference to factual criteria. The traditional pattern of diplomatic protection is in essence the protection of the rights of the claimant State. This requires construing this field of law as requiring the effectiveness of nationality of the physical person whose rights are vindicated through the exercise of diplomatic protection. The International Court in *Nottebohm* had to refer to the factual aspect of the legal relation of nationality. Without such reference, the nationality rule would not in this case be sufficiently determinate to enable the Court adjudicating the case, or prevent abuse. The Court referred to the criteria that governed the determination of dominant nationality in arbitral practice: family ties, participation in public life, the locus of the centre of interests, and habitual residence.[167] The Court required the existence of a 'genuine connection' between the individual and the State of nationality. Other States will be bound to recognise such nationality, as the 'legal bond having as its basis a social fact of attachment, a genuine connection of existence, interests and sentiments, together with reciprocal rights and duties'. Such factual attachment to the State justifies the entitlement to protection.[168]

The broad legal principle is that international law leaves each State to determine who its nationals are. Further recognition as a matter of international law of the nationality thus conferred requires examination of the circumstances in which the nationality was conferred. Above all this relates to the real and effective preference of the relevant individuals.[169] Nottebohm's only purpose in acquiring

[167] *ICJ Reports*, 1955, 22.
[168] *Id*, 23.
[169] *Id*, 24.

the nationality of Liechtenstein was to obtain protection, and Guatemala was not obliged to recognise this nationality.[170]

Judge Klaestad insisted on a more black letter approach. If the State can regulate its nationality, then other States cannot object to this regulation.[171] Similarly, Judge Read insisted that once naturalisation had taken place in accordance with Liechtenstein's law, Guatemala had the burden to contest and prove that it was not valid. The abuse of the right to determine nationals could not be proved in this case.[172] The individual's subsequent conduct was not relevant either.[173] And yet, Judge Read referred to the considerations of genuine link. Upon his naturalisation, Nottebohm had spent nine years in Liechtenstein, four years in Guatemala and two years in the United States.[174] A*d hoc* Judge Guggenheim referred to the objective criteria of nationalisation which the Court, according to him, replaced by the subjective criteria of the genuineness of application, attachment and loyalty to the new State, central point of economic interests, and the intention to become integrated in the new country. Judge Guggenheim also emphasised that the concept of the 'bond of attachment' is not defined anywhere.[175]

It is arguable that in such a case the factual requirement such as a genuine link provides the rationale for the rule, legitimates connection, and prevents abuses generated by excessive formalism. At the same time, the factual criterion of the bond of attachment can itself be indeterminate. The balancing of different factors demonstrating the genuineness of the link appearing on different sides may be difficult.

According to the *Lotus* criteria, if Liechtenstein had acted in the absence of the prohibitive rule related to the conferment of nationality, Guatemala was bound to accept its exercise of the right to do so. One response to this is that the exercise of sovereign right has an international aspect of regulation, as affirmed in the *Fisheries* case. Another response is that the rule itself incorporated the (factual) limitation as to the exercise of this right so as to make it inapplicable to other States.

Similar to the International Court's approach in *Nottebohm*, the arbitral practice manifests support for the fact-oriented approach in determining the nationality of corporations. The prevailing approach is that the nationality of a corporation is the State where it has its head office, as opposed to the nationality of shareholders.[176] The International Law Commission's Draft Articles 4 and 6, dealing with diplomatic protection in general and against third States in particular, abandon the effective or genuine link test that was required in

[170] *Id*, 25.
[171] *Id*, 28.
[172] *Id*, 35–36, 39–40.
[173] *Id*, 44.
[174] *Id*, 45.
[175] *Id*, 55–56.
[176] For an overview of arbitral practice see, S Alexandrov, The 'Baby Boom' of Treaty-Based Arbitrations and The Jurisdiction of ICSID Tribunals: Shareholders as 'Investors' and Jurisdiction *Ratione Temporis*, 4 *LPICT* (2005), 19 at 34–35.

Nottebohm.[177] While it is understandable to refuse to imply the factual element in the legal rule under which States in principle are free to determine the criteria under which they grant nationality to individuals, it is equally problematic that the Commission's approach does not offer any practical safeguard against the exercise of diplomatic protection on behalf of nominal nationals, including those who acquire nationality in bad faith.

In some cases, the factual element in legal regulation may be inherently necessary to escape the deadlock that the relevant context may otherwise produce. This relates, above all, to situations where the relevant individual holds more than one nationality, which may complicate finding which State can exercise diplomatic protection in relation to him. The solution that international practice has found for these situations is that of the dominant or active nationality. This requires examining, as a matter of fact, which of the individual's nationalities is predominant, in the sense of reflecting his link to and presence within the relevant State.

This approach is further confirmed by the ILC's Articles on Diplomatic Protection, Article 7 of which specifies that 'A State of nationality may not exercise diplomatic protection in respect of a person against a State of which that person is also a national unless the nationality of the former State is predominant, both at the date of injury and at the date of the official presentation of the claim.'[178] The predominant nationality test was also applied by the Iran-US Claims Tribunal in the case of *Esphahanian v Bank Tejarat*, in which the claimant's long and consistent links with the United States were emphasised.[179]

Although the predominant nationality test has merits, it raises questions not only in terms of the factual condition implied in the legal rule being justified, but also about the nature of this factual condition itself. The requirement of predominant nationality does not fully fit within, nor can be explained by, the principle of effective nationality. It is one thing that the relevant nationality must be effective in absolute terms; it is another thing that it has to be predominant in relevant terms. The nationality which is effective in absolute terms can fall short of being predominant in relative terms. The effective nationality test under *Nottebohm*

[177] Articles 4 and 6, and Commentary thereto, see ILC's *Draft Articles on Diplomatic Protection, ILC Report* 2006, 22, at 31ff, 41ff.

[178] Article 7 and Commentary thereto, see ILC's *Draft Articles on Diplomatic Protection, ILC Report* 2006, 22 at 43ff. The Commission refrained from describing in this Article the factors of predominance to be taken into account, but the Commentary specifies that these include 'habitual residence, the amount of time spent in each country of nationality, date of naturalization (i.e., the length of the period spent as a national of the protecting State before the claim arose); place, curricula and language of education; employment and financial interests; place of family life; family ties in each country; participation in social and public life; use of language; taxation, bank account, social security insurance; visits to the other State of nationality; possession and use of passport of the other State; and military service. None of these factors is decisive and the weight attributed to each factor will vary according to the circumstances of each case.' See the Commentary, *id*, at 46, para 5. The Commission's last observation seems to indicate that none of these factual considerations can entail a legal outcome on their own.

[179] *Esphahanian v Bank Tejarat*, 2, *IUSCT Reports* (1983), 157.

operates by denying the standing to exercise diplomatic protection to the State of nominal nationality. The dominant nationality test extends the same to States of effective nationality. This could cause denying the State of effective nationality the right to protect its national just because the link of that individual is stronger with its other State of nationality. This is not to say that the test of predominant nationality is wrong; it is practically the only solution to avoid the deadlock of double claims. But the predominant nationality link has to be applied with caution to ensure that the State of nationality is not excluded from protecting its national against the other State of nationality unless the contrast in effective link is wide and evident. At the same time, it is rather curious that the International Law Commission's Draft Articles on Diplomatic Protection disregard the factual requirement of effective nationality, but adhere to the factual requirement of predominant nationality.

In *M/V Saiga* before the International Tribunal for the Law of the Sea Guinea objected to the admissibility of the St Vincent and Grenadines claim by submitting that the ship, although registered with the latter, had no genuine connection with it. The argument developed around Article 91 of the Law of the Sea Convention, according to which 'Every State shall fix the conditions for the grant of its nationality to ships, for the registration of ships in its territory, and for the right to fly its flag. Ships have the nationality of the State whose flag they are entitled to fly. There must exist a genuine link between the State and the ship.' St Vincent and Grenadines opposed Guinea's assertion about the lack of genuine link by submitting that such a link was not required and that it had such a link with the ship anyway.[180]

The Tribunal proceeded with identifying the requirements under Article 91 of the 1982 Law of the Sea Convention, which was deemed not to provide the answer. The Tribunal explained that the relevant clause in the draft convention on the high seas, subsequently adopted as the 1958 High Seas Convention, provided that, apart from the nationality requirement, 'for purposes of recognition of the national character of the ship by other States, there must exist a genuine link between the State and the ship'. The actual Article 5 of the 1958 Convention no longer contained such a requirement. In other words, there was a requirement of genuine link, but it was not crucial for recognising the nationality of ships registered with other States. The 1982 Convention followed this approach.[181] Thus, the matter turned upon the construction of the clauses in the 1958 and 1982 Conventions, as opposed to identifying the state of general international law. The Tribunal maintained that 'the purpose of the provisions of the Convention on the need for a genuine link between a ship and its flag State is to secure more effective implementation of the duties of the flag State, and not to establish criteria by reference to which the validity of the registration of ships in a flag State may be

[180] *M/V Saiga* (Saint Vincent and the Grenadines v Guinea), Judgment of 1 July 1999, paras 75ff.
[181] *Id*, paras 80–81.

challenged by other States'.[182] But this stops short of resolving the problem. If the requirement of genuine link serves the need of the effective implementation of the duties of the flag State, this is meant to establish legal certainty in relation to other States in the sense that they are aware of who is responsible for meeting those duties in the relevant case. It is quite logical that recognition of the nationality of a ship must be premised on that condition.

Another principle incorporating the factual requirement in international legal rules is the principle of *uti possidetis juris* applicable to territorial title. This is a regulatory principle referring to facts that were not originally, at the time of their occurrence, meant to produce the regime of sovereign frontiers. This regime is subsequently construed for the sake of systemic stability, thus providing for an example of systemic effectiveness.

In *Burkina-Faso v Mali*, the International Court identified the primary aim of the *uti possidetis* rule as 'securing respect for the territorial boundaries at the moment when independence [of the State] is achieved'. This means that former colonial borders become international boundaries.[183]

As a rule, it is recognised that *uti possidetis juris* disposes of the need to ascertain the basis of the territorial title in the factual effectiveness of the exercise of State authority. However, in some cases, the same rule can itself refer to the criterion of effective possession. In *El Salvador/Honduras*, the Chamber of the Court affirmed that 'possession backed by the exercise of sovereignty may be taken as evidence confirming the *uti possidetis juris* title. The Chamber does not find it necessary to decide whether such possession could be recognised even in contradiction of such a title, but in the case of the islands, where the historical material of colonial times is confused and contradictory, and the accession to independence was not immediately followed by unambiguous acts of sovereignty, this is practically the only way in which the *uti possidetis juris* could find formal expression so as to be judicially recognised and determined.'[184]

Therefore, the subsequent conduct and attitudes of the parties displaced the issue of sovereignty over the islands. Sovereignty could not be ascertained on the basis of colonial titles. Hence, the effective possession by Honduras, coupled with the lack of protest and acquiescence by El Salvador, established that the relevant islands were under the sovereignty of Honduras.[185]

In *Benin–Niger*, the claims of *effectivités* were argued in relation to *uti possidetis juris*. Benin argued for the taking into account of the physical realities subsequent to independence, to ensure that the Chamber's judgment would have meaningful significance in the relations between the parties. Niger, on the other hand, insisted on the strict application of *uti possidetis juris*. The Chamber observed that 'present-day physical realities', especially the emergence of certain islands in the

[182] *Id*, para 83.
[183] *ICJ Reports*, 1986, 586–587.
[184] *El Salvador/Honduras*, *ICJ Reports*, 1992, 566 (para 347).
[185] *Id*, 569–570 (paras 354–355), 574 (para 362), 579 (para 367).

area in question were to be taken into account.[186] This suggests that there is some degree of factual inter-temporality whereby subsequent factual, in this case physical, developments are allocated within the application of the general principle of *uti possidetis juris*.

Thus, the general relevance of *uti possidetis juris* as the principle independent of external facts has not been doubted either in general nor on this specific occasion. But the lack of some factual prerequisites on which the validity of this principle could rely in this case required assessing other, supplementary, factual data to ensure the judicial manageability and determinacy of this principle in this case. This would by no means apply to land boundaries, as demonstrated above, but was solely applied to the island frontiers, and only due to the specific circumstances.

In the law of the European Convention on Human Rights, the content of and compliance with certain Convention standards cannot be ascertained without reference to some considerations of fact. This context is not just about judging the conduct of the State in terms of the Convention, but also examining the features of the systemically designated fact which, according to the Convention, produces a certain legal effect.

Articles 8 to 11 of the Convention give States a certain degree of freedom, within the framework of the margin of appreciation, to take certain actions dictated by public interest at a national level. Such action must be 'in accordance with the law', that is national legislation which is a fact in terms of international law. Thus, compliance with the factual requirement becomes the condition of legality of the State action. On a number of occasions, the European Court of Human Rights has judged the compliance of States with Articles 8 to 11 by reference to this requirement.

In *Malone v UK*, the Court addressed the issue of intercepting telephone conversations in contravention of Article 8, and found that there was interference with the scope of this provision.[187] In judging 'accordance with the law', the Court emphasised that the Convention 'does not merely refer back to domestic law but also relates to the quality of the law. This required it to be compatible with the rule of law, which is expressly mentioned in the preamble to the Convention.' In this context, the Court observed that 'The phrase thus implies—and this follows from the object and purpose of Article 8 that there must be a measure of legal protection in domestic law against arbitrary interferences by public authorities with the rights safeguarded by paragraph 1.'

Furthermore, 'where a power of the executive is exercised in secret, the risks of arbitrariness are evident'. 'The law must be sufficiently clear in its terms to give citizens an adequate indication as to the circumstances in which and the conditions on which public authorities are empowered to resort to this secret and

[186] *Case concerning the Frontier Dispute* (Benin/Niger), Chamber of the Court, Judgment of 12 July 2005, *ICJ Reports*, 2005, 90 at 108–109.

[187] *Malone v UK*, Application No 8691/79, Judgment of 2 August 1984.

potentially dangerous interference with the right to respect for private life and correspondence.'[188] In applying this principle to the case, the Court concluded that the law on the 'interception of communications for police purposes is somewhat obscure and open to differing interpretations'. It could not 'be said with any reasonable certainty what elements of the powers to intercept are incorporated in legal rules and what elements remain within the discretion of the executive'. In view of the attendant obscurity and uncertainty as to the state of the law in this essential respect, the Court concluded that the interference with the right under Article 8 constituted a breach of the European Convention.[189]

In *Kruslin v France*, the Court addressed the issue of telephone tapping by the French authorities and ruled that it constituted interference with the inviolability of private life under Article 8. In examining whether the interference was 'in accordance with law', the Court emphasised that it 'requires firstly that the impugned measure should have some basis in domestic law; it also refers to the quality of the law in question, requiring that it should be accessible to the person concerned, who must moreover be able to foresee its consequences for him, and compatible with the rule of law'.[190] In examining 'the quality of the law' the Court concentrated on 'the law's "foreseeability" as to the meaning and nature of the applicable measures'.[191] The Court stated that 'it must inevitably assess the relevant French "law" in force at the time in relation to the requirements of the fundamental principle of the rule of law. Such a review necessarily entails some degree of abstraction. It is none the less concerned with the "quality" of the national legal rules applicable.'[192] An interference with privacy as serious as telephone tapping had to be based on law that is sufficiently precise, and this was not the case. The system did 'not for the time being afford adequate safeguards against various possible abuses'. For instance, the categories of people liable to have their telephones tapped by judicial order and the nature of the offences which may give rise to such an order were nowhere defined. Nothing obliges a judge to set a limit on the duration of telephone tapping.[193] Therefore, the Court found a breach of Article 8.

It is noteworthy that the European Court of Human Rights repeatedly refuses to take the normative implication of the normative fact at its face value. The consideration of 'the quality of the law' is introduced as the criterion of legality of national action at international level. The relevance of fact is judged in terms of its compatibility with the aims and rationale of the relevant legal framework, in this case the European Convention.

Another aspect of the law of the European Convention on Human Rights where the operation of the Convention rule depends on factual circumstances

188 *Id*, para 67.
189 *Id*, paras 79–80.
190 *Kruslin v France*, Application No 11801/85, Judgment of 24 April 1990, paras 26–27.
191 *Id*, para 30.
192 *Id*, para 32.
193 *Id*, paras 33–36.

relates to the concept of 'family' under Article 8. In *Abdulaziz, Cabales and Balkandali*, the European Court emphasised that the meaning of 'family' in Article 8 'must at any rate include the relationship that arises from a lawful and genuine marriage'.[194] The family thus established had the claim to be protected under Article 8. This is similar to the requirement of genuine nationality in *Nottebohm*, to allow the exercise of diplomatic protection by the State of nationality. In *Kroon v Netherlands*, the European Court found a breach of Article 8 in a dispute as to what kind of unit can be considered as family. Under Dutch law certain procedural rights extended only to those who were in a marriage and the Government argued that the relationship of applicants did not amount to family life. The Court examined the concept of 'family' under Article 8 in terms of factual effectiveness, observing that:

> the notion of 'family life' in Article 8 is not confined solely to marriage-based relationships and may encompass other de facto 'family ties' where parties are living together outside marriage. Although, as a rule, living together may be a requirement for such a relationship, exceptionally other factors may also serve to demonstrate that a relationship has sufficient constancy to create de facto 'family ties'; such is the case here, as since 1987 four children have been born to Mrs Kroon and Mr Zerrouk.[195]

The further relevance of factual analysis was underlined in the Court's more general observation as to the Convention-specific concept of family. The policy behind the preference of factual analysis seems to be the rationale of Article 8. In terms of this rationale 'A solution which only allows a father to create a legal tie with a child with whom he has a bond amounting to family life if he marries the child's mother cannot be regarded as compatible with the notion of 'respect' for family life.'[196] 'Consequently, "respect" for "family life" requires that biological and social reality prevail over a legal presumption which, as in the present case, flies in the face of both established fact and the wishes of those concerned without actually benefiting anyone.'[197] Therefore, the Court found that Article 8 had been violated.

7. The Prescription of *De Facto* Outcomes by Legal Rules

There is substantial judicial practice that sees treaty regulation in the factually oriented perspective. This refers to the performance of international obligations both *de jure* and *de facto*. This is presumably required by the effectiveness of legal regulation. To illustrate, the Permanent Court of International Justice took the factually-oriented approach in *Minority Schools in Albania*, opposing

[194] *Abdulaziz, Cabales and Balkandali v UK*, Application Nos 9214/80, 9473/81 and 9474/81, Judgment of 28 May 1985, paras 62–63.

[195] Application No 18535/91, Judgment of 27 October 1994, para 30.

[196] *Id*, para 38.

[197] *Id*, para 40.

laws discriminating in practice against minorities not in their fact but in their effect. The Court observed that 'Equality in law precludes discrimination of any kind; whereas equality in fact may involve the necessity of different treatment in order to attain a result which establishes an equilibrium between different situations.'[198] The European Court of Human Rights in the *Pine Valley* case adopted a similar approach in relation to the right to property under Article 1 of Protocol I to the European Convention on Human Rights. Under this approach, the protection of the right to property has both a formal and a factual aspect. Article 1 can be violated not only by formal expropriation, but also by *de facto* deprivation of property.[199]

The investment arbitration practice has developed the concept of creeping expropriation. This, although falling short of direct and straightforward expropriation, can still amount to expropriation in practice. This approach is used to construe the relevant conventional and customary rules that prohibit expropriation of foreign investment.[200] A similar phenomenon is accepted in WTO law. In *EC–Bananas*, the WTO Appellate Body enquired into whether the obligation contained in Article II:1 GATS to extend 'treatment no less favourable' applies not only to *de jure* but also to *de facto* discrimination. The Appellate Body concluded that the ban on *de facto* discrimination was included.[201]

In *Korea–Beef*, Korea argued before the WTO Appellate Body that its dual retail system applicable to the distribution of imported meat did not result in *de jure* or *de facto* discrimination. 'With regard to *de jure* discrimination, Korea's dual retail system assures perfect regulatory symmetry between imports and domestic products. Imported beef is sold only in stores that choose to sell imported beef, and domestic beef is sold only in stores choosing to sell domestic beef. In addition, there is total freedom on the part of retailers to switch from one category of shops to the other.' Furthermore, 'To demonstrate the presence or absence of *de facto* discrimination, the Panel should have undertaken an analysis of the market as part of an examination of the "total configuration of the facts". Instead, the Panel resorted to "speculation". An examination of the facts of the Korean beef market demonstrates that imported and domestic goods experience equal competitive conditions.'[202] The Appellate Body did not expressly address these arguments, which would have presented a good opportunity to clarify further issues in this contested field.

[198] *PCIJ Series* A/B, No 64, Advisory Opinion of 6 April 1935, 19.

[199] *Pine Valley Developments Ltd and others v Ireland*, No 12742/87, 29 November 1991, paras 55–56.

[200] On this see Chapter 15 below on the interpretation of customary rules.

[201] *European Communities–Regime for the Importation, Sale and Distribution of Bananas*, WT/DS27/AB/R, Report of the Appellate Body, 9 September 1997, paras 229–234.

[202] *Korea–Measures Affecting Imports of Fresh, Chilled and Frozen Beef*, AB-2000–8, Report of the Appellate Body, WT/DS161/AB/R, WT/DS169/AB/R, 11 December 2000, paras 17–18.

8. Requirements of Fact as Part of the Structural Framework of International Law

In certain fields of international law, facts are systemically assigned a crucial role in determining the operation and continuation in force of, requirement of compliance with, and termination of legal obligations. In contrast to facts referred to in a specific legal rule, systemic facts relate to principles governing the systemic structure of international law. Thus, this structural operation is to some extent dependent on the presence or absence of systemically designated factual considerations. Systemic principles refer to the factual situations that justify non-compliance with or termination of the relevant international obligations. The ascertainment of the required fact is part of the process of the application of law, that is the systemic principles, to facts. It is not the fact itself that justifies the non-compliance with or termination of the specific legal obligation, but the systemic principle from which the fact derives such relevance.

(a) The Law of State Responsibility

Several rules of the law of State responsibility relate to the ways in which law should be applied to facts. This relates to the characteristics of the concept of internationally wrongful acts of the State, as dealt with in Part I of the ILC's Articles of State Responsibility. Most provisions of Draft Articles, such as the rules on attribution of wrongful acts and the character of wrongful acts, deal with the application of law to facts and the appreciation of facts in the context of legal obligations. They proceed from the assumption that once there is legal obligation, it has to be enforced through international responsibility. Some of the rules of State responsibility, however, relate to defining the relevance of facts in construing and determining the relevance of the legal obligation itself. Circumstances precluding wrongfulness address situations where the relevant legal obligations are generally applicable, but some factual events are justified in making them inapplicable to the specific case. These rules relate to situations which, though not challenging the general validity of relevant obligations, justify non-compliance with them.

Article 23 of the ILC draft exculpates the wrongdoer State in the case of '*force majeure*, that is the occurrence of an irresistible force or of an unforeseen event, beyond the control of the State, making it materially impossible in the circumstances to perform the obligation'. Paragraph 2 of the same Article specifies that this defence does not apply if 'the situation of *force majeure* is due, either alone or in combination with other factors, to the conduct of the State invoking it'. Therefore, *force majeure* refers to objective facts and occurrences that are not due to the wrongdoer States' will, and this is confirmed in the Commentary.[203] In terms

[203] ILC's Articles on State Responsibility, Commentary to Article 23, para 9.

of characterising the required factual situation, the Commentary specifies that 'impossibility of performance giving rise to *force majeure* may be due to a natural or physical event (eg, stress of weather which may divert State aircraft into the territory of another State, earthquakes, floods or drought) or to human intervention (eg, loss of control over a portion of the State's territory as a result of an insurrection or devastation of an area by military operations carried out by a third State), or some combination of the two'.[204] The simple increase of burden on the State will not justify its claims as *force majeure*, as affirmed in the *Rainbow Warrior* case.[205]

Article 24 provides for exculpation in the case of distress, when 'the author of the act in question has no other reasonable way, in a situation of distress, of saving the author's life or the lives of other persons entrusted to the author's care'. As the Commentary specifies, in this case 'a person acting under distress is not acting involuntarily, even though the choice is effectively nullified by the situation of peril'.[206] The Commentary specifies that this mostly applies to distress experienced by ships and aircraft justifying them in entering the area of the other State's sovereignty.[207] The plea of distress is 'limited to cases where human life is at stake'. 'The problem with extending Article 24 to less than life-threatening situations is where to place any lower limit.'[208]

Article 25 refers to a state of necessity which enables the State not to comply with its obligation if this 'is the only way for the State to safeguard an essential interest against a grave and imminent peril; and does not seriously impair an essential interest of the State or States towards which the obligation exists, or of the international community as a whole'. As the Commentary specifies, these stringent conditions ensure that necessity will rarely be available as the circumstance precluding wrongfulness.[209] As the International Court specified in the *Gabcikovo-Nagymaros* case, 'the state of necessity can only be invoked under certain strictly defined conditions which must be cumulatively satisfied; and the State concerned is not the sole judge of whether those conditions have been met'.[210]

A general look at the circumstances precluding wrongfulness confirms that we are dealing here not with exculpation due to facts as such. This happens because of facts that for systemic reasons objectively justify non-compliance in carefully selected circumstances. These are systemically arranged facts, and they cannot serve the argument of the law-creating or law-modifying force of facts. At the same time, the strict conditions for the use of these defences confirm

[204] ILC's Articles on State Responsibility, Commentary to Article 23, para 3.

[205] Case concerning the difference between New Zealand and France concerning the interpretation or application of two agreements, concluded on 9 July 1986 between the two States and which related to the problems arising from the *Rainbow Warrior* Affair, XX *RIAA* 21, at 253.

[206] ILC's Articles on State Responsibility, Commentary to Article 24, para 1.

[207] ILC's Articles on State Responsibility, Commentary to Article 24, paras 2–4.

[208] *Id*, para 6.

[209] ILC's Articles on State Responsibility, Commentary to Article 25, para 2.

[210] *ICJ Reports* 1998, 40.

that they are available only in rare cases, which in turn obviates the need for a comprehensive consideration of the impact of facts on the operation of law.

(b) The Law of Treaties

In the law of treaties, there are a number of systemically designated facts that can justify the termination of treaty obligations, provided that their stringent requirements are met. These are impossibility of performance, material breach of a treaty, and *rebus sic stantibus*. Article 60 of the 1969 Vienna Convention on the Law of Treaties justifies the State in terminating a treaty in response to its material breach. A material breach is defined in the same article as 'a repudiation of the treaty not sanctioned by the present Convention; or the violation of a provision essential to the accomplishment of the object or purpose of the treaty'. As the ILC emphasised in its 1966 Final Commentary on the draft convention, these acts could interact with the factors that induced the State to enter into treaty obligations and therefore constitute material breaches.[211]

Under Article 61 of the Vienna Convention, a treaty can be terminated 'if the impossibility results from the permanent disappearance or destruction of an object indispensable for the execution of the treaty. If the impossibility is temporary, it may be invoked only as a ground for suspending the operation of the treaty.' Article 61 requires, as is acknowledged in the ILC Commentary on State Responsibility, more than ILC's Article 23 on *force majeure*.[212] This is so because more is at stake in the case of treaty termination than in the case of a simple one-off finding that no responsibility was owed. To justify the termination of a treaty, Article 61 requires the 'permanent disappearance or destruction of an object indispensable for the execution'. As the ILC's Final Commentary specified, the reasons must be extremely serious, such as the drying-up of the river or the destruction of a dam or hydro-electric installation indispensable for the execution of the treaty.[213]

Under Article 62 of the Vienna Convention, a treaty can be terminated in the case of *rebus sic stantibus*, that is the existence of circumstances which 'constituted an essential basis of the consent of the parties to be bound by the treaty'. Here 'the effect of the change is radically to transform the extent of obligations still to be performed under the treaty'. At the same time, Article 62 specifies that *rebus sic stantibus* cannot be invoked 'if the fundamental change is the result of a breach by the party invoking it either of an obligation under the treaty or of any other international obligation'. In *Fisheries Jurisdiction*, the International Court specified that at the jurisdictional stage, when *rebus sic stantibus* was pleaded, it did not need to pronounce on this question of fact, but would deal with it, if need be, at the stage of merits. These alleged changes could not affect the jurisdiction

[211] Commentary to Article 57, para 9, II *YBILC*, 1966, 255.

[212] ILC's Articles on State Responsibility, Commentary to Article 23, para 4.

[213] Commentary to Article 58, para 2, II *YBILC*, 1966, 256.

of the Court as established under the 1961 Exchange of Notes.[214] The factual consideration could not prejudice the operation of the legal instrument.

It is also noteworthy that the free-standing impact of facts on treaty termination, desuetude, is not recognised under the Vienna Convention on the Law of Treaties. The International Law Commission treated this as an incidence of the termination of treaties by consent of the parties. It is consent of the parties and not the factual non-application of the treaty that causes its termination.[215]

The impact of these systemically arranged facts is recognised because these are facts that are not due to the influence or action of the relevant State, but facts with objective reason and justification. Such defences, both under the law of treaties and the law of State responsibility, are very unlikely to succeed in practice. They are normally rejected, as illustrated by the cases of *Fisheries Jurisdiction*, *Rainbow Warrior* and *Gabcikovo/Nagymaros*. This entire context once again confirms the anomalous nature of the Court's finding in the *Oil Platforms* case, based on the factual situation brought about by the intentional conduct of a State-party. In *Oil Platforms*, the Court accorded relevance to the facts in terms of substantive legal regulation as opposed to the secondary framework of non-compliance or structural aspects of continuation of validity of treaty obligations.[216] *Oil Platforms* not only stands alone in its approach, but also fails to locate its approach within any recognised framework in which factual considerations are permitted to affect the operation of treaty obligations.

9. Evaluation

The foregoing analysis demonstrates that the relevance of facts in the international legal system is highly relative. The significance of the principle *ex factis jus oritur* must not be overemphasised. In most relevant cases, the emergence of rights is due not to factual effectiveness as such but to its being complemented by the factors of will and consent. In other contexts, factual considerations can be useful in ensuring the determinacy and fairness of rules. But they cannot externally qualify the content of the rule agreed on and accepted by States. On the other hand, facts may possess normative or systemic relevance if they are designated as the systemic element of legal regulation.

[214] *ICJ Reports*, 1973, 19–20; similarly, in examining the 1955 Iran–US Treaty, the International Court emphasised in the *Tehran Hostages* case that 'although the machinery for the effective operation of the 1955 Treaty has, no doubt, now been impaired by reason of diplomatic relations between the two countries having been broken off by the United States, its provisions remain part of the corpus of law applicable between the United States and Iran', *ICJ Reports*, 1980, 28.

[215] II *YBILC* 1966, 237.

[216] See below Part V.

6

Interest as Non-Law

1. Conceptual Aspects

Before proceeding with examining the legal relevance of interest as non-law, it is necessary to elaborate upon the distinction between such interest and what is normally denoted as 'legal interest'. 'Legal interest' generates the standing to present the legal claim, within a judicial framework or otherwise. Legal interest is the legally protected interest, or interest recognised under a legal rule. The concept of interest, as a category of non-law, relates, however, to the question of whether and to what extent having an interest in a particular subject-matter implies having legal rights in relation to it.

In terms of 'legal interest', several categories are developed in doctrine and practice. Our attention is drawn to the notions of actual interest (*interet né et actuel*), or concrete interest, which is an interest in the specific outcome of the relevant legal dispute. In this sense, the notion of interest is cognate to that of damage or injury, which will be a corollary of the existence of the injured or damaged State's interest in the relevant subject-matter.[1] This is an interest in the observance of the relevant legal rule in the relevant context. Legal interest may conceptually be categorised as a material or tangible interest in order to have legal standing. Broadly speaking, all these notions relate to the concept of 'legal interest'. The main aspect of this relates to the enforcement perspective of international law and focuses on who can demand compliance and remedies. This issue is part of the law of State responsibility and is reflected in Articles 42 and 48 of the International Law Commission's Articles.[2]

It is thus generally accepted that 'legal interest' relates to existing legal regulation and addresses the issue of who is legally interested in the operation and enforcement of the relevant legal rule or regime. Thus, in the *Wimbledon* case the Permanent Court of International Justice held that several States had a legal interest in open access to the Kiel Canal because they all operated merchant fleets.[3] In some cases, the notion of legal interest appears in judicial proceedings.

[1] K Mbaye, L'intérêt pour agir devant la Cour Internationale de Justice, 209 *RdC* (1988-II), 223 at 262.

[2] This has been examined elsewhere. See A Orakhelashvili, *Peremptory Norms in International Law* (2006), Chapters 8 and 16.

[3] *Wimbledon*, *PCIJ Series* A, No 1, 15.

This happens, for instance, in terms of the absent third-party doctrine, according to which the International Court cannot adjudicate on a dispute if its subject-matter affects the legal interests of a State not present in the proceedings. Legal interest is likewise involved in the framework of third-party intervention in the International Court's proceedings.[4] In some cases the legal rule or regime may be distinguished as embodying some sort of specific or heightened interest. For instance, the International Court of Justice held that the Genocide Convention embodies not individual interests of States but interests of the international community.[5]

In certain cases, the existence of an interest of a State in a legal outcome related to the operation of the relevant legal regime may lead to stipulation of its right to be informed and notified by another State in relation to this problem. For instance, LOSC Article 198 stipulates that 'When a State becomes aware of cases in which the marine environment is in imminent danger of being damaged or has been damaged by pollution, it shall immediately notify other States it deems likely to be affected by such damage, as well as the competent international organizations.'[6]

The interest focused upon in this study is, however, not 'legal interest', but interest as non-law. 'Our' interest focuses not on the implementation of existing legal frameworks, issues of standing and dispute settlement, but on claims as to substantive legal regulation, substantive rights and obligations of States.

If international law is understood as the body of rules agreed upon and accepted by States to guide their conduct, the key to clarifying the legal position of the relevant interest shall always be the evidence that demonstrates its acceptance by States. A different view from the positivist perspective, Georges Scelle's social solidarity doctrine, conceives of law as existing in terms of legal necessity to enable legal persons to achieve security and satisfaction of their basic needs. According to Scelle, the dictates of social necessity, which contribute to the process by influencing the content and direction of legal rules, consist of social and material factors and of considerations of justice and morality.

Scelle perceives justice in terms of individual utility and the consequent understanding of interest. Legal order ends up expressing the interest of legal persons as a pre-conceived social ideal. For Scelle, positive laws are an expression of basic social laws in the development of society. If positive law were to conflict with what Scelle denotes as objective natural law, a rupture of social solidarity possibly leading to revolution would ensue. Effectively, Scelle advocates the idea of judging positive law in the light of natural law reflecting the dynamics of society.[7]

[4] JP Quenedec, La notion d'Etat Intéressé en droit international, 255 *RdC* (1995-V), 339 at 356ff.

[5] Mbaye (1998-II), 295–323, on the variety of this and related phenomena.

[6] Quenedec (1995–18), 378–389.

[7] G Scelle, *Précis de droit des gens* (1923), 2–5.

On the other hand, Lauterpacht's analysis confirms that interest on its own cannot have a free-standing legal impact on the creation, operation and extinction of international legal rules, rights and obligations. As Lauterpacht observes, 'the ultimate purpose of law is to serve the interests subjected to its sway. But that cannot mean that every important interest, so deemed by the State in question, can claim superiority over rights, recognised by international law, of other States'.[8] The task of international tribunals is to apply law, not to assess interests.[9] This problem is further corroborated by the subjective connotation and manipulability of the relevant interest, which is inherent in this notion. As Lauterpacht assesses this problem, 'any doctrine which, in relations between States, postulates the individual interest of the single State as the ultimate standard of values and of legal obligation, amounts to a negation of international law'.[10] This should apply to the notion of the interest of a group of States too. The most important point here is, however, that if interest is to have any relevance in the international legal system, this cannot be the interest of the State(s) that are present on a single side of a particular international controversy. In other words, the key might lie with the notion of the balance of interests.

This approach of measuring the acceptability of positive law by reference to the socially recognised interest has not been accepted in the framework of international law. Moreover, it is incompatible with the essence of this framework. Nevertheless, the concept of interest as a legally relevant concept often arises in the process of application of international law and can affect the legal outcome.

The interest-based category of non-law is the one that has attracted substantial doctrinal attention. A number of writers deal with the concept and relevance of interest in international law.[11] The relevance of the concept of interest for the construction and application of international legal rights has long since found its acceptance in jurisprudence. Arbitrator Max Huber has repeatedly referred to the relevance of legal interest in allocating international rights and obligations, at the same time placing an emphasis on the legal standing of interest. In the *Island of Palmas* case relating to the allocation of territorial sovereignty, Huber observes that:

> International law, like law in general, has the object of assuring the coexistence of different interests which are worthy of legal protection. If, as in the present instance, only one of two conflicting interests is to prevail, because sovereignty can be attributed to but one of the Parties, the interest which involves the maintenance of a state of things having offered at the critical time to the inhabitants of the disputed territory, and to other States, a certain guarantee for the respect of their rights ought, in doubt, prevail over an interest which—supposing it to be recognised in international law—has not yet received any concrete form of development.[12]

[8] *Function of Law* (1933), 430. [9] *Cf* Lauterpacht (1933), 353. [10] *Id.*

[11] See, for instance, the overviews in Fitzmaurice, *The Law and Procedure of the International Court of Justice* (1986), 138ff, 199ff; Brownlie, *Principles of Public International Law* (2003), 27–28; Thirlway, The Law and Procedure of the International Court of Justice, *BYIL* (1990), 15ff.

[12] 22 *AJIL* (1928), 911.

Therefore, it is not interest *per se*, according to Huber, that deserves legal protection, but the interest with legal standing which must at least be given preference over interests that are not similarly privileged.

In another award, regarding the *British Claims in the Spanish Zone of Morocco*, Arbitrator Huber reiterated that:

every law aims at assuring the coexistence of interests deserving of legal protection. That is undoubtedly true also in international law. The conflicting interests in this case, in connection with the question of indemnification of aliens, are, on the one hand, the interest of the State it the exercise of authority in its own territory without interference of supervision by foreign States, and, on the other hand, the interest of the State in seeing the rights of its nationals in a foreign country respected and and effectively protected.

In this process, Huber emphasises, 'there will always remain . . . a fairly considerable margin or a subjective element of appreciation which cannot be removed'.[13] Along similar lines, Judge Jessup emphasised in *Barcelona Traction* that law constantly balances conflicting interests.[14]

These conclusions raise the question of the notion of balance of interests and whether this process of balancing already finds its expression in the accepted content of the relevant rule, or in the process of the application of the rule and whether, in this latter case, the content and scope of the rule can be compromised. Furthermore, the question is whether the relevance of interest arises primarily in a context where the applicable rule itself is not sufficiently determinate and consequently includes a reference to the relevant interest. Another question to be raised is whether the interest can be determined objectively, through objective standards, or whether there is some room for an appreciation based on subjectivism.

As Fitzmaurice observes, interests of States can be the inspiration or motive power behind legal rules. But the rules themselves emerge not through the interest but through the ordinary modes of law-making, acquiescence or prescription.[15] Brownlie states that 'the law is inevitably bound up with the accommodation of the different interests of States, and the rules often require an element of appreciation', examples of this being the excuses for delictual conduct, and the various compromises in the law of war between the considerations of necessity and humanity.[16] This raises the separate problem of interests that are referred to in legal rules and thus given legal standing, as opposed to interests *per se*.

It may also happen that interest may exist externally to a legal rule yet aspire to impact on its scope and operation. In other words, can the interest by itself provide rights and obligations in the legal system where rules are created by the

[13] *Affaire das biens britanniques au Maroc espagnol*, Espagne *contre* Royaume-Uni. La Haye, 1er Mai 1925, II *RIAA* 615 at 640; English translation of the relevant passage in Lauterpacht (1933), 121.

[14] Separate Opinion, *ICJ Reports*, 1970, 207.

[15] Fitzmaurice (1986), 199–200.

[16] Brownlie (2003), 28.

consent and agreement of States? The cardinal division that analysis of the legal relevance of interest requires is that between the claims of immediate relevance of interest in impacting on international rights and obligations, and the relevance of interest as referred to in the relevant legal rule. This latter category refers to an interest with legal standing. The rule expressing a legitimate interest is not the same as the immediate relevance of interest.

2. Claims of Independent Legal Relevance of Interest

Early arbitral practice displays some attention to the category of interest and its legal implications, but always emphasises its subordination to the accepted categories of law-making in the international legal system. In the *Behring Sea* Award, the Arbitral Tribunal emphasised that the regulations it adopted for the preservation of fur seal in the Behring Sea did not apply to Indians dwelling on the coasts of the territory, provided that they were in not in the employment of other persons.[17]

In *Grisbådarna*, the Arbitral Tribunal's reasoning shows some consideration of the relevance of interest, by pointing out that 'fishing is, in general, of more importance to the inhabitants of Koster than to those of Hvaler [in Norway], the latter having, at least until comparatively recent times, engaged in navigation rather than fishing'.[18] This finding accompanied, however, the ascertainment by the Tribunal of the correlation of the attitudes of the parties as to the ownership of the relevant maritime areas.

In the *Lake Lanoux* Award, which dealt with the diversion by France of the waters in the Lake Lanoux area, the Arbitral Tribunal formulated, in general terms, the correlation between the rights and interests of the parties, by observing that 'France is entitled to exercise her rights; she cannot ignore Spanish interests. Spain is entitled to demand that her rights be respected and that her interests be taken into consideration.' The Tribunal emphasised that 'States are today perfectly conscious of the importance of the conflicting interests brought into play by the industrial use of international rivers, and of the necessity to reconcile them by mutual concessions.' But the Tribunal continued that 'The only way to arrive at such compromises of interests is to conclude agreements on an increasingly comprehensive basis.'[19] Therefore, the Tribunal refused to imply that an interest of the State can independently affect rights and obligations under international law.

The gist of this argument is that interest may evolve and develop. But law will not follow it unless States agree that it should reflect the relevant interest. This is

[17] Award of the Tribunal of Arbitration constituted under the Treaty concluded at Washington, 29 February 1892, between US and UK, 15 August 1893, 6 *AJIL* (1912), 233 at 239.

[18] *Grisbådarna* (Norway v Sweden), Award of 23 October 1909, G Wilson (ed), *The Hague Arbitration Cases* (1915), 111 at 129.

[19] 12 *RIAA* 316, 318.

further manifest in the pertinent observation of Hersch Lauterpacht which contrasts the rigidity of the law with the comparative dynamism of interests:

> It is sufficient to mention the rigidity with which [international law] adheres to the three miles' limit of territorial sea regardless of the large variety of interests to be protected by the littoral State, or to the rule of jurisdictional immunities of States regardless of the nature of particular State activity.[20]

In today's international law, both legal standards Lauterpacht mentions are different: not because they adapted to changing interests *per se*, but because consistent State practice demonstrated the concordant will of States that they were no longer willing to be governed by such regulation of their rights in these areas.

In the field of territorial jurisdiction and sovereignty, the assertion that interests may have free-standing legal impact will always remain contestable. In a way, the very notion of territorial jurisdiction and sovereignty already implies that other States may have their legitimate interest in whatever is done within the State's territorial domain. This is above all expressed in the principle that jurisdiction of States is always concurrent, and territorial jurisdiction of one State does not exclude other jurisdictional titles available to other States. This was affirmed in the cases of *Casablanca* and *Lotus* among others.

But it is quite another question whether and to what extent the State's exercise of its territorial jurisdiction should yield to the interests of other States. Certain rules of international law are arguably meant to balance the interest of territorial and other States in the exercise of jurisdiction over persons. The rules on diplomatic immunity impose wide-ranging restrictions on the jurisdiction of the host State in favour of that of the sending State. This is, however, balanced by the final say the host State retains under the 1961 Vienna Convention on Diplomatic Relations on whether the relevant immunities shall be conferred and continue (Articles 2, 4 and 9). In the final analysis, no individual can obtain immunity without the approval of the host State. The host State not only generally accepts that diplomats should have immunity, but it also has to give its consent to a specific diplomat enjoying the relevant immunity. It is on these conditions that the standards of the 1961 Convention can be viewed as part of general international law.

The situation is more complicated in the cognate area of State immunity, where it is doubtful that general international law regulation exists on its scope, with the consequent limitation on the sovereignty and jurisdiction of the territorial State. After the disappearance of the absolute immunity rule, it is presumably right to assume that general international law has not elaborated upon the alternative regulation. The consensus required for the formation of such regulation is lacking.[21]

[20] Lauterpacht (1933), 74.

[21] M Karagiannakis, State Immunity and Fundamental Human Rights, 11 *Leiden Journal of International Law* (1998), 9 at 12; for multiple references and more extensive analysis regarding the absence of customary law on State immunity see A Orakhelashvili, State Immunity and

This problem possesses certain acuteness in relation to territorial jurisdiction and sovereignty, because the potential general international law on State immunity would, as it were, be self-operating. It would directly and without the requirement of further agreement of the territorial State impose wide-ranging limitations on its territorial jurisdiction as a matter of international legal duty. Now it is true that immunity to foreign States is frequently granted by the forum States. But this is done not because those States feel legally obliged to do so as a matter of international law, but because they choose to do so either on the basis of comity, the discretionary exercise of territorial jurisdiction, or pursuant to their national legal instruments.

Some fields of international law have developed and exist as the balance and compromise between the relevant interests of States. For instance, humanitarian law is generally understood as balancing military necessity with humanity. It is perfectly correct to say that certain aspects of the law of the sea, such as the law of delimitation, are the product of balancing the interests of coastal and other States, or adjacent coastal States. As the International Court put it in *Fisheries Jurisdiction*, 'the rules of international maritime law have been the product of mutual accommodation, reasonableness and co-operation'.[22] But the Court added that its task is to apply the law as it stands. Historically, the rules on range of vision, cannon shot and fixed numerical limits were adopted in State practice under the twofold pressure of the interest of the coastal State and the interest of the other States in the high seas. They represented a compromise of interests. 'The fundamental rule has not therefore been the interest of the coastal State in adjacent waters. It has been the consent of States which has operated to reconcile the conflicting interests of the individual coastal State and of the international community.'[23] The legal framework on maritime delimitation certainly evidences the balance of interests that potentially arise in the process of delimitation.

As demonstrated in the comprehensive enquiry, the law of continental shelf, as it stands currently, is the product of compromise and accommodation of State interests arising at different periods of historical evolution of the law of the sea.[24] As Judge Tanaka emphasised in the *North Sea* case, the concept of the continental shelf acquired legal significance exactly because of its link to the economic interests of States. This institution combines the interest of coastal States in exploration and exploitation of the relevant area with that of other States in the freedom of maritime communication.[25] Thus, it is hardly disputable that the interest can

International Public Order Revisited, 49 *German YIL* (2006), 327 at 338–343; and *id*, State Immunity and International Public Order, 45 *German YIL* (2002), 227 at 243–251.

[22] *Fisheries Jurisdiction*, *ICJ Reports*, 1974, 23.

[23] H Waldock, The Anglo-Norwegian Fisheries Case, 28 *BYIL* (1951), 113 at 129.

[24] C Rozakis, Compromises of State Interests and their Repercussions upon the Rules of Delimitation of the Continental Shelf: From the Truman Proclamation to the 1982 Convention on the Law of the Sea, in CL Rozakis and CA Stephanou (eds), *The New Law of the Sea* (1983), 155.

[25] Dissenting Opinion, *ICJ Reports*, 1969, 171.

enhance the formation and evolution of international legal rules and standards. The principal question addressed here is, however, what is the role and relevance of interest when it operates in parallel to, on the basis of, or in conflict with, the established legal rule or standard. The interests already protected under the legal rules have no significance of their own. The bare interest, whether of the State or the non-State actor, does not generate a legal impact on rights and obligations under international law. There can, however, be interests that are not part of the accepted legal rule but can nevertheless be invoked as impacting on the legal position. This can be either the interest external to the relevant applicable rules, or the interest referred to, though not specified, in one of those rules.

It is true that the International Court in *Anglo-Norwegian Fisheries* referred to the factor of the interest of Norwegian coastal communities—their economic interests being manifested by long usage.[26] This happened against the background of Norway claiming the immediate relevance of interest in producing legal rules, titles and rights. Norway claimed that the coastal State had the power to appropriate the adjacent waters in regard to which its legitimate interests justify its appropriation. Norway asserted that all the formulae of different epochs, such as the cannon shot rule, have given expression to the fundamental rules of the coastal State's legitimate interests. Under this theory, any delimitation by the coastal State would be binding on other States without their acquiescence unless it was manifestly unreasonable, that is disproportionate to the interests claimed.[27] On the other hand, the UK maintained that Norway's 'legitimate interests' theory was not law at all.[28]

However, at the oral hearings, Norway abandoned its claim to expand its maritime spaces pursuant to its economic and social interest. Instead, Norway insisted that the case concerned the baselines and confined its legitimate interest theory solely to delimitation. However, the need for other States' acquiescence is relevant.[29] The basis of the decision likewise rested on consensual factors. The Court stated that the 'vital needs of the population' involved in the case had to be considered in the context of the long-term usage and acquiescence of other States.[30] The Court based its decision on the acceptance of the Norwegian straight baselines system by the United Kingdom by its long-standing lack of opposition, as opposed to the recognition of any direct relevance of the factor of interest.

As Judge McNair emphasised in *Anglo-Norwegian Fisheries*, the process of delimitation of maritime spaces is objective. The coastal State cannot manipulate its maritime frontier with a view to enhancing its economic and other social interests.[31] It seems that McNair's point most precisely links the limits on the

[26] *ICJ Reports*, 1951, 141.
[27] Waldock (1951), 113 at 128.
[28] *Id*, 129.
[29] *Id*, 130.
[30] *ICJ Reports*, 1951, 142.
[31] *Id*, 1951, 161.

notion of interest to the integrity of legal obligations and the need to avoid auto-interpretation by States of their obligations. Furthermore, as Fitzmaurice stated in the context of the *Fisheries* case, the International Court rejected the idea that the legitimate interests of the State can justify the non-application of the applicable legal rule, or the deviation from its uniformity. To uphold such a line of reasoning 'would indeed be totally subversive of the rule of law in international relations'.[32] Fitzmaurice especially sees the rejection of the independent relevance of interests as confirmation of the presumption of the existence of international legal regulation on the given subject-matter.[33] The Court took economic interest into account, but it was not willing to justify the Norwegian baselines system on economic grounds alone, in the absence of legal justification.[34] In addition, Fitzmaurice follows Judge McNair's line of reasoning that 'the manipulation of the limits of territorial waters for the purpose of protecting economic and other social interests has no justification in law'. Such practice would be dangerous in encouraging States 'to adopt a subjective appreciation of their rights instead of conforming to a common international standard'.[35]

The *Barcelona Traction* case, dealing with the issue of diplomatic protection in the context of the rights of shareholders of a company by the State of nationality of shareholders, clarifies that there is a distinction between injury in respect of a right and injury to a simple interest. As the Judgment specifies, 'Not a mere interest affected, but solely a right infringed involves responsibility, so that an act directed against and infringing only the company's rights does not involve responsibility towards the shareholders, even if their interests are affected.'[36] The identification of international legal standing of the applicant State to protect individual shareholders was impossible and hence the intervention of the State was not allowed.

In this case, Judge Fitzmaurice advanced the interest-based reasoning in favour of allowing shareholders to take advantage of the State's right of diplomatic protection. Fitzmaurice in the first place refers to the cases where the company has the nationality of the defendant State and hence the company becomes *de facto* incapable of protecting its interests internationally.[37] Similarly, Fitzmaurice suggests that if international law is to remain faithful to the concept of the company, it has to allow for cases where the national State of the company refuses to intervene in the case of breach of the shareholders' rights.[38] More generally, Fitzmaurice argues that international law is underdeveloped in comparison with private law, in that it fails to provide a mechanism for effective protection not

[32] Fitzmaurice (1986), 151, 199.
[33] *Id*, 141, 151.
[34] *Id*, 230–231.
[35] *ICJ Reports*, 1951, 169.
[36] *ICJ Reports*, 1970, 36.
[37] Separate Opinion, *id*, 72.
[38] *Id*, 76.

only of shareholders but also the company itself. While the management of the company is obliged to act in the interest of the company, the governments have no legal obligation to do so. Therefore, Fitzmaurice attempts to construct an 'enlightened' rule, according to which where the company's national State has no interest in intervening, the shareholders' national State must be allowed to do so.[39] Consequently, Fitzmaurice concludes that 'the present state of international law leads to the inadmissible consequence that important interests may go wholly unprotected'.[40]

Judge Tanaka similarly emphasised 'the existence of an interest worthy of protection by the shareholders' national State'.[41] The shareholders, in Judge Tanaka's opinion, are the real cause of interest and must be considered as the object of diplomatic protection. The company itself only has a fictive existence and serves the shareholders' interests.[42] Therefore, Judge Tanaka upheld the option of the shareholders' national State exercising diplomatic protection.[43] Similarly, Judge Jessup emphasised that shareholders represented the real interest in the cause and international law did not prohibit the exercise of their diplomatic protection.[44] Judge Jessup highlights that States set up corporations because of their real national interests and not for reasons of nationality link. Hence, 'the primacy of general economic interests of the State in protecting private investments abroad' constitutes 'one essential test justifying diplomatic protection'.[45]

As can be seen, the three learned judges effectively advanced the thesis that the existence of interest in the relevant subject-matter justifies the relevant legal entitlement, in this case that of diplomatic protection. However, this argument could not be accepted by the Court, which was in the first place guided by rights as distinct from interests. It had to deliver a ruling that would be consistent with the inter-State structural designation of international law. The existence of the legal rule on nationality link between the State and the relevant entity, which is one expression of this structural designation, precluded the use of the concept of interest to overturn the established legal position.

In *Fisheries Jurisdiction*, the Court considered as part of customary law 'the concept of preferential rights of fishing in adjacent waters in favour of the coastal State in a situation of special dependence on its coastal fisheries, this preference operating in regard to other States concerned in the exploitation of the same fisheries'. State practice on the subject of fisheries revealed increasing and widespread acceptance of the concept of preferential rights of the coastal States, particularly when they depended on coastal fisheries.[46] The Court explained this

39 *Id*, 76–77.
40 *Id*, 84.
41 Separate Opinion, *ICJ Reports*, 1970, 128.
42 *Id*, 132.
43 *Id*, 133, 135.
44 Separate Opinion, *id*, 188.
45 *Id*, 196–197.
46 *Fisheries Jurisdiction*, *ICJ Reports*, 1974, 23, 26.

preference as the 'special consideration [that] should be given to the coastal State whose population is overwhelmingly dependent on the fishing resources in its adjacent waters'. The Court noted that the requisite proposal of Iceland did not obtain majority support at the 1958 Geneva Conference. But the Convention adopted the declaration, emphasising the need in certain cases, where the total catch is limited 'when an intensification in the exploitation of fishery resources makes it imperative to introduce some system of catch-limitation and sharing of those resources, to preserve the fish stocks in the interests of their rational and economic exploitation', for 'establishing agreed measures which shall recognize any preferential requirements of the coastal State resulting from its dependence upon the fishery concerned while having regard to the interests of the other States'. Similarly, the 1960 Conference affirmed that 'the faculty of claiming preferential fishing rights in any area of the high seas adjacent to its exclusive fishing zone when it is scientifically established that a special situation or condition makes the exploitation of the living resources of the high seas in that area of fundamental importance to the economic development of the coastal State or the feeding of its population'.[47] The Court concluded that 'The contemporary practice of States leads to the conclusion that the preferential rights of the coastal State in a special situation, are to be implemented by agreement between the States concerned, either bilateral or multilateral.' The Court referred to agreements that 'assign an additional share to the coastal State on the ground of its preferential right in the fisheries in its adjacent waters'. In particular, 'The Faroese agreement takes expressly into account in its preamble "the exceptional dependence of the Faroese economy on fisheries" and recognizes "that the Faroe Islands should enjoy preference in waters surrounding the Faroe Islands".'[48]

As for the exceptional dependence of Iceland on its coastal fishing, the Court referred to the recognition of this dependence by the United Kingdom.[49] Therefore, translating interest into entitlement requires agreement between the relevant States or their recognition. Interest by itself does not provide or affect legal regulation.

When the coastal State obtains preferential rights, it 'has to take into account and pay regard to the position of such other States, particularly when they have established an economic dependence on the same fishing grounds'.[50] Thus, interests recognised by law are not absolute, but are limited by the similar interests of other States. However, in addressing this aspect of interest in the *Fisheries Jurisdiction* case, the Court again referred to the normative aspect of the problem. This was that 'Iceland has for its part admitted the existence of the Applicant's historic and special interests in the fishing in the disputed waters' through the relevant Exchange of Notes and discussion. Iceland thus also recognised that

[47] *Id*, 24–25, 27.
[48] *Id*, 25–26.
[49] *Id*, 26–27.
[50] *Id*, 28.

fisheries conservation and efficient exploitation was not only in its own interest but also in that of the United Kingdom.[51] Thus, the Court in no aspect of this problem treated the mere interest as generating a legal position by itself. In every case, the agreement between, and recognition by, the interested State of each other's interest is the crucial factor.

Given the due recognition of both sides' interests, preferential rights of the coastal State and the established rights of other States were considered as continuing to coexist.[52] As the Court emphasised:

> Due recognition must be given to the rights of both Parties, namely the rights of the United Kingdom to fish in the waters in dispute, and the preferential rights of Iceland. Neither right is an absolute one: the preferential rights of a coastal State are limited according to the extent of its special dependence on the fisheries and by its obligation to take account of the rights of other States and the needs of conservation; the established rights of other fishing States are in turn limited by reason of the coastal State's special dependence on the fisheries and its own obligation to take account of the rights of other States, including the coastal State, and of the needs of conservation.[53]

The notion of State interest was advanced in the *Tunisia–Libya* case in which Tunisia claimed that the delimitation of the continental shelf should be affected by its position of relative poverty vis-à-vis that of Libya. The Court responded that economic considerations and interests could not be taken into account. They were extraneous factors, as 'a country might be poor today and become rich tomorrow as a result of an event such as the discovery of a valuable economic resource'.[54] Similarly, in *Libya–Malta*, the Court emphasised that considerations of economic interest were 'totally unrelated to the underlying intention of the applicable rules of international law'.[55]

In *El Salvador/Honduras*, the Chamber of the Court dealt with the notion of interest in the context of the *uti possidetis juris* principle. The Chamber understood this principle as the reference principle that does not impose a substantive solution on its own but merely confers validity on solutions that conform to certain criteria. As the Chamber specified, demographic pressures as regards the need for territory were involved, but the Court thought them insufficient to generate or displace the territorial title. The question was not whether the colonial province needed wide boundaries to accommodate its population, but where the boundaries actually were. As for the argument of inequality of natural resources, the Court reiterated, by reference to the *Libya–Tunisia* case, that this was not relevant in allocating the maritime boundaries. Still less could it be relevant in terms of the land boundaries.[56]

[51] *Id*, 28–29.
[52] *Id*, 30.
[53] *Id*, 31.
[54] *ICJ Reports*, 1982, 77.
[55] *ICJ Reports*, 1985, 41.
[56] *ICJ Reports*, 1990, 396.

From time to time, judicial practice witnesses the reliance of States on their security interests as the reason for the particular construction of the legal position they consider favourable. In general, the relevance of security interests is not altogether denied, but in specific cases it is not very likely that they can impact on the relevant legal position. To make a parallel with the concept of economic interests, such are deemed irrelevant in judicial practice unless catastrophic consequences threaten the relevant States and communities. If this parallel is right, then the State can only plead its security interest in matters of maritime delimitation if the proposed outcome drastically affects its security. This goes hand in hand with the indeterminacy of the law of delimitation and the potential role of security interests as a factor in equity.

In the context of maritime delimitation, this issue was raised in the *Libya–Malta* case. Libya claimed that the drawing of the maritime boundary in a certain way would jeopardise its security interests. The Court dismissed this argument by responding that the relevant line would not be close enough to the Libyan border to trigger its security concerns.[57]

In other fields, where legal rules are straightforward and determinate, security interests can be accorded no role. The relevance of interest was examined by the International Court in a number of cases related to highly contingent political situations involving serious political interests. For instance, in *Nicaragua*, the Court faced the argument that it could not determine the legality of US claims and actions of collective self-defence in support of El Salvador. This would involve judging the appreciation by the US of the necessity of forcible action to protect its own security. This arguably involved political and security matters on which the Court was unable to judge. The Court responded that its only task was to determine whether the US actions were preceded by armed attack and whether these actions constituted the appropriate reaction as a matter of collective self-defence. These issues were independent of the military and security considerations the US could have been concerned with. This consequently delimited the field within which the Court could adjudicate.[58] Similarly, in the *Congo–Uganda* case, dealing with the forcible action of Uganda against the Congo, the Court faced arguments that the situation in the Congo had security implications for its neighbouring States. The Court acknowledged that such security implications may exist, but stated that its function was to decide only in accordance with international law.[59] In other words, non-legal considerations should not influence the Court's decisions.[60] After all, the political and security justifications are subjective questions while the Court has to hand down the judgment which responds to the applicable legal framework.

[57] *ICJ Reports*, 1985, 42, 52.

[58] *ICJ Reports*, 1986, 27–28.

[59] *Case Concerning the Armed Activities on the Territory of the Congo* (Democratic Republic of the Congo v Uganda), Judgment of 19 December 2005, General List No 116, para 26.

[60] See the Separate Opinion of Judge Onyeama in the *Namibia* case, *ICJ Reports* 1971, 132–134, observing that the Court's function is not to render decisions that are politically acceptable.

In *M/V Saiga*, the International Tribunal for the Law of the Sea examined the law of the nationality of claims in relation to the nationality of ships and crew. After examining the scope of Articles 94 and 217 of the Law of the Sea Convention, the Tribunal observed that 'the Convention considers a ship as a unit, as regards the obligations of the flag State with respect to the ship and the right of a flag State to seek reparation for loss or damage caused to the ship by acts of other States and to institute proceedings under Article 292 of the Convention. Thus the ship, every thing on it, and every person involved or interested in its operations are treated as an entity linked to the flag State. The nationalities of these persons are not relevant.'[61] Here the Tribunal made an observation that arguably refers to the relevance of interest:

> The Tribunal must also call attention to an aspect of the matter which is not without significance in this case. This relates to two basic characteristics of modern maritime transport: the transient and multinational composition of ships' crews and the multiplicity of interests that may be involved in the cargo on board a single ship. A container vessel carries a large number of containers, and the persons with interests in them may be of many different nationalities. This may also be true in relation to cargo on board a break-bulk carrier. Any of these ships could have a crew comprising persons of several nationalities. If each person sustaining damage were obliged to look for protection from the State of which such person is a national, undue hardship would ensue.[62]

In this context, it is open to question whether the considerations of interest independently lead to that construction of the rule of the nationality of ships, or whether this outcome is due to the regulation under the treaty. On balance it appears that the latter assumption is more correct. (At the same time, while the *M/V Saiga* case does not directly recognise the legal implications of interest, some questions may arise regarding its construction of the law of nationality. This especially concerns the fact that the jurisdiction and enforcement rights and duties over the ship and its crew do not inherently, and without more, imply an entitlement to exercise diplomatic protection over each and every person present on the ship.)

The conclusion following from practice is that the interest of a State of any possible kind is not in a position to affect or overturn outcomes following from legal regulation on the subject. In a legal system where rules are produced by consent of States, the extra-legal concept of interest cannot have normative standing on its own.

3. References to Interest in Legal Rules

Apart from the general relevance of interest in international law, a separate issue that arises is the scope of relevance of interest which forms part of legal regulation,

[61] *M/V Saiga*, paras 103–106.
[62] *Id*, para 107.

eg is referred to in a legal rule. This can be seen from the thesis advanced by Fitzmaurice. According to Fitzmaurice, 'When the legitimacy of an act depends as a matter of law on its reasonableness, the existence of special interests such as economic ones may be a justificatory factor, or at any rate the factor to be taken into account.'[63] At the same time, the problem of determinacy arises in such cases, because interests thus referred to can be indeterminate and open-ended. The legal regulation that refers to interest is no longer straightforward but indeterminate.

In some fields of international law, there exist 'statutory' requirements to respect the interests of other States. Several treaty provisions foresee legal regulation that refers to the interest of the relevant States as a factor influencing the legal outcome to be reached on the basis of that regulation. For instance, Article 2 of the 1958 Geneva Convention on the High Seas provides that the freedoms of navigation, fishing, overflight and the laying of submarine cables, and other freedoms 'which are recognized by the general principles of international law, shall be exercised by all States with reasonable regard to the interests of other States in their exercise of the freedom of the high seas'. A similar clause is included in Article 87 of the 1982 Law of the Sea Convention.

As O'Connell's analysis suggests, these clauses are attributable to the relativity of the freedom of the high seas and the doctrine of its reasonable use. In the codification process in the International Law Commission the test of reasonableness was deemed to be too subjective. The Commission, however, affirmed that all the relevant freedoms must be exercised by respecting the interests of all.[64] But, while this is the desirable objective, its application to situations on the ground cannot take place without further specifications.

The International Court emphasised in its judicial application of this principle that it is 'the principle enshrined in Article 2 of the 1958 Geneva Convention on the High Seas which requires that all States, including coastal States, in exercising their freedom of fishing, pay reasonable regard to the interests of other States'. The Court judged the Icelandic Regulations and their unilateral implementation in disregard of the fishing rights of the United Kingdom as an infringement of the principle enshrined in Article 2. Consequently, these Regulations were not applicable to the United Kingdom.[65]

This, however, took place in the context where Iceland had admitted that the United Kingdom had historic and special interests in fishing in the disputed waters. In addition, such interest was also admitted in relation to conservation of fish stocks.[66] Therefore, Article 2 could be invoked to protect the interests of the United Kingdom as these interests were otherwise admitted to exist. Thus, it seems that the effect of such clauses can only be case-specific. This clause falls short of protecting the interest in general, that is without the interest being

[63] Fitzmaurice (1986), 200.
[64] DP O'Connell, *The International Law of the Sea* (1984), vol II, 796–798.
[65] *Fisheries Jurisdiction*, *ICJ Reports*, 1974, 29.
[66] *Id*, 28–29.

mutually agreed to exist or to be relevant. If the existence of the relevant interest is not duly demonstrated, as would be the case, for instance, with the common heritage of mankind or some comparable doctrines of environmental protection, the freedom of action of States remains unlimited by the consideration of the interest of others. This is in line with the traditional *Lotus* approach to the operation of international rights and duties.

That the mere interest of another State or the alleged lack of reasonableness of the relevant measure does not affect the legal entitlement to perform that measure is confirmed by the following statement related to Article 2 of the 1958 Convention and Article 87 LOSC:

> There are high-seas activities alleged by some States to constitute freedoms, but denied this status by other States. The principle on which such disputes should be resolved is that any use compatible with the status of the high seas—that is the use which involves no claim to appropriation of parts of the high seas—should be admitted as a freedom unless it is excluded by some specific rule of law.[67]

According to Article 59 of the 1982 Law of the Sea Convention:

> In cases where this Convention does not attribute rights or jurisdiction to the coastal State or to other States within the exclusive economic zone, and a conflict arises between the interests of the coastal State and any other State or States, the conflict should be resolved on the basis of equity and in the light of all the relevant circumstances, taking into account the respective importance of the interests involved to the parties as well as to the international community as a whole.

Thus, this clause makes reference to a relevant interest where the allocation of jurisdiction is not defined, that is where there is some sort of *non liquet*. It does not apply to situations where the legal basis for the rights and obligations of States is duly present. As is emphasised, 'examination of the text of Article 59 soon reveals that, in fact, it is only concerned with cases where the Convention does *not* attribute rights or jurisdiction to the coastal State or to other States within the EEZ'. This clause reflects the fact that some uses of the EEZ do not fall within the scope of rights and jurisdiction defined in other specific provisions of the Law of the Sea Convention. These uses, the Convention falling short of defining them, may consist in military training and exercises, archaeological measures, or some aspects of ocean research.[68] In relation to military exercises, some States have claimed that these require obtaining the coastal State's consent, while other States have opposed such an approach and denied the need for such consent.[69] As Collier and Lowe suggest, in the case of these unattributed rights, there is no presumption in favour of any State, and every situation will have to be assessed on its merits.[70] The balancing test is suggested in terms of clarifying whether

[67] R Churchill and AV Lowe, *The Law of the Sea* (1999), 206.

[68] ED Brown, *The International Law of the Sea* (1994), vol I, 239 (emphasis original).

[69] *Id*, 240–242.

[70] Churchill and Lowe (1999), 176.

the relevant measure interferes with the rights of the coastal State in the EEZ.[71] While this would be so anyway, this falls short of providing the criteria of how interests should be balanced against each other—that is the criteria that would guide the dispute settlement bodies under the Convention. What is clear beyond doubt is that the interest of one State cannot undermine the operation of legal entitlement of the coastal State. On a case-specific basis, the measure of affecting the interest of the coastal State can also be tested, for instance by asking whether the military exercise is conducted too close to the coast of the State, given all the relevant factors, such as the size of the contingent and weapons deployed.

4. The Systemic Relevance of Interest: State of Necessity in the Law of State Responsibility

The International Law Commission, while introducing the concept of State necessity into the law of State responsibility, justified it as the tool 'by means of which States can escape the inevitably harmful consequences of trying at all costs to comply with the requirements of rules of law'. Compliance with the law must not result in situations characterised by the maxim *summum jus summa injuria*.[72] The International Court has in principle shared this justification of the concept.[73] Therefore, both the Commission and the International Court perceive this concept as justifying the non-application of applicable law. It is obvious that such a concept must be defined most precisely and transparently. All that is offered, however, by both versions of the ILC Draft is that the action of necessity must be the only means of safeguarding 'an essential interest' of the State, and shall not 'seriously impair an essential interest' of the State in favour of which the relevant obligation exists. Thus, the concept of State necessity has been defined as repeatedly referring to indeterminate categories. This may perhaps explain the description of this concept as controversial by the Arbitral Tribunal in *Rainbow Warrior*.

The Commission clarified that 'essential interest' is not restricted to the existence of the State. But the Commission considered it unfeasible to specify the categories of 'essential interest' and preferred to leave this to case-by-case clarifications.[74] At the same time, the Commission insisted that the interest of the other State which is sacrificed to the defence of the 'essential interest' of the first State must be 'a less essential interest'.[75] The Draft adopted by the second reading reiterates the same and further specifies that 'the interest relied on must outweigh

[71] Brown (1994), 244.

[72] Commentary to Article 33, para 31, II *YbILC* 1980.

[73] *Gabcikovo-Nagymaros Project*, 25 September 1997, General List No 92, para 57.

[74] Commentary to Article 33, para 32, II *YbILC* 1980; Commentary to Article 25, para 15, in *ILC Report* 2001; *Gabcikovo-Nagymaros*, para 53.

[75] Commentary to Article 33, para 35, II *YbILC* 1980.

all other considerations, not merely from the point of view of the acting State but on reasonable assessment of competing interests, whether these are individual or collective'.[76] The Commission identifies no criteria for measuring these categories in practice, nor works out its own criteria and adds yet another indeterminate criterion—that of 'reasonable' assessment.

The Articles adopted by the second reading refer to the 'essential interest' of the State in question, but also of the international community as a whole. A very apt illustration of this is given by the Commission—the preservation of the natural environment by avoiding the extermination of fur seals, as dealt with in the *Fur Seal* case.[77] At the same time, it must be noted that the reference to the essential interest of the international community as a whole does not in this case mean the reference to *jus cogens*, despite the similar conceptual basis of the latter and the contrary appearance in the Commission's Commentary.[78] *Jus cogens* does not raise the issue of necessity in justifying non-compliance with the conflicting obligation but the issue of normative hierarchy. In fact, as the ILC's Article 26 affirms, the operation of the necessity plea is not admitted in the field of *jus cogens*.

During the first reading of the Draft, the Commission expressly stated that 'the State invoking the state of necessity is not and should not be the sole judge of the existence and necessary conditions in the particular case concerned'. The initial determination would be left with the State. But the matter is beyond its discretion and must be determined within the dispute settlement arrangements.[79] The International Court concurred with this conclusion, which was reflected in the Articles adopted by the second reading.[80]

In terms of defining 'essential' interest specifically, the Court's judgment on *Gabcikovo-Nagymaros* does not take the matter much further. The Court mentions the requirement of 'essential interest'[81] but then circumvents its content and proceeds with analysis of other requirements of the state of necessity.[82] When examining Hungary's actions in relation to the Gabcikovo dam, the Court concentrated on judging them in terms of there being 'grave peril' to its interest,[83] without evaluating that interest as such.

The Court's treatment of this issue assumes that there can be criteria by which the 'essential interest' can be determined in specific cases. But this does not prove that other cases will be similarly straightforward. There is so far no case decided in which the plea of necessity was upheld on account of 'essential interest'. In addition, there is no case yet decided in which the 'essential interests' of two

[76] Commentary to Article 25, para 17.
[77] Commentary to Article 25, para 6.
[78] Such as in Commentary to Article 25, para 18.
[79] Commentary to Article 33, para 36, II *YbILC* 1980.
[80] *Gabcikovo-Nagymaros*, para 51; Commentary to Article 25, para 16.
[81] *Gabcikovo-Nagymaros*, para 52.
[82] Such as addressing the considerations of ecological balance in para 53.
[83] *Gabcikovo-Nagymaros*, paras 55ff.

States are compared with and balanced against each other. Overall, the Court's treatment of the state of necessity is correct in outcome. But it is problematic in taking the balanced approach and falling short of explaining how the individual elements of the concept of necessity work. Fortunately, the inherent problems this concept is ridden with are mitigated by the complexity of its qualifications which make the practical application of this concept leading to precluding the responsibility of a State quite unlikely.

5. Evaluation

The entire doctrinal and jurisprudential framework developed around the concept of interest in international law confirms the elusiveness and indeterminacy of this notion. Therefore, the accepted approach is that interest will be given no free-standing relevance in assessing the claims of States or legality of their conduct. Interest may be embodied in a legal rule either by the rule balancing the interests of States or by making an open-ended reference to interest. In such cases, it is the agreed legal rule as opposed to interest as such that governs the conduct of States and provides for the legal outcome.

7

Values as Non-Law

1. General Aspects

Values constitute a separate category of non-law that possess certain normative relevance in the international legal system. There may be values that underlie certain institutions in the international legal system or aims to which international law aspires in one or another field. The focus here is restricted to values that have, so to speak, certain normative standing, if not normative status, in the sense that they are referred to as guiding principles and factors in international instruments or practice. This standing is, again, not the same as producing a definite impact on the rights and duties of international legal persons.

Consequently, this analysis is not meant as an examination of the values that guide and underlie international legal relations in general, but focuses only on values to the extent that they have or try to have an impact on the interpretation and application of international legal rules. The function of this chapter is less to present a solution as to the relevance and impact of the relevant values and more to present what these relevant values themselves are. The intention behind doing so is to clear the way for examining, in subsequent chapters, the more specific incidences of those values in interpreting and applying the relevant international legal rules and instruments.

Values refer to goals to be achieved. The standards of actual conduct of States, whether embodied in binding rules or declaratory standards, are not the same as values. The conduct required or desired in a rule or standard may serve a certain goal and hence the relevant value, but this very fact underlines the distinction just drawn. This distinction is instrumental in projecting the limits of the present analysis.

That values as such are not the same as law can be seen from Lauterpacht's observation that 'the social ideal is not law, but justice', and 'ultimately law is the more effective guarantee to secure that end'.[1] That law indeed aspires to meet various ends expressed in the relevant values is clear from the recognition of the standing of these values in legal instruments, such as treaty preambles. At the same time, this means that values remain non-law, and at most they can be a

[1] *The Function of Law in the International Community* (1933), 346.

guide in understanding the content of legal rules that exist independently of these values, that is on the basis of inter-State agreement. For instance, the value of sustainable development is recognised as a goal under the WTO Agreement.[2] Thus it potentially forms part of the WTO object and purpose. But its relevance is limited to aiding clarification of the scope of specific WTO rules, as opposed to independently providing for rights and obligations. The same would hold true for the value of peace and security under the United Nations Charter.

These are the values that are referred to in preambles of treaties, and hence possess interpretative relevance as elements of their object and purpose. These are also presumably the values that can affect the balance when assessing whether the relevant State possesses a certain right, or is properly exercising its otherwise existing right, within the relevant legal framework. The question of how far these values are relevant as values *per se* is prompted not only by their lack of fixed normative status, but also by the lack of their normative definition. With this in mind, specific values relevant to the international legal system should be examined.

2. Peace and Security

The concept of international peace and security is referred to as a goal of the United Nations Organization in Article 1 of its Charter, and as both a goal and a guiding principle in Chapters VI and VII of the Charter, respectively dealing with the settlement of disputes endangering peace and security, and enforcement action in relation to threats to peace and security. In none of these cases is the concept of peace and security itself defined. There is thus no established meaning of peace and security, although there is consensus that this concept relates to more than just absence of war. This follows from an attempt by the UN Security Council to define the parameters of the concept of peace.[3]

In some cases the concept of peace and security as a goal can influence the construction of the relevant treaty obligations, and consequently the institutional powers based on the treaty. Thus, in the *Certain Expenses* Advisory Opinion the International Court of Justice construed the scope of implied powers in such a way as to encompass the establishment of peace-keeping forces and to ajudge that

[2] The Preamble of the 1994 WTO Agreement attempts to allow 'for the optimal use of the world's resources in accordance with the objective of sustainable development, seeking both to protect and preserve the environment and to enhance the means for doing so in a manner consistent with their respective needs and concerns at different levels of economic development'.

[3] Statement of the Heads of States and Governments of Members of the Security Council, 31 January 1992: 'The absence of wars and military conflicts among States does not in itself ensure international peace and security. The non-military sources of instability in the economic, social, humanitarian and ecological fields have become threats to peace and security. The United Nations membership as a whole, working through the appropriate bodies, needs to give the highest priority to the solution of these matters.' UN doc S/PV.3046.

the expenses incurred in this process were valid United Nations expenses.[4] 'Peace and security' did not by itself determine whether the relevant institutional action was lawful. But, as one of the aims of the Charter, it did impact on the choice from the range of options available in terms of judging the legality of that institutional action.

This instance is not a case of the independent and free-standing impact of the concept of peace and security. The key to this approach was that the United Nations Charter had as a matter of positive law declared peace and security as a priority goal and established the collective security mechanism to pursue that goal. The impact of the concept of peace and security has only been the construction of the otherwise existing institutional powers in such a way as to foster the treaty-designated goal. This position is very different from arguing that peace and security can independently affect the rights and obligations of international legal persons, for instance by constructing, on its own, the rights and obligations of States.

3. Sustainable Development

The notion of sustainable development is referred to in a number of international instruments, mostly in the field of international environmental law and international economic law. The 1972 UN Declaration on the Human Environment does not directly mention the concept of sustainable development. On the other hand, the 1992 Rio Declaration on Environment and Development is riddled with references to this concept. This instrument perceives sustainable development as a goal to be achieved. Pursuant to this, Principles 8 and 9 of the Declaration state the goals of reducing unsustainable means of production and of strengthening the respective capacity-building. Some environmental law conventions also refer to sustainable development as a goal and objective. This holds true, for instance of the 1992 Convention on Biological Diversity.[5]

The International Court in the *Gabcikovo-Nagymaros* case dealt with the concept of sustainable development, but did not clarify its scope or normative status. Having emphasised that throughout the ages mankind has been interfering with the environment with serious or irreversible impact, the Court specified that 'Th[e] need to reconcile economic development with protection of the environment is aptly expressed in the concept of sustainable development.'[6] The context of the case related to the implications for the construction of the Gabcikovo dam of the evolving standards of international environmental law. The Court's response to this situation was that 'the Parties together should look afresh at the effects on

[4] *Certain Expenses*, Advisory Opinion, *ICJ Reports*, 1962.

[5] For an overview see P Birnie and A Boyle, *International Law and the Environment* (2002), 84ff, and P Sands, *Principles of International Environmental Law* (2003), 252–256.

[6] *Gabcikovo-Nagymaros Project* (Hungary/Slovakia), Judgment of 25 September 1997, *ICJ Reports*, 1997, 7 at 78.

the environment of the operation of the Gabcikovo power plant. In particular they must find a satisfactory solution regarding the volume of water to be released into the old bed of the Danube and into the side-arms on both sides of the river.'[7] This fell substantially short of specifying any concrete and determinate obligation that the relevance of the concept of sustainable development could impose on the parties.

The Court indeed emphasised that the outcome of this process depends on the agreement between the Parties:

> It is not for the Court to determine what shall be the final result of these negotiations to be conducted by the Parties. It is for the Parties themselves to find an agreed solution that takes account of the objectives of the Treaty, which must be pursued in a joint and integrated way, as well as the norms of international environmental law and the principles of the law of international watercourses.[8]

On the other hand, this passage also shows that in conducting negotiations the Parties are not completely free but subject to the objectives of the 1977 Treaty and of applicable international law. As an alternative to what has been stated above, or perhaps as an implication thereof, one may also be inclined to suggest that the Court's reference to the agreed solution between the Parties relates to the modalities and arrangements to emerge out of such an agreed solution, and does not imply that the Parties are under no normative obligations in this process. This reading can tentatively suggest that the Court implied the normative status of sustainable development as an aspirational category which at the same time can produce framework-type legal limitations, but not specific rights and obligations applicable, without more, to the conduct of States. Another reference to the concept of sustainable development took place in the *US–Shrimp* case where the WTO Appellate Body considered it as part of the object and purpose of the WTO Agreement. Sustainable development thus weighed in the process of interpretation of Article XX GATT.

The independent relevance of the value of sustainable development or its antecedent concepts has also been dealt with in jurisprudence. The *Fur Seal* Award decided that the limitation on the high sea freedoms of fishing was not justified in the name of preservation of maritime species to ensure their sustainable use. In short, the *Fur Seal* approach was that the sustainable use did not affect existing law. The legal position today is not too far away from that approach, because no developments in the century following the *Fur Seal* decision have conferred independent normative relevance to the values in question.[8a]

Birnie and Boyle consider that an impact of the concept of sustainable development is that, for the first time, it makes a State's management of its domestic resources and environment a matter of international concern in a systematic

[7] *Id.*

[8] *Id.*

[8a] Award of the Tribunial of Arbitration constituted under the Treaty concluded at Washington, 29 February 1982, between US and UK, 15 August 1893, 6 AJIL (1912), 233.

way.[9] Sands similarly argues that this concept can be found attractive in other fields of international litigation to enable incorporation of environmental standards into the field of international economic law.[10]

As Lowe suggests, the concept of sustainable development has no normative status in the sense of sources of international law under Article 38 of the International Court's Statute.[11] The concept of sustainable development does not satisfy the conditions of emergence of customary rules. Instead, Lowe suggests that sustainable development can have a normative status as part of judicial reasoning.[12] It presumably exists as a legal concept, as opposed to a legal rule, and needs no confirmation in State practice and *opinio juris* in the way legal rules do.[13] Birnie and Boyle likewise doubt that sustainable development is a legal rule, and emphasise that it is a goal that influences the outcome of cases and interpretation of treaties, and generally guides the activities of States in relation to the global environment.[14]

There is also some doctrinal argument regarding the normative status of specific implications of the concept of sustainable development. Birnie and Boyle argue that in international practice, in particular in the *Fisheries Jurisdiction* case between UK and Iceland, the International Court upheld the existence of a customary law obligation to cooperate for the preservation of fishing resources on the high seas.[15] The Court's real emphasis, however, was on the agreement achieved in bilateral practice between UK and Iceland on their mutual recognition of each other's interests in the relevant fisheries, and the consequent limitation on their fishing freedoms. This was due to that agreement and not to the operation of developmental concepts as such.

What is certain in any case is that sustainable development has no determinate meaning. More importantly, there is no inter-State consensus as to the status of any possible meaning it may have. Consequently, sustainable development, although being a juridical category having its standing recognised under international law, is not part of international law in the sense of producing an independent impact on the rights and obligations of States.

4. Democracy and 'Democratic Society'

The notion of democracy is considered relevant in a number of international legal frameworks. In certain non-binding instruments, such as the major declarations

[9] Birnie & Boyle (2002), 85.

[10] P Sands, International Courts and the Application of the Concept of 'Sustainable Development', 3 *Max Planck YBUN* (1999), 389 at 404–405.

[11] V Lowe, Sustainable Development and Unsustainable Arguments, in Boyle & Freestone (eds), *International Law and Sustainable Development* (1999), 19 at 21.

[12] *Id*, 24, 31.

[13] *Id*, 33.

[14] Birnie & Boyle (2002), 96–97.

[15] *Id*, 88 (without reference to the specific passage of the case).

of the Organization for Security and Co-operation in Europe (OSCE), democracy figures as the major foundational concept. But these instruments have no binding force and cannot, without more, be seen as conferring direct normative status to the notion of democracy. There is substantial doctrinal discourse regarding the emergence of the right to democracy, or democratic governance, in international law. Franck speaks of 'new international law, requiring democratization to validate governance', and this rule allegedly expresses 'a universal sense of fairness'.[16] This entitlement allegedly derives from textual sources, but only non-binding declarations are referred to in support of this thesis.[17] In another, later, contribution, Franck suggests that 'democracy is *becoming* an entitlement in international law', and refers to the increased number of States having adopted democracy.[18]

However, despite the waves of democratisation in different parts of the world over the last two decades, international law is still unfamiliar with the general rule that would oblige States to adopt the democratic form of governance. Nor is there any binding definition of democracy that would specify to which areas of public and social life the required democratic governance would have to extend. The legal position remains the same as was declared by the International Court in the *Nicaragua* case, in which the Court could not 'find an instrument with legal force, whether unilateral or synallagmatic, whereby Nicaragua has committed itself in respect of the principle or methods of holding elections'. The Court's analysis upheld the approach that the governance of Nicaragua was for the Nicaraguan people to decide. As the Court observed in more general terms, 'A State's domestic policy falls within its exclusive jurisdiction, provided of course that it does not violate any obligation of international law. Every State possesses a fundamental right to choose and implement its own political, economic and social systems.'[19] This approach is still valid today, as there have been no normative developments in terms of the emergence of the binding rule of international law which, unlike non-binding declarations, would commit States to adopt the democratic form of government.

At the same time, the Court's approach effectively highlights the contradiction between the inter-State structure of international law and the potential rule obliging States to adopt a certain form of governance. If States are sovereign and if peoples are entitled to self-determination, this conceptually implies that the people of the State have the right to govern themselves. However, the imposition of any specific legal duty on the State to adopt a particular form of government would negate the very freedom of the people to decide on the form of their governance. Consequently, the current system of international law does not tolerate

[16] T Franck, *Fairness in International Law and Institutions* (1995), 85.

[17] *Id*, 112–117, 138.

[18] T Franck, Legitimacy and Democratic Entitlement, in G Fox & B Roth (eds), *Democratic Governance and International Law* (2001), 25 at 27 (emphasis original).

[19] *ICJ Reports*, 1986, 14 at 131–132.

the existence of any obligation or rule committing the State to a particular form of government unless that particular State were to specifically undertake the respective obligation. The diversity of States in terms of their political, economic or social systems makes it impossible for international law to accommodate and tolerate a principle obliging the States to commit themselves to one particular form of government.

Within certain treaty frameworks the elements of democratic governance are embodied in the legal standards. Article 3 of Protocol 1 of the European Convention on Human Rights and Article 23 of the American Convention on Human Rights provide for the human right to take part in the conduct of public affairs and to vote and to be elected in genuine periodic elections held at reasonable intervals, by universal and equal suffrage and by secret ballot. It is noteworthy that these treaty obligations do not stipulate a commitment to democracy or democratic government in general, but lay down specific requirements regarding the conduct of and participation in elections. This may be yet another confirmation of the difficulty of transforming the broad democratic entitlement into a rule of international law, because such entitlement cannot feasibly be defined. Where legal commitments as to democratic governance are undertaken, they are always specific and relate to particular modalities of political participation in government. Apart from such clauses, there is hardly any determinate and specific legal rule obliging States to have democracy as their form of government or to act in accordance with democratic principles.

International law, being the body of rules accepted by sovereign States, definitionally cannot attach specific legal implications to the domestic form or style of governance of the State. The adherence of the State or its government to one or other ideology cannot affect their legal status and rights. According to the liberal theory of international law, such a distinction has to be drawn with the outcome of relative but increasing isolation of non-democratic States and governments. The creed of liberal theory is expressed as follows:

> The most distinctive aspect of Liberal international relations theory is that it permits, indeed mandates, a distinction among different types of States based on their domestic political structure and ideology. In particular, a growing body of evidence highlights the distinctive quality of relations among liberal democracies, evidence collected in an effort to explain the documented empirical phenomenon that liberal democracies very rarely go to war with one another. The resulting behavioural distinctions between liberal democracies and other kinds of States, or more generally between liberal and non-liberal States, cannot be accommodated within the framework of classical international law.[20]

But the reality of international law is that the behavioural difference between liberal and non-liberal States does not, without more, translate into differentiating between their legal status and rights. With the specific contrary legal regulation

[20] A-M Slaughter, International Law in a World of Liberal States, 6 *EJIL* (1995), 503 at 504.

absent, all States, whatever their domestic form of governance or ideology, enjoy similar legal personality and rights within the international legal system. The liberal theory does not provide legally relevant evidence to establish that this is not the case. Such evidence has to be drawn not from doctrinal and political opinion, but from the agreed and accepted legal position, which falls short of favouring the liberal theory premises. The identification of international law with one particular ideology inherently risks misunderstanding the basic structural and substantive parameters of this legal system, and has no reasonable prospect of being accepted in the international legal community that accommodates the multiplicity of political, economic and social ideologies.

The reaction of States or groups of States, or indeed of the United Nations, against the States and governments that do not observe democratic standards and do not possess democratic credentials has to be explained not on the basis of some sort of right to democratic governance or liberal international law, but on the basis of specific systemic frameworks that relate to these processes. The adoption of sanctions against non-democratic States has to be explained either by reference to the operation of collective security mechanisms such as Chapter VII measures of the United Nations Charter or, where the conduct of the non-democratic regime involves breaches of international law, to the law of countermeasures as an aspect of State responsibility.[21] As for the general process of adoption of attitudes towards, or conducting relations with, non-democratic States and governments, this is a matter of free choice of the relevant States inherent in their own sovereignty. States are sovereign not only within their territory but also, as far as they are not positively subject to legal limitations, in international relations. The decision of States to reduce or abandon bilateral relations with non-democratic States and governments is a decision based on their sovereignty.

To recapitulate the argument as to the legal position in this field, the right or entitlement to democracy can only exist to the extent that States specifically commit themselves to it. This is not really an issue of theoretical discourse regarding traditional versus modern international law. This legal system, whether traditional or modern by whatever measure, is the product of agreement and consensus between States.

While the notion of democracy falls short of forming part of international legal rules that impose on States specific obligations, it can in certain cases assume important interpretative relevance. The concept of 'democratic society' pervades the entire framework of the European Convention on Human Rights and serves as a criterion for the assessment of legality of State action, in particular in the exercise by a State of its margin of appreciation under Articles 8 to 11 of the Convention. 'Democratic society' thus appears as a potential guage of the

[21] On countermeasures see Articles 49 to 54 of the ILC Articles on State responsibility, Report of the International Law Commission on the work of its Fifty-third session (2001), *Official Records of the General Assembly, Fifty-sixth session, Supplement No. 10* (A/56/10).

necessity of measures undertaken by States-parties in the exercise of the margin of appreciation.

'Democratic society' has relevance, mostly together with other factors, for construing the scope of the Convention rights. But the relevance of 'democratic society' arguably extends beyond the ambit of provisions in which it is expressly mentioned, and could extend to the right of personal liberty under Article 5 of the Convention. As the European Court of Human Rights put it in the *Brogan* case:

> The Court has regard to the importance of this Article [5] in the Convention system: it enshrines a fundamental human right, namely the protection of the individual against arbitrary interferences by the State with his right to liberty. Judicial control of interferences by the executive with the individual's right to liberty is an essential feature of the guarantee embodied in Article 5(3), which is intended to minimise the risk of arbitrariness. Judicial control is implied by the rule of law, 'one of the fundamental principles of a democratic society ..., which is expressly referred to in the Preamble to the Convention.[22]

The Court was effectively referring to what is already mentioned in the text of the Convention.

In relation to the rights under Articles 8 to 11, the notion of 'democratic society' can assume greater interpretative importance. In *United Communist Party v Turkey*, the Court further elaborated upon the notion of 'democratic society' as an interpretative factor. It specified why a 'democratic society' is essential for the enjoyment of the Convention rights:

> the participation of a plurality of political parties representing the different shades of opinion to be found within a country's population. By relaying this range of opinion, not only within political institutions but also—with the help of the media—at all levels of social life, political parties make an irreplaceable contribution to political debate, which is at the very core of the concept of a democratic society.[23]

The Court observed that 'Democracy is without doubt a fundamental feature of the European public order. That is apparent, firstly, from the Preamble to the Convention, which establishes a very clear connection between the Convention and democracy by stating that the maintenance and further realisation of human rights and fundamental freedoms are best ensured on the one hand by an effective political democracy and on the other by a common understanding and observance of human rights.' Furthermore, 'the Convention was designed to maintain and promote the ideals and values of a democratic society. ... In addition, Articles 8, 9, 10 and 11 of the Convention require that interference with the exercise of the rights they enshrine must be assessed by the yardstick of what is "necessary in a democratic society". The only type of necessity capable of justifying

[22] *Brogan v UK*, para 58.
[23] *United Communist Party*, para 44.

an interference with any of those rights is, therefore, one which may claim to spring from "democratic society". Democracy thus appears to be the only political model contemplated by the Convention and, accordingly, the only one compatible with it.'[24] These principles were used by the Court to assess and condemn the dissolution of a political party in violation of Article 11 of the Convention.[25]

In the *Lingens* case, the European Court elaborated upon the parameters of the notion of 'democratic society' in relation to the freedom of speech and expression. As the Court put it:

> freedom of expression, as secured in paragraph 1 of Article 10, constitutes one of the essential foundations of a democratic society and one of the basic conditions for its progress and for each individual's self-fulfilment. Subject to paragraph 2, it is applicable not only to 'information' or 'ideas' that are favourably received or regarded as inoffensive or as a matter of indifference, but also to those that offend, shock or disturb. Such are the demands of that pluralism, tolerance and broadmindedness without which there is no 'democratic society'.[26]

The Court added that 'freedom of political debate is at the very core of the concept of a democratic society which prevails throughout the Convention'.[27] This case further demonstrates that 'democratic society' as a value falls short of binding States as a legal rule. Instead it appears as one of the interpretative factors in the exercise of margin of appreciation under Article 10 of the Convention. In this case, the European Court found a breach of this provision contributed to by the interpretation based on the implications of the notion of 'democratic society'.

5. Considerations of Humanity

Humanitarian considerations constitute an important value relevant in several fields of international law, and above all in the areas that deal with the protection of the individual in peacetime and wartime. International humanitarian law is obviously based on the balance of military necessity and humanitarian considerations. But both the criteria of military necessity and humanitarian considerations on their own are vague and undefined, and they themselves cannot constitute criteria for the rights and duties of the belligerent or occupying power.[28] The legality of belligerent action in humanitarian law depends more on compliance with specific prescriptions as to individual aspects of the belligerent's or occupant's conduct.

[24] *United Communist Party*, para 45.
[25] See below Chapter 8.
[26] *Lingens v Austria*, Application No 9815/82, Judgment of 8 July 1986, para 41.
[27] *Id*, para. 42.
[28] The concept of necessity in international law is dealt with below in Chapter 8.

Still, practice has witnessed some instances of judicial treatment of humanitarian values. In the *Corfu Channel* case, the International Court examined the legality of minelaying in the territorial waters of Albania which had the effect of damaging British vessels. The pertinent paragraph of the Court's judgment describes the relevance of humanitarian values in this context:

The obligations incumbent upon the Albanian authorities consisted in notifying, for the benefit of shipping in general, the existence of a minefield in Albanian territorial waters and in warning the approaching British warships of the imminent danger to which the minefield exposed them. Such obligations are based, not on the Hague Convention of 1907, No. VIII, which is applicable in time of war, but on certain general and well-recognized principles, namely: elementary considerations of humanity, even more exacting in peace than in war; the principle of the freedom of maritime communication; and every State's obligation not to allow knowingly its territory to be used for acts contrary to the rights of other States.[29]

Thus, humanitarian considerations constituted one of the factors that influenced the characterisation of Albania's failure to warn British ships of the forthcoming danger as unlawful. The Court treated humanitarian considerations as a 'general and well-recognised principle'. The Court's judgment does not clarify whether such a principle of humanity operates across the field of international law. In *M/V Saiga*, the International Tribunal for the Law of the Sea was more specific in stressing that 'Considerations of humanity must apply in the law of the sea, as they do in other areas of international law.'[30] This factor was one of the causes, though not the only and direct one, for judging the relevant uses of force on the seas as illegal.

In the *South-West Africa* case, the International Court encountered a reference to humanitarian considerations as entailing the existence of judicial standing of the applicant States to vindicate, in judicial proceedings against South Africa, the rights of the population of the League of Nations mandated territory. The Court rejected the argument that the sacred trust of civilisation embodied in the Mandate Agreement entailed the judicial standing of all interested States:

The Court must examine what is perhaps the most important contention of a general character that has been advanced in connection with this aspect of the case, namely the contention by which it is sought to derive a legal right or interest in the conduct of the mandate from the simple existence, or principle, of the 'sacred trust'. The sacred trust, it is said, is a 'sacred trust of civilization'. Hence all civilized nations have an interest in seeing that it is carried out. An interest, no doubt; but in order that this interest may take on a specifically legal character, the sacred trust itself must be or become something more than a moral or humanitarian ideal. In order to generate legal rights and obligations, it must be given juridical expression and be clothed in legal form.[31]

29 *ICJ Reports*, 1949, 4 at 22.
30 *M/V Saiga*, para 155.
31 *ICJ Reports*, 1966, 6 at 34.

The Court went further to distinguish moral and legal factors from each other in defining the legal parameters of the 'sacred trust':

In the present case, the principle of the sacred trust has as its sole juridical expression the mandates system. As such, it constitutes a moral ideal given form as a juridical regime in the shape of that system. But it is necessary not to confuse the moral ideal with the legal rules intended to give it effect. ... To sum up, the principle of the sacred trust has no residual juridical content which could, so far as any particular mandate is concerned, operate per se to give rise to legal rights and obligations outside the system as a whole; and, within the system equally, such rights and obligations exist only in so far as there is actual provision for them. Once the expression to be given to an idea has been accepted in the form of a particular regime or system, its legal incidents are those of the regime or system. It is not permissible to import new ones by a process of appeal to the originating idea—a process that would, *ex hypothesi*, have no natural limit.[32]

In broader conceptual terms, the Court emphasised that:

Throughout this case it has been suggested, directly or indirectly, that humanitarian considerations are sufficient in themselves to generate legal rights and obligations, and that the Court can and should proceed accordingly. The Court does not think so. It is a court of law, and can take account of moral principles only in so far as these are given a sufficient expression in legal form. Law exists, it is said, to serve a social need; but precisely for that reason it can do so only through and within the limits of its own discipline. Otherwise, it is not a legal service that would be rendered. Humanitarian considerations may constitute the inspirational basis for rules of law, just as, for instance, the preambular parts of the United Nations Charter constitute the moral and political basis for the specific legal provisions thereafter set out. Such considerations do not, however, in themselves amount to rules of law.[33]

The outcome of the case did not crucially depend on the 'sacred trust' argument. The question whether Ethiopia and Liberia had standing to sue South Africa for breaches of the Mandate was more contingent on the interpretation of the specific clauses of the Mandate Agreement. The Court's refusal to allow standing has widely been regarded as a step backwards; it was based on improper construction of the compromissory clause under the Mandate Agreement, and fails to fit with the understanding of legal interest and consequent judicial standing in the rest of the Court's jurisprudence.[34] However, in terms of general analysis of the relationship between established legal rules and humanitarian considerations as extra-legal values, the Court's analysis correctly draws a line of separation between the two. But it is questionable whether the upholding of the relevance of 'sacred trust' in terms of judicial standing was contingent upon the status of that 'sacred trust' as an established legal rule. The applicants did not seek to establish their judicial standing merely on the basis of 'sacred trust' and in the absence

[32] *Id*, 33–35.
[33] *Id*, 34.
[34] For detail see A Orakhelashvili, *Peremptory Norms in International Law* (2006), Chapter 16.

of other factors. Their case was predominantly based on the construction of the compromissory clause in the Mandate Agreement.[35] The relevance of humanitarian considerations in this case was not to provide for judicial standing by themselves, but to weigh as an interpretative factor in construing the ambit and scope of pertinent legal provisions, including the compromissory clause. The factor of 'sacred trust' as part of the object and purpose of the Mandate Agreement was significant in construing the specific provisions of the Agreement, such as its jurisdictional clause. The Court's distinction between rules and values is correct on a general plane. The problem with the Court's reasoning is that the case before it did not call for using values as a substitute for legal regulation—it called for using values for construing the *existing* legal regulation.

6. Security and Survival of States

There are also certain values which do not as such serve the purposes of international law, but the purposes that are national priorities in the first place. This refers to the values referred to in derogation or margin of appreciation clauses under several treaty instruments varying from human rights treaties to the WTO Agreement. Examples are the considerations of prevention of disorder or crime, protection of health or morals, or natural resources, the interests of national security, territorial integrity or public safety, or war or other public emergency threatening the 'life of the nation'. These are values that international law accepts and recognises in order to accommodate the basic needs of States. Some related values, for instance the preservation of human, animal or plant health under Article XX(g) GATT, are extra-State in character.

As the analysis in the following chapters demonstrates, the acceptance of such values and their endowment with international standing results, in international judicial practice, in their recognition as a way of stating the presumptive and conditional legality of State action undertaken in pursuance of upholding and preserving these values. On the other hand, the involvement of the relevant value will not by itself predetermine the outcome of the case. The legality of the relevant action will ultimately be judged on grounds additional to the values that are involved in the case. These will be grounds to test the compatibility of State action with its treaty obligations.

This is further confirmed in the example of the modern problem of terrorism, combating which acquires ever-increasing significance in the international legal system. That said, the security needs of the State in combating terrorism

[35] Article 7 of the Mandate Agreement reads as follows: 'The Mandatory agrees that, if any dispute whatever should arise between the Mandatory and another Member of the League of Nations relating to the interpretation or the application of the provisions of the Mandate, such dispute, if it cannot be settled by negotiation, shall be submitted to the Permanent Court of International Justice provided for by Article 14 of the Covenant of the League of Nations.'

does not by itself justify or require any specific conduct under international law. Combating terrorism is justified only if it is exercised through the means allowed by international law, and does not conflict with its rules. Terrorist acts, condemnable as they are, do not justify any deviation from human rights and humanitarian law standards. As affirmed widely, especially in Article 15 of the 2005 Inter-American Convention against Terrorism and the UN Security Council Resolutions 1456(2003) and 1566(2004), the fight against terrorism must be conducted in strict compliance with the applicable human rights and humanitarian law. Therefore, the issue of terrorism, even if it had been more extensively dealt with by the Court, would hardly have an impact on its legal findings. The same holds true for the issue of self-defence, because terrorism does not constitute a free-standing aspect of *jus ad bellum* and the response to it is justified, as Abi-Saab has emphasised, only to an extent that accords with the otherwise applicable framework of the law of self-defence.[36]

Arguably 'life of the nation' is also a value that has international legal significance. The survival of States is served by much of the international legal framework. The inherent right to self-defence under Article 51 of the UN Charter and the relevant customary law is but one example of this. Along similar lines, the International Court of Justice elaborates upon the notion of the 'survival of States' by which it qualifies the restrictions that international law may impose on States in terms of their use of nuclear weapons.[37] The Court's Opinion is clear that its approach is concerned only with situations that also fall within the legitimate ambit of the right to self-defence.

There are doctrinal objections to the Court's use of the notion of State survival. It is claimed that the concept of State survival is not referred to in any international instruments and consequently those instruments, whether treaties against aggression or General Assembly resolutions such as the Friendly Relations Declaration (Resolution 2625 of 1970) or the Definition of Aggression (Resolution 3314 of 1974), protect merely the independence and territorial integrity of the State, but not its survival. Under this approach, international law does not recognise the right of the State to survive.[38] A further analogy is sought in the emergency clauses in human rights treaties, such as Article 4 ICCPR, which authorises emergency derogation if the 'life of the nation' is threatened, but subject to compliance with additional conditions, such as proportionality and non-discrimination. Hence, it is claimed that the notion of State survival is not supported in this context either.[39]

[36] G Abi-Saab, The Proper Role of International Law in Combating Terrorism in A Bianchi (ed), *Enforcing International Law Norms against Terrorism* (2004), xxvii–xxviii.

[37] The operative paragraph 2E of the Opinion states that 'in view of the current state of international law, and of the elements of fact at its disposal, the Court cannot conclude definitively whether the threat or use of nuclear weapons would be lawful or unlawful in an extreme circumstance of self-defence, in which the very survival of a State would be at stake'.

[38] M Cohen, The Notion of 'State Survival' in L Boisson de Chazournes & P Sands (eds), *International Law, the International Court of Justice and Nuclear Weapons* (1999), 293 at 296, 302.

[39] *Id*, 297.

In relation to the first objection, it must be emphasised that danger to the survival of the State will necessarily endanger the territorial integrity and independence of that State. As for human rights emergency clauses, their ambit is of little utility to define the meaning and merits of State survival. The fact that treaty regimes require subjecting State action undertaken in relation to its citizens to some additional conditions does not mean that the same conditions would also be inherently present in *jus ad bellum*. State survival has its own normative basis, which is Article 51 of the Charter, together with its customary counterpart. It is not a free-standing right.

The Court's reference to State survival may be open to criticism from some quarters. However, it is clear that it is not an independent notion based on indeterminate and undefined values, but follows from the right to self-defence and is strictly confined to the area to which that right applies. Consequently, the reference to State survival does not imply the revival of older concepts of self-preservation or similar extra-legal categories that have been used as justification for forcible action at various stages of development of the international legal system. This is a category that justifies the relevant action not in terms external to legal regulation, but as part of an established legal right. More so, as survival is the ultimate aim of any defence of the State and consequently State survival relates to the most essential core of the inherent right to self-defence.

7. Evaluation

The foregoing analysis demonstrates that values that possess relevance in the international legal system do not by themselves establish, modify or abolish legal rules, rights or obligations. Consequently, values do not by themselves limit the sovereign freedom of action of States, but leave it unaffected in line with the *Lotus* pronouncement on residual sovereignty. At the same time, values can gain recognition as part of customary law, subject to the requirements of custom-generation, or be part of treaty arrangements, expressly or by implication. In such cases values do impact on the existing legal position not externally, but as part of that very legal position. If the relevant value constitutes part of the rationale or object and purpose of the treaty framework, it can impact on the rights and obligations of States-parties to the relevant treaty.

8

Quasi-Normative Non-Law

1. General Introduction

The term 'quasi-normative' serves to denote standards that cannot be straightforwardly formulated, but follow from legal rules and have normative aspiration in terms of multiple and indiscriminate applicability. This refers to the concepts of margin of appreciation, equity, 'fair and equitable treatment', proportionality, legitimate expectations, or necessity.[1] These concepts impact on the legality of State actions over a range of fields such as the law of the sea, law of investment, law of reparation, human rights law or the law of armed conflict. Each of the categories of quasi-normative non-law has been the subject of separate academic studies and much can be said to analyse them from different perspectives. This study will be limited to analysing the categories of quasi-normative non-law in terms of their ability to imitate the law, that is the degree of their normativity.

Analysis of this kind of non-law involves examining the relevance of fact, interest or value. In essence, the categories of quasi-normative law indeed embody considerations of fact, interest and value. As distinct from analysis of the independent relevance facts, interests or values may possess in relation to legal rules, their relevance as quasi-normative non-law focuses on observing their imitation of normative quality. There is no evidence of agreement by States as to the exact scope of this normative quality. Yet, the outcome reached through the use of quasi-normative non-law is deemed to realise the intendment behind the legal rules agreed as between States. These are the rules that refer to quasi-normative non-law and make it relevant. From this perspective, the categories of quasi-normative law, despite having no determinate content and meaning, are intended to impact on the rights and obligations under international law. The basis for their ability to do so follows from the very consent of States, which simultaneously fails to determine their meaning and scope.

The existence and operation of these various headings of quasi-normative non-law raise several basic problems in terms of the main argument of this study. The wide-ranging rule-based categories of quasi-normative non-law refer to the

[1] The analysis of this chapter relates to the content and scope of non-law elements as such. At later stage, in Part V, non-law elements are considered in the context of interpretation of treaty instruments of which they are part.

multiple categories of policy and interest. This may provoke a question as to the relevance of policy in the construction of legal rules. The question could be raised as to whether this sort of non-law introduces policy, or political, elements that impact on rights and obligations under international law. Another, related problem is that the lack of determinacy of the categories of quasi-normative non-law raises the question as to who is in charge of applying them to facts. In other words, the problem of subjectivity arises. The essence of this problem is that if individual States, or tribunals, are to be allowed to exercise subjective appreciation of the relevant factors, such subjectivism will have to be related not only to non-law elements, but also to the entire rule from which the relevant non-law element derives.

These problems illustrate the possible implications of the lack of determinacy in the relevant fields of international law. Even though the relevant non-law categories are indeterminate on their face, the intendment behind the rules is that they have to be applied to facts and produce a result as a matter of application of international law. This seems to be a serious dilemma: the rules of international law provide the legal basis for indeterminate non-law elements and thus make them part of binding international law, yet fall short of defining their meaning and scope. In the absence of clearer guidance and parameters, the decision-maker would have no option but to adopt such objectively justifiable and explainable decisions as would be based on legal rules and principles accepted by all parties to the relevant legal dispute.

This factor requires ascertaining the parameters within which the non-law elements can operate, the stage at which they can and should be resorted to, the limits beyond which they cannot extend, and any possible competing factors that are relevant in the context in which they are applied for determining the final outcome. In other words, the following analysis will demonstrate that the process of application of quasi-normative non-law is that of balancing all the relevant factors. This process of balancing is quite specific to this category of non-law, not only because of its indeterminacy, which more or less characterises all categories of non-law, but also because it is legal rules which direct the decision-maker to apply non-law elements and pronounce on their scope and effect.

The actual, potential or claimed relevance of all categories of quasi-normative non-law relates to the outer limit of legal norms with indeterminate content. The doctrine of margin of appreciation provides the institutional arrangement for assessing State conduct in terms of the relevant treaty requirements. Equity follows the fundamental norm on maritime delimitation and regulates the issues to which that norm does not extend. Necessity and proportionality as indeterminate requirements to be satisfied sequentially and cumulatively arise in several fields of international law. They relate to the justification and type of action of States that is claimed to be performed under the relevant norm of international law. Two other kinds of quasi-normative non-law—'fair and equitable treatment' and legitimate expectations—also resemble equity in claiming autonomous content.

But their independent relevance is much more difficult to identify through the use of appropriate evidence.

2. The Doctrine and Essence of the Margin of Appreciation

(a) General Aspects

The margin of appreciation can be denoted as an institution, or a doctrine, which is not crucial for the legal implications of this notion. A general analysis of the margin of appreciation as operating within several fields of international law has not yet been undertaken. Still, the general concept of the margin of appreciation controls the overall conception of quasi-normative non-law, by entitling States to act, under institutional supervision, in deviation from their ordinary treaty obligations.

The generic concept of the margin of appreciation denotes the arrangement within the legal framework established by a treaty according to which the State-party to such treaty has the initial freedom to determine the scope of its obligations. This is done by characterising the relevant conduct in terms of the number of circumstances referred to in the same treaty. These circumstances of non-law normally relate to the overriding policy reasons that are essential for the existence and functioning of States, their national policy priorities, or their ability to deal with emergencies that are expressly mentioned in the relevant treaty and solely for this reason they qualify the scope of treaty obligations. To avoid arbitrariness, the grounds on which the relevant State may qualify its action as legitimate form only one, indeed the initial, part of the process. The rest of the process is determined by systemic factors which are applied to the conduct of the State irrespective of its attitude, such as necessity or proportionality. In this sense, the margin of appreciation is designed to avoid arbitrariness in the form of auto-determination. At the same time, as will be seen, the margin of appreciation arrangement operates in the context where treaty-based organs are designed to safeguard the purposes and rationale of the relevant treaty framework. To achieve this, a set of presumptions is brought into play which ensures that State discretion is kept in check and arbitrary assertions of the freedom of action are avoided.

International law contains no general principle on the margin of appreciation that would entitle States to claim its exercise in terms of their compliance with international law, although there are doctrinal calls to the contrary.[2] The structure of the international legal system renders this construct unsustainable. As international law is a system based on consensual agreement, international obligations must be construed and implemented in accordance with what the relevant States have agreed on. The freedom of action reserved through the margin

[2] Y Shany, Toward a General Margin of Appreciation Doctrine in International Law? 16 *EJIL* (2005), 907–940.

of appreciation is possible only where such margin of appreciation is based on express agreement between the parties to the relevant treaty framework. The margin of appreciation can only exist where it has been admitted, in relation to the specific context, by the agreement of States.

The margin of appreciation is only possible when the obligation to which it relates is indeterminate, that is it has an undefined outer limit. With regard to norms and obligations that straightforwardly require or prohibit certain conduct, the phenomenon of the margin of appreciation is irrelevant. This is due to the inherent nature of the margin of appreciation which in all cases stems from the norm agreed upon by the States. The margin of appreciation can have no abstract, free-standing or autonomous existence. It can only regulate or justify actions referred to in the relevant norm; it cannot regulate the actions of States externally to, or independently of, the relevant norm. In other words, the margin of appreciation cannot be a tool undermining the rule of law.

The margin of appreciation is not the same as the points which can be argued. All points of law, regardless of the character of norms and legal relations involved, whether absolute or limited by the margin of appreciation, are decided on the basis of the parties' arguments which will often represent the issue in a way favourable to them. The specificity of the margin of appreciation is that in the limited circumstances in which it applies, the initial assessment of fact and law by the State will be taken as a point of reference. On this basis further analysis of the lawfulness of relevant State action will be developed. The relevant conduct of the State will qualify as violation if it does not satisfy the requirements specified or implied in the relevant norm that admits the margin of appreciation in the first place. The overall philosophy behind the margin of appreciation is that the categories of non-law referred to in it have no autonomous relevance. They are relevant in so far as they serve the rationale of the relevant treaty regime.

The margin of appreciation cannot be equated with bare discretion. It is instead a complex and multi-level arrangement which includes initial determination by the State that may well include an element of discretion, and the consequent third-party review of this determination. The complex and multi-level profile of the margin of appreciation arrangements is meant to ensure the application of international legal rules which have no *a priori* defined outer limit to facts in a way to produce the legal outcome under which the relevant conduct is characterised as lawful or unlawful. Even if the relevant treaty rule referring to the margin of appreciation is open-ended and indeterminate, the result obtained through the use of the margin of appreciation involves the straightforward determination of whether this rule is or is not violated.

Situations to which the margin of appreciation relates differ from those falling within the category of circumstances precluding wrongfulness of an internationally wrongful act.[3] While the latter relate to the secondary norms framework of

[3] *Cf* ILC Articles on State Responsibility, Articles 20–27.

the law of State responsibility, the former relate to primary and substantive legal obligations. Even though both categories may look similar on the surface, the margin of appreciation analysis enquires into whether the conduct of the State is lawful under the substantive obligation. Circumstances precluding wrongfulness enquire into whether, the original breach of an international obligation being established, it can be excused on the basis of circumstances external to the scope of the relevant substantive norm. In short, the margin of appreciation is a condition of lawfulness of the relevant State action and part of substantive legal regulation under primary norms. Circumstances precluding wrongfulness relate to situations already involving illegality.

The confusion between the margin of appreciation and circumstances precluding wrongfulness, namely the state of necessity, was witnessed in the Arbitral Award on *CMS/Argentina*. The Arbitral Tribunal used the criteria for this area of the law of State responsibility to assess the content of the primary, or substantive, regulation of the margin of appreciation under Article IX of the 1991 Treaty between the United States of America and the Argentine Republic Concerning the Reciprocal Encouragement and Protection of Investment. The Tribunal concluded that the Treaty, which included emergency clauses did, by its object and purpose, exclude reliance on the state of necessity. This was in accordance with the ILC's Article 25 on State responsibility, which deals with the conditions under which the state of necessity can be invoked.[4] What the Arbitral Tribunal misunderstood was the clear and cardinal difference between the substantive emergency clause as *lex specialis* under the 1991 Treaty, and the general international law regulation of the state of necessity. The fact that the Treaty allegedly excluded reliance on the general international law rule of necessity does not prejudice the validity and continued relevance of the clause expressly included in the Treaty and enabling the State-party to take appropriate measures.

(b) The European Convention on Human Rights[5]

Action in the exercise of margin of appreciation under the European Convention on Human Rights must be undertaken in pursuance of legitimate aims specified

[4] *CMS Gas Transmission Company and the Argentine Republic*, Case No ARB/01/8, Award, 12 May 2005, paras 332ff. According to Article IX of the aforementioned Treaty, 'This Treaty shall not preclude the application by either Party of measures necessary for the maintenance of public order, the fulfilment of its obligations with respect to the maintenance or restoration of international peace or security, or the protection of its own essential security interests.'

[5] See, in general, A McHarg, Reconciling Human Rights and the Public Interest: Conceptual Problems and Doctrinal Uncertainty in the Jurisprudence of the European Court of Human Rights, 62 *Modern Law Review* (1999), 671; HC Yourow, The Margin of Appreciation Doctrine in the Dynamics of European Human Rights Jurisprudence, 3 *Connecticut Journal of International Law* (1987–1988), 111; L Helfer, Consensus, Coherence and the European Convention on Human Rights, 26 *Cornell International Law Journal* (1993), 133; J Sweeney, Margins of Appreciation: Cultural Relativity and the European Court of Human Rights, 54 *ILCQ* (2005), 459; K Cavanaugh,

in the Convention, Articles 8 to 11. These refer to considerations of national security, territorial integrity of States, public safety, prevention of disorder, protection of health or morals, public order, protection of the rights and reputation of others, prevention of disclosure of information received in confidence and maintenance of the independence and impartiality of the judiciary. Most of these notions have no precise meaning from the viewpoint of international law and cannot be given a straightforward definition. In short, these headings of legitimate aim relate to one or another dimension of public interest at national level, which can potentially justify interference with the relevant right. If the requirement of legitimate aim is not met, the interference with the right becomes its violation and hence breach of the European Convention.

The indeterminacy notwithstanding, States-parties to the Convention can normally defend their actions in terms of Convention-derived justifications. As Van Dijk and Van Hoof observe, the Convention organs have very rarely found a violation of the Convention by reference to the legitimate aim standard.[6]

The essence of the margin of appreciation is described by the European Court of Human Rights in its analysis of the dimensions of the right to private life under Article 8 of the European Convention:

> Whilst the State is required to give due consideration to the particular interests, the respect for which it is obliged to secure by virtue of Article 8, it must in principle be left a choice between different ways and means of meeting this obligation. The Court's supervisory function being of a subsidiary nature, it is limited to reviewing whether or not the particular solution adopted can be regarded as striking a fair balance...
>
> Whether in the implementation of that regime the right balance has been struck in substance between the Article 8 rights affected by the regime and other conflicting community interests depends on the relative weight given to each of them.[7]

The same Court defined the relevant criteria also in *Buckley*:

> The scope of this margin of appreciation is not identical in each case but will vary according to the context. Relevant factors include the nature of the Convention right in issue, its importance for the individual and the nature of the activities concerned.[8]

In other words, the more severe the interference with individual interests, the lesser the role the margin of appreciation would have to play in justifying that interference.

As the relevant clauses of the European Convention are applied in a domestic context, it is open to the European Court to consider domestic circumstances

Policing the Margins: Rights Protection and the European Court of Human Rights, *EHRLR* (2006), 422; T Lewis, What Not To Wear: Religious Rights, The European Court, and the Margin of Appreciation, 56 *ICLQ* (2007), 395.

[6] Van Dijk & Van Hoof, *Theory and Practice of the European Convention on Human Rights* (2006), 340.

[7] *Hatton v UK*, GC, Case No 36022/97, Judgment of 7 August 2003, paras 124–125.

[8] *Buckley*, No 20348/92, Judgment of 25 September 1996, para 74.

and it does not require absolute uniformity among the States-parties.[9] To illustrate, in the *Gillow* case, the Court held that the United Kingdom could enact housing regulations on Guernsey Island, as required for the economic well-being of that area. This was considered a legitimate aim and the Court did not find it 'to be established that the legislation pursued any other purpose'.[10]

(c) WTO Law

In WTO law too, the exercise of the margin of appreciation may depend on the relative balance of interests. One field in which the margin of appreciation is heavily resorted to and discussed in the WTO jurisprudence is the areas where States can take certain measures to protect their interests, such as public order, protection of natural resources, security or public morals, as regulated under Article XX of the 1947 Agreement on Tariffs and Trade (GATT).[11] A similar clause is included in Article XIV of the General Agreement on trade in Services (GATS), which allows States-parties to deviate from their obligations under the Agreement if certain

[9] *Sunday Times*, Case No 6538/74, Judgment of 26 April 1979, para 61.

[10] *Gillow v UK*, No 9063/80, Judgment of 24 November 1986, para 54.

[11] Article XX (General Exceptions) stipulates that:

Subject to the requirement that such measures are not applied in a manner which would constitute a means of arbitrary or unjustifiable discrimination between countries where the same conditions prevail, or a disguised restriction on international trade, nothing in this Agreement shall be construed to prevent the adoption or enforcement by any contracting party of measures:

(*a*) necessary to protect public morals;
(*b*) necessary to protect human, animal or plant life or health;
(*c*) relating to the importations or exportations of gold or silver;
(*d*) necessary to secure compliance with laws or regulations which are not inconsistent with the provisions of this Agreement, including those relating to customs enforcement, the enforcement of monopolies operated under paragraph 4 of Article II and Article XVII, the protection of patents, trade marks and copyrights, and the prevention of deceptive practices;
(*e*) relating to the products of prison labour;
(*f*) imposed for the protection of national treasures of artistic, historic or archaeological value;
(*g*) relating to the conservation of exhaustible natural resources if such measures are made effective in conjunction with restrictions on domestic production or consumption;
(*h*) undertaken in pursuance of obligations under any intergovernmental commodity agreement which conforms to criteria submitted to the CONTRACTING PARTIES and not disapproved by them or which is itself so submitted and not so disapproved;
(*i*) involving restrictions on exports of domestic materials necessary to ensure essential quantities of such materials to a domestic processing industry during periods when the domestic price of such materials is held below the world price as part of a governmental stabilization plan; *Provided* that such restrictions shall not operate to increase the exports of or the protection afforded to such domestic industry, and shall not depart from the provisions of this Agreement relating to non-discrimination;
(*j*) essential to the acquisition or distribution of products in general or local short supply;

Provided that any such measures shall be consistent with the principle that all contracting parties are entitled to an equitable share of the international supply of such products, and that any such measures, which are inconsistent with the other provisions of the Agreement shall be discontinued as soon as the conditions giving rise to them have ceased to exist. The CONTRACTING PARTIES shall review the need for this sub-paragraph not later than 30 June 1960.

pressing needs of public health, morality, public order, environment, or the need to prevent fraudulent practices require such action.[12]

The Appellate Body Report in *US–Gasoline*[13] relates to US measures to control toxic and other pollution caused by the combustion of gasoline manufactured in or imported into the United States. The issue arising in terms of the margin of appreciation was whether the baseline establishment rules regarding gasoline were justified under Article XX(g) of the General Agreement, as a measure related to the conservation of exhaustible natural resources.[14] More specifically, the issue was whether clean air was a natural resource that could be depleted. The Appellate Body affirmed that the baseline establishment rules can be regarded as primarily aimed at the conservation of natural resources for the purpose of Article XX(g).[15] Thus, the margin of appreciation of the State to assess the relevant situation as falling within the relevant exception clause was reviewed and its determination upheld.

In *Korea–Beef*, the Appellate Body examined the legality of a Korean measure to establish the dual retail system of imported beef to prevent retailers from presenting imported beef as a domestic product.[16] In *US–Gambling*, the issue before the Appellate Body was US measures affecting the cross-border supply of gambling justified by the US as designed to protect public morals and public order under Article XIV(a) GATS.[17]

[12] According to Article XIV GATS (General Exceptions):

Subject to the requirement that such measures are not applied in a manner which would constitute a means of arbitrary or unjustifiable discrimination between countries where like conditions prevail, or a disguised restriction on trade in services, nothing in this Agreement shall be construed to prevent the adoption or enforcement by any Member of measures:

(a) necessary to protect public morals or to maintain public order; [according to the footnote to this sub-paragraph, 'The public order exception may be invoked only where a genuine and sufficiently serious threat is posed to one of the fundamental interests of society.']
(b) necessary to protect human, animal or plant life or health;
(c) necessary to secure compliance with laws or regulations which are not inconsistent with the provisions of this Agreement including those relating to:
    (i) the prevention of deceptive and fraudulent practices or to deal with the effects of a default on services contracts;
    (ii) the protection of the privacy of individuals in relation to the processing and dissemination of personal data and the protection of confidentiality of individual records and accounts;
    (iii) safety;
(d) inconsistent with Article XVII, provided that the difference in treatment is aimed at ensuring the equitable or effective imposition or collection of direct taxes in respect of services or service suppliers of other Members;
(e) inconsistent with Article II, provided that the difference in treatment is the result of an agreement on the avoidance of double taxation or provisions on the avoidance of double taxation in any other international agreement or arrangement by which the Member is bound.

[13] *United States–Standards for Reformulated and Conventional Gasoline*, AB-1996–1, Report of the Appellate Body, WT/DS2/AB/R, 29 April 1996.

[14] *Id*, at 2–12. [15] *Id*, at 10, 17.

[16] *Korea–Measures Affecting Imports of Fresh, Chilled and Frozen* Beef, AB-2000–8, Report of the Appellate Body, WT/DS161/AB/R, WT/DS169/AB/R, 11 December 2000.

[17] *United States–Measures Affecting the Cross-Border Supply of Gambling and Betting Services*, AB-2005–1, Report of the Appellate Body, WT/DS285, AB/R, 7 April 2005.

In *US–Gasoline*, the Appellate Body formulated general conditions for the exercise of the margin of appreciation in relation to GATT:

In order that the justifying protection of Article XX may be extended to it, the measure at issue must not only come under one or another of the particular exceptions—paragraphs (a) to (j)—listed under Article XX; it must also satisfy the requirements imposed by the opening clauses of Article XX. The analysis is, in other words, two-tiered: first, provisional justification by reason of characterization of the measure under XX(g); second, further appraisal of the same measure under the introductory clauses of Article XX.[18]

The rationale of the exception measures is further highlighted in the same case:

The chapeau is animated by the principle that while the exceptions of Article XX may be invoked as a matter of legal right, they should not be so applied as to frustrate or defeat the legal obligations of the holder of the right under the substantive rules of the General Agreement. If those exceptions are not to be abused or misused, in other words, the measures falling within the particular exceptions must be applied reasonably, with due regard both to the legal duties of the party claiming the exception and the legal rights of the other parties concerned.[19]

Therefore, the essence of margin of appreciation in the WTO law is to allow States to take exceptional measures deviating from their mainstream obligations if that is required by their essential interests. They could do so only in the circumstances specified in GATT and under the close scrutiny of the WTO dispute settlement bodies.

In *US–Shrimp*, the Appellate Body addressed the US import ban on shrimp harvested with commercial fishing technology capable of adversely affecting sea turtles. Reliance was placed on Article XX(g) GATT which entitles States to take measures to protect exhaustible natural resources. As the Appellate Body remarked, clarification of this issue required looking 'into the relationship between the measure at stake and the legitimate policy of conserving exhaustible natural resources'. The US measures related 'clearly and directly to the policy goal of conserving sea turtles'.[20] It was undisputed that the harvesting of shrimp by commercial shrimp trawling vessels with mechanical retrieval devices in waters where shrimp and sea turtles coincide is a significant cause of sea turtle mortality.[21] Therefore, the Appellate Body upheld the US qualification of its measures as protective of natural resources under Article XX(g).

In terms of compliance with US measures, with the chapeau of Article XX, the Appellate Body stated that 'The policy goal of a measure at issue cannot provide its rationale or justification under the standards of the chapeau of Article XX.' The legitimacy of policy measure can only provide provisional justification under

[18] *US–Gasoline*, at 20.

[19] *Id.*

[20] *US–Import Prohibition of Certain Shrimp and Shrimp Products*, AB-1998–4, Report of the Appellate Body, WT/DS58/AB/R, 12 October 1998, paras 135ff.

[21] *Id*, para 140.

Article XX(g). But compliance with the chapeau requirements is an autonomous and additional standard.[22] Judging the US import ban from this perspective, the Appellate Body found that it constituted an arbitrary discrimination between countries where the same conditions prevail. Hence it was not justified as a measure under Article XX. The basis for discrimination was that the procedure in the United States regarding certification of harvesting States for import was not fair and transparent.[23]

This confirms that the margin of appreciation in the WTO law is conditional upon the fulfilment of some preceding conditions as determined in the chapeau. This seems to be the feature of margin of appreciation in all relevant treaty regimes.

In *US–Gambling*, the Appellate Body construed the requirements of the margin of appreciation under Article XIV GATS in a way similar to that under Article XX GATT. The analysis of compatibility with Article XIV GATS:

> requires that the challenged measure address the particular interest specified in [the relevant] paragraph and that there be a sufficient nexus between the measure and the interest protected. The required nexus—or 'degree of connection'—between the measure and the interest is specified in the language of the paragraphs themselves, through the use of terms such as 'relating to' and 'necessary to'. Where the challenged measure has been found to fall within one of the paragraphs of Article XIV, a panel should then consider whether that measure satisfies the requirements of the chapeau of Article XIV.[24]

In terms of presumptions, the State invoking the exception must prove that the measure invoked under one of the paragraphs of Article XX does not constitute an abuse of such exceptions.[25]

(d) Bilateral Treaties

The emergency clauses in some bilateral treaties entitle States-parties to deviate from their obligations in pursuance of their essential security interests. In the *Nicaragua* case, the International Court faced a defence raised by the United States as to its military and paramilitary actions in and against Nicaragua on the basis of Article XX(1)(d) of the 1956 FCN Treaty between the United States and Nicaragua. According to this provision, the State-party can deviate from its other obligations under the Treaty if this is rendered necessary by the risk to its 'essential security interests'.

The Court ruled that this clause was not self-judging and it would have to rule on whether the US invocation of this clause was justified.[26] The US claimed

22 *Id*, para 149.
23 *Id*, para 184.
24 *US–Gambling*, AB Report, para 292.
25 *US–Gasoline*, at 20–21.
26 *ICJ Reports*, 1986, 116.

that Article XXI(1)(d) entitled it to act in self-defence. The Court determined that the concept of 'essential security interests' was broader than the concept of self-defence. The issue thus was whether the measures presented as protective of the above-mentioned interests were not only useful but necessary.[27] In the end, the United States could not use this clause as justifying the use of force against Nicaragua. The Court examined the various actions of the United States, such as the mining of Nicaraguan ports, arming the *contras* and blockade. But the Court was unable to conclude that they could fall within the scope of actions authorised under Article XXI. The finding by the US President that the Nicaraguan policies contravened the national security of the United States was not sufficient to trigger Article XXI.[28]

The essence of why such clauses cannot be used in the field of *jus ad bellum* is further clarified in the International Court's decision in *Oil Platforms* (Iran v USA).[29] According to Article XX of the 1955 Iran–US Treaty, 'The present Treaty shall not preclude the application of measures: ... *(d)* necessary to fulfil the obligations of a High Contracting Party for the maintenance or restoration of international peace and security, or necessary to protect its essential security interests.' The US invoked this provision to justify its bombing of Iranian oil platforms as a measure protective of its 'essential security interest'. The Court was unable to follow this line of reasoning. The relevant actions of the United States were governed not exclusively by the 1955 Treaty but also by rules of general international law on the use of force that could not be displaced by the terms of the Treaty. The margin of appreciation claimed in relation to the *Oil Platforms* case relates not only to the use of treaty prerogatives under Article XX, but also the use of such prerogative in defiance of norms on the use of force in relation to which the 1955 Treaty cannot validly constitute *lex specialis*.[30]

Most crucially, however, the Court observed that it did not 'have to decide whether the United States interpretation of Article XX, paragraph 1 *(d)*, on this point is correct, since the requirement of international law that measures taken avowedly in self-defence must have been necessary for that purpose is strict and objective, leaving no room for any "measure of discretion"'.[31] Therefore, the Court did not allow the margin of appreciation in this case. The clear-cut regulation of *jus ad bellum* excluded even the initial assessment by the United States of the appropriateness of its military actions in the Persian Gulf. The Court concluded that:

> the actions carried out by United States forces against Iranian oil installations on 19 October 1987 and 18 April 1988 cannot be justified, under Article XX, paragraph 1 *(d)*,

[27] *Id*, 117.
[28] *Id*, 141.
[29] *Oil Platforms* (Islamic Republic of Iran v United States of America), Merits, Judgment of 6 November 2003, General List No 90.
[30] On details see A Orakhelashvili, case review on *Oil Platforms*, *ICLQ* 2004, 753–761.
[31] *Oil Platforms*, para 73.

of the 1955 Treaty, as being measures necessary to protect the essential security interests of the United States, since those actions constituted recourse to armed force not qualifying, under international law on the question, as acts of self-defence, and thus did not fall within the category of measures contemplated, upon its correct interpretation, by that provision of the Treaty.[32]

Judge Koojmans suggested that the question whether the forcible actions of the US against Iranian oil installations were justified by 'essential security interests' under Article XX of the 1955 Treaty must be judged by a test of reasonableness. Such a test would follow from the political nature of the issues covered by Article XX and 'only when the political evaluation is patently unreasonable... is a judicial ban appropriate'.[33] The use of such a test cannot, however, be extended to subject-matter on which the content of the Treaty cannot have the final word.

In the arbitral case of *CMS/Argentina*, the claimant argued that emergency clauses such as the one embodied in the 1991 US-Argentine Treaty provide very narrow and specific exceptions to liability. They do not allow the respondent to invoke a state of emergency. The respondent argued that such emergency clauses provide *lex specialis* which enables the government to maintain public order, protect its essential security interests and re-establish its connections with the international economic system.[34] The Arbitral Tribunal affirmed the general relevance of emergency clauses and their inclusion of the field of economic interests. As the Tribunal put it the question was:

whether Article XI of the Treaty can be interpreted in such a way as to provide that it includes economic emergency as an essential security interest. While the text of the Article does not refer to economic crises or difficulties of that particular kind, as concluded above, there is nothing in the context of customary international law or the object and purpose of the Treaty that could on its own exclude major economic crises from the scope of Article XI.

It must also be kept in mind that the scope of a given bilateral treaty, such as this, should normally be understood and interpreted as attending to the concerns of both parties. If the concept of essential security interests were to be limited to immediate political and national security concerns, particularly of an international character, and were to exclude other interests, for example, major economic emergencies, it could well result in an unbalanced understanding of Article IX.

Thus far, the Tribunal's approach is quite even-handed and perceptive of the State-parties' need to exercise their margin of appreciation in relation to extreme situations contemplated in the Treaty.

A further issue in the Arbitration was to establish how grave the relevant economic crisis was. As the Tribunal emphasised, the crisis at some level could lead to disruption and disintegration of society, and total breakdown of economy.

[32] *Id*, para 78.
[33] Separate Opinion of Judge Koojmans, *id*, paras 44ff.
[34] *CMS/Argentina*, paras 336, 344.

Therefore, the meaning of emergency acquired a different sense when such was the case.[35] The respondent argued that the emergency clause in the Treaty was self-judging and it could alone determine the existence of the relevant emergency situation.[36] The Tribunal confirmed that the clause was not self-judging and stated its interpretative policy in the following terms:

> The Tribunal must conclude next that this judicial review is not limited to an examination of whether the plea has been invoked or the measures have been taken in good faith. It is a substantive review that must examine whether the state of necessity or emergency meets the conditions laid down by customary international law and the treaty provisions and whether it thus is or is not able to preclude wrongfulness.[37]

Having done this, the Tribunal failed to proceed with identifying whether the relevant requirements were objectively satisfied. Instead, it turned to the general international law notion of a state of necessity. Thus, the Tribunal found that the requirements of a state of necessity were not met, and ruled against the State.

One should note the Tribunal's questionable characterisation of the emergency clause, that the relevant 'Article does not derogate from the Treaty rights but rather ensures that any measures directed at offsetting or minimizing losses will be applied in a non-discriminatory manner'.[38] It is very difficult to square this with the text of Article IX of the 1991 Treaty. The Tribunal in fact made a straightforward error of confusion in the matter of applicable law. It thereby avoided an examination of the merits of the respondent's rights under Article IX, in terms of the assessment of its margin of appreciation. This effectively is to fail giving proper effect to Article IX.

(e) Evaluation

As Van Dijk and Van Hoof observe in the example of the European Convention on Human Rights, there is no definite meaning of the margin of appreciation. In addition, there is no authoritative definition of any of the categories mentioned in ECHR or GATT and WTO instruments. These categories have no determinate content to enable *a priori* definition. The relevant State possesses initial freedom to determine that the relevant situation is covered by one of those notions. The propriety of such determination is eventually assessed in terms of compliance by that State with its treaty obligations. Even though there is no determinate content of these notions, it is still possible, and indeed happens in practice, that a review of the determination initially made by the State takes place. The principal implication of this process is that the non-law in treaty frameworks is allowed to operate under careful and multilevel scrutiny which prevents it from undermining the rationale of the relevant legal rules.

[35] *CMS/Argentina*, paras 354, 359–361.
[36] *Id*, para 367. [37] *Id*, para 374.
[38] *Id*, para 375.

3. Necessity

The standard of necessity relates to the application of the relevant international legal norms in the field not initially and straightforwardly defined in these norms.[39] Yet it relates to authorisation to undertake certain steps on multiple occasions. The content of authorisation is not defined in the relevant legal norms and instruments but has to be identified on a case-by-case basis in terms of the relevant factual circumstances. Still, in all relevant legal frameworks there are guiding criteria elaborated to determine the limits of when and how the concept of necessity can operate. The concept of necessity should not promote subjectivism in application of international legal standards.

(a) The Law of the European Convention on Human Rights

In the law of the European Convention on Human Rights, the concept of necessity controls recourse to the margin of appreciation. As the European Court emphasised in *Sunday Times*, it is not sufficient that the interference with the Convention right 'belongs to that class of the exceptions' listed in the relevant provision of the Convention. What matters is that, in addition to the classification of the interference under the relevant Convention clause on legitimate aim, it has to be necessary having regard to the facts and circumstances prevailing in the specific case.[40]

One interesting feature of the concept of necessity is that it cannot come into play just because the relevant measure can be seen as necessary. It can do so only *after* the precondition is fulfilled that the relevant measure of the State is in accordance with law as required in Articles 8 to 11 of the European Convention. In *Malone*, the European Court ruled that interception of the applicant's correspondence was not in accordance with the law as required under Article 8(2) of the Convention. The Court stated in abstract terms that 'the resultant interference can only be regarded as "necessary in a democratic society" if the particular system of secret surveillance adopted contains adequate guarantees against abuse'. However, as the condition of the legal basis was not met, the Court considered it irrelevant to rule on necessity, and pronounced that there was a breach of Article 8.[41]

[39] This analysis relates to the concept of necessity as part of the relevant substantive regulation, and not to that which forms one of the circumstances precluding wrongfulness in the secondary rules framework of the law of State responsibility. On this latter concept of necessity see above Chapter 6.

[40] *Sunday Times UK*, Case No 6538/74, Judgment of 26 April 1979, para 65.

[41] *Malone v UK*, Judgment No 8691/79, 2 August 1984, paras 80–82.

The European Court has described the normative side of the concept of necessity, stressing that:

whilst the adjective 'necessary', within the meaning of Article 10(2), is not synonymous with 'indispensable' (cf., in Articles 2(2) and 6(1), the words 'absolutely necessary' and 'strictly necessary' and, in Article 15(1), the phrase 'to the extent strictly required by the exigencies of the situation'), neither has it the flexibility of such expressions as 'admissible', 'ordinary', 'useful', 'reasonable' or 'desirable'. Nevertheless, it is for the national authorities to make the initial assessment of the reality of the pressing social need implied by the notion of 'necessity' in this context.[42]

Therefore, States-parties can make the initial assessment of whether the relevant measure is necessary, but the final assessment will be made by the Court. Another characteristic feature of necessity under the European Convention is that:

the Court's supervision is [not] limited to ascertaining whether a respondent State exercised its discretion reasonably, carefully and in good faith. Even a Contracting State so acting remains subject to the Court's control as regards the compatibility of its conduct with the engagements it has undertaken under the Convention.[43]

Thus, on the one hand, the concept of necessity implies the initial freedom of the State-party to determine the permissibility of its own action in those aspects of its treaty obligation that cannot be defined *a priori* and straightforwardly. On the other hand, the same concept of necessity requires the Court's assessment of the State-party's compliance with those undefined aspects of treaty obligation. In other words, this involves the review of discretionary judgement of States. The compliance of the State-party with the Convention means in such cases the proper exercise of their discretion as to the necessity of certain measures.

In *Sunday Times*, the Court emphasised the autonomous, Convention-specific character of necessity. This case involved the invocation of the legitimate aim to maintain the authority of the judiciary under Article 10(2) of the Convention. The defendant State argued that this condition was inserted in the Convention because of the institution of contempt which is unique to common law countries. The Court responded that the national legal institution cannot by itself be taken as the measure of whether the relevant action of the State-party is necessary in the sense of the Convention. As the Court summed up:

the reason for the insertion of those words would have been to ensure that the general aims of the law of contempt of court should be considered legitimate aims under Article 10(2) but not to make that law the standard by which to assess whether a given measure was 'necessary'. If and to the extent that Article 10(2) was prompted by the notions underlying either the English law of contempt of court or any other similar domestic institu-

[42] *Handyside v UK*, No 5493/72, Judgment of 7 December 1976, para 48; see also *Silver v UK*, Nos 5947/72; 6205/73; 7052/75, Judgment of 25 March 1983, para 97.

[43] *Sunday Times v UK*, para 59.

tion, it cannot have adopted them as they stood: it transposed them into an autonomous context. It is 'necessity' in terms of the Convention which the Court has to assess, its role being to review the conformity of national acts with the standards of that instrument.[44]

As to whether the relevant measure is necessary, account must be taken of any public interest of the case as balanced against the importance of the relevant Convention right.[45] The requirement of necessity is not considered in all cases. In *Hatton*, both the Third Section and Grand Chamber of the European Court decided the case on the basis of a fair balance struck between the public interest and individual right. At no stage did they examine whether the relevant measures were necessary under Article 8(2) of the Convention.

But in most relevant cases, the standard of necessity is rigorously applied. In *Klass*, the European Court addressed the issue of whether the surveillance of telephones that was pursued as part of the Government's policy of protecting free democratic constitutional order was compatible with the Convention. The Court found that a legitimate aim was indeed present in the Government's action. It still decided to examine whether 'the means provided under the impugned legislation for the achievement of the above-mentioned aim remain in all respects within the bounds of what is necessary in a democratic society'.[46] In other words, the examination of necessity related to the means used to meet the legitimate aim.

The Court emphasised that in identifying the legitimate aim the Government enjoyed certain discretion. It was not for the Court 'to substitute for the assessment of the national authorities any other assessment of what might be the best policy in this field'. Nevertheless, the Court affirmed 'that the Contracting States may not, in the name of the struggle against espionage and terrorism, adopt whatever measures they deem appropriate'.[47] As a measure of whether the necessity test was fulfilled, the Court stressed that when surveillance operates, there must be 'adequate and effective guarantees against abuse'. Whether this is the case 'depends on all the circumstances of the case, such as the nature, scope and duration of the possible measures, the grounds required for ordering such measures, the authorities competent to permit, carry out and supervise such measures, and the kind of remedy provided by the national law'.[48]

The Court noted that there was an administrative procedure regulating in strict terms the use and authorisation of the surveillance measures, and prescribing the time limit within which the material thus obtained could be stored. The applicants considered that the absence of judicial control in this case caused this process to operate in reality as political control.[49] The Court held that although judicial control was in principle desirable, its exclusion did not 'exceed the limits

[44] *Id*, para 60.
[45] *Id*, para 65.
[46] *Klass v FRG*, No 5029/71, Judgment of 6 September 1978, para 46.
[47] *Id*, para 49.
[48] *Id*, para 50.
[49] *Id*, paras 51–54.

of what may be deemed necessary in a democratic society'. The process was controlled by the Parliamentary body, which included wide political representation, and this reduced the risk of politically motivated surveillance.[50] Therefore, the Court held that there were enough safeguards to consider that the German Government identified its measures as necessary in a democratic society.

In *Sunday Times*, the Court found that the injunction granted in relation to the relevant publication was not necessary within the meaning of Article 10(2) of the Convention. That publication would not, contrary to the Government's assertion, have the effect of undermining the authority of the judiciary.[51]

That the relevance of necessity is controlled by the nature of the right can be seen in the *United Communist Party* case. The Court in this case found that freedom of association under Article 11 is a very fundamental right, indispensable in a democratic society. Consequently, 'in determining whether a necessity within the meaning of Article 11(2) exists, the Contracting Parties possess only a limited margin of appreciation, which goes hand in hand with rigorous European supervision embracing both the law and the decisions applying it'.[52] The Court concluded that neither the name nor the programme of the party made out a case for the necessity of Government interference.

In *Otto-Preminger Institut*, the European Court affirmed that 'as a matter of principle it may be considered necessary in certain democratic societies to sanction or even prevent improper attacks on objects of religious veneration'. This may be justified in relation to 'possible expressions that are gratuitously offensive to others and thus an infringement of their rights, and which therefore do not contribute to any form of public debate capable of furthering progress in human affairs'.[53] The Court considered that by the seizure of the offensive film in the Tyrolean region dominated by Catholicism 'the Austrian authorities acted to ensure religious peace in that region and to prevent that some people should feel the object of attacks on their religious beliefs in an unwarranted and offensive manner'. These authorities were 'better placed than the international judge, to assess the need for such a measure in the light of the situation obtaining locally at a given time'. Thus, their action was in accordance with Article 10(2) as a measure aimed at the protection of morals.[54]

The case of *Wingrove v UK* dealt with restrictions on circulation of video work. The applicant complained of a breach of Article 10. The Court concluded that the national authorities are in a better position to judge the necessity of interfering with such exercise of this right as will 'cause substantial offence to persons of a particular religious persuasion'. The relevant video work clearly had offensive content and the British authorities were justified in imposing limitations on it.[55]

[50] *Id*, paras 55–56. [51] *Sunday Times*, para 62.

[52] *United Communist Party v Turkey*, No 19392/92, Judgment of 30 January 1998, paras 45–46.

[53] *Otto-Preminger Institut v Austria*, No 13470/87, Judgment of 25 November 1994, para 50.

[54] *Id*, para 56.

[55] *Wingrove v UK*, No 17419/90, Judgment of 25 November 1996, paras 58 and 61.

(b) WTO Law

In *Korea–Beef*, the WTO Appellate Body examined the issue of whether the dual retail system established by Korea in relation to imported beef was necessary to ensure compliance with its laws of market regulation.[56] The Appellate Body proceeded to specify the characteristics of the concept of necessity under GATT:

> as used in the context of Article XX(d), the reach of the word 'necessary' is not limited to that which is 'indispensable' or 'of absolute necessity' or 'inevitable'. Measures which are indispensable or of absolute necessity or inevitable to secure compliance certainly fulfil the requirements of Article XX(d). But other measures, too, may fall within the ambit of this exception. As used in Article XX(d), the term 'necessary' refers, in our view, to a range of degrees of necessity. At one end of this continuum lies 'necessary' understood as 'indispensable'; at the other end, is 'necessary' taken to mean as 'making a contribution to'. We consider that a 'necessary' measure is, in this continuum, located significantly closer to the pole of 'indispensable' than to the opposite pole of simply 'making a contribution to'.[57]

The necessity of the action is measured on the one hand by 'the extent to which the measure contributes to the realisation of the end pursued, the securing of compliance with the law or regulation at issue. The greater the contribution, the more easily a measure might be considered to be "necessary". ' On the other hand, 'the extent to which the compliance measure produces restrictive effects on international commerce' must be considered. This means that 'A measure with a relatively slight impact upon imported products might more easily be considered as "necessary" than a measure with intense or broader restrictive effects.'[58]

The relevance and appropriateness of every measure under Article XX depends on 'the relative importance of the common interests or values that the law or regulation to be enforced is intended to protect. The more vital or important those common interests or values are, the easier it would be to accept as "necessary" a measure designed as an enforcement instrument.' The evaluation of measures which are not indispensable but still may be necessary involves an assessment of the relative importance of the relevant interests.[59] Similarly, in *US–Gambling*, the Appellate Body emphasised that the relative value of the interests must be weighed and balanced. The Appellate Body reiterated the two requirements for judging the necessity of the relevant measure: its contribution to the realisation of the ends it pursues, and its restrictive impact on international commerce.[60]

In this process, as is emphasised in *Korea–Beef*, it is relevant whether there are other measures available to the State that it could be reasonably expected to employ, and through which it could meet its aims with less impact on trade.[61]

[56] *Korea–Beef*, AB Report, para 159.
[57] *Id*, para 161; further confirmed in *US–Gambling*, AB Report, para 310.
[58] *Korea–Beef*, AB Report, para 163.
[59] *Id*, para 162.
[60] *US–Gambling*, AB Report, para 306.
[61] *Korea–Beef*, AB Report, paras 165–170.

Korea argued that the alternative measures must not only be available but also guarantee the level of enforcement it sought through the introduction of the dual retail system, that is the elimination of fraud. The Appellate Body thought it unlikely that Korea sought to establish a system that would totally eliminate fraud, and other WTO-consistent measures were still available and relevant. The Appellate Body was not convinced that Korea could not achieve the same result through police enforcement measures, such as well-targeted measures of control.[62] Hence, the Appellate Body ruled against Korea.

In assessing US measures to protect public morality and public order in the *US–Gambling* case, the Appellate Body treated this issue in terms of the required necessity of the relevant measures.[63] Above all, the Appellate Body emphasised that 'the standard of "necessity" provided for in the general exceptions provision is an *objective* standard'. The dispute settlement bodies are not bound by the State-party's characterisations of the relevant measures as necessary.[64]

The Appellate Body referred to the finding of the Panel in the same case that the United States had identified legitimate interests that made its measures restrictive of gambling practices necessary under Article XIV GATS, but these measures still were not necessary because the United States did not hold consultations on this issue with Antigua—the other party to the case. The Panel had identified no other viable alternative to the US measures. The consultations suggested would not have been comparable to the measures that the US adopted.[65] Therefore, the Appellate Body ruled on this issue in favour of the United States.

In terms of proving the necessity of the relevant measures, as the Appellate Body ruled in *US–Gambling*, 'a responding party invoking an affirmative defence bears the burden of demonstrating its measure'. Therefore, 'the responding party must show that its measure [under Article XIV GATS] is "necessary" to achieve objectives relating to public morals or public order'. Nevertheless, there are some limitations as to how far the respondent's burden of proof goes. The respondent is not obliged to show that 'there are *no* reasonably available alternatives to achieve its objectives. In particular, a responding party need not identify the universe of less trade-restrictive alternative measures and then show that none of those measures achieves the desired objective. The WTO agreements do not contemplate such an impracticable and, indeed, often impossible burden.'[66]

(c) Bilateral Treaties

The security interest exception clauses in some bilateral treaties refer to the concept of necessity as the measure of lawfulness of action undertaken under those

[62] *Id*, paras 175, 178, 180.
[63] *US–Gambling*, AB Report, paras 301–302.
[64] *Id*, para 304 (emphasis original).
[65] *Id*, paras 321–326.
[66] *Id*, para 309 (emphasis original).

clauses. In the *Nicaragua* case, the International Court accepted the determination of the United States that the situation in Central America in the 1970s and 1980s raised issues in terms of their 'essential security interests' under Article XXI of the 1956 FCN Treaty between the US and Nicaragua. For instance, the measure of blockade against Nicaragua was an economic one and fell within the purview of Article XXI. However, the Court concluded that this clause was not self-judging. The Court had to determine whether the relevant actions were 'necessary' to satisfy the essential security interests of the United States. The Court was unable to conclude that this was the case. There was no evidence to show how the Nicaraguan policies became a threat to the 'essential security interests' of the United States.[67]

In *Oil Platforms*, the United States claimed that it considered in good faith that the attacks on the platforms were necessary to protect its essential security interests. This meant that a measure of discretion should be afforded to a party's good faith application of measures to protect its essential security interests under Article XX of the 1955 Iran–US Treaty.[68] The Court noted that Iran was prepared to recognise some of the interests referred to by the United States—the safety of United States vessels and crew, and the uninterrupted flow of maritime commerce in the Persian Gulf—as its reasonable security interests. But Iran denied that the United States' actions against the platforms could be regarded as 'necessary' to protect those interests. The Court, as seen above, refused to use the test of necessity and to admit the margin of appreciation.[69]

(d) Humanitarian Law

In international humanitarian law, the concept of necessity, or military necessity, determines the appropriateness of combat action by a State. It is often assumed that humanitarian law balances the considerations of military necessity against humanitarian considerations. This can only be true in a descriptive sense. Military necessity is no general principle accepted as such in the framework of humanitarian law. It is a defence admitted only in the specific norms which by their nature can admit the relevance of military necessity, such as the norms on attack, or property destruction. It could never be enough to state in general terms that the law of armed conflict confronts the 'built-in tension' between military necessity and humanitarian considerations, balances them against each other, and does not lose sight of any of these factors.[70] This position leaves open the question as to what the regulation should be in specific contexts. The answer to this question

[67] *ICJ Reports*, 1986, 141.
[68] *Oil Platforms*, para 73.
[69] *Id*, para 73.
[70] *Cf*, Y Dinstein, *The Conduct of Hostilities under the Law of International Armed Conflict* (2004), 17.

depends on the content of individual rules of humanitarian law regulating the specific types of belligerent action. As for balancing necessity against humanity, it has to be borne in mind that treaties such as the 1949 Geneva Conventions and their 1977 Additional Protocols have been adopted as instruments facilitating the protection of individuals, with corresponding limitations on the freedom of belligerents. Thus, the core of legal regulation of military necessity does not place the interest of the belligerent and the interest of the protected individual on the same footing.

The plea of necessity can only be relevant in the case of rules which by their nature admit the operation of this concept. Rules on the selection of military or civilian objects in targeting during combat operations essentially control the operation of the requirements of necessity and proportionality. Whether or not an attack on the relevant object is justified is basically the same as whether it is necessary to attack it and whether the attack would be proportionate.

Humanitarian law establishes criteria for distinguishing between military and civilian targets. According to Article 52(1) of the I Additional Protocol of 1997, 'all objects which are not military objects' are civilian objects. Military objects in their turn are defined as those 'which by their nature, location, purpose or use make an effective contribution to military action and whose total or partial destruction, capture or neutralization, in the circumstances ruling at the time, offers a definite military advantage'. According to Article 52(3), in case of doubt as to whether an object normally dedicated to civilian purposes, such as a place of worship, a house or other dwelling, or a school is being used to make an effective contribution to military action, it shall be presumed not to be so used. These treaty clauses are particularly important as State practice, including national court decisions both before and after the entry into force of the relevant treaties, suggest different outcomes. Reliance on State practice as such can often result in affirming the lack of definite regulation on the issue of military necessity as a matter of humanitarian law. Therefore, it is vital to bear in mind the inherent link between the concept of necessity and the distinction between military and civilian targets as affirmed in the relevant conventions which would override any conflicting practice as *lex specialis* in the first place and possibly also as customary law.

Judicial practice on the application of humanitarian law conforms to the above legal framework of necessity. This presumption that the object in question is not used as a military object was treated as an imperative of international humanitarian law by the ICTY Appeals Chamber in *Kordic*.[71] In *Galic*, the ICTY Trial Chamber held that 'For the purpose of the protection of victims of armed conflict, the term "civilian" is defined negatively as anyone who is not a member of the armed forces or of an organized military group belonging to a party to

[71] *Kordic*, Appeals Chamber, IT-95–14/2-A, Judgment of 17 December 2004, para 53.

the conflict.'[72] The Trial Chamber defined the concept of civilian population in *Strugar*:

> members of the civilian population are people who are not taking any active part in the hostilities, including members of the armed forces who laid down their arms and those persons placed *hors de combat* by sickness, wounds, detention or any other cause.[73]

In *Blaskic*, the Trial Chamber held that 'civilian property covers any property that could not be legitimately considered a military objective'.[74] Furthermore, in *Naletilic*, the Trial Chamber rejected the argument that in order to be protected as civilian objects, the relevant institutions 'must not have been in the vicinity of military objectives'. The Chamber did not concur with the view that the mere fact that an institution is in the 'immediate vicinity of military objective' justifies its destruction.[75] In *Galic*, the Appeals Chamber observed that the presence of individual combatants in civilian areas does not necessarily change the legal status of the civilian population. The proportion of combatants and civilians in the area, as well as the question of whether combatants are on duty or on leave will count in the determination of this issue.[76]

Once the categories of the relevant objects and targets are delimited, the scope of operation of the factor of necessity can be duly identified. Necessity can only be invoked in relation to military objects. In *Blaskic*, the Appeals Chamber observed that 'there is an absolute prohibition on the targeting of civilians in customary international law'.[77] As the Appeals Chamber observed in *Kordic*:

> The prohibition against attacking civilians stems from a fundamental principle of international humanitarian law, the principle of distinction, which obliges warring parties to distinguish *at all times* between the civilian population and combatants, between civilian objects and military objectives and accordingly to direct military operations only against military objectives.

Here, the Appeals Chamber follows the International Court's jurisprudence in affirming the intransgressible character of these principles.[78] The Trial Chamber in *Galic* also discussed limits on military necessity, observing that 'civilians and the civilian population as such should not be the object of attack. [Article 51 of the I Additional Protocol] does not mention any exceptions. In particular, it does not contemplate derogating from this rule by invoking military necessity.'[79] The Appeals Chamber also reiterated that targeting civilians cannot be justified by military necessity, because the prohibition against targeting civilians is absolute.[80]

[72] *Galic*, Trial Chamber, IT-98–29-T, Judgment of 5 December 2003, para 47.

[73] *Strugar*, Trial Chamber, IT-01–42-T, Judgment of 31 January 2005, para 282.

[74] *Blaskic*, Trial Chamber, IT-95–14-A, Judgment of 3 March 2000, para 180.

[75] *Naletilic*, Trial Chamber, IT-98–34-T, Judgment of 31 March 2003, para 604.

[76] *Galic*, Appeals Chamber, paras 136–137.

[77] *Blaskic*, Appeals Chamber, IT-95–14-A, Judgment of 29 July 2004, para 109; reaffirmed in *Strugar*, Trial Chamber, para 280; *Galic*, Appeals Chamber, IT-98–29-A, Judgment of 30 November 2006, para 130.

[78] *Kordic*, para 54 (emphasis added).

[79] *Galic*, Trial Chamber, para 44.

[80] *Galic*, Appeals Chamber, para 130.

The character of actions undertaken in an attack can define the profile of that attack and hence be indicative of whether the military necessity can be invoked in relation to it. In *Strugar*, the Trial Chamber identified the attack on civilians in the blockade organised at Dubrovnik by the Yugoslav armed forces:

> one apparent objective of the JNA blockade of Dubrovnik was to force capitulation of the Croatian defending forces by the extreme hardship the civilian population was being compelled to endure by virtue of the blockade.
>
> In the Chamber's finding it is particularly obvious that the presence of a large civilian population in the Old Town, as well as in the wider Dubrovnik, was known to the JNA attackers, in particular the Accused and his subordinates, who variously ordered, planned and directed the forces during the attack.

At the same time, JNA was proved not to have targeted any military target while shelling the Old Town in Dubrovnik. Due to these factors, the Chamber was in a position to find that 'the elements of the offence of attacks on a civilian population and civilian objects have been established'.[81] In *Galic*, the Trial Chamber affirmed that 'indiscriminate attacks, that is to say, attacks which strike civilians or civilian objects and military objectives without distinction, may qualify as direct attacks against civilians'.[82] The Appeals Chamber also affirmed that 'direct attack can be inferred from the indiscriminate character of the weapon used'.[83]

It follows that if not all precautions are taken and risks assessed, what would otherwise be an attack against a legitimate military object becomes an attack against civilians. It is punishable under international criminal law as a grave breach of international humanitarian law.

A plea of necessity will be allowed only against military objects when collateral casualties are not excessive in relation to the military advantage gained. In *Blaskic*, the Appeals Chamber developed criteria for judging whether the relevant attack can be justified by military necessity. The Chamber dealt with the attack of 16 April 1993 on Stari Vitez, and noted that this town had at that time a large presence of Bosnian forces and the attack resulted in a battle. There was no proof that the attack was directed against the civilian population. Therefore, the attack was not unlawful *per se*.[84] The operation of necessity in relation to military targets was dealt with in *Hadjihasanovic*, where the Trial Chamber observed that:

> collateral damage to civilian property may be justified by military necessity and may be an exception to the principles of protection of civilian property. Relying primarily on the principles set out in Articles 57 and 58 of Additional Protocol I, the Chamber in *Kupreškić* held that the protection of civilians and civilian property provided by modern international law may cease entirely, or be reduced or suspended, when the target of a

[81] *Strugar*, paras 285–289.

[82] *Galic*, Trial Chamber, para 57.

[83] *Galic*, Appeals Chamber, para 132.

[84] *Blaskic*, Appeals Chamber, paras 438, 466; the Appeals Chamber also reversed the Trial Chamber's finding that the majority of the victims were civilians, on the basis of the evidence presented to it, *id*, para 441.

military attack is comprised of military objectives and belligerents cannot avoid causing collateral damage to civilians.[85]

Consequently,

the offence of wanton destruction of towns and villages is constituted when acts of destruction not justified by military necessity are committed deliberately and on a large scale. The criterion of large scale must be evaluated according to the facts of the case.[86]

In the same case, the Trial Chamber held, by reference to the kind of weapons used, and the number of houses destroyed, that the attack did not result in wanton destruction not justified by military necessity.[87] In other cases, where destruction was on a large scale and the damage was caused intentionally, the Trial Chamber did rule in the same case that the destructions was wanton and not justified by military necessity.[88]

This practice confirms that necessity in international humanitarian law is not a free-standing and autonomous principle. It can only be relevant where the specific context of legal regulation allows this. The law before the adoption of the 1949 Geneva Conventions and the 1977 Additional Protocols allegedly admitted of the free-standing and general principle of necessity, capable on its own of justifying certain combat actions. The US Military Tribunal in Nuremberg gave the following description of the essence of military necessity:

Military necessity permits a belligerent, subject to the laws of war, to apply any amount and kind of force to compel the complete submission of the enemy with the least possible expenditure of time, life, and money. ... It permits the destruction of life of armed enemies and other persons whose destruction is incidentally unavoidable by the armed conflicts of the war; it allows the capturing of armed enemies and others of peculiar danger, but does not permit the killing of innocent inhabitants for purposes of revenge or the satisfaction of a lust to kill. The destruction of property to be lawful must be imperatively demanded by the necessities of war. Destruction as an end in itself is a violation of international law. There must be some reasonable connection between the destruction of property and the overcoming of the enemy forces. It is lawful to destroy railways, lines of communication, or any other property that might be utilised by the enemy. Private homes and churches may be destroyed if necessary for military operations.[89]

This description does not distinguish between types of military attack against objects in different categories. In addition, it admits that anything that 'might' be used by the adversary can be the object of lawful military attack. This approach can no longer be valid after the above-mentioned treaties, and customary law established pursuant to them, has replaced the law that existed before. This development has definitely limited the relevance of military necessity only to purely

[85] *Hadjihasanovic*, IT-01–47-T, Trial Chamber, Judgment of 15 March 2006, para 45.
[86] *Id*, para 48.
[87] *Id*, paras 1797, 1830.
[88] *Id*, paras 1844–1845.
[89] *In re List (Hostages Trial)*, US Military Tribunal at Nuremberg, 15 *AD* 636–637.

military objects as defined by modern law. The law codified in Articles 51 and 52 of the 1977 I Additional Protocol, as applied in jurisprudence, clearly confirms that the plea of necessity as a free-standing and wide-ranging principle can no longer find a valid place in humanitarian law.

The normative framework and its application in practice demonstrate the limits on the concept of military necessity and limit this only to where military targets are attacked. The requirement of assessment of the adequacy of military advantage against civilian losses applies only in cases where the object attacked is a legitimate military object in the first place. In relation to attacks against civilians or indiscriminate attacks, there can be no balancing tests. The prohibition on attacking civilians is absolute, without any regard to the requirement of military necessity. With these attacks, claims about incidental or collateral damage are simply irrelevant. With regard to attacks against military objects, the normative framework refers to the verifiable factual element. This is the presence in the relevant area of military personnel and equipment. Thus, necessity refers not to the common sense necessity to ensure military victory and submission by the enemy. This is the specialised meaning of necessity to achieve military advantage in relation to and through targeting a legitimate military objective.

As was seen above, in human rights law, notably under the ECHR, and in WTO law, necessity does not equate to indispensability. But in humanitarian law, there is no such measure for necessity. It is either allowed or it is not. In humanitarian law, necessity is not systemic permission for the State to justify its non-compliance with or deviation from its obligations under a treaty. The freedom of action allowed in armed conflict does not conflict with the prohibition of attacks of a certain kind. When the attack or destruction is prohibited, no necessity, even as presented as essential or inevitable, can justify it or make it lawful. When the attack is allowed, the State does not have to justify it by invoking certain degrees of necessity—it is simply a lawful act of war.

(e) The Law of the Use of Force

In the law of the use of force, the requirement of necessity operates in relation to the exercise by the State of its inherent right to self-defence under Article 51 of the United Nations Charter. Just as in other fields of international law, the concept of necessity is not autonomous but can only be invoked after certain preconditions established in law are met. Necessity in *jus ad bellum* is not a commonsense necessity generally measuring the actions that may be necessary to deal with the adversary and win the war. Necessity in the context of self-defence can only be invoked after the State suffers an armed attack, as determined by Article 51 of the Charter. Consequently, necessity shall be assessed in terms of what is necessary to repel that specific armed attack, as opposed to some broader objectives. The question relates to the permissible types and extent of the action in response to the armed attack. This latter requirement ensures that action taken in alleged self-defence does not take the shape of reprisal but remains a preventive action to repulse the actual armed attack.[90]

The International Court's jurisprudence repeatedly affirms that lawfulness of action in self-defence always depends on compliance with the requirements of necessity and proportionality.[91] In *Nicaragua*, the Court dealt with the argument that US mining of Nicaraguan ports was lawful as the alleged exercise of its right to collective self-defence in support of El Salvador. The conditions for the resort to collective self-defence were not fulfilled in this case. Thus, the US action would not become lawful even if carried out in strict compliance with the requirements of necessity and proportionality. However, if the US actions were not in accordance with these canons, this could constitute an additional ground of wrongfulness. Therefore, the Court went on to examine the actual US actions in terms of their necessity and proportionality. The Court concluded that they were not necessary because they were performed months after the Salvadorian Government repulsed the major opposition attack. Nor were they proportionate because the scale of the Nicaraguan aid to Salvadorian rebels, if established, would not match the scale of mining by the US of Nicaraguan ports and attacks on ports and oil installations.[92] Therefore, the US plea of collective self-defence could not be sustained.

In *Oil Platforms*, the Court judged that US attacks on Iranian oil installations could not be regarded as necessary. It is also noteworthy that the Court did not consider as proved that Iran had attacked the US. The Court characterised the US actions in the following passages:

> The Court is not sufficiently convinced that the evidence available supports the contentions of the United States as to the significance of the military presence and activity on the Reshadat oil platforms; and it notes that no such evidence is offered in respect of the Salman and Nasr complexes. However, even accepting those contentions, for the purposes of discussion, the Court is unable to hold that the attacks made on the platforms could have been justified as acts of self-defence. ... In the case both of the attack on the *Sea Isle City* and the mining of the USS *Samuel B. Roberts*, the Court is not satisfied that the attacks on the platforms were necessary to respond to these incidents. In this connection, the Court notes that there is no evidence that the United States complained to Iran of the military activities of the platforms, in the same way as it complained repeatedly of minelaying and attacks on neutral shipping, which does not suggest that the targeting of the platforms was seen as a necessary act. The Court would also observe that in the case of the attack of 19 October 1987, the United States forces attacked the R-4 platform as a 'target of opportunity', not one previously identified as an appropriate military target.[93]

[90] See, for details, A Orakhelashvili, Legal Stability and Claims of Change: the International Court's Treatment of *Jus ad Bellum* and *Jus in Bello*, 75 *Nordic JIL* (2006), 371–407.

[91] The Court affirmed this in its earlier jurisprudence, notably in the *Nicaragua* case, *ICJ Reports*, 1986, 194; the *Nuclear Weapons* Advisory Opinion, *ICJ Reports*, 1996, 245 (where the Court considered this requirement as part of customary law), and the *Oil Platforms* Judgment, General List No 90, paras 51, 76.

[92] *ICJ Reports*, 1986, 122–123.

[93] *Oil Platforms*, para 76.

Thus, the Court examined both the objective situation and subjective side of the US calculation to determine whether the attack on the platform was necessary in terms of *jus ad bellum*.

Similarly, in the *Congo–Uganda* case it was not crucial for the outcome of the case to ascertain whether Uganda's action in its claimed self-defence was necessary to repel the original attack and proportionate to it for there had been no armed attack in the first place. The Court observed that:

> since the preconditions for the exercise of self-defence do not exist in the circumstances of the present case, the Court has no need to enquire whether such an entitlement to self-defence was in fact exercised in circumstances of necessity and in a manner that was proportionate. The Court cannot fail to observe, however, that the taking of airports and towns many hundreds of kilometres from Uganda's border would not seem proportionate to the series of transborder attacks it claimed had given rise to the right of self-defence, nor to be necessary to that end.[94]

Thus the Court emphasised the order in which the issues of self-defence should be examined. But it touched upon the issue of necessity and proportionality which was, strictly speaking, not necessary or crucial in this case. The Court set quite strict requirements in this field as well: the purpose was to contain the violence and allow it only to the extent necessary to repel the armed attack.

(f) Conclusion

In each of the fields examined, the concept of necessity is context-specific. Yet, there is some inherent concept of necessity controlling its application in the variety of fields. Above all, this relates to the predetermined legal conditions after the fulfilment of which necessity comes into play. In human rights law this is the requirement for the State to act 'in accordance with the law'; in the law of self-defence this is the requirement of armed attack; in humanitarian law this is the predetermined qualification of the object of attack as a military object.

Both under *jus ad bellum* and *jus in bello* the meaning of necessity is specialised and strictly functional. Law admits of the necessity to repel armed attack, and the necessity to eliminate the relevant military target. At the same time, the two concepts of necessity relate to different subject-matters. One relates to the necessity of the use of force and the second to the necessity of attack. Under *jus in bello*, necessity cannot imitate the *jus ad bellum* necessity and justify acts that are generally necessary to overcome the enemy. The *jus ad bellum* necessity relates to the necessity of the overall effort countering armed attack. The *jus in bello* necessity relates to the justification of individual acts within the terms of conducting that overall effort.

[94] *Case Concerning the Armed Activities on the Territory of the Congo* (Democratic Republic of the Congo v Uganda), Judgment of 19 December 2005, General List No 116, para 147.

4. Equity

(a) General Aspects of Relevance

Equity has an actual or potential role in different fields of international law. Although much has been written on equity, its relevance in terms of the relationship between law and non-law has not yet been properly and straightforwardly addressed. The crucial question that this analysis addresses is why equity as distinct from or complementary to law is there to impact on the rights and obligations of States, and how far it can go in doing so, either complementing the law or in parallel to it. This analysis identifies as basic issues the normative basis of equity, the scope of relevance of equity, and factors informing equity.

In the fields of international law in which equity is, or can be, resorted to, the response has not been homogenous. In the law of the sea, the delimitation of maritime spaces is widely conducted by reference to equity. The relevance of this concept has been accepted in every single case of delimitation of maritime boundaries in the continental shelf and exclusive economic zones since the Truman Declaration on the continental shelf.[95] In international investment law, the concept of 'fair and equitable treatment', which is based on considerations similar to equity and embodied in hundreds of bilateral investment treaties, is actively used by arbitral tribunals with the result of achieving diverse, sometimes mutually exclusive outcomes.[96] Equity has been given some relevance in assessing compensation to redress the consequences of an internationally wrongful act, for instance in the jurisprudence of the International Court and the European Court of Human Rights. However, in some fields where equity could have potential application due to the nature of the relevant procedures, it has never been used. This holds true for WTO law.[97] For instance, in the non-violation complaints procedure in the WTO, related to adjudication in the absence of determined legal rules and called on to weigh up burdens and benefits, equity is never

[95] M Evans, *Relevant Circumstances and Maritime Delimitation* (1989), 69; further on equity in the law of the sea, see M Evans, Maritime Delimitation and Expanding Categories of Relevant Circumstances, 40 *ICLQ* (1991), 1; AV Lowe, The Role of Equity in International Law, 12 *Australian Yearbook of International Law* (1992), 54; RY Jennings, Equity and Equitable Principles, 42 *Annuaire Suisse De Droit International* (1986), 27; *id*, The Principles Governing Maritime Boundaries in Hailbronner, Ress & Stein (eds), *Staat und Völkerrechtsordnung, Festschrift für Karl Doehring* (1989), 397; R Higgins, *Problems and Process: International Law and How We Use It* (1995), 218–228; H Thirlway, The Law and Procedure of the International Court of Justice, *BYIL* (1989), 49–62; T Rothpfeffer, Equity in the North Sea Continental Shelf Cases, 42 *Nordic Journal of International Law* (1972), 81; M Akehurst, Equity and General Principles of Law, 25 *ICLQ* (1976), 801; R Lapidoth, Equity in International Law, 22 *Israel Law Review* (1987), 161; LDM Nelson, The Roles of Equity in the Delimitation of Maritime Boundaries, 84 *AJIL* (1990), 837; M Mendelson, On the Quasi-Normative Effect of Maritime Boundary Agreements, in N Ando, E McWhinney & R Wolfrun (eds), *Liber Amicorum for Judge Shigeru Oda* (2002), 1069.

[96] Because of the extent of this issue, it is examined separately in the next section.

[97] M Pannizon, *Good Faith in the Jurisprudence of the WTO* (2006), 24.

used. Similarly, equity has never been used in the field of diplomatic protection of nationals. To illustrate, Judge Fitzmaurice in *Barcelona Traction* concluded that the current state of international law is unsatisfactory because it does not allow the State to protect the interests of shareholders as opposed to those of the company. Judge Fitzmaurice advanced the thesis that 'a strict view of the law' as it stood *de lege lata* had to be mitigated and corrected by the use of equity which would allow protection by the State of the nationality of shareholders. Therefore, Judge Fitzmaurice suggested that a 'less inelastic' approach was required in determining standing. Equity should have been deployed to resolve the impasse that this case involved.[98] Similarly, Judge Jessup advanced the idea of this field of law being governed by equity and thus free of strict requirements.[99] The Court itself dealt with the plea of equity in this case, but concluded that equity had no impact on this situation. The potential relevance of equity would not contribute to the clarity and determinacy of the legal position: 'it would be difficult on an equitable basis to make distinctions according to any quantitative test: it would seem that the owner of 1 per cent or the owner of 90 per cent of the share-capital should have the same possibility of enjoying the benefit of diplomatic protection'.[100] The adoption of a position in which to admit the possibility of competing diplomatic claims would cause 'confusion and insecurity in international economic relations'.[101] The legal test on the other hand is straightforward and creates a predictable framework by admitting of the protection of those entities only which are linked to the State of nationality through their separate legal personality, in relation to the wrongs suffered in that capacity. And in general, it is quite unusual to characterise as an impasse the position that looks most natural from the structural perspective of international law as the law governing inter-State relations.

The relevance of equity for the law of diplomatic protection was pleaded but rejected in the *Ahmadou Sadio Diallo* case. The applicant attempted to obtained protection of a shareholder of the company with which it was unable to establish a nationality link. The Applicant, Guinea, did not advance any argument based on the legal rule, but relied on 'considerations of equity' in order to justify the right to exercise its diplomatic protection in favour of Mr. Diallo and, by substitution for Africom-Zaire and Africontainers-Zaire, independently of the violation of the direct rights of the former.[102] The Respondent, the DRC, observed that Guinea was trying to exercise diplomatic protection in a manner contrary to international law. Consequently, the DRC requested the Court to dismiss any possibility of resorting to equity *contra legem*.[103] Guinea for its

[98] *ICJ Reports*, 1970, 84–86.
[99] *Id*, 1970, 199.
[100] *Id*, 1970, 48 (para 94).
[101] *Id*, 1970, 49 (para 96).
[102] *Ahmadou Sadio Diallo*, Preliminary Objections, General List No 103, Judgment of 24 May 2007, para 77.
[103] *Id*, para. 79.

part argued that the equity in this case was *infra legem*, aimed at the reasonable application of the rules on diplomatic protection. This consisted in affording protection to shareholders of the company of the respondent State's nationality in order not to deprive them of all possibility of protection.[104] Guinea's reasoning presumably demonstrates the parties' agreement that equity cannot be used to contradict the established rules of law. The Court's own reasoning does not mention equity, being instead based on the lack of the shareholders' exception to the general international law principles of diplomatic protection. Thus, by requiring the existence of specific exception duly established in customary law instead of assessing the equitability of the result, the Court presumably sent the message that the likelihood of equity being applied to the law of diplomatic protection is very slight.

Equitable considerations have no part to play in human rights law either. The European Court of Human Rights in *Poltoratskiy v Ukraine* encountered the claim that the death row detention of the applicant in dire conditions was to be excused because the State 'encountered serious socio-economic problems in the course of its systemic transition and . . . [was] struggling under difficult economic conditions'. The Court responded that 'lack of resources cannot in principle justify prison conditions which are so poor as to reach the threshold of treatment contrary to Article 3 of the Convention. Moreover, the economic problems faced by Ukraine cannot in any event explain or excuse the particular conditions of detention . . . unacceptable in the present case.'[105]

The position of the WTO law, the law of diplomatic protection and human rights law militate against assuming that equity could ever have a corrective role in relation to the established international legal position. In general, equity can only be relevant in a context where it is referred to in the relevant legal regulation. Absent that, equity can play no role even if the relevant legal context is by its substance allegedly conducive to the use of equity.

International jurisprudence, which extensively elaborates upon aspects of equity, confirms that equity emanates from law and forms part of the idea of law. The principal question at the normative level relates to the normative basis of equity. This is the issue whether equity is based on positive law or forms a transcendent and independent body of equitable norms accepted and incorporated as such in the international legal system. A consequential, and related, question is to what extent courts are inclined to base their reasoning on equity as non-law, especially how the threshold of applying equity must be approached. Instead

[104] *Id*, para 82.

[105] *Poltoratskiy v Ukraine*, Application No 38812/97, Judgment 29 April 2003, paras 145 and 148; in *Broniowski*, the European Court was acting in the context of margin of appreciation and the respective need to strike a fair balance between public and private interests when it made some allowance for the general political and economic situation to be considered in assessing the legality of the position of the Government in relation to certain property claims. *Broniowski v Poland*, 31443/96, Judgment of 22 June 2004, paras 162–163. Therefore, this case does not involve the application of equity.

of focusing, as several contributions do, on preconceived categories of equity *infra legem*, *praeter legem* and *contra legem*, this analysis will focus on that concept of equity which is accepted in international jurisprudence. It will examine the practical aspects of interaction between law and equity and their reciprocal influence.

The problem of equity as non-law and its relationship with law has two principal aspects. The first aspect is the legal basis of equity, namely the question whether equity is based on law or has an independent basis. The second aspect is the extent to which non-law in the shape of equity affects rights and duties of States, by reference to the use in practice of individual equitable criteria.

To understand the proper role of equity, it is necessary to study it in comparison with the related phenomenon of deciding the case *ex aequo et bono*. As Sir Robert Jennings puts it, 'a decision *ex aequo et bono* could well be made without the need of specifically legal training or skill; indeed may perhaps be made better by one with a different skill'.[106] The relationship between equity and deciding the case *ex aequo et bono* is discussed doctrinally and judicially. The International Court's Statute allows a case to be decided using the latter option if the parties expressly empower the Court to that effect. The same would be required with regard to other tribunals. Still, there is a doctrinal trend equating the two categories. Sir Robert Jennings refers to the 'classical role of equity' meant 'to modify a rule of law when it might if strictly applied work injustice'. Thus, law and justice work 'together serving the ends of justice by introducing flexibility, adaptability, and even limitations upon the application and meaning of legal rules'. As there is no straightforward rule on delimitation methods, equity is not really modifying or mitigating any existing rule. What the litigants get 'is in effect a decision *ex aequo et bono* whether they wanted it or not'.[107] It is further observed that 'if equity is not to modify the law, it can have no role to play other than to complicate and confuse the juristic terminology'.[108]

This approach raises several issues. In the first place, it is not clear what the 'classical role of equity' is. Equity in international law functions not because of its 'classical' connotations, but because of and in the way the international legal system accepts it. The 'classical role' of modifying strict law is only one version of equity accepted in various legal systems. This particular version is not accepted in international law. Thus, equity in international law has, in conceptual terms, to be something which does not modify or mitigate strict law, and at the same time can be used by tribunals as a matter of applicable law, as opposed to contractual authorisation *in casu*.

The equation between the two equitable categories is consistently rejected in practice. The Arbitral Tribunal in the *Rann of Kutch* case dealt with the

[106] Jennings (1986), 30.
[107] Jennings (1989), 400–401.
[108] *Id*, 404.

relationship between equity and deciding the case *ex aequo et bono*. The question was whether the 1965 Arbitration Agreement conferred the power to decide the case *ex aequo et bono*. The Tribunal emphasised that equity is part of international law and the parties were free to develop their cases with reliance on equity. However, the wider power to adjudicate *ex aequo et bono* could be exercised by the Tribunal 'only if such power has been conferred on it by mutual agreement between the Parties'. This was not the case with the 1965 Arbitration Agreement.[109] In *Tunisia–Libya*, the Court expressly distinguished equity from a decision *ex aequo et bono*.[110] In *Burkina-Faso/Mali*, the parties had agreed that the application of *ex aequo et bono* was not possible without the International Court's Chamber being specifically authorised to act in this way, even though Mali urged the Chamber to apply that equity which was in its view inseparable from international law.[111] Thus, practice confirms that the two equitable concepts are not identical. The proper role of equity has to be explained by other factors.

That the application of equity is not the same as deciding the case *ex aequo et bono* can be seen from the practice of using equity in assessing compensation for internationally wrongful acts. The International Court emphasised in the *ILO Administrative Tribunal* Advisory Opinion that the application of equity in calculating compensation was not a deviation from applicable law. The application of equitable criteria was instead due to the absence of precise positive legal regulation of the amount of compensation for internationally wrongful acts. The relevance of equity related merely to the determination of true measure of compensation.[112] Significantly enough, the International Court in the *North Sea* case referred to this practice as supportive of its approach that 'it is precisely a rule of law that calls for the application of equitable principles'.[113] The award of 'equitable' compensation by the European Court of Human Rights should also be seen from this perspective. All in all, the role of equity in the assessment of compensation is not an aspect of substantive regulation of rights and obligations in international law. It merely relates to applying law to facts as a way of calculating damage, injury and the amount to be awarded. Equity in this sense relates to the enforcement of legal prescriptions and hardly specifically raises the question of indeterminacy.

While equity is essential in the law of maritime delimitation, it is disputed whether equitable considerations can find application in the law of territorial boundaries as well. The argument runs not only as affirming or rejecting the relevance of equity, but also as attempting to differentiate among its various

[109] *Rann of Kutch Arbitration* (India and Pakistan), The Indo-Pakistan Western Boundary Case Tribunal, Award of 19 February 1968, 7 *ILM* (1968), 633 at 642–643.

[110] *ICJ Reports*, 1982, 60.

[111] *ICJ Reports*, 1986, 567.

[112] *Judgments of the ILO upon Complaints Made against UNESCO*, Advisory Opinion, *ICJ Reports*, 1956, 100.

[113] *ICJ Reports*, 1969, 48.

aspects. As the International Court's Chamber recapitulated in *Burkina-Faso/Mali*, Burkina-Faso 'emphasized that in the field of territorial boundary delimitation there is no equivalent to the concept of "equitable principles" so frequently referred to by the law applicable in the delimitation of maritime areas. Mali did not question this statement; it explained that what it had in mind was simply the equity which is a normal part of the due application of law.'[114] Mali's position could be a subtle plea in favour of equity while expressly refusing to plead in its favour. This could also be an attempt, if impliedly, to distinguish to between equity and deciding the case *ex aequo et bono*, in a way pleading the former and rejecting the latter. As the Chamber specified:

the Chamber cannot decide *ex aequo et bono* in this case. Since the Parties; have not entrusted it with the task of carrying out an adjustment of their respective interests, it must also dismiss any possibility of resorting to equity *contra legem*. Nor will the Chamber apply equity *praeter legem*. On the other hand, it will have regard to equity *infra legem*, that is, that form of equity which constitutes a method of interpretation of the law in force, and is one of its attributes. As the Court has observed: "It is not a matter of finding simply an equitable solution, but an equitable solution derived from the applicable law." (*Fisheries Jurisdiction, I. C.J. Reports 1974*, p. 33, para. 78; p. 202, para. 69.) How in practice the Chamber will approach recourse to this kind of equity in the present case will emerge from its application throughout this Judgment of the principles and rules which it finds to be applicable.[115]

In general, as Thirlway puts it, 'One would not expect equity to play any role in the judicial determination of a land frontier: unlike a continental shelf boundary, a land frontier is simply the product of historical processes—agreement, occupation of *uti possidetis*—that produce a defined result as a matter of law, no matter how inequitable that result may seem from some points of view.'[116] The approach of the Chamber in *Burkina-Faso/Mali* indeed inaugurates this approach:

The Chamber would however stress more generally that to resort to the concept of equity in order to modify an established frontier would be quite unjustified. Especially in the African context, the obvious deficiencies of many Frontiers inherited from colonization, from the ethnic, geographical or administrative standpoint, cannot support an assertion that the modification of these frontiers is necessary or justifiable on the ground of considerations of equity. These frontiers, however unsatisfactory they may be, possess the authority of the *uti possidetis* and are thus fully in conformity with contemporary international law.[117]

Equity, then, could step in where a frontier has not been agreed through treaty or *effectivités* that also imply an element of agreement. As the Chamber stated, 'in the

[114] *ICJ Reports*, 1986, 567.

[115] *Id*, 567–568, 633.

[116] H Thirlway, The Law and Procedure of the International Court of Justice 1960–1989: Supplement, 2005, *BYIL* 2005, 1 at 27.

[117] *Id*, 633.

absence of any precise indication in the texts of the position of the frontier line, the line should divide' the relevant frontier area 'in two, in an equitable manner'.[118] The unsuitability of equity to affect treaty-based regulation or the operation of the *uti possidetis* rule is demonstrated by the approach of the Court's Chamber in the *El Salvador/Honduras* case, in which 'even equity *infra legem*, a recognised concept of international law, could not be resorted to in order to modify an established frontier inherited from colonisation, whatever its deficiencies'.[119]

This consistent approach of the International Court demonstrates the unsuitability of claims voiced in doctrine or practice in favour of modifying, disregarding or abandoning established legal positions because of their deficiency, unreasonability or social unacceptability. As international rules are based on what States agree on, subjective considerations of equity, rationality or reasonableness do not impact on international rights and duties. They belong to the field of non-law.

(b) The Indeterminacy of Equity

Equity, it is said, serves achieving 'justice according to the rule of law'.[120] As Judge Ammoun stated in the *North Sea Continental Shelf* case, 'To do no more than declare that agreement should be reached on an equitable delimitation is not to resolve the question, for the Parties may well be divided as to what is an equitable delimitation and as to the means of determining it. The Court should therefore... state the rule which is capable of being adopted by application of the principle of equity.'[121] As the Chamber of the International Court emphasised in *Gulf of Maine*, there is 'no systematic definition of the equitable criteria' applicable to maritime delimitation and it would be very difficult to make such definition *a priori*.[122] Judge Shahabuddeen also emphasised in *Jan Mayen* that equity and equitable solution are indeterminate legal concepts.[123]

There are a number of circumstances that contribute to such indeterminacy. The International Court of Justice has consistently refused to identify equity with any concept, value, or principle that would have given it independent and straightforward applicability. In the first place, the International Court refuses to identify equity with equality. According to the Court, the application of equity in matters of maritime delimitation does not necessarily ensure equality of the relevant States in terms of the maritime spaces allocated. Secondly, the International Court refuses to identify equity with distributive justice. While impacting on

[118] *Id*, 633.
[119] *ICJ Reports*, 1992, 396.
[120] *Case concerning Continental Shelf* (Libyan Arab Jamahiriya/Malta), Judgment of 3 June 1985, *ICJ Reports*, 1985, 13 at 39.
[121] *ICJ Reports*, 1969, 145.
[122] *Gulf of Maine* (Canada v USA), *ICJ Reports*, 1984, 246 at 312.
[123] Separate Opinion, *ICJ Reports*, 1993, 152.

the allocation of spaces and resources in the international legal system, equity does not require the correction of disadvantages or making a State better off than it actually is.[124] Thirdly, equity should not be understood as contradicting the nature of the relevant legal institutions. It is repeatedly affirmed in jurisprudence that the application of equity in maritime delimitation should not distort the legal nature of the legal institution of the continental shelf.

Thus equity is no absolute justice, but justice as applied in and to, and permitted by, the relevant factual and legal context. This is one of the implications of denoting equity as individualised justice. Equity provides no independent yardstick for assessing what is or is not just. Thus, equity can make no straightforward and independent impact on the ground, which means that it has no capability to duplicate or imitate the operation of law.

True, as the International Court emphasised in *Libya–Malta*, consolidating earlier findings in jurisprudence, there are some straightforward and determinate standards related to the operation of equity:

That equitable principles are expressed in terms of general application, is immediately apparent from a glance at some well-known examples: the principle that there is to be no refashioning of geography, or compensating for the inequalities of nature; the related principle of non-encroachment by one party on the natural prolongation of the other, which is no more than the negative expression of the positive rule that the coastal State enjoys sovereign rights over the continental shelf to the full extent authorised by international law in the relevant circumstances.[125]

In *Gulf of Maine*, the Court also delivered its perception equity:

There is, for example, the criterion expressed by the classical formula that the land dominates the sea; the criterion advocating, in cases where no special circumstances require correction thereof, the equal division of the areas of overlap of the maritime and submarine zones appertaining to the respective coasts of neighbouring States; the criterion that, whenever possible, the seaward extension of a State's coast should not encroach upon areas that are too close to the coast of another State; the criterion of preventing, as far as possible, any cut-off of the seaward projection of the coast or of part of the coast of either of the States concerned; and the criterion whereby, in certain circumstances, the appropriate consequences may be drawn from any inequalities in the extent of the coasts of two States into the same area of delimitation.[126]

Other cases have also suggested some straightforward principles. As was specified in the *St Pierre/Miquelon* Arbitration, a proposal which would deprive a coast or islands of any maritime area beyond the territorial sea is not equitable.[127]

[124] *Case concerning Continental Shelf* (Libyan Arab Jamahiriya/Malta), Judgment of 3 June 1985, *ICJ Reports*, 1985, 13 at 39–40.

[125] *ICJ Reports*, 1985, 39.

[126] *ICJ Reports*, 1984, 312–313, para 157.

[127] *Case Concerning the Delimitation of Maritime Areas between Canada and the French Republic*, 31 ILM (1992), 1169.

Furthermore, it cannot be equitable to deprive a territory of the exclusive economic zone altogether.

What is missing in this reasoning is the positive content of equity. Despite these straightforward and direct formulations, these passages only clarify what equity cannot do, and what the limitations on equity are. They do not say what equity means and what the equitable standards are. We can see from this that equity, whatever its content, is subject to inherent limitations. On the one hand, some factual preconditions, whatever the degree of their normative status, qualify and prevail over the considerations of equity. On the other hand, equity is simply of no avail against the strict legal norms following from the territorial sovereignty of States. Few positive aspects of these statements, especially in *Gulf of Maine*, elaborate on questions of law, such as the basis of entitlement to maritime areas. These are the facts which are accorded law-making relevance by the legal system, to determine the content of equity and its reach. One positive principle influencing the choice of equitable methods, though providing no method in itself, is enunciated in the *Guinea/Guinea-Bissau* Arbitral Award. It affirms that each party shall have control over the maritime territory opposite to and in the vicinity of its coast.[128] But this does not translate into the delimitation method. In fact, the Tribunal in this case rejected the equidistance method.

(c) The Essence of the Quasi-Normative Character of Equity

The role of equity in international law is unique, as is consistent with the character of this legal system. More specifically, equity is not a system which exists separately from international law, or imitates independent legal solutions, or is meant to correct the existing legal position. The relevance of equity follows either from treaty stipulation or from the fundamental rule that requires equitable delimitation. There are still doctrinal attempts to portray equity as modifying the existing legal position in a case. As Jennings suggests, the very relevance of equity consists in modifying what legal rules require.[129]

This argument notwithstanding, there is nothing in the content of equity which could contradict or attempt to modify the content of any accepted legal norm. Equity simply covers the field on which consensually agreed legal norms are silent. In practice too, it is consistently acknowledged that the modifying or corrective role of equity is irrelevant. As Judge Hudson observed in the case of *Diversion of Water from the Meuse River*, 'a sharp division between law and equity, such as prevails in the administration of justice in some States, should find no place in international jurisprudence'.[130] As the International Court emphasised

[128] *Delimitation of Maritime Boundary between Guinea and Guinea-Bissau*, Award of 14 February 1985, para 98.

[129] Jennings (1989), 404.

[130] *PCIJ Series* A/B, No 70, at 76.

in *Tunisia/Libya*, international law does not accept the concept of equity recognised in some national legal systems, which is meant to mitigate the severity of the rules of positive law.[131] Similarly, Judge Weeramantry observed in *Jan Mayen* that the attitude of equity as corrective of legal norms is inapplicable to international law.[132]

In terms of defining equity, Lowe considers equity as a body of general principles of justice as opposed to fixed rules of law.[133] As the International Court observes in *North Sea Continental Shelf*, 'it is not a question of applying equity simply as a matter of abstract justice, but of applying the rule of law which itself requires the application of the equitable principles'.[134] Although, as illustrated below, equitable criteria themselves are not law, equity, as the International Court affirmed in *Tunisia–Libya*, is a legal concept and a direct emanation of justice, 'the legal concept of equity is a general principle directly applicable as law'.[135] Similarly, as the Arbitral Tribunal emphasised in *Guinea/Guinea-Bissau*, the application of equity is not a decision *ex aequo et bono*, but the 'findings must be based on considerations of law'.[136] In *Libya–Malta*, the International Court pointed to the 'normative character of equitable principles applied as a part of general international law'.[137] In *Gulf of Maine*, the Chamber of the Court referred to 'the equitable criteria whose application is called for by the law itself'.[138]

The basic dilemma is that while equity has no straightforwardly determinate content and value, it is still treated as a concept of general applicability that impacts on the rights and duties of States. In other words, as Judge Shahabuddeen observes, equity is in essence 'the individualisation of justice, through the application of legal norms framed in terms of standards, in such a way as to reconcile a tolerable degree of predictability with the need to adjust to the peculiarities of a special situation'.[139] According to Judge Weeramantry, the International Court in applying equity 'should concentrate on the variable facts of each separate case rather than on a search for overriding rules which are common to all'.[140]

As Judge Arechaga emphasised in *Tunisia–Libya*, equity should not be viewed as 'a correction or moderation of a non-existent rule of law, but as a "lead rule" well adapted to the shape of the situation to be measured'. It is based on 'the need to maintain consistency and uniformity in the legal principles and rules applicable to a series of situations which are characterised by their multiple diversity'.[141]

[131] *Case concerning Continental Shelf* (Tunisia/Libyan Arab Jamahiriya), Judgment of 24 February 1982, *ICJ Reports*, 1982, 18 at 60.
[132] Separate Opinion, *ICJ Reports*, 1993, 250.
[133] Lowe (1992), 54.
[134] *ICJ Reports*, 1969, 47.
[135] *ICJ Reports*, 1982, 60.
[136] *Guinea/Guinea-Bissau*, para 88.
[137] *ICJ Reports*, 1985, 39.
[138] *ICJ Reports*, 1984, 343.
[139] Separate Opinion, *ICJ Reports*, 1993, 195.
[140] *Id*, 1993, 257.
[141] *Id*, 1993, 106.

This means providing a degree of legitimacy through the use of initially undefined standards and criteria. On the one hand this emphasises the overarching goal of equitable solution. On the other hand, this places the whole process within the framework of law through acknowledging the limits imposed by law in the field of application of equitable principles.

The dual essence of equity described above is most conveniently explained in the *Libya–Malta* Judgment. The Court explains the starting-point nature of equity in an attempt to combine its indeterminacy with the fact that it exists and impacts on the rights of States:

> the justice of which equity is an emanation, is not abstract justice but justice according to the rule of law; which is to say that its application should display consistency and a degree of predictability; even though it looks with particularity to the peculiar circumstances of an instant case, it also looks beyond it to principles of more general application. This is precisely why the courts have, from the beginning, elaborated equitable principles as being, at the same time, means to an equitable result in a particular case, yet also having a more general validity and hence expressible in general terms.[142]

Thus, as the Court affirmed, 'equitable principles are expressed in terms of general application'.[143] Thus, equity is something we do not know on its face, yet it must be applied predictably and consistently to multiple situations. This begs the question of the identifiable general content of equity.

(d) The Non-Law Character of Equitable Criteria

The basic rule of international law on delimitation of maritime boundaries is not the most determinate one. In *Gulf of Maine*, the Chamber of the Court explained the requirements of this rule:

> any agreement or other equivalent solution should involve the application of equitable criteria, namely criteria derived from equity which—whether they be designated 'principles' or 'criteria', the latter term being preferred by the Chamber for reasons of clarity—are not in themselves principles and rules of international law.[144]

As further reiterated in the same case, 'the criteria in question are not themselves rules of law and therefore mandatory in the different situations, but "equitable", or even "reasonable", criteria, and that what international law requires is that recourse be had in each case to the criterion, or the balance of different criteria, appearing to be most appropriate to the concrete situation'.[145] On balance, the use of 'criteria' instead of principles or standards to denote equitable categories further mirrors the non-law character of equity.

[142] *ICJ Reports*, 1985, 39. [143] *Id.*
[144] *ICJ Reports*, 1984, 292.
[145] *Id*, 313, para 158; Sir Robert Jennings likewise considers it odd to try and convert a method into a rule of law, Jennings (1989), 398.

It is also repeatedly emphasised in jurisprudence that 'There has been no systematic definition of the equitable criteria that may be taken into consideration for an international maritime delimitation, and this would in any event be difficult *a priori*, because of their highly variable adaptability to different concrete situations.' In other words, the relevant method should be judged not in the abstract but with reference to its application to a specific situation.[146]

The background against which the relevance of equity has to be viewed relates to the kind of legal regulation of the relevant aspects of the law of the sea. In delimitation matters, equity is there not because it is sensible, useful, fair or appropriate, but because there is no determinate norm straightforwardly resolving the pertinent situations, and because equity is itself referred to in legal norms. Thus, the basis of relevance of equity is twofold. Equity operates in the absence of a norm that would otherwise resolve the situation in specific terms, and it is provided for in the legal norm. Equity *per se* generates no legal regulation.

Given the absence of the corrective role of equity, it is there not to mitigate the rigours of law, but the rigours of abstract legal regulation, which, if it existed, would entail an outcome so inequitable as to make States unable to agree to such legal regulation. The resort to equity can compensate for this through providing case-specific solutions.

Presumably, the absence of straightforward legal regulation in the general international law of continental shelf and exclusive economic zone delimitation is due to the multiplicity of factors observable in maritime spaces and the ensuing diversity of specific situations. This makes it highly difficult if not impossible for States to achieve a greater consensus by agreeing on a norm that would express the uniform standard embodying equitable, just and uniform principles applicable to all situations. Hence the fundamental norm pointing to an equitable result is the most States can agree upon.

The Court in *North Sea* observed that the 'international law of continental shelf delimitation does not involve any imperative rule and permits resort to various principles or methods, as may be appropriate, or a combination of them, provided that, by the application of equitable principles, a reasonable result is arrived at'.[147] The Court further emphasised in *Tunisia–Libya* 'that in international law there is no single obligatory method of delimitation and that several methods may be applied to one and the same delimitation'.[148] In addition, there is no mandatory rule of customary law requiring the application of the equidistance method.[149] As Judge Gros pointed out in this case, equity is resorted to in the absence of the straightforward determinate rule of delimitation. In 'the absence of any one method of delimitation solely applicable, the need to balance the equities' arises, necessitating, among other things, a consideration 'of the effects of particular

[146] *Id*, 312, 319, paras 157, 174; see also *Tunisia–Libya*, *ICJ Report*, 1982, 59, para 70.
[147] *ICJ Reports*, 1969, 49.
[148] *ICJ Reports*, 1982, 79.
[149] *Id*, 88.

geographical features, examination of the physical and geological structure and of the natural resources'.[150] As the Joint Separate Opinion of Judges Ruda, Bedjaoui and Arechaga suggests, 'the law of the sea is still quite rudimentary and comprises few rules, and more especially because the entire process of maritime delimitation law is dominated by a "fundamental norm", that of the equitable result, which is as uninstructive as it is all-embracing'.[151] And this is the point at which the legal regulation in this field stops.

As the Chamber of the Court emphasised in *Gulf of Maine*, the parties 'in the current state of the law governing relations between them, are not bound, under a rule of treaty-law or other rule, to apply certain criteria or to use certain particular methods for the establishment of a single maritime boundary for both the continental shelf and the exclusive maritime fishery zone'.[152] The relevance of equitable criteria in allocating international rights and obligations is explained by the fact that, as the *Gulf of Maine* Judgment affirms, customary law:

> can of its nature only provide a few basic legal principles, which lay down guidelines to be followed with a view to an essential objective. It cannot also be expected to specify the equitable criteria to be applied or the practical, often technical, methods to be used for attaining that objective—which remain simply criteria and methods even where they are also, in a different sense, called 'principles'. Although the practice is still rather sparse, owing to the relative newness of the question, it too is there to demonstrate that each specific case is, in the final analysis, different from all the others, that it is monotypic and that, more often than not, the most appropriate criteria, and the method of combination of methods most likely to yield a result consonant with what the law indicates, can only be determined in relation to each particular case and its specific characteristics.

In other words, these criteria are meant to implement the relevant rules of international law *in concreto*.[153] The Chamber affirms that denoting equitable criteria as principles is only descriptive and cannot be identified with the use of the same notion with regard to norms that embody the established legal standard. The purpose these criteria serve is that laid down by law, not the equitable purpose *per se*. These criteria are meant to implement that overarching purpose in conditions of specificity that each case displays.

Most importantly, as the Chamber observes, the situation of diversity of individual situations 'precludes the possibility of those conditions arising which are necessary for the formation of principles and rules of customary law'.[154]

Therefore, the very relevance of equitable criteria as non-law in maritime delimitation lies with the definitional impossibility of the existence of legal norms that would be determinate and specific enough to provide a ready-made solution.

[150] *Id*, 148.
[151] Joint Separate Opinion, *id*, 90.
[152] *ICJ Reports*, 1984, 312, para 155.
[153] *Id*, 290.
[154] *Id*, 290.

(e) The Normative Basis of Equity

The general legal basis of resort to equity in maritime delimitation is the reference to it in the relevant international legal instrument, or the fundamental rule prescribing equitable delimitation.[155] For instance, according to Article 83 of the 1982 Law of the Sea Convention, 'The delimitation of the continental shelf between States with opposite or adjacent coasts shall be effected by agreement on the basis of international law, as referred to in Article 38 of the Statute of the International Court of Justice, in order to achieve an equitable solution.' This means that the delimitation process has to be based on and remain within the realm of the norms of international law. Equitable solution is the purpose the use of international law establishes.

In various litigation, the role of equity is provided for in Special Agreements, as can be seen from the *Tunisia–Libya* case. As the Separate Opinion of Judge Jimenez de Arechaga clarifies in this case, the basis for the Court's power to apply equitable principles was the authorisation in the Special Agreement. This provided the legal basis for equity in this case, especially in defining the geographical area in which equitable principles would affect delimitation.[156]

The second sentences in paragraphs 1 and 2 of Article 6 of the 1958 Convention on Continental Shelf deal with the delimitation of the continental shelf between adjacent and opposing coasts. They stipulate that 'In the absence of agreement, and unless another boundary line is justified by special circumstances, the boundary is the median line, every point of which is equidistant from the nearest points of the baselines from which the breadth of the territorial sea of each State is measured.' The approach to identifying 'special circumstances' under Article 6 of the 1958 Convention with equity originates from the *Anglo-French* case. This was the first case to adjudicate on continental shelf delimitation on the basis of Article 6 of the 1958 Convention.

Under Article 6 of the 1958 Geneva Convention, as the Arbitral Tribunal determined, 'the equidistance principle ultimately possesses an obligatory force which it does not have in the same measure under the rules of customary law. For Article 6 makes the application of the equidistance principle a matter of treaty obligation for parties to the Convention.' Nevertheless, the Tribunal pointed to the content of the norm embodied in Article 6 and observed that the equidistance principle was good so long as special circumstances did not justify the use of another method. The role of these 'special circumstances' was 'to ensure an equitable delimitation'. The combined 'equidistance-special circumstances rule' in effect gives particular expression to a general norm that, absent agreement, the boundary between States abutting on the same continental shelf is to be determined on equitable principles.[157] In this case, therefore, equitable delimitation

[155] This is dealt with in Chapter 4 above. [156] *ICJ Reports*, 1982, 105.
[157] *UK–French Continental Shelf* case (1977), 54 *ILR* 303, para 70.

was required by the express provision of the treaty, as opposed to the fundamental norm on delimitation.

The Arbitral Tribunal observed that even where the method of equidistance has normative force, it is, in the overall normative context, only one of the factors whose relevance depends on the assessment and appreciation of geographical and other considerations.[158]

The similarity between Article 6 'special circumstances' and equitable considerations was emphasised by the International Court in *Jan Mayen*, in such a way that 'it must be difficult to find any material difference—at any rate in regard to delimitation between opposite coasts—between the effect of Article 6 and the effect of the customary rule which also requires a delimitation based on equitable principles'.[159] As the Court emphasised, the concept of 'special circumstances' originates from the 1958 Convention, while 'relevant circumstances' are a general international law phenomenon. There is 'inevitably a tendency towards assimilation between the special circumstances of Article 6 of the 1958 Convention and the relevant circumstances under customary law, and this if only because both are intended to enable the achievement of an equitable result'.[160] As Judge Shahabuddeen emphasises, special circumstances are narrower than relevant circumstances. While the latter can justify the use of the equidistance method, the former can only operate to exclude it.[161]

Under such perspective, 'special circumstances' become a mere sub-species of equity and its 'relevant circumstances'. 'Special circumstances' are special in relation to equidistance. 'Relevant circumstances' include equidistance as one of the circumstances. Nevertheless, the entire legal framework ends up being the same, in that there is no single method of delimitation that can dispose of disputed cases.

Article 6 of the 1958 Geneva Convention was treated as a unity in *Gulf of Maine*. As the Chamber observed, the second sentences of paragraphs 1 to 2 of Article 6 do not 'enunciate a principle or rule of international law, but contemplate, *inter alia*, the use of a particular practical method for the actual implementation of the delimitation process. ... The applicability of this method is, however, subject to the condition that there are no special circumstances in the case which would make that criterion inequitable, by showing such division to be unreasonable and so entailing recourse to a different method or methods or, at the very least, appropriate correction of the effect produced by the application of the first method.'[162] Furthermore, the Chamber notes that the parties, 'in the current state of the law governing relations between them, are not bound, under a rule of treaty-law or other rule, to apply certain criteria or use certain

[158] *Anglo-French*, 55.
[159] *Jan Mayen*, *ICJ Reports*, 1993, 58.
[160] *Id*, 62.
[161] Separate Opinion, *id*, 148.
[162] *ICJ Reports*, 1984, 300–301.

particular methods for the establishment of a single maritime boundary both for the continental shelf and the exclusive maritime fishery zone, as in the present case. Consequently, the Chamber also is not so bound.'[163] Thus, the Chamber went on to state that in this condition it would select the range of criteria capable of delimiting the single maritime boundary and select from them the most equitable ones from that range.

Therefore, not only customary law, but also conventional law fall short of providing a single and straightforward rule applicable to the delimitation of maritime spaces in such a way as to provide a straightforward and ready-made outcome. Here, equity is referred to in both sets of norms.

(f) The Scope of Relevance of Equity

The relevance of equity relates to the field of the relevant international legal relation which is not governed strictly by legal norms. Thus, equity as such cannot affect the established legal position and encroach on what has been already allocated to the relevant State by a legal norm. Equity can only be relevant in terms of the delimitation of maritime spaces. Entitlement to and ownership of the relevant maritime space is exclusively governed by law. This is in accordance with the position that equity governs those fields in which there is no sufficient or detailed legal regulation.

This phenomenon is illustrated in the International Court's distinction between the title to the area and delimiting its outer boundary in the *North Sea* case. The Court addressed the German submission that the Court should simply award the equitable share of the relevant area to each relevant State. This submission effectively aimed at displacing the legal entitlement of each State to its continental shelf, that is at removing the whole question from law to the realm of equity, which is non-law.

The Court considered that 'its task in the present proceedings relates essentially to the delimitation and not to the apportionment of the areas concerned, or their division into converging sectors. Delimitation is a process which involves establishing the boundaries of an area already, in principle, appertaining to the coastal State and not the determination *de novo* of such an area. Delimitation in an equitable manner is one thing, but not the same thing as awarding a just and equitable share of a previously undelimited area, even though in a number of cases the results may be comparable, or even identical.' Consequently, 'the notion of apportioning an as yet undelimited area, considered as a whole (which underlies the doctrine of the just and equitable share) is quite foreign to, and inconsistent with, the basic concept of continental shelf entitlement, according to which the process of delimitation is essentially one of drawing a boundary line between areas which already appertain to one or other of the States affected.

[163] *Id*, 312.

The delimitation itself must indeed be equitably effected, but it cannot have as its object the awarding of an equitable share, or indeed of a share, as such, at all, for the fundamental concept involved does not admit of there being anything undivided to share out.'[164]

As the *North Sea Continental Shelf* case confirms in its entirety, equity in maritime delimitation does not serve as the basis for legal rights to maritime areas. It only serves as the basis for determining the limits of the rights of one State to the relevant maritime area in relation to similar rights of another State.

As the Court emphasised in *Jan Mayen*, equity is applied to delimit 'the areas which each State would have been able to claim had it not been for the presence of the other State'.[165] Furthermore, 'the sharing-out of the area is therefore the consequence of the delimitation, not vice versa'.[166] As Judge Oda characterised this finding, 'The Court seems to have found it an implicit consequence of [the doctrine of continental shelf] that the areas of continental shelf falling under the jurisdiction of each party were predetermined *ab initio*, each being mutually exclusive of the other, so that the function of the delimitation of the continental shelf consisted "merely" in discerning and bringing to light a line already in potential existence.'[167] The context of maritime delimitation, as can be seen from Judge Oda's observations in *Libya–Tunisia*, involves situations where each relevant State has in principle the right to claim any area within a 200-mile radius. There is no absolute, that is the only possible, legal line, deviation from which by one State would mean the encroachment on the maritime areas of another State. Judicial decision-making should thus be based on ascertaining the preferable claim which possesses greater cogency than other claims, in relation to the area which both parties could in principle claim.[168]

The application of equity to issues of entitlement to the continental shelf would distort the legal framework. As Judge Tanaka emphasised in *North Sea*, the apportionment demanded by Germany was effectively an alternative to delimitation. Delimitation of maritime spaces is an act of a bilateral nature, a combination of bilateral relationships, based on highly individualistic considerations. The method of apportionment suggested by Germany was, on the other hand, collectivistic. It implied 'the concept that delimitation is not demarcation of two sovereign spheres already belonging to two different States, but an act of division, or sharing among more than two States of *res nullius* or *res communis*. Therefore, the concept of apportionment is necessarily constitutive and multilateral. ...It can be said abstractly that the apportionment should be just and equitable; however, it is not easy to demonstrate in what way apportionment is, under given circumstances, in conformity with justice and equitableness.'[169] Judge Morelli

[164] *ICJ Reports*, 1969, paras 19–20.
[165] *ICJ Reports*, 1993, 64. [166] *Id*, 67.
[167] *Jan Mayer, ICJ Reports*, 1982, 254.
[168] *Id*, 253.
[169] *ICJ Reports*, 1969, 187.

also asserted that the rule of equitable sharing could not automatically effect the sharing out of the continental shelf among the various States.[170] This approach illustrates that equity has no free-standing relevance.

Judge Tanaka's reasoning clarifies two points. First, delimitation, even if carried out among more than two States, is essentially an act carried out between them individually. Speaking in legal terms, there is no maritime space common to them. Secondly, such common maritime space cannot be constructed to exist even as between individual States in the area and equity certainly cannot help to construct this. For law, through inherent rules, has already formed its approach to appurtenance and prolongation as the criteria which make up the continental shelf as the prolongation of the land territory of the relevant States.[171] Within that field, equity is simply irrelevant. Its relevance begins when the determinate legal norms have no more to say regarding the required outcome, that is the outer limit of the relevant maritime area.

The statement of the Court in *Tunisia/Libya* that equity is not distributive justice[172] further confirms that equity cannot affect legal entitlements. Furthermore, as can be seen from *North Sea* and *Anglo-French* cases, the relevance of equity in delimitation should never obscure the relevance of the fact that the continental shelf is based on the entitlement of natural prolongation. The outcome equity can suggest must comply with the factor of natural prolongation. More specifically, a State with restricted coastline cannot claim equality with a State with extensive coastline. Therefore, equity cannot possibly require the refashioning of geography or remedy natural inequalities, but could only succeed in 'abating the effects of an incidental special feature from which an unjustifiable difference of treatment could result'.[173]

This illustrates the essence of equity as quasi-normative non-law. Unlike legal norms which either enable facts to have legal effect or proscribe them from having it, equity does not in principle affect the legal effects of the factual situation. It merely serves as a balancing factor, in the absence of strict legal regulation, against certain effects that can otherwise result from such factual situations.

(g) The Will of States and the Role of Tribunals

An equitable solution is not a solution of compromise between the parties. It is resorted to when there is no compromise and agreement between them. In other words, equity is a means of providing the standards for resolving a dispute. But it is not possible to identify such standards in a straightforward *a priori* manner.

[170] *Id*, 207.
[171] See, above, Chapter 4.
[172] *ICJ Reports*, 1982, para 71.
[173] *ICJ Reports*, 1969, 50.

On the other hand, equitable considerations can be dispensed with if States so agree. As Judge Shahabuddeen emphasised in *Jan Mayen*, States can enter into delimitation agreements which will be binding as a treaty yet fall short of being based on the relevant equities.[174] This can be seen as another side of the coin in relation to the argument that equity is relevant where there is no straightforward legal regulation on the relevant subject-matter. Equity is relevant where parties are not agreed with each other and a solution has to be imposed on them.

In equity, just as in law, the role of tribunals is more limited than that of States. States apparently can on a bilateral basis agree on the principles of delimitation they choose, but judicial organs do not enjoy a similar broad freedom in choosing the applicable methods. Therefore, judicial application of equity requires demonstrating greater legitimacy in choosing the relevant methods than would be the case with agreement between the parties.

As the Court emphasised in *Libya–Malta*:

> although there may be no legal limit to the considerations which States may take account of, this can hardly be true for a court applying equitable procedures. For a court, although there is assuredly no closed list of considerations, it is evident that only those that are pertinent to the institution of the continental shelf as it has developed within the law, and to the application of equitable principles to its delimitation, will qualify for inclusion.[175]

This more limited nature of the Court's choice of equitable considerations is linked with the Court being bound by the law, in this case the legal character of the relevant maritime areas.

Thus, judicial bodies can choose only those considerations of equity that clearly follow from the nature of the relevant institution as a legal institution. These are considerations emanating from law, even though it may involve these organs in some interpretation and deduction in terms of what the nature of the relevant institution entails. In choosing an equitable principle just because it is equitable and not because it appertains to the legal institution, courts would risk assuming law-making function that would greatly undermine their legitimacy in the legal society which knows of no central authority over States.

(h) Equity and the Risk of Subjectivism

Equity, with its indeterminate content, can potentially involve the risk of subjectivism in decision-making. This risk has caused significant scepticism about and criticism of the relevance of equity. As Judge Koretsky emphasised in *North Sea*, the concept of what is equitable can be subject to debate, and 'to introduce

[174] Separate Opinion, *ICJ Reports*, 1993, 149–150.
[175] *ICJ Reports*, 1985, 40.

so vague a notion into the jurisprudence of the International Court may open the door to make subjective and at times arbitrary evaluations, instead of following the guidance of established general principles and rules of international law'.[176] As the Joint Separate Opinion of Judges Ruda, Bedjaoui and Arechaga in *Libya–Malta* points out, a judge in such cases must struggle to see how he can escape from subjectivism. 'The finest legal dissertations on equity will never succeed in completely eliminating what is perhaps the irreducible core of the judicial subjectivism ... The utmost, in all honour, that a judge can do is modest: to summon up all his resources with a view to reducing its scope and effects to a minimum.'[177]

As Sir Robert Jennings observed in relation to the *North Sea* case, equity is not really based on subjectivism. In fact, the Court demonstrated by simple geometry why the application of equidistance was inequitable and unfair.[178] As for the positive content of equity, the Court elaborated upon the relevant equitable methods and directed the parties to negotiate with a view to implementing them. The impossibility of stating *a priori* what sort of principles should form part of an equitable decision has to do with the indeterminacy of equity, not subjectivism.

The link between equity and the fundamental norm of maritime delimitation requires adopting objectively justifiable decisions. Subjectivism in general would refer either to the parties' own joint decision on delimitation, which is solely their bilateral affair assuming no rights and interests of third States are affected, and hence would not raise any issue of (the lack of) equity; or to the parties' unilateral judgment which has no prospect of being recognised as part of the legal position; or, finally, the subjective appreciation of the relevant circumstances by the relevant tribunal. One safeguard against such subjectivism is the above-mentioned difference between the capacity of States and tribunals in selecting equitable principles. By limiting themselves to choosing those equitable principles that emanate from the nature of the relevant legal institution and consequently are likely to be seen as just and fair from the perspective of all litigants, courts can avoid a great deal of subjectivism that could otherwise materialise.

Although there may be a discretionary element involved, courts have to ensure, as Judge Shahabuddeen suggests, that their application of equity is defensible on rational grounds, in terms of what is fair and just, as opposed to the mere use of discretion. The latter option would lead to government by judges which no State would accept. As can be seen from Judge Shahabuddeen's analysis, one safeguard against the arbitrary use of equity is that the process of equitable delimitation cannot depart from established rules of law.[179] Another safeguard is the structural limit on the delimitation process, consisting in its relevance for delimiting

176 *ICJ Reports*, 1969, 166.
177 *ICJ Reports*, 1985, 90.
178 Jennings (1986), 32–33.
179 Separate Opinion, *ICJ Reports*, 1993, 193–194.

the areas already appertaining to States, as opposed to the apportioning of the common area.[180] As the Court emphasised in *Tunisia–Libya*, even though equitable criteria are not governed by strict legal norms, the task of application of these criteria is not an exercise of discretion or conciliation. It is part of the process of application of international law.[181] As Judge Weeramantry stated in *Jan Mayen*, 'What principles a court adopts from the range of choice available is determined by a weighing of considerations such as those of relevance, immediacy to the problem, practical value in the particular circumstances, and the degree of authority of the principle.' An additional guide is, 'within the limits of choice available in law, the court's sense of justice, fairness and equity'.[182]

Evans pleads for excluding or reducing the role of subjectivism in the process of the application of equity in maritime delimitation:

> The equitable solution is a result of the delimitation process; of correctly applying the applicable norms of international law. Nevertheless, the greater the perceived arbitrariness of that determination, the greater will be the scope for claiming that the resulting delimitation is not an equitable solution. There is a fine line between a subjective and objective characterisation of the result as equitable. It is important to exclude as much subjectivity from the process leading to that result as possible.[183]

If equity results in subjective appreciation and discretion, it definitionally ceases to be equity. An equitable result is that which is objectively acceptable as equitable. In *Guinea/Guinea-Bissau*, the Arbitral Tribunal stressed that delimitation must be based on 'equitable and objective principles'. Everything possible should be done 'to apply objective factors offering the possibility at an equitable result', and 'objective legal reasoning' is required.[184] This approach seems to pervade the entire jurisprudence on maritime delimitation. Only those factors that are objectively comprehensible, implying either equality or reliance on geographical situation or shared practice, are accepted as bases of delimitation. This excludes factors that express the interests of individual States not shared by other parties.

The same approach seems to dominate the distinction between relevant equitable factors and irrelevant ones. The dominance of objectivism requires tribunals to limit their references to factors that are contemporary and will also last. The *Guinea/Guinea-Bissau* Award, for instance, refuses to consider economic factors, namely the reliance of both parties on receiving fair profits from the maritime areas. These are not permanent circumstances on whose relevance the Tribunal can pronounce through 'a contemporary evaluation'.[185] This is yet another confirmation of the preference for objective evaluation.

180 *Id*, 196.
181 *ICJ Reports*, 1982, 60.
182 *ICJ Reports*, 1993, 250.
183 Evans (1989), 91.
184 *Guinea/Guinea-Bissau* Award, paras 91, 102.
185 *Id*, para 122.

Thus, jurisprudence consistently avoids basing decisions on factors merely embodying subjective considerations and individual interests. It instead concentrates, in terms of starting-point principles at least, on factors deriving their legitimacy from their reference to objective factors. Thus, the initial basis of equity is found in objective factual situations, objectively verified practice of parties expressing their attitude in terms of *de facto* existence of the relevant situation and its toleration for the time being, or the criterion of equidistance. Factors which objectively exist, such as resource deposits and economic or security interests, but affirming impact of which on delimitation would involve granting preference to the interests or perception of one party over that of another party, are considered at later stages of analysis. This is to ensure that the use of initial criteria does not entail too inequitable a result. At the final stage of analysis, the criterion of proportionality steps in to ensure that the combination of criteria and factors used does not allocate burdens and benefits disproportionately.

(i) Factors Informing Equity

As the International Court emphasised in *Tunisia–Libya*, 'no rigid rules exist as to the exact weight to be attached to each element in the case'.[186] This is the specificity of the (quasi)normative impact of non-law such as equity. It can provide no single or straightforward criterion determining the legal outcome, but instead it requires a balanced outcome through the use of relevant criteria. As the *Gulf of Maine* Judgment affirms, 'there is no single method which intrinsically brings greater justice or is of greater practical usefulness. ... The greater or lesser appropriateness of one method or another can only be assessed with reference to the actual situations in which they are used, and the assessment made in one situation may be entirely reversed in another.'[187]

When equity is used, all relevant factual, geographical, historical and other factors are considered. This becomes a matter of balancing these equitable factors. The matter is not about non-law qualifying law, but the relevance of non-law in the absence of straightforward legal regulation. These factors do not relate to entitlement to the relevant maritime area but only to delimitation. They are relevant only because the law does not exclude them through more straightforward regulation. At the same time, these factors are relevant not *per se* but only if on balance judged equitable.

The International Court warns against putting an emphasis on the equitableness of equitable criteria as such. As the Court emphasised in *Tunisia–Libya*, the reference to 'equitable principles' is not entirely satisfactory, because they tend 'to characterise both the result to be achieved and the means to be applied to reach that result'. This, according to the Court, should not detract from the real essence

[186] *ICJ Reports*, 1982, 60.
[187] *ICJ Reports*, 1984, 315, paras 162–163.

of the problem, namely that it is the equitable goal, as opposed to the criteria, that matters.[188] As the Court earlier emphasised in *North Sea*, 'It is necessary to seek not one method of delimitation but one goal.'[189] As *Tunisia–Libya* further confirms, the aim of the application of equitable principles is to ensure an equitable result. It is the result that is predominant, and 'the equitableness of a principle must be assessed in the light of its usefulness for the purpose of arriving at an equitable result'.[190] Therefore, 'what is reasonable and equitable in any given case must depend on its particular circumstances'.[191] Furthermore, 'It is not every [equitable] principle which is itself equitable; it may acquire this quality by reference to the equitableness of the solution. The principles... have to be selected according to their appropriateness for reaching an equitable result. From this consideration it follows that the term "equitable principles" cannot be interpreted in the abstract; it refers back to the rules and principles which may be appropriate in order to achieve an equitable result.'[192]

The same approach prevails in the opinions of individual judges. As Judge Gros emphasises, 'equity is a goal, and the way to reach that goal is to apply to the relevant facts such legal methods and reasoning' as are suited to the situation dealt with in the relevant case.[193] As Judge Jimenez de Arechaga observed, 'All the relevant circumstances are to be considered and balanced; they are to be thrown together into the crucible and their interaction will yield the correct equitable solution of each individual case.'[194]

As the Arbitral Tribunal emphasised in *Guinea/Guinea-Bissau*, equitable factors 'result from legal rules, although they evolve from physical, mathematical, historical, political, economic or other facts. However, they are not restricted in number and none of them is obligatory for the Tribunal, since each case of delimitation is a *unicum*.'[195]

Thus, individual equitable criteria possess no normative value on their own and to give straightforward weight to any equitable method of delimitation is effectively to treat them as legal requirements. As the Arbitral Tribunal emphasised in *Anglo-French*, even under Article 6 of the 1958 Convention, 'it is the geographical and other circumstances of any given case which indicate and justify the use of the equidistance method as the means of achieving an equitable solution rather than the inherent quality of the method as a legal norm of delimitation'.[196]

The *North Sea* judgment clarifies that 'there is no legal limit to the considerations which States may take account of for the purpose of making sure that they

[188] *ICJ Reports*, 1982, 59.
[189] *ICJ Reports*, 1969, 50.
[190] *Tunisia–Libya*, *ICJ Reports*, 1982, 59.
[191] *ICJ Reports*, 1982, 60.
[192] *Id*, 59; see also Evans (1989), 73.
[193] *ICJ Reports*, 1982, 152.
[194] *Id*, 109.
[195] *Guinea/Guinea-Bissau*, para 89.
[196] *Anglo-French*, para 70.

apply equitable procedures, and more often than not it is the balancing-up of all such considerations that will produce this result rather than reliance on one to the exclusion of all others'.[197] As Judge Weeramantry also emphasises, no complete list of equitable considerations can be made because one can never foretell which factors will surface in individual cases. In addition, each item, such as State conduct or national security, is infinitely variable.[198] Thus, one of the individual criteria will be given standing not on its own, but in a balance that produces the outcome seen as equitable from the perspective of both parties.

According to *Gulf of Maine*, there is no equitable method which deserves priority application. The relevant method can be equitable at the outset but its correction may be necessary if it proves inequitable at subsequent stages, and other methods must be found. 'Above all there must be willingness to adopt a combination of different methods' if circumstances so require.[199]

The further reasoning of the Court in *Libya–Malta* equally evidences the interaction between law and non-law. The Court emphasises that the median line adopted as the provisional solution due to the opposite location of the coasts of the parties cannot be the final solution. This would be:

> conferring on the equidistance method the status of being the only method the use of which is compulsory in the case of opposite coasts. As already pointed out, the existing international law cannot be interpreted in this sense; the equidistance method is not the only method applicable to the present dispute, and it does not even have the benefit of a presumption in its favour. Thus, under existing law, it must be demonstrated that the equidistance method leads to an equitable result in the case in question.[200]

The reason that the equidistance principle cannot dispose of the case follows from the fact that this principle lacks the legal status of a compulsory principle. It therefore cannot be used under the guise of equity to produce a solution which it cannot produce due to a lack of legal status. Therefore, equity cannot here be used to achieve a result that cannot be achieved under the law.

In the same case, the Court rejected the use of proportionality as exclusive of other considerations, observing that:

> to use the ratio of coastal lengths as of itself determinative of the seaward reach and area of continental shelf proper to each Party, is to go far beyond the use of proportionality as a test of equity, and as a corrective of the unjustifiable difference of treatment resulting from some method of drawing the boundary line. If such a use of proportionality were right, it is difficult indeed to see what room would be left for any other consideration; for it would be at once the principle of entitlement to continental shelf rights and also the method of putting that principle into operation.[201]

[197] *North Sea*, *ICJ Reports*, 1969, 50.
[198] Separate Opinion, *ICJ Reports*, 1993, 261–262.
[199] *ICJ Reports*, 1984, 315, para 163.
[200] *ICJ Reports*, 1985, 47.
[201] *Id*, 45.

Thus, the non-legal character of the relevant equitable criterion and its lack of straightforward value in individual cases go hand in hand with the need to ensure the achievement of an equitable result as opposed to the mere use of equitable criteria. This general framework of equitable principles must be borne in mind when the utility of individual factors informing equity is appreciated.

In the end, the concept of equity as referring to various non-law categories (geography, conduct, economy, security, proportionality) operates to balance these non-law categories against each other. The reason is that no category of non-law can on its own determine the outcome of the application of the relevant legal norms.

If any of the headings of equity could predetermine a case then it would be that particular kind of non-law which would determine the legal outcome. Equity instead works in terms of excluding those kinds of non-law that are not overtly relevant, and then balancing the rest of the relevant circumstances. If one single equitable principle were considered as controlling and decisive, other principles would be excluded. The solution would then be not that of equity but of projecting upon the relevant institution the rule endorsing the straightforward method of delimitation—the very rule that does not exist in the law of delimitation.

Every equitable circumstance is potentially relevant but none of them is *per se* endowed with the standing and shape of law. This is, furthermore, why the goal is the equitable result; equitable principles themselves command no normative consensus. They are relevant only in so far as being useful in bringing about an equitable solution. Even if equitable in one case, the standing of the same method in another case is uncertain until the situation on the ground is examined.

(j) Continuous Relevance of Law at the Stages of Application of Equity

The fundamental rule on maritime delimitation is very basic, general and indeterminate. But it still operates as a legal rule and impacts on every single stage of maritime delimitation. As observed in the *Gulf of Maine* case, 'The Chamber has evidently to keep in mind its obligation to comply with the fundamental norm provided by general international law.'[202]

Generally, the methods of equity in maritime delimitation can be divided into the initial, operative and corrective. In *North Sea*, in selecting the relevant equitable factors, the Court began with those that had legal standing as generative of the legal entitlement of States to the continental shelf. These were considerations of fact that were systemically treated as derivative of legal entitlements. The Court emphasised that the institution of the continental shelf had arisen out of the recognition of a physical fact of extension of the coastal territory of the State.

[202] *ICJ Reports*, 1982, 326.

Geological factors are thus to be considered as relevant in achieving an equitable delimitation. The same holds true for the configuration of the relevant coasts.[203] The Court's analysis does not suggest in this case any hierarchy or priority among the equitable criteria.

As *Gulf of Maine* suggests, the process of the application of equitable criteria to delimitation consists of two phases. The first phase is preliminary and consists in choosing equitable criteria; the next phase consists in the application of these criteria in the sense of drawing the particular line of delimitation.[204] In this case, the Chamber first delimited the area through reference to the geographical configuration of the relevant areas. The Chamber then adjusted the line by reference to the relevant circumstances. It finally verified the outcome in terms of its equitability by reference to its impact in terms of economy and resources.

In *Libya–Malta*, the Court faced a situation where the achievement of an equitable result was a complex task and could not be performed in a single-stage exercise. Therefore, the Court decided to make provisional delimitation first by using the method that would contribute to the equitableness of the final result. Then the Court examined the initial outcome in the light of other equitable criteria which might call for the correction of the initial result.[205]

There seems to be no established rule as to which equitable considerations must be used for drawing a preliminary line—in several cases the median line has indeed been used—or for correcting that preliminary line. It is, however, certain that the most practicable way of drawing an equitable maritime boundary is to specify the *prima facie* line first by reference to the legitimate criteria in the relevant situation, and then verify its implications by reference to the other—equally legitimate—factors. It is clear that the selection of any, including initial, criteria of equity can give rise to thoughts and doubts as to its suitability and propriety in the sense that the method chosen is better than other methods. There is in principle neither established evidence nor empowered agency for reaching such conclusions.

This fits perfectly with the Court's decision in the *Libya–Malta* case to link the initial criteria of equitable delimitation to the legal standards related to the continental shelf. Thus the Court's choice commands increased legitimacy by referring to the established legal criteria as far as they go, as opposed to the solely Court-determined criteria of equity.

The Court began by pointing out that the modern law of continental shelf is based on the entitlement to the 200-mile area guided by the criterion of distance from the coast, as opposed to geological factors. Therefore, it was 'logical to the Court that the choice of the criterion and the method which it is to employ in the first place to arrive at a provisional result should be made in a manner consistent

[203] *ICJ Reports*, 1969, 51.
[204] *ICJ Reports*, 1984, 328–329.
[205] *ICJ Reports*, 1985, 46.

with the concepts underlying the attribution of legal title'.[206] The Court confronted the legal position that had evolved following *North Sea*. In delimiting the continental shelf, the Court found that the rules and principles underlying the concept of exclusive economic zone also had to be taken into account. These two institutions 'are linked together in modern law'. Consequently, distance from the coast as the factor common to both the exclusive economic zone and continental shelf had to be relevant in this case.[207]

Thus, the relevance of legal considerations does not stop even after equity assumes its role in the context of the absence of legal regulation beyond the fundamental rule prescribing the equitable delimitation. The relevance of law continues to inject guidance into equity even where it would not *prima facie* appear as pre-determinative of the equitable result. To an important extent, equitability means complying with legal requirements.

The relevance of the legal basis for entitlement to the relevant maritime area is reflected in the choice of delimitation methods in other cases as well. In *Guinea/Guinea-Bissau*, the Arbitral Tribunal emphasised that the rule of natural prolongation, relied upon in the 1969 *North Sea* Judgment, was no longer the only relevant factor of entitlement to the continental shelf. The 1982 Law of the Sea Convention also incorporated the 200 miles distance principle.[208]

In *Gulf of Maine*, the Chamber, having noted the geographical factors, considered it inevitable that its 'basic choice should favour a criterion long held to be as suitable as it is simple, namely that in principle, while having regard to the special circumstances of the case, one should aim at an equal division of areas' in which the maritime projections of coasts overlap.[209] After this, the correct application of the fundamental rule required the use of auxiliary criteria based on geography. Only geometrical methods could serve as appropriate for both the continental shelf and superjacent waters.[210] The Chamber had to 'prevent the partial relationship of adjacency from ultimately predominating over the partial relationship of oppositeness'.[211] In theory the delimitation of each of these spaces could require applying the methods and criteria corresponding to the characteristics of the relevant area. However, the choice made by the parties through the Special Agreement resulted in their foregoing claiming the best equities specifically applicable to each space, in favour of the combined equity applied to both spaces. This is a further instance of the impact of legal choice on the relevance of non-law.

During the final stage of delimitation in *Gulf of Maine*, the Chamber emphasised the need to comply with the fundamental norm.[212] Thus, the interaction

[206] *Id*, 45–46.
[207] *Id*, 33.
[208] *Guinea/Guinea-Bissau* Award, para 115.
[209] *ICJ Reports*, 1984, 327, para 327.
[210] *Id*, 328–329, paras 197–199.
[211] *Id*, 324, para 187.
[212] *Id*, 326, para 191.

between law and non-law is present at every step in the background of the Court's analysis of selection and application of equitable methods. If there can be no equitable criteria applicable to the entire area of delimitation, the relevant court would be justified in splitting the area into sectors, depending on the latter's geographical characteristics. This was done by the Arbitral Tribunal in the *St Pierre and Miquelon* case.[213] As the International Court emphasised in *Jan Mayen*, international law does not prescribe adopting a single line of delimitation over the entire area of delimitation as an equitable method. If needed, various methods of delimitation can be applied to various parts of the relevant area.[214]

(k) Individual Factors of Equity

(i) Geographical Factors

In *North Sea*, the Court emphasised the relevance of geographical factors as a matter of equity, but added that the exaggeration of the consequences of natural geographical features must be remedied through the use of other methods.[215] As the *Tunisia-Libya* case suggests, the identification of natural prolongation of the continental shelf in the appropriate geographical circumstances may have an important role to play in defining the equitable result. 'But the two considerations—the satisfying of equitable principles and the identification of natural prolongation—are not to be placed on a plane of equality.'[216] Similarly, the Judgment of the Court considers the coastal configuration as one of the basic criteria of equity.[217] Therefore, considerations of fact can contribute to reaching an equitable solution, but cannot by themselves explain or predetermine it. If they could do so, this would undermine the broader principle that considerations of fact cannot by themselves bring about the legal position. This would be the outcome of allowing facts to determine the legal position through their straightforward role in equity.

But this does not result in any straightforward limit on the relevance of geographical factors. As Judge Gros points out, 'a court of justice does not modify a delimitation because it finds subjectively that it is less advantageous to one party than to the other, for this would embark upon the vain task of equalizing the facts of nature; it notes, having taken into consideration all the factors contemplated by the applicable law, that some of those factors, which are relevant, have disproportionate or inordinate effects which, perhaps, may generate inequity'.[218]

[213] *Case Concerning the Delimitation of Maritime Areas between Canada and the French Republic*, 31 *ILM* (1992), 1169.

[214] *Jan Mayen*, *ICJ Reports*, 1993, 77.

[215] *ICJ Reports*, 1969, 49.

[216] *Tunisia–Libya*, *ICJ Reports*, 1982, 47.

[217] *Id*, 85–87.

[218] *Id*, 150.

(ii) Practice and Conduct of the Parties

In *Tunisia–Libya*, the Court addressed a situation involving the practice of both parties regarding the enactment of petroleum concession licences. This had caused the emergence of the *de facto* line that both parties regarded as the temporary solution of their disagreement on the continental shelf delimitation. The Court was careful enough to emphasise that no finding of tacit agreement between the parties was being made, but only that the solution temporarily achieved supplied some sense of what may be the equitable delimitation in the parties' perception.[219] At law this temporary solution would have no validity. In equity the same solution could provide evidence of the parties' attitudes as to what they regarded as equitable.

At the same time, the direction of this *de facto* line could not be good apart from within the area in relation to which it was accepted as the temporary solution.[220]

In *Gulf of Maine*, the Chamber faced the US claim that the practice of it and its nationals should be considered as the relevant circumstance. The US claim relied on historical rights, but also included fisheries management, rescue, research and defence. Canada, on the other hand referred to socio-economic factors, namely the interest of the local fishing communities. The Chamber rejected all these submissions. Especially regarding the US practice, the Court emphasised that it had developed when the relevant areas were still part of the high seas, that is before the emergence of the legal institution of EEZ. The achievement of US predominance in fisheries took place in a different legal regime, and 'whatever preferential situation the United States may previously have enjoyed, this cannot constitute in itself a valid ground for its now claiming the incorporation into its exclusive fishery zone of any area which, in law, has become Canada's'.[221] In *Jan Mayen*, the Court held that the conduct of States could not constitute relevant circumstance for delimiting the maritime area between Norway and Denmark.[222]

The Court is generally careful, as a matter of the application of equity, not to duplicate or imitate the legal character of factors that would not, on their own, grant legal entitlement to any of the parties. When the factual background would not by itself generate legal title, equity cannot be applied as if it would.

(iii) Interests of Coastal States

The most likely outcome in relation to economic interest is that respective activities such as fishing, navigation, petroleum exploration or exploitation, or defence, cannot be taken into account as a relevant circumstance for selecting equitable criteria. Dependence on fisheries could only be considered in terms of equity if deprivation thereof would entail catastrophic repercussions for the

[219] *Id*, 84.
[220] *Id*, 87.
[221] *Gulf of Maine, ICJ Reports*, 1984, 340–342, paras 232–235.
[222] *ICJ Reports*, 1993, 77.

livelihood and economic well-being of the countries concerned.[223] In addition, as both *Libya–Malta* and *Jan Mayen* confirm, the consideration of economic resources and interest cannot affect the relevant delimitation, because these are only temporary considerations. The economic condition of States as well as the state of the resource deposits can evolve over the relevant periods of time. As the Court emphasised in *Jan Mayen*, maritime delimitation by its nature is bound to be permanent and its outcome cannot be affected by factors that are liable to change over time.[224]

The relevance of security interests was rejected both in *Tunisia–Libya* and *Guinea/Guinea-Bissau* because the relevant delimitation line would not get close enough to the party's coast to raise any security concerns. Especially in *Guinea/Guinea-Bissau*, the Tribunal emphasised that as the continental shelf and EEZ were not areas of sovereignty, as opposed to the territorial sea, the relevance the security factor could have was reduced.[225] The *St Pierre & Miquelon* Award emphasises the accessory relevance of economic interest in terms of equitable considerations. As the Arbitral Tribunal noted, after having performed the delimitation based on geographical factors, it had to ascertain whether the outcome would be 'radically inequitable' economically, in the sense of the *Gulf of Maine* criterion of catastrophic repercussions. The Tribunal found that in that case such a radical impact would not ensue.[226]

(iv) Equidistance

In the case of opposite coasts equidistance can be applied more readily than in the case of adjacency. This was initially recognised by the International Court in *North Sea*, and went hand in hand with, and perhaps also explains, the Court's rejection of the status of equidistance as the general rule of the customary law of delimitation.

As the Court emphasised in *North Sea*, 'in certain geographical circumstances which are quite frequently met with, the equidistance method, despite its known advantages, leads unquestionably to inequity'.[227] In *North Sea*, Judge Morelli clarified the relationship between equity and the rule of equidistance in a way that anticipated the further developments in jurisprudence. According to Judge Morelli, accepting the relevance of equity would require excluding the relevance of equidistance as the straightforward rule, reducing it instead to 'one possible method of arriving at the result of equitable sharing out aimed at by the legal rule'.[228]

223 *Gulf of Maine*, *ICJ Reports*, 1984, 342, para. 237.
224 *Libya–Malta*, *ICJ Reports*, 1985, 41; *Jan Mayen*, *ICJ Reports*, 1993, 74.
225 *Guinea/Guinea-Bissau* Award, para 124.
226 *St Pierre & Miquelon*, paras 84–85.
227 *ICJ Reports*, 1969, 49.
228 *ICJ Reports*, 1969, 207.

In *Anglo-French*, the Arbitral Tribunal decided that under Article 6 of the 1958 Geneva Convention, 'the question whether the use of the equidistance principle or some other method is appropriate for achieving an equitable delimitation is very much a matter of appreciation in the light of geographical and other circumstance. In other words, even under Article 6 it is the geographical and other circumstances of any given case which indicate and justify the use of the equidistance method as the means of achieving an equitable solution rather than the inherent quality of the method as a legal norm of delimitation.'[229]

In *Tunisia–Libya*, the Court emphasised that although the equidistance method was not based on the mandatory customary norm, it still had the virtue (which under the circumstances could just as well be a weakness) that it reflected the changes in the coastal configuration. As the coastal correlation between Tunisia and Libya was initially that of adjacency and then changed into oppositeness, in this latter part the equidistance principle could become an equitable factor of increased weight.[230] The normative characteristic of equidistance in the context of equity is most eloquently emphasised by Judge Jimenez de Arechaga who points out that equidistance as an aspect of equity 'is a method and not a principle'. Like other principles, 'it must be judged by its success in achieving an equitable solution'.[231]

In *Guinea/Guinea-Bissau* equidistance was also not suitable as it would seriously disadvantage the third country situated in the middle—Sierra-Leone—by preventing it from extending its maritime territory seaward to the extent permitted by international law.[232]

That equidistance can be a useful equitable method, at least a good starting point, is demonstrated in the cases of *Libya–Malta*, *Gulf of Maine* and *Jan Mayen*—the cases where equidistance was taken as the starting-point of delimitation. But its merits will always depend on its equitability in the context of other possible criteria.

In *Libya–Malta*, equidistance was corrected by proportionality. The Joint Separate Opinion in this case observes that 'To assert, as Malta has done, that the equidistance method should be applied, even if it produces a delimitation which is grossly disproportionate to the length of the relevant coasts, is an attempt to subordinate the equitable result to be achieved, to the method adopted.'[233]

In *Gulf of Maine*, the Chamber adjusted the provisionally used median line, as 'The difference in length is a special circumstance of some weight, which, in the Chamber's view, justifies a correction of the equidistance line, or any other line.'[234]

229 *Anglo-French*, para 70.
230 *ICJ Reports*, 1982, 88.
231 *Id*, 109.
232 *Guinea/Guinea-Bissau* Award, para 104.
233 Joint Separate Opinion, *Libya/Malta*, *ICJ Reports*, 1985, 82.
234 *ICJ Reports*, 1984, 322, para 184.

In *Jan Mayen*, the Court examined the state both of conventional and customary law of the continental shelf and concluded that drawing a provisional line of equidistance was entirely appropriate. This result was acceptable both under Article 6 of the 1958 Convention and the general international law rule requiring an equitable solution. Under Article 6, equidistance applied unless special circumstances required another option, and the Court considered it acceptable to use it as the provisional line. For similar reasons, the Court thought the median line an appropriate provisional solution for the fishery zone. As the Court further emphasises, especially in the case of opposite coasts, the median line *prima facie* expresses the equitable result.[235]

The Court's preference in *Jan Mayen* for the provisional use of a median line was linked to the Court's ascertainment of the legal basis of the continental shelf entitlement in terms of distance from the coast. Thus, the original legal entitlement to the maritime space impacts the choice of equitable means of delimitation.

As Judge Shahabuddeen pointed out in *Jan Mayen*, equidistance in terms of Article 6 of the 1958 Geneva Convention was applicable because there were no other special circumstances that could modify its impact. Judge Shahabuddeen continued:

> By contrast, under customary international law, the equidistance method applies only where the 'relevant circumstances' require its application. Combining these two perspectives, one may say that, whereas 'relevant circumstances' may well require the application of equidistance, 'special circumstances' can only operate to exclude it, and never to apply it.[236]

In the end, both regimes can be seen as similar, if Article 6 of the 1958 Convention is seen as a unity which perceives the equidistance principle merely as a criterion that is applied when the factor of special circumstances requires this. Whether or not special and relevant circumstances are the same, the ultimate relevance of equidistance depends on whether it is equitable in the final analysis.

(l) Evaluation

The foregoing analysis demonstrates that equitable methods are those that need to give effect to legal principles governing the entitlement to maritime areas. Law is present at every stage of equitable delimitation. Equity serves the purpose of the law and has its legal basis determined under the law. At the same time, the very use and selection of equitable methods is impacted on by the legal considerations governing entitlement to the maritime areas.

The selection and use of equitable criteria above all depends on their link to the legal basis of the entitlement of the State to the relevant maritime area. In

[235] *ICJ Reports*, 1993, 61–62.
[236] Separate Opinion, *id*, 148.

most cases it is just equidistance and proportionality that dispose of the dispute. These are the most straightforward, simple and transparent methods whose equitableness is not very likely to be doubted. This approach excludes or significantly reduces the risk and impression of subjectivity.

Thus, there is very little in the original content of equity. On the whole, the methods selected by the Court as compared to the rejected methods convey the impression that the equitable delimitation should be more than something seen as equitable by the Court. It should relate to some objective factor, law or systemic fact, to command the required degree of legitimacy.

5. The Standard of 'Fair and Equitable Treatment' in International Investment Law

(a) Conceptual Aspects

'Fair and equitable treatment' is a standard applicable in international investment law against which the treatment of foreign investors by the State is judged. The legal basis of 'fair and equitable treatment' is the reference to it in the relevant treaty provisions.

The requirement of equitable treatment raises the issue of whether this concept is yet another aspect of equity or even the requirement to resolve situations *ex aequo et bono*. There have been several attempts to define 'fair and equitable treatment' or illuminate its content. The OECD Committee pointed out in 1967 that 'fair and equitable treatment' relates to the protection standard set by international law. The standard requires the protection that is generally accorded by a State to its own nationals. But this standard will be more exacting if national law and administrative practice fall short of the requirements of international law.[237]

The content and meaning of 'fair and equitable treatment' has been the subject of extensive analysis.[238] This, however, has not produced any authoritative definition. The precise meaning of the 'fair and equitable standard' is normally not defined in the respective treaties. The ICSID Arbitration Tribunal in *CMS/Argentina* emphasised that 'The [US-Argentine Bilateral investment] Treaty, like most bilateral investment treaties, does not define the standard of fair and equitable treatment and to this extent Argentina's concern about it being somewhat vague is not entirely without merit.'[239] Similarly, the Tribunal in *Lauder* noted

[237] OECD, *ILM* 1967, 120.

[238] For comprehensive and detailed analysis see OECD, *Fair and Equitable Treatment Standard in International Investment Law* (September 2004); UNCTAD, *Investor-State Disputes arising from in Investment Treaties: A Review* (2005), 37–41.

[239] *CMS Gas Transmission Company and the Argentine Republic*, Case No ARB/01/8, Award, 12 May 2005, para 273.

that there is no definition in the 1991 US-Slovak BIT of the 'fair and equitable treatment' standard it could adjudicate upon.[240] The ICSID Tribunal in *Genin* also affirmed that 'the exact content of this standard is not clear'.[241] Some tribunals, such as the Arbitral Tribunal in *Occidental*, decide on breaches of 'fair and equitable treatment' without clarifying it. The Tribunal found the breach of 'fair and equitable treatment' standard in the breach of legitimate expectations.[242]

As the ICSID Award on *Azurix* suggests, 'The question whether fair and equitable treatment is or is not additional to the minimum treatment requirement under international law is a question about the substantive content of fair and equitable treatment.'[243] At the same time, this is also a question of the normative basis of each of the standards. In other words, it matters not only whether the relevant standard covers certain conduct, but whether that standard is duly accepted and recognised as covering that conduct.

The important question relates to whether 'fair and equitable treatment' refers to some general homogenous standard of conduct, or the sum of specific proscribed conducts. In the *ADF* Award, the NAFTA Tribunal emphasised that the Investor did not discharge the burden of proving a violation of Article 1105(1) NAFTA, which provides for the requirement to accord investors 'fair and equitable treatment'. The respondent did not have to prove that 'current customary international law concerning standards of treatment consists only of discrete, specific rules applicable to limited contexts'. Nevertheless, the Tribunal refused to imply that 'the customary international law on the treatment of aliens and their property, including investments, is bereft of more general principles or requirements, with normative consequences, in respect of investments'.[244]

The standard of 'fair and equitable treatment' is incorporated in hundreds of investment treaties.[245] Yet there is no independent evidence that, apart from being embodied in conventional provisions, this standard has achieved the status of a general, or customary, norm of international law. The mere fact of this standard being enshrined in numerous treaties does not evidence its customary status. There are doctrinal claims that 'fair and equitable treatment' as embodied in bilateral investment treaties has penetrated the body of customary law.[246] The

[240] *Ronald S. Lauder and the Czech Republic*, Final Award, UNCITRAL Arbitration, 3 September 2001, para 292.

[241] *Alex Genin, Eastern Credit Limited, Inc. and A.S Baltoil and the Republic of Estonia*, Case No ARB/99/2, para 367.

[242] *Occidental Exploration and Production Company v The Republic of Ecuador*, LCIA Case No UN3467 (US/Ecuador BIT), 1 July 2004, paras 180ff.

[243] *Azurix Corp. and the Argentine Republic*, ICSID Case No ARB/01/12, Award of 14 July 2006, para 364.

[244] *ADF Group and USA*, Case No ARB(AF)/00/1, 9 January 2003, para 185.

[245] S Vascianne, The Fair and Equitable Treatment Standard in International Investment Law and Practice, *BYIL* (1999), 99 at 127.

[246] S Schwebel, Investor-State Disputes and The Development of International Law, *ASIL Proceedings* (2004), 27.

better view still is that this standard is not part of customary law, as there is no sufficient evidence of *opinio juris* among States.[247]

As the OECD Guide confirms, the meaning of 'fair and equitable treatment' varies from treaty to treaty.[248] This effectively undermines the thesis that the standard as embodied in treaties has become part of customary international law. But apart from this factor, it is highly doubtful that such an indeterminate notion can be part of customary law.

In *ADF*, the NAFTA Tribunal emphasised that the investor did not demonstrate the existence in customary international law of 'a general and autonomous requirement (autonomous, that is, from specific rules addressing particular, limited, contexts) to accord fair and equitable treatment and full protection and security to foreign investments'. Although hundreds of bilateral treaties included such a requirement, this was not the same as the existence of the similar general international law standard.[249]

There are some doctrinal attempts to clarify the meaning of 'fair and equitable treatment'. FA Mann views the 'fair and equitable treatment' standard as an autonomous standard independent of the standard of general international law, suggesting that:

> A tribunal would not be concerned with a minimum, maximum or average standard. It will have to decide whether in all the circumstances the conduct in issue is fair and equitable or unfair and inequitable. No standard defined by other words is likely to be material. The terms are to be understood and applied independently and autonomously.[250]

This approach militates in favour of viewing 'fair and equitable treatment' as independent from, and higher than, the standard of treatment normally accorded to investors under international law. Under this perspective, the question whether the 'fair and equitable treatment' standard is part of customary law becomes irrelevant.

The autonomous nature of the 'fair and equitable treatment' standard can mean different things. One meaning of autonomous standard is that it differs from other standards for treatment of investors, such as the minimum standard and most-favoured nation standard.[251] This is not the same as viewing the 'fair and equitable treatment' standard as including in itself completely autonomous requirements that can govern legal relations without being supported by evidence in terms of the sources of international law.

A similar perspective relates to viewing the 'fair and equitable treatment' standard as an objective standard: that is a standard that applies objectively, that

[247] Vascianne (1999), 160–161.

[248] OECD, Fair and Equitable Treatment Standard in International Investment Law (September 2004), 40.

[249] *ADF*, para 183.

[250] FA Mann, British Treaties for the Promotion and Protection of Investments, 5 *BYIL* (1982), 244.

[251] R Kreindler, 'Fair and Equitable Treatment'—A Comparative International Law Approach, 3 *Transnational Dispute Management* (2006), Issue 3.

is to say, does not depend on the choice of parties. This is not necessarily a standard that includes a set of objectively accepted, or acceptable, principles, whatever the state of the rest of international law. This further raises the issue of whether there is an objective standard that can be inferred from international law. Finally, as can be seen from some parts of arbitral practice, objective standard also could mean that it applies to the particular investor covered by the clause whatever the standard applicable to other investors.

(b) Indeterminacy and the Quasi-Normative Character of 'Fair and Equitable Treatment'

The meaning of 'fair and equitable treatment' is mostly context-dependent. As the *Mondev* Tribunal emphasised:

> A judgment of what is fair and equitable cannot be reached in the abstract; it must depend on the facts of the particular case. It is part of the essential business of courts and tribunals to make judgments such as these. In doing so, the general principles referred to in Article 1105(1) and similar provisions must inevitably be interpreted and applied to the particular facts.[252]

The *Lauder* Arbitration Award goes further by suggesting that 'In the context of bilateral investment treaties, the "fair and equitable" standard is subjective and depends heavily on a factual context.'[253] In addition, the *Mondev* Tribunal emphasises that Article 1105(1) NAFTA does not give a NAFTA tribunal an unfettered discretion to decide for itself, on a subjective basis, what is 'fair' or 'equitable' in the circumstances of each particular case. The Tribunal can make its determination, but is bound by the minimum standard as established in State practice and in the jurisprudence of arbitral tribunals: 'It may not simply adopt its own idiosyncratic standard of what is "fair" or "equitable", without reference to established sources of law.' Consequently:

> the standard of treatment, including fair and equitable treatment and full protection and security, is to be found by reference to international law, i.e., by reference to the normal sources of international law determining the minimum standard of treatment of foreign investors.[254]

The NAFTA Tribunal in *ADF* also confirmed that the standard of 'fair and equitable treatment' does not have any autonomous and free-standing content. As the Tribunal noted, 'any general requirement to accord "fair and equitable treatment" and "full protection and security" must be disciplined by being based upon State practice and judicial or arbitral caselaw or other sources of customary or general

[252] *Mondev International Ltd and USA* (Award), 11 October 2002, para 118.
[253] *Ronald S. Lauder v The Czeck Republic*, UNCITRAL Arbitration, 3 September 2001, para 292.
[254] *Mondev*, paras 119–120.

international law'.[255] Furthermore, Articles 5(1) and 5(2) of the 2004 US Model Bilateral Investment Treaty conceives 'fair and equitable treatment' as part of the international minimum standard under general international law. As Article 5(1) specifies, 'Each Party shall accord to covered investments treatment in accordance with customary international law, including fair and equitable treatment and full protection and security.' This may be further evidence that 'fair and equitable treatment' lacks a meaning and content of its own and is accepted as part of international law. Article 5(2) even more notably suggests that '"fair and equitable treatment" includes the obligation not to deny justice in criminal, civil, or administrative adjudicatory proceedings in accordance with the principle of due process embodied in the principal legal systems of the world'.

(c) The General Content of 'Fair and Equitable Treatment'

The general problem of content relates to the measuring of State conduct in order to assess whether it can be subsumed within the 'fair and equitable treatment' standard. In terms of general judicial policy in examining the 'fair and equitable treatment' standard, the *SD Myers* Award treats 'fair and equitable treatment' as part of the structure of the international legal system. This cannot have content that neglects the characteristics of that structure, and the ways in which the norms of international law are established. As the Tribunal stresses:

> a breach of Article 1105 occurs only when it is shown that an investor has been treated in such an unjust or arbitrary manner that the treatment rises to the level that is unacceptable from the international perspective. That determination must be made in the light of the high measure of deference that international law generally extends to the right of domestic authorities to regulate matters within their own borders. The determination must also take into account any specific rules of international law that are applicable to the case.[256]

But this definition is circular. It claims that the treatment is unfair and inequitable if it is unacceptable. In reality, the unacceptability is a consequence, not the cause, of the breach of 'fair and equitable treatment'.

Further guidance in terms of the content of this standard as related to the requirements of international law can be seen in the Tribunal's pronouncement that:

> In some cases, the breach of a rule of international law by a host Party may not be decisive in determining that a foreign investor has been denied 'fair and equitable treatment', but the fact that a host Party has breached a rule of international law that is specifically designed to protect investors will tend to weigh heavily in favour of finding a breach of Article 1105.[257]

[255] *ADF*, para 184.

[256] *SD Myers and Government of Canada* (Partial Award, NAFTA Arbitration under the UNCITRAL Rules), 13 November 2000, para 263.

[257] *SD Myers*, para 264.

Tribunals also pronounce on what should be the basic characteristics if the conduct can be seen as a breach of fair and equitable treatment. If 'fair and equitable treatment' is understood literally, then it arguably encompasses more than just egregious or arbitrary conduct by the host State. Being inequitable can presumably relate to conduct that is not necessarily arbitrary. As the *Mondev* Award specifies, 'To the modern eye, what is unfair or inequitable need not equate with the outrageous or the egregious. In particular, a State may treat foreign investment unfairly and inequitably without necessarily acting in bad faith.'[258] *Mondev* also attempts to describe the positive content of the 'fair and equitable treatment' standard, but suggests only a very loose and indeterminate definition:

> The test is not whether a particular result is surprising, but whether the shock or surprise occasioned to an impartial tribunal leads, on reflection, to justified concerns as to the judicial propriety of the outcome, bearing in mind on the one hand that international tribunals are not courts of appeal, and on the other hand that Chapter 11 of NAFTA (like other treaties for the protection of investments) is intended to provide a real measure of protection. In the end the question is whether, at an international level and having regard to generally accepted standards of the administration of justice, a tribunal can conclude in the light of all the available facts that the impugned decision was clearly improper and discreditable, with the result that the investment has been subjected to unfair and inequitable treatment.[259]

This formulation is as vague as it is circular, in suggesting that treatment is unfair and inequitable when the relevant evidence suggests that it is unfair and inequitable. In addition, it does not define in relation to what the relevant conduct should be improper and discreditable and what standard should be applied to judging this process. More specifically, the core question—does the relevant conduct have to be at variance with international law to be considered inequitable?—is not addressed.

The *Mondev* Tribunal in the same paragraph accepts that 'This is admittedly a somewhat open-ended standard, but it may be that in practice no more precise formula can be offered to cover the range of possibilities.' This is the issue of determining applicable law to judge the State conduct. The *Mondev*-style identification of indeterminate standard susceptible of subjective manipulation fails to guarantee the legal certainty and transparency so much needed in the context where States agree to submit to treaty-based arbitral jurisdiction.

The Award in *Waste Management* professes to follow *Mondev*, but upholds a narrower definition of 'fair and equitable treatment' which is more acceptable in terms of the general structure of international law:

> the minimum standard of treatment of fair and equitable treatment is infringed by conduct attributable to the State and harmful to the claimant if the conduct is arbitrary, grossly unfair, unjust or idiosyncratic, is discriminatory and exposes the claimant

[258] *Mondev*, para 116.
[259] *Mondev*, para 127.

to sectional or racial prejudice, or involves a lack of due process leading to an outcome which offends judicial propriety—as might be the case with a manifest failure of natural justice in judicial proceedings or a complete lack of transparency and candour in an administrative process. In applying this standard it is relevant that the treatment is in breach of representations made by the host State which were reasonably relied on by the claimant.[260]

In *Thunderbird*, the investor limited its claim under Article 1105(1) to the traditional general international law understanding of 'fair and equitable treatment'. As the Investor submitted, 'three international law doctrines—detrimental reliance, denial of justice, and abuse of rights—can be used to inform the Tribunal's interpretation of how "fair and equitable treatment" was not provided to Thunderbird or its investments'.[261] The Tribunal conceived of the 'fair and equitable treatment' standard as limited to the general international law protection of investors. It decided to 'measure the Article 1105(1) of the NAFTA minimum standard of treatment against the customary international law minimum standard, according to which foreign investors are entitled to a certain level of treatment, failing which the host State's international responsibility may be engaged'.[262]

The ICSID Award in *CMS/Argentina* suggests that 'fair and equitable treatment is inseparable from stability and predictability'.[263] But it still falls short of providing any predictable standard. It fails to clarify what is the legal standard defining the scope of the required conduct in relation to which the investor can expect 'stability and predictability'. Is this limited to the requirement that rights specifically defined in the treaty will not be violated, or does it go beyond that?

The *CMS* Tribunal includes the concept of arbitrariness in 'fair and equitable treatment', stating that 'The standard of protection against arbitrariness and discrimination is related to that of fair and equitable treatment. Any measure that might involve arbitrariness or discrimination is in itself contrary to fair and equitable treatment.' But after this relatively predictable standard, the Tribunal proceeds to argue that 'The standard is impairment: the management, operation, maintenance, use, enjoyment, acquisition, expansion, or disposal of the investment must be impaired by the measures adopted.'[264] If arbitrariness is a requirement that must be satisfied in relation to impairment, this is a relatively predictable standard; if the two are separate then it is not. Still, there is no evidence that the notion of impairment is built into the treaty-based notion of 'fair and equitable treatment', or that the latter is restricted to the former. The *CMS* Tribunal's exercise consists in developing original notions instead of referring to established law.

260 *Waste Management Inc and United Mexican States* (Award), 2 June 2000, para 98.

261 *International Thunderbird Gaming Corporation and the United Mexican States* (Award), 26 January 2006, para 186.

262 *Thunderbird*, para 193.

263 *CMS/Argentina*, para 276.

264 *CMS*, para 290.

In *Tecmed*, the NAFTA Tribunal viewed the observance of the 'fair and equitable treatment' standard in terms of the absence of arbitrariness in terms of *Neer* and the International Court's decision in *ELSI*.[265] At the same time, the Tribunal considered that the 'fair and equitable treatment' standard under the 1996 Spanish-Mexican BIT incorporates the legitimate expectations standard. This requires 'the host State to act in a consistent manner, free from ambiguity and totally transparently in its relations with the foreign investor, so that it may know beforehand any and all rules and regulations that will govern its investments, as well as the goals of the relevant policies and administrative practices or directives, to be able to plan its investment and comply with such regulations. Any and all State actions conforming to such criteria should relate not only to the guidelines, directives or requirements issued, or the resolutions approved thereunder, but also to the goals underlying such regulations.'[266] Furthermore, 'the Claimant was entitled to expect that the government's actions would be free from any ambiguity that might affect the early assessment made by the foreign investor of its real legal situation or the situation affecting its investment and the actions the investor should take to act accordingly'.[267]

This is again a very general, far-reaching and all-comprehensive standard, making the State accountable to the investor in all dimensions. It does not require that the abuse of power, denial of justice, or bad faith be present in the State conduct. The breaches that the Tribunal identified would not be subsumable within the *Neer/ELSI* standard. They did not cross the threshold of inappropriateness depicted in these two cases—the very same cases which were taken by the *Tecmed* Tribunal as a starting point.

(d) Specific Elements of the 'Fair and Equitable Treatment' Standard

The principal question in relation to the specific content of 'fair and equitable treatment' is whether arbitral tribunals enunciate any link between the standard of 'fair and equitable treatment' and the legal norms that govern the rights of investors or host States, for instance the norm on expropriation or the prohibition on discrimination. The indeterminacy of this notion causes duplication in arbitral practice and the adoption of different assessments by tribunals in relation to similar facts.[268] In general, it seems that the whole standard as developed in one part of arbitral jurisprudence relates to the common-sense understanding of

[265] *Tecnicas Medioambientales Tecmed S.A v The United Mexican States*, Case No ARB (AF)/00/2, Award of 29 May 2003, para 154. *L.F.H. Neer and Pauline Neer (U.S.A.) v United Mexican States*, 4 *RIAA* 60.

[266] *Tecmed*, para 154.

[267] *Id*, para 167.

[268] Discussion on 'Fair and Equitable Treatment under NAFTA's Investment Chapter', 96 *ASIL Proceedings* (2002), 9 at 16.

what is useful and advantageous for the investor, not what effective operation of the relevant legal norms requires. Such a common-sense approach by tribunals to 'fair and equitable treatment' is based on no authority other than the reference to previous arbitral decisions. The evolution of the relevant principle, particularly its significant expansion in scope, is repeatedly claimed in arbitral practice without demonstrating the evidence normally required for the evolution of legal norms. In addition, the adherence to the 'evolutionary' standard does not necessarily mean that breach of 'fair and equitable treatment' will be found.

In *Mondev*, the Tribunal applied the 'evolutionary' concept of 'fair and equitable treatment', that is, that shaped, as a matter of customary law, by the investment treaties. The Tribunal concluded that there was no breach of that standard in the conduct of the United States. More specifically, the retrospective application of the new rule in civil cases and statutory immunity of the public authorities did not constitute a breach of that standard. Furthermore, no breach of that standard was found in the failure of the Supreme Judicial Court's dismissal of and failure to remand the contract claim. In this area the Arbitral Tribunal reasoned in terms of the requirements of the rule on the denial of justice and arbitrariness.[269]

The *ADF* Tribunal also examined the conduct of the US authorities in the light of the 'fair and equitable treatment' standard. The Tribunal refused to see the application of domestic procurement measures as breaching this standard. The reason was that the NAFTA Treaty does not exclusively provide a list of such measures and leaves some of them to the freedom of national authorities. Nor was a breach of this standard found in the reversal of previous national case law. Nor did the alleged contradiction with US administrative law have such a result. As the Tribunal emphasised, 'An unauthorized or ultra vires act of a governmental entity of course remains, in international law, the act of the State of which the acting entity is part, if that entity acted in its official capacity. But, even under the Investor's view of Article 1105(1), something more than simple illegality or lack of authority under domestic law is necessary to render an act or measure inconsistent with the customary international law requirements embodied in that Article. This "something more" has not been shown by the Investor.'[270]

Furthermore, an allegation of breach of good faith is not enough to prove a breach of the 'fair and equitable treatment' standard. As the Tribunal emphasised, 'An assertion of breach of a customary law duty of good faith adds only negligible assistance in the task of determining or giving content to a standard of fair and equitable treatment.'[271] This demonstrates that in terms of breaches of the 'fair and equitable treatment' standard, tribunals are looking for breaches that will by themselves amount to breaches of international law.

269 *Mondev*, paras 129–156.
270 *ADF*, para 190.
271 *Id*, para 191.

The *Waste Management* Award ruled, consistently with its definition of 'fair and equitable treatment' in accordance with general international law standards, that Article 1105 was not breached. The case involved no arbitrariness, no denial of justice, and the other conduct of the authorities did not involve breach of an international legal obligation.[272]

In *Thunderbird*, the Tribunal failed to see the manifest arbitrariness in the Government's conduct, given that the Thunderbird company was given a full opportunity to be heard in administrative proceedings. Hence, the treatment of the company did not attain the minimum level of severity to trigger Article 1105(1).[273]

The *Methanex* Award holds that the Article 1105 treatment does not exclude discrimination between nationals and aliens.[274] The *Genin* Award does not regard the withdrawal of a licence from a company as a breach of BIT. There was no evidence of discrimination against the investor. Furthermore, 'any procedural irregularity that may have been present would have to amount to bad faith, a wilful disregard of due process of law or an extreme insufficiency of action'.[275]

The *Lauder* Award refuses to see the actions of the Czech Republic as breaches of the 'fair and equitable treatment' standard.[276] In *Azinian*, the Tribunal criticised the claimant's attempt to cloak the expropriation claim covered by Article 1110 NAFTA under the 'fair and equitable treatment' standard enshrined in Article 1105, noting that 'There has not been a claim of such a violation of international law other than the one more specifically covered by Article 1110.' The Tribunal thus denoted the claimant's attempt to maintain its claim under Article 1105 as feeble and paraphrasing the Article 1110 claim. Therefore, the Tribunal concluded that there was no breach of the 'fair and equitable treatment' standard under Article 1105.[277] One should be careful to note also that the absence of an Article 1105 claim due to the absence of an Article 1110 claim does not mean that, should the Article 1110 claim be present, the Article 1105 requirements will also be met.

In *Azurix*, the claimant alleged breach of the 'fair and equitable treatment' standard by referring to administrative delays, refusal to provide information, assertion of policy reasons, manipulation of contract language and administrative fines. In addition, the claimant referred to the good faith requirement as part of the 'fair and equitable treatment' standard.[278] The Tribunal viewed as breach of the 'fair and equitable treatment' standard the Government's decision to terminate the concession, its tariff and zoning regime and the call of the regional

[272] *Waste Management*, paras 128 ff.
[273] *Id*, paras 197 ff.
[274] *Methanex Corporation and United States of America* (NAFTA/UNCITRAL Rules), Final Award on Jurisdiction and Merits, 3 August 2005, Part 4(C), para 14.
[275] *Genin*, para 371.
[276] *Lauder*, para 293.
[277] *Azinian*, para 92.
[278] *Azurix*, paras 330, 342.

Governor for non-payment of bills by customers.[279] In reality, hardly any of these measures had any direct legal impact on investment.

Azurix interprets previous decisions, including *Waste Management*, as not requiring the presence of bad faith or malicious intention in the actions of the State.[280] As seen above, *Genin* does not unconditionally require bad faith, but on further reflection, it is difficult to see how 'arbitrary, grossly unfair, unjust or idiosyncratic [or] discriminatory' conduct can be performed without bad faith or malicious intention. If the explanation were that the measure of review relates to the outcome of the conduct rather than its motivation, this could be understood, but less so if the arbitrariness and bad faith were seen in this context either as separate or mutually exclusive.

In *Tecmed*, a breach of 'fair and equitable treatment' was found in the refusal to renew the annual permit for the operation of the company, and the ensuing uncertainty.[281] Without attempting to link this refusal to the breach of some other specific standard, the Tribunal's approach suggests that anything and everything that does not suit the investor can be seen as a breach of the 'fair and equitable treatment' standard.

The *Saluka* Award finds a breach of the 'fair and equitable treatment' standard in the failure of Government institutions to adequately communicate with investors.[282] The *CMS/Argentina* Award finds that Argentina breached the 'fair and equitable treatment' standard when it altered the investment climate.[283] The Tribunal made this finding in the context of its other, more general, finding that the 'fair and equitable treatment' standard did not differ from the international law minimum standard. Thus, the Tribunal is very presumptive in assuming that the general international law standard has developed to include alterations of the investment climate.

Under such an expansive understanding of 'fair and equitable treatment', anything that adversely affects investments and is economically unfavourable to their owners can constitute a breach of the relevant provisions of the bilateral investment treaties. That very part of jurisprudence which argues in favour of perceiving the 'fair and equitable treatment' standard as an autonomous standard independent from other international law standards confirms, by its reference to the unsubstantiated connections between the relevant acts of governments and the investment, that the 'fair and equitable treatment' standard cannot have any consistent content if it is perceived as essentially 'autonomous'.

This analysis demonstrates that arbitral practice offers very little in identifying the 'independent' or 'autonomous' content of the 'fair and equitable treatment' standard. Any 'autonomous' standard, if it does exist, can differ from the general international law standard only in marginal aspects, but not in terms of

279 *Id*, paras 374–376.
280 *Azurix*, para 372.
281 *Tecmed*, paras 161ff, 172.
282 *Saluka*, para 407.
283 *CMS/Argentina*, paras 267, 281.

mainstream substantive content. At the same time, arbitral practice is not in the least agreed as to the basic content of this projected 'autonomous' standard.

(e) Evaluation

It must be admitted that the narrower conception of the 'fair and equitable treatment' standard which limits the scope of 'fair and equitable treatment' to the classical international law requirements of refraining from abuse, discrimination and denial of justice, is by far a more consistent, transparent and predictable standard than the broader, so-called autonomous conception of the same notion. This latter conception has no consistent or predictable content and is potentially likely to encompass anything that governments do to the dislike of investors, without the need to prove that the relevant actions contradict the standards of international law.

One controversial aspect of this process is the tribunals' reference to each others' decisions in ascertaining what the 'fair and equitable treatment' standard means, while none of the previous decisions are completely faultless or consistent. The use of previous decisions, which for their part fall short of identifying the intrinsic content of 'fair and equitable treatment', to deal with the 'fair and equitable treatment' standard with no defined content, as if it had such content, is in fact an attempt to compensate for the absence of evidence of such defined content. This approach is not compatible with the framework of international law-making which requires demonstrating the content of legal norms through evidence of agreement between States.

In many cases, tribunals are generally unable to find breach of 'fair and equitable treatment' in cases where it is identified with the requirements of general public international law. In some awards tribunals adhere to the so-called 'evolutionary' concept of 'fair and equitable treatment', yet apply it to the facts in a way compatible with the general international law understanding. Other tribunals, mostly within the ICSID and UNCITRAL framework, feel freer to go beyond what international law requires in measuring 'fair and equitable treatment', as was seen above, and arrive at inconsistent outcomes.

Given the rarity of breaches of the 'fair and equitable treatment' standard found in decisions treating it as part of general international law, the content of the 'fair and equitable treatment' standard, if considered as going beyond the general international law standard, is not only indeterminate but also arbitrary. By detaching this standard from what general international law requires, one places it in a context where there are no coherent standards of identification, their place being taken by the subjective discretion of the decision-maker.

The unacceptability of such an outcome requires viewing the 'fair and equitable treatment' standard as strictly limited to what the general international law requirements are. On its own, 'fair and equitable treatment' lacks the consistency and recognition necessary for viewing it as a free-standing, quasi-normative non-law. It may embody some considerations of equity, but these are mostly what are already recognised under international law. The fact that the 'fair and equitable treatment' standard is derived from treaty clauses is also a relevant factor. Consequently, and in the final analysis, we are dealing not with the content of the 'fair and equitable treatment' standard as such, but with the content of the treaty provisions that happen to incorporate this standard. The matter, then, becomes one of treaty interpretation as opposed to one of the identification of some free-standing and autonomous rule, which is the subject of the next stage of analysis of this area.[284]

6. Proportionality

(a) General Aspects

The requirement of proportionality implies that the relevant action of the State has to be commensurate with the ends it pursues. This is not a universal principle applicable to all international law. Proportionality is nevertheless used in various fields where the limits on the freedom of action of States are evaluated in the absence of a determinate outer limit of the relevant legal regulation. The consideration of proportionality cannot impact on the legal outcome in the case of determinate legal regulation, unless the pertinent rule requires that the legality of the action of the State has to be measured by its proportionality. In this sense, proportionality is not a free-standing rule agreed upon by the international society, but a tool by which the compliance of States with their particular obligations is determined; or the tool which is used in assessing the result in applying other indeterminate concepts such as equity.

Some doubts are expressed as to whether the principle of proportionality is a general principle of law. As Higgins suggests, in the law of the sea the relevance of proportionality is different from other fields; in laws of war its existence is doubtful; and in human rights law it hardly has an existence separate from necessity.[285] Still, the concept of proportionality arises and is dealt with in jurisprudence on a regular basis, and impacts on the outcome. As non-law, proportionality is referred to in the relevant legal frameworks, either as an aspect of equity or of the margin of appreciation. The crucial question is whether this aspect of non-law, which it is, if it is not to be regarded as a general principle of law, operates similarly or differently in several fields of international law. Another key question is whether proportionality is a substantive principle determining whether some action or conduct is proportionate in the first place, or a corrective principle judging the proportionality of the outcome arrived at through the use of other principles and criteria.

Proportionality serves as a measure of actions that are otherwise deemed to be authorised in the relevant legal frameworks. Thus, its preferred meaning should be corrective rather than substantive. The following analysis demonstrates that

[284] This latter aspect constitutes a further stage of analysis, to be dealt with in Part V of this study.

[285] Higgins (1995), 236.

while in certain fields of law proportionality is expressly allocated a corrective role, in other fields such a role follows implicitly.

(b) The Law of the Sea

In the law of the sea, as the International Court emphasised in *Tunisia–Libya*, proportionality operates as an aspect of equity.[286] In maritime delimitation, proportionality has a corrective role. This means that tribunals have to assess the equitability of delimitation in terms of the disproportion in the delimitation effected through other criteria. This is not the substantive proportionality that impacts on the delimitation in the first place.

As the Arbitral Tribunal emphasised in the *Anglo-French* case, in delimiting the continental shelf of the States with opposite coasts, 'it is disproportion rather than any general principle which is the relevant criterion or factor'. Were it otherwise, the delimitation of the continental shelf would be merely the process of apportioning the equitable/proportionate share to the relevant States. This, the International Court in *North Sea* observed, was not the case. To accord primary relevance to proportionality 'would be to substitute for the delimitation of boundaries a distributive apportionment of shares'.[287] Furthermore, as Judge Arechaga observes, proportionality is meant 'to test the equitable character of the method of delimitation used, in the light of the results to which it leads. It constitutes a test to be applied *ex post facto* to the results obtained through the appreciation of the relevant circumstances, and not a relevant circumstance, or independent factor in itself.'[288] Judge Oda similarly affirms that proportionality does not by itself inform the process of delimitation.[289] As Judge Weeramantry affirmed, the disproportion factor constitutes both a special circumstance under Article 6 of the 1958 Convention, and a relevant circumstance under customary international law.[290] This reinforces the thesis that proportionality in the law of the sea is an aspect of equity.

The question thus posed in connection with the relevant delimitation is not whether the delimitation is proportionate given the size of areas and coasts. It is, instead, whether the delimitation effected through the other relevant equitable criteria is overtly disproportionate as regards the size of a certain area or in relation to the coast of a certain length.

Proportionality is not meant to impact on or modify the substantive nature of the relevant legal institutions. Its normative status as law cannot be proved with the required evidence. Thus it cannot by itself provide entitlement to the maritime area. This entitlement is based on legal norms and proportionality can only step in among the range of equitable factors to verify the final result.

[286] *ICJ Reports*, 1982, 91. [287] *Anglo-French*, para 101.
[288] *Tunisia–Libya*, *ICJ Reports*, 1982, 138.
[289] Dissenting Opinion, *Tunisia–Libya*, *ICJ Reports*, 1982, 258.
[290] Separate Opinion of Judge Weeramantry, *ICJ Reports*, 1993, 273.

As specified in the *Libya–Malta* Judgment, the use of proportionality as the substantive factor would exclude the relevance of other factors.[291] The Court goes on to explain that 'The use of proportionality as a method in its own right is wanting of support in the practice of States...or in the jurisprudence.'[292] More straightforwardly in *Gulf of Maine*, the Chamber stressed that 'it in no way intends to make an autonomous criterion or method of delimitation out of the concept of "proportionality," even if it be limited to the aspects of the length of coastline'. Proportionality could only be used to correct the inequitable consequences of applying the main method of median line.[293]

But even in this way, proportionality still serves to maintain the integrity of law. As the *Libya–Malta* case confirms, the need for a proportionality assessment may arise when the use of some other method does not duly respect the coastal configuration. If, for instance, the raw equidistance method is used, some elements of coastal configuration may be obscured. Thus, the relevance of proportionality arises from the requirement that nature must be respected.[294] Thus, the relevance of proportionality follows from the need to respect the legal basis for entitlement to the relevant maritime area.

Judge Arechaga suggests that the basic premises to consider are the area of delimitation and the length of the coast.[295] This further accords with the Arbitral pronouncement in the *Anglo-French* case that the fundamental principle that the continental shelf is based on natural prolongation places inherent limits on the relevance of proportionality in delimitation.[296] Thus, the continental shelf entitlement as law determines the limits on the relevance of proportionality as non-law.

(c) The European Convention on Human Rights

Proportionality often appears as the ultimate factor controlling the propriety and legality of action of the State in the exercise of its margin of appreciation under Articles 8 to 11 of the European Convention on Human Rights. It is stated that the margin of appreciation extends to the assessment of proportionality of the measures undertaken by the State.[297] The proportionality factor comes into play once the State's margin of appreciation is affirmed in the relevant situation, that is the requirements of necessity and legitimate aim are considered to have been met.

According to Higgins, the concept of proportionality is not expressly mentioned in the European Convention and hence in some cases the European Court seemingly analyses proportionality in the same context as necessity.[298] But still,

[291] *ICJ Reports*, 1985, para. 45.
[292] *Id*, 45.
[293] *ICJ Reports*, 1984, 335.
[294] *ICJ Reports*, 1985, 44, para 56.
[295] *Tunisia–Libya*, *ICJ Reports*, 1982, 138.
[296] *Anglo-French*, para 101.
[297] P Leach, *Taking the Case before the European Court of Human Rights* (2005), 163.
[298] Higgins (1995), 234–236.

the identity of the two concepts in the law of the European Convention cannot be assumed. The requirement is that action in the exercise of the margin of appreciation of States under the European Convention must be necessary in pursuing the legitimate aim to respond to 'pressing social need', as well as proportionate to the aim pursued. Jurisprudence is not absolutely uniform, and sometimes necessity and proportionality are examined in terms of the individual factual background. Still, in categorical terms the difference between the two requirements is visible. One determines the basis of the action. The other relates to the type and extent of that action, the initial choice of which lies with the State-party.

In *Young, James and Webster*, the concepts of necessity and proportionality are dealt with in the same context. In this case the Court was examining whether the closed shop trade union arrangements in British Rail were necessary in terms of enabling the unions to protect the interests of the employees. The Court noted that in areas other than British Rail such arrangements were not considered necessary. It had 'not been informed of any special reasons justifying the imposition of such a requirement in the case of British Rail'. The unions would still be able to protect the members' interests without the obligation for the latter to join the specific trade unions. Therefore, the Court emphasised that 'the detriment suffered by Mr. Young, Mr. James and Mr. Webster went further than was required to achieve a proper balance between the conflicting interests of those involved and cannot be regarded as proportionate to the aims being pursued'.[299]

Thus, under certain circumstances proportionality can arguably be an aspect of necessity. Nevertheless, the normal pattern is the separate profile of the two categories. Necessity relates to the reasons justifying the relevant measure, while proportionality relates to the assessment of the exercise of that measure. In *Otto-Preminger*, the European Court ruled that the relevant necessary measures will be lawful provided that they are also proportionate, though it did not directly pronounce on the issue of proportionality.[300] In the *Gillow* case, having ascertained the economic well-being of the relevant area as a legitimate aim, the Court addressed the related but qualitatively different question of whether the manner in which the housing regulation was exercised was proportionate to the legitimate aim pursued. The Court found that the measures complained of were disproportionate.[301] In *United Communist Party*, the Court, having earlier found no link between the relevant political party and terrorist activities, declared its dissolution as disproportionate. As the Court put it, 'a measure as drastic as the immediate and permanent dissolution of the TBKP, ordered before its activities had even started and coupled with a ban barring its leaders from discharging any other political responsibility, is disproportionate to the aim'.[302]

[299] *Young, James & Webster*, Nos 7601/76; 7806/77, Judgment of 13 August 1981, paras 64–65.
[300] *Otto-Preminger*, para 56.
[301] *Gillow v UK*, paras 57–58.
[302] *United Communist Party v Turkey*, para 61.

In *Pine Valley*, the Court established that governmental action was taken pursuant to the legitimate aim of applying planning legislation. The Court thus emphasised that the applicants were engaged in a business venture which by its nature involved risk. They were aware of the relevant zoning plan and the attitude of the local authority to implement it. Therefore, the annulment of the permission could not be seen as disproportionate.[303]

(d) WTO Law

In this field too, the concept of proportionality is the ultimate measure and outer limit of the legality of measures adopted under the exception clauses of GATT and GATS. Although in *US–Gasoline* the Appellate Body held that the US baseline establishment rules were subsumable under Article XX(g) of the GATT, 'There was more than one alternative course of action available to the United States in promulgating regulations.' Those alternative measures could have avoided discrimination at all. Consequently, the Appellate Body ruled 'that the baseline establishment rules, although within the terms of Article XX(g), are not entitled to the justifying protection afforded by Article XX as a whole'.[304] It seems that here the impact of measures, that is discrimination, caused a finding that the claim under Article XX(g) GATT must fail.

US–Shrimp further demonstrates the features of the proportionality principle in the WTO law. In this case, the Appellate Body considered that the US measure of a ban on shrimp imports was not 'a simple, blanket prohibition of the importation of shrimp imposed without regard to the consequences (or lack thereof) of the mode of harvesting employed upon the incidental capture and mortality of sea turtles'. It was not disproportionately wide in scope and reach in relation to the policy objection it stated. In other words, 'the means are, in principle, reasonably related to the ends. The means and ends relationship between Section 609 and the legitimate policy of conserving an exhaustible, and, in fact, endangered species, is observably a close and real one', every bit of that relationship being substantial.[305]

(e) International Humanitarian Law

As we have seen above, in humanitarian law the concept of military necessity can only be used in relation to a belligerent attack against military objects. In this context, the legality of incidental civilian damage is judged in terms of proportionality and the requirements of precaution in attack. The absolute prohibition in international humanitarian law on attacking civilians, either directly, or indiscriminately, constitutes an inherent limitations on the relevance not only of military necessity, but also proportionality.

[303] *Pine Valley Developments Ltd and others v Ireland*, No 12742/87, Judgment of 29 November 1991, para 59.

[304] *US–Gasoline*, at 23, 27.

[305] *US–Shrimp*, para 141.

In humanitarian law necessity and proportionality are separate requirements. Necessity defines the situations in which the law authorises attack. Proportionality relates to the action in authorised attack and the implications of such attack. Certain norms of humanitarian law are designed to give specific expression to the broader principle of proportionality in particular instances, being framed in such a way as to stipulate required actions and choices. One such important regulation is included in Article 57 I AP which deals with the obligation of military commanders to prevent attacks that will cause disproportionate civilian damage and to cancel the attack if such disproportionate damage is likely. Proportionality as general requirement will be applied in any relevant case.

The ICTY emphasised in *Kupreskic* the 'principle of proportionality, whereby any incidental (and unintentional) damage to civilians must not be out of proportion to the direct military advantage gained by the military attack'.[306] The proportionality of military action is measured, among other things, in terms of the time factor, 'which entails not only that the reprisals must not be excessive compared to the precedent unlawful act of warfare, but also that they must stop as soon as that unlawful act has been discontinued'.[307] In the *Blaskic* case, the Tribunal engaged with the assumption that 'Before the retreat of the Muslims, it was not clear that the criteria of proportionality of a military attack against positions defended by the military had not been met as regards the destruction of property.' However, the Tribunal noted that 'much of the destruction and damage occurred after the assaults on the villages were over and the HVO had taken control of the villages'. The civilian homes were burned by Croatian forces after the Bosnian inhabitants had left, and no one made an effort to put out the fires. Thus, after the relevant date the houses in that area could no longer be considered as military targets and consequently 'these events were large-scale destruction or devastation with no military necessity'.[308] Similarly, in the *Stakic* case, the Tribunal referred to proportionality in terms of launching 'what can only be described as planned, co-ordinated, and sustained armed attacks on civilian settlements'. This did 'not meet the requirements imposed by the fundamental principle of proportionality, particularly when considering the eyewitness testimony that fire was also opened with heavy weapons on the fleeing civilian population. The disproportionality and the use of armed force against civilian population rendered both attacks illegal.'[309]

Furthermore, the principle of proportionality can also govern attacks on targets that can, on their face, be of mixed civilian and military composition. As observed in *Kupreskic*:

Even if it can be proved that the Muslim population of Ahmici was not entirely civilian but comprised some armed elements, still no justification would exist for widespread and

[306] *Kupreskic*, IT-95–16-T, Judgment of 14 January 2000, para 524.
[307] *Id*, para 535.
[308] *Blaskic*, Trial Chamber, para 543–544.
[309] *Stakic*, Trial Chamber, IT-97–24-T, 31 July 2003, para 153.

indiscriminate attacks against civilians. Indeed, even in a situation of full-scale armed conflict, certain fundamental norms still serve to unambiguously outlaw such conduct, such as rules pertaining to proportionality.[310]

In *Galic*, the Trial Chamber examined the requirement of proportionality in conjunction with the duty of precaution under the I Additional Protocol and the consequent obligation to cancel the attack. It stated that 'The practical application of the principle of distinction requires that those who plan or launch an attack take all feasible precautions to verify that the objectives attacked are neither civilians nor civilian objects, so as to spare civilians as much as possible.'[311] Furthermore:

> In determining whether an attack was proportionate it is necessary to examine whether a reasonably well-informed person in the circumstances of the actual perpetrator, making reasonable use of the information available to him or her, could have expected excessive civilian casualties to result from the attack.[312]

Here, proportionality is in fact a condition that characterises the type of the relevant attack. As the Trial Chamber specified, 'certain apparently disproportionate attacks may give rise to the inference that civilians were actually the object of attack'.[313]

Furthermore, the requirement of proportionality is absolute and does not depend on the conduct of the other side in the conflict. The parties in conflict are under an obligation to remove civilians from the vicinity of military objects. But 'the failure of a party to abide by this obligation does not relieve the attacking side of its duty to abide by the principles of distinction and proportionality when launching an attack'.[314]

(f) The Law of the Use of Force

The requirement of proportionality in *jus ad bellum* has historically developed to enable the crystallisation of the concept of self-defence as distinguished from the broader claims to the right to self-preservation.[315] Although the issue of proportionality has received extensive doctrinal treatment, it has rarely been pronounced upon in judicial practice.

As Dinstein observes, the concept of proportionality in the context of self-defence has special meaning, and requires comparing the quantum of force and counter force used.[316] Dinstein also argues that the requirement of proportionality is not genuinely relevant in terms of all-out armed attack.[317]

310 *Kupreskic*, para 513.
311 *Galic*, Trial Chamber, para 58.
312 *Id*, para 58.
313 *Id*, para 60.
314 *Id*, para 61.
315 I Brownlie, *International Law and the Use of Force by States* (1963), 261.
316 Y Dinstein, *War, Aggression and Self-Defence* (2005), 237.
317 Dinstein (2005), 238–241.

Nevertheless, in practice the criteria of *jus ad bellum* in relation to proportionality are strict and have never in judicial practice justified the use of force. As seen above, in the *Oil Platforms* case the International Court did not accept the plea of the United States that its attacks on Iranian oil platforms were necessary. As for proportionality, the Court could not:

> close its eyes to the scale of the whole operation, which involved, *inter alia*, the destruction of two Iranian frigates and a number of other naval vessels and aircraft. As a response to the mining, by an unidentified agency, of a single United States warship, which was severely damaged but not sunk, and without loss of life, neither 'Operation Praying Mantis' as a whole, nor even that part of it that destroyed the Salman and Nasr platforms, can be regarded, in the circumstances of this case, as a proportionate use of force in self-defence.[318]

A similar approach was taken by the Court in the above-quoted passage from the *Congo–Uganda* case in terms of the assessment of proportionality of Ugandan actions on the territory of the Congo.[319]

A special problem of proportionality has been raised regarding the use of nuclear weapons in self-defence. As the International Court emphasised in the *Nuclear Weapons* Advisory Opinion, 'The submission of the exercise of the right of self-defence to the conditions of necessity and proportionality is a rule of customary international law. ... This dual condition applies equally to Article 51 of the Charter, whatever the means of force employed.' However, the Court added that 'The proportionality principle may thus not in itself exclude the use of nuclear weapons in self-defence in all circumstances. But at the same time, a use of force that is proportionate under the law of self-defence, must, in order to be lawful, also meet the requirements of the law applicable in armed conflict which comprise in particular the principles and rules of humanitarian law.'[320] Thus, the Court viewed this aspect of proportionality under *jus ad bellum* as referring to the operation of proportionality under *jus in bello*. The pertinent question is whether the former can be measured independently of the latter, which question is essentially which of the two bodies of law prevail in the relevant situation.

The Court also addressed the submission that:

> the very nature of nuclear weapons, and the high probability of an escalation of nuclear exchanges, mean that there is an extremely strong risk of devastation. The risk factor is said to negate the possibility of the condition of proportionality being complied with. The Court does not find it necessary to embark upon the quantification of such risks; nor does it need to enquire into the question whether tactical nuclear weapons exist which are sufficiently precise to limit those risks: it suffices for the Court to note that the very nature of all nuclear weapons and the profound risks associated therewith are further considerations to be borne in mind by States believing they can exercise a nuclear response in self-defence in accordance with the requirements of proportionality.[321]

318 *Oil Platforms*, para 77.
319 See above Section III(5).
320 *ICJ Reports*, 1996, 258.
321 *Id.*

One explanation of the use of nuclear weapons as proportionate measure of self-defence is that the use of nuclear weapons can be permitted when the conventional forces of the attacked State fail to check the aggressor.[322] This understanding is neither approved nor disapproved in practice, although it would not be easy to prove that this would be disproportionate. It must also be noted that in its Advisory Opinion the International Court still left some uncertainty in terms of the proportionality, and more generally legality, of the use of nuclear weapons. It referred to the situations in which the requirement of State survival may preclude the unambiguous characterisation of the use of nuclear weapons as illegal.[323] Therefore, in the end, the Court's examination of proportionality in this field does not really clarify the matter. For the Court refers the originally *jus ad bellum* issue to *jus in bello* and then again provides for a *jus ad bellum* ground which could in the final analysis preclude the unambiguous illegality of the disproportionate use of nuclear weapons. Although the Court has arguably left this issue unresolved, it could be suggested, though perhaps not definitely established, that the very reference to State survival as an element of the right to self-defence under Article 51 of the Charter and the relevant customary law, entails the primacy of the *jus ad bellum* regulation over that of *jus in bello*. The proportionality of the use of nuclear weapons has in such a case to be determined by its relationship to the need for State survival as a matter of self-defence, as distinguished from the proportionality of its impact under *jus in bello*. This reading is supported by the Court's initial statement in the Operative Part of the Opinion that the use of nuclear weapons has to satisfy the requirements of Article 51 of the UN Charter, its subsequent statement that the use of nuclear weapons is generally contrary to humanitarian law, and its ultimate reference to the extreme circumstances of State survival, which prevent the ambiguous characterisation of the use of nuclear weapons as illegal.

(g) Evaluation

Even though several authors treat the determination of issues of necessity and proportionality as a single process, the two concepts are still separate. Necessity relates to what is necessary in the first place, in the sense that a pressing social need requires something to be done. Proportionality relates to the *a posteriori* assessment of the measures taken. Viewed from this perspective, necessity and proportionality are in principle separate in all relevant fields of international law.

Whether or not proportionality can be seen as a general rule or principle of international law, it operates in a variety of fields in this legal system and can provide the limitation and the measure of legality of the action of States, sometimes to the extent of detail. Tribunals use this criterion frequently and rigorously. In

[322] Brownlie (1963), 263.
[323] *ICJ Reports*, 1996, 266, Operative Paragraph 1(E).

other words, proportionality is the adverse limitation on the relevance and effect of non-law on rights and obligations under international law. While indeterminate on its face, proportionality can be quite specific in enabling tribunals to assess the legality of State actions in various fields.

7. Legitimate Expectations

In a way, the protection of legitimate expectations relates to the operation of any legal obligation. Literally speaking, the party to any legal obligation has a legitimate expectation that it will be reciprocated. The meaning of legitimate expectations as an autonomous concept is more complex, and has been raised in different fields of international law. It is not straightforwardly clear what can be expected in an area in which legitimate expectations are relevant: the observance of legal norms, or favours and benefits going beyond what the legal norms require?

Some indications as to the legal position in this field can be seen in the jurisprudence of the European Court of Human Rights, most notably with regard to the application of Article 1 of Protocol I to the European Convention regarding the right to peaceful enjoyment of possessions. In some cases, the concept of legitimate expectations is used to define whether a particular situation is covered by the concept of 'possession' that triggers the applicability of Article 1 to the facts. At the same time, the Court's jurisprudence is clear that relevant expectations should be more than a reasonable hope. They should follow from the relevant domestic legislation or judicial practice, that is they must largely be expectations created by the conduct of the State.

The *Malinovskiy* case related to the issue of housing and was adjudicated against the legal background that, as the Court defined it, 'the right to any social benefit is not included as such among the rights and freedoms guaranteed by the Convention' and 'a right to live in a particular property not owned by the applicant does not as such constitute a "possession" within the meaning of Article 1'.[324] But the Court stated that pecuniary assets and benefits in relation to which the applicant has 'legitimate expectation' may well be subsumable within this concept of 'possession'.[325] The facts of the case disclosed that the judgment of the Russian court obliged the town council to put at the applicant's disposal a flat. This generated the applicant's 'legitimate expectation' of acquiring this asset, which in its turn became covered by the concept of 'possession' under Article 1.[326] Thus, in this case legitimate expectations derived from the Government's action which created these expectations on the part of the applicant.

[324] *Malinovskiy v Russia*, No 41302/02, Judgment of 7 July 2005, para 42.
[325] *Id*, para 43.
[326] *Id*, paras 44–46; see also *Shpakovskiy v Russia*, No 41307/02, Judgment of 7 July 2005, paras 32–38.

In *Stretch*, the Court reaffirmed that under Article 1 of Protocol 1, '"possessions" can be "existing possessions" or assets, including claims, in respect of which the applicant can argue that he has at least a "legitimate expectation" of obtaining effective enjoyment of a property right'.[327] The legitimate expectation was inferable from the fact that the applicant and the Dorchester local authority had agreed that the applicant would have the possibility of extending the lease of the relevant object. As it turned out, this agreement contradicted domestic legal requirements and was *ultra vires*, without the parties being familiar with this. Therefore, the applicant:

> clearly expected to be able to renew the option and continue to obtain the benefit of rent from the occupation of those premises which he had sub-let. He reached in negotiations with the local authority the stage of preparing a draft renewal lease with an agreed increased ground rent, already signed on his side and had proceeded to enter into agreements with his sub-lessees. The local authority, West Dorset, itself only raised the problem of invalidity at a very late stage.

Consequently, the applicant was 'regarded as having at least a legitimate expectation of exercising the option to renew' and the governmental action constituted interference with the rights under Article 1.[328]

In terms of whether the interference with the applicant's rights was justified, the Court focused on the improper application of the doctrine of *ultra vires*. The local authority's powers did not include the possibility of agreeing to an option for renewal of the lease. The Court emphasised that 'Since however the local authority itself considered that it had the power to grant an option, it does not appear unreasonable that the applicant and his legal advisers entertained the same belief.' Therefore, 'The applicant not only had the expectation of deriving future return from his investment in the lease but, as was noted in the Court of Appeal, the option to renew had been an important part of the lease for a person undertaking building obligations and who otherwise would have had a limited period in which to recoup his expenditure.' Consequently, the Court found that the interference with the applicant's possessions was disproportionate and Article 1 had been violated.[329] Thus, in this case the concept of legitimate expectations was applied in terms of defining the concept of possessions, of determining the existence of interference with the right, and of the assessment of proportionality of Governmental measures. In all these dimensions, the Court examined the same factual matter of the applicant's expectation of having the possibility of lease renewal due to the lack of knowledge that the local authority had acted *ultra vires*. The Court's approach implies that the uncertainty created by authorities will weigh in the assessment of proportionality of government measures.

[327] *Stretch v UK*, 44277/98, Judgment of 24 June 2003, para 32.
[328] *Id*, paras 34–35.
[329] *Id*, paras 39–41.

In *Oneryildiz*, the Court likewise emphasised that 'The concept of "possessions" is not limited to "existing possessions" but may also cover assets, including claims, in respect of which the applicant can argue that he has at least a reasonable and "legitimate expectation" of obtaining effective enjoyment of a property right.'[330] It was established that the applicant's dwelling had been erected in breach of Turkish town-planning regulations and had not conformed to the relevant technical standards. The applicant stated that no steps were taken to prevent him from taking ownership of the land. The Court emphasised that the applicant's hope of having the land in issue transferred to him one day did not constitute a claim of a kind that was sufficiently established to be enforceable in the courts, and hence distinct 'possession' within the meaning of the Court's case law.[331] In terms of the applicant's dwellings on the land, the Court was able to see that the authorities acknowledged the applicant's proprietary interest in this object. On this point the Court stated, significantly enough, that it could not:

> accept that they can be criticised in this way for irregularities of which the relevant authorities had been aware for almost five years.
>
> It does, admittedly, accept that the exercise of discretion encompassing a multitude of local factors is inherent in the choice and implementation of town and country planning policies and of any resulting measures. However, when faced with an issue such as that raised in the instant case, the authorities cannot legitimately rely on their margin of appreciation, which in no way dispenses them from their duty to act in good time, in an appropriate and, above all, consistent manner.
>
> That was not the case in this instance, since the uncertainty created within Turkish society as to the implementation of laws to curb illegal settlements was surely unlikely to have caused the applicant to imagine that the situation regarding his dwelling was liable to change overnight.

Therefore, the applicant could have had a legitimate expectation that the interference would not take place the way it did. Consequently, the applicant's proprietary interest having been sufficiently established, the Court found that the situation was included within the concept of 'possession' under Article 1.[332] In terms of compliance with a duty to protect possessions from the harm caused by an explosion that occurred nearby, the Court emphasised that:

> Genuine, effective exercise of the right protected by that provision does not depend merely on the State's duty not to interfere, but may require positive measures of protection, particularly where there is a direct link between the measures an applicant may legitimately expect from the authorities and his effective enjoyment of his possessions.
>
> In the present case there is no doubt that the causal link established between the gross negligence attributable to the State and the loss of human lives also applies to the engulfment of the applicant's house. In the Court's view, the resulting infringement amounts

[330] *Oneryildiz v Turkey*, No 48939/99, Judgment of 30 November 2004, para 124.
[331] *Id*, para 126.
[332] *Id*, paras 127–129.

not to 'interference' but to the breach of a positive obligation, since the State officials and authorities did not do everything within their power to protect the applicant's proprietary interests.[333]

The Court further rejected the argument that a legitimate aim could offset the need to perform the positive obligation to take practical steps to avoid destruction of the applicant's house. Therefore, the Court ruled that Article 1 had been violated.[334] It is also significant that the *Oneryildiz* case relates not to the Government's arbitrary interference with property such as expropriation, but its negligence which resulted in harm to the applicant's possessions. This explains why legitimate aim could not be invoked by the Government. The harm caused by negligence could not be said to be caused pursuant to the legitimate aim.

In *SA Dangeville*, the applicant invoked the concept of legitimate expectations in terms of the recovery of tax paid as a result of a situation which the French Administrative Court of Appeal and the Government Commissioner in the *Conseil d'Etat* considered to be unlawful.[335] The Court concluded that the applicant's claim to the tax paid in error constituted an asset subsumable within the concept of 'possession' and 'the applicant company had at least a legitimate expectation of being able to obtain the reimbursement of the disputed sum'.[336] As distinct from *Malinovskiy*, in this case the Court first identified the existence of the asset covered by the concept of 'possession' and on the basis of this it ruled that legitimate expectations existed.

In *Pine Valley*, the European Court affirmed that the applicant had 'at least a legitimate expectation' of developing land which could have been the subject of an interference with the right under Article 1 of Protocol 1. The land thus constituted part of its property covered under Article 1.[337] However, the Court applied the doctrine of margin of appreciation to this case. It found that the interference was 'in accordance with the general interest' as an application of the relevant planning legislation.[338] Therefore, the factor of 'legitimate expectations' was not critical.

In assessing the general concept of 'legitimate expectations', the Grand Chamber of the European Court in the *Kopecky* case emphasised some features of this notion as inferable from previous practice. In terms of *Pine Valley* and *Stretch*, the Grand Chamber emphasised that this doctrine related to the definition of protected possessions under Article 1, as:

the persons concerned were entitled to rely on the fact that the legal act on the basis of which they had incurred financial obligations would not be retrospectively invalidated to their detriment. In this class of case, the 'legitimate expectation' is thus based on a

[333] *Id*, paras 134–135.
[334] *Id*, paras 136–137.
[335] *S.A. Dangeville v France*, No 36677/97, Judgment of 16 April 2002, para 44.
[336] *Id*, para 48.
[337] *Pine Valley Developments Ltd and others v Ireland*, No 12742/87, Judgment of 29 November 1991, para 51.
[338] *Id*, paras 57–59.

reasonably justified reliance on a legal act which has a sound legal basis and which bears on property rights.[339]

While the existence of 'possessions' does not automatically generate legitimate expectations, 'It was however implicit that no such expectation could come into play in the absence of an "asset" falling within the ambit of Article 1 of Protocol No. 1.' In other words, legitimate expectations were not themselves constitutive of the relevant legal right to property.[340] They only arise in relation to an otherwise existing entitlement to property or other possessions subsumable within Article 1.

What, then, is the normative status of the protection of 'legitimate expectations' under the law of the European Convention? On the one hand, these expectations relate to the factual situation and the conduct of States in the light of the concepts included in Article 1 of Protocol 1. They relate, among others, to the expectations created and conveyed to the individual by governmental action. The concept of 'legitimate expectations' does not define the normative standard nor influence the level of protection under it. What it does is to help clarify whether the standard as it exists has been interfered with. On the other hand, 'legitimate expectations' having been found to be breached does not necessarily entail a finding of breach of the Convention. 'Legitimate expectations' relate to determining whether there is interference with the exercise of the right—the very same interference that can be justified by the legitimate aim. Therefore, the law of the European Convention on Human Rights does not envisage the protection of legitimate expectations as an autonomous quasi-normative standard that impacts on the content of applicable law.

There have been frequent references to the protection of legitimate expectations in the practice of WTO dispute settlement bodies. The Panel Report in *Korea–Government Procurement* perceives the notion of legitimate expectations as going beyond the duty to respect the object and purpose of the treaty, and comprising the general requirement of good faith in competition.[341] The Appellate Body in *India–Patent* achieved a different outcome. India questioned the Panel's determination that the protection of legitimate expectations of Members regarding the conditions of competition was a well-established GATT principle, which derived in part from Article XXIII GATT.[342] The Appellate Body referred to two related concepts. One was 'the concept of protecting the expectations of contracting parties as to the competitive relationship between their products and the products of other contracting parties'. The second was 'the concept of the

[339] *Kopecky v Slovakia*, No 44912/98, Judgment of 28 September 2004, para 47.

[340] *Id*, para 49.

[341] *Korea–Measures Affecting Government Procurement*, Report of the Panel, WT/DS163/R, 1 May 2000, para 7.95.

[342] *India–Patent Protection for Pharmaceutical and Agricultural Chemical Products*, AB-1997–5, Report of the Appellate Body, WT/DS50/AB/R, 19 December 1997, paras 33ff.

protection of the reasonable expectations of contracting parties relating to market access concessions'.[343]

In the context of violation complaints, the relevance of the reasonable expectations of States is often stated in relation to equal competition between imported and domestic products. But this is done after the violation of the relevant legal provision is found. However, with regard to non-violation complaints, which, 'In the absence of substantive legal rules in many areas relating to international trade, . . . [are] aimed at preventing contracting parties from using non-tariff barriers or other policy measures to negate the benefits of negotiated tariff concessions,' complaints can be brought before the WTO bodies whether or not the relevant measure is inconsistent with the covered agreements. The ultimate goal of this is not the withdrawal of a measure but 'achieving a mutually satisfactory adjustment, usually by means of compensation'.[344] More specifically, on the nature of legitimate expectations, the Appellate Body stated that 'The legitimate expectations of the parties to a treaty are reflected in the language of the treaty itself.' The Appellate Body rejected the Panel's development of legitimate expectations as a specific and free-standing interpretative principle.[345]

As emphasised in doctrine, the protection of legitimate expectations is a judge-made principle originated in the jurisprudence of the WTO panels and the Appellate Body has yet to accept its full enforceability.[346] Presumably, the non-violation complaints in WTO law and the notion of legitimate expectations as to conditions of competition 'have been brought into relation with good faith and completeness of WTO as a legal system'.[347] Nevertheless, the relevance of the notion of legitimate expectations depends on the adjudicatory use of the interpretation principles under the Vienna Convention on the Law of Treaties, and within the Appellate Body the restrictive approach prevails.[348]

Another field where the notion of legitimate expectations has found expression is international investment arbitration. The NAFTA Tribunal in *ADF* referred to the investor's submission that the relevant US Governmental body 'refused to follow and apply pre-existing caselaw in respect of ADF International in the Springfield Interchange Project, thus ignoring the Investor's legitimate expectations generated by that caselaw'. But the Tribunal dismissed this claim by placing the issue of legitimate expectations in the context of appreciating whether the relevant conduct was 'grossly unfair or unreasonable'. Furthermore, 'any expectations that the Investor had with respect to the relevancy or applicability of the caselaw it cited were not created by any misleading representations made by authorized officials of the US Federal Government but rather, it appears probable, by legal advice received by the Investor from private U.S. counsel'.[349]

[343] *India–Patent*, para 36.
[344] *Id*, paras 40–41.
[345] *Id*, paras 45–48.
[346] Pannizon (2006), 129.
[347] *Id*, 143.
[348] *Id*, 174–175.
[349] *ADF*, para 189.

Thus the Tribunal seems to have refused to view the legitimate expectations standard as the autonomous requirement against which the State conduct could be judged, whatever the investor's perception of this. Expectations can be seen as breached when the elements of the denial of justice are present, or when the government seems to be estopped in relation to the investor.

In *Tecmed*, the ICSID Tribunal considered the issue of legitimate expectations in the context of allegations of breaches of the 'fair and equitable treatment' standard. It claimed that these expectations were breached even though the claimant could not in these circumstances expect the relevant favours either as a matter of national or international law. The matter related to the relevant political and social circumstances 'shown with all their magnitude after a substantial part of the investment had been made and could not have reasonably been foreseen by the Claimant with the scope, effects and consequences that those circumstances had'. There was no doubt for the Tribunal that, even if the investor did not have an indefinite permit for its operations but a permit renewable every year, 'the Claimant's expectation was that of a long-term investment relying on the recovery of its investment and the estimated return through the operation of the landfill during its entire useful life'.[350]

The ICSID Award in *Azurix* addressed the issue of legitimate expectations in the context of the expropriation of property. It referred to 'the frustration of the investor's legitimate expectations when a State repudiates former assurances, or refuses to give assurances that it will comply with its obligations depriving the investor in whole or significant part, of the use or reasonably-to-be-expected economic benefit of its investment'.[351] The Tribunal also addressed the issue of legitimate expectations in the set of State actions which did not contradict any legal standard *per se*, but allegedly were 'unhelpful' to the investor and damaged its image.[352] The Tribunal was unable to identify the relevant conduct as expropriation. Hence no independent, or otherwise, breach of legitimate expectations was identified. Further, in the context of 'fair and equitable treatment', the claimant referred to the alleged breach of legitimate expectations.[353] But the Tribunal judged the 'fair and equitable treatment' issue without pronouncing on the issue of legitimate expectations.

The *Saluka* Award treats the principle of legitimate expectation as an aspect of 'fair and equitable treatment', and hence as an issue of compliance by the host State with treaty obligations. While this is so conceptually, problems arise in terms of application of this standard in view of the indeterminacy of the 'fair and equitable treatment' standard and its susceptibility to be manipulated subjectively.

According to the Award, the Claimant was entitled to expect even-handed and consistent action by the State.[354] The claim of the investor that it should not have been treated differently was also seen by the Tribunal as an aspect of

350 *Tecmed*, para 149.
351 *Azurix*, para 316.
352 *Id*, paras 319–320.
353 *Id*, at 120–124.
354 *Saluka*, para 323.

'fair and equitable treatment'. In relation to another claim, the Tribunal held that the Company could not have reasonably expected that the Czech legislature would fix certain legal shortcomings in the field where the investor was active. The investor knew in advance that Czech legal regulation on loan security was not effective.[355]

Similarly, *Occidental* addressed the issue of legitimate expectations in the context of 'fair and equitable treatment', as part of Article II(1) BIT. The claim was that the revocation of previous decisions relied upon by the investor breached its legitimate expectations. The respondent argued that there was no legitimate expectation in the matter of a VAT refund.[356] The Tribunal referred to the fact that Occidental's clarification request received from the Ecuadorian Government was 'a wholly unsatisfactory and thoroughly vague answer'. By reference to the breach of legitimate expectations it found that the 'fair and equitable treatment' standard was breached.[357] The Tribunal's reasoning is dubious. In this case one could at least expect that the Tribunal would clarify whether the Government's reply was well founded on its merits. Deriving breach of legitimate expectations from the vague answer on what could not otherwise produce legitimate expectations is rather odd.

This practice suggests that the NAFTA jurisprudence identifies the protection of legitimate expectations with the breach of treaty obligations. Other tribunals pronounce on this notion in a wide variety of contexts, without identifying its normative basis. They use it to identify various breaches of the treaty standards without making a convincing case that the conduct allegedly covered by 'legitimate expectations' indeed breaches the relevant legal obligation. Therefore it seems that in arbitral jurisprudence the notion of 'legitimate expectations' has become jargon. This jurisprudence raises, but does not clarify, thoughts as to the nature of the principle of legitimate expectations and whether it can have any content without being linked to the breach of some other rule related to expropriation or 'fair and equitable treatment'. While suggesting no uniform formulation of the principle they advocate, the arbitral tribunals seem to be suggesting that the notion of legitimate expectations can cover anything that would be disadvantageous or disagreeable to the investor even without raising it to the rank of breach of pertinent clause in the relevant investment treaty, or a rule of general international law.

Thus, the concept of legitimate expectations, if properly applied in different areas of international law, is a concept that expresses or gives effect to other principles or norms of international law, including *pacta sunt servanda*, good faith, and presumably also equity. If the protection of legitimate expectations relates to what States are expected to do in terms of their international obligations, then it just expresses the binding force of law rather than the separate category of non-law.

[355] *Id*, paras 352–360.

[356] *Occidental Exploration and Production Company v The Republic of Ecuador*, LCIA Case No UN3467 (US/Ecuador BIT), Award of 1 July 2004, para 181.

[357] *Occidental*, paras 184–186.

PART IV

THE REGIME AND METHODS OF INTERPRETATION IN INTERNATIONAL LAW

9

Conceptual Aspects of Interpretation

1. The Limits on the Process of Interpretation

Interpretation is indispensable for understanding the content and effects of international acts and instruments and is therefore extensively treated both in doctrine and in jurisprudence. As a legal tool, interpretation is concerned with the clarification of the meaning of legal acts and rules. In literary sense, interpretation means explanation or exposition.[1] As a synonym of interpretation, the term 'construction' is also often used.[2] As the Permanent Court of International Justice observed, 'to construe' means to give a precise definition of the meaning and scope.[3]

The purpose of interpretation is to specify the ambit and normative content of the relevant instrument.[4] Interpretation is also denoted as the exercise that clarifies the sense of the treaty (*Vertragssinn*) and its effect;[5] or ascertains the intention of the parties from the text,[6] their common intention.[7] As emphasised repeatedly, interpretation is closely linked with the application and enforcement of treaties. The application of a treaty is necessarily preceded by its conscious or subconscious interpretation, to clarify its ambit before it can be applied.[8]

It is axiomatic that international law is the body of rules produced by consent and agreement between sovereign States. It is also important to understand that

[1] 5 *Oxford English Dictionary* (1989), 414–415.

[2] Construction is defined as 'interpretation put upon conduct, action, facts, words etc.; the way in which these are taken by onlookers'. 2 *Oxford English Dictionary* (1989), 880–881.

[3] *Interpretation of Judgments Nos. 7 and 8*, Judgment No 13 of 16 December 1927, *PCIJ Series* A, No. 13, 4 at 10.

[4] R Bernhardt, *Die Auslegung völkerrechlicher Verträge* (1963), 32; S Sur, *L'interprétation en droit international public* (1974), 194; MK Yasseen, L'interprétation des traités d'après la Convention de Vienne sur le Droit des Traités, 151 *Recueil des Cours* (1976-III), 1 at 9.

[5] W Karl, *Vertrag und spätere Praxis in Völkerrecht—Zum Einfluß der Praxis auf Inhalt und Bestand völkerrechlicher Verträge* (1983), 22; M Heymann, *Einseitige Interpretationserklärungen zu multilateralen Veträgen* (2005), 38.

[6] L Ehrlich, L'interprétation des traités, 24 *Recueil des cours*, (1928-IV), 1 at 53–54; P Reuter, *Introduction to the Law of Treaties* (1985), 74.

[7] I Voïcu, *De l'interprétation authentique des traités internationaux* (1968), 19; Ehrlich (1928), 64.

[8] Harvard Draft on the Law of Treaties, 29 *AJIL Supplement* (1935), 938; G Schwarzenberger, *International Law and Order* (1971), 116.

the existence of consensual rules is premised not on the general capacity of States to give or withhold their sovereign consent, but on the consent that they have already and actually given in relation to the relevant rule or instrument. Thus, the content and scope of rules has to be identified by reference to the pre-determined methods of interpretation that clarify the parameters of the original consent. The scope of the consensual rule, as opposed to its emergence, is independent from the (capacity to give or withhold) the original consent.

Interpretation is linked to the structural profile of international law based on consent and agreement. All international acts embody State consent and agreement, expressed in one or another form. Therefore, interpretation methods must be those which deduce the meaning exactly of what has been consented to and agreed. In addition, interpretation methods must be consistent, transparent and possess general applicability. In other words, they must fit within the general legal framework of applying law to facts. A case-by-case analysis of interpretative outcomes cannot be an adequate alternative. Legal positivism in international law implies consensualism in terms of the existence of original consent and agreement. If positivism were to be identified also with consent to the use of interpretation methods or interpretative outcome, then the process of interpretation and its pre-established rules would lose their meaning and relevance. This would require going back, in every instance of interpretation, to clarifying the original or actual will of the States bound by the rule, which would hardly be possible in the context of a dispute that inherently implies the opposition of views and claims. In other words, such positivism-plus would entail legal chaos. At the same time, the legal regime of interpretation warrants in certain cases going back to factors reflecting the will and action of States, but such resort is permissible only where that legal regime expressly allows this, or where sufficient evidence can be provided that the original consensual agreement has been modified as between the relevant States.[9]

The task of interpretation is to ensure that the determinate meaning of provisions in acts and instruments is not neglected or hijacked. Situations of legal indeterminacy, as Richard Falk acknowledged, open the door for value-inputs by the interpreter.[10] This approach involves the risk of blurring the distinction between law and non-law, with the consequent perversion of the parameters of the will and consent of States in relation to the relevant instruments.

Interpretation in international law is likewise independent of whatever rules and methods of interpretation may be applicable in the domestic law of the relevant State. As early as in the *Asylum* case the International Court accepted the approach. Interpretation is also independent of the state of national law of the relevant State. The case concerned the grant of asylum under the 1928 Havana

[9] On this latter issue see below Chapter 10.

[10] R Falk, On Treaty Interpretation and the New Haven Approach: Achievements and Prospects, 8 *Virginia JIL* (1967–1968), 323 at 352.

Convention on Political Asylum. The Court stated that 'interpretation, which would mean that the extent of the obligation of one of the signatory States would depend upon any modifications which might occur in the law of another, cannot be accepted'.[11] This accords, on the one hand, with the irrelevance of sovereignty in construing treaty obligations,[12] and on the other hand, with the primacy of treaties over facts and practices that do not validly qualify as subsequent practice under Article 31 of the Vienna Convention.

International acts and instruments do not produce their effect just because they exist, but because their effect follows from their content and scope. Interpreting legal rules and instruments as opposed to merely acknowledging their existence is what distinguishes international lawyers from stamp collectors. Interpretation must be able to lead to a concrete and conclusive outcome, which dictates the need to search for and identify its methods. Consequently, the practice of international tribunals extensively engages with interpretation arguments. The only codified set of rules on treaty interpretation is provided in Articles 31 and 32 of the 1969 Vienna Convention on the Law of Treaties.[13] But interpretation also relates to the broader category of international acts and rules, including statements, declarations, actions, judgments, institutional decisions, and customary rules.

International legal rules and instruments express the will and intention of States which are meant to make a difference in the existing legal position. The selection of interpretative methods requires acknowledging that international

[11] *Asylum Case* (Colombia/Peru), Judgment of 20 November 1950, *ICJ Reports*, 1950, 266 at 275–276.

[12] See above Chapter 2 and below Chapter 11.

[13] According to Article 31:

1. A treaty shall be interpreted in good faith in accordance with the ordinary meaning to be given to the terms of the treaty in their context and in the light of its object and purpose.
2. The context for the purpose of the interpretation of a treaty shall comprise, in addition to the text, including its preamble and annexes:
   (*a*) any agreement relating to the treaty which was made between all the parties in connection with the conclusion of the treaty;
   (*b*) any instrument which was made by one or more parties in connection with the conclusion of the treaty and accepted by the other parties as an instrument related to the treaty.
3. There shall be taken into account, together with the context:
   (*a*) any subsequent agreement between the parties regarding the interpretation of the treaty or the application of its provisions;
   (*b*) any subsequent practice in the application of the treaty which establishes the agreement of the parties regarding its interpretation;
   (*c*) any relevant rules of international law applicable in the relations between the parties.
4. A special meaning shall be given to a term if it is established that the parties so intended.

According to Article 32,

Recourse may be had to supplementary means of interpretation, including the preparatory work of the treaty and the circumstances of its conclusion, in order to confirm the meaning resulting from the application of Article 31, or to determine the meaning when the interpretation according to Article 31:

(*a*) leaves the meaning ambiguous or obscure; or
(*b*) leads to a result which is manifestly absurd or unreasonable.

legal rules are not what academics, legal advisers or politicians want or perceive them to be, or what could under certain circumstances be sensible, sound, reasonable or agreeable, but what is *agreed* by and as between States in one way or another. Once the relevant rule is agreed and accepted, the process of interpretation has to consider that it is meant to make a difference in relation to what would be the legal position had that rule or instrument been non-existent. This has to be the case if the original will, consent and agreement of the author of the instrument is to be given legal effect. The legal rule is supposed to make a difference on the ground through serving its rationale, that is to impact the freedom, rights and obligations of States. Rules cannot achieve this purpose unless given full effect in terms of what they suggest at face value, not least because giving consent to a rule is a psychological and intellectual process. Consent is not easily given, but given only for a reason, which is to obtain benefits in exchange for burdens. When States consent to a rule that suggests X at face value, they undergo the intellectual process of understanding the implications of that rule as construed at face value. Therefore, the process of interpretation has structural limits. It is a process composed, so to speak, of solid materials that possess particular shape, and designed to look at the evidence of what was originally agreed. The fluidity or elusiveness of the elements of interpretation can only contribute to confusing or perverting the outcome of the original expression of will.

Interpretation of legal acts, as a task limited to the clarification of meaning, must be distinguished from their revision or amendment.[14] Judge Alvarez asserted in the *Admissions* case that 'it is possible, by way of interpretation, to effect more or less important changes in treaties', if they lead to unreasonable consequences.[15] This, however, has never been an accepted task of interpretation. In the *Peace Treaties* case, the Court asserted that its task was to interpret treaties, not to revise them.[16]

The problem of the relationship between treaty interpretation and treaty amendment or modification has been addressed in the *Gabcikovo-Nagymaros* case. The Court's judgment is not very explicit on this issue, because it eventually upheld the state of treaty relations in a way not requiring or endorsing their amendment. But the Separate Opinion of Judge Bedjaoui clarifies the interpretative approach that is in principle responsible for the entire Court's approach:

[14] Yasseen (1976-III), 1 at 45; C de Visscher *Problèmes d interprétation judiciaire en droit international public* (1963), 24–25; for the overview of the relevant early practice confirming this thesis see G Schwarzenberger, *International Law* (1957), vol I, 488–489.

[15] Dissenting Opinion, *Second Admissions* case, *ICJ Reports*, 1950, 18.

[16] *Interpretation of Peace Treaties with Bulgaria, Hungary and Romania* (Second Phase, Advisory Opinion), 18 July 1950, *ICJ Reports*, 1950, 221 at 229; see also *Differend sur le trace de la ligne frontière entre la Borne 62 et le Mont Fitz Roy* (Argentine/Chili), Sentence du 21 octobre 1994, *RGDIP* (1996), 521 at 552.

An interpretation of a treaty which would amount to substituting a completely different law to the one governing it at the time of its conclusion would be a *distorted revision*. The '*interpretation*' is not the same as the '*substitution*' for a negotiated and approved text, of a completely different text, which has neither been negotiated nor agreed.[17]

In some contexts the notion of reinterpretation is advanced. Reinterpretation is effectively a legal change, that is an amendment or abrogation of the relevant rule.[18] On the other hand, reinterpretation can be accommodated within the factors that are normally perceived as part of the process of interpretation. This could happen in the context of the interpretative relevance of subsequent practice under Article 31 of the 1969 Vienna Convention, provided that the relevant subsequent practice survives the rigorous test as required under Article 31 and is applied in practice.[19]

A related question is that of the relationship between interpretation and the doctrine of approximate application of treaties. Originally, this doctrine was developed by Judge Lauterpacht in the *Admissibility of Hearings* case.[20] In the *Gabcikovo-Nagymaros* case, the International Court confronted the argument that, given the new series of facts that had made it difficult to apply the 1977 Treaty between Hungary and Slovakia in literal terms, the approximate application of that Treaty must be found. In other words, it should be applied in a way to be compatible with these factual situations. The Court saw no need to resort to and examine this doctrine because it could decide the case on other grounds. However, Judge Bedjaoui's reaction was more straightforward:

The theory of '*approximate application*' or '*close approximation*' relied on by Slovakia in order to justify the construction and commissioning of Variant C is unconvincing. There is no such theory in international law. The 'precedents' advanced in favour of this theory are worthless. At least because of its dangers, this theory deserved wholehearted censure, which I find lacking in the Judgment.

Were this theory to be accepted, it would be to the detriment of *legal certainty* in relations between States and in particular of the certainty of treaties and of *the integrity of the obligations* properly entered into. The consolidation of this theory would virtually signal the end of the cardinal principle *pacta sunt servanda,* since a State which undertakes a specific obligation is left free to fulfil another, which it would be quite cunning to present as being very close to the first obligation. The State would only have to observe that its '*approximate application*' was allowed since, according to it, the conduct of the other party placed it in the impossibility of performing its obligations under the treaty and

[17] Separate Opinion of Judge Bedjaoui, *ICJ Reports*, 1997, 123 (emphasis original).

[18] To illustrate, the calls in the 1980s to reinterpret the ABM Treaty in terms of accommodating the US Strategic Defence Initiative were received and opposed as calls for its abrogation. See I Johnstone, Treaty Interpretation: The Authority of Interpretive Communities, 12 *Michigan JIL* (1990–91), 405–406.

[19] See below Chapter 10.

[20] See for details above Chapter 5.

since it had no other remedy. All breaches of the obligations of the State would thus run the risk of being presented as an '*approximate application.*'[21]

Judge Bedjaoui also emphasises the difficulty of determining what degree of proximity or approximation is required in this situation. The most important problem with the doctrine of 'approximate application' is that 'What the theory of "approximate application" lacks in order to be a valid "*reinterpretation*" of the treaty is quite obviously the basic condition of the consent of the other State. ... The "*approximate application*" may only be recognized as valid and may only constitute a "*reinterpretation*" if the other party to the Treaty has *given its consent.*'[22]

Another allegedly similar concept is that of evolutive interpretation, the essence of which is that treaties and their surrounding environment are not static but develop continuously.[23] Although relevant in different fields of treaty interpretation, this concept is not independent or free-standing. To illustrate, in its practice, the European Court of Human Rights has affirmed that the European Convention on Human Rights is a 'living instrument which ... must be interpreted in the light of present-day conditions'. Consequently, the Convention's provisions 'cannot be interpreted solely in accordance with the intentions of their authors as expressed more than forty years ago'.[24] Similarly, the UN Human Rights Committee emphasised in *Judge v Canada* that the International Covenant on Civil and Political Rights 'should be interpreted as a living instrument and the rights protected under it should be applied in context and in the light of present-day conditions'. The Committee was, however, quick to add that 'as required by the Vienna Convention on the Law of Treaties, a treaty should be interpreted in good faith and in accordance with the ordinary meaning to be given to the terms of the treaty in their context and in the light of its object and purpose'. The Committee in fact applied a textual approach to interpreting the parameters of the right to life under Article 6 of the Covenant.[25] Similarly, in the *Soering* case, where the European Court had to examine the legality of submitting individuals to death row, it affirmed in the first place that it had to interpret the European Convention 'in the light of present-day conditions' and could not remain uninfluenced by commonly accepted standards in the penal policy of the member States of the Council of Europe in this field. Still, the outcome of the case turned on the actual prescription under Article 3 not to subject individuals to torture. The Court was unable to infer that the evolution of a common

[21] Separate Opinion of Judge Bedjaoui, *ICJ Reports*, 1997, 127–128 (emphasis original).

[22] *Id*, 128 (emphasis original).

[23] See R Berhnardt, Evolutive Treaty Interpretation, Especially of the European Convention of Human Rights, 42 *GYIL* (1999), 11.

[24] *Tyrer v UK*, Application No 5856/72, Judgment of 25 April 1978, para 31; *Loizidou v Turkey*, Application No 15318/88, Judgment of 29 March 1995, para 71.

[25] *Roger Judge v Canada*, Communication No 829/1998, paras 10.3–10.4.

European attitude had imposed a specific obligation on States in this field. What mattered was whether the potential treatment on death row would cross the test of severity under Article 3 itself.[26]

As the context of these cases demonstrates, evolutive interpretation does not imply the exemption of the relevant treaty from the normal regime of interpretation. The evolution in question could refer to a variety of factors such as the (literal) meaning of terms included in the treaty, expansion of its object and purpose, or the rules of general international law governing the fields not covered by the relevant treaty that could be relevant for determining how that treaty applies. Evolutive interpretation does not imply treating the content of original agreement as evolved over time. It can only relate to those aspects of the treaty which are open and adaptable in a way to reflect the evolution and development of certain rules and regimes in the surrounding international legal system. In other words, evolutive interpretation cannot allow modifying or re-interpreting the relevant treaty; it can only lead to interpreting that treaty by reference to those factors whose relevance the treaty itself does not exclude. Therefore, the merits of evolutive interpretation can be best clarified by reference to individual interpretative methods as their specificities can also help to explain the merit of this concept in individual cases.[27]

The relevance and outcomes of the interpretative process also interact with the concept of State sovereignty.[28] This is a field in which the concept of sovereignty is neither seen nor contested in categorical terms. Instead this field deals with sovereignty in action. As affirmed in the classical dictum of the *Lotus* case, sovereignty is not given up unless to the extent it is established to have been given up. On the other hand, and as the *Wimbledon* judgment of the Permanent Court confirms, international obligations are incurred in the exercise of State sovereignty.[29] The latter coexists, in the background, with those relevant obligations, but does not prejudice their existence or scope. The content of rules and obligations depends not on sovereignty as such, but on the pre-determined methods of interpretation designed to discern that content.

The *Wimbledon* framework of interaction between sovereignty and obligation is maintained in subsequent jurisprudence. In *Japan–Alcoholic Beverages*, the WTO Appellate Body took an approach similar to that of the Permanent Court in *Wimbledon*:

> The WTO Agreement is a treaty—the international equivalent of a contract. It is self-evident that in an exercise of their sovereignty, and in pursuit of their own respective national interests, the Members of the WTO have made a bargain. In exchange for the

[26] *Soering v UK*, No 14038/88, Judgment of 7 July 1989, paras 102–104.
[27] See below Chapter 10.
[28] See above Chapter 2.
[29] *SS Wimbledon*, Judgment of 17 August 1923, *PCIJ Series* A, No 1, 15 at 24–25.

benefits they expect to derive as Members of the WTO, they have agreed to exercise their sovereignty according to the commitments they have made in the WTO Agreement.[30]

These factors and the consequent legitimate expectations of States require giving international acts the meaning that they have on the basis of their independent and free-standing examination. Pre-determined interpretative methods are used for clarifying the meaning of the legal act—the meaning which itself is not predetermined but depends solely on the outcome that the open-ended use of interpretative methods will entail.[31] Not even perceptions about the nature and structure of international law should be allowed to upset the interpretative process. To illustrate, in the *Danzig Courts* case, the Permanent Court of International Justice examined the question whether, contrary to the dominant legal sentiment, the international agreement could create rights for individuals, and observed that:

The answer to this question depends upon the intention of the contracting Parties. It may be readily admitted that, according to a well established principle of international law, the *Beamtenabkommen*, being an international agreement, cannot, as such, create direct rights and obligations for private individuals. But it cannot be disputed that the very object of an international agreement, according to the intention of the contracting Parties, may be the adoption by the Parties of some definite rules of creating individual rules and obligations and enforceable by the national courts.[32]

Therefore, whatever the general structural pattern of international law, international legal instruments have the meaning that is inferable from their content, their object as intended by the author States, even though, in the absence of the given instrument, the legal position could be substantially and even radically different. That international instruments are meant to make such a difference was recognised, with the example of treaties, by the Permanent Court in *Wimbledon*, where Article 380 of the Versailles Peace Treaty was interpreted as being unaffected by the rules of neutrality under international law.[33] The

[30] *Japan—Taxes on Alcoholic Beverages*, AB-1996–2, WT/DS8/AB/R, 4 October 1996, 13.

[31] Some factors can nevertheless impose limits on the open-endedness of interpretative process and on interpretative outcomes, such as *jus cogens*. This issue is examined elsewhere. See A Orakhelashvili, *Peremptory Norms in International Law* (2006), Chapters 6 and 12. But such limits on interpretation are dictated by the limits of treaty-making power of States and cannot be generalised throughout the overall field of interpretation.

[32] *Jurisdiction of the Courts of Danzig*, Advisory Opinion of 3 March 1928, *PCIJ Series* B, No 15, 4 at 17–18. Similarly, in *Acquisition of Polish Nationality*, the Permanent Court observed that even under general international law States are entitled to decide who are and who are not their nationals, this principle was applicable only subject to treaty obligations of States, *Acquisition of Polish Nationality*, Advisory Opinion of 15 September 1923, *PCIJ Series* B, No 7, 6 at 15–16. Lauterpacht argues that in the *Danzig Courts* case the main issue was whether the general international law made it possible that individuals acquire rights through a treaty, H Lauterpacht, *Development* (1958), 28. However, as the above passage confirms, the Court's real approach was that the specific outcome of endowing individuals with rights followed from the specific treaty provisions. The Court referred to the intention of parties to the treaty, as opposed to general international law.

[33] *SS Wimbledon*, Judgment of 17 August 1923, *PCIJ Series* A, No 1, 15 at 24–25.

outcome of interpretation has to be independent of the general state of the relevant field of international law; otherwise the principles of interpretation would have no free-standing relevance. The use of predetermined methods of interpretation is required for the legitimacy of the interpretative process. An alternative could be the reference to past decisions but in the international legal system that recognises no sovereign authority over States and knows of no doctrine of precedent, this could not provide a sufficiently legitimate explanation.

If interpretation is meant to clarify the content of law that has crossed the threshold of legal regulation, it naturally follows that the process of interpretation has to be independent of non-legal considerations. As the International Court described in the *Certain Expenses* case, interpretation is a purely legal, not political, task.[34] There may be politically motivated attempts by States to have the relevant instrument interpreted in one or another way. This may be opposed by the equally political attempts of other States to have the same instrument interpreted in a different way. As Maarten Bos observes, the adjective 'political' denotes the process of organising human life and administering public affairs. As interpretation in international law is part of that process, it is in this sense political. But Bos also specifies that there are degrees to which public affairs can be political. If interpretation were to be identified with politics, all difference between law and pure politics would fall to the ground. This requires rejecting the option of purely political interpretation. Interpretation is thus a legal activity.[35]

In the international arena, nearly all State attitudes are inherently political, guided by whether and to what extent the original agreement suits the political interest of the relevant State at the time of interpretation. If these attitudes are accorded decisive importance, the outcome very often will be the absence of legal regulation which may be conducive to the political interests of certain States, but not reflective of what was originally agreed in the relevant instrument, and hence incompatible with the basic principle of the observance of international obligations. States may agree on political grounds on interpreting or even reinterpreting the relevant instrument (just as they agree on concluding agreements), but this (re)interpretation would take place because the States in question so agreed, not because it is a political phenomenon.

As Visscher observes, the security afforded by the treaty to States-parties is measured by its capability to resist the pressure that can be exercised on it by the intervening transformations relating to interests and force.[36] This confirms that the process of interpretation aimed at clarifying the content of law has to be seen as independent of the influence of non-law.

The consistency of interpretation methods has been subjected to a number of doctrinal attacks. An attempt to question the reliance of pre-established methods of interpretation in favour of a more situational interpretation is presented by

[34] *Certain Expenses of the United Nations* (Advisory Opinion), *ICJ Reports*, 1962, 151 at 155.
[35] M Bos, *A Methodology of International Law* (1984), 132.
[36] Visscher (1963), 54.

Franck, particularly in the context of the operation of the UN collective security mechanism. This is asserted in relation to various instances of the use of force not authorised under the UN Charter, and consequent attempts to see the Charter, especially its prohibition of the use of force, interpreted and reinterpreted in individual cases. Franck, taking this as the starting point, submits that in certain instances the use of force not explicitly sanctioned under the UN Charter was tolerated by what he calls 'the system', and this arguably happened in cases of anticipatory self-defence, countermeasures, or humanitarian intervention. This situational approach is, according to Franck, more useful than what he denotes as 'textual literalism'.[37]

However, as the examination of specific methods of interpretation will demonstrate, that 'textual literalism' is the principal method of treaty interpretation as confirmed by the 1969 Vienna Convention on the Law of Treaties, which in all certainty applies to the constituent instruments of international organisations, such as the UN Charter. There would be little point in associating this basic interpretative principle with a restricted, possibly narrow-minded, attitude involving a propensity to neglect a wider context of State practice and international politics. After all, interpretation methods are meant to disclose the content of the original agreement.

A comparable approach is taken by Koskenniemi in an analysis which, it must be stated, pays little attention to the practice of application of the principles of interpretation. Koskenniemi questions the coherence of the Vienna Convention methods, above all that of plain and ordinary meaning, and attempts to take as the starting point the various theoretical approaches to clarify the genuine relevance of interpretation. Koskenniemi's main argument relates to comparing and reconciling objective and subjective approaches to interpretation.[38] This approach is effectively an attempt to return to the state of doctrine that existed before the adoption of the Vienna Convention on the Law of Treaties. The current state of international law admits of no doubting of the thesis that the process of interpretation should be conducted in accordance with fixed rules arranged in hierarchical order. Whether one or another rule reflects the consent of the State, subjective intention or objective agreement is not a matter that influences the interpretative process. The relevant rules of interpretation apply because the Vienna Convention so establishes, independently of what an academic or political assessment would make of them.

Along these lines, the problem of the consistent use of interpretation methods was confronted in the *Brogan* case, in which the European Court of Human Rights found a violation of Article 5(3) of the European Convention on Human Rights on the basis of literal interpretation of the requirement to 'promptly, bring the detained person before the national court'. The case was adjudicated in the context of alleged terrorist activities of the relevant individuals. The Court still

[37] T Franck, *Recourse to Force* (2002), and the review on it, 52 *ICLQ* (2003), 827–829.

[38] M Koskenniemi, *From Apology to Utopia* (2004), 333–345.

adhered to the textual approach and textual meaning of 'promptness'.[39] The dissenting Judge Martens, considering the threat terrorism poses to national societies, suggested that 'the Court should remain free to adapt the interpretation of the Convention to changing social conditions and moral opinions. That calls for methods of interpretation that do not stop, prematurely, at the wording of a provision.'[40] Thus, Judge Martens opposed the Court's consistent use of the principles of interpretation and expressly suggested the use of extra-legal socio-political factors that bypass the principles and outcome of legal interpretation.

This approach includes a great deal of subjectivism under which the identification of the transparent meaning of the relevant treaty provision becomes difficult if not impossible. The broader issue Judge Martens' dissent involves is its difference to the European Court's approach to the relationship between the plain meaning of the treaty provision and the balancing of interests and values within the field that provision covers. The Court's general approach is that the balancing of values and interests legitimately belongs to the field of those of the Convention provisions which include indeterminate notions. These indeterminate notions are not defined in a straightforward manner and consequently the identification of their meaning and impact requires the fair balancing of relevant interests and values.[41] However, when the meaning of treaty provisions is determinate, they have to be applied in terms of what they say on their face, and there is no room for the additional exercise of balancing values and interests that is likely to distort the textual meaning of the treaty which is the guide of the content of the agreement between States-parties.[42]

The European Court referred to the notion of fair and just balance between the relevant values and interests in the context of the right to education under Article 2 of Protocol 1 of the European Convention. This clause does not immediately incorporate the reference to margin of appreciation, nor refer to the concept of non-law, and for this reason an understanding of the proper essence of the Court's approach is essential. The Court emphasised that the aim of the Convention 'implies a just balance between the protection of the general interest of the Community and the respect due to fundamental human rights while attaching particular importance to the latter'.[43] The specific question was whether the refusal of regional authorities in Belgium to subsidise schools not instructing in the language of the region in question contradicted Article 2. The Court held that the text of Article 2 did not go as far as to require government-subsidised education in the language of the minority in the region in question. The Court

[39] See below Chapter 10.

[40] *Brogan v UK*, Nos 11209/84, 11234/84, 11266/84 & 11386/85, Judgment of 29 November 1988, Dissenting Opinion of Judge Martens, para 5.

[41] See for detail below Part V.

[42] See for detail below Chapter 10.

[43] *Belgian Linguistics*, Application Nos 1474/62, 1677/62, 1691/62, 1769/63, 1994/63, 2126/64, Judgment of 23 July 1968, Section 1.B, para 5.

noted the argument of this regulation 'bearing hard' on the relevant minority pupils and their families, but responded that, whatever their severity, the relevant legal and administrative measures did not amount to a distinction in treatment of an arbitrary and therefore discriminatory nature that would contradict Article 14 of the Convention. These measures did not really restrict what individuals could do under the Convention, but only affected the State subsidising the relevant activities. The relevant individuals and their groups could organise and fund the education in their language privately. After this, the Court observed that 'the legal and administrative measures in question create no impediment to the exercise of the individual rights enshrined in the Convention with the result that the necessary balance between the collective interest of society and the individual rights guaranteed is respected'.[44]

This reasoning demonstrates that in the *Belgian Linguistics* case the Court was not concerned with values and interests that existed, as it were, outside the Convention. It based its decision on the textual scope of the relevant clauses in the first place. The Court accepted the hardship and severity of the measures of the Government, but it did not proceed to examine the merits of this hardship and severity on its own, and as compared to other options for mitigating it, or with values and interests that were to be balanced against it. What mattered was that these hard or severe measures did not violate the text of the Convention. If these measures would be so hard or severe as to restrict an individual's choice of his language of education as such, they would presumably contradict Article 2; but they would be illegal not for their hardship or severity, but because of nullifying the free choice of education as expressly stipulated in Article 2.

In general, the consistency of interpretative methods, as seen in terms of their hierarchical sequence, best expresses the nature of international obligations which are based on consent and agreement, and also is indispensable for stability and predictability of international legal rules. Any argument that interpretation methods are not rigorously consistent or are situation-dependent implies the denial of consistent and predictable application of international law to the conduct of States. Nearly all attempts to upset the sequence of interpretation methods and especially the primacy of plain meaning are motivated either by dissatisfaction with the positivist background of international law as based on agreement between States, by desire to subordinate law to political factors, or to evade the operation of treaties as *lex specialis*.

Therefore, this analysis is concerned with the use of interpretative methods; in other words, with *interpretation as a process* as it operates in the variety of fields. This study is bound to be generalist and thus fill the gaps in the previous studies which either relate only to the interpretation of treaties, or have been written at earlier stages and do not consider the practical developments in the last few decades.

[44] *Id*, Section 2.B.4.

2. Acts and Rules Interpreted

International acts are different from each other in their form and structure. Some of them are produced by a single international person while others are produced jointly. Some acts have a simple structure and are adopted with a simple procedure, while others have a more complex structure and are adopted through a complex procedure. These structural and formal differences notwithstanding, all international acts are supposed to confirm, contest or modify legal positions. Therefore, different acts, such as treaties, unilateral acts, institutional decisions, jurisdictional instruments, judicial submissions and others produce effects and consequences in which international persons can place confidence. Different legal acts have in common that they are based on the will and intention of States that make them. Intention, originally a subjective factor to be objectively evidenced to take effect, can and must be identified with regard to all acts by reference to all intrinsic and extrinsic evidence.

While the legal character of certain international acts is beyond dispute, that of some other international acts is widely debated. It is important to understand that acts and instruments may differ from each other in form but nevertheless share fundamental features of their nature. For instance, it is difficult to make an absolutely clear distinction between a treaty, and an institutional or collective decision such as the waiver in the WTO legal system, or a Security Council resolution. All of them are agreements expressing the will of States in written form. Similarly, it is difficult to distinguish the substance of treaties from that of Optional Clause declarations under the International Court's Statute, and the latter from that of Schedules of Commitments in WTO law. These latter instruments are allegedly unilateral in origin or form but have an important contractual dimension.[45] Declarations under the Optional Clause are sometimes characterised as treaties and sometimes as unilateral acts. Institutional decisions, such as the UN Security Council resolutions, are from various perspectives considered as agreements, 'statutory' instruments or administrative acts.

The similarity in nature between treaties and Optional Clause declarations is frequently noted. In *Anglo-Iranian Oil Co*, the Court noted that 'the text of the Iranian Declaration is not a treaty text resulting from negotiations between two or more States. It is the result of unilateral drafting by the Government of Iran.'[46] However, the words 'It is the result of unilateral drafting' refer not to the legal nature of an instrument but to the circumstances of its adoption.[47] Thus, as

[45] On Schedules of Commitments under the GATS see *A Handbook on the GATS Agreement* (2005), 16–20.

[46] *Anglo-Iranian Oil Co*, *ICJ Reports*, 1952, 105.

[47] 'The statement means no more than that the declaration is the result not of negotiations but of unilateral drafting,' Separate Opinion of Judge Lauterpacht, *Norwegian Loans*, *ICJ Reports*, 1957, 48–49; See also Fitzmaurice, *The Law and Procedure of the International Court of Justice* (1986), 366, noting that there is a difference between assuming that a given instrument is not a treaty text and assuming that the same instrument is not a 'text resulting from negotiations between two or more States', being 'the result of unilateral drafting' by a State.

Lauterpacht remarks, 'the declarations under Article 36(2) of the Statute, made as they are at different times and by different States, are not in all aspects exactly like a treaty. But they are essentially a treaty'.[48]

In *Nicaragua*, although the Court characterised declarations under the Optional Clause as 'facultative, unilateral engagements that States are absolutely free to make or not to make', it did not hesitate to apply the principles of the law of treaties to the interpretation and application of such declarations.[49] The Court, moreover, emphasised that 'declarations, even though they are unilateral acts, establish a series of bilateral engagements'. The Court gave the further clarification: 'interested States may take cognisance of unilateral declarations and place confidence in them, and are entitled to require that the obligation thus created be respected'.[50] In *Fisheries Jurisdiction*, the Court referred to the circumstance in which a declaration under the Optional Clause 'establishes a consensual bond' between States.[51] Earlier, in *Right of Passage*, the Court referred to 'contractual relations between the Parties' which arise out of 'the fact of making declaration'.[52]

In fact, however the Court might have characterised them on particular occasions, the nature and legal effects of the declarations of acceptance dictate that they should be considered as international agreements under Article 2(1)(a) of the Vienna Convention on the Law of Treaties, stipulating that an international treaty shall consist of the single or several interconnected acts and whatever is its particular designation. Moreover, declarations under the Optional Clause are registered as international agreements under Article 102 of the United Nations Charter.

Lastly, the treaty character of jurisdictional declarations has been affirmed in the process of judicial treatment of the issue of their unilateral and immediate termination. The issue of termination of an agreement may undoubtedly be an issue agreed upon *inter partes*. Moreover, in *Nicaragua*, the International Court applied the law of treaties to the issue of termination of declarations;[53] and at the provisional measures stage in the same case, the Court totally agreed with the applicant's suggestion on the notion and extent of applicability of the law of treaties to declarations.[54]

In some cases the precise nature of legal acts and instruments cannot be identified easily and straightforwardly. In the *Jaworzina* case the Permanent Court had to interpret the Decision of the Conference of Ambassadors of July 28,

[48] H Lauterpacht, *The Development of International Law by the International Court* (1958), 345–346.

[49] *Nicaragua*, Jurisdiction and Admissibility, *ICJ Reports*, 1984, 420; Judge Schwebel, Dissenting Opinion, *id*, 620.

[50] *Id*, 418.

[51] *Fisheries Jurisdiction* (Spain v Canada), *ICJ Reports*, 1998, 432 at 453.

[52] *Right of Passage*, *ICJ Reports*, 1957, 146.

[53] *ICJ Reports*, 1984, 418ff.

[54] *Id*, 178ff.

1920, adopted pursuant to the decision of the Allied Supreme Council, and for this purpose clarify the precise legal nature of this instrument. Apart from the Council's decision, the Decision of Conference was based on the consent of the relevant parties: Poland and Czechoslovakia. Therefore, the Court concluded that 'it has much in common to arbitration'.[55] Thus, the Court had to deal with a hybrid document, which simultaneously had the features of a treaty, an award and an institutional decision, and it is noteworthy that it applied to it interpretative principles which it normally applied to treaties.

Distinctive characteristics of acts are often caused by the legal framework within which they are made. At the same time, every act has, to some extent, its inherent nature as it expresses the will of author States or institutions, affects the hitherto existing legal position, and gives rise to the expectations of other relevant entities. All international acts, despite their form, are meant to make a difference in the existing legal position. Even though serious conclusions ought to be made only after analysis, the starting-point assumption may nevertheless be formulated at this stage, namely that the rules applicable to all international acts are similar if not identical. An intelligent approach requires not merely seeing differences in nature and form, but also similarities and commonalities of different acts. Once this is acknowledged, the next question is whether these similarities have to be disregarded in the process of interpretation, or whether these essential characteristics ought to be taken into account by the interpreter. The outcome depends not least on the state of the relevant practice that applies the methods of interpretation.

According to Kelsen, the principles of treaty interpretation are the same as apply to interpretation of other instruments.[56] In addition, the object of interpretation can be an instrument, or a rule. Just like written instruments, individual rules have their content and rationale, the identification of which has to take place through interpretation based on transparent methods. The parallelism between the construction of a rule and interpretation of an instrument is inferable, among others, from the treatment of the equidistance/special circumstances rule in the law of continental shelf delimitation, namely under Article 6 of the 1958 Geneva Convention on Continental Shelf, in the Separate Opinion of Judge Shahabuddeen in the *Jan Mayen* case:

The provision was formulated in terms of providing, exceptionally, for a non-equidistance line (including a modified equidistance line) where the existence of special circumstances

[55] *Question of Jaworzina (Polish-Czechoslovakian Frontier)*, Advisory Opinion of 6 December 1923, *PCIJ Series* B, No 8, 6 at 26–29, 38; similarly, in the *Treaty of Lausanne* case, the Permanent Court affirmed that the decision of the Council of the League of Nations on the determination of the Iraqi-Turkish border on the basis of authorisation under the Treaty of Lausanne can be considered as an arbitral award, due to its character, even as the complete similarity between the League Council and an arbitration tribunal cannot be affirmed. *Article 3, Paragraph 2, of the Treaty of Lausanne*, Advisory Opinion of 21 November 1925, *PCIJ Series* B, No 12, 6 at 26.

[56] H Kelsen, *The Principles of International Law* (R Tucker, ed, 1967), 459–460.

justified such a line as opposed to an equidistance line. The necessary assumption was that special circumstances would not exist in all cases. Were it otherwise, the foundation of the main rule would largely disappear and, with it, the usefulness of the rule itself; such a consequence stands excluded by the principle that an interpretation which would deprive a treaty of a great part of its value is inadmissible.[57]

Furthermore, Judge Shahabuddeen argues that 'However widely the exception relating to special circumstances may be construed, it cannot be read so as to decapitate the clear intendment of the rule that, when the two prescribed conditions are satisfied, the equidistance method automatically and compulsorily applies to define the boundary.'[58] This reasoning emphasises the priority of preserving the object, purpose and intendment of the relevant rule, and largely affirms that the rationale for interpreting an individual rule overlaps with that for interpreting a written instrument.

[57] *ICJ Reports*, 1993, 148–149, referring to PCIJ cases that affirmed the need for effective interpretation of treaties.

[58] *Id*, 158.

10

Treaty Interpretation: Rules and Methods

1. Early Views on Treaty Interpretation

Early views on treaty interpretation refer to the approaches developed from the classical period of international legal doctrine until the adoption of the 1969 Vienna Convention on the Law of Treaties. Strictly speaking, early views are not directly relevant for clarifying the pertinent regime of interpretation. Yet these views illustrate the evolution of doctrinal attitudes and how different factors of interpretation were considered at different stages of doctrinal development.

Although the period covered is quite long, it is characterised by the absence of codified rules on interpretation, and the prevailing propensity to resort to logic, common sense, natural law or principles of national law to justify the relevant interpretative approaches.[1] Being based on, indeed being an implication of, the principle of good faith, interpretation was also treated as having an equitable dimension.[2] Although views on interpretation can be found as early as in the writings of Gentili and Grotius, it was Vattel who formulated the approach to interpretation in a way intelligible from the modern perspective, among other things by emphasising the rationale behind interpretation rules.

Vattel considered treaties as a means of adjusting the pretensions of States, and that the establishment of fixed rules of conduct under treaties must lead to ascertaining what they are entitled to expect.[3] Giving predominant importance to the need to secure good faith through treaties, Vattel observed that the principle of good faith is infringed when treaties are intentionally drafted in equivocal terms and ambiguous expressions are introduced 'to look for opportunities of quibbling, to outwit those with whom we are dealing, and outdo them in cunning and duplicity'. Hence, interpretative principles are very important in preserving the good faith embodied in treaties: 'a clearly false interpretation as contrary to good faith as anything could be imagined to be'.[4]

[1] For an overview of early views on treaty interpretation see R Bernhardt, *Die Auslegung der völkerrechlicher Verträge* (1963), 4–7.

[2] Bos (1984), 116–117.

[3] E de Vattel, *The Law of Nations or the Principles of Natural Law applied to the Conduct and to the Affairs of Nations and of Sovereigns* in Scott (ed), *Classics of International Law* (1916), 188.

[4] *Id*, 191.

Consistently with this priority, Vattel considered it 'necessary to lay down rules founded upon reason, and authorized by the natural law and adapted to throw light upon what is obscure, decide what is uncertain, and frustrate the designs of one who enters into the contract in bad faith'.[5] These rules are meant 'to discover not only what one of the parties had the intention of promising, but also what the other reasonably and in good faith believed was being promised to him—what was sufficiently expressed to him and on which his acceptance was based'. Consequently, treaties must be interpreted by 'fixed rules'. Otherwise, 'no agreement can be safely relied upon'.[6] This view of Vattel prioritises the need to construe legal instruments as clear and straightforward, and contradicts subsequently developed views of so-called deliberate ambiguity. Vattel's textual view is clearly motivated by his priority to safeguard the legitimate expectations parties have in treaty obligations:

> The first general rule of interpretation is that it is not permissible to interpret what has no need of interpretation. When a deed is worded in clear and precise terms, when its meaning is evident and leads to no absurdity, there is no ground for refusing to accept the meaning which the deed naturally presents. To have recourse to conjectures in order to restrict or extend its meaning is to attempt to elude it. Once allow so dangerous a practice and there is no deed which it will not render ineffectual. However clearly the provisions of an act be worded, however definite and precise its terms, all will be of no avail, if it be permissible to argue from extraneous sources that the deed is not to be taken in the sense which it naturally bears.

In addition, Vattel did in fact anticipate the principle of effectiveness in the interpretation of treaties and advocated giving to treaty clauses the full effect following from their content:

> If he who could and should have explained himself clearly and fully has not done it, so much the worse for him; he can not afterwards be admitted to prove restrictions which he has not admitted.[7]

Vattel advocates objective standards of treaty interpretation: parties cannot be allowed to interpret the treaty according to their fancy and thus render treaty obligations illusory.[8]

The later stages of doctrinal development witnessed a reluctance towards both the relevance of fixed rules of interpretation and the textual approach. The range of writers in the nineteenth and twentieth centuries—Westlake, Lawrence, Fenwick, and Oppenheim—argued against the primacy of text and held that the purpose of interpretation was to ascertain the real intention of the parties. They argued that international law did not contain fixed rules on treaty

[5] *Id*, 199.
[6] *Id*, 200–201.
[7] *Id*, 199.
[8] *Id*, 200.

interpretation. The approach of these writers anticipated the attitude embodied in the Harvard codification of the law of treaties. Not only did the Harvard Draft not suggest any hierarchy among the interpretative methods, but it also expressly argued against the utility of interpretative rules.[9] In general, rule-scepticism in the field of treaty interpretation has been well represented in all relevant periods of doctrinal development, as well as within different political systems.[10]

At the outset of his rather sketchy and perfunctory analysis of interpretation, Westlake asserts that the rules of interpretation elaborated upon are not of much practical use. The important point for Westlake was 'the real intention of the parties'.[11] Westlake did not take his analysis much further than that and certainly did not suggest any approach that could fit within the current framework of treaty interpretation. In particular, Westlake avoided the issue of how this 'real intention' is ascertained, and where it is has to be derived from. In similar terms, and in the most unusual and eccentric way, Hyde asserts at the outset that there is no single set of interpretation standards and the contracting States are free to adopt any one they choose.[12] In his early contribution on the subject, Hyde claimed that as all circumstances probative of the sense of the terms of agreement are admissible, 'the formation of rules of interpretation can hardly serve a useful purpose'.[13] This approach, again, has never been accepted in practice. In addition, if all facts 'probative' of meaning can be admissible, the failure of according hierarchical preference to some methods over others can result in approving diverse, even mutually exclusive, interpretations, and thus in legal chaos.

Yü referred to 'the fundamental difficulty in prescribing a system of rules' that among others followed from the imperfection of human language.[14] In his substantial analysis of early judicial practice of interpretation, this writer was generally sceptical about rules of interpretation and advocated a view that would admit all the relevant, including extraneous, evidence in this process. Another contemporary author, Chang, also argued against the suitability of the rules of interpretation.[15] Similarly, McNair in his magisterial work also argued against the 'so-called rules' of interpretation, considering them as 'merely prima facie guides of the intention of the parties', they face 'gradual devaluation' and the true task of the interpreter should be to ascertain the real intention of the parties.[16]

[9] See especially Article 19 of the Harvard Draft and its commentary, 29 *AJIL Supplement* (1935), 937–939. The approaches of the abovementioned writers are summarised *id*, 944.

[10] For an overview see G Haraszti, *Some Fundamental Problems of the Law of Treaties* (1973), 195–207.

[11] J Westlake, *International Law* (1910), vol I, 293.

[12] CC Hyde, *International Law, Chiefly as Interpreted and Applied by the United States* (1922), vol II, 61.

[13] CC Hyde, *Concerning the Interpretation of Treaties*, 3 *AJIL* (1909), 46 at 54.

[14] TC Yü, *The Interpretation of Treaties* (1927), 28.

[15] YT Chang, *The Interpretation of Treaties by Judicial Tribunals* (1933), 19.

[16] AD McNair, *The Law of Treaties* (1961), 365–366.

Nevertheless, nineteenth- and early twentieth-century thinking was not limited to the perception of rule-scepticism. Some prominent scholars from this period emphasised the necessity of fixed rules to guide treaty interpretation as a precondition for the stability of treaty relations. Phillimore begins his analysis on interpretation by observing that 'all International Treaties are covenants *bonae fidei*, and are, therefore, to be equitably and not technically construed'. Phillimore emphasises that the imperfection of language as an instrument for expressing intention renders interpretation necessary.[17] Despite his introductory observation on equitable interpretation, it soon becomes clear that Phillimore adheres to the approach of textual meaning to be discovered on the basis of fixed rules of interpretation, these rules being demanded by the necessities of international society.[18] WE Hall similarly supports the interpretation of treaties on the basis of established rules.[19] The adherence to the rule-based approach to interpretation is also demonstrated in the work of Ehrlich.[20] Sir Eric Beckett likewise supported the approach that the interpretation of treaties is guided by pre-determined rules, observing that 'it is not correct as a matter of practice and experience to state that the meaning of a treaty provision cannot be clear or otherwise the States concerned would not be going to the trouble and expense of litigating about it'.[21] Visscher considered the rules of interpretation as working hypotheses which can be verified at subsequent stages of analysis.[22]

The doctrinal divergence on this subject was so explicit that, shortly before the adoption of the 1969 Vienna Convention, Bernhardt was induced to proclaim, after having examined the relevant doctrine, that there was no general international agreement as to the interpretation rules applicable to international treaties.[23] At the same time, the issue of the rules of interpretation had to be answered not only on the basis of doctrinal contributions, but also on the basis of the then existing judicial practice. This requires an acknowledgement that the pre-Vienna Convention rule-scepticism as to treaty interpretation had been premised on considering only part of the available evidence.

In this context, the approach to interpretation developed by Fitzmaurice has peculiar connotations. Fitzmaurice emphasised the relevance of various schools of interpretation: the textual school which puts overriding emphasis on the treaty text; the teleological school which is guided by the objects of the treaty; and the intentions school which considers the intention of States-parties as paramount.[24]

[17] R Phillimore, *Commentaries upon International Law* (1855), vol II, 70.
[18] *Id*, 71.
[19] Hall, *A Treatise on International Law* (1895), 350.
[20] L Ehrlich, L'interprétation des traités, 24 *Recueil des cours*, (1928-IV), 1 at 78.
[21] Comments by Sir E Beckett, 43 *Annuaire de L'institut de Droit International* (1950), 435, 440.
[22] Visscher (1963), 70.
[23] Bernhardt (1963), 28; see also Yü (1927), 43.
[24] G Fitzmaurice, The Law and Procedure of the International Court of Justice: Treaty Interpretation and Certain Other Treaty Points, *BYIL* (1951), 1 at 7–10; G Fitzmaurice, The Law

More importantly, Fitzmaurice also elaborated upon certain rules of interpretation: the rules of textuality, subsequent practice, effectiveness. But his analysis does not suggest any order which should guide the relationship between these principles.[25] Fitzmaurice acknowledged the view that the last resort in the process of interpretation should be 'the exercise of common sense by the judge, applied in good faith and with intelligence'.[26] This is the view of the subjective discretion of the judge not subjected to any definable and identifiable criteria. Fitzmaurice considered it inevitable that the interpretation of treaties must be guided by a coherent set of rules.[27]

Each 'school' of treaty interpretation is arguably sound in placing an emphasis on the factor that is, on its own, relevant in locating the meaning of the treaty. At the same time, the reliance on various 'schools', which have no authority other than doctrinal writings, cannot answer the question of what the interpretative outcome should be when the factors emphasised by various 'schools' are in mutual conflict. While these 'schools' reflect, as can be seen from Fitzmaurice's writings, the trends crystallised in judicial practice, they only point to different factors of interpretation without specifying their order of priority. The question of which 'school' holds the key to interpretative outcomes is thus left open. This is even more necessary because, as will be shown, the jurisprudence of international tribunals on the basis of which the 'schools' of interpretation have been defined and elaborated upon, expressly specifies which interpretative factors must enjoy priority over others. This answer is instead provided by the rules of interpretation which, as Bernhardt aptly specifies, are in essence conflict rules. They are meant to settle the difference of views as to the content of rules.[28]

In evaluating the merit of these approaches, it has to be emphasised that the advantage of 'technical' and fixed rules of interpretation is that they search for the original consensus of parties, and in this way safeguard stability and predictability in treaty relations. The attempts of lawyers, diplomats or academics to downplay 'fixed' methods of interpretation in favour of a more 'dynamic', 'flexible' or 'realist' approach, or political interpretation, is in reality part of wider attempts to sell their perception or interest as an accepted legal position, or to manipulate the content of a treaty in the interest of power. International law is a system of agreed rules, from which it inherently follows that it has to be interpreted according to an agreed, fixed and predictable set of rules aimed at discovering the parameters of an original agreement.

and Procedure of the International Court of Justice 1951–1954, *BYIL* (1957), 203 at 204–209; on the description and comparison of the different 'schools' of interpretation see F Jacobs, Varieties of Approach to Treaty Interpretation: With Special Reference to the Draft Convention on the Law of Treaties before the Vienna Diplomatic Conference, 18 *ICLQ* (1969), 318.

[25] Fitzmaurice (1957), 211.

[26] Fitzmaurice (1951), 2–3.

[27] *Id*, 6.

[28] Bernhardt (1963), 46.

In general, one common feature of different doctrinal approaches opposed to the understanding of the process of interpretation as guided by fixed rules is that none of these schools of thought come up with a constructive alternative. None of those doctrinal approaches address the basic question of how, in the alleged absence or lack of relevance of fixed rules of interpretation, it can be ensured that the process of interpretation properly reflects the parameters of the original agreement between the States-parties. Doctrinal references to the factors of 'real intention' and community values effectively promote subjectivism and the consequent manipulation and hijacking of the established meaning of treaty obligations in the political interest.

Subjective reasons may lead States to consent to treaties. Yet the treaty so concluded acquires objective content and existence. It objectively exists even if some parties were to deny its legal status; it also has objective content that can be established even if one or more parties to it did not share its understanding. This leads to ascertaining the inherent deficiency of the notion of 'intention'.

In contrast to McNair, Fitzmaurice disapproved of the concept of 'intention,' which he considered an unstable notion that is difficult to identify in the interpretative process because of its uncertainty. In every dispute States can advance different interpretations and also claim to have different intentions. States that join the treaty subsequently do so not on the basis of what the parties originally intended, but what the text itself says. In any case, treaty interpretation is related not to the intention of the State but to the common or joint intention of parties. Thus, tribunals can derive intention either from the text, and 'in effect ascribe a common intention to the parties accordingly, whether they profess to have had it or not', or from the object and purpose of the treaty.[29] In general terms, as Visscher specifies, declared will takes priority over internal volition.[30]

Scepticism towards the relevance of the factor of intention has also been expressed by Sir Eric Beckett, emphasising that the task of tribunals is to interpret the written text. Beckett further observed that 'it is unrealistic to attempt to find a common intention of the parties when, in fact, they never had a common intention on the point that has arisen, but simply agreed on a text'.[31]

Lauterpacht addresses the cases in which the common intention of States-parties is allegedly lacking. This may be due, for instance, to the fact that the parties did not intend the same result and attached different meaning to the same clause, or used ambiguous non-committal expressions to leave the divergence of views to be resolved on a later occasion. In all such cases, although the common intention of the parties may be to avoid giving definite meaning to the relevant clauses, that is adopting a clear-cut and straightforward solution

[29] Fitzmaurice (1951), 3–4; Fitzmaurice (1957), 205–206.
[30] Visscher (1963), 17.
[31] Beckett (1950), 435 at 438.

on the relevant matter, it is the right and duty of tribunals to impart an effect to these clauses.[32] These observations address the potential cases in which some may be inclined to plead the disagreement in writing. In effect, what makes Lauterpacht's argument viable is that the ordinary methods of treaty interpretation do not actually refer to the intention of States as an independent factor, but merely specify particular methods of interpretation deemed to express that intention. In the end what matters is not what the actual intention of States-parties was, but what meaning is inferable from the treaty when it is interpreted according to ordinary methods.

Lauterpacht's analysis also demonstrates that the process of interpretation serves the more general task of ensuring the completeness of the international legal system. This approach follows from the premise that:

> the treaty is law; it is part of international law. As such it knows of no gaps. The completeness of the law when administered by legal tribunals is a fundamental—the most fundamental—rule not only of customary but also of conventional international law. It is possible for the parties to adopt no regulation at all. They may expressly disclaim any intention of regulating the particular subject-matter. But, in the absence of such explicit precaution, once they have clothed it in the form of a legal rule and once they have found themselves in a position in which that subject-matter is legitimately within the competence of a legal tribunal, the latter is bound and entitled to assume an effective common intention of the parties and to decide the issue. That common intention is no mere fiction.[33]

This approach is a reflection of Lauterpacht's more general thesis of the completeness of the international legal system within the field of its regulation. At the same time, the completeness of legal regulation implies that subjectivism can have no valid place in treaty interpretation. What the treaty regulation is depends not on what the parties subjectively intended, but on what appears to be the case from the available evidence that qualifies under the ordinary methods of interpretation.

Julius Stone opposes Lauterpacht's thesis that the task of interpretation is to ascertain the common intention of the parties. Stone is inclined to portray this process as that of the exercise of institutional rule-creation and states that to conceal this process behind assumed intention is to exercise power without the acceptance of responsibility for it. Stone is sceptical as to whether the intention of parties can exist independently of the perception of the interpreter.[34] But Stone's thesis fails to appreciate that evidence of the intention of parties follows from those interpretative factors which are relevant under the rules of interpretation. If the relevant outcome follows from the text, the parties must be taken as having indeed intended it.

[32] Lauterpacht, *BYIL* (1949), 76–78.
[33] Lauterpacht, (1949), 78–79.
[34] J Stone, Fictitional Elements in Treaty Interpretation—A Study in the International Judicial Process, 1 *Sydney Law Review* (1953–1955), 344 at 348–349, 358.

Stone's argument effectively supports judicial subjectivism under the veil of applying predetermined legal rules. As soon as the rules are there and applied, the way in which judges reach their decision, their mental position, is not crucially material.

2. The Relevance of the Vienna Convention

During the work of the International Law Commission, doctrinal resistance to fixed rules of interpretation was acknowledged, above all by Special Rapporteur Waldock but, as is the case with every codification, the aim still was to elaborate upon these fixed rules, because the interpretation of treaties without arbitrariness and according to the principles of law is the necessary implication of the *pacta sunt servanda* principle. The Commission expressed an identical attitude.[35] In the Commission's Final Draft, the priority was expressed to codify a few general principles that would constitute the general rules of interpretation.[36] The Commission also upheld the approach that the aim was to search for the objectively ascertainable intention of the parties as manifested in the treaty text, as opposed to the subjective intention of the party.[37] Articles 31 and 32 of the 1969 Vienna Convention on the Law of Treaties are the products of this approach.

The Vienna Convention regime is an elaboration and codification of the principles and practices that dominated the field at least from the period of the work of the Permanent Court and the International Court. It seems that the doctrinal works contemporary to this practice did not properly describe the applicable principles and there was a wide gap between practice and doctrine. The adoption of the Vienna Convention represented a choice in favour of the principles developed in practice, as will be seen through the examination of individual interpretative principles.

This is even clearer considering that in the process of adoption of the Vienna Convention at the Vienna Conference in 1968, the ILC's approach to codifying the fixed and straightforward rules on interpretation met with serious resistance from the United States, which was represented, for this purpose, by Myres McDougal, the founder of the New Haven School of a policy-oriented approach to international law. McDougal extensively criticised the Commission's approach and called upon the Conference to abandon this approach, especially the primacy of the text and hierarchy among the methods of interpretation, in favour of

[35] II *YbILC* 1964, 53–54, 200.
[36] II *YbILC* 1966, 218–219.
[37] *Id*, 220.

a single rule that would place all methods—text, context, preparatory work, subsequent practice and others—at the same level.[38]

According to the New Haven school, the objective of interpretation is to construe agreements that reflect as closely as possible the genuine shared expectations of the parties and broader community policies. If the outcome of interpretation does not yield obvious 'expectation' or 'intention' then recourse must be had, according to the New Haven School, to more general community policies and purposes.[39] The major problem with the New Haven approach to treaty interpretation is that it contradicts the concept of interpretation as the process that aims not at the particular result as such, but at such result as will follow from the application of the rules of interpretation. Interpretation is a process of applying pre-determining rules, not of prescribing what the outcome as such should be. As Fitzmaurice rightly observed regarding the New Haven approach, this school subordinates the process of interpretation to the attainment of certain 'policy goals'. As for the New Haven approach that the decision-maker should supplement express stipulations in the treaty by the 'basic constitutive prescriptions of the larger community', Fitzmaurice comments that this, 'however excellent, is not law but sociology'. In practice this would have the effect of substituting the will of the adjudicator for that of the parties, because the adjudicator would accord to the text such meaning as he thinks would be good for the community. This approach has little chance of being adopted in practice.[40]

As is clear, the Vienna Conference rejected this approach and proceeded with adopting the provisions embodying fixed interpretative rules based on textual primacy. Thus, the view that the rules of the Vienna Convention are merely working assumptions[41] is misguided, being a mere assertion unsupported by any evidence. The text of the Vienna Convention, the process of its drafting and the practice of its application are all unanimous in affirming that the rules of treaty interpretation are fixed rules and do not permit the interpreter a free choice among interpretative methods.

The impact of the Vienna Convention on the law in this field has been threefold. In the first place, the Vienna Convention conclusively and definitively

[38] Statement of Professor Myres S McDougal, US Delegation, to the Committee of the Whole, April 19, 1968, 62 *AJIL* (1968), 1021; for McDougal's further criticism of the ILC's approach see McDougal, The International Law Commission's Draft Articles Upon Interpretation: Textuality *Revidivus*, 61 *AJIL* (1967), 992. For opposition at the Vienna Conference to McDougal's statement by Uruguay, represented by E Jimenez de Arechaga, and the UK, represented by Sir Ian Sinclair, see I Sinclair, Vienna Conference on the Law of Treaties, 19 *ICLQ* (1970), 47 at 62–63.

[39] MS McDougal, HD Lasswell & JC Miller, *The Interpretation of International Agreements and World Public Order* (1967), 93, 156; see also R Falk, On Treaty Interpretation and the New Haven Approach: Achievements and Prospects, 8 *Virginia JIL* (1967–1968), 323 at 341.

[40] G Fitzmaurice, *Vae Victis* or Woe to the Negotiators! Your Treaty or Our Interpretation of It (Review Article), 65 *AJIL* (1971), 358 at 370, 372.

[41] D French, Treaty Interpretation and the Incorporation of Extraneous Legal Rules, 55 *ICLQ* (2006), 281.

replaced the relevance of various 'schools' of interpretation by formulating a single regime of interpretation based on rules. As the European Court of Human Rights emphasised in *Golder*, the Vienna Convention regime, especially its Article 31, lays down a single interpretative rule which operates as 'a unity, a single combined operation'.[42] This leaves no visible room for opting between various 'schools'. The International Law Commission, as has rightly been noted on a number of occasions, identified the General Rule of Interpretation as a single consistent rule.[43] This however relates to the single nature of the regime under Article 31, and does not impact on the allocation of priorities as between individual methods within that single rule. The rule in general being a single rule does not mean that all methods embodied in it have the same interpretative value.

The attempt to portray the interpretation regime under Article 31 as a 'holistic' single regime can be met in the Panel jurisprudence of the WTO. As the Panel claimed in *US—Sections 301–310 of Trade Act 1974*:

> Text, context and object-and-purpose correspond to well established textual, systemic and teleological methodologies of treaty interpretation, all of which typically come into play when interpreting complex provisions in multilateral treaties. For pragmatic reasons the normal usage, and we will follow this usage, is to start the interpretation from the ordinary meaning of the 'raw' text of the relevant treaty provisions and then seek to construe it in its context and in the light of the treaty's object and purpose. However, the elements referred to in Article 31—text, context and object-and-purpose as well as good faith—are to be viewed as one holistic rule of interpretation rather than a sequence of separate tests to be applied in a hierarchical order. Context and object-and-purpose may often appear simply to confirm an interpretation seemingly derived from the 'raw' text. In reality it is always some context, even if unstated, that determines which meaning is to be taken as 'ordinary' and frequently it is impossible to give meaning, even 'ordinary meaning', without looking also at object-and-purpose.[44]

What stands out in this approach is the prejudice against the relevance of the text, manifested by the use of the adjective 'raw'. There is in reality no legal concept of raw text. There is instead the concept of plain and ordinary meaning under Article 31 of the Vienna Convention. This provision speaks of 'the ordinary meaning to be given to the terms of the treaty in their context and in the light of its object and purpose'. Thus, the ultimate task is to use context and object and purpose to find the meaning of the text. This is substantially different from the Panel's projection of 'one holistic rule of interpretation rather than a sequence of separate tests to be applied in a hierarchical order'. As for the Panel's observation that 'Text, context and object-and-purpose correspond to

[42] *Golder v UK*, 4451/70, Judgment of 21 February 1975, para 30.

[43] *YbILC* 1966, 219–220.

[44] *US–Sections 301–310 of Trade Act 1974*, Report of the Panel, W/DS152/R, 22 December 1999 (99–5454), para 7.22.

well established textual, systemic and teleological methodologies of treaty interpretation', these relevant factors of interpretation do not really refer to different methods that operate independently from, or as an alternative to, each other. These factors refer only to the methods of interpretation that are laid down in strict order of hierarchy under Articles 31 and 32 of the Vienna Convention. As the consistent jurisprudence of the Appellate Body demonstrates, neither context nor object and purpose are viewed as an alternative to the plain textual meaning of words, which they would have to be unless their relevance was subordinated to that of the ordinary meaning of words.

The danger that attends the use of a 'holistic' approach is that, advocating dynamism and a contextual approach, could on occasions result in attempts to justify presenting the relevant treaty provision in a way different from what it says on its face, and consequently from what the parties have really agreed on.

The essence of a 'holistic' approach seems to be the balance of interpretative outcomes under particular methods of interpretation. The 'holistic' approach in essence reflects the possibility of political factors impacting on the process of interpretation, and also the possibility that the decision-maker replaces the outcome of consensual agreement between States with what this outcome should be according to his own perception. In other words, the essence of the 'holistic' approach is about blurring the distinction between law and politics, and about promoting subjectivism in the process of interpretation.

The reason why tribunals do not adopt so-called 'holistic' interpretation relates to the consensual nature of international treaties. As the aim of interpretation is to discover the parameters of original consensus, each method of interpretation relates to discovering those parameters in the data that are relevant within the profile of that particular method. The interpretative outcome can be accepted if the data qualifying under the particular method point to it in terms of discovering that the States-parties to the treaty are indeed agreed on it. The particular methods of interpretation are also arranged in the order of preference that gives priority to those methods which reflect the original agreement better and more authentically than other methods. The 'holistic' method instead admits of the likelihood of, if not necessarily implies, the projecting of the agreement between States-parties where such agreement cannot be established in terms of the data subsumable within individual methods of interpretation. Under this approach, clarification of the basic question of the existence and parameters of the original agreement between States-parties is not necessarily the principal consideration. For these reasons, the resort to a 'holistic' approach is inimical both to the consensual nature of international treaties in general, and the structure and sequence of the methods of interpretation under the Vienna Convention in particular.

The second impact of the Vienna Convention is that it consolidated, pursuant to previous developments in jurisprudence, the distinction between the General Rule of Interpretation embodied in Article 31 and the Supplementary

Methods of Interpretation embodied under Article 32. As Sir Ian Sinclair writes:

> The distinction between the general rules of interpretation and the supplementary means of interpretation is intended rather to ensure that supplementary means do not constitute an alternative, autonomous method for interpretation, divorced from the general rule.[45]

Even within the framework of the General Rule, the interpretative methods are further classified into those which guide the interpretative process (plain meaning, context, object and purpose), and those which 'shall be taken into account' together with the context of the treaty (subsequent practice, general rules of international law), which must be understood as a further allocation of priorities.[46]

The third impact of the Vienna Convention regime is that it no longer allows considering the intention of States as an independent and free-standing factor of interpretation, and its Articles 31 and 32 do not even mention the concept of intention.[47] Intention has instead to be ascertained from specific interpretative factors included in the Convention, such as the text, object and purpose or other factors. This is clear from the attitude of the International Law Commission at the codification stage, emphasising that 'the starting point of interpretation is the elucidation of the meaning of the text, not an investigation *ab initio* into the intentions of the parties'.[48] That locating intention as such cannot be the prevailing aim of treaty interpretation is clear from the presence within the Vienna Convention of certain methods that do not relate to the original intention of the parties. These methods relate to extraneous factors like the subsequent practice of States-parties and the relevant rules of general international law under Article 31.

The approach of the International Law Commission as further embodied in the Vienna Convention was also accepted at earlier stages. The intention factor is resorted to in practice, but never separately from the normal methods of interpretation. As the Permanent Court had emphasised in the *Polish War Vessels* case, it was ' not prepared to adopt the view that the text of the Treaty of Versailles can be enlarged by reading into it stipulations which are said to result from the pro-claimed intentions of the authors of the Treaty, but for which no provision is made in the text itself'.[49] As Paul Reuter has emphasised, it is essential to identify in what way the intention of parties was expressed and give precedence to its

[45] I Sinclair, *The Vienna Convention on the Law of Treaties* (1984), 116.

[46] Even though *Golder* (para 30) suggests that the interpretative factors under Article 31 are placed on the same footing.

[47] The Vienna Convention uses the term 'intention' about 15 times, but never in Articles 31 and 32.

[48] II *YbILC* 1966, 220.

[49] *Access to, or Anchorage in, the port of Danzig, of Polish War Vessels*, Advisory Opinion No 22 of 12 November 1931, *PCIJ Series* A/B, No 43, 144.

most immediate expression.[50] In general, manipulating with words and notions such as 'intention', or 'expectations', as New Haven School does, is not a position from which to clarify problems in the process of interpretation, but can only introduce extra superfluous elements which are not essential or necessary for the governing legal framework as defined under Articles 31 and 32 of the Vienna Convention.

The relevance of the Vienna Convention is universally accepted as the general guide of treaty interpretation, extending to fields from trade and investment to human rights, from bilateral transactions to multilateral 'law-making treaties'. In *Libya-Chad Boundary Dispute*, the International Court affirmed that Article 31 of the Vienna Convention reflects the rules of customary international law on treaty interpretation,[51] and reiterated this conclusion in *LaGrand*.[52] In *Kasikili/Sedudu*, the Court's task was, according to the Special Agreement concluded between Botswana and Namibia, to interpret the 1890 Treaty between Britain and Germany. As the Court pointed out in terms of the law governing interpretation, 'neither Botswana nor Namibia are parties to the Vienna Convention on the Law of Treaties of 23 May 1969, but that both of them consider that Article 31 of the Vienna Convention is applicable inasmuch as it reflects customary international law. The Court itself has already had occasion in the past to hold that customary international law found expression in Article 31 of the Vienna Convention.'[53] In *Ligitan/Sipadan*, the Court noted that Indonesia was not a party to the 1969 Vienna Convention, and reaffirmed that Article 31 thereof, with its priority for textual and teleological interpretation, was part of customary international law.[54]

A similar approach prevails in the arbitral practice. The Arbitral Tribunal in the *Young Loan* Award,[55] as well as the Arbitral Tribunal in the *Iron Rhine* Award, emphasised the unanimity of judicial bodies in considering the Vienna Convention interpretation regime as universally applicable as general (customary) international law. As the Tribunal put it, there was no tribunal to have disputed this position.[56]

According to Article 102(2) of the NAFTA Agreement, it shall be interpreted 'in accordance with the applicable rules of international law'. As the NAFTA Arbitral Tribunal pointed out in *Pope & Talbot*, 'NAFTA is a treaty, and the

[50] P Reuter, *Introduction to the Law of Treaties* (1985), 75.

[51] *Libya–Chad Boundary Dispute, ICJ Reports*, 1994, 21.

[52] *LaGrand* (Germany v USA), Merits, Judgment of 27 June 2001, *ICJ Reports*, 2001, 466, para 99.

[53] *Kasikili/Sedudu* (Botswana v Namibia), Judgment of 13 December 1999, General List No 98, para 18.

[54] *Sovereignty over Pulau Ligitan and Pulau Sipadan*, Judgment of 17 December 2002, para 37.

[55] *Belgium et al v Federal Republic of Germany (Young Loan Arbitration)*, Award of 16 May 1980, 19 ILM (1980), 1357 at 1370.

[56] *Arbitration Regarding Iron Rhine Railway* (Belgium/Netherlands), Award of 24 May 2005, para 45.

principal international law rules on the interpretation of treaties are found in the Vienna Convention on the Law of Treaties'.[57] The Tribunal reaffirmed that Articles 31 and 32 of the Vienna Convention reflect the generally accepted rules of customary international law.[58] The relevance of the interpretation methods under the Vienna Convention was also affirmed in *Metalclad*[59] and *Waste Management*.[60] The Arbitral Tribunals in *Thunderbird* and *SD Myers* also maintained that they would construe the terms of Chapter 11 NAFTA in accordance with its plain meaning, context and object and purpose as required by the Vienna Convention.[61]

The same holds true for human rights treaties. In *Golder*, the European Court of Human Rights examined how the European Convention should be interpreted. The Court stated that it should be guided by the Vienna Convention, because 'its Articles 31 to 33 enunciate in essence generally accepted principles of international law'.[62] Therefore, even as interpretation of treaties is undertaken in diverse treaty frameworks regulating different subject matters, it is the same regime of the Vienna Convention that applies—the regime that refers to multiple interpretative factors that can explain diverse outcomes depending on the character of treaty relations.

As is emphasised in the example of the WTO practice, the connection between the interpretation requirements of Article 3.2 DSU and Articles 31 and 32 of the Vienna Convention had become so fundamental that any WTO Panel deviating from these requirements would have its decisions reversed.[63]

The WTO jurisprudence confirms that the process of interpretation of treaties must be placed strictly within the framework of the Vienna Convention on the Law of Treaties and governed by its methods exclusively. The practice of the Appellate Body not only affirms the formal exclusivity of the Vienna Convention rules, but also explains the substantive essence of these rules. In *India–Patent*, the WTO Appellate Body addressed the issue of interpretation of the Agreement on Trade-related Aspects of Intellectual Property (TRIPS). The WTO Panel had addressed this issue before and suggested that the interpretative process must be governed by the principle of legitimate expectations, the standards developed in past panel reports and the principle of the protection of conditions of

[57] *Pope & Talbot Inc and the Government of Canada* (Interim Award, NAFTA Chapter 11 Arbitration), 26 June 2000, para 65.

[58] *Id*, para 66.

[59] *Metalclad Corporation and the United Mexican States* (Award), 30 August 2000, para 70.

[60] *Waste Management Inc and United Mexican States* (Award), 2 June 2000, para 9; see also *S.D. Myers and Government of Canada* (Partial Award, NAFTA Arbitration under the UNCITRAL Rules), 13 November 2000, paras 199–200.

[61] *International Thunderbird Gaming Corporation and the United Mexican States* (Award), 26 January 2006, para 91; *S.D. Myers*, para 202.

[62] *Golder* , paras 29–30.

[63] D Shanker, The Vienna Convention on the Law of Treaties, the Dispute Settlement System of the WTO and the Doha Declaration on the TRIPs Agreement, 36 *Journal of World Trade* (2002), 721 at 727.

competition.[64] This approach did not refer to any objectively recognised authority regarding interpretation. The Panel also relied on the principles of the Vienna Convention and recognised their customary law status. The Panel proceeded to state that 'good faith interpretation requires the protection of legitimate expectations derived from the protection of intellectual property rights provided for in the Agreement'. As the Appellate Body emphasised, the Panel misapplied Article 31 of the Vienna Convention. It misunderstood the concept of legitimate expectations in the context and as part of customary rules on interpretation. These legitimate expectations were reflected in the language of the treaty itself, and the duty of a treaty interpreter was 'to examine the words of the treaty to determine the intentions of the parties'. The principles of the Vienna Convention 'neither require nor condone the imputation into a treaty of words that are not there or the importation into a treaty of concepts that were not intended'. The Panel had created its own interpretative principle which was not compatible with the Vienna Convention and established jurisprudence. The WTO organs must be guided by the Vienna Convention and can neither add to nor diminish existing treaty rights.[65]

In *EC–Computer Equipment*, the Appellate Body emphasises the need for rigorous application of the Vienna Convention regime in the process of interpretation. In this regard, the Appellate Body criticises the Panel for abandoning the effort to interpret the relevant Schedule of Commitments in accordance with Articles 31 and 32 of the Convention.[66] Similarly, the Appellate Body is quite rigorous in asserting the relevance of every applicable method of interpretation:

> As already discussed above, the Panel referred to the context of Schedule LXXX as well as to the object and purpose of the WTO Agreement and the GATT 1994, of which Schedule LXXX is an integral part. However, it did so to support its proposition that the terms of a Schedule may be interpreted in the light of the 'legitimate expectations' of an exporting Member. The Panel failed to examine the context of Schedule LXXX and the object and purpose of the WTO Agreement and the GATT 1994 in accordance with the rules of treaty interpretation set out in the Vienna Convention.[67]

The Appellate Body also rejected the conclusion that the meaning of a tariff concession in a Member's Schedule may be determined in the light of the 'legitimate expectations' of an exporting Member.[68] Furthermore, nothing in Article II:5 GATT suggested that the expectations of the exporting Member only can be the basis for interpreting a concession in a Member's Schedule for the purposes of determining whether that Member has acted consistently with its

[64] *India–Patent, Protection for Pharmaceutical and Agricultural Chemical Products*, AB-1997-5, Report of the Appellate Body, WT/DS 50/AB/R, 19 December 1997, para 33.

[65] *Id*, paras 43–46.

[66] *European Communities–Customs Classification of Certain Computer Equipment*, WT/DS62/AB/R, AB-1998–2, Report of the Appellate Body, 5 June 1998, para 87.

[67] *Id*, paras 88, 90; see further para 97 reiterating this conclusion.

[68] *Id*, para 80.

obligations.[69] In terms most noteworthy for the philosophy underlying interpretation, it was:

> especially unacceptable that the maintenance of the security and predictability of tariff concessions allows the interpretation of a concession in the light of the 'legitimate expectations' of exporting Members, i.e., their subjective views as to what the agreement reached during tariff negotiations was. The security and predictability of tariff concessions would be seriously undermined if the concessions in Members' Schedules were to be interpreted on the basis of the subjective views of certain exporting Members alone.[70]

Against this background of rejecting the relevance of subjectivism and auto-interpretation by the State of the scope of international obligations, the Appellate Body proceeds to formulate the interpretative regime based on the Vienna Convention. The Appellate Body consequently rejects the argument 'that interpreting the meaning of a concession in a Member's Schedule in the light of the "legitimate expectations" of exporting Members is consistent with the principle of good faith interpretation under Article 31 of the Vienna Convention'.[71]

The Appellate Body's approach proceeds from the premise of stability of treaty obligations and the consequent need to facilitate the parties' reliance on the objectively identifiable content of their treaty obligations. The treaty interpreter has to take the treaty obligations on their face; neither enhancing nor diminishing their scope can be condoned in this process.

There is no substantial doctrinal contradiction to the universal relevance and customary law status of the Vienna Convention rules of interpretation, apart from the objections voiced by Schwebel. As Schwebel argues, the hierarchical structure of Articles 31 and 32 of the Vienna Convention is unreal, and preparatory work cannot be a supplementary means of interpretation.[72] Schwebel does not seem to conceal his disagreement with the existing legal position. He argues that because of the above circumstance, Articles 31 and 32 of the Vienna Convention could hardly be reflective of customary international law, 'for there is simply too much State practice and judicial precedent that accords preparatory work a greater place'.[73] That said, the above analysis of judicial practice has confirmed that there can be no meaningful objection to the customary status of Articles 31 and 32. At the same time, the analysis of practice regarding *travaux*

[69] *Id*, para 81.
[70] *Id*, para 82.
[71] *Id*, para 83.
[72] S Schwebel, May Preparatory Work be Used to Correct Rather than Confirm the 'Clear' Meaning of a Treaty Provision? in J. Makarczyk (ed), *Theory of International Law at the Threshold of the 21st Century: Essays in Honour of Krzysztof Skubiszewski* (1996), 541 at 543.
[73] *Id*, 547.

preparatoires demonstrates that the attitude dominating practice is far removed from the perspective depicted by Schwebel.[74]

The rules of treaty interpretation are meant to serve the observance of treaty obligations in good faith. Good faith is a governing factor both under Article 26 of the Vienna Convention, dealing with *pacta sunt servanda*, and under its Article 31, formulating the General Rule of Interpretation. The exclusivity of the Vienna Convention rules on interpretation, including the hierarchy between its methods, is dictated by the need for stability of treaty obligations, of avoiding their mutually exclusive construction, and subjectivism in the process of interpretation of treaty obligations. The Vienna Convention methods of interpretation, as the practice consistently demonstrates, are not only treaty-based methods but also constitute the generally accepted legal framework of constitutional significance. Attempts to distort the sequence of interpretation methods, with or without professing this as an interpretative task, and thus achieve an interpretative outcome that cannot be accommodated within the Vienna Convention framework, can be undertaken in practice to portray solutions that are conducive to the decision-maker's perception of power and politics or with a view to providing the relevant national government with freedom of action and deferring to the will of the political branches of government. In other words, these approaches promote subjectivism in the process of treaty interpretation. These approaches, whether or not expressly so professing, proceed from the understanding of mixing law with politics and accept modification of the relevant legal outcomes in the interests of power.

Principles of interpretation must be distinguished from interpretation maxims. There are several maxims that, on the whole, convey rational ideas in clarifying the meaning of written provisions, such as *expressio unius est exclusio alterius*, *ejusdem generis*, or *contra proferentem*.[75] These maxims differ from principles of interpretation in that the latter derive their legitimacy from the Vienna Convention which is also part of customary law. The latter have been developed on a case-by-case basis or in doctrine, and have no independent legitimacy. Although resorted to in several cases, the maxims of interpretation are valuable only in so far as they constitute the application of the principles of interpretation. Where a recognised principle of interpretation disposes of the issue, the maxims of interpretation are irrelevant. Another factor preventing the maxims of interpretation from having direct normative impact is that they are so specific in scope that, given the context of individual situations of interpretation, they can lead to mutually incompatible outcomes in different cases.

[74] See below Section 8 and see further Chapter 12.

[75] McNair (1961), 393ff, 464.

3. Plain and Ordinary Meaning of Words

(a) The Logical and Normative Primacy of Plain and Ordinary Meaning

The terms used in doctrine and practice refer to the ordinary, clear, plain and natural meaning of words and provisions. All these terms have in common that they refer to the literal and linguistic meaning of words embodied in a particular treaty. Even though it has been argued that the purpose of interpretation is to give meaning to dead words,[76] the governing legal framework views the clarification of the ordinary meaning of treaties as a primary mean of treaty interpretation. The primacy or plain and ordinary meaning follows directly from the need for an interpreter to establish and preserve the original consensus between States-parties.

Doctrinal support for the method of ordinary meaning dates much further back than the adoption of the Vienna Convention. The method of ordinary and plain meaning is upheld by Phillimore, who observed that 'the principal rule' is 'to follow the ordinary and usual acceptation, the plain and obvious meaning of the language employed'.[77] Phillimore also endorsed some specific elements of the textual approach, namely 'That the contracting party, who might and ought to have expressed himself clearly and fully, must take the consequences of his carelessness, and cannot, as a general rule, introduce subsequent restrictions or extensions of his meaning. That what is sufficiently declared must be taken to be true, and to have been the true intention of the party entering into the engagement.'[78] In this respect, Phillimore follows Vattel's understanding of the textual approach. WE Hall likewise endorsed the ordinary meaning rule as a rule to which no objection can be urged, observing that:

> When the language of a treaty, taken in the ordinary their plain meaning of the words, yields a plain and reasonable sense, it must be taken as intended to be read in that sense, subject to the qualifications, that any words which may have a customary meaning in treaties, differing from their common signification, must be understood to have that meaning.[79]

In the process of the ILC codification, Special Rapporteur Waldock accepted the fundamental character of the textual interpretation rule and the International Law Commission approved this approach at different stages of its work, stating that the text is the most recent and authentic expression of the common will of the parties.[80] By recognising the need to interpret the clear text, the Vienna Convention distances itself from the Vattelian approach. As Judge Weeramantry

[76] Yü (1927), 40.
[77] Phillimore (1855), vol II 73.
[78] *Id* (1855), vol II 79.
[79] Hall (1895), 350.
[80] II *YbILC* 1964, 56, 202; II *YbILC* 1964, 220.

put it in the *Arbitral Award* case, 'we have moved far away from the Vattelian principle that... it is not permissible to interpret what has no need of interpretation. Though followed by some eminent international jurists even into the early days of this century, the need for even the simplest words to require interpretation has been highlighted both by scholars and by modern linguistic studies.'[81] As further emphasised, interpretation is needed where the text of the treaty is capable of misunderstanding or does not speak for itself. At the same time, the statement that the text is unclear cannot be the ultimate outcome of interpretation.[82]

Article 31(1) of the Vienna Convention places the predominant emphasis on the plain and natural meaning of treaty provisions. Although it is doctrinally contended that clarity of words does not guarantee clarity of ideas,[83] the Vienna Convention, and the practice that followed it, place the predominant emphasis on the plain and ordinary meaning precisely of words and phrases. The linguistic debate as to whether there is such a thing as clear and established meaning of words is beside the point in this analysis. The principal factor is that, according to the attitude of the international community as expressed in Article 31 of the Vienna Convention and the respective judicial practice, words do have established meaning and interpreters are able to find it on a regular basis. This exercise is complete as soon as the meaning is objectively and intelligibly identifiable, whether or not it is seen as reasonable, satisfactory or sound.

There are doctrinal approaches contradicting the plain meaning method as the primary method of treaty interpretation. Authors such as Hyde and McNair are sceptical about the plain meaning method of treaty interpretation. McNair considers this method as a mere *prima facie* guide in identifying the real intention of parties.[84] Kelsen argues that the wording of a legal instrument may not be in conformity with the ascertainable intention of the parties. It may go beyond, or stay behind, that intention, in which case restrictive or extensive interpretation would follow.[85] Hyde considers that the search for linguistic natural meaning is unscientific and unhelpful, and prefers the emphasis on the thought and conduct of parties.[86] Hyde further asserts that 'linguistic clearness is not necessarily identical with clearness of design on the part of the contracting parties', and the function of words is merely to give expression to that design.[87] But Hyde does not provide for any criteria to locate the parameters of that design. If the text as the most immediate reflection of that design is disregarded, the interpreter will be

[81] *Arbitral Award* (Guinea-Bissau v Senegal), *ICJ Reports*, 1989, 112 (Dissenting Opinion), referring in particular to Schwarzenberger.

[82] HF Köck, *Vertragsinterpretation und Vertragsrechtskonvention. Zur Bedeutung der Artikel 31 und 32 der Wiener Vertragsrechtskonvention 1969* (1976), 60.

[83] Visscher (1963), 56.

[84] McNair (1961), 367–368.

[85] H Kelsen, *The Principles of International Law* (R Tucker, ed, 1967), 459.

[86] CC Hyde, *International Law, Chiefly as Interpreted and Applied by the United States* (1945), vol II, 1470.

[87] CC Hyde, Judge Anzilotti on the Interpretation of Treaties, 27 *AJIL* (1933), 502 at 503.

left only with the option to speculate on the basis of subjective appreciation. Such an exercise cannot ensure faithful adherence to the parameters of the original agreement.

Chang also sceptically assessed the relevance of the plain meaning rule, asserting that in judicial practice this method was usually supported by external considerations, there having been no real conflicts between the two.[88] What is crucial, however, is what is responsible, in the final analysis, for the outcome reached in the case: plain meaning itself or those external factors. As the analysis of practice will demonstrate, plain meaning is regularly the crucial factor responsible for the outcome of interpretation, and can make extraneous evidence irrelevant. In fact, another early study on treaty interpretation affirms that even in the period of the Permanent Court, judicial practice was already based on the primacy of the text.[89]

Lauterpacht focuses on early arbitral awards which arguably departed from the method of plain meaning.[90] He accepts the natural meaning of treaty provisions as the starting-point of interpretation, not to be given the 'complexion of finality'. It has to be treated as rebuttable *presumptio juris*, not as an irrefutable *presumptio juris et de jure*.[91] Lauterpacht poses the question: 'What is meant by saying that the meaning of the treaty is "clear"? A phrase or word is seldom, if ever, clear in itself.' The clarity of words relates to the mind of the judge which assesses all relevant circumstances.[92] This approach implies some degree of subjectivism on the part of the decision-maker as opposed to the application of what the relevant States have agreed on. Similarly, Julius Stone is sceptical as to the notion of plain and natural meaning of treaty provisions. Stone argues that only insofar as no other common intention can be found, can tribunals apply treaty provisions in accordance with their ordinary meaning.[93]

There are further doctrinal suggestions that words are not absolutes but have to be evaluated in the context from which they derive their meaning. The literal meaning of words is thus not considered to be decisive.[94] This argument may prove correct in individual cases but there is little merit in arguing on a general plane that words cannot have a determined meaning of their own. Taking this approach *a priori* would force the interpreter to adopt the shifted presumption

[88] Chang (1933), 39–40.

[89] M Jokl, *De l'interprétation des traités normatifs d'après de la doctrine et la jurisprudence internationales* (1936), 24.

[90] H Lauterpacht, *Development* (1958), 56–58, mainly the awards in the 1910s and 1920s.

[91] *Id*, 58.

[92] *Id*, 139; see also H Lauterpacht, Some Observations on Preparatory Work in the Interpretation of Treaties, 48 *Harvard Law Review* (1934–1935), 549 at 572; Lauterpacht's scepticism towards the principle of plain meaning is visible from his report on the interpretation of treaties, at the Institute of International Law, De l'interpretation des traités, 43 *Annuaire de L'institut de Droit International* (1950), 366, 378ff.

[93] Stone (1953–1955), 355–356.

[94] M Matsushita, T Schoenbaum & P Mavroidis, *The World Trade Organization: Law, Practice and Policy* (2006), 38.

that none of the words in the treaty text should be taken at their face value. This could be the case only after the context, as well as the object and purpose of the treaty, are specifically studied and affirmative reasons are identified why the relevant word should not be given its strict literal meaning and must be seen as influenced by its context.

In a further attempt to dispute the relevance of the plain meaning rule, Johnstone argues that the interpretive process is the balancing of the understanding of one party with that of another. Meaning is, according to this approach, not a product of explicit agreement, but of the underlying reciprocal process. The meaning can be clarified by reference to the situation in which the meaning-related communication takes place.[95] Furthermore, Johnstone argues that 'agreement is far from automatic, because many words (and the rules, principles, purposes and policies they convey) are ambiguous and manipulable, and the interests of the parties will remain, in some respects, different'.[96] As can be seen, this view effectively attempts to negate the relevance of the plain meaning rule, and it has never been reflected in judicial or arbitral practice. In addition, this approach confirms that the opposition to the plain meaning rule to some extent implies the rejection of the determinacy of legal regulation under treaties.

Koskenniemi likewise disputes the relevance of plain meaning, submitting that this is 'not a rule of interpretation at all. It assumes what has to be proved; that the expression has a certain meaning instead of another one'.[97] This argument involves a logical error. The interpretative method of plain meaning is not by itself about ascribing a specific meaning to individual words. It is merely a direction to the interpreter that the meaning the words possess must be sought; if they are contested they must be clarified, so that the treaty provision can be applied to facts. Finding specific meaning of words is an exercise to be undertaken only after the applicability of the plain meaning method is acknowledged. The need to establish the meaning of individual words and phrases does not negate, but instead directly follows from, the interpretative method that accords primary significance to that meaning.

Another shortcoming of Koskenniemi's argument on the plain meaning method relates to the distortion of the role it occupies in the Vienna Convention framework. Koskenniemi presents the framework as if the meaning of words were merely a vehicle for carrying and demonstrating what has been agreed originally and separately from those words.[98] This approach cannot be accommodated either within the Vienna Convention text, or the International Law Commission's approach, or, as we shall see, the judicial practice of application of Article 31 of the Vienna Convention.

[95] I Johnstone, Treaty Interpretation: The Authority of Interpretive Communities, 12 *Michigan JIIL* (1990–91), 371, 378, 384.

[96] Johnstone (1991), 387.

[97] M Koskenniemi, *From Apology to Utopia* (2004), 333–334.

[98] *Id*, 334.

Koskenniemi's further, linguistically oriented, argument relates to the alleged non-existence of objective meaning from a linguistic perspective. According to this argument, interpretation allegedly creates meaning instead of discovering it.[99] This thesis neglects the basic object of interpretation, which is the ascertaining of *original* consensus, instead of projecting what it could be. This is why in practice the plain meaning method is regularly applied as the most important one, and considerations of linguistic theory do very little to upset this position.

The deficiency of these views relates to their failure to duly consider the consensual character of treaties. The intention to be searched for in the process of interpretation is the agreed intention. The primacy of text is dictated by the fact that it constitutes the most suitable and straightforward evidence of that agreement. If the text suggests the identifiable meaning of agreed rules, this has to be the end of the matter. It is obviously possible that the uncertainty of the text can direct the interpreter to other methods of interpretation. However, the uncertainty is never to be presumed, but to be ascertained only if it positively exists. At the same time, the uncertainty and ambiguity is the absence of definable meaning, not the existence of the meaning that one may consider unsatisfactory, unacceptable or unsuitable for one's interests.

(b) The Resort to Plain and Ordinary Meaning in Judicial Practice

As the Permanent Court of International Justice emphasised in the *Wimbledon* case, the plain meaning of treaty provisions applies even if it could be seen by some as unreasonable or unacceptable. The Court decided that the duty to grant free passage to vessels under the Versailles Treaty prevailed over conflicting claims under the rest of international law. In a vigorous dissent, Judges Anzilotti and Huber argued that:

> Though it is true that when the wording of a treaty is clear its literal meaning must be accepted as it stands, without limitation or extension, it is equally true that the words have no value except in so far as they express an idea; but it must not be presumed that the intention was to express an idea which leads to contradictory or impossible consequences or which, in the circumstances, must be regarded as going beyond the intention of the parties. The purely grammatical interpretation of every contract, and more especially of international treaties, must stop at this point.[100]

International law in the final analysis is not what is seen as reasonable on occasions, but what is agreed by States. The reasonableness of the relevant provision plays no role in determining the meaning of treaty provisions in defiance of their natural and ordinary meaning.

[99] *Id*, 530–532.
[100] Dissenting Opinion, 1923 *PCIJ Series* A, No 1, 36.

The 1969 Vienna Convention was adopted against a background of both the doctrinal resistance to the concept of plain and natural meaning of treaty provisions as the basic rule of interpretation, and the prevailing recognition of this approach in judicial practice. Apart from the fact that it follows what international tribunals have been consistently deciding for decades, the approach of the International Law Commission and the Vienna Conference in favour of the plain meaning rule has to be explained by the best reflection in this rule of the authenticity of State consent and agreement on which international treaties are based. Those writers who doubt or oppose the relevance of the plain meaning rule do not properly address the issue of how else the authenticity of the agreement between States is to be preserved.

The Vienna Convention's preference for the plain meaning of terms follows the long-standing development of this principle in judicial practice. As the Permanent Court specified in *Acquisition of Polish Nationality*, when the text of a treaty clause is clear, the Court 'is bound to apply this clause as it stands, without considering whether other provisions might with advantage have been added to or substituted for it.... To impose an additional condition not provided for in the Treaty of June 28th, 1919, would be equivalent not to interpreting the Treaty, but to reconstructing it.'[101] In other words, the task of interpretation is to ascertain what the treaty provision says, not how sensible it is from one or another perspective, or how it could be improved.

Similarly, in *Polish Postal Service* the Court asserted, as a 'cardinal principle of interpretation that words must be interpreted in the sense which they would normally have in their context, unless such interpretation would lead to something unreasonable or absurd'.[102]

In the *Night Work* case, the Court had to interpret a provision in the ILO convention, according to which 'women without distinction of age shall not be employed in any public or private industrial undertaking', to answer the question whether this only applied to female manual workers. Having emphasised the predominance of textual interpretation, the Court rejected any need for restrictive interpretation, because 'this would be tantamount to saying that, as no such contrary intention is shown to exist in the case of this Convention, Article 3 must be regarded as applying only to manual workers. The Court holds that it would not be sound to argue this.'[103]

The International Court adopted the textual approach to the interpretation of the UN Charter in the *Admissions* case, where it dealt with the question of whether, under Article 4(2), the General Assembly can admit to the UN membership a State which has not been recommended by the Security Council. On

[101] *Acquisition of Polish Nationality*, Advisory Opinion of 15 September 1923, *PCIJ Series* B, No 7, 6 at 20.

[102] *Polish Postal Services in Danzig* (Advisory Opinion), *PCIJ Series* B, No 11, 39.

[103] *Interpretation of the Convention of 1919 Concerning Employment of Women During the Night*, Advisory Opinion of 15 November 1932, *PCIJ Series* A/B, No 50, 365 at 372–374.

the basis of textual analysis of this provision, the Court concluded that the recommendation of the Council was the basis for the Assembly's decision. The Court reiterated again that if 'the words in their natural and ordinary meaning make sense in their context, this is an end of the matter', and added that 'it may not interpret the words by seeking to give them some other meaning'.[104]

In the *IMCO* case, the International Court applied the plain meaning method to the notion of 'largest ship-owning nations' under Article 28(a) of the IMCO Convention. The Court observed that the Convention intended that the Maritime Safety Committee was to be under the control of the largest ship-owning nations.[105] The *IMCO* case deals in this respect with the plain meaning of the treaty clause in relation to claims of the institutional discretion of the IMCO Assembly to elect the Committee members and assess their qualification to be elected. The Court observes that:

> The argument based on discretion would permit the Assembly, in use only of its discretion, to decide through its vote which nations have or do not have an important interest in maritime safety and to deny membership on the Committee to any State regardless of the size of its tonnage or any other qualification. The effect of such an interpretation would be to render superfluous the greater part of Article 28(a) and to erect the discretion of the Assembly as the supreme rule for the constitution of the Maritime Safety Committee. This would in the opinion of the Court be incompatible with the principle underlying the Article.[106]

Consequently, the institutional discretion argument had to give way to the need to read treaty clauses in terms of their plain meaning.

The Court noted the suggestion 'that the word "elected" where it first appears in Article 28(a) was deliberately chosen in order to confer on the Assembly

[104] *Competence of the General Assembly for the Admission of a State to the United Nations* (Advisory Opinion), 3 May 1950, *ICJ Reports* 1950, 4 at 7–8. In the *First Admissions* Advisory Opinion, in another manifestation of its unconditional support for the primacy of the text over other methods of interpretation, the Court likewise adhered to the textual method of interpretation when it dealt with conditions for admission to the UN membership. The Court emphasised, in relation to the conditions listed in Article 4 of the Charter, that 'The text of this paragraph, by the enumeration which it contains and the choice of its terms, clearly demonstrates the intention of its authors to establish a legal rule which, while it fixes the conditions of admission, determines also the reasons for which admission may be refused for the text does not differentiate between these two cases and any attempt to restrict it to one of them would be purely arbitrary.' The Court went on to emphasise that 'The natural meaning of the words used leads to the conclusion that these conditions constitute an exhaustive enumeration and are not merely stated by way of guidance or example. The provision would lose its significance and weight, if other conditions, unconnected with those laid down, could be demanded. The conditions stated in paragraph I of Article 4 must therefore be regarded not merely as the necessary conditions, but also as the conditions which suffice. … If the authors of the Charter had meant to leave Members free to import into the application of this provision considerations extraneous to the conditions laid down therein, they would undoubtedly have adopted a different wording.' *ICJ Reports*, 1947–48, 62–63.

[105] *Constitution of the Maritime Safety Committee of the Inter-Governmental Maritime Consultative Organisation*, Advisory Opinion of 8 June 1960, *ICJ Reports*, 1960, 150 at 159ff.

[106] *Id*, 160.

a wide authority to appraise the relative qualifications of Member States for election to the Committee'. But the Court responded that whatever the margin of choice or individual appraisal which existed in the Assembly in relation to the election of any Member of the Council, that margin of choice or appraisal was one which was no greater than was permitted by the terms of the relevant Articles of the IMCO Constitution. The words 'elect' and 'elected' had to be construed accordingly.[107] The Court concluded that:

> What Article 28*(a)* requires the Assembly to do is to determine which of its Members are the eight 'largest ship-owning nations' within the meaning which these words bear. That is the sole content of its function in relation to them. The words of the Article 'of which not less than eight shall be the largest ship-owning nations' have a mandatory and imperative sense and precisely carry out the intention of the framers of the Convention.[108]

The Court's approach rejects that expressed in Judge Kleastad's dissent, that the imposition of this 'automatic text' on the electing body would deprive that body of the freedom of choice.[109] In general, the Court's approach confirms that the relevance of plain meaning of treaty provisions affects not only the process of interpretation as such, but also locates the scope of institutional powers within that process.

The Court in *IMCO* had further to examine the meaning of the words 'the largest ship-owning nations'. The Court noted the UK and Netherlands suggestion that 'The expression "the largest ship-owning nations" has no apparent clear-cut or technical meaning ... the intention of those words was to enable the Assembly in the process of election to look at the realities of the situation and to determine according to its own judgment, whether or not candidates for election to the Maritime Safety Committee could properly be regarded as the "largest ship-owning nations" in a real and substantial sense.' The Court observed that according to this submission the phrase 'the largest ship-owning nations' would merely be a guide enabling the Assembly to exercise discretion in assessing the true situation and realities. The Assembly would be bound by no ascertainable criteria, and its members could be guided by any considerations they thought relevant. Thus, the Assembly would be 'uncontrolled by any objective test of any kind'. The Court was unable to accept such a result.[110]

Having rejected the argument of discretionary decision-making, the Court went on to determine the plain meaning of the phrase 'the largest ship-owning nations'. The Court observed that 'it is apparent that some basis of measurement must be applied'. The rationale of the situation was that Article 28(*a*), when

[107] *Id*, 159.
[108] *Id*, 165.
[109] Dissenting Opinion, *id*, 173–174.
[110] *Id*, 165–166.

speaking of the largest ship-owning nations, had meant the comparative size of one nation's fleet to that of another nation.[111]

The *IMCO* Opinion thus provides a straightforward case of determining the plain meaning of a treaty provision by applying legal requirements to a factual situation. In particular, the *IMCO* Opinion indicates that when the meaning of words is contested, the reality test must be applied. It has to be tested what these words mean in real terms on the ground.

In *Jan Mayen*, Norway pleaded that the Norwegian–Danish Agreement of 8 December 1965 had established the boundary of their maritime spaces according to the principle of median line. The Agreement did not refer specifically to the maritime boundary between Greenland and Jan Mayen. Norway contended that the agreement was of a general nature and hence the median line maritime boundary operated between the two States without restrictions as to the area of operation. Denmark argued that the Agreement merely related to Norway's mainland coast and the North Sea area, and moreover the reference to this region was included in Article 2 of the Agreement. The Court upheld the reasoning of Denmark and held that the area of Jan Mayen was not included in the Agreement.[112]

In *Libya–Chad*, the International Court adopted the interpretative policy of relying on the ordinary meaning of the 1955 Treaty between France and Libya, in the light of its object and purpose, pursuant to Article 31 of the Vienna Convention. As the Court put it, 'interpretation must be based above all upon the text of the treaty'.[113] The treaty clause to be interpreted related to the recognition of frontiers between Libya and Chad. Libya contended that the 1955 Treaty recognised the frontiers that were determined under other instruments but did not itself establish or determine such frontiers. The Court refused to accept this view, reiterating its mission to ascertain the natural and ordinary meaning of the Treaty and giving effect to it. To hold that some frontiers between the two States were defined but others were left unsettled would contradict the ordinary meaning of Article 3 of the Treaty. The fact that Article 3 referred to frontiers 'that result from the international instruments' means all the frontiers mentioned in these instruments. 'Any other construction would be contrary to the actual terms of Article 3.'[114] As the Court put it, 'there is nothing to prevent the parties from deciding by mutual agreement to consider a certain line as a frontier, whatever the previous status of that line'.[115] Therefore, the Court presumed, by reference to the actual terms of Article 3, that the parties' intention was to consider all the

[111] *Id*, 166.

[112] *Case concerning Maritime Delimitation in the Area of Jan Mayen* (Denmark v Norway), Judgment of 14 June 1993, *ICJ Reports*, 1993, 38 at 49.

[113] *Boundary Dispute between Libya and Chad, ICJ Reports*, 1994, 21–22.

[114] *Id*, 22–23.

[115] *Id*, 23.

listed instruments as being in force for the purpose of Article 3, since otherwise they would not have referred to them.[116]

The Court's reasoning in this case is based on the nature of the treaty as *lex specialis* adopted on a bilateral plane and consequently gives effect to the intention of the parties as evidenced by the text. The frontiers fixed in earlier unratified treaties were considered valid on the basis of the will and intention of the parties as embodied in the text of the 1955 Treaty.

In *Kasikili/Sedudu*, the Court restated its task to interpret the 1890 Treaty, as the Vienna Convention requires it, in terms of its plain meaning and object and purpose. Consequently, the Court found that the boundary between Namibia and Botswana was on the 'main channel' of the River Chobe,[117] and the identification of this main channel led to the conclusion that the island of Kasikili/Sedudu belonged to Botswana. In *Ligitan/Sipadan*, the Court's task was to interpret the 1891 Anglo-Dutch Convention to establish whether it allocated the boundary between Malaysia and Indonesia, as successors of Britain and the Netherlands, in such a way as to enable it to be established which of them owned the islands in dispute. The crucial issue was the interpretation of Article IV which allocated the boundary 'across' the island of Sebattik. The question was whether this was limited to the boundary around Sebattik or extended, as Indonesia put it, 'so far as was necessary to achieve the Convention's purposes'.[118] The Court stated that the Parties differed as to how 'across' should be interpreted. It 'acknowledge[d] that the word is not devoid of ambiguity and is capable of bearing either of the meanings given to it by the Parties. A line established by the Treaty may indeed pass "across" an island and terminate on the shores of such island or continue beyond it.' The Court observed that the ambiguity could have been avoided had the Convention stipulated expressly that the line defined in Article IV constituted, beyond the east coast of Sebattik, the line separating the islands under British sovereignty from those under Dutch sovereignty. The silence of the text could not be ignored and it supported the position of Malaysia, which meant that the line was without prejudice to the sovereignty over Ligitan/Sipadan.[119]

The predominance of the plain meaning methods has also been affirmed by the European Court of Human Rights. The possible controversies around giving words their plain meaning are highlighted by the European Court of Human Rights in the *Lawless* case, in its treatment of the right of detained persons to be brought promptly before a court under Articles 5(1)(c) and 5(3) of the European Convention.[120] In this case, Ireland argued that the right to be brought before a

[116] *Id*, 25.

[117] Judgment of 13 December 1999, General List No 98, paras 20–21.

[118] *Sovereignty over Pulau Ligitan and Pulau Sipadan*, (Indonesia/Malaysia), Judgment of 17 December 2002, General List No 102, paras 39–40.

[119] *Ligitan/Sipadan*, paras 41–42.

[120] Article 5(1)(c) of the European Convention authorises 'the lawful arrest or detention of a person effected for the purpose of bringing him before the competent legal authority on reasonable suspicion of having committed an offence or when it is reasonably considered necessary to prevent

judge related only to persons who were detained for the purpose of being tried and not to those detained for the purpose of preventing crime.[121] The Court responded that the wording of Article 5 was sufficiently clear, the words 'effected for purpose of bringing him before the competent legal authority' applied to both categories of detainees, and Article 5(3) 'plainly entail[ed] the obligation to bring everyone arrested or detained in any of the circumstances contemplated by the provisions of paragraph 1(c)'. Such was the plain and natural wording of both the first and third paragraphs of Article 5.[122]

In *Belgian Linguistics*, the European Court dealt with Article 2 of Protocol 1 of the European Commission which provides, in its relevant part, that 'In the exercise of any functions which it assumes in relation to education and to teaching, the State shall respect the right of parents to ensure such education and teaching in conformity with their own religions and philosophical convictions.' The Court interpreted this provision textually, emphasising that:

> This provision does not require of States that they should, in the sphere of education or teaching, respect parents' linguistic preferences, but only their religious and philosophical convictions. To interpret the terms 'religious' and 'philosophical' as covering linguistic preferences would amount to a distortion of their ordinary and usual meaning and to read into the Convention something which is not there.[123]

The preference for the textual approach has also been evident in arbitral practice for a long time. The Arbitral Tribunal in *North Atlantic Fisheries* adhered to the textual method in assessing the parameters of the stipulation that British and American nationals had to conduct fishing 'in common' under the 1818 London Convention. As the Tribunal put it, 'these words are such as would naturally suggest themselves to the negotiators of 1818 if their intention had been to express a common subjection to regulations as well as a common right'.[124]

The Tribunal in *North Atlantic Fisheries* refused to apply the *expressio unius* principle to the interpretation of the 1818 London Convention. The US contention was that 'as the liberty to dry and cure on the Treaty coasts and to enter bays and harbours on the non-treaty coasts are both subjected to conditions, and the latter to specific restrictions, it should therefore be held that the liberty to fish should be subjected to no restrictions, as none are provided for in the Treaty'. The Tribunal responded that 'these [other] restrictions of the right to enter bays and harbours applying solely to American fishermen must have been expressed in

his committing an offence or fleeing after having done so'; according to Article 5(3), 'Everyone arrested or detained in accordance with the provisions of paragraph 1(c) of this Article shall be brought promptly before a judge or other officer authorised by law to exercise judicial power and shall be entitled to trial within a reasonable time or to release pending trial'.

[121] *Lawless v Ireland*, No 332/57, Judgment of 1 July 1961, para 10.

[122] *Lawless* para 14.

[123] *Belgian Linguistics*, Application Nos 1474/62, 1677/62, 1691/62, 1769/63, 1994/63, 2126/64, Section I.B, para 6.

[124] JB Scott, *Hague Court Reports* 163.

the Treaty, whereas regulations of the fishery, applying equally to American and British, are made by right of territorial sovereignty'.[125]

Another provision the interpretation of which was at stake in *North Atlantic Fisheries* related to the renunciation of US fishing rights in certain British maritime areas. Britain argued that this renunciation applied to all maritime bays, while the US asserted that it applied only to bays of certain class or condition. The Tribunal observed, adhering to the plain meaning textual method, that:

> Now, considering that the Treaty used the general term 'bays' without qualification, the Tribunal is of opinion that these words of the Treaty must be interpreted in a general sense as applying to every bay on the coast in question that might be reasonably supposed to have been considered as a bay by the negotiators of the Treaty under the general conditions then prevailing, unless the United States can adduce satisfactory proof that any restrictions or qualifications of the general use of the term were or should have been present to their minds.[126]

As the notion of 'bays' was contested, the Tribunal emphasised that it was 'unable to understand the term "bays" in the renunciation clause in other than its geographical sense, by which a bay is to be considered as an indentation of the coast'.[127]

More recent arbitral practice likewise follows the primacy of the textual approach. At one point the Arbitral Tribunal in *Iron Rhine* considered plain meaning as the 'starting point for interpretation'.[128] As the NAFTA Tribunal emphasised in *Pope & Talbot*, 'the analysis and interpretation of Article 1106 of NAFTA is initially informed by the ordinary meaning of its terms'.[129] It consequently based its decision on a textual analysis of the requirements as to access for foreign investment to the territory of the party of the NAFTA Agreement.

The investor submitted to the NAFTA Tribunal that Article 1110 NAFTA went beyond the scope of the customary international law prohibiting expropriation and encompassed 'measures of general application which have the effect of substantially interfering with the investments of investors of NAFTA Parties', because Article 1110 encompassed 'measures... tantamount to expropriation'. The Tribunal adopted the textual approach, pointing out that '"tantamount" means nothing more than equivalent. Something that is equivalent to something cannot logically encompass more.' Therefore, measures that have regulatory character or impair the economic value of the property were not considered as expropriation that could breach Article 1110. As the Tribunal emphasised, 'measures are covered only if they achieve the same results as expropriation'.[130]

125 *Id*, 165.
126 *Id*, 181.
127 *Id*, 187.
128 *Iron Rhine*, para 47.
129 *Pope & Talbot* (Interim Award), para 69; see also *S.D. Myers* (Partial Award), para 202.
130 *Pope & Talbot* (Interim Award), paras 103–104.

The WTO jurisprudence states its strong preference for the textual approach. As the Appellate Body emphasised in *India–Patent*:

The duty of a treaty interpreter is to examine the words of the treaty to determine the intentions of the parties. This should be done in accordance with the principles of treaty interpretation set out in Article 31 of the Vienna Convention. But these principles of interpretation neither require nor condone the imputation into a treaty of words that are not there or the importation into a treaty of concepts that were not intended.[131]

This pronouncement was made in response to the argument that interpretation must be conducted in accordance with the principle of legitimate expectations. The Appellate Body's approach implies that only those expectations can be validly invoked that are inferable from the intention of the parties ascertainable from the text.

In *EC–Hormones*, the Appellate Body reiterated that 'The fundamental rule of treaty interpretation requires a treaty interpreter to read and interpret the words actually used by the agreement under examination, and not words which the interpreter may feel should have been used.'[132] In this case, the Appellate Body objected to the panel's interpretation of Article 3.2 of the Agreement on the Application of Sanitary and Phytosanitary Measures (SPS Agreement) in a way to equate the reference to the measures based on international standards with those conforming to those standards. As the Appellate Body observed, 'based on' is not the same as 'conforming to':

The implication arises that the choice and use of different words in different places in the SPS Agreement are deliberate, and that the different words are designed to convey different meanings. A treaty interpreter is not entitled to assume that such usage was merely inadvertent on the part of the Members who negotiated and wrote that Agreement.[133]

The Appellate Body is here resorting to interpretative presumptions militating against assuming that States-parties would have agreed that the relevant international standards are vested with binding force. But this presumption goes hand in hand with the reference to the textual meaning. The Appellate Body's analysis is based on the text of the relevant treaty provision:

It is clear to us that harmonization of SPS measures of Members on the basis of international standards is projected in the Agreement, as a *goal*, yet to be realized *in the future*. To read Article 3.1 as requiring Members to harmonize their SPS measures *by conforming those measures with international standards*, guidelines and recommendations, *in the here and now*, is, in effect, to vest such international standards, guidelines and recommendations (which are by the terms of the Codex *recommendatory* in form and nature) with *obligatory* force and effect. The Panel's interpretation of Article 3.1 would, in other words,

[131] *India–Patent*, AB Report, para 45.

[132] *EC Measures concerning Meat and Meat Products* (*Hormones*), WT/DS26/AB/R, AB-1997-4, Report of the Appellate Body, 16 February 1998, para 181.

[133] *Id*, para 164.

transform those standards, guidelines and recommendations into binding *norms*. But, as already noted, the SPS Agreement itself sets out no indication of any intent on the part of the Members to do so. We cannot lightly assume that sovereign states intended to impose upon themselves the more onerous, rather than the less burdensome, obligation by mandating *conformity* or *compliance with* such standards, guidelines and recommendations. To sustain such an assumption and to warrant such a far-reaching interpretation, treaty language far more specific and compelling than that found in Article 3 of the SPS Agreement would be necessary.[134]

The Appellate Body went on to examine what 'based on' means, and specified that 'A panel is authorized only to determine whether a given SPS measure is "based on" a risk assessment. . . . this means that a panel has to determine whether an SPS measure is sufficiently supported or reasonably warranted by the risk assessment.'[135] As for the specific meaning:

The term 'based on', when applied as a 'minimum procedural requirement' by the Panel, may be seen to refer to a human action, such as particular human individuals 'taking into account' a document described as a risk assessment. Thus, 'take into account' is apparently used by the Panel to refer to some subjectivity which, at some time, may be present in particular individuals but that, in the end, may be totally rejected by those individuals. We believe that 'based on' is appropriately taken to refer to a certain *objective relationship* between two elements, that is to say, to an *objective situation* that persists and is observable between an SPS measure and a risk assessment. Such a reference is certainly embraced in the ordinary meaning of the words 'based on' and, when considered in context and in the light of the object and purpose of Article 5.1 of the SPS Agreement, may be seen to be more appropriate than 'taking into account'. We do not share the Panel's interpretative construction and believe it is unnecessary and an error of law as well.[136]

The Appellate Body in *Japan–Beverages* again emphasised that 'the words actually used in the Article provide the basis for an interpretation that must give meaning and effect to all its terms. The proper interpretation of the Article is, first of all, a textual interpretation.'[137] In *US–Shrimp*, in relation to the interpretation of General Exceptions under Article XX GATT, the Appellate Body criticised the Panel for not having properly followed through the interpretative exercise as required under the Vienna Convention. What was required was:

an examination of the ordinary meaning of the words of a treaty, read in their context, and in the light of the object and purpose of the treaty involved. A treaty interpreter must begin with, and focus upon, the text of the particular provision to be interpreted. It is in the words constituting that provision, read in their context, that the object and purpose of the states parties to the treaty must first be sought.[138]

[134] *Id*, para 165 (emphasis original).
[135] *EC–Hormones*, para 186.
[136] *Id*, para 189 (emphasis original).
[137] *Japan–Taxes on Alcoholic Beverages*, AB-1996-2, WT/DS8/AB/R, Report of the Appellate Body, 4 October 1996, 17.
[138] *US–Import Prohibition of certain shrimp and shrimp products*, AB-1998-4, Report of the Appellate Body, WT/DS58/AB/R, 12 October 1998, para 114.

After this the Appellate Body went on to criticise the various elements of the Panel's interpretative exercise. In particular, the Panel was censored for focusing on the design as opposed to the application of the measures of the Member State in light of the introductory clauses of Article XX GATT.

There may be a variety of opinions as to how the textual approach can be used when the meaning of the clause is arguably ambiguous or uncertain. Early doctrinal attempts to confront this problem emphasised the need to prevent this problem from obstructing the interpretative process. As Phillimore emphasised as early as in the nineteenth century:

> However different these forms of doubt, arising from the incompleteness or ambiguity of an instrument, may be, they have this feature in common, that they offer an obstacle to the full understanding of the intention of the framers of the Treaty in which they occur. Whether this obstacle has arisen from the want of clearness in the thoughts, or in an imperfect mastery over language in the provisions of the Treaty, a logical interpretation is equally needed; and for this purpose the application of the general rules, already laid down, must be first resorted to.[139]

There are a number of instances of applying textual method to interpret the meaning of contested or contestable notions included in treaties. This was clarified in the *Brogan* case where the European Court had to interpret the meaning of 'promptness' under Article 5(3) of the European Convention. As the Court emphasised, 'the scope for flexibility in interpreting and applying the notion of "promptness" is very limited'. Even a few days of detention fell short of the Convention requirements, because 'To attach such importance to the special features of this case as to justify so lengthy a period of detention without appearance before a judge or other judicial officer would be an unacceptably wide interpretation of the plain meaning of the word "promptly".' The plain meaning of 'promptness' did not allow any additional balancing of interests and values to be undertaken in order to clarify the meaning of that very same notion.[140] This outcome would undermine the essence of the rule of law. On that basis, the Court found that Article 5(3) had been breached.

The importance of the textual approach to clarifying the meaning of Convention provisions is witnessed by the divergence of the approaches taken by the European Court and some dissenting Judges. Judge Evans considered that the meaning of 'promptness' was not the same as 'immediacy'. The object and purpose of Article 5(3) required some degree of flexibility in assessing the meaning of 'promptness'. Judge Evans referred to the fact that 'the Court has consistently recognised that States must, in assessing the compatibility of their laws and practices with the requirements of the Convention, be permitted a "margin of appreciation" and that inherent in the whole Convention is the search for a fair balance

139 Phillimore (1855), vol II, 79.

140 *Brogan v UK*, Nos 11209/84, 11234/84, 11266/84, 11386/85, Judgment of 29 November 1988, paras 59–62.

between the demands of the general interest of the community and the protection of the individual's fundamental rights'. Judge Evans emphasised that this margin of appreciation serves the compromise between defending democracy and individual rights. However, in supporting this thesis Judge Evans referred only to such jurisprudence as deals with the Convention provisions expressly admitting the margin of appreciation.[141]

Similarly, Judge Martens argued that, in the process of balancing values and interests in interpreting 'promptness', it was 'undesirable to attach a degree of importance to the wording of this Convention that excludes application of a principle [of the balancing of values and interests] which seems fundamental in this context and, under the Court's established case-law, is inherent in the Convention as a whole'. Instead, changing social and economic conditions required 'methods of interpretation that do not stop, prematurely, at the wording of a provision'.[142]

It could hardly have been unclear that adopting the two judges' approach would have promoted an important degree of subjectivity in interpretation under which courts could hardly arrive at consistent and transparently interpretative outcomes. At the same time, the approach suggested by the two judges would have upset the framework of treaty interpretation and the sequence of its methods, and would allow the undefined non-law to hijack the established meaning of the determinate treaty clause. The Court's approach is in line with the primacy of the text of the treaty over other factors, such as socio-political extra-legal factors, in the process of clarifying what the agreed treaty provisions could mean. The textual approach, combined with the principle of effectiveness, excludes the balancing of values and interests in the case of treaty provisions that have determinate meaning and in relation to which the margin of appreciation is not designated to operate. Treaty clauses such as Article 5(3) of the European Convention already include in themselves the balance of the relevant interests and values, and they are adopted with that in mind. Attempts to qualify treaty obligations by recourse to extraneous interests and values would undermine the consistent application of treaty obligations.

In *US–Shrimp*, the Appellate Body examined the arguably contestable notion of 'exhaustible' natural resources, and still treated this as a matter of textual interpretation. According to the Appellate Body:

> One lesson that modern biological sciences teach us is that living species, though in principle, capable of reproduction and, in that sense, 'renewable', are in certain circumstances indeed susceptible of depletion, exhaustion and extinction, frequently because of human activities. Living resources are just as 'finite' as petroleum, iron ore and other non-living resources.[143]

141 *Id*, Dissenting Opinion of Judge Sir Vincent Evans, paras 3–5.
142 *Id*, Dissenting Opinion of Judge Martens, para 5.
143 *US–Shrimp*, AB Report, para 128.

This approach demonstrates that the textual interpretation method is perfectly capable of accommodating the interpretive tasks that require resorting to the facts and phenomena of the real world. More generally, this practice confirms that the constructive use of the plain meaning method can resolve problems of interpretation in situations where initial assumptions of ambiguity or contestability of concepts are made.

While international tribunals normally respect the primacy of plain meaning, this is not always true in the case of national courts, as was the case in the House of Lords' treatment of Article 14 of the UN Convention against Torture in the *Jones* case. The case related to the scope of State immunity in relation to torture. Article 14 of the Torture Convention prescribes that victims of torture shall be entitled to civil remedy, including compensation, and does not impose any limitation as to the place where the original act of torture occurred. The House of Lords nevertheless asserted that Article 14 gives entitlement to a judicial remedy only if the original torture has been committed in the territory of the forum State.[144]

There is no evidence whatsoever in the text that such a reading of Article 14 is well founded. It is true that two States shared the view, at the time of ratification, that Article 14 extended only to acts of torture committed within the forum State. But this is hardly enough to impact the real meaning of Article 14 which, contrary to what the House of Lords asserted, does not include any limitation of territoriality. The House of Lords ought to have considered the observation of the Permanent Court in the *Polish Nationality* case that 'to impose an additional condition not provided for in the Treaty...would be equivalent not to interpreting the Treaty, but to reconstructing it'.

A similar problem is involved in the Judgment of the Israeli Supreme Court regarding the lawfulness of targeted killing of suspected terrorists.[145] The two principal concerns raised by this judgment relate to the law that applies to targeted killings, and the definition of the category of combatants that can be attacked. With regard to the first issue, the Supreme Court found that the starting point was that between Israel and the various terrorist organisations active in Judea, Samaria, and the Gaza Strip, there was continuous and constant armed conflict.[146]

One striking point of the Supreme Court's judgment is that having considered humanitarian law to apply, the Supreme Court paid no attention to Common Article 3 which prohibits violence to life and person 'at any time'. In addition, having avoided the analysis of human rights law, the Supreme Court examined the issue of whether the suspected terrorists could be legitimate targets under

[144] *Jones v Ministry of Interior Al-Mamlaka Al-Arabyia AS Saudiya (the kingdom of Saudi Arabia)* [2006] UKHL 26, Decision of 14 June 2006, para 25 (*per* Lord Bingham).

[145] *The Public Committee against Torture in Israel et al. v The Government of Israel*, HCJ 769/02, 11 December 2005.

[146] *Id*, paras 16–20.

Article 51(3) I 1977 Protocol according to which civilians enjoy protection from attack 'unless and for such time as they take a direct part in hostilities'. This is a key provision serving the I Protocol's overall framework of distinguishing between legitimate and illegitimate targets in hostilities. Having confronted the provision which is as clear in its meaning as it could possibly be, the Supreme Court surprisingly asserted that 'regarding the scope of the wording "and for such time" there is no consensus in the international literature. ... With no consensus regarding the interpretation of the wording "for such time", there is no choice but to proceed from case to case.'[147] In the end, the Supreme Court accepted that targeted assassinations in situations not subsumed within Article 2 of the 1949 Geneva Conventions could in the relevant cases be lawful under humanitarian law.

This approach on the one hand contradicts the applicable principles of interpretation, as embodied in Article 31 of the 1969 Vienna Convention on the Law of Treaties. According to the Vienna Convention regime, the plain meaning of the treaty provision by itself constitutes sufficient consensus and there is no need to find additional consensus in literature which moreover has no authoritative force. On the other hand, the Supreme Court's approach undermines the careful balance drawn in humanitarian law regarding the operability of the concept of military necessity. The temporal limitation included in Article 51(3) of the I Protocol is absolutely crucial to maintaining the entire system of civilian/military targets distinction intact. In order to be workable, this distinction must be straightforward in terms of which targets can be attacked and which cannot. This, in turn, is possible only if such a distinction can be made at the moment of attack. If anything or anybody that is potentially or prospectively viewed as a military target or unlawful combatant can be attacked, then any civilian target can be attacked because it can always potentially become, or has in the past been, a part of combat action. This outcome is hardly acceptable in terms of the cardinal distinction drawn between civilian and military targets under international humanitarian law.[148]

(c) The Concept of Autonomous Meaning

It is accepted in jurisprudence that the plain meaning of treaty provisions has to be considered as their autonomous meaning, that is their meaning as part of the relevant treaty arrangement and not, for instance, the same meaning as the relevant word would possess under the national law of the State-party. Broadly speaking, the concept of autonomous meaning could be the implication of the need to understand words in the light of the context or the object and purpose of the treaty. This means that the meaning attached to a word or phrase is the

[147] HCJ 769/02, para 39.
[148] See further Chapter 8 above.

one serving the rationale of the treaty. Autonomous meaning is not the same as special meaning under Article 31(4) of the Vienna Convention.[149] There is a presumption in the law of treaties against the relevance of special meaning, as was confirmed in the *Eastern Greenland* case.[150]

Autonomous meaning signifies the meaning of a phrase or provision treaty which is independent of what the same phrase or provision may mean in another context, and in this respect it is an expression of the plain meaning approach. Special meaning, on the other hand, is a reversion of the plain meaning after adducing adequate evidence of this being justified. The autonomous meaning with its independence from domestic law may be necessary to avoid auto-interpretation which can take place because the State can always change its law.

The doctrine of autonomous meaning has been developed to an important extent to prevent treaty obligations from being influenced in their content by the legal position under the national law of the State. The link between autonomous meaning and the independence of treaty provisions from the state of national law was affirmed as early as in the case of *Exchange of Greek and Turkish Populations* before the Permanent Court. The question was the meaning of Article 2 of the 1923 Lausanne Convention, according to which 'established' persons would be exempted from the exchange of population. The Turkish submission was that the determination of who was 'established' should be made by reference to Turkish legislation, and 'a contrary solution would involve consequences affecting Turkey's sovereign rights'. The Court responded that it was 'impossible to admit that a convention which creates obligations of this kind, construed according to its natural meaning, infringes the sovereign rights of the High Contracting Parties'. The Court further rejected the argument that national courts had to decide which persons were 'established' under Article 2.[151]

In *Engel*, the European Court of Human Rights dealt with the issue of interpretation of terms as autonomous concepts. This was required for preserving the viability of the Convention provisions. The issue in question related to the meaning of 'criminal charges' for the purposes of the fair trial guarantees under Article 6. As the Court put it, 'Does Article 6 cease to be applicable just because the competent organs of a Contracting State classify as disciplinary an act or omission and the proceedings it takes against the author, or does it,

[149] *Legal Status of Eastern Greenland, PCIJ Series* A/B, No 53, 1934. This provision, as the ILC's Final Commentary on the law of treaties explains, 'provides for the somewhat exceptional case where, notwithstanding the apparent meaning of a term in its context, it is established that the parties intended it to have a special meaning'. The burden of proof lies on the party invoking the special meaning of the term. II *YbILC* 1966, 222.

[150] *PCIJ Series* A/B, No 53, 49.

[151] *Exchange of Greek and Turkish Populations (Lausanne Convention VI, January 30th, 1923, Article 2), PCIJ Series* B, No 10, 1925, 6 at 21–22.

on the contrary, apply in certain cases notwithstanding this classification?'[152] Although the Convention normally allowed States to decide on the criminalisation of offences:

> If the Contracting States were able at their discretion to classify an offence as disciplinary instead of criminal, or to prosecute the author of a 'mixed' offence on the disciplinary rather than on the criminal plane, the operation of the fundamental clauses of Articles 6 and 7 would be subordinated to their sovereign will. A latitude extending thus far might lead to results incompatible with the purpose and object of the Convention.[153]

In this sense, the meaning of 'criminal charge' was autonomous and the Court would decide this issue in terms of the Convention as such, instead of deferring to the classification of offences by the State.

In *Lawless*, the European Court interpreted Article 5(3) of the European Convention autonomously and independently from the national law of the respondent State. Ireland contended that Article 5(3) safeguards extended only to persons to be prosecuted and not to those detained to prevent crime; and also that 'this interpretation is supported by the fact that in Common Law countries a person cannot be put on trial for having intended to commit an offence'.[154] The Court's upholding of the textual approach in this case is dismissive of the argument that treaty obligations must be construed by reference to the law of the State. Instead, these clauses have an autonomous meaning.

Along similar lines, the European Court emphasised in the *Sunday Times* case that the concept of contempt under English law did not determine the meaning of the requirement to ensure the independence of the judiciary as a matter of margin of appreciation under Article 10(2) of the European Convention. The Court observed that:

> the reason for the insertion of those words would have been to ensure that the general aims of the law of contempt of court should be considered legitimate aims under Article 10(2) but not to make that law the standard by which to assess whether a given measure was 'necessary'. If and to the extent that Article 10(2) was prompted by the notions underlying either the English law of contempt of court or any other similar domestic institution, it cannot have adopted them as they stood: it transposed them into an autonomous context. It is 'necessity' in terms of the Convention which the Court has to assess, its role being to review the conformity of national acts with the standards of that instrument.[155]

Similarly, the autonomous meaning of the requirement of 'prompt' bringing of detained persons before the judiciary under Article 5(3) of the European Convention was affirmed in *Brogan v UK*. In this case, Judge Martens, along with his general opposition to the consistent use of the principles of interpretation,

[152] *Engel and Others v the Netherlands*, 5100/77, Judgment of 8 June 1976, paras 79–80.
[153] *Id*, para 81.
[154] *Lawless*, para 10.
[155] *Sunday Times v UK*, Case No 6538/74, Judgment of 26 April 1979, para 60.

also opposed the autonomous viewing of 'promptness'. Thus, Judge Martens suggested that 'a (rather) short period, but nevertheless a period which may last some days, to be fixed in the national laws of the High Contracting States'. Under this perspective, the 'promptness' requirement implies that 'the national legislature has a certain margin of appreciation and is free to fix the period it thinks most suitable to the specific conditions of the country in question, although subject to the ultimate control of the Convention organs'.[156] Had the Court adopted this approach, it would have deprived 'promptness' of any intelligible independent meaning and tied it to the national law of the relevant State, that is subordinated the meaning of the Convention provision to national discretion. As for Judge Martens' reference to ultimate supervision by the Convention organs, it is unclear how such supervision could be enforced unless Article 5(3) has a meaning that is independent of what national law and national bodies determine.

(d) The Reality and Implications of Textual Ambiguity in General

Ambiguity is a general problem which arises in circumstances where the method of plain meaning does not yield a straightforward result. The problem of the ambiguity of text is essential for determining the conditions for resort to extra-textual factors. Ambiguity can be of a different kind and degree. Parties to a treaty may include a certain notion in their agreement yet fall short of defining it. In other cases, it may be difficult to grasp the precise meaning of the treaty provision or phrase. In that case the Vienna Convention provides for a number of interpretative factors to be resorted to. As Visscher emphasises, the task of interpretation is to deal with obscure, equivocal or contradictory phrases through the use of available methods.[157]

Ambiguity can be clarified by reference to the context, object and purpose of the treaty, or the relevant rules of general international law. If all those factors fail to yield a result, recourse to supplementary methods of interpretation can be justified. Fitzmaurice's observations regarding the problem of ambiguity and the available alternatives are pertinent in this context:

> There are perhaps few texts to which it is not *possible*, by a greater or lesser manipulation of language, to attribute more than one not implausible meaning, even if one of them is strained or otherwise improbable. If this were a ground for immediate recourse to extraneous sources of interpretation, the principle of interpreting texts as they actually stand, and according to the natural and ordinary meaning of their terms, in the context in which they occur, would have little scope or reality. It is therefore not sufficient in itself that a text is *capable* of bearing more than one meaning. These meanings must be equally valid meanings, or at any rate, even if one may appear more possible and likely than the

[156] Dissenting Opinion of Judge Martens, para 10.
[157] Visscher (1963), 14.

other, both must attain a reasonable degree of possibility and probability, not only grammatically but as a matter of substance and sense.

Only in such cases will there be real ambiguity justifying recourse to extraneous material.[158] The clarification of ambiguity with the aid of factors available within the treaty text is illustrated by the *IMCO* Advisory Opinion, in which the International Court clarified, by reference to the context in which the words are used, the meaning of the word 'elected' in relation to the constitution of the Maritime Safety Committee. The Permanent Court's approach in *Wimbledon*, especially as contrasted with the above-quoted dissenting opinion, is also in line with the approach that alleged lack of clarity or reasonableness will not be enough to deprive treaty provisions of their meaning. It would be subversive of the rule of law to allow notions that are subjectively manipulable to impact on the outcome of an objectively identifiable agreement.

Ambiguity of treaty provisions is not the same as the absence of legal regulation of the subject-matter covered by the relevant provision. Resorting to external factors of interpretation in this case involves an admission that the treaty does not itself regulate the relevant subject matter. Instead, if ambiguity is resolved within the treaty, then it is a relative problem capable of being removed by reference to the context and the object and purpose of the treaty. Seen from this perspective, the factor of ambiguity does not carry with it any interpretative presumption in terms of expanding or restricting the ambit of treaty-based legal regulation. It is only a factor that opens the door for other factors of interpretation that are available within the framework of the relevant treaty.

4. Context

(a) The Relevance and Limits of Context

The reference to the interpretative relevance of context is in effect a ramification of the textual approach. This is clear from Phillimore's observation that 'The construction is to be derived from a due consideration of the language of the whole instrument, and not from that of particular portions or sentences(s) of it.'[159] Article 31(1) of the Vienna Convention requires interpreting treaty provisions in their context, and specifies that:

The context for the purpose of the interpretation of a treaty shall comprise, in addition to the text, including its preamble and annexes: (a) any agreement relating to the treaty which was made between all the parties in connexion with the conclusion of the treaty; (b) any instrument which was made by one or more parties in connexion with the

158 Fitzmaurice (1957), 216, (emphasis original).
159 Phillimore (1855), vol II, 74.

conclusion of the treaty and accepted by the other parties as an instrument related to the treaty.[160]

Given the way Article 31 of the Vienna Convention defines 'context', it is clear that this 'context' does not include the general, or common-sense, still less political, context in which the relevant treaty is concluded and operates. The 'context' refers to the textual aspect of treaty provisions other than those directly at stake in the interpretative process. The aim of this factor is to ensure that the meaning ascribed to the treaty clause does not contradict the meaning that other clauses of the same treaty may possess, so that the treaty does not prescribe mutually contradictory outcomes. Thus, the 'contextual' approach is a variety of textual approach, and for this reason context is rated, under Article 31, among the primary methods of interpretation.

At the same time, context has no primary relevance in interpreting the treaty text. It cannot be resorted to by default to clarify or verify the meaning of each and every word inserted in the treaty. Such resort is justified only in cases where the meaning of the word or phrase positively admits of more than one signification, raises the issue of compatibility with the object and purpose, or undermines the meaning of another clause in the same treaty. There is no other way in which the law of treaties, as codified in the Vienna Convention, would recognise the relevance of the contextual approach.

Therefore, only in this narrow 'context' can the possible evidence justify deviating from what otherwise is the standard and natural meaning of words. All this requires taking cautiously the doctrinal calls for a broad contextual approach that may include a number of factors external to the treaty and the will of States-parties expressed in it. In particular, context under the Vienna Convention is certainly not the same as the contextual factors identified by the New Haven approach, which views the relevant treaty as part of the broader context within which it operates.[161]

(b) The Resort to Context in Practice

As the Permanent Court of International Justice considered in the advisory opinion on the *ILO Competence*,[162] the significance of context is that treaty phrases must be interpreted in the light of it, and should not be detached from it. This statement puts clear limits on the relevance of context, which is relevant only in so far as the phrase can mean different things if removed from the context.

160 As the International Law Commission specified, 'a unilateral document cannot be regarded as forming part of the "context"', II *YbILC* 1966, 221.

161 For this approach see McDougal, Laswell & Miller (1967), 11.

162 *Competence of the ILO to Regulate Agricultural Labour*, Advisory opinion of 12 August 1922, *PCIJ Series* B, Nos 2 and 3, 23.

An interesting use of context can be found in the *IMCO* Advisory Opinion. The Court was examining the legality of the process through which the IMCO Assembly had elected the members of the Maritime Safety Committee, and the meaning of the word 'elected' was at issue. The Court acknowledged that by itself 'elected' means 'a notion of choice which was said to imply an individual judgment on each member to be elected and a free appraisal as to the qualifications of that member'. However, Article 28(a) of the IMCO Convention stipulated that the fourteen-member Committee should include the eight largest ship-owning nations. The autonomous literal understanding of 'elected' would place that condition in a subordinated position. In this regard, the Court observed that:

> The meaning of the word 'elected' in the Article cannot be determined in isolation by recourse to its usual or common meaning and attaching that meaning to the word where used in the Article. The word obtains its meaning from the context in which it is used. If the context requires a meaning which connotes a wide choice, it must be construed accordingly, just as it must be given a restrictive meaning if the context in which it is used so requires.[163]

The Court emphasised that the use of the words 'shall be' in relation to the election of the eight largest ship-owning nations to the Committee was mandatory. Therefore, if these words involved an obligatory designation, there was an evident contrast between such a designation and a free choice. Consequently, the Court observed that:

> If the words 'of which not less than eight shall be the largest ship-owning nations' do involve an obligatory designation of such nations that satisfy that qualification, the use of the word 'elected' to cover the designation of two categories, one of which would be determined on the basis of a definite and pre-established criterion whilst the other would be a matter of choice, cannot convert the designation of the eight nations into an elective procedure which would be contrary to the pre-established criterion.[164]

The *Libya–Chad* case also demonstrates the interpretative relevance of the context of a treaty. Having ascertained the meaning of Article 3 of the 1955 Treaty between France and Libya as determining all borders between them, the Court went on to confirm this interpretative outcome by reference to the context of the 1955 Treaty. As the Court specified, the Convention of Good Neighbourliness between France and Libya, concluded between the parties at the same time as the 1955 Treaty, provided evidence that the parties at the time of the conclusion of the 1955 Treaty considered their relevant boundaries as delimited. This was implied by the parties' commitments to grant rights

[163] *Constitution of the Maritime Safety Committee of the Inter-Governmental Maritime Consultative Organisation*, Advisory Opinion of 8 June 1960, *ICJ Reports*, 1960, 150 at 158.
[164] *Id*, 159.

of passage to nomads over the frontier which was thus established. As the Court put it:

> it is difficult to deny that the 1955 Treaty provided for a frontier between Libya and French Equatorial Africa, when one of the appended Conventions contained such provisions governing the details of the trans-frontier movements of the inhabitants of the region.[165]

The recourse to the interpretative relevance of context in the WTO jurisprudence also reflects the approach codified in the Vienna Convention. In *India–Patent*, the Appellate Body emphasised that for interpreting Article 70.8(a) TRIPS, paragraphs (b) and (c) of the same Article provided the context.[166] In *US–Gambling*, the Appellate Body disapproved the panel's use of the negotiating documents related to the Uruguay Round as part of the context, having seen difficulties with the Panel's characterisation of these documents as context. In the first place, the relevant documents did not constitute an agreement made between all the parties or an instrument made between some parties and accepted by the others as such. The document was drafted by the GATT Secretariat and not by States that participated in the negotiations. As the Appellate Body specified:

> on its own, authorship by a delegated body would not preclude specific documents from falling within the scope of Article 31(2). However, we are not persuaded that in this case the Panel could find W/120 and the 1993 Scheduling Guidelines to be context. Such documents can be characterized as context only where there is sufficient evidence of their constituting an 'agreement relating to the treaty' between the parties or of their 'acceptance by the parties as an instrument related to the treaty'.[167]

The Appellate Body referred to the relationship of the US Schedule to those of other States-parties to GATS. Several States in their schedules had, unlike the United States, expressly used the words 'gambling and betting services'. The failure of the US to use the same language undercut its assertion that it intended to single out such services for exclusion from the scope of its commitment. Other States had specified that their commitment in relation to 'sporting' did not include gambling. At the same time, the United States did not point to any example in another Member's Schedule where the category of 'sporting services' clearly included gambling and betting services.[168] The Appellate Body in the final analysis was unable to infer any definitive solution as to the meaning of the US Schedule from its context, particularly the schedules of other States. It was unclear whether the US Schedule placed gambling services within 'sporting'.[169] This finding reinforces the view that the meaning of words in an instrument

[165] *ICJ Reports*, 1994, 26–27.
[166] *India–Patent*, AB Report, para 56.
[167] *US–Gambling*, paras 174–175.
[168] *Id*, para 184.
[169] *Id*, para 186.

issued by one State can rarely be determined by that in instruments issued by other States. The Vienna Convention requirement that the relevant instruments embody the agreement between States holds the key for considering them as part of context as an interpretative factor.

5. Object and Purpose of the Treaty[170]

(a) Interpretative Relevance of the Object and Purpose

Object and purpose refers to the rationale of the treaty, its general design. It refers to reasons for which States-parties have adopted the relevant treaty and the aim they desire to achieve through it. The object and purpose does not directly create rights and obligations for States-parties, but its interpretative relevance means that the scope of rights and obligations stipulated in the treaty will be significantly impacted upon by its object and purpose. The object and purpose of the treaty almost inevitably embodies some values or interests shared by the parties, thus giving these concepts of non-law some legal standing under the treaty.[171] However, such legal standing is necessarily limited as the object and purpose relates not to the realisation of certain purposes, values and ideals in a general and abstract way, but through the provisions and machinery in the relevant treaty. Thus, the primary relevance of the object and purpose is not to produce legal regulation on its own, but to assist in construing the existing treaty regulation in such a way that its object and purpose is not endangered. In this sense, object and purpose may constitute a categorical limit on what the relevant treaty clauses could mean.

The object and purpose of the treaty is ascertained either from its text, including its preamble,[172] and the general design of the treaty as understood on its own or in comparison with that of other treaties. According to Sinclair, object and purpose is a test for the ordinary meaning of the words as identified from the text.[173] The interpretation of a treaty in accordance with its object and purpose is normally denoted as teleological interpretation.[174] An 'extreme' form of teleological interpretation refers to the 'emergent purpose' of the treaty, as developed in the writings of Fitzmaurice. This is the approach according to which 'the notion of object and purpose is itself not a fixed and static one, but is liable to change, or rather develop as an experience gained in the operation and working of the convention'.

[170] For a useful analysis of this concept in a variety of contexts of the law of treaties see V Crnic-Grotic, Object and Purpose of Treaties in the Vienna Convention on the Law of Treaties, 7 *Asian Yearbook of International Law* (1997), 141–174.

[171] See further Chapter 7 above.

[172] MK Yasseen, L'interprétation des traités d'après la Convention de Vienne sur le Droit des Traités, 151 *Recueil des Cours* (1976-III), 1, 57.

[173] Sinclair (1984), 130.

[174] Fitzmaurice (1951), 7–8; Fitzmaurice (1957), 207–208.

Treaties have to be interpreted by reference to their object and purpose at the time of interpretation. Alternatively, the relevant object or purpose may emerge after the treaty enters into force. The element of teleology thus has a legitimate place in the law of treaty interpretation.[175]

The emphasis on emerging or evolving object and purpose also underlines the potential of evolutive interpretation by reference to changes experienced, after the entry of the treaty into force, in the framework of international law or that surrounding the treaty in general. The genuineness of such potential is evident from the jurisprudence of the International Court, such as in the *Namibia* case regarding the interpretation of the Mandate Agreement, or from a number of decisions of the European Court of Human Rights in which it adopted the approach of construing the European Convention on Human Rights as a living instrument and not a reference to the attitudes prevailing when the Convention was adopted.[176] In *Iron Rhine*, the Arbitral Tribunal emphasised that the Iron Rhine Treaty between Belgium and the Netherlands was not of fixed or limited duration, and nor, consequently, was its object and purpose. Therefore, the latter had to be understood as aimed at resolving the tasks of ongoing and evolving significance.[177]

The phenomenon of emerging purpose could raise questions in terms of the threshold of legal regulation,[178] in terms of whether the object and purpose of the treaty at the moment of interpretation is what States-parties agreed on at the moment of the conclusion of the treaty. At the same time, the problem of the threshold of legal regulation would not arise in this case if it were to be shown that States-parties had not intended to have the object and purpose of their treaty fixed in time.

The concept of the object and purpose of a treaty has multiple implications for the process of interpretation. In the first place, it can help in specifying what the treaty is intended to achieve. In this process, object and purpose can influence the meaning of words and phrases when they can, on their own, have more than one defensible meaning. It can also define the ambit of the treaty and serve as a guide to establish which matters are and which matters are not regulated by the treaty. It can be a factor enhancing the ambit of the treaty, and also a factor that imposes limits on its scope.

The relevance of object and purpose was acknowledged at the early stages of doctrinal debate, but with a certain caution. Phillimore referred to 'The rule of considering the ground or reason (*ratio legis*) in which the Treaty originated, and the object of those who were parties to it. This is a less safe and less certain mode of interpretation, and one which requires more caution in its use and

[175] Fitzmaurice (1957), 208.
[176] See Chapter 9 above.
[177] *Iron Rhine*, paras 82–83.
[178] See above Part II.

application.'[179] WE Hall specifically emphasised the relevance of the treaty's object and purpose in eliminating or reducing ambiguity. Hall advocated the 'recourse to the general sense and spirit of the treaty as shown by the context of the incomplete, improper, ambiguous, or obscure passages, or by the provisions of the instrument as a whole'.[180] But Hall was more enthusiastic about this rule, observing that 'if the result afforded by it is incompatible with that obtained by any other means except proof of the intention of the parties, such other means must necessarily be discarded'.[181]

It is observed that in some cases the object and purpose may be too broadly and uncertainly expressed and thus be unable to meaningfully contribute to the interpretative process.[182] While international adjudication has dealt with object and purpose on multiple occasions, its alleged ambiguity or generality has hardly ever by itself caused a stalling of the process of interpretation. Courts and tribunals normally use the object and purpose of the relevant treaty as part of their constructive exercise of interpretation.

The object and purpose of the treaty belongs to the primary interpretative methods, as specified in Article 31(1) of the Vienna Convention.[183] In the codification process, although Special Rapporteur Waldock practically attached to the object and purpose merely secondary significance,[184] the International Law Commission placed the relevance of the object and purpose at a higher level, just after the relevance of plain meaning.[185]

(b) Resort to Object and Purpose in Practice

In practice, the relevance of the object and purpose has been raised in multiple contexts. In *Night Work*, Judge Anzilotti opposed the interpretative outcome the Court reached on the basis of textual interpretation of the ILO Convention, that the text of the Convention applied to all female workers, whether manual or not. Judge Anzilotti argued that it is not possible to 'say that an article of a convention is clear until the subject and aim of the convention have been ascertained'. The references to 'workers' in the convention justified reading the limitation on night work as applicable to manual workers only.[186] But it seems that Judge Anzilotti was trying to put the cart before the horse, and in fact upheld the

179 Phillimore (1855), vol II, 76.

180 Hall, 353–354.

181 *Id*, 354.

182 M Lennard, Navigating by the Stars: Interpreting the WTO Agreements, 5 *JIEL* (2002), 19 at 27.

183 In the commentary to its final draft, the International Law Commission emphasised that international courts 'more than once had recourse to the statement of the object and purpose of the treaty in the preamble in order to interpret a particular provision', II *YbILC* 1966, 221.

184 See Waldock's Article 70, Third Report on the Law of Treaties, II *YbILC*, 1964, 52.

185 See the Commission's Article 69, II *YbILC*, 1964, 199.

186 *Night Work*, 383ff (Dissenting Opinion).

restrictive interpretation of the plain meaning of the Convention on the basis of what he perceived as its object and purpose. Such contentions cannot hold water because they go against the textual meaning of the treaty.

In *US Nationals in Morocco*, the International Court rejected the plea of the United States that the 1880 Madrid Convention recognised US capitulatory rights in Morocco. However, the Court noted that this did not follow from the text of the Convention, and its object and purpose did not allow conceiving it as inclusive of capitulatory rights. The Court could not 'adopt a construction by implication...which would go beyond the scope of its declared purposes and objects'; this would involve 'radical changes and additions' to the Convention.[187]

The Court also interpreted the 1906 Algeciras Act, which, according to the US plea, recognised and confirmed the regime of capitulations in Morocco. The Court observed that the Act presupposed the existence of the capitulations regime. The object and purpose of the Act was quite general, but was not about the capitulations regime; nor did the Act include any specific provision to that effect; nor was it possible to assume that the capitulations regime was included implicitly:

> An interpretation, by implication from the provisions of the Act, establishing or confirming consular jurisdiction would involve a transformation of the then existing treaty rights of most of the twelve Powers into new and autonomous rights based upon the Act. It would change treaty rights of the Powers, some of them terminable at short notice... into rights enjoyable for an unlimited period. Neither the preparatory work, nor the Preamble gives the least indication of any such intention. The Court finds itself unable to imply such fundamental a change.[188]

The Court however confirmed that the maintenance of consular jurisdiction can 'be justified as based upon the necessary intendment of the provisions of the Act', to the extent necessary to give effect to those specific provisions, and 'render effective' these clauses. The Court could not derive the general consular jurisdiction from the Act, but could not disregard particular provisions that needed such jurisdiction to operate effectively.[189] This approach confirms the link between the object and purpose of the treaty and the principle of effectiveness.

In the *IMCO* Advisory Opinion, the Court emphasised that contestable provisions in treaties have to be construed by reference to the object and purpose of the treaty. The Court had determined that the eight largest ship-owning nations to be elected to the IMCO Maritime Safety Committee under Article 28(a) of the

[187] *ICJ Reports*, 1952, 196.

[188] *Id*, 197–198; similarly, the Court found that the 1880 Madrid Convention merely referred to the existing tax regime by presupposing its existence and did not incorporate or confirm it. Thus, no independent basis for tax immunity was provided, *id*, 205–206; see further Chapter 11 below.

[189] *Id*, 198–199; along similar lines, the Court noted that no general inference of tax immunity could be drawn from the 1880 Madrid Convention which merely referred to the limited class of protected persons. *Id*, 206.

IMCO Constitution were, as defined according to the ordinary meaning of the relevant clauses, those nations that owned the largest tonnage of fleet. The Court emphasised that altering this outcome would pervert the object and purpose of the IMCO Convention. It was thus unable to:

subscribe to an interpretation of 'largest ship-owning nations' in Article 28*(a)* which is out of harmony with the purposes of the Convention and which would empower the Assembly to refuse Membership of the Maritime Safety Committee to a State, regardless of the fact that it ranks among the first eight in terms of registered tonnage.[190]

Thus, in this case the object and purpose of the treaty was seen as corroborating the relevance of the plain meaning method of interpretation.

In *South-West Africa*, the International Court further adopted the approach that the object and purpose should guide the meaning of treaty provisions. Where the outcome of literal interpretation 'results in a meaning incompatible with the spirit, purpose and context of the clause or instrument in which the words are contained, no reliance can be validly placed on it'.[191]

In *Jan Mayen*, the International Court determined that the 1965 Norwegian-Danish Agreement allocating continental shelf boundaries had to be interpreted in the light of its object and purpose. Having examined the preamble and text, the Court concluded that the object and purpose of the Agreement was to simply provide for the delimitation in the North Sea area. The 1965 Agreement was concluded having in mind the 200 metres depth limit of continental shelf under the 1958 Geneva Convention on Continental Shelf. In the North Sea area the seabed is less than 200 metres deep and hence the parties could not have envisaged that the Agreement would apply to other areas such as that of Jan Mayen.[192] Thus, the object and purpose was ascertained from the context of the conclusion of the Agreement.

In interpreting, in the *Boundary Dispute* case, the 1955 Treaty between France and Libya, the Court examined its object and purpose. As the Preamble of the Treaty expressed the will of the parties to settle all questions that arose in terms of their geographical location, the Treaty was aimed at definite settlement of boundaries between the two States. The object and purpose of the Treaty supported the interpretation on the basis of the text.[193]

A very peculiar treatment of the object and purpose of the treaty took place at the jurisdictional stage of the *Oil Platforms* case. During the proceedings, the United States suggested that Article I of the 1955 Iran–US Treaty on Amity, which requires that 'There shall be firm and enduring peace and sincere friendship

[190] *ICJ Reports*, 1960, 171.

[191] *South-West Africa* (Ethiopia and Liberia v South Africa), Preliminary Objections, Judgment of 21 December 1962, *ICJ Reports* 1962, 319 at 336 (the natural meaning of words referred to in this case was the reference in Article 7 of the Mandate Agreement to the standing of the already dissolved League of Nations members).

[192] *ICJ Reports*, 1993, 50–51.

[193] *ICJ Reports*, 1994, 25–26.

between the United States…and Iran,' had no independent meaning but just served the need to interpret other provisions of the Treaty. Article I was merely a 'statement of aspiration'.[194] Iran called this attitude 'astounding', because it argued that Article I was inserted into the Treaty 'to say nothing'. In addition, the US attitude ignored the principle of effectiveness.[195]

The Court approached the issue from the perspective of the object and purpose of the 1955 Treaty, and observed that this object and purpose was not to regulate peaceful and friendly relations between the two States in a general sense. Rather the two States intended to stress that peace and friendship constituted the precondition for a harmonious development of their commercial, financial and consular relations and that such a development would in turn reinforce that peace and that friendship. It followed that Article I must be regarded as fixing an objective, in the light of which the other Treaty provisions were to be interpreted and applied.[196] As further specified:

> The spirit and intent set out in this Article animate and give meaning to the entire Treaty and must, in case of doubt, incline the Court to the construction which seems more in consonance with its overall objective of achieving friendly relations over the entire range of activities covered by the Treaty.[197]

Nevertheless, the Court held that Article I, taken in isolation, could not be a basis for its jurisdiction, because it had been drafted in terms so general that by itself it was not capable of generating legal rights and obligations.[198] While the Court's approach arguably accords with the textual approach accepted as dominant from the *Night Work* case onwards, it can also be asked why, in the context of adjudication of armed attacks against Iranian oil platforms, the provision could not, like Article I, have its independent meaning. If the 1955 Treaty can generally cover the situations of armed attack, it is unclear why its provision under which such attacks generically fall cannot be properly applied. The Court's allegedly textual approach potentially conflicts with the principle of effectiveness and endorses, in a way which is not declared, the use of restrictive interpretation. The Court's stated interpretative policies are correct, but its actual use of interpretative methods does not result in what those methods actually require.

In *Kasikili/Sedudu*, the Court considered how and to what extent the object and purpose of the treaty can clarify the meaning to be given to its terms. The Treaty in question was not the boundary treaty proper, but the treaty determining spheres of influence. The parties nevertheless accepted it as the boundary treaty. This was clear from Article VII of the Treaty, which prohibited nationals and companies of one party from acting in the exercise of sovereign rights

[194] *Oil Platforms* (Iran v US), Preliminary Objections, Judgment of 12 December 1996, para 26.
[195] Observations of Iran on the US Preliminary Objections, para 3.10.
[196] Judgment of 12 December 1996, para 28.
[197] *Id*, para 52.
[198] *Id*, para 32.

in the other party's sphere of influence.[199] Consequently, the parties chose to refer to the main channel of the Chobe River as the frontier, in terms of both navigation and their desire 'to delimit as precisely as possible their respective spheres of influence'.[200] In other words, the need for certainty formed part of the object and purpose of the 1890 Treaty and this provided a guide for its interpretation.

In *LaGrand*, the Court examined the interpretative relevance of the object and purpose of the treaty in the context of the binding force of its provisional measures under Article 41 of the Court's Statute.[201] The French version of the text of Article 41 included the words 'indiquer' and 'l'indication', which were deemed by the Court to be neutral as to the mandatory character of the measure concerned. By contrast, the Court found that the words 'doivent être prises' in the same Article have an imperative character. On the other hand, the use in the English text of the words 'ought' and 'measures suggested' meant that the Court's provisional measures were not binding. The Court decided to rely on the text which best reflected the object and purpose of the Statute and hence it had to examine what this object and purpose was.[202] Its approach regarding this issue is worth following at length:

> The object and purpose of the Statute is to enable the Court to fulfil the functions provided for therein, and in particular, the basic function of judicial settlement of international disputes by binding decisions in accordance with Article 59 of the Statute. The context in which Article 41 has to be seen within the Statute is to prevent the Court from being hampered in the exercise of its functions because the respective rights of the parties to a dispute before the Court are not preserved. It follows from the object and purpose of the Statute, as well as from the terms of Article 41 when read in their context, that the power to indicate provisional measures entails that such measures should be binding, inasmuch as the power in question is based on the necessity, when the circumstances call for it, to safeguard, and to avoid prejudice to, the rights of the parties as determined by the final judgment of the Court. The contention that provisional measures indicated under Article 41 might not be binding would be contrary to the object and purpose of that Article.[203]

Therefore, the Court's approach affirmed that the notion of the object and purpose of a treaty is not just an ancillary notion having a marginal value. On the contrary, it guides the process of interpretation and plays a major role in understanding the very textual meaning of treaty provisions. The rules on treaty interpretation apply equally to substantive and institutional treaty provisions.

The *LaGrand* approach resembles, at the level of principle, the observation of Judge Anzilotti that the text has no meaning without the aim of the treaty being

199 *Kasikili/Sedudu*, para 43.
200 *Id*, para 45.
201 *LaGrand*, Judgment of 27 June 2001, paras 98–99.
202 *Id*, Judgment of 27 June 2001, paras 100–101.
203 *Id*, Judgment of 27 June 2001, para 102.

ascertained. But in *LaGrand* the Court construed the disputable readings of the text as conducive to the object and purpose of its Statute, while Anzilotti's attitude in *Night Work* required restricting clear textual provisions by the alleged dictates of object and purpose. The impermissibility of restrictive interpretation militates in favour of differentiating between the interpretative outcomes reached in the two cases.

In *Ligitan/Sipadan*, the Court had to examine the object and purpose of the 1891 Anglo-Dutch Convention. Indonesia suggested that the aim of the Convention was to resolve the uncertainties once and for all to avoid future disputes. Indonesia argued that the line under the Convention covered several islands; it did not extend indefinitely but only as far as required by the purpose of the Convention, which was to effect the settlement, once and for all, of possible Anglo-Dutch territorial differences in the region.[204] Malaysia put forward its own vision of the object and purpose of the 1891 Convention, namely to define boundaries around the islands that were under British protection. As the Convention was intended as a land boundary treaty, nothing suggested that it was intended to divide sea areas or to allocate distant offshore islands.[205] The Court referred to the preamble of the Convention, which provided that the parties were 'desirous of defining the boundaries between the Netherlands possessions *in* the Island of Borneo and the States *in that island* which are under British protection'. The Court did not find anything in the Convention intended to define the boundaries in areas not mentioned in it.[206]

The object and purpose of the treaty has been an important interpretative factor also for other international tribunals. In *Iron Rhine*, the Arbitral Tribunal formulated the practical relevance of the treaty's object and purpose for interpretation thus:

> It is clear that a Belgian claim to what is now the Netherlands province of Limburg was forfeited and at the same time the commercial proximity that Belgium would otherwise have had to Germany was retained by the road and canal prolongation provisions. In this way (among others) was the overall object and purpose of the 1839 Treaty to be achieved. What may certainly be said is that this object and purpose requires the careful balancing of the rights allowed to each party in Article XII.[207]

On this basis the Tribunal examined whether the Netherlands was obliged to consult Belgium regarding the designation of ecological zones in areas potentially covered by road and canal extensions. The Tribunal concluded that as the existing Dutch measures were not of sufficient magnitude to interfere with the transit rights of Belgium, the Netherlands was not under such a duty. Had they been of such magnitude, the matter would have been different.[208]

204 *Ligitan/Sipadan*, paras 48–49.
205 *Id*, para 50.
206 *Id*, para 51 (emphasis to the treaty text added by the Court).
207 *Iron Rhine*, para 91.
208 *Id*, paras 92–96.

The European Court of Human Rights identified in *Golder* the rule of law as one of the elements of the object and purpose of the European Convention. This was instrumental to arrive at the outcome that the right to access to a court without which the rule of law is unimaginable, and which was not expressly stated in Article 6, was nevertheless implied to be part of it.[209] In *Lawless*, the European Court of Human Rights upheld its finding as to the textual interpretation of Article 5 by reference to the object and purpose of the European Convention. As the Court observed:

> the purpose of the Convention . . . is to protect the freedom and security of the individual against arbitrary detention or arrest; . . . if the construction placed by the Court on the aforementioned provisions were not correct, anyone suspected of harbouring an intent to commit an offence could be arrested and detained for an unlimited period on the strength merely of an executive decision without its being possible to regard his arrest or detention as a breach of the Convention; . . . such an assumption, with all its implications of arbitrary power, would lead to conclusions repugnant to the fundamental principles of the Convention.[210]

In *Soering*, the European Court applied the object and purpose of the European Convention to construe its Article 3 prohibiting torture not only as outlawing actual torture, but also extradition to a third country where the individual in question could face death row. The Court treated this question as one relating to the values underlying the Convention, in effect its object and purpose. As the Court observed:

> It would hardly be compatible with the underlying values of the Convention, that 'common heritage of political traditions, ideals, freedom and the rule of law' to which the Preamble refers, were a Contracting State knowingly to surrender a fugitive to another State where there were substantial grounds for believing that he would be in danger of being subjected to torture, however heinous the crime allegedly committed.[211]

The Court's approach balances the pertinent values in such way as to accord primacy to those values which are protected under the Convention over other values that come into play in the relevant situation, in this case punishment for a serious crime.

Object and purpose has been used as an interpretative factor in WTO jurisprudence as well. The Appellate Body Report in *Japan–Beverages* emphasises that the concept of object and purpose can be used to determine the meaning of the terms of the treaty but not as an independent means of interpretation.[212] In *US–Shrimp*, the Appellate Body emphasises that the object and purpose of GATT cannot be broadly construed, criticises the Panel for resorting to it too

[209] *Golder*, para 34.
[210] *Lawless*, para 14.
[211] *Soering*, Application No 14038/88, Judgment of 7 July 1989, para 88.
[212] *Japan–Beverages*, 20.

quickly and emphasises the need to keep the interpretative exercise linked to the treaty text.[213]

In *US–Shrimp*, the Appellate Body delineated the relevance of object and purpose as an interpretative tool, stressing that 'Where the meaning imparted by the text itself is equivocal or inconclusive, or where confirmation of the correctness of the reading of the text itself is desired, light from the object and purpose of the treaty as a whole may usefully be sought.'[214] In the same case, the relevance of object and purpose is presented as relatively modest, and accords with the perspective that object and purpose does not produce legal regulation on its own. The Appellate Body stated that:

> Maintaining, rather than undermining, the multilateral trading system is necessarily a fundamental and pervasive premise underlying the WTO Agreement; but it is not a right or an obligation, nor is it an interpretative rule which can be employed in the appraisal of a given measure under the chapeau of Article XX.[215]

Instead the Appellate Body emphasised that the purpose of the chapeau of Article XX was to prevent abuses by members of the specific exceptions stipulated in that Article.

In another part of its *US–Shrimp* Report, the Appellate Body was more receptive to the relevance of object and purpose. It identified sustainable development (which is among other things linked to the protection of living natural resources) as part of the object and purpose of the WTO Agreement, and concluded that Article XX(g) GATT could not be read as referring only to the conservation of exhaustible mineral or other non-living natural resources.[216] Living resources were also included in exhaustible resources, a reading which was required by the dictates of sustainable development.

In *US–Gambling*, the Appellate Body referred, for the purposes of interpretation of the US GATS Schedule, to the object and purpose of the WTO Agreement, which includes the need for transparency and clarity of the members' obligations in relation to access to their markets. Nevertheless, this did not provide any guidance as to where gambling services fell in the context of the US Schedule.[217]

The common feature of the approaches of different tribunals is that the relevance of object and purpose comes after the meaning of text is dealt with. The object and purpose cannot produce meaning by itself. It can only confirm the textual meaning, or influence it, and consequently the scope of obligations, where some residual ambiguity requires such adjustment.

[213] *US–Shrimp*, AB Report, paras 116–117.
[214] *Id*, para 114.
[215] *Id*, para 116.
[216] *Id*, para 131.
[217] *US–Gambling*, paras 188–189.

(c) Object and Purpose of Individual Treaty Provisions

The reference to the object and purpose of specific treaty provisions rather than the treaty as a whole is not alien to international jurisprudence, as can be seen from the above-examined *LaGrand* case. But there has been very little doctrinal argument as to the essence of this concept and its relationship to the object and purpose of the treaty as a whole. One doctrinal suggestion is that if the object and purpose of individual provisions reflects the general purpose of the treaty, recourse to it would involve no great harm.[218]

In practice too the object and purpose of individual treaty clauses is understood as a ramification of the general object and purpose of the treaty. The treatment of this issue in judicial practice demonstrates that the object and purpose of individual treaty clauses normally complements that of the entire treaty by reflecting such specific rationale or aim that is certainly conducive to, but does not inherently follow from, the latter.

In *IMCO*, the International Court implicitly referred to the object and purpose of Article 28(a) of the IMCO Convention dealing with the constitution of the IMCO Maritime Safety Committee. The Court emphasised that the 'underlying principle' of this clause required an interpretation affirming the presence on the Committee of the eight largest ship-owning nations. This underlying principle was that those eight nations had to have predominance in the Committee.[219]

In *Brogan*, the European Court of Human Rights interpreted Article 5(3) of the European Convention requiring that detained persons shall be brought 'promptly' before the judicial authority. The Court approached the interpretation of the requirement of 'promptness' from the perspective of object and purpose of Article 5. The Court observed that 'Judicial control of interferences by the executive with the individual's right to liberty is an essential feature of the guarantee embodied in Article 5(3), which is intended to minimise the risk of arbitrariness.' Judicial control was furthermore essential to the principle of democratic society which inspires the entire Convention system.[220] This reasoning was conducive to the finding of breach of the Convention, but not crucial. The principal factor responsible for the outcome was textual interpretation of 'promptness'.

In the *Sakik* case the European Court refused to infer from Article 15 of the European Convention that the emergency situation duly proclaimed under that Article justified the derogation measures from Article 5 of the Convention safeguarding freedom from arbitrary detention in areas to which

[218] Lennard (2002), 26.
[219] *ICJ Reports*, 1960, 160–161.
[220] *Brogan v UK*, para 58.

the derogation thus proclaimed did not extend. The Court emphasised that it:

> would be working against the object and purpose of that provision if, when assessing the territorial scope of the derogation concerned, it were to extend its effects to a part of Turkish territory not explicitly named in the notice of derogation. It follows that the derogation in question is inapplicable *ratione loci* to the facts of the case.[221]

In this case, the Court's treatment of the object and purpose of Article 15 was crucial for identifying the incompatibility of Article 15. The Court's reasoning is not based on strict textual analysis because the Convention does not directly pronounce on the spatial limits of a valid state of emergency. The Court's exercise here is teleological, and infers these spatial limits from the rationale of the Convention system. A more conservative reading, indefensible on the grounds of teleology, could have involved the affirmation that as soon as a state of emergency exists, the measures undertaken pursuant to it do not breach Article 15 requirements regardless of the factor of space.

In *US–Gasoline*, the WTO Appellate Body considered it 'important to underscore that the purpose and object of the introductory clauses of Article XX is generally the prevention of "abuse of the exceptions" ' under Article XX GATT.[222] This interpretative policy largely underlies the Appellate Body's application of Article XX exceptions.

In *Japan–Beverages*, the WTO Appellate Body specified that 'The broad and fundamental purpose of Article III [of GATT, on national treatment] is to avoid protectionism in the application of internal tax and regulatory measures. More specifically, the purpose of Article III "is to ensure that internal measures will 'not be applied to imported or domestic products so as to afford protection to domestic production' ".' Consequently, 'The Article III national treatment obligation is a general prohibition on the use of internal taxes and other internal regulatory measures so as to afford protection to domestic production.' The Appellate Body observed that 'Members of the WTO are free to pursue their own domestic goals through internal taxation or regulation so long as they do not do so in a way that violates Article III or any of the other commitments they have made in the WTO Agreement.' Finally, the Appellate Body emphasised that 'The broad purpose of Article III of avoiding protectionism must be remembered when considering the relationship between Article III and other provisions of the WTO Agreement.'[223]

[221] *Sakik* v *Turkey*, Application No 23878/94, Judgment of 26 November 1997, para 39.
[222] *US–Gasoline*, WT/DS2/AB/R, Report of 20 May 1996, 22.
[223] *Japan–Beverages*, 16–17.

6. Subsequent Agreement and Subsequent Practice

(a) Conceptual and Structural Characteristics of Subsequent Practice

Article 31(3)(a) of the Vienna Convention refers to 'any subsequent agreement between the parties regarding the interpretation of the treaty or the application of its provisions' while Article 31(3)(b) refers to 'any subsequent practice in the application of the treaty which establishes the agreement of the parties regarding its interpretation'. There seems to be no clear-cut distinction between the concepts of subsequent agreement and subsequent practice, either in terms of the nature of the concepts or their place in terms of the structure of international law-making. For the purposes of treaty interpretation, there is hardly any substantial difference between these two elements, both of them referring to the agreement as to interpretation, except perhaps the fact that the former presumably refers to straightforward (express) agreement between the parties, while the latter seeks to infer such agreement from the practice of the application of the treaty.

Subsequent agreement requires the positive agreement of all States-parties, as the International Law Commission specified in its final commentary.[224] The conventional meaning of subsequent agreement makes this notion perfectly operable even if only some parties accept it. In judicial practice, the existence of subsequent agreement as an interpretative factor is rarely found as such. For instance, it is emphasised that the WTO Appellate Body would be very reluctant to find subsequent agreement unless it is reached through the WTO formal procedures.[225] However, finding a qualitative difference, in terms of effect, between subsequent agreement and subsequent practice is hardly possible. The inclusion of the reference to the subsequent agreement factor in the Vienna Convention can be explained by its formal element of straightforwardly expressing agreement, and by the broader structural dimension of international law under which an agreement between States can be reinterpreted by their subsequent agreement. Still, the relevant practice mainly deals with the element of subsequent practice.

Subsequent practice does not illustrate the original intention of States-parties, but the parties' subsequent shared understanding of the terms of their original agreement. A distinction must be drawn between different types of treaty-related practice. Some practice conforms to the text of the treaty while its other instances may contradict it. Practice can be unilateral, or cover two or more, even all

[224] II *YbILC* 1966, 222.
[225] Lennard (2002), 30.

parties to the treaty. Eventually, practice can lead to modification of the treaty regime.[226]

The relevance of subsequent practice as a factor in interpretation has long been recognised. Fitzmaurice distinguished between the interpretation aspect of this notion and the subsequent practice that brings about the revision of the treaty and shall therefore not be treated as an interpretative method.[227] Throughout the ILC codification process the relevance of subsequent practice was recognised as a factor that could shed light on the meaning of the treaty. However, the precise character of this interpretative method could mean different things in terms of different approaches. For instance, Article 73 proposed by Special Rapporteur Waldock placed subsequent practice at the same level as subsequent customary rules and subsequent agreements; Waldock's subsequent practice is the practice 'evidencing the consent of all the parties to an extension or modification of the treaty'.[228] This refers not just to interpretation but to modification of treaties. At later stages, as is known, the issue of overriding subsequent custom was excluded from the codification of the law of treaties, and subsequent practice retained its interpretative relevance. The Commission's Article 69, adopted in the same year as Waldock's proposals were presented, did not refer to the relevance of custom, but merely to subsequent practice 'in the application of the treaty which clearly establishes the understanding of all the parties regarding the interpretation'.[229] As the Commission specified at the final stage of codification, 'the value of subsequent practice varies according as it shows the common understanding of the parties as to the meaning of the terms'.[230] The Commission also stated that subsequent practice 'constitutes objective evidence of the understanding of the parties as to the meaning of the treaty'.[231] This makes clear that the Commission perceived these factors only as relevant for interpretation of the treaty, not for its revision, amendment or modification.

Subsequent practice in terms of Article 31 is not practice *per se* but practice establishing agreement, whether explicit or implicit. The potential of this method can never be underestimated as it reflects the decentralised nature of international law-making, the implications of which are apparent in the framework of treaty interpretation as well.

The International Law Commission specified that the participation of all States-parties in the relevant State practice is not a necessary condition of its validity. What is required is that some States must have participated in practice

[226] Köck (1976), 43–44; MK Yasseen, L'interprétation des traités d'après la Convention de Vienne sur le Droit des Traités, 151 *Recueil des Cours* (1976-III), 1 at 51.

[227] Fitzmaurice (1986), 345–346.

[228] II *YbILC* 1964, 53.

[229] *Id*, 199.

[230] II *YbILC* 1966, 222.

[231] II *YBILC* 1966, 221–222.

and others must have knowingly acquiesced in or accepted it.[232] The Commission 'omitted the word "all" merely to avoid any possible misconception that every party must individually have engaged in the practice where it suffices that it should have accepted the practice'.[233] Thus, the Commission still emphasises the role that all States-parties have to play in terms of expressing will. At the same time, there seems to be no obstacle to such subsequent practice as will (re)interpret the treaty as between the limited number of parties, provided that such is possible in terms of the nature of the relevant treaty obligations.[234]

Subsequent practice in general can involve diverse acts and processes, such as protests, reward for compliance with the treaty, or tacit consent to actions and declarations. If judicial decisions express attitudes vis-à-vis the content of the treaty, they too can count as part of subsequent practice.[235] In order to constitute relevant subsequent practice, it has to relate to the provision that is being interpreted. Thus, the WTO Panel in *Brazil–Coconut* rejected the view that the Tokyo Round Security and Countervailing Measures (SCM) Code could serve as valid subsequent practice in this case. It was not related to Article VI GATT and hence had no bearing on the interpretation of that clause.[236]

In the *Russian Indemnities* Award, often referred to in literature in the context of subsequent practice, the Arbitral Tribunal emphasised that the execution of

[232] II *YbILC* 1966, 222.

[233] *Id.*

[234] Thus it is problematic that Canadian and English courts have considered that 'subsequent practice' of two States could have modified the ambit of Article 14 of the 1984 Torture Convention, which stipulates universal civil jurisdiction over torture. Canadian and English courts subscribed to the exclusively territorial character of jurisdiction under Article 14 by reference to the practice of certain States, namely the US attitude on territoriality met by the response of Germany which can only ambiguously, if at all, be considered as the acceptance of the US view, and the silence of other States-parties. The courts did not make any effort to prove that the silence of other States-parties was necessarily meant to establish agreement to reduce the scope of Article 14 to a provision that provides merely for territorial jurisdiction. See *Bouzari* v *Islamic Republic of Iran* (Court of Appeal for Ontario), 30 June 2004, Docket: C38295; *Jones v Saudi Arabia*, 16. What the US-German exchange can show at most is the possible bilateral agreement reached between the two States-parties to interpret restrictively, as between themselves, the jurisdictional clause contained in Article 14. But this is not the end of the matter, because the Torture Convention is a human rights treaty. It requires objective application and cannot be split into bilateral agreements such as that allegedly reached between the US and Germany. It has to operate uniformly in relation to all States-parties, even in cases where some of them do not actually comply with its terms. It is generally accepted that human rights and humanitarian treaties embody objective obligations, not reducible to bilateral inter-State relations, see *Austria v Italy*, Eur Comm HR, 4 *Yearbook of the European Convention on Human Rights* (1961), 140; *Ireland v UK*, ECtHR, 58 ILR 188, at 291; *Effect of Reservations*, IACtHR, para 27, 67 ILR 568. See also G Fitzmaurice, Judicial Innovation: Its Uses and Its Perils, Cambridge Essays in International Law (1965), 24, 33–34. See for detail A Orakhelashvili, State Immunity and International Public Order Revisited, 49 *German YIL* (2006), 327–365, and *id*, *Peremptory Norms* (2006), Chapter 4.

[235] W Karl, *Vertrag und spätere Praxis in Völkerrecht—Zum Einfluß der Praxis auf Inhalt und Bestand völkerrechlicher Verträge* (1983), 115.

[236] *Brazil–Measures affecting Desiccated Coconut*, Report of the Panel, WT/DS22/R, 20 March 1997, para 256.

the agreement by the State-party is proof of its view as to its binding character.[237] A similar approach was taken by the International Court in the advisory opinion regarding South-West Africa, where it examined a declaration by the South African Government that it would continue to comply with the League of Nations mandate agreement on South-West Africa. The Court stated that 'Interpretations placed upon legal instruments by the parties to them, though not conclusive as to their meaning, have considerable probative value when they contain recognition by a party of its own obligations under an instrument.'[238] However, this jurisprudence contains nothing to indicate, and should not be seen as indicating, that the status of treaty obligations can depend on the view and attitude of a single State.[239] Such an understanding would further be incompatible with the concept of subsequent practice which the Vienna Convention recognises. Indeed the Court itself emphasised in its advisory opinion that the relevant declarations were not conclusive as to the meaning of treaty obligations. They can confirm the meaning the obligations otherwise have, but they cannot alter that meaning unilaterally.

A crucial question that the factor of subsequent agreement and subsequent practice raises in the context of interpretation is that of the relationship between the principles of interpretation and the agency that has the power to interpret.[240] States-parties to the relevant treaty are obviously among the principal agencies that have the power to interpret a treaty. The context of subsequent practice is specific in its reference to practice and agreement that does not inherently relate to the original treaty text and its context and rationale. States-parties could in principle subsequently adopt a divergent attitude in relation to any of those elements.

As the International Law Commission emphasised, the subsequent agreement is authoritative interpretation and must be read into the relevant treaty.[241] This presumably implies that this factor can displace other outcomes required by the application of the principles of interpretation. Consequently, valid subsequent practice could potentially achieve the same substantive result as amendment of the treaty. This is due to the structural similarity between subsequent practice and other phenomena of State practice in general whereby States modify and develop their mutual legal relations.

The relevance of subsequent practice as a method of treaty interpretation is among other things dictated by structural factors in the international legal system in which the practice of States accounts for much of the process which ultimately results in creation, modification and abolition of international

[237] *Russian Indemnities Arbitration*, G Wilson (ed), *The Hague Arbitration Cases* (1915) 11 *RIAA* 433.

[238] *International Status of South-West Africa*, Advisory Opinion of 11 July 1950, *ICJ Reports* 1950, 128 at 135–136.

[239] McNair argues along similar lines (1961), 431.

[240] See below Chapter 16.

[241] II *YbILC*, 1966, 221.

legal rules. But precisely because State practice is an element of international law-making, its relevance in the process of treaty interpretation has to be considered on those very same conditions on which State practice can be part of international law-making in general. This is especially true in the present context where the practice is displayed not in a normative vacuum, but against the background of already existing treaty regulation.[242] In short, subsequent practice matters not as such, but because relevance is accorded to it by the general structural framework of international law and the particular framework of the Vienna Convention. Article 31(3)(b) of the Vienna Convention duly considers these structural factors and attaches interpretative relevance to such subsequent practice as embodies the agreement of States-parties to a treaty as to its interpretation.

The issue of subsequent practice in the interpretation of treaties combines the relevance of interpretation and amendment of treaties, as well as raising a number of issues related to the general international law concepts of acquiescence, estoppel, recognition and State practice in general. Keeping this concept within the framework of interpretation, but also taking into account the broader legal framework and the need to respect the intention of the parties to a treaty, is both a complex and delicate task. As the Ethiopia-Eritrea Boundary Commission has emphasised:

> The function of [subsequent] practice is not... relevant exclusively to the interpretation of the Treaties. It is quite possible that practice or conduct may affect the legal relations of the Parties even though it cannot be said to be practice in the application of the Treaty or to constitute an agreement between them. ... Thus, the effect of subsequent conduct may be so clear in relation to matters that appear to be the subject of a given treaty that the application of an otherwise pertinent treaty provision may be varied, or may even cease to control the situation, regardless of its original meaning.[243]

In other words, the conduct or practice of contracting parties embodying the correlation of their attitudes subsequent to the conclusion of the relevant treaty, whether related to its interpretation, or aimed at changing the legal regime it establishes, can be relevant for determining what the scope and ambit of that treaty is. The reason for this is that the parties, being masters of the treaty, could impact on its content either by interpreting it, or amending it.

(b) Resort to Subsequent Practice in Jurisprudence

In *Jan Mayen*, the Court examined the practice subsequent to the 1965 Norwegian-Danish Agreement on Continental Shelf. Such practice was provided by the 1979 Agreement between the two States on delimitation of the continental

[242] See above Chapter 5.

[243] Award of the Commission, paras 3.6 and 3.8.

shelf between the coasts of Norway and the Danish Faroe Islands. The method of delimitation chosen in the Agreement was the median line, and the Agreement did not refer to the 1965 Agreement which it would have done had the latter been relevant for the area covered by the 1979 Agreement. This proved the unity of attitude of the Parties that the 1965 Agreement was not meant to apply to their maritime boundaries irrespective of their location.[244] This aspect of the *Jan Mayen* case provides us with the most straightforward example of how the requirements of subsequent practice should be met.

In the *Libya–Chad* case, the Court observed that no subsequent agreement had called into question the frontier established by the 1955 Treaty. The frontier determined under the 1955 Treaty was acted upon.[245] As for the subsequent attitudes of the parties, Chad had consistently held that it had a frontier with Libya, and Libya also confirmed before the Organisation of African Unity that the frontier was valid.[246] However, it should also be noted that the Court, while referring to subsequent events and instruments, did not directly state that it was doing so in terms of the interpretative task under Article 31(3) of the 1969 Vienna Convention.

In *Kasikili/Sedudu*, the Court examined extensively the parties' arguments about the conduct of the relevant States subsequent to the 1890 Treaty, and in this case it expressly stated that it acted pursuant to Article 31(3), subparagraphs (a) and (b) of the 1969 Vienna Convention.[247] As for the actual relevance of subsequent practice, the Court made a number of findings. Botswana submitted a number of arguments on the issue of subsequent practice. In the first place, the Court found that the Eason Report did not constitute subsequent practice because as an internal document it was never made known to Germany. Further events sometimes reflected the agreement between the relevant States that the main channel of the Chobe River was the southern channel, and sometimes reflected numerous disagreements between them. Overall, these declarations and correspondence evidenced disagreement and could not qualify as subsequent practice in terms of the Vienna Convention because they did not give rise to 'agreement between the parties regarding the interpretation of the treaty or the application of its provisions'.[248] The 1984 border shooting incident also gave rise to differences as to the interpretation of the location of the boundary between Botswana and South Africa. After that the decision was taken to effect the joint survey to determine where the main channel, and consequently the boundary,

[244] *ICJ Reports*, 1993, 51. The other aspect of 'subsequent practice' noted by the Court was the declaration of the Norwegian Storting that the 1965 Agreement did not cover the area of the Faroe islands, *id* 51. However, this has only a unilateral dimension and therefore the Court would have done better to have qualified this as an aspect of estoppel rather than of subsequent practice as a matter of the law of treaties.

[245] *ICJ Reports*, 1994, 35.

[246] *Id*, 36–37.

[247] *Kasikili/Sedudu*, paras 47–49.

[248] *Id*, paras 55–61, especially paras 62–63.

was located. The conclusion was that the main channel was in the north of the Kasikili/Sedudu Island, which outcome was communicated by Botswana to South Africa through a Note. But South Africa never responded to this Note. Therefore, the Court could not 'conclude therefrom that in 1984–1985 South Africa and Botswana had agreed on anything more than the despatch of the joint team of experts. In particular, the Court cannot conclude that the two States agreed in some fashion or other to recognize themselves as legally bound by the results of the joint survey carried out in July 1985.'[249]

Namibia's arguments on subsequent practice related to the alleged effective exercise of State authority by Namibia and the corresponding silence of Botswana's authorities and their predecessors in the face of an almost century-old situation. The Court pointed out that to establish subsequent practice under Article 31 of the Vienna Convention, 'the long-standing, unopposed, presence' in the relevant territory should meet two criteria:

first, that the occupation of the Island by the Masubia was linked to a belief on the part of the Caprivi authorities that the boundary laid down by the 1890 Treaty followed the southern channel of the Chobe; and, second, that the Bechuanaland authorities were fully aware of and accepted this as a confirmation of the Treaty boundary.

While the Court acknowledged the existence of maps confirming such territorial presence, these maps did not officially interpret the 1890 Treaty and this could not be linked to the claim of territorial title. The presence of Namibian tribes on the Island was tolerated merely because, as the Court put it, it 'did not trouble anyone and was tolerated, not least because it did not appear to be connected with interpretation of the terms of the 1890 Treaty'.[250] Therefore, the Court rejected the relevance of subsequent practice in this case as well. In its general conclusion on this issue, the Court ruled that the subsequent practice argument would fail, even though the practice of the parties included some acts and actions that confirmed the textual interpretation of the 1890 Treaty.[251]

In *Ligitan/Sipadan*, the Court refused to treat the map produced by the Dutch Government as a subsequent agreement in terms of Article 31(2)(a) of the Vienna Convention. The map was transmitted to the diplomatic agent of Britain in The Hague, but the British Government did not react to this transmission. Such lack of reaction could not be deemed to constitute acquiescence in the line of the frontier depicted on that map.[252] The Court also examined a number of Agreements concluded after the 1891 Convention and dealing with the boundaries in one or another region, between the two parties or their predecessors. The Court did not see anything in any agreement that disposed of the boundary in

[249] *Id*, paras 64–66, 68.
[250] *Id*, paras 71, 73–74.
[251] *Id*, para 79.
[252] *Ligitan/Sipadan*, paras 48, 59–61.

the Ligitan/Sipadan area.[253] But, most interestingly, the Court also examined, as it was requested to do, the practice of the two States regarding oil concessions in the area. Indonesia submitted that in granting oil concessions, both parties had observed the line determined in Article IV of the 1891 Convention as the limit to their respective national jurisdiction. But Malaysia argued, and the Court agreed, that the limits of the oil concessions granted by the parties in the area to the east of Borneo did not encompass the islands of Ligitan and Sipadan.[254] Therefore, the Court stated that it could not draw any conclusion for the purposes of interpreting Article IV of the 1891 Convention from the practice of the parties in awarding oil concessions.

The Court's treatment of these issues evidences how high the threshold is for establishing the existence of subsequent practice. In essence, subsequent practice under the Vienna Convention has a similar nature and requirements to international law-making in general, whether through agreements, custom, acquiescence or unilateral acts: it has to involve concordance of actions and attitudes. Therefore, it is not surprising that the burden of proof in the case of establishing subsequent practice is as high as in the case of establishing other law-making processes. In the end, it is the treaty which is interpreted and in which the parties place confidence; the proof of any deviation therefrom must meet a high threshold of evidence.

In the jurisprudence of the European Court of Human Rights, the relevance of subsequent practice is limited only to that practice which expresses agreement between States-parties. In *Soering*, the European Court refused to take an evolutive approach in terms of affirming that the death penalty was prohibited by the Convention due to the evolution of a common European attitude to it, namely the 'virtual consensus in Western European legal systems that the death penalty is, under current circumstances, no longer consistent with regional standards of justice'. The fact that States-parties had adopted a separate protocol regarding the death penalty evidenced that if they so desired they would 'adopt the normal method of amendment of the text in order to introduce a new obligation to abolish capital punishment in time of peace and, what is more, to do so by an optional instrument allowing each State to choose the moment when to undertake such an engagement'. Thus, the Convention could not be interpreted as generally prohibiting the death penalty.[255] The resort to common European attitudes is permissible in the European Court's practice of defining the ambit of certain indeterminate concepts under the margin of appreciation clauses of Articles 8 to 11,[256] but this is a matter of definition of concepts as opposed to the reinterpretation of existing obligations.

[253] *Id*, paras 62–74.
[254] *Id*, paras 78–79.
[255] *Soering v UK*, paras 102–103.
[256] See below Part V.

In *North Atlantic Fisheries*, the Arbitral Tribunal assessed the relevance of subsequent practice sceptically. The facts at issue were alleged expressions by Britain that were inconsistent with its right to regulate fishing in coastal waters. The Tribunal observed that 'such conflicting or inconsistent expressions as have been exposed on either side are sufficiently explained by their relations to ephemeral phases of a controversy of almost secular duration, and should be held to be without direct effect on the principal and present issues'.[257]

The WTO Appellate Body is cautious in accepting the relevance of subsequent practice.[258] In *Japan–Beverages*, the Appellate Body examined the relevance of subsequent practice focusing on the status of the GATT and WTO Panel reports. The Appellate Body stressed that for constituting valid subsequent practice, an isolated act is not sufficient. There has to be a sequence of acts or pronouncements that is concordant, common and consistent and establishes agreement between the parties.[259] In the GATT context, Panel reports were approved by the contracting parties. Yet according to the Appellate Body, this approval did not constitute an agreement of contracting parties on the legal reasoning of the report. The Panel reports bound States-parties to the case, but had no such effect in subsequent cases.[260] The Appellate Body did not believe that in adopting a Panel report the contracting parties intended that their decision would constitute a definitive interpretation of the relevant provisions of GATT.[261] As a crucial part of its argument the Appellate Body observed that:

> Adopted panel reports are an important part of the GATT *acquis*. They are often considered by subsequent panels. They create legitimate expectations among WTO Members, and, therefore, should be taken into account where they are relevant to any dispute. However, they are not binding, except with respect to resolving the particular dispute between the parties to that dispute. In short, their character and their legal status have not been changed by the coming into force of the WTO Agreement.

Therefore, the Appellate Body rejected the argument that the Panel reports constituted 'subsequent practice' for interpreting GATT.[262]

The questionable aspect of this reasoning relates to the Appellate Body's seeming equation of the legal force of Panel reports with their relevance as subsequent practice. Obviously the WTO law, just like the rest of international law, knows of no doctrine of precedent. Subsequent panels are by no means bound to follow previous decisions. But by virtue of developing the WTO *acquis* and consequently interpreting the covered agreements on the basis of their exercise of powers delegated by States-parties, panels do indeed express agreement between

257 Scott, 166.
258 Lennard (2002), 35.
259 *Japan–Beverages*, AB Report, 11.
260 *Id*, 12.
261 *Id*, 12.
262 *Id*, 13.

States-parties as to the meaning of the relevant treaty provisions. This role of dispute settlement bodies warrants, at least, according to their decisions the presumptive value of representing the valid subsequent practice, unless it can be shown that the relevant panel report distorts the textual meaning of these treaty provisions.

That said, the Appellate Body, for which the review and overruling of panels' reports is part of its daily work, does not feel inclined to accept that these reports are independent factors in interpretation. Given that the appellate procedure is provided, the panels' determinations are never final. The Appellate Body's reports, on the other hand, are more suitable to constitute an independent interpretative factor.

There are instances which confirm the relevance of institutional pronouncements as subsequent practice. In *US–Shrimp*, the Appellate Body observed that the 'two adopted GATT 1947 panel reports previously found fish to be an "exhaustible natural resource" within the meaning of Article XX(g)' of GATT. This was used as a relevant factor for interpretation of this clause.[263] It is unclear on what basis this could be the case if not as 'subsequent practice'. On the other hand, it has to be reiterated that the relevance of decisions of treaty-based organs as subsequent practice has to be taken with caution, and always verified in terms of its compliance with the original meaning of the treaty, to avoid the risk of exercising legislative power that has not been delegated.

In *EC–Computer*, the Appellate Body further refined the conditions under which subsequent practice can validly count in the process of treaty interpretation. The Appellate Body emphasised that:

> The purpose of treaty interpretation is to establish the *common* intention of the parties to the treaty. To establish this intention, the prior practice of only *one* of the parties may be relevant, but it is clearly of more limited value than the practice of all parties. In the specific case of the interpretation of a tariff concession in a Schedule, the classification practice of the importing Member, in fact, may be of great importance. However, the Panel was mistaken in finding that the classification practice of the United States was *not* relevant.[264]

Without more, this approach does not clarify where the line must be drawn to distinguish valid subsequent practice from the rest of State practice related to the context of the treaty operation. Nor is it clear what 'relevant' means in this context and what the implications of such 'relevance' are.

The Appellate Body proceeds to point out that 'Then there is the question of the *consistency* of prior practice. Consistent prior classification practice may often be significant. Inconsistent classification practice, however, *cannot* be relevant in interpreting the meaning of a tariff concession.' In this context, the Appellate Body emphasised that the Panel had drawn its conclusions on the interpretation

[263] *US–Shrimp*, AB Report, para 131.

[264] *EC–Computer*, para 93 (emphasis original).

of the schedule of commitment by reference to the practice of only five of the twelve members of the European Communities.[265] As a consequence, the Appellate Body disapproved the Panel's interpretative exercise.

In *US–Gambling*, the Appellate Body addressed the issue of subsequent practice for interpreting US Schedules of Commitment. Antigua pleaded that the 2001 Scheduling Guidelines adopted by the Council for Trade in Services constituted such subsequent practice. The Appellate Body emphasised that in order to qualify as subsequent practice under Article 31(3)(b) of the Vienna Convention, the relevant practice had to evidence the agreement between the parties on the relevant issue. Therefore, the Appellate Body had:

> difficulty accepting Antigua's position that the 2001 Scheduling Guidelines constitute 'subsequent practice' revealing a common understanding that Members' specific commitments are to be construed in accordance with W/120 and the 1993 Scheduling Guidelines. Although the 2001 Guidelines were explicitly adopted by the Council for Trade in Services, this was in the context of the negotiation of future commitments and in order to assist in the preparation of offers and requests in respect of such commitments. As such, they do not constitute evidence of Members' understanding regarding the interpretation of existing commitments.[266]

Other documents involved in the case did not constitute subsequent practice either. Although they might have been relevant in identifying the United States' practice, they did not establish a common, consistent, discernible pattern of acts or pronouncements by the Membership as a whole. Nor did they demonstrate a common understanding among Members that specific commitments are to be interpreted by reference to W/120 and the 1993 Scheduling Guidelines.[267] This demonstrates that the standard of proof of relevance of subsequent practice is considerably higher. Practice *per se* will not do.

7. The 'Relevant Rules' of International Law

Article 31(3)(c) of the Vienna Convention specifies that 'any relevant rules of international law applicable in the relations between the parties' can contribute to the interpretation of treaties. During the ILC codification process, both the Special Rapporteur and initially the Commission itself envisaged for general rules of international law a considerably higher interpretative relevance than it has in the current text of the Vienna Convention. Draft Article 70(1)(b) suggested by Waldock and later adopted by the Commission as draft Article 69(1)(b) placed the relevance of general rules at the same level as the object and purpose of the treaty: the plain meaning was to be construed not just in terms

[265] *EC–Computer*, para 95 (emphasis original).
[266] *US–Gambling*, paras 190–193.
[267] *Id*, para 194.

of the object and purpose but also in terms of general rules of international law.[268] This approach does not correspond to the *lex specialis* character of treaties which are meant to make the difference in relation to the otherwise existing legal position. The Vienna Convention adopts the approach by placing the relevance of general rules one level below the treaty's plain meaning and object and purpose: general rules do not guide interpretation; they merely 'shall be taken into account'.

The rules to be taken into account under Article 31(3)(c) must meet the relevant qualifications. In the first place, Article 31(3)(c) covers only established rules of international law, to the exclusion of principles of uncertain or doubtful legal status, so-called evolving legal standards, policy factors or more generally related notions.[269] In addition, Article 31(3)(c) covers all relevant sources of international law, whether treaties, customary norms or general principles of law.

Whatever the required effect under Article 31(3)(c), its applicability cannot be assumed to be straightforward and ready-made. This provision always applies subject to the textual meaning and the object and purpose of the relevant treaty. General rules of international law under Article 31(3)(c) are an interpretative tool to aid the interpretation of a treaty, as opposed to the interpretation of extraneous rules as such. The mere presence of the 'relevant rules' of international law does not mean that they have to be applied as if they formed part of treaty relations. These rules are inherently capable of being excluded from bilateral relations by the parties to a treaty and any construction of the treaty by reference to those rules must duly respect this factor. If extraneous rules under Article 31(3)(c) were to warrant interpretation of the treaty in defiance of the outcome required under its text and object and purpose, the Vienna Convention would end up requiring mutually exclusive interpretative outcomes, by approving that extraneous rules under Article 31(3)(c) can modify the outcome that follows from the application of the interpretative methods embodied in Article 31(1).

According to the *Mox Plant* Award, the interpreter must apply the relevant extraneous rules of customary and conventional law, unless and to the extent that the parties to the relevant treaties have created *lex specialis*.[270] Consequently, within the realm covered by the treaty the general rules of international law are irrelevant.

This method of interpretation can be useful on some occasions, but on other occasions it may raise some concerns in terms of doctrinal and practice-based

[268] II *YbILC* 1964, 52, 199.

[269] For instance, the Arbitral Tribunal in *Mox Plant* refused to apply extraneous rules, because the ones in question were 'evolving international law', Ireland v UK, Final Award of 2 July 2003, paras 99–105. The Tribunal distinguished the case of *Libya–Malta Continental Shelf Delimitation*, where the compromise incorporated the law *in statu nascendi*, which was not the case in the proceedings at hand.

[270] *Mox Plant*, para 84.

inclinations to find grounds on which States can evade their treaty obligations, motivated by various, including political, grounds.

The notion of 'systemic integration' is resorted to in some contributions.[271] It is emphasised that 'the principle of systemic integration goes further than merely restate the applicability of general international law in the operation of particular treaties. It points to a need to take into account the normative environment more widely.'[272] But the use of this notion does not by itself clarify the essence of the process, in terms of what is integrated, how and on what conditions. More importantly, integration relates to a result, while interpretation methods definitionally relate to methods and means. From the perspective of the law of interpretation, reference to the relevant rules of international law will in some cases produce the result of integration while in other cases it will not. The positive or negative outcome in each case will in its turn be produced by circumstances more specific to the relevant interpretative method and context than is the general notion of 'systemic integration'. All these factors require some degree of caution in advancing such a far-reaching notion. Although the integration of extraneous rules into a treaty can be an interpretative outcome in some cases, it is certainly not a principle, still less a principle that applies across the board.

Consequently, the real question is not whether the extraneous rules should be systemically integrated into the relevant treaty, but rather it involves some specific questions. It is one—preliminary—question what Article 31(3)(c) by itself requires or warrants. It is another—consequential—question how the requirements of Article 31(3)(c) are properly applied in individual cases.

The relevance of general international law for the interpretation of treaties has been raised in different contexts and different outcomes have been suggested. The analysis of practice leads to the conclusion that cases that are generally believed to have been decided in the context of Article 31(3)(c) of the Vienna Convention, whether the Arbitral decision on *Mox Plant*, the European Court's decision on *Al-Adsani*, the International Court's decisions on *Gabcikovo* and *Oil Platforms*, or a number of Reports of the WTO Appellate Body, do not in reality constitute instances of the consistent application of the single principle of interpretation. In some cases tribunals refer to extraneous rules to clarify a meaning or definition not expressly specified in a treaty, or to explain aspects not covered in it. In other cases, such as *Oil Platforms*, a reference to extraneous rules has been due to a specific factor, namely the peremptory status of the rules on recourse to force. Given the insistence by Judge Higgins

[271] *Fragmentation of International Law: Difficulties Arising from the Diversification and Expansion of International Law*, Report of the Study Group of the International Law Commission, Finalized by Martti Koskenniemi, A/CN.4/L.682, 13 April 2006, 206ff; C McLachlan, The Principle of Systemic Integration and Article 31(3)(c) of the Vienna Convention, 54 *ICLQ* (2006), 279.

[272] ILC Fragmentation Report, 209, para 415.

in this case that the 1955 Iran–US Treaty had to be applied in terms of its ordinary meaning, which meant that no reference should be made to rules on the use of force not mentioned in it, hardly any basis that could have prompted the Court's decision other than peremptory law can be identified.[273] In this sense, *Oil Platforms* is not a case that can explain the mainline aspect of the operation of Article 31(3)(c). The *Al-Adsani* decision of the European Court of Human Rights in turn resulted in a restrictive interpretation of the right to access to a court under Article 6 of the European Convention on Human Rights.

Article 31(3)(c) of the Vienna Convention does not specify whether the 'relevant rules', in order to contribute to the process of treaty interpretation, have to be binding on all parties to the relevant treaty. The phrase 'applicable in the relations between the parties' could be understood as pointing in either direction. This question is not frequently confronted in doctrine. It is argued that in the WTO context the Vienna Convention reference to the 'applicable rules' of international law relates to the rules that apply to all parties to the WTO, not just to the parties to the dispute. This arguably follows from each treaty having an objectively ascertainable meaning in relation to all its parties. Furthermore, it is asserted that 'we need to ensure that we do not have the same WTO obligations and rights having a different meaning in the contexts of different WTO Parties, because of their non-WTO relationships. That would create great uncertainty as to the nature of WTO rights and obligations.'[274] On the other hand, it must be accepted that every WTO party may be in a different bilateral treaty relation with another WTO party and this has to be considered if these two parties happen to be parties in the WTO dispute settlement procedures. This process is not exclusively about the meaning of the treaty clause. The purpose of 'relevant rules' is not to clarify the intention of the parties embodied in the treaty. This process is instead about the external evidence capable of affecting that meaning.

Pauwelyn stresses the 'distinction between interpreting WTO rules (and the prohibition to add or detract from those rules in the process) and examining

[273] French (2006), 281 at 291 claims that the Court's analysis in this case was not motivated by *jus cogens* as such or exclusively, but some 'more intricate' issues raised by Article 31(3)(c), but without explaining what those intricate reasons could be. This analysis is not concerned with the issue of *jus cogens* in general or its particular application in *Oil Platforms*, which has been dealt with by this author in *Peremptory Norms in International Law* (2006), Chapters 6 and 15. Note also that the *Mox Plant* Award conceives of this phenomenon as involving the relevance of *jus cogens*, observing that it should defer the application of the relevant treaty to the applicable *jus cogens* with which the relevant *lex specialis* may be inconsistent. The Tribunal further emphasised that 'as long as it is not inconsistent with *jus cogens*, Parties may also instruct a tribunal to apply *lex specialis* that is not part of general international law at the time'. A similar role is reserved to the *jus cogens* which subsequently emerged; see paras 84, 100, 103. A comparison of these two decisions only confirms that one of them expressly states what is necessarily implied in another.

[274] Lennard (2002), 19 at 37.

WTO claims in the context of other applicable international law'.[275] Pauwelyn continues that:

> most obviously, these other rules must be binding on both disputing parties (and be invoked by either of them). If either of the two parties is not so bound, these other rules cannot be held against it. In technical terms, this means that one either applies other rules binding on the disputing parties as part of the applicable law on the ground that the WTO agreement, as a treaty under public international law, must be applied in the context of such other treaties; or that one interprets the relevant WTO rules in the context of such other treaties based on, for example, Article 31.3(c) of the Vienna Convention referring to 'any elevant rules of international law applicable in the relations between the parties'.

Pauwelyn is quick and careful enough to add that:

> The disadvantage of this approach is, however, that one risks giving too broad a meaning to the term interpretation. Indeed, what one is effectively doing when dis-applying a WTO norm to the advantage of another, non-WTO norm agreed upon only by the disputing parties (or even when applying a rule of general international law to solve a question on which the WTO treaty itself remains silent) is not so much interpreting WTO terms in the light of other norms agreed upon by WTO Members. Rather, one is then applying WTO norms together with such other norms as they are binding (only) in the relationship between the disputing parties.[276]

As Pauwelyn emphasises, WTO dispute settlement bodies are reluctant to make findings that the customary rules impact on the content and scope of covered treaty obligations. This is linked to the more complicated character of custom-generation in comparison with the more straightforward process of treaty-making. In practice, it is rare for custom to emerge notwithstanding the continuing existence of a contradictory treaty norm. Pauwelyn further clarifies that:

> even if new custom does emerge in the face of a treaty dealing with the same subject matter, given the often vague and general nature of custom, a genuine conflict between custom and treaty is exceptional: in most cases it will be possible to interpret the treaty in line with the new custom. Finally, in those cases where a genuine conflict does arise, the treaty is most likely to prevail as *lex specialis* based on its often more specific and explicit expression of state will.[277]

Pauwelyn's approach accurately reflects the limits on the interpretative relevance of general international law—the very limits that inherently follow from the structural characteristics of international law based on consent and agreement between States. In general, there are different ways in which the 'relevant rules' can enter the field of treaty interpretation. In some cases general international law

[275] J Pauwelyn, How to Win a WTO Dispute Based on Non-WTO Law? 37 *Journal of World Trade* (2003), 997 at 1003.

[276] Pauwelyn (2003), 1003–1004.

[277] Pauwelyn (2003), 1025.

rules can serve the purpose of completeness of legal regulation under treaties. If, for instance, the relevant concept in a treaty is not defined, the treaty regulation cannot be complete and apply to facts without such definition. The use of other rules of international law can usefully fill this gap.

One field in which general international law may assume an interpretative role relates to the structural framework of international law within which a treaty operates. This field is somehow related to that involving the definition of the concepts embodied in the treaty. Resort to the general law of treaties may be necessary to identify the applicability of treaty obligations. The rules of State responsibility may have to be resorted to for clarifying the legal consequences of violations of treaties. To illustrate, the jurisprudence under the European Convention on Human Rights is familiar with examples by reference to which the Convention organs have identified the status of an applicant or respondent, or have given effect to some overarching principles such as that of non-recognition of illegal territorial changes.[278] However, this field is not strictly as much one of interpretation of substantive rules embodied in a treaty as that of the application of structural principles of general law which support the operation of the treaty framework as it stands, without determining or influencing the meaning and scope of substantive treaty obligations.

A similar phenomenon of the relevance of general international law was witnessed in the *Ethiopia–Eritrea Boundary Delimitation* case. Article 4 of the 2000 Agreement between Ethiopia and Eritrea entitled the Boundary Commission to use not only the treaties that determined the boundary between them, but also the 'applicable international law.' The Commission emphasised, by reference to the International Court's decision in *Kasikili/Sedudu*, that this reference was not limited in its effect to the international law applicable to the interpretation of treaties. It also required the Commission to take into consideration any rules of customary international law that might have a bearing on the case, for example, prescription and acquiescence, even if such rules might involve a departure from the position prescribed by the relevant treaty provisions.[279] Consequently, the Commission observed that:

> it finds itself unable to accept the contention advanced by Ethiopia that the Commission should determine the boundary exclusively on the basis of the three specified Treaties as interpreted in accordance with the rules of international law governing treaty interpretation. The Commission considers that it is required also to apply those rules of

[278] Such a resort to general international law may be necessary to clarify the status of the applicant or respondent, 6780/74 & 6950/75, *Cyprus v Turkey*, 2 *DR*, 145ff, 8007/77, *Cyprus v Turkey*, 13 *DR*, 146ff, *An v Cyprus*, 13 *HRLJ*, 153, *Loizidou* (Preliminary Objections), para 57; to clarify the role of reciprocity in jurisdictional issues, *Turkish* (Admissibility), paras 35–43, 4 *HRLJ*, 555–557; to clarify the issue of permissibility of reservations to the Convention, *Loizidou*, paras 65–73; to clarify the legal force of provisional measures, *Cruz Varas*, (Judgment by the Court), para 101. See generally also J Charney, International Law and Multiple International Tribunals, 271 *RdC* 1998, 210–216, 241–244.

[279] Award of the Commission, para 3.14.

international law applicable generally to the determination of disputed borders including, in particular, the rules relating to the effect of conduct of the parties.[280]

It must be emphasised that such a mandate to apply general international law is substantially different from specifying that the treaty should be construed in accordance with general international law. According to the Commission's approach, the treaty provisions would mean whatever they mean. However, room would be left for verifying whether the contracting parties had agreed in practice to modify them. This is essentially a question of amendment or modification of the treaty, as opposed to treaty interpretation.

Given the nature of treaties as *lex specialis*, the relevance of the rest of international law in interpreting them must be viewed as limited to two fields. The first field is the clarification of meaning of the terms employed in the treaty, or the examination of how the relevant concept evolves over time. It is considered, quite correctly, that general international law can be used for clarifying the meaning of the terms of a treaty (unless they have treaty-specific or autonomous meaning). Thus, it could be quite permissible to refer to customary law to clarify, in the context of international investment law, the meaning of expropriation or denial of justice; or, in the context of the law of the sea, the meaning of continental shelf. As Visscher specifies, even where the treaty establishes legal regulation separate or different from general international law, it may still borrow from the latter concepts and categories.[281]

The European Court of Human Rights in *Selmouni* referred to the 1984 UN Convention against Torture to clarify the meaning of torture for the purposes of application of Article 3 of the European Convention on Human Rights.[282] A reference to general rules of international law under Article 31(1)(c) of the Vienna Convention was also made in *Golder*. The European Court observed that 'The principle whereby a civil claim must be capable of being submitted to a judge ranks as one of the universally "recognised" fundamental principles of law; the same is true of the principle of international law which forbids the denial of justice. Article 6(1) must be read in the light of these principles.'[283] However it should be noted that *Golder* referred to this rule along with the use of other interpretative methods, and with the purpose of preserving the broader reading of Article 6.

In *Council of Civil Service Unions v UK* the European Commission on Human Rights had to address the interpretation of Article 11(2) of the European Convention in the light of other international agreements invoked in the case. The Commission referred to Article 22(1) ICCPR which imposes limitations on forming trade unions applicable to members of the police and armed forces, and

[280] *Id*, para 3.16.
[281] Visscher (1963), 92.
[282] *Selmouni v France*, Application No 25803/94, Judgment of 28 July 1999, paras 97–98.
[283] *Golder*, para 35.

Article 8(2) of the International Covenant on Economic, Social and Cultural Rights, which restates the same limitation in more general terms in relation to 'members...of the administration of the State'. The Commission thus refused to be guided by the rest of international law in interpreting Article 11(2) of the European Commission. As the European Commission stated, 'there can be no settled view under international law as to the position of members of the "administration of the State" in respect of trade union rights'. Other treaties could not be of assistance to the Commission's interpretative exercise.[284]

In the *IMCO* case, the International Court upheld the presumption that the meaning of the notion included in the treaty reflects, unless the opposite is stated, the meaning of the same notion included in other treaties. The Court was unable to accept:

> the view that when the Article was first drafted in 1946 and referred to 'ship-owning nations' in the same context in which it referred to 'nations owning substantial amounts of merchant shipping', the draftsmen were not speaking of merchant shipping belonging to a country in the sense used in international conventions concerned with safety at sea and cognate matters from 1910 onwards. It would, in its view, be quite unlikely, if the words 'ship-owning nations' were intended to have any different meaning, that no attempt would have been made to indicate this. The absence of any discussion on their meaning as the draft Article developed strongly suggests that there was no doubt as to their meaning; that they referred to registered ship tonnage.[285]

In *US–Shrimp* the WTO Appellate Body examined the meaning of 'exhaustible natural resources' under Article XX(g) GATT. After concluding that textually this clause was not limited to the conservation of 'mineral' or 'non-living' natural resources, the Appellate Body resorted to other rules and standards of international law. The Appellate Body emphasised that 'The words of Article XX(g), "exhaustible natural resources", were actually crafted more than 50 years ago. They must be read by a treaty interpreter in the light of contemporary concerns of the community of nations about the protection and conservation of the environment.' The generic term 'natural resources' was not static but evolutionary in its content, as could be seen from the modern international conventions and declarations. For instance, Article 56 of the 1982 Law of the Sea Convention referred both to living and non-living resources; its Articles 61 and 62 referred to 'living resources' in specifying the rights and duties of the coastal State in its Exclusive Economic Zone; and so did other conventions.[286]

The only concern that may be raised in relation to this line of reasoning is that the relevant conventions did not confirm the judgment that the relevant resource was exhaustible. Although this is not contestable as a matter of fact and has in the same case been clarified through textual interpretation, interpretation by ref-

[284] *Council of Civil Service Unions v UK*, 50 *DR* (1987), 228.
[285] *ICJ Reports*, 1960, 170.
[286] *US–Shrimp*, AB Report, paras 129–130.

erence to the 'relevant rules' could not alone have led to this outcome. But the outcome is not too grave, because it follows the outcome of the use of the textual method of interpretation which the Appellate Body upheld in this case.

The second field of reference to 'relevant rules' is where the meaning of treaty rules is qualified by external factors. This may either be a situation where the parties to a particular bilateral dispute are also parties to another treaty that prevails over the first treaty as *lex posterior* or *lex specialis*; or the situation where the meaning of the treaty clause offends public policy. The relevance of general international law rules does not fall within any of the above categories, and it leaves untouched the treaty regulation as *lex specialis*. This aspect relates this issue, arguably that of interpretation, to that of the hierarchy of norms; for there must be a clear reason why the provision of a treaty with clearly ascertainable content should not be applied to the facts in the way in which it was intended.[287]

The basic principle of textual interpretation requires interpreting treaty provisions as overriding customary rules whenever their application conflicts with these rules. To interpret the clear wording of text which, on its face, dispenses with requirements under general international law, as not doing so, just because it fails to specifically mention that specific customary rule, is to refuse to give effect to the intention of the parties which formulated the rule that is meant to override the general international law rule through its operation, and operating as *lex specialis* or *lex posterior*. After all, parties to a treaty are aware of the *lex specialis* principle and they cannot be expected to state, with regard to each and every treaty rule, which non-treaty rules they intend to override.

In WTO law, there has been little reliance on customary law to interpret WTO agreements.[288] The WTO Panel Report in *Korea–Procurement* emphasises the role of customary law in regulating the principles of interpretation applicable to WTO agreements. The Report continues that:

> the relationship of the WTO Agreements to customary international law is broader than this. Customary international law applies generally to the economic relations between the WTO Members. Such international law applies to the extent that the WTO treaty agreements do not 'contract out' from it. To put it another way, to the extent there is no conflict or inconsistency, or an expression in a covered WTO agreement that implies differently, we are of the view that the customary rules of international law apply to the WTO treaties and to the process of treaty formation under the WTO.[289]

In *EC–Hormones* the Appellate Body considered it unnecessary and imprudent to assess the question whether the precautionary principle constitutes part of customary law. The Appellate Body acknowledged that this principle could have

[287] See above note 273 and the accompanying text.

[288] Matsushita, Schoenbaum & Mavroidis (2006), 78–79.

[289] *Korea–Measures Affecting Government Procurement*, Report of the Panel, WT/DS163/R, 1 May 2000, para 7.96.

interpretative value in assessing the propriety of State conduct. But 'the precautionary principle does not, by itself, and without a clear textual directive to that effect, relieve a panel from the duty of applying the normal (i.e. customary international law) principles of treaty interpretation'.[290]

The Appellate Body further observed that the precautionary principle that had been invoked adversely in the SPS Agreement would be relevant in interpreting that Agreement. This principle 'has not been written into the SPS Agreement as a ground for justifying SPS measures that are otherwise inconsistent with the obligations of Members set out in particular provisions of that Agreement'.[291] Had the precautionary principle been embodied in the SPS Agreement itself, it could have qualified its main provisions, and justified conduct that would not be justified under those provisions as such. That not being the case, the precautionary principle could not affect the scope of the SPS Agreement as *lex specialis*.

This is a clear statement that WTO agreements as *lex specialis* retain their independent meaning and the rules of general international law cannot by themselves influence their content. General, or customary, international law is relevant only in so far as it does not contradict WTO rules.

In arbitral practice the issue has been dealt with of whether Article 1121 NAFTA, which deals with the preconditions for recourse to arbitration, dispenses with the requirement to exhaust local remedies. As the Arbitral Tribunal pointed out in *Loewen*, 'an important principle of international law [in this case the local remedies rule] should not be held to have been tacitly dispensed with by international agreement, in the absence of words making clear an intention to do so. Such an intention may be exhibited by express provisions which are at variance with the continued operation of the relevant rules of international law.' As the Tribunal further specified, 'It would be strange indeed if *sub silentio* the international rule were to be swept away.'[292] Therefore, the Tribunal found that Article 1121 did not exclude the duty to exhaust local remedies.

This approach has two implications. It should not be presumed that a treaty is overriding customary international law norms unless the intention of parties to this effect can be demonstrated. On the other hand, there can be no restrictive interpretation of wording that does override the customary rule; it does not have to be the words that directly and expressly dispense with the customary rule; it is rather required, as the *Loewen* Tribunal pointed out, to identify 'express provisions which are at variance with the continued operation of the relevant rules of international law'. As the Arbitral Tribunal emphasised in *George Pinson*,

[290] *EC–Hormones*, paras 123–124.

[291] *Id*, para 124.

[292] *The Loewen Group, Inc. and Raymond L. Loewen and United States of America* (Award, Case No ARB(AF)/98/3), 26 June 2003, 42 *ILM* (2003), 811 paras 159 and 162, at 837.

a treaty must be seen as referring to general international law 'for all questions which it does not itself resolve expressly and in a different way'.[293] Therefore, it is implied in the Tribunal's reasoning that the treaty can derogate from general international law both in express and implicit ways.

The *Haya de la Torre* case highlights an interesting situation in which the general international law background can be relevant. The case involved the 1928 Havana Convention on Asylum, which was silent on the surrender of political offenders. This silence could not 'be interpreted as imposing an obligation to surrender the refugee in case the asylum was granted to him contrary to the provisions of Article 2 of the Convention'. This silence further coexisted with the Latin American tradition of non-surrender of political refugees. There was nothing in this tradition to require the surrender of persons who irregularly obtained asylum. Furthermore:

> If it has been intended to abandon that tradition, an express provision to that effect would have been needed, and the Havana Convention contains no such provision. The silence of the Convention implies that it was intended to leave the adjustment of the consequences of this situation to decisions inspired by considerations of convenience or of simple political expediency.[294]

The background against which the Court decided that the extra-conventional legal background determined the outcome was closely linked to the non-regulation of the relevant field under the 1928 Treaty. The Treaty was silent on that particular issue and thus the Latin American tradition had a crucial role. The Court did not strictly speak of general or customary law, but its finding is relevant for understanding the relevance of customary law as well.

The silence of a treaty instrument in relation to a specific matter can have different implications depending on the general purpose and design of the treaty. In some instances the silence of a treaty on a particular subject can mean the lack of treaty regulation,[295] while in other cases silence can imply legal regulation on the basis of the interpretative principle of effectiveness.[296] The relevance of general international law as a factor of interpretation can vary accordingly.

Thus, in order to clarify whether and how the 'relevant rules' apply in relation to the subject matter covered by the treaty, the following questions have to be clarified in every specific situation. In the first place, it has to be clarified whether the 'relevant rule' conflicts with treaty regulation. This question can only be answered after the textual meaning of relevant treaty provisions is identified, possibly also by reference to the principle of effectiveness which can, under cer-

[293] *Georges Pinson* (*France v United Mexican States*) Award of 13 April 1928, V *RIAA*, 422.

[294] *Haya de la Torre Case* (Colombia/Peru), Judgment of 13 June 1951, *ICJ Reports*, 1951, 71 at 80–81.

[295] See above Chapter 3.

[296] See below Chapter 11.

tain circumstances, justify the assumption that the treaty does regulate certain aspects on which its text as such is silent. If the conclusion is reached that silence in a particular case equates to non-regulation, then the *lex specialis* principle does not come into play and the 'relevant rules' of general international law continue to govern the relevant area or question. If, however, there is legal regulation under the treaty, either in express terms or by implication on the basis of the principle of effectiveness, that regulation is applicable whatever the state of general international law. The latter law can however be relevant if the treaty regulation includes some concepts the essence of which may be defined and clarified by reference to general international law.

The *Namibia* case offers an instance of treatment of extraneous rules in the context where the text of the treaty itself mandates their relevance. The treaty text may be open-ended or receptive to further evolution of general law. In this spirit, the Court approached the issue of the interpretation of Article 22 of the League of Nations:

> Mindful as it is of the primary necessity of interpreting an instrument in accordance with the intentions of the parties at the time of its conclusion, the Court is bound to take into account the fact that the concepts embodied in Article 22 of the Covenant—'the strenuous conditions of the modern world' and 'the well-being and development' of the peoples concerned—were not static, but were by definition evolutionary, as also, therefore, was the concept of the 'sacred trust'. The parties to the Covenant must consequently be deemed to have accepted them as such. That is why, viewing the institutions of 1919, the Court must take into consideration the changes which have occurred in the supervening half-century, and its interpretation cannot remain unaffected by the subsequent development of law, through the Charter of the United Nations and by way of customary law. Moreover, an international instrument has to be interpreted and applied within the framework of the entire legal system prevailing at the time of the interpretation.

The few decades preceding the Court's rendering of the Opinion had brought important developments relating to the law governing the position of non-self-governing people. The principle of self-determination was among these developments and thus constituted the 'ultimate objective of the sacred trust'.[297] Consequently, the whole issue was the content of the 'sacred trust' under the League Covenant, as opposed to the free-standing impact of extraneous legal rules—a notion accepted by States-parties under the Mandate agreement as an evolving one, as opposed to the deference of the Mandate agreement to the rest of international law.

A similar approach is observable in the *Gabcikovo-Nagymaros* case, in which Hungary claimed that the application of the 1977 Treaty between Hungary and Slovakia had to be qualified by reference to rules of international environmental law which had emerged subsequently. Here again, the relevance of extraneous

[297] *ICJ Reports*, 1971, 31.

rules, to the extent they were established under international law, derived from the mandate under the text of the 1977 Treaty. As the Court observed:

> newly developed norms of environmental law are relevant for the implementation of the Treaty and that the parties could, by agreement, incorporate them through the application of Articles 15, 19 and 20 of the Treaty. These articles do not contain specific obligations of performance but require the parties, in carrying out their obligations to ensure that the quality of water in the Danube is not impaired and that nature is protected.[298]

Articles 15, 19 and 20 of the 1977 Treaty already contained a direction to the parties to protect the quality of water, nature and fishing.[299] In this way the Treaty itself required the parties to protect the relevant aspects of the environment.[300]

A more detailed and specific analysis of this problem of interpretation is included in the Separate Opinion of Judge Bedjaoui, which agrees with the outcome that the Court reached, but refuses to accord any blanket relevance to evolutive interpretation. As Judge Bedjaoui emphasises, 'The intentions of the parties are presumed to have been influenced by *the law in force at the time the Treaty was concluded,* the law which they were supposed to know, and not by future law, as yet unknown.' At the same time, this factor could not affect the plain meaning of treaty clauses under Article 31 of the Vienna Convention.[301]

Judge Bedjaoui's reasoning develops further by drawing a distinction between the definition of concepts included in the treaty and the law applicable to that concept. Judge Bedjaoui begins with a reference to the evolutionary concept of 'sacred trust' in *Namibia*, emphasising that this factor was treaty-specific, correctly emphasising that 'the Court patently knew that it was pursuing this approach because the situation was special. Nowhere did it state that its method of mobile reference was subsequently to become mandatory and extend to all cases of interpretation.'[302] Consequently, Judge Bedjaoui had to conclude that:

> Although there is no need to abandon the '*evolutionary interpretation*', which may be useful, not to say necessary in very limited situations, it must be said that it cannot automatically be applied to any case. In general, it is noteworthy that the classical rules of

[298] *ICJ Reports*, 1998, 67.

[299] *Id*, 22–23; according to the ILC Fragmentation Report, this demonstrates that the parties had committed themselves to progressive development, at 242–243, para 478(a).

[300] Had this not been so, environmental rules could have been relevant only if their peremptory status could be established, enabling them to qualify the *lex specialis* principle. For one of such options see Orakhelashvili, *Peremptory Norms* (2006), Chapter 2. Likewise, the new peremptory law on self-determination would have retrospectively voided Article 22 of the League Covenant if that provision had not offered room to accommodate the principle of self-determination.

[301] Separate Opinion of Judge Bedjaoui, *ICJ Reports*, 1997, 121 (emphasis original).

[302] *Id*, 122.

interpretation do not require a treaty to be interpreted *in all circumstances* in the context of the entire legal system prevailing at the time of the interpretation.

This went hand in hand with his more general thesis that interpretation of treaties is not the same as substitution of the negotiated and mutually approved text.[303] On this basis, Judge Bedjaoui emphasised that the 1977 Treaty was not to be interpreted evolutively:

Indeed, it is quite the opposite that these rules of interpretation prescribe, seeking as they do to recommend an interpretation consonant with the intentions of the parties at the time the Treaty was concluded. In general, in a treaty, a State incurs specific obligations contained in a body of law as it existed on the conclusion of the treaty and *in no wise incurs evolutionary und indeterminate duties.* A State cannot incur unknown obligations whether for the future or even the present.[304]

In general, the new rules of environmental law could be incorporated into the treaty, but on the basis of the consent of the parties to it, which would be a revision of the treaty, not its interpretation. In the specific case of the 1977 Treaty, Articles 15, 19 and 20 were, 'fortunately' as Judge Bedjaoui put it, drafted in vague terms. Consequently, and 'In the absence of any other specification, respecting the autonomy of the will implies precisely that provisions of this kind are interpreted in an evolutionary manner, in other words, taking account of the criteria adopted by *the general law* prevailing in each period considered.'[305] It was this factor, and not any free-standing relevance of extraneous rules, that opened the way for evolutive interpretation according to the new law. Judge Bedjaoui expressly stated that:

in applying the so-called principle of *the evolutionary interpretation* of a treaty in the present case, the Court should have clarified the issue more and should have recalled that the general rule governing the interpretation of a treaty remains that set out in Article 31 of the 1969 Vienna Convention.[306]

The matter was consequently resolved by the treaty text, not by general international law. It was the former that made the latter relevant. As Judge Bedjaoui further specified:

the classical rules of interpretation do not require a treaty to be interpreted *in all circumstances* in the context of the entire legal system prevailing at the time of the interpretation, in other words, in the present case, that the 1977 Treaty [between Hungary and Slovakia] should be interpreted '*in the context*' and in the light of the new contemporary law of the environment or of international watercourses. Indeed, it is quite the opposite that these rules of interpretation prescribe, seeking as they do to recommend an interpretation consonant with the intentions of the parties at the time the Treaty was concluded.

[303] *Id*, 123.
[304] *Id*, 123.
[305] *Id*, 123–124 (emphasis original).
[306] *Id*, (emphasis original).

In other words, 'the new law might have played a role in the context of a *"reinterpretation"* of the Treaty but only provided it did so *with the consent* of the other Party'.[307]

However, sometimes the more predominant role for customary norms is suggested. Lauterpacht suggests that treaties must be interpreted against the background of customary law, and 'often it is custom that will vitally affect the treaty, and not conversely'.[308] The ascertainment of the intention of parties through interpretation cannot be a process divorced from the application and development of customary international law. Intention cannot be elicited by mere logical and grammatical interpretation. If the intention is not clear, it must be assumed that the intended result is in conformity with general international law.[309] Such views contradict the *lex specialis* principle and can also result in a restrictive interpretation at the expense of the clear meaning of treaties.

That general rules of international law cannot by themselves impact interpretation, but can merely provide a source for clarifying the meaning of ambiguous terms, was affirmed by the Permanent Court in *River Oder*. The relevant provision of the Versailles Treaty was unclear and the Court had to examine the applicable principles of general law. The Court stated its interpretative policy to examine the 'principles governing international fluvial law in general and consider what position was adopted by the Treaty of Versailles in regard to these principles'.[310] In other words, the Court acted in line with the *lex specialis* status of the regulation under the Versailles Treaty. The principles of general law were needed to clarify what the Versailles Treaty actually prescribed, not to provide legal regulation on their own or override the provisions of the Treaty.

Likewise, *The Diversion of Water from the Meuse* offers a cautious attitude to the relevance of general international law in the interpretation and application of treaties. The Permanent Court dealt with the rights and duties of riparian States in relation to water diversion from the river. The issue in this case was regulated by specific agreements. The Court faced a submission as to the applicability of general rules of international law as regards rivers. As the Court observed, the context of the case did not 'entitle it to go outside the field covered by the Treaty of 1863. The points at issue must all be determined solely by the interpretation and application of that Treaty.'[311]

[307] *Id*, *ICJ Reports*, 1997, 123 (emphasis original).

[308] H Lauterpacht, *Collected Papers* (1970), vol I, 224–225.

[309] Lauterpacht (1958), 27–28.

[310] *Territorial Jurisdiction of the International Commission of the River Oder*, Judgment of 10 September 1929, *PCIJ Series* A, No 23, 5 at 26.

[311] *The Diversion of Water from the Meuse*, Series A/B, No 70, Judgment of 28 June 1937, 4 at 16; the question whether the 1886 Anglo-Greek Treaty incorporated the general principles on the treatment of foreigners and denial of justice was raised in the *Ambatielos* case but not pursued because it was not fully argued, *Ambatielos* (Preliminary Objections), *ICJ Reports*, 1952, 45.

In *Al-Adsani v UK*, which stands out as deviating from the regular pattern of treating the impact of general international law on treaties, the European Court referred to general international law to restrict the scope of operation of Article 6 of the European Convention. The Court asserted that Article 6 tolerates granting immunity to foreign States for torture, even if the text of Article 6 does not contain any such condition.[312] The Court thus unjustifiably adopted a restrictive interpretation of Article 6,[313] and used the method of interpretation by reference to general international law as if it were the only method. Most notably, the Court gave no consideration in this respect to the object and purpose of the European Convention. Thus, the use of extraneous rules under Article 31(3)(c) of the Vienna Convention took place in the context of overlooking the outcomes that Article 31(1) of the same Convention required the Court to uphold.

In *Iron Rhine*, the Arbitral Tribunal had to interpret the 1839 Treaty between Belgium and the Netherlands, and assess the impact on it of the subsequently developed rules of international environmental law. The Tribunal emphasised that:

> provisions of general international law are also applicable to the relations between the Parties, and thus should be taken into account in interpreting Article XII of the 1839 Treaty of Separation and Article IV of the Iron Rhine Treaty. Further, international environmental law has relevance to the relations between the Parties. There is considerable debate as to what, within the field of environmental law, constitutes 'rules' or 'principles'; what is 'soft law'; and which environmental treaty law or principles have contributed to the development of customary international law.

The duty to prevent or mitigate environmental harm had become a principle of general international law. More specifically, this applied to the obligation to mitigate or avoid harm to the environment. This applied, according to the Tribunal, as a principle of general international law, 'not only in autonomous activities but also in activities undertaken in implementation of specific treaties between the Parties', although the Tribunal was careful to note that the mere invocation of those principles would not determine the outcome.[314] This finding was above all possible because the Treaty did not by itself authorise any action that would be harmful to the environment.

In addressing the relevance of these principles of extraneous law for the interpretation of Article XII of the 1839 Separation Treaty, the Tribunal referred to the intertemporal rule, but also stressed that later legally relevant developments that were important for the effective application of the Treaty could not be disregarded either. The Tribunal emphasised that 'an evolutive interpretation, which would ensure an application of the treaty that would be effective in terms of its object and purpose, will be preferred to a strict application of the intertemporal

[312] *Al-Adsani v UK*, Judgment of 21 November 2001, 34 EHRR 11(2002); as the ILC Fragmentation Report also emphasises, 'the Court used Article 31(3)(c) so as to set aside, in this case, the rules of the [European] Convention, at 221, para 438'; see for further details Orakhelashvili, *EJIL* (2003), the references in Chapter 6 (note 21), and Chapter 2 above.

[313] See, on restrictive interpretation, below Chapter 11.

[314] *Iron Rhine*, paras 58–60.

rule'.[315] The Tribunal's preference for the evolutive approach for the sake of promoting the object and purpose of the Treaty must be noted. As a consequence, the Tribunal stated that 'It may therefore be necessary to read into Article XII, so far as the allocation of contemporary costs for upgrading is concerned, the provisions of international law as they apply today.' These were the above-mentioned rules of environmental law.[316]

However, the context of the case is broader than this. The relevant issue of nature protection, that is the Netherlands' designation of a nature reserve in the area where the relevant treaty-based works had to be conducted, was seen by the Tribunal as an emanation of its remaining territorial sovereignty which the Treaty did not affect. Thus, 'the relationship between Belgium's right of transit and the Netherlands' rights of sovereignty remained in balance as intended under Article XII'.[317]

The conclusion on the *Iron Rhine* case should be that what eventually was responsible for the interpretative outcome was not the relevance of extraneous rules as such and in the first place, but the textual outcome following from the Treaty itself that the Netherlands had not given up its sovereign right to designate the nature reserve in that area. This was possibly not due to extraneous environmental law, but due to the fact that the Treaty text did not restrict the sovereignty of the Netherlands in that way. Nor did the existence of the nature reserve contradict the Treaty. Consequently, the outcome could have been the same whether or not the extraneous rules had been resorted to.

In cases where rules of general international law do not contradict the treaty-based *lex specialis*, their application inherently falls within the treaty-based jurisdiction of the relevant tribunals to ensure the proper exercise of their judicial function through the complete resolution of the dispute and full-fledged application of law to it. The jurisdiction of dispute settlement bodies to interpret and apply a treaty implies jurisdiction to judge the field within which it applies.[318] This mandate cannot authorise the interpretation of the treaty in a way to make it applicable where it does not apply. In *Oil Platforms*, the International Court took it as read that its jurisdiction under the 1955 Iran–US Treaty extended to the application of the general international law of *jus ad bellum*, because the latter set of rules was crucial for understanding whether the relevant provisions of the 1955 Treaty, Articles X and XX, had been observed. A similar approach has been taken by the International Tribunal for the Law of the Sea. In *M/V Saiga*, the Tribunal observed that it:

> must take into account the circumstances of the arrest in the context of the applicable rules of international law. Although the Convention does not contain express provisions

[315] *Id*, paras 79–80.
[316] *Id*, para 85.
[317] *Id*, paras 93, 95; see for more detail below Chapter 11.
[318] On judicial jurisdiction to apply extraneous legal rules see in particular J Pauwelyn, *Conflict of Norms in Public International Law* (2003), Chapter 8.

on the use of force in the arrest of ships, international law, which is applicable by virtue of article 293 of the Convention, requires that the use of force must be avoided as far as possible and, where force is unavoidable, it must not go beyond what is reasonable and necessary in the circumstances.[319]

The Tribunal added that the use of force was permissible only as a last resort after warning had been given, and consequently ruled the relevant forcible action as illegal. It found 'no excuse for the fact that the officers fired at the ship itself with live ammunition from a fast-moving patrol boat without issuing any of the signals and warnings required by international law and practice'.[320]

To conclude, in order to affect the content of treaty rules, other 'relevant rules' of international law must be unambiguously established in terms of the sources of law criteria, and be applicable specifically to the dispute as to the interpretation in question. There is no single principle which would apply in all cases. In particular, there is very little utility in advancing dubious notions such as 'systemic integration' which is bound to complicate matters in a field which already consists of multiple factors and elements. Furthermore, in case of divergent regulation under the treaty and other rules, those other rules must have the hierarchical capacity to qualify the scope of the rules under the treaty. The rarity of the application of 'relevant rules' for construing treaty provisions with the actual impact and occasional insufficiency of reasoning in the pertinent decisions suggests that 'relevant rules' are not normally able to qualify the meaning of treaty obligations.

8. Preparatory Work

(a) Essence and Admissibility

According to Article 32 of the Vienna Convention, recourse to the circumstances of conclusion of the treaty[321] and its preparatory work is justified if the treaty text as interpreted in terms of Article 31 produces a result that is ambiguous, obscure or absurd. It should be noted that ambiguity in this context means not ambiguity of the text *per se*. When the text as such is ambiguous, the General Rule of Interpretation offers a variety of ways to ascertain what the parties intended, and consequently in practice recourse is made to the object and purpose of the

[319] *M/V Saiga* (Saint Vincent and the Grenadines v Guinea), Judgment of 1 July 1999, Merits, para 155.

[320] *Id*, paras 156–157.

[321] Circumstances of conclusion of the treaty may include immediately surrounding circumstances. They can also refer to historical circumstances of objective character which may have influenced the process of the conclusion of a treaty. On this latter factor see Visscher (1963), 74.

treaty, its context, general rules of international law, and subsequent practice. Only such ambiguity as persists even after exhaustion of all methods listed in Article 31 of the Vienna Convention will justify recourse to the preparatory work or the circumstances of conclusion of the treaty. Without meeting the requirements in this order, preparatory work is simply irrelevant.

Similarly, the absurdity of the interpretative outcome is not something that is just uncongenial, disagreeable or unacceptable from some points of view, unacceptable to a party, or not conducive to its interests, but something that renders the treaty clause unworkable, inconsistent with the object and purpose of the treaty or its other clauses, or any superior legal rule.

In general, preparatory work (*travaux*) embodies numerous statements, many of which have nothing to do with legal obligation, being made for political purposes or courtesy, as is the case in the normal course of treaty preparation. Recourse to the *travaux*, which requires interpreting each statement of this kind to ascertain its effect, is no doubt complicated and may ultimately prove useless if these statements cannot evidence the agreement, and must be avoided if at all possible.

In the work of the International Law Commission, the secondary status of the *travaux* and their irrelevance in the face of the clear text has been repeatedly emphasised, both by the Special Rapporteur and the Commission itself.[322] As the Commission emphasised at the final stage of codification, preparatory work does not, unlike the plain meaning and the object and purpose of the treaty, have an authentic meaning in interpretation. The Commission classified the *travaux* as a 'supplementary' method, which means that it 'does not provide alternative, autonomous, means of interpretation but only means to aid an interpretation governed by the principles' embodied in the General Rule of Interpretation.[323]

Defining preparatory work is a complicated question. The International Law Commission refused to specify examples of preparatory work, explaining this by the need to avoid excluding evidence not mentioned.[324] Article 32 does not determine whether the relevant preparatory work has to be publicly available, at least in a way to be accessible to the relevant parties in dispute, both at the time of the preparatory stage and of interpretation. In terms of the formal element of preparatory work, there is no guidance on this specific question either, although the Arbitral Tribunal in the *Young Loan* case has stated that preparatory work is normally limited to written documents materially available at a later date. The value of oral statements is limited and can be admitted in exceptional cases where they are made in an official context and during the negotiations themselves.

[322] II *YbILC* 1964, 57, 204–205.
[323] II *YbILC* 1966, 220.
[324] II *YBILC* 1966, 223.

A further requirement is that the material should be accessible and known to all the parties.[325] In any case, as Visscher specifies, only those materials which evidence the common intention of States-parties can rank as preparatory work for treaty interpretation.[326]

Preparatory work can evidence the views and intention of States at the preparatory stage, but it cannot establish their intention as to the agreed treaty obligations. In addition, the relevance of exchange of positions at the preparatory stage cannot displace the meaning of the finally adopted instrument. As the International Court emphasised in a different but related context, 'The fact that a particular proposal is not adopted by an international organ does not necessarily carry with it the inference that a collective pronouncement is made in a sense opposite to that proposed.'[327]

The process of adoption of the Vienna Convention was accompanied by the sceptical perception of the role of preparatory work as an element of treaty interpretation. For instance, the United Kingdom expressed a negative attitude in terms of the relevance of preparatory work, considering it as incomplete and misleading. As Sir Ian Sinclair representing the United Kingdom observed, preparatory work could evidence the intention of the relevant State delegation at the moment when the pertinent expression is made, but this does not necessarily bear any relation to the ultimate text of the treaty.[328]

There are few authors who defend the relevance of preparatory work. Klabbers demonstrates a sympathetic approach to the relevance of preparatory work, yet acknowledges that it is not among the most important elements of treaty interpretation. Klabbers especially acknowledges that statements made at the preparatory stage may be self-serving. Curiously enough, Klabbers doubts the existing allocation of interpretative priorities under Articles 31 and 32 of the Vienna Convention and argues that preparatory work should be consulted even where the text is sufficiently clear.[329] Taking this approach further, Schwebel is the only writer to argue that preparatory work can be viewed not only as conforming to but also as overriding the plain meaning of the treaty.[330] By this argument Schwebel effectively acknowledges the point he seeks to contradict: the irrelevance of preparatory work when treaty text is clear and intelligible.

[325] *Belgium et al. v Federal Republic of Germany (Young Loan Arbitration)*, Award of 16 May 1980, 19 ILM (1980), 1357 at 1380.

[326] Visscher (1963), 115.

[327] *Namibia*, *ICJ Reports*, 1971, 36, para 69.

[328] Official Records, Vienna Conference on the Law of Treaties (1968), 178.

[329] J Klabbers, International Legal Histories: Declining Importance of *Travaux Préparatoires* in Treaty Interpretation? *NILR* (2003), 267 at 279, 285.

[330] S Schwebel, May Preparatory Work be Used to Correct Rather than Confirm the 'Clear' Meaning of a Treaty Provision? in J Makarczyk (ed), *Theory of International Law at the Threshold of the 21st Century: Essays in Honour of Krzysztof Skubiszewski* (1996), 541 at 545.

Lauterpacht offered some positive but balanced observations regarding the role of preparatory work in treaty interpretation. His earlier contribution accorded a far stronger significance to the preparatory work, observing that 'in no circumstances ought preparatory work to be excluded on the ground that the treaty is clear in itself'. Tribunals should attach importance to the discrepancy between natural meaning of words and that suggested by preparatory work. Such assumption 'shifts the burden of proof upon the party who, basing himself on preparatory work, alleges a discrepancy between the natural meaning and the true one as it appears to him'.[331] Later, in his monograph, Lauterpacht noted that the International Court in a number of cases, 'without making even a negative reference to preparatory work, dispensed with it altogether'.[332]

As for general characteristics:

> Preparatory work is often lengthy, repetitive and contradictory. In relation to multilateral treaties it frequently reveals the views of the more articulate rather than the more important, the better instructed and the more influential participants. The record of preparatory work is on occasions incomplete and faulty. Much depends in this connection on the adequacy of the secretarial arrangements of the Conference. It frequently happens that in the heat or enthusiasm of the debate views are advanced or expressions used which it is subsequently deemed wiser to modify or to qualify in the written word—and yet it is the spoken word which provokes the answers and supplies the substance of the debate. Moreover, in the course of negotiations the participating States change their views as expressed on previous occasions, and the examination of any particular stage of the preparatory work, to the exclusion of others, is therefore liable to be incomplete and misleading.[333]

Yet, frequently 'there may be no effective alternative to the laborious unravelling of the sequence and the inconsistencies of preparatory work whenever such is available'. There is arguably 'all the difference' between disregarding preparatory work altogether and examining it and finding that because of its incompleteness or contradictions it offers no clue of the intention of the parties, and does not support the claim of the relevant party.[334] The suggested solution is the one 'which lies half-way between the finality of the text and the indiscriminate use of preparatory work'.[335]

Lauterpacht's points are constructive. The genuine problem in the relevance of preparatory work is *when* resort to it is justified. The Vienna Convention has a clear approach to this question, assigning to the *travaux* the role of supplementary means of interpretation.

331 Lauterpacht (1934–1935), 549 at 571, 573.
332 Lauterpacht (1958), 123–124.
333 *Id*, 130.
334 *Id*, 131.
335 *Id*, 140.

There are further repeated expressions of doubt and scepticism as to the interpretative relevance of preparatory work. Sir Eric Beckett in his observations at the Institute of International Law specified the factors which preclude preparatory work from acquiring primary significance in the interpretation of treaties. The crucial factor is the principal relevance of the text:

> The text of the treaty, when once signed, assumes, if I may so put it, a sort of life of its own. It is soon found that half of the points which trouble people during negotiation are of little importance but a whole lot of new points which were hardly thought of then are those which seem to matter. As time goes on less and less thought is ever given to the *travaux preparatoires*. Indeed, a perusal of them after an interval of years rather leads to the reflection that everybody was then worrying about the things that did not matter and most of the things that did escaped their attention. To hark back to the *travaux preparatories* for the purposes of interpretation may operate like bringing a dead hand from the grave or subjecting a grown mature man to the paternal injunctions of his boyhood.[336]

Bernhardt considers that preparatory work should have a particularly minor role with regard to multilateral treaties.[337] In another contribution, Bernhardt likewise points out that 'For very good reason, preparatory work always has had a doubtful place in treaty interpretation.'[338] In sum, 'The special nature of the European Convention on Human Rights means that particular caution is necessary in relying on the preparatory work of the Convention. Preparatory work is notoriously unreliable as a general guide to treaty interpretation.'[339]

In an early and so far most comprehensive work analysing the relevance of preparatory work in treaty interpretation, Spencer characterises preparatory work as possessing rather qualified relevance. To the extent that preparatory work does not reflect the authentic intention of the parties, it lacks evidentiary value.[340] In addition, there is no presumption in favour of resorting to the preparatory work, and if the text is clear, there is no need to resort to it anyway; indeed, such resort is prohibited.[341]

There is a further doctrinal argument that the drafters of the Vienna Convention 'thought it sensible to leave it to the adjudicating bodies to decide

[336] Beckett (1950), 435 at 444.

[337] Bernhardt (1963), 120.

[338] Bernhardt (1999), 14. See also Judge Spender in *Guardianship of Infants*, *ICJ Reports*, 1958, suggesting that caution must be exercised in any recourse to preparatory work, because one is always presented with the danger of interpreting preparatory work instead of interpreting a treaty.

[339] Ovey & White, *The European Convention on Human Rights* (2006), 40. *Travaux* are not often helpful according also to D Harris, M O'Boyle & C Warbrick, *The Law of the European Convention on Human Rights* (1995), 17.

[340] JH Spencer, *L'interprétation des traités par les travaux préparatoires* (1934), 125–127.

[341] *Id*, 165, 167, 196.

when such recourse [to preparatory work] should be made'.[342] In fact, the Vienna Convention does not give adjudicators any such freedom or discretion. What the Vienna Convention does is to lay down clear guidance as to when preparatory work should be used. International judicial bodies do not perceive themselves as endowed with discretionary powers but follow carefully the sequence laid down in the Convention.

(b) Preparatory Work in Judicial Practice

The approach whereby preparatory work is accorded only secondary importance has enjoyed long-standing support in jurisprudence. In *Agricultural Labour* the Permanent Court refused to examine the preparatory work, considering that the construction of the treaty text enabled it to reach an outcome.[343] In *Treaty of Lausanne*, the Permanent Court rejected the outcome that would follow from recourse to the *travaux*: if the *travaux* affirmed that the League of Nations Council could not decide on the frontier between Turkey and Iraq without the agreement of the parties, the Council's role would be reduced to mere mediation and would eliminate the possibility of a definite decision. Such an attitude contradicted the text of Article 3 of the Lausanne Treaty and was therefore inadmissible.[344]

In the *Admissions* case, the International Court stated that if 'the words in their natural and ordinary meaning are ambiguous or lead to an unreasonable result, then, and only then, must the Court, by resort to other methods of interpretation, seek to ascertain what the parties really did mean when they used these words'. In this case some States had invited the Court to resort to the *travaux preparatoires* to ascertain the meaning of the relevant UN Charter provision. However, the Court considered that due to the clarity of the text 'it is not permissible, in this case, to resort to *travaux preparatoires*'.[345] Judge Alvarez in his Dissenting Opinion suggested that it is necessary to exclude *travaux preparatoires* from consideration when interpreting treaties, because they embody changing and inconsistent attitudes, States are often not familiar with them and they may prevent treaties from being in harmony with the new conditions of social life.[346] Even after resorting to the *travaux*, no guarantee of clarity and certainty can be

[342] Matsushita, Schoenbaum & Mavroidis (2006), 39.

[343] *Question of Jaworzina (Polish-Czechoslovakian Frontier)*, Advisory Opinion of 6 December 1923, *PCIJ Series* B, No 8, 6 at 41.

[344] *Article 3, Paragraph 2, of the Treaty of Lausanne*, Advisory Opinion of 21 November 1925, *PCIJ Series* B, No 12, 6 at 22–23.

[345] *Admissions* (Advisory Opinion), *ICJ Reports*, 1950, 8; in the *IMCO* case, the Court also referred to the *travaux preparatoires* of the IMCO constitution to confirm the outcome of textual interpretation, *ICJ Reports*, 1960, 162–165; see also *Ambatielos* (Preliminary Objections), *ICJ Reports* 1952, 45, and the *Night Work* case, 378–380.

[346] *Admissions*, 18 (Dissenting Opinion).

provided. As the Court observed in *US Nationals in Morocco*, the *travaux* of the 1906 Conference of Algeciras did not provide much guidance.[347]

In the *IMCO* Advisory Opinion, the International Court examined the *travaux* of Article 28(a) of the IMCO Convention to confirm the meaning of this article it inferred from textual, contextual and purposive interpretation.[348] In *Libya–Chad*, the International Court considered that 'it is not necessary to refer to the *travaux preparatoires* to elucidate the content of the 1955 Treaty; but, as in previous cases, it finds it possible by reference to the *travaux* to confirm its reading of the text, namely, that the Treaty constitutes an agreement between the parties which, *inter alia,* defines the frontiers', ie the outcome that had already been identified by the Court through resort to the text, context and the principle of effectiveness. The relevant *travaux* demonstrated that the parties intended to determine the frontier as well as recognise the boundaries determined through their earlier treaties.[349]

In *Kasikili/Sedudu*, the International Court examined the circumstances of the conclusion of the 1890 British-Germany Treaty and arrived at the same conclusion as followed from examination of the text. The Court pointed out that the British side suggested inserting into Article III a reference to the main channel of the River Chobe and the German side accepted that.[350] In *Libya–Chad* the International Court considered that it was not necessary to refer to the *travaux preparatoires* to elucidate the content of the 1955 French-Libyan Treaty. But the Court found the *travaux* helpful for confirming the outcome of the textual interpretation that it had reached earlier in the case. The evidence that the parties did not wish to end negotiations without a settlement of the frontiers issue and that the records mentioned the 'demarcation' of the frontiers proved that the parties viewed the frontiers as effected in terms of the text of the Treaty.[351]

In *LaGrand*, the Court, having affirmed the binding force of its provisional measures under Article 41 of the Statute on the basis of its object and purpose, held that 'it does not consider it necessary to resort to the preparatory work in order to determine the meaning of that Article'. Nevertheless, the Court decided to examine the *travaux*, pointing out that 'the preparatory work of the Statute does not preclude the conclusion that orders under Article 41 have binding force'. In examining the *travaux*, the Court acknowledged that 'the preparatory work of Article 41 shows that the preference [was] given in the French [authentic] text to "*indiquer*" over "*ordonner*" ', but explained this by the consideration that the Court did not have the means to assure the execution of its decisions. 'However,'

[347] *ICJ Reports,* 1952, 209; in *Danube Commission*, preparatory work was confidential and the Court was not called upon to take it into account, *Jurisdiction of the European Commission of the Danube*, Advisory Opinion of 8 December 1927, *PCIJ Series* B, No 14, 5 at 32.

[348] *ICJ Reports*, 1960, 161ff.

[349] *ICJ Reports*, 1994, 27–28.

[350] *Kasikili/Sedudu*, para 46.

[351] *ICJ Reports*, 1994, 27–28.

the Court continued, 'the lack of means of execution and the lack of binding force are two different matters. Hence, the fact that the Court does not itself have the means to ensure the execution of orders made pursuant to Article 41 is not an argument against the binding nature of such orders.'[352]

But whatever the motivation behind replacing '*ordonner*' by '*indiquer*', the fact remains that such replacement did take place. It is perfectly arguable that the terminology in Article 41 was chosen on the basis of the approach that as the Court has no means to enforce its orders, it should not have the power to order binding provisional measures. Even if unacceptable to the present writer as an argument, this could be a defensible reading of the *travaux*. Therefore, the *travaux* did at least potentially conflict with the Court's interpretative outcome reached on the basis of the text and the aim of the Statute. The Court thus implicitly adopted the view that *travaux* that conflict with the text and aim of the treaty shall not be treated as relevant.

In addition, it is noteworthy that the Court used the words 'not preclude' in relation to the outcome of textual and teleological interpretation, instead of the word 'confirm' that is used in Article 32 of the Vienna Convention in relation to the interpretative outcomes arrived at through the use of the General Rule of Interpretation under Article 31. This may be an implicit acknowledgment by the Court that the *travaux* did not positively 'confirm' its interpretation of Article 41, and also strengthens the view that the Court is ready to overrule the *travaux* if they contradict the text and aim of the treaty.

As in other cases, the Court did not find it necessary to resort to preparatory work in the *Ligitan/Sipadan* case. But the Court decided to resort to the *travaux* to 'seek a possible confirmation of its interpretation of the text of the [1891 Anglo-Dutch] Convention'.[353] The Court found that once the parties to the Convention agreed on the partition of Sebatik, they were only interested in the boundary on the island of Borneo and did not exchange views on an allocation of the islands in the open seas to the east of Sebatik. Therefore, the *travaux* did not support the position of Indonesia when it contended that the parties agreed not only on a land boundary but also on an allocation line beyond the east coast of Sebatik.[354]

The Arbitral Tribunal in *Iron Rhine* described some limitations as to what may validly constitute preparatory work for the purpose of interpretation. The Tribunal noted that the parties had provided extracts of prolonged diplomatic negotiations leading to the conclusion of the 1839 Separation Treaty between Belgium and the Netherlands, but these did not have the character of *travaux preparatoires* on which the Tribunal could safely rely in terms of Article 32 of the Vienna Convention. In particular, these extracts possibly showed 'the desire

352 *LaGrand*, Judgment of 27 June 2001, para 107.
353 *Ligitan/Sipadan*, para 53.
354 *Id*, paras 57–58.

or understanding of one or other of the Parties at particular moments in the extended negotiations, but [did] not serve the purpose of illuminating a common understanding as to the meaning of the various provisions of Article XII [of the 1839 Treaty]'.[355] In the *Young Loan* arbitration, the Tribunal used the *travaux* to confirm the meaning of the treaty provision established under Article 31(1) of the Vienna Convention.[356]

The European Court of Human Rights is consistently sceptical as to the role of preparatory work. In *Golder*, the European Court refused to resort to the *travaux* under Article 32 of the Vienna Convention, because it had already interpreted the European Convention in terms of its object and purpose.[357] In *Lawless*, the Irish Government referred to the *travaux* of the European Convention on Human Rights which arguably upheld the position that individuals can be detained for the purpose of prevention of crime without the requirement of being brought before a judge. The European Commission submitted that 'in accordance with a well-established rule concerning the interpretation of international treaties, it is not permissible to resort to preparatory work when the meaning of the clauses to be construed is clear and unequivocal',[358] which certainly applied with regard to Article 5(3) involved in the case. The Court did not take the preparatory work into account. It observed that 'having also found that the meaning of this text is in keeping with the purpose of the Convention, the Court cannot, having regard to a generally recognised principle regarding the interpretation of international treaties, resort to the preparatory work'.[359]

The WTO law regime of treaty interpretation emphasises the modest role of preparatory work in this process. As the WTO Panel emphasised in *Korea–Government Procurement*, the reference to the customary law of interpretation in Article 3.2 DSU is due to the fact that in past practice 'reliance on negotiating history was being utilized in a manner arguably inconsistent with the requirements of the rules of treaty interpretation of customary international law'.[360] This confirms that the difference between hierarchical order of the General Rule and supplementary means of interpretation acquires primary importance in WTO law.

In *US–Shrimps* the Appellate Body confirmed, by resorting to the 1946 International Trade Organisation (ITO) negotiating history, the interpretative result achieved by the use of the General Rule. The preparatory work thus confirmed the Appellate Body's understanding that the exception clauses under Article XX GATT require assessment of the conduct of the State both under

355 *Iron Rhine*, para 48.

356 Belgium et al. v Federal Republic of Germany (*Young Loan Arbitration*), Award of 16 May 1980, 19 ILM (1980), 1357.

357 *Golder*, para 36.

358 *Lawless*, paras 10–11.

359 *Id*, para 14.

360 *Korea–Measures affecting Government Procurement*, Report of the Panel, WT/DS163/R, 1 May 2000 (00–1679), para 7.96 (fn. 753).

specific exceptions and its general chapeau.[361] In *US–Section 211*, the Appellate Body reversed the Panel's interpretative outcome, following its use of the preparatory work, as contrary to the ordinary meaning of the relevant treaty clause. According to the Appellate Body, the recourse to the negotiating history was not decisive.[362] In *US–Gasoline*, the Appellate Body evaluated the relevance of the preparatory documents thus:

> We do not accept, as the Panel appears to have done, that, simply by requesting the preparation and circulation of these documents and using them in preparing their offers, the parties in the negotiations have accepted them as agreements or instruments related to the treaty. Indeed, there are indications to the contrary.

The Panel, most importantly, had invoked no evidence to prove that these documents were meant not merely as preparatory but also interpretative tools for interpreting GATS and schedules of commitments.[363]

In *US–Gambling*, the Appellate Body resorted to preparatory work because none of the other interpretative factors, such as the plain meaning, context and the object and purpose of the US Schedule of Commitments revealed its clear meaning.[364] The Appellate Body considered certain documents as part of preparatory work after having rejected their role as context under Article 31 of the Vienna Convention. As the Appellate Body stated:

> W/120 and the 1993 Scheduling Guidelines were prepared and circulated at the request of parties to the Uruguay Round negotiations for the express purpose of assisting those parties in the preparation of their offers. These documents undoubtedly served, too, to assist parties in reviewing and evaluating the offers made by others. They provided a common language and structure which, although not obligatory, was widely used and relied upon. In such circumstances, and in the light of the specific guidance provided in the 1993 Scheduling Guidelines, it is reasonable to assume that parties to the negotiations examining a sector of a Schedule that tracked so closely the language of the same sector in W/120 would—absent a clear indication to the contrary—have expected the sector to have the same coverage as the corresponding W/120 sector.[365]

On that basis, the Appellate Body concluded that the inclusion of gambling and betting as 'other recreational services' in subsector 10.D of the US Schedule was dictated by the treatment under W/120 of gambling and betting as part of these 'other recreational services'.[366]

Thus there appears to be only one international case decided through the use of preparatory work. This is the *US–Gambling* case in which the

[361] *US–Shrimp*, paras 152–157.
[362] *US–Section 211 Omnibus Appropriations Act of 1998*, Appellate Body Report, WT/DS176/AB/R, 1 February 2001, paras 339–340.
[363] *US–Gambling*, paras 176–177.
[364] *Id*, para 197.
[365] *Id*, para 204.
[366] *Id*, para 208.

preparatory work was used after all other methods failed, and only through rigorous evaluation of all materials. When an interpretative outcome is arrived at on the basis of treaty text and its object and purpose, the preparatory work is simply irrelevant, as follows from the interpretative policy repeatedly stated in the Vienna Convention and in jurisprudence.

11

Treaty Interpretation: Effectiveness and Presumptions

1. The Principle of Effectiveness

(a) Essence and Reach

A preliminary question likely to arise, quite apart from the affirmation of the principle of effectiveness by all relevant authorities, is why this principle needs to guide the treaty interpretation process at all. If we take as a starting point the approach of Brierly and Lauterpacht that international law is as binding in the international society as national law is within the State, then we should also accept that international legal rules should apply and operate with effectiveness relating to their scope and intendment. Without the principle of effectiveness the clarification of the real scope of treaty obligations would be difficult, and the narrowing down of treaty obligations through political manipulation would become possible. The principle of effectiveness is indispensable for ensuring that treaties have their proper effect. Arguments related to the structure of international law as a decentralised system operating between sovereign equals could provide no viable objection. This explains why the need for effective interpretation of treaties was recognised at early stages of doctrinal development. As Phillimore emphasised, 'When a provision or clause in a Treaty is capable of two significations, it should be understood in that one which will allow it to operate, rather than in that which will deny to it effect.' Furthermore 'When the same provision or sentence expresses two meanings, that one which most conduces to carry into effect the end and object of the Convention, should be adopted.'[1] An attempt at ineffective interpretion of a treaty can in some circumstances be equal to breach of the treaty, thus triggering the remedies available to the contracting parties under Article 60 of the Vienna Convention on the Law of Treaties.

Another, more practical, question relates to the way presumptions should operate in the context of effective interpretation. What should be effective: obligations, rights, primary provisions, exceptions to those primary provisions, or object and purpose?

[1] R Phillimore, *Commentaries upon International Law* (1855), vol II, 76–77.

As we can see from today's legal position, the effectiveness requirement operates not in a free-standing way, but as part of the General Rule of Interpretation under Article 31(1) of the Vienna Convention. This requirement concerns the effectiveness of treaty obligations embodied in the text, in light of the object and purpose of the treaty. What should be effective is the enterprise included in the treaty. The requirement of effectiveness cannot make treaty obligations expand to other objects or aspects of life, or justify inroads into State sovereignty that do not relate to that object. A treaty clause operating effectively in pursuing and safeguarding the object of the treaty is not the same as its contribution to making, in general terms, the international legal system or the life of international society more efficient. The principle of effectiveness is aimed at construing the original consent and agreement of States-parties effectively and not as unreal and illusory.

McNair considered the principle of effectiveness as limited in its importance, merely emphasising that the treaty must have some purpose.[2] The treatment of this issue both in doctrine and practice demonstrates that the implications of the principle of effectiveness are considerably wider. According to Thirlway, the principle of effectiveness can have two possible manifestations. One option is to ensure that none of the provisions in the treaty is deprived of meaning. The other option is to secure that the treaty is effective in achieving its objects.[3] As further analysis of the jurisprudence demonstrates, the genuine essence of the principle of effectiveness combines both those characteristics.

The scholar who championed the doctrine of effective interpretation of international treaties was Hersch Lauterpacht. His analysis of international practice links the principle of effectiveness to the finality of international adjudication and of boundary and territorial settlements, in the sense that no issue covered by the relevant treaty must be left unsettled.[4] The International Court is determined in its practice 'to secure a full degree of effectiveness of international law, in particular of the obligations undertaken by parties to treaties'.[5]

Lauterpacht considers that the principle of effectiveness is threatened by the thesis of restrictive interpretation and the deliberate inconclusiveness of a treaty embodying a compromise attempted but not actively achieved. He also objects to treating interpretation as a political issue and states that in the absence of adequate standards, treaties concluded by governments 'may become political instruments safeguarding their freedom of action instead of being source of their legal obligations'.[6]

[2] AD McNair, *The Law of Treaties* (1961), 385.

[3] H Thirlway, The Law and Procedure of the International Court of Justice 1960–1989, *BYIL* (1994), 1 at 44.

[4] H Lauterpacht, *The Development of International Law by the International Court* (1958), 231ff.

[5] *Id*, 227.

[6] *Id*, 227.

Arguably there may be cases where there is no intention of rendering the treaty fully effective, but:

> it is in relation to that contingency that the principle *ut res magis valeat quam pereat* assumes a complexion of urgency and importance. This is a major principle, in the light of which the intention of the parties must be interpreted even to the extent of disregarding the letter of the instrument and of reading into it something which, on the face of it, it does not contain—so long as that 'something' is not contradicted by available and permissible evidence of the intention of the parties.[7]

Thus, the effectiveness of treaty regulation can be assumed to exist if it follows from the purpose and general design of the treaty, and even in the face of the silence of the treaty regarding the particular matter in question. At the same time, not every single piece of evidence of the intention of parties can undermine the effectiveness and completeness of treaty regulation. This would above all concern the extraneous manifestation of intention[8] or preparatory work.

Lauterpacht's approach has several implications. In the first place, it addresses the issue of silence of treaty regulation and thereby follows the more general thesis on completeness of international legal regulation in general.[9] In addition, Lauterpacht's approach has indeed guided much judicial practice of different tribunals at later stages, including the effectiveness approach adopted by the European Court of Human Rights, as well as the approach of the International Court of Justice regarding the implied powers of international organisations and inherent powers of international tribunals which are not expressly specified in the relevant constituent instrument, yet are necessary to enable the relevant institution to perform its functions.[10]

According to Lauterpacht, the principle of effectiveness requires rejecting an interpretation that results in maintaining an uncertain and precarious position. As is specified, 'the object of the law is order, not perpetuation of disagreements.'[11] This approach goes hand in hand with the more general approach that an alleged lack of common intention shall not render treaty obligations unworkable.[12] According to this thesis, if the relevant subject matter falls within international legal regulation, no attitude can be taken in favour of the absence of rules that regulate it. Consequently, if the relevant matter is covered by a treaty, and if the situation in relation to that matter is related to the meaningful operation of the treaty's structure and object and purpose, it has to be seen as providing rules to regulate that matter.

[7] *Id*, 228.

[8] As Lauterpacht emphasised, governments are likely to argue that the relevant legal obligation does not correspond to their intention. In response the International Court will 'extract from them every reasonable measure of effectiveness', *id*, 228.

[9] See above Chapter 1.

[10] See below Section 5.

[11] Lauterpacht (1958), 233–234.

[12] See above Chapters 9 and 10.

Lauterpacht also elaborates upon the interaction between effective interpretation and sovereignty of States, observing that 'Interpretation resulting in effectiveness, as distinguished from ineffectiveness or limited effectiveness, of treaty obligations implies a limitation of sovereignty—although such limitation may be the consequence of an obligation freely undertaken.'[13] In essence, the principle of effectiveness is no more than a requirement of good faith, and provides that 'good faith requires no more than the effect be given, in a fair and reasonable manner, to the intention of the parties'. On occasion 'good faith may require that the effectiveness of the instrument should fall short of its apparent and desirable scope'[14] and thus, the principle of effectiveness is implied in the consensual basis of treaties.

Bernhardt considers that the principle of effectiveness has to be recognised to the extent that it gives expression to the text, in a way that its construction is conducive to the purposes of the treaty. But this principle can be a source of concern if the point of departure for effectiveness is not the treaty text but its general objects and purposes with the desire to achieve the most effective regulation. This approach could result in creating new rights and obligations that were not intended by the parties.[15]

The principle of effectiveness can either mean that the common intention of parties, even if allegedly incomplete, must be rescued. It could also give rise to an assumption that the parties desired the widest possible treaty regulation in order to avoid future disputes. This would require an interpretation according to which the treaty covers all issues within its reach (*alle irgendwie erreichbare Fälle*).[16] At the same time, the use of the effectiveness principle cannot justify going beyond the treaty regulation.[17] If the principle of effectiveness is given too large a scope, it can amount to a broad teleological approach and cause matters to be read into the treaty in pursuing the perceived object and purpose. This would not amount to a good faith textual interpretation.[18]

This analysis confirms that the principle of effectiveness is essentially an incidence of the requirement of completeness of legal regulation. As is known, completeness of legal regulation relates not to international law governing the entirety of international relations, but to the completeness of the actually adopted

[13] Lauterpacht (1958), 298.

[14] Lauterpacht (1958), 292; this version, however, is not Lauterpacht's principal version of the principle of effectiveness. Under this version, Lauterpacht refers, among other things, to the construction of non-binding instruments. As judicial practice demonstrates, more acceptance is gained by that version of effectiveness which gives treaty provisions the maximum scope deducible from their textual meaning and object and purpose.

[15] Bernhardt (1963), 96.

[16] HF Köck, *Vertragsinterpretation und Vertragsrechtskonvention. Zur Bedeutung der Artikel 31 und 32 der Wiener Vertragsrechtskonvention 1969* (1976), 49–50.

[17] *Id*, 50.

[18] M Lennard, Navigating by the Stars: Interpreting the WTO Agreements, 5 *JIEL* (2002), 19 at 60.

legal regulation in relation to its subject matter.[19] Thus, the completeness of treaty regulation presupposes the principle of effectiveness which ensures that the relevant treaty applies to the complete subject matter which it covers and regulates. It does not imply the use of 'methods' plural to create a new legal regulation which does not follow from the original agreement.

Effectiveness of interpretation relates to the effectiveness of what has been agreed between the parties, not to supplementing the product of agreement by whatever would make it more effective. It could be argued in specific cases that if the parties had agreed to assume more complex obligations than they actually did the entire treaty enterprise would have been more effective. But this is not what the interpretative principle of effectiveness is about. It is about construing effectively what the parties actually agreed on. Seen from this perspective, it is definitionally impossible for the parties to have agreed on rendering the treaty not fully effective.

Fitzmaurice defines the principle of effectiveness by stating that 'treaties are to be interpreted with reference to their declared or apparent objects and purposes; and particular provisions are to be interpreted so as to give them their fullest weight and effect consistent with the normal sense of the words and with other parts of the text, and in such a way that a reason and a meaning can be attributed to every part of the text'.[20] During the ILC codification work, Special Rapporteur Waldock proposed formulating the effectiveness rule so as to give effect to the plain meaning and the object and purpose of the treaty. This followed from the recognition of textual primacy in jurisprudence. The Commission accepted this approach, and reinforced it by placing the relevance of the object and purpose of the treaty just after the treaty's plain meaning.[21] At the final stage of codification, the Commission affirmed that the rule of effectiveness is reflected in the rule that a treaty shall be interpreted in accordance with its plain meaning and its object and purpose. The Commission further stated that 'when a treaty is open to two interpretations one of which does and the other does not enable the treaty to have appropriate effects, good faith and the objects and purposes of the treaty demand that the former interpretation should be adopted'.[22] Given that the Commission adopted this approach even for cases where the meaning of the text admits of two different interpretations, it should not be difficult to understand how cogent the principle of effectiveness becomes when the meaning of the treaty text is clear and straightforward on its face.

The Commission adopted the version of effectiveness that locates it in terms of the text of the treaty. It fell short of encouraging liberal or extensive interpretation

[19] See above, Chapter 2.

[20] G Fitzmaurice, *Law and Procedure of the International Court* (1986), 345.

[21] II *YbILC* 1964, 60–61, 199, 201.

[22] II *YbILC* 1966, 219; see also Ch de Visscher *Problèmes d'interprétation judiciaire en droit international public* (1963), 86.

of treaties for ensuring their 'effectiveness', because this could encourage attempts to expand illegitimately the meaning of treaty provisions.[23]

It is presumably right to say that the principle of effectiveness is reinforced by the principle of good faith, as is duly mentioned in Article 31(1) of the Vienna Convention. The principle of good faith indeed relates both to fulfilment of treaty obligations and interpretation of treaty provisions. In relation to this latter field, its function is to preclude States-parties from adopting views and positions that misrepresent the genuine content of what they have undertaken through the treaty. But effectiveness is more than adherence to good faith, and relates to the understanding of the actual content of treaty provisions. In this sense, the relevance of the principle of good faith is consequential upon the effective construction of treaty provisions and interpretative outcome thus obtained. The effective construction itself follows from the need to favour the interpretation conducive to that object and purpose over that which is likely to curtail it.

(b) Application in Jurisprudence

The principle of effectiveness has found multiple application in jurisprudence. In its Advisory Opinion on *Agricultural Labour*, the Permanent Court examined the question whether the competence of the International Labour Organisation included the regulation of agriculture. The Court examined the meaning of the term 'industry' as used in ILO instruments and concluded that it covered agriculture. Most importantly, the Court observed that 'every argument used for the exclusion of agriculture might with equal force be used for the exclusion of navigation and fisheries'.[24] This would unjustifiably restrict the competence of the Organisation.

In *Treaty of Lausanne*, the Permanent Court affirmed that the purpose of Article 3, paragraph 2, of the Lausanne Treaty had been 'to bring about a definitive and binding settlement of the [Iraqi-Turkish] frontier'. Therefore, the decision of the League of Nations Council on the basis of that provision could not be seen as a recommendation. Such a recommendation would not settle the dispute.[25] In the *Night Work* case as well, the plain meaning of the treaty was used for effective interpretation.

In *Acquisition of Polish Nationality*, the Permanent Court had to interpret a clause from the minorities' treaty, according to which Poland undertook to recognise as its nationals persons of German, Austrian, Russian and Hungarian origin who were born in the territory or whose parents habitually resided there. Poland argued that only those Germans could claim its nationality whose parents were resident in Poland both on the date of the birth of the individual and at the date of the entry into force of the Treaty. The Court observed that such

[23] II *YbILC* 1966, 219.

[24] *Agricultural Labour*, Advisory Opinion of 12 August 1922, *PCIJ Series* B, Nos 2 & 3, 6 at 41.

[25] *Article 3, Paragraph 2, of the Treaty of Lausanne*, Advisory Opinion of 21 November 1925, *PCIJ Series* B, No 12, 6 at 28.

an interpretation would diminish greatly the value of the treaty and was inadmissible.[26] The construction was preferred that required the presence of parents in Poland only when the child was born. This is a classic illustration of how the principle of effectiveness prevails over the restrictive interpretation.

In *US Nationals in Morocco*, the International Court referred to the principle of 'economic liberty without any inequality' fixed in a number of treaties and observed that this principle was intended as a binding principle, not merely an empty phrase.[27] In *Libya–Chad*, the Court adhered to the principle of effectiveness, by reference to *Treaty of Lausanne*. The Court observed that the manifest intention of the parties was that the instruments referred to in the 1955 Treaty 'would indicate, cumulatively, all the frontiers between the parties, and that no frontier taken in isolation would be left out of that arrangement'. Article 3 conveyed the intention to settle all frontiers definitively, and 'any other construction would be contrary to one of the fundamental principles of interpretation of treaties, consistently upheld by international jurisprudence, namely that of effectiveness'.[28] It was not crucial whether the relevant treaties were ratified earlier. To be effective, Article 3 of the 1955 Treaty had to be seen as encompassing all frontiers between Libya and Chad, not just those *per se* deriving from earlier ratified treaties.

In *Ligitan/Sipadan*, Indonesia pleaded the principle of effectiveness, pointing out in line with the *Treaty of Lausanne* case that treaty provisions allocating boundaries must be interpreted as conclusive and complete. Therefore, the 1891 Anglo-Dutch Convention which dealt with the boundary in the north-eastern region of Borneo, should be interpreted as doing so in all relevant areas.[29] The Court itself did not comment on the principle of effectiveness in this case, which is a question-begging approach. If the principle of effectiveness was relevant, the Court ought to have applied it; if it was immaterial, the Court ought to have stated this. The shortcomings in the Court's reasoning are presumably mitigated by the Court's reference to the object and purpose of the 1891 Convention to support its interpretation.[30] Still, the silence on this issue in the Judgment signifies the failure to confront one of the most important interpretative principles and leaves unanswered the question whether it is arguable that the case should have been decided otherwise.

The *Peace Treaties* case offers a very peculiar treatment of the principle of effectiveness. In this case, the International Court had to interpret a treaty clause providing that the two States had to appoint one member each of the arbitration commission and the third member, if the parties could not agree on his identity,

[26] *Acquisition of Polish Nationality*, Advisory Opinion of 15 September 1923, *PCIJ Series* B, No 7, 6 at 13, 16–17.

[27] *Rights of Nationals of United States of America in Morocco* (France v USA), Judgment of 27 August 1952, *ICJ Reports*, 1952, 176 at 184, 191.

[28] *ICJ Reports*, 1994, 24–25.

[29] *Sovereignty over Pulau Ligitan and Pulau Sipadan* (Indonesia/Malaysia), Judgment of 17 December 2002, General List No 102, para. 49.

[30] See above Chapter 10.

was to be appointed by the UN Secretary-General. The Court was asked to determine the legal consequences of the failure of a State to appoint an arbitrator and whether the Secretary-General was entitled to appoint the third member.[31] The Court rejected the argument that the 'third member' was merely a neutral member to be distinguished from party-appointed arbitrators, and concluded that the Secretary-General was not entitled to select the third member just because the parties had not selected him before:

> The Court considers that the text of the Treaties does not admit of this interpretation. While the text in its literal sense does not completely exclude the possibility of the appointment of the third member before the appointment of both national commissioners, it is nevertheless true that according to the natural and ordinary meaning of the terms it was intended that the appointment of both the national commissioners should precede that of the third member. This clearly results from the sequence of the events contemplated by the article: appointment of a national Commissioner by each party; selection of a third member by mutual agreement of the parties; failing such agreement within a month, his appointment by the Secretary-General. Moreover, this is the normal order followed in the practice of arbitration, and in the absence of any express provision to the contrary there is no reason to suppose that the parties wished to depart from it. . . .
>
> The rule of effectiveness cannot justify the Court in attributing to the provisions for the settlement of disputes in the Peace Treaties a meaning which, as stated above, would be contrary to their letter and spirit.[32]

The Court admitted that the text can have two different meanings. In such cases it had to resort to the object and purpose and the principle of effectiveness. But in the passage excluding the relevance of the principle of effectiveness the Court proceeds from the assumption that the text has only one established meaning, which is not quite consistent. While it is perfectly true that the principle of effectiveness does not justify the revision of treaties as opposed to their interpretation, the choice between the two alternatives in *Peace Treaties* did not present such a risk.

As for the 'normal order' followed in the practice of arbitration, the treaty is *lex specialis* and aimed to achieve its object and purpose. That in other cases a certain order of appointment is provided for does not mean that the Treaty cannot lead to a different outcome if its object and purpose so require and moreover its text admits this as one of the possibilities. The Court's approach, instead of the stated preference for the textual approach, is in fact based on restrictive interpretation, as confirmed by this passage from the Opinion:

> The Secretary-General's power to appoint a third member is derived solely from the agreement. . . . by its very nature such a clause must be strictly construed and can be applied only in the case expressly provided therein.[33]

[31] *ICJ Reports*, 1950, 226.
[32] *Id*, 227, 229.
[33] *Id*, 227.

Peace Treaties is also incompatible with the outcome the Court arrived at in *Admissibility of Hearings*, where the Court established that, due to the failure of the Mandatory for South-West Africa to cooperate with the Committee for South-West Africa in conducting the consideration of petitions, the Committee was entitled to conduct the hearing of petitions, even if this was not originally part of the agreement. The Mandatory was bound by its obligations and this required the 'effective supervision' of performance and the 'real protection' of the relevant rights. The Committee had to work effectively and the lack of cooperation from the Mandatory prevented that. Therefore, the Committee had the right to conduct hearings.[34]

The principle of effectiveness found unconditional acceptance with the European Court of Human Rights. In *Wemhoff*, the European Court examined the permissible length of detention of individuals under Article 5(3) of the European Convention. The Court had to 'ascertain whether the end of the period of detention with which Article 5(3) is concerned is the day on which a conviction becomes final or simply that on which the charge is determined, even if only by a court of first instance'. In choosing between the two possible understandings of the clause in Article 5 of the European Convention, the European Court held that it was necessary:

> to seek the interpretation that is most appropriate in order to realize the aim and achieve the object of the treaty, not that which would restrict to the greatest possible degree the obligations undertaken by the Parties.[35]

The *Golder* case before the European Court involved a situation in which the Home Secretary had not allowed the Applicant to consult a solicitor with a view to bringing a civil action. The question was whether this violated the Applicant's rights under Article 6, even though this provision does not expressly admit of the right to access to a court.[36] The Court observed that:

> Were Article 6(1) to be understood as concerning exclusively the conduct of an action which had already been initiated before a court, a Contracting State could, without acting in breach of that text, do away with its courts, or take away their jurisdiction to determine certain classes of civil actions and entrust it to organs dependent on the

[34] *Admissibility of Hearings of Petitioners by the Committee on South-West Africa*, Advisory Opinion, 1 June 1956, *ICJ Reports*, 1956, 23 at 27–28, 30–32.

[35] *Wemhoff*, ECtHR Judgment of 27 June 1968, Series A, No 7, para 8. More specifically, the Court pointed out in para 7, in relation to choosing between the versions of the text in different languages, that 'The Court cannot accept this restrictive interpretation. It is true that the English text of the Convention allows such an interpretation. The word "trial", which appears there on two occasions, refers to the whole of the proceedings before the court, not just their beginning; the words "entitled to trial" are not necessarily to be equated with "entitled to be brought to trial", although in the context "pending trial" seems to require release before the trial considered as a whole, that is, before its opening. But while the English text permits two interpretations the French version, which is of equal authority, allows only one. According to it the obligation to release an accused person within a reasonable time continues until that person has been "jugée", that is, until the day of the judgment that terminates the trial. Moreover, he must be released "pendant la procédure", a very broad expression which indubitably covers both the trial and the investigation.'

[36] *Golder v UK*, 4451/70, Judgment of 21 February 1975, para 26.

Government. Such assumptions, indissociable from a danger of arbitrary power, would have serious consequences which are repugnant to the aforementioned principles and which the Court cannot overlook.

It would be inconceivable, in the opinion of the Court, that Article 6(1) should describe in detail the procedural guarantees afforded to parties in a pending lawsuit and should not first protect that which alone makes it in fact possible to benefit from such guarantees, that is, access to a court. The fair, public and expeditious characteristics of judicial proceedings are of no value at all if there are no judicial proceedings.[37]

Therefore, the right of access constituted an inherent element of the right to a fair trial. The Court also observed that its interpretation was not an extensive interpretation but interpretation on the basis of the text and the object and purpose of the treaty.[38]

The Court's reasoning was opposed by Judge Fitzmaurice, who accused the Court of confusing access to a court with a fair hearing after such access. As the right to access to a court was an important right, that very importance required its explicit recognition in the Convention.[39] As for interpretative policy, Fitzmaurice argued that:

These various factors could justify even a somewhat restrictive interpretation of the Convention but, without going as far as that, they must be said, unquestionably, not only to justify, but positively to demand, a cautious and conservative interpretation, particularly as regards any provisions the meaning of which may be uncertain, and where extensive constructions might have the effect of imposing upon the contracting States obligations they had not really meant to assume, or would not have understood themselves to be assuming.[40]

It can only be asked what real difference persists between restrictive interpretation and the so-called 'cautious and conservative interpretation' that Fitzmaurice advocated. It hardly needs emphasising that this approach has never been adopted by the European Court.

In *Belgian Linguistics*, the European Court adopted the effective interpretation of Article 2 Protocol 1 to the European Convention. The Court emphasised that:

For the 'right to education' to be effective, it is further necessary that, inter alia, the individual who is the beneficiary should have the possibility of drawing profit from the education received, that is to say, the right to obtain, in conformity with the rules in force in each State, and in one form or another, official recognition of the studies which he has completed.[41]

Such requirement of official recognition is not stipulated in Article 2, yet it has to be observed if the right to education is construed effectively.

[37] *Id*, para 35.

[38] *Id*, para 36.

[39] *Id*, Separate Opinion, paras 21, 32.

[40] *Id*, Separate Opinion, para 39.

[41] *Belgian Linguistics*, Application Nos 1474/62, 1677/62, 1691/62, 1769/63, 1994/63 & 2126/64, Judgment of 23 July 1968, Section I.B, para 4.

In several other cases, the European Court stated its policy to interpret the Convention safeguards so as to make them practical and effective, not theoretical and illusory. In *Artico*, the European Court found that Article 6 of the Convention required granting free legal aid to the Applicant.[42] In *Soering*, this interpretation enabled the Court to construe the prohibition of torture under Article 3 as extending not just to actual torture but also to extradition to the State in which the observance of Article 3 was at risk.[43] The Court faced the plea of absence in Article 3 of an indication that an extradition likely to lead in another country to a result outlawed under Article 3 would itself be prohibited by that Article. References were even made to other treaties, such as the 1984 UN Convention against Torture, Article 3 of which—unlike Article 3 of the European Convention—prohibits such extradition in express terms. The Court responded that 'The fact that a specialized treaty should spell out in detail a specific obligation attaching to the prohibition of torture does not mean that an essentially similar obligation is not already inherent in the general terms of Article 3 of the European Convention.' The Court further adopted a teleological perspective and noted that 'Extradition in such circumstances, while not explicitly referred to in the brief and general wording of Article 3, would plainly be contrary to the spirit and intendment of the Article.'[44] The effectiveness of the treaty clause was thus upheld despite its silence on the particular point at issue.

In *Brogan v UK*, the European Court assessed the meaning of 'promptness' under Article 5(3) to exclude an interpretation which would reduce the relevant right to fiction:

> Whereas promptness is to be assessed in each case according to its special features, the significance to be attached to those features can never be taken to the point of impairing the very essence of the right guaranteed by Article 5(3), that is to the point of effectively negativing the State's obligation to ensure a prompt release or a prompt appearance before a judicial authority.[45]

This interpretation 'would import into Article 5(3) a serious weakening of a procedural guarantee to the detriment of the individual and would entail consequences impairing the very essence of the right protected by this provision'.[46] In *United Communist Party*, the European Court of Human Rights formulated the principle of effectiveness to ascertain the meaning of the freedom of association under Article 11 of the European Convention:

> The Court reiterates that the Convention is intended to guarantee rights that are not theoretical or illusory, but practical and effective. The right guaranteed by Article 11 would be largely theoretical and illusory if it were limited to the founding of an association, since the national authorities could immediately disband the association without having

[42] *Artico*, Application No 6694/74, Judgment of 13 May 1980, para 33.
[43] *Soering*, Application No 14038/88, Judgment of 7 July 1989, paras 87–88.
[44] *Id*, para 88.
[45] *Brogan*, para 59.
[46] *Id*, para 62.

to comply with the Convention. It follows that the protection afforded by Article 11 lasts for an association's entire life.[47]

In some cases the effectiveness of treaty provisions implies the existence of positive obligations in addition to what the text plainly states. Regarding the example of the right to life under the European Convention, the European Court of Human Rights emphasised in *Cyprus v Turkey* that 'the obligation to protect the right to life under Article 2 of the Convention, read in conjunction with the State's general duty under Article 1 to "secure to everyone within [its] jurisdiction the rights and freedoms defined in [the] Convention", requires by implication that there should be some form of effective official investigation when individuals have been killed as a result of the use of force by agents of the State'. To further enhance the effectiveness of Article 2, the European Court emphasised that the operation of this procedural obligation was not contingent upon proof of violation of the primary duty under Article 2. As the Court put it, 'the above-mentioned procedural obligation also arises upon proof of an arguable claim that an individual, who was last seen in the custody of agents of the State, subsequently disappeared in a context which may be considered life-threatening'.[48]

In the case of prohibition on torture and ill-treatment, the European Court construes the relevant positive obligations, emphasising that 'where an individual raises an arguable claim that he has been subjected to ill-treatment by agents of the State unlawfully and in breach of Article 3 of the Convention... that provision,... requires by implication that there should be an effective official investigation'.[49] This is meant to ensure that actual breaches are not left outside the primary prohibition on torture and ill-treatment when the violations are not yet proved beyond doubt.

The principle of effectiveness requires interpreting treaties so as to make them have an impact on the ground. In other words, treaty provisions have to be effective in terms of their factual implications.[50] This is clear from the treatment of the issue of expropriation by the European Court of Human Rights in the light of Article 1 of Protocol I. In *Sporrong and Lönnorth*, the European Court emphasised that in assessing the legality of the respondent Government's measures, 'it must look behind the appearances and investigate the realities of the situation complained of'. By reference to the principle that the Convention provisions must be construed so as to be practical and effective, 'it has to be ascertained whether that situation amounted to a de facto expropriation', even if the formal expropriation had not been undertaken. The Court emphasised that:

> all the effects complained of [following from the system of relevant permits and prohibitions] stemmed from the reduction of the possibility of disposing of the properties

[47] *United Communist Party v Turkey*, No 19392/92, 30 January 1998, para 33.
[48] *Cyprus v Turkey*, Application No 25781/94, Judgment of 10 May 2001, paras 131–132.
[49] *Poltoratskiy v Ukraine*, Application No 38812/97, Judgment of 29 April 2003, para 125.
[50] See also above Chapter 5.

concerned. Those effects were occasioned by limitations imposed on the right of property, which right had become precarious, and from the consequences of those limitations on the value of the premises. However, although the right in question lost some of its substance, it did not disappear. The effects of the measures involved are not such that they can be assimilated to a deprivation of possessions. The Court observes in this connection that the applicants could continue to utilise their possessions and that, although it became more difficult to sell properties in Stockholm affected by expropriation permits and prohibitions on construction, the possibility of selling subsisted.[51]

This means that there is a limit on the relevance of understanding the factual situation on the ground. It is not the factual situation that *per se* impacts the characterisation of the legality of the relevant government action. A factual situation can only have such impact as is subsumable within the legal concepts embodied in the relevant treaty clause. More specifically, in this particular case there was a serious factual impact on the property of the applicants. But the effective interpretation of Article 1 of the Protocol I encompassed only such factual impact as would fit within the notion of deprivation under that provision. Thus, the Government's action was not outlawed under the effective prohibition on expropriation in Protocol I.

A similar approach was affirmed in *Broniowski v Poland*. The Court formulated its task to judge the legality of the action of a State-party in its exercise of margin of appreciation as covering the entirety of actual activities of all pertinent organs of the State. As the Court emphasised:

In assessing compliance with Article 1 of Protocol No. 1, the Court must make an overall examination of the various interests in issue, bearing in mind that the Convention is intended to safeguard rights that are 'practical and effective'. It must look behind appearances and investigate the realities of the situation complained of. That assessment may involve not only the relevant compensation terms—if the situation is akin to the taking of property—but also the conduct of the parties, including the means employed by the State and their implementation. In that context, it should be stressed that uncertainty—be it legislative, administrative or arising from practices applied by the authorities—is a factor to be taken into account in assessing the State's conduct. Indeed, where an issue in the general interest is at stake, it is incumbent on the public authorities to act in good time, in an appropriate and consistent manner.[52]

This passage demonstrates that the Court would verify the conduct of the State-party in dynamic terms covering all its relevant organs and action at all relevant stages where the exercise of the pertinent Convention rights would be at stake. In this case, the assessment of the exercise of property rights included the assessment of legislation, as well as the state of its implementation.

[51] *Sporrong and Lönnorth*, Application Nos 7151/75 & 7152/75, Judgment of 23 September 1982, para 63.

[52] *Broniowski v Poland*, Application No 31443/96, Judgment of 22 June 2004, para 151.

The obvious and predominant relevance of the principle of effectiveness is confirmed by its application in relation to treaty provisions which fall short of imposing specific immediate obligations but only stipulate the obligations that depend on 'progressive realisation'. In interpreting Article 2 of the 1966 International Covenant on Economic, Social and Cultural Rights, which stipulates that States-parties shall take certain steps and measures 'with a view to achieving progressively the full realization of the rights recognized' in the Covenant, the UN Committee on Economic, Social and Cultural Rights admitted that 'The concept of progressive realization constitutes a recognition of the fact that full realization of all economic, social and cultural rights will generally not be able to be achieved in a short period of time.' Still, the Committee emphasised that flexibility notwithstanding:

> the phrase must be read in the light of the overall objective, indeed the *raison d'être*, of the Covenant which is to establish clear obligations for States parties in respect of the full realization of the rights in question. It thus imposes an obligation to move as expeditiously and effectively as possible towards that goal. Moreover, any deliberately retrogressive measures in that regard would require the most careful consideration and would need to be fully justified by reference to the totality of the rights provided for in the Covenant and in the context of the full use of the maximum available resources.[53]

The Committee goes even further and emphasises 'that even where the available resources are demonstrably inadequate, the obligation remains for a State party to strive to ensure the widest possible enjoyment of the relevant rights under the prevailing circumstances'.[54] The Committee thus subscribes to the maximum possible effectiveness of the obligations under the Covenant.

The principle of effectiveness has been recognised and applied in international arbitration. In *Iron Rhine*, the Arbitral Tribunal noted that the principle of effectiveness is a well-established principle and is linked to the object and purpose of the Treaty. It does not authorise revising the Treaty.[55] In NAFTA arbitration, the interpretation of Article 1110 on expropriation in *Pope & Talbot* can be characterised as a textually inclusive application of the principle of effectiveness: whatever the general purposes of free trade, Article 1110 did not cover any measure that fell short of expropriation, but it covered *anything* that achieves the same result as expropriation. This suggests that a reference to the formal character of State action in relation to assets would be irrelevant.[56]

In *Loewen*, the NAFTA Tribunal did not accept that the applicant had the necessary standing before it, because his nationality was not that which was

[53] General Comment No 3, The nature of States parties' obligations (Fifth session, 1990), UN Doc E/1991/23, annex III at 86 (1991), *Compilation of General Comments and General Recommendations Adopted by Human Rights Treaty Bodies*, UN Doc HRI/GEN/1/Rev.6 at 14 (2003), para 9.

[54] *Id*, para 10.

[55] *Iron Rhine*, para 49.

[56] See above Chapter 10.

required in terms of the continuous nationality rule.[57] The *Loewen* Award is criticised in terms of the Tribunal's reference to customary rule on continuous nationality due to the Treaty's silence on the point of nationality. It is suggested that the Tribunal should have referred to the purpose that NAFTA Chapter 11 sets out to achieve. Once the Treaty was silent, the 'argument of justice was arguably very relevant'. The object and purpose of NAFTA is to increase trade and investment between the member States and encourage investment through the system which is more effective than the old State-to-State system of diplomatic protection.[58]

Thus, the argument seems to be that the object and purpose of the NAFTA system is different from the traditional model of diplomatic protection. But in reality it is difficult to characterise NAFTA as much more than an institutionalised system of diplomatic protection. The above argument in fact suggests that the Tribunal should not have resorted to general international law because the object and purpose provided for the end of the matter. While this is generally quite possible and rational, this can only happen where the text allows, which was not the case in *Loewen*.

Effectiveness as an interpretative principle does require safeguarding and guaranteeing certain purposes, aims and values not as such and on their own, but only to the extent that their observance and achievement follow from the plain meaning of treaty provisions. In other words, effectiveness is not a free-standing principle, and it cannot justify interpretation in a way that is not admissible under the Vienna Convention. Effectiveness cannot enlarge the meaning of treaty rules, or transform them into substantially different rules. It is about effectiveness of what has been agreed *in casu*, not about what is effective in terms of common sense.

The WTO Appellate Body affirmed in *Japan–Beverages* that 'A fundamental tenet of treaty interpretation flowing from the general rule of interpretation set out in Article 31 is the principle of effectiveness (*ut res magis valeat quam pereat*).'[59] In *US–Shrimp*, the Appellate Body upheld the principle of effectiveness in terms of interpreting the meaning of 'exhaustible natural resources' under Article XX(g) GATT. As the Appellate Body put it, 'in line with the principle of effectiveness in treaty interpretation, measures to conserve exhaustible natural resources, whether *living* or *non-living*, may fall within Article XX(g)'.[60]

In *India–Patent*, the WTO Appellate Body located the relevance of effectiveness of treaty obligations in the light of the object and purpose of the TRIPS Agreement. The preamble of this Agreement referred to 'the need to promote

[57] See below Chapter 15.

[58] M Mendelson, Runaway Train: The 'Continuous Nationality' Rule from *Panevezys-Saldutiskis Railway* case to *Loewen* in T Weiler (ed), *International Investment Law Arbitration: Leading Cases from the ICSID, NAFTA, Bilateral Treaties and Customary International Law* (2005), 46. See further Chapter 15 below.

[59] *Japan—Taxes on Alcoholic Beverages*, AB-1996-2, WT/DS8/AB/R, Report of the Appellate Body, 4 October 1996, 11.

[60] *US–Import Prohibition of Certain Shrimp and Shrimp Products*, AB-1998-4, Report of the Appellate Body, WT/DS58/AB/R, 12 October 1998, para 131.

effective and adequate protection of intellectual property rights'. Therefore, the obligation to provide procedures for patent applications under Article 70.8(a) TRIPS included the obligation to provide for priority dates in relation to applications covered by that Article, in order to preserve their novelty. This followed necessarily from Article 70.8.[61] However, the Appellate Body refused to see Article 70.8 as implying an obligation by India to provide the means for eliminating doubts as to the likelihood of rejection of applications on the ground that the relevant matter was not patentable. India's obligations were limited to procedural aspects, and did not include the substantive aspects of the outcome of patent applications.[62]

Another application of the principle of effectiveness in the *India–Patent* case relates to the obligation to provide a sound legal basis, as an aspect of 'means' of filing patent applications under Article 70.8 TRIPS, for preserving the novelty and priority of these applications. India claimed that its domestic administrative regulations provided this 'sound legal basis'. The Appellate Body had thus to examine these administrative regulations and their place in the Indian legal system to find out whether they satisfied the requirements of India's treaty obligations. The Appellate Body concluded that the regulations were incompatible with India's patent legislation and would not survive, under domestic law, a legal challenge on the basis of that legislation. Hence, 'sound legal basis' was not provided and India was in breach of Article 70.8 TRIPS.[63]

The *Japan–Beverages* Report of the Appellate Body emphasises the link between textual interpretation and the principle of effectiveness as an example of interpretation of Article III GATT:

> Article III:1 articulates a general principle that internal measures should not be applied so as to afford protection to domestic production. This general principle informs the rest of Article III. The purpose of Article III:1 is to establish this general principle as a guide to understanding and interpreting the specific obligations contained in Article III:2 and in the other paragraphs of Article III, while respecting, and not diminishing in any way, the meaning of the words actually used in the texts of those other paragraphs. In short, Article III:1 constitutes part of the context of Article III:2, in the same way that it constitutes part of the context of each of the other paragraphs in Article III. Any other reading of Article III would have the effect of rendering the words of Article III:1 meaningless, thereby violating the fundamental principle of effectiveness in treaty interpretation. Consistent with this principle of effectiveness, and with the textual differences in the two sentences, we believe that Article III:1 informs the first sentence and the second sentence of Article III:2 in different ways.[64]

In *EC–Bananas*, the Appellate Body interpreted Article I:1 GATS on a textual basis and in accordance with the principle of effectiveness. The issue was the reach

[61] *India–Patent Protection for Pharmaceutical and Agricultural Chemical Products*, AB-1997-5, Report of the Appellate Body, WT/DS50/AB/R, 19 December 1997, para 57.

[62] *Id*, para 58.

[63] *Id*, paras 57, 60ff.

[64] *Japan–Alcohol*, AB Report, 18.

of the phrase that '[t]his Agreement applies to measures by Members affecting trade in services'. The Appellate Body considered that:

the use of the term 'affecting' reflects the intent of the drafters to give a broad reach to the GATS. The ordinary meaning of the word 'affecting' implies a measure that has 'an effect on', which indicates a broad scope of application. This interpretation is further reinforced by the conclusions of previous panels that the term 'affecting' in the context of Article III of the GATT is wider in scope than such terms as 'regulating' or 'governing'.[65]

Thus, the ordinary meaning of words was given the widest meaning it could literally and textually accommodate.

In *EC–Bananas*, the Appellate Body faced similar content in Articles II and XVII GATS, one of which relates to Most Favoured Nation treatment and the other to the national treatment standard. The Appellate Body rejected the plea that 'treatment no less favourable' had the same meaning in relation to both standards, because Article XVII paragraphs 2 and 3 referred to 'formally identical treatment or formally different treatment' which was not the case in Article II. Article II did not expressly exclude *de facto* discrimination. As the Appellate Body pointed out:

The obligation imposed by Article II is unqualified. The ordinary meaning of this provision does not exclude *de facto* discrimination. Moreover, if Article II was not applicable to *de facto* discrimination, it would not be difficult—and, indeed, it would be a good deal easier in the case of trade in services, than in the case of trade in goods—to devise discriminatory measures aimed at circumventing the basic purpose of that Article.[66]

Consequently, the WTO jurisprudence follows that understanding of the principle of effectiveness which requires giving such effect to treaty obligations as will make them effective on the ground.

An important application of the principle of effectiveness was witnessed in the jurisprudence of the International Criminal Tribunal for the Former Yugoslavia in the context of application of the requirement of Article 4 of the IV Geneva Convention of 1949 that 'Persons protected by the Convention are those who, at a given moment and in any manner whatsoever, find themselves, in case of a conflict or occupation, in the hands of a Party to the conflict or Occupying Power of which they are not nationals.' The Tribunal was addressing the conflict in the former Yugoslavia which, although essentially an international conflict, did not particularly fit within the types of conflict to which Convention IV applies according to its Article 2, namely cases of 'declared war or of any other armed conflict which may arise between two or more of the High Contracting Parties, even if the state of war is not recognized by one of them'. The question was whether the war crimes committed by the defendants tried before the

[65] *European Communities–Regime for the Importation, Sale and Distribution of Bananas*, AB-1997-3, Report of the Appellate Body, WT/DS27/AB/R, 9 September 1997, para 220.

[66] *Id*, para 233.

Tribunal could lead to their being responsible by amounting to crimes covered by the ICTY Statute despite the fact that the distinct nationality requirement under Article 4 of the Geneva Convention was not satisfied.

The ICTY Trial Chamber examined this question in *Tadic*, where the outcome was contingent on the rejection of the argument that the armed forces of the *Republika Srpska* could be considered as *de facto* organs or agents of the Government of the Federal Republic of Yugoslavia. Thus, the victims were under the protection of the Common Article 3 of the Geneva Conventions, but not of the more specific grave breaches provisions of Geneva Convention IV. Thus, the victims were not protected persons under Article 4 of the Convention and the defendants were consequently acquitted on a number of charges regarding grave breaches.[67]

The Appeals Chamber observed that this 'approach, hinging on substantial relations more than on formal bonds, becomes all the more important in present-day international armed conflicts'. In conflicts like that in the former Yugoslavia:

> ethnicity rather than nationality may become the grounds for allegiance. Or, put another way, ethnicity may become determinative of national allegiance. Under these conditions, the requirement of nationality is even less adequate to define protected persons. In such conflicts, not only the text and the drafting history of the Convention but also, and more importantly, the Convention's object and purpose suggest that allegiance to a Party to the conflict and, correspondingly, control by this Party over persons in a given territory, may be regarded as the crucial test.[68]

As the Appeals Chamber had proved that the Bosnian Serb forces acted as *de facto* organs of the FRY, the victims were 'protected persons' under Article 4. Even if the perpetrators and victims had the same nationality of Bosnia-Herzegovina, the position would not change from a legal point of view. This was so, because:

> Article 4 of Geneva Convention IV, if interpreted in the light of its object and purpose, is directed to the protection of civilians to the maximum extent possible. It therefore does not make its applicability dependent on formal bonds and purely legal relations. Its primary purpose is to ensure the safeguards afforded by the Convention to those civilians who do not enjoy the diplomatic protection, and correlatively are not subject to the allegiance and control, of the State in whose hands they may find themselves. In granting its protection, Article 4 intends to look to the substance of relations, not to their legal characterisation as such.[69]

Thus, the Chamber concluded that 'even if in the circumstances of the case the perpetrators and the victims were to be regarded as possessing the same nationality, Article 4 would still be applicable'. The victims did not owe allegiance to and did not receive the diplomatic protection of the FRY on whose behalf the Bosnian

[67] *Prosecutor v Tadic*, IT-94-1, Trial Chamber, Judgment of 7 May 1997, paras 607–608.
[68] *Prosecutor v Tadic*, IT-94-1, Appeals Chamber, Judgment of 19 July 1999, para 166.
[69] *Id*, para 167–168.

Serb armed forces had been fighting.[70] Consequently, the Appeals Chamber found the defendant guilty on charges of which he had been acquitted by the Trial Chamber.

On balance, the Appeals Chamber's effective interpretation of Article 4 of the Geneva Convention is a matter of applying normal rules of interpretation and fits perfectly within the description by the International Law Commission of the role of the principle of effectiveness to support out of those options available that option of interpretation which secures the effectiveness of the undertaking. The restrictive interpretation would have upheld the view that the nationality of captors as such is relevant in the same way as the nationality of State captors is effectively represented. The Appeals Chamber applied the wording of Article 4 without reading additional conditions into it. As soon as there is an international armed conflict, the effective interpretation of Article 4 requires applying it in terms of who actually directs the fighting, that is in terms of the identity of belligerents as opposed to that of individual captors. Both the wording and object and purpose of the Convention would be seriously curtailed if it were not to extend to conduct directed by the belligerent just because the actual perpetrators have the same nationality as the victims.

In the *Aleksovski* decision, the Appeals Chamber faced the defendant's submission that the treatment of Bosnian Muslims by Croats was outside the scope of Article 4 because the conflict in question was internal. The Chamber accepted the position of the Prosecution that 'if it is established that the conflict was international by reason of Croatia's participation, it follows that the Bosnian Muslim victims were in the hands of a party to the conflict, Croatia, of which they were not nationals and that, therefore, Article 4 of Geneva Convention IV is applicable'. This was the case where 'Article 4 may be given a wider construction so that a person may be accorded protected status, notwithstanding the fact that he is of the same nationality as his captors.' The Chamber based this approach on a teleological approach to the interpretation of Article 4 of Geneva Convention IV. Such extended application of Article 4 met the object and purpose of the Convention.[71]

The same approach was taken in the *Delalic* case, where the Appeals Chamber engaged with the issue of determining the nationality of victims for the purpose of applying Article 4. This case likewise approved the teleological interpretation of Article 4. The Chamber countered the appellants' view that the 'strict' interpretation of Article 4 was mandated by traditional rules of treaty interpretation.[72] The Chamber reiterated that it was bound to interpret the Geneva Convention in accordance with Articles 31 and 32 of the 1969 Vienna Convention. It was seen as crucial that the nationality requirement in Article 4 of Geneva Convention IV should therefore be ascertained within the context of the object and purpose of

[70] *Id*, para 169.

[71] *Prosecutor v Aleksovski*, Appeals Chamber, Judgment of 24 March 2000, paras 147–152.

[72] *Prosecutor v Delalic et al.*, IT-96–21-A, Appeals Chamber, Judgment of 20 February 2001, paras 56–59.

humanitarian law, which 'is directed to the protection of civilians to the maximum extent possible'.[73] Here the Appeals Chamber took the approach of the autonomous meaning of the nationality requirement under Article 4, thereby contradicting the defendants' argument that the victims as well as the perpetrators had Bosnian nationality. The relevant nationality link was 'a nationality link defined for the purposes of international humanitarian law, and not as referring to the domestic legislation as such'.[74] Thus, the Chamber observed that 'the formal national link with Bosnia and Herzegovina cannot be raised before an international tribunal to deny the victims the protection of humanitarian law'. The Chamber continued that:

> who arguably are of the same nationality under domestic law as their captors, of the protection of the Geneva Conventions solely based on that national law would not be consistent with the object and purpose of the Conventions. Their very object could indeed be defeated if undue emphasis were placed on formal legal bonds, which could also be altered by governments to shield their nationals from prosecution based on the grave breaches provisions of the Geneva Conventions.[75]

In some cases, according to the Chamber, 'ethnicity may reflect more appropriately the reality of the bonds. ... In today's ethnic conflicts, the victims may be "assimilated" to the external State involved in the conflict, even if they formally have the same nationality as their captors, for the purposes of the application of humanitarian law, and of Article 4 of Geneva Convention IV specifically.'[76] Formal legal bonds on the basis of nationality were considered by the Chamber in the light of the principle that domestic laws granting nationality are merely facts whose effect had to be ascertained in the international context.

In the *Blaskic* case the Appeals Chamber faced the argument that under the express language of Article 4 of Geneva Convention IV, 'because the Bosnian Muslims were held captive by the HVO [of Croatian origin], each possessing Bosnian nationality, they could not be deemed protected persons in terms of the Geneva Conventions'.[77] The Tribunal observed that 'The Bosnian Muslims were held captive by the HVO and they owed no allegiance to Croatia. Given that the HVO was operating *de facto* as Croatia's armed forces, the Bosnian Muslim victims found themselves in the hands of a Party to the conflict of which they were not nationals.'[78]

Given that nationality laws of the State are mere facts under international law,[79] and that the meaning of nationality has to be determined in an international context

[73] *Id*, para 73.
[74] *Id*, paras 74–77.
[75] *Id*, para 81.
[76] *Id*, paras 82–83.
[77] *Prosecutor v Tihomir Blaskic*, IT-95-14-A, Appeals Chamber, Judgment of 29 July 2004, para 167.
[78] *Id*, para 175.
[79] See Chapter 5 above.

independently of national legal prescriptions, the Appeal Chamber's treatment of the nationality requirement in Article 4 is justified. Article 4 thus refers to the nationality bond as a factual matter that can be a starting point of reference in terms of which persons can be 'protected persons', but not a strict legal requirement to exclude individuals from enjoying this status and thus curtail the protection offered by the object and purpose of the Convention. The autonomous meaning of nationality link entails construing Article 4 as requiring the absence of a nationality link in the final analysis, and not in all pertinent aspects.

The Appeals Chamber's approach is guided by the principle of effectiveness, which is meant to ensure that treaty provisions are construed so as to make a difference on the ground as required by the language and object and purpose of the relevant treaty. To some extent, the Appeals Chamber's approach also constitutes evolutive interpretation referring to the nature of modern conflicts. But from the viewpoint of the regime of interpretation, this approach relies on the textual meaning of the treaty provision and prefers that approach to other options which promote rather than curtail the protection derived from the object and purpose of the treaty.

2. Restrictive Interpretation

(a) Essence and Doctrinal Treatment

The terminology used in jurisprudence and doctrine involves the notions of restrictive, strict or narrow interpretation. The common feature of these similar but not necessarily identical terms is that they aim at qualifying what the relevant treaty provision may suggest on its face. In each of these cases, the essence of the process matters more than terminology. The restrictive interpretation properly so called relates to the restriction of the meaning of treaty clauses identified through the use of normal interpretative methods.

The notion of restrictive, as well as extensive, interpretation implies the possibility that the duly established meaning of the treaty clause can be modified by the interpreter. These notions are therefore incompatible with the aim to ascertain the meaning of treaty clauses and the intention of parties. At the same time, restrictive interpretation can take place not only as a matter of declared policy, but also as a disguised and unprofessed interpretative exercise.

Haraszti assesses the merit of claims favouring restrictive or extensive interpretation by adverting to the basic task of interpretation to clarify the intention of States-parties. On this ground:

> It follows that this intention has to become fully known. In such a knowledge a treaty cannot be applied by way of interpretation beyond the limits intended by the parties, nor can the effect of a treaty be limited by some sort of an arbitrarily restrictive interpretation to a narrower sphere. It is on this understanding that those rejecting the notion of

extensive and restrictive interpretation altogether are right; that is, in the case of treaties an interpretation extending or restricting the intention of the parties is out of the question.[80]

Thus, extending or restricting the meaning of the treaty directly contradicts the thesis that treaty interpretation is different from its amendment. The required choice can never be between restrictive and extensive interpretations, because both these approaches pervert the meaning of treaties and thus of the original agreement between States.

As Visscher specifies, the issue of restrictive interpretation may be raised where a treaty is seen as derogating from general international law or what he describes as the normal order of things.[81] Doubts about the quality of restrictive interpretation were expressed at the early stages of doctrinal development. Phillimore observed that:

these assumed qualities cannot found any safe rules of interpretation. That the same characteristics may seem odious to one party and favourable to another, according to the dispositions of each, and the point of view from which they regard them. That they are incapable therefore of a certain definition; that it is admitted that the two qualities are often blended together in one and the same subject; and, above all, that without having recourse to this distinction, sound rules of interpretation may be always obtained.[82]

Restrictive interpretation and the approach of *in dubio mitius* raise the issue of the interaction between the interpretation of obligations and State sovereignty. The crucial question arising is whether sovereignty is residual to treaty obligations, or whether it continues impacting their content once these obligations are assumed. At the same time, sovereignty may be a reinforcing idea or principle triggering the adoption of restrictive interpretation. The real essence of restrictive interpretation is taking obligations for less than they mean on their face and in the light of the object and purpose of the treaty. The sovereignty factor has no independent relevance in interpreting treaties. The extent of sovereign freedom *in casu* is merely a consequence of the position that obtains through and after the interpretation of a treaty by using normal interpretative methods.

The merit and normative status of restrictive interpretation is examined in the works of Hersch Lauterpacht. The principle of effectiveness inherently contradicts the notion of restrictive interpretation of treaties,[83] which is not part of international law. This proposition is reaffirmed in practice, as can be seen from the divergence of the approaches in the *Golder* case between the European Court of

[80] G Haraszti, *Some Fundamental Problems of the Law of Treaties* (1973), 151; G Schwarzenberger, *International Law* (1957), vol I, 510, also describes both these options as rudimentary.

[81] Visscher (1963), 91.

[82] Phillimore (1855), vol II, 89.

[83] H Lauterpacht, Restrictive Interpretation and Effectiveness in the Interpretation of Treaties, *BYIL* (1949), 50–51, 69; Yasseen likewise confirms that the role of the effectiveness principle is to counter the invocation of restrictive interpretation: MK Yasseen, L'interprétation des traités d'après la Convention de Vienne sur le Droit des Traités, 151 *Recueil des Cours* (1976-III), 1 at 72.

Human Rights and Judge Fitzmaurice. Fitzmaurice himself later abandoned his point of view. In *Belgian Police*, he emphasised that he was not 'suggesting that a Convention such as the Human Rights Convention should be interpreted in a narrowly restrictive way', and that the liberal construction of the Convention's provisions should be undertaken in the light of the legal environment prevailing at the time of interpretation.[84] As Lauterpacht further observes, 'restrictive interpretation of treaty obligations finds no support in the practice of the Court and is indefensible on grounds of principle'.[85] Restrictive interpretation is a threat to the principle of effectiveness.[86] The factor of sovereignty, however fundamental in international law, cannot affect interpretation by directing presumptions in this process. The paramount principle of good faith requires that:

> the party upon which the treaty has conferred benefits in return for valuable consideration should not have its rights whittled away as the result of restrictive interpretation of the obligations of the party which obtained the consideration. A restrictive interpretation of the obligations of one party implies a restrictive interpretation of the rights of the other party. Undue regard for the sovereignty of one State implies undue disregard of the sovereignty of another.[87]

This illustrates that the fact of sovereignty cannot on its own be a relevant factor in interpretation. This applies to all categories of treaties, including those establishing the jurisdiction of international tribunals.[88]

Brownlie also finds that the principle of restrictive interpretation has no support under the Vienna Convention on the Law of Treaties.[89] Doctrinal support for restrictive interpretation is minimal. Although the New Haven School asserts that the authoritative character of restrictive interpretation 'has seldom been questioned',[90] the fact remains that since the establishment of the Permanent Court of International Justice this principle, in the sense of restricting what the treaty means on its face, has never been judicially implemented. On the other hand, the consistent jurisprudential use of the principle of effectiveness has resulted in repeated rejection of restrictive interpretation.

(b) Application in Jurisprudence

In *River Oder*, the Permanent Court rejected the restrictive interpretation favouring a 'solution which imposes least restriction on the freedom of States', if the text

[84] Separate Opinion of Judge Sir Gerald Fitzmaurice, *Belgian Police*, Application No 4464/70, Judgment of 27 October 1975, para 10.

[85] Lauterpacht (1958), 338–340.

[86] *Id*, 227.

[87] *Id*, 306.

[88] See below Chapter 12.

[89] I Brownlie, *Principles of Public International Law* (2003), 606.

[90] MS McDougal, HD Lasswell & JC Miller, *The Interpretation of International Agreements and World Public Order* (1967), 173.

is doubtful. The Court observed that restrictive interpretation cannot be automatically applied if the grammatical construction of the text produces no definite results. Only if all pertinent considerations including the applicable principles of general law fail to clarify the issue and the text still remains doubtful, should 'interpretation . . . be adopted which is most favourable to the freedom of States'.[91]

The thesis of restrictive interpretation aspires to find conceptual support in the concept of State sovereignty. Under this approach, State sovereignty retains its continuous relevance and operates, as it were, parallel to treaty obligations, retaining its capability to influence their content and operation. Judicial practice provides the guidance as to why and in which circumstances the use of restrictive interpretation is unjustified. The Permanent Court in *Wimbledon* emphasised the interpretative relevance of sovereignty in cases where the extent of treaty limitations of sovereignty is doubtful. The case involved the treaty-based consent of Germany to allow free passage of belligerents through the Kiel Canal in wartime. The argument was advanced that the literal construction of the Treaty 'would imply the abandonment by Germany of a personal and imprescriptible right, which forms an essential part of her sovereignty and which she neither could nor intended to renounce by anticipation'. The Court was urged that:

> like all restrictions or limitations upon the exercise of sovereignty, this servitude must be construed as restrictively as possible and confined within its narrowest limits, more especially in the sense that it should not be allowed to affect the rights consequent upon neutrality in an armed conflict.[92]

The Court's reasoning indeed considers the factor of the scale of restriction on the sovereignty of the State, acknowledging that the limitation of sovereignty in question was of important character. However, the Court was clear that the factor of sovereignty was of no appeal if the treaty provision was clear. As the Court put it, it would 'feel obliged to stop at the point where the so-called restrictive interpretation would be contrary to the plain terms of the article and would destroy what has been clearly granted'.[93]

The significance of the Court's rejection of restrictive interpretation of the Versailles Treaty is illustrated in the Dissenting Opinion of Judges Anzilotti and Huber, who in fact opposed the textual approach that the Court preferred. As the Judges stated:

> for the purposes of the interpretation of contracts which take the form of international conventions, account must be taken of the complexity of interstate relations and of the fact that the contracting parties are independent political entities.

The judges continued that a purely grammatical interpretation must stop where it 'leads to contradictory or impossible consequences or which, in the

[91] *Territorial Jurisdiction of the International Commission of the River Oder*, Judgment of 10 September 1929, *PCIJ Series* A, No 23, 5 at 26.

[92] *Wimbledon*, 1923, *PCIJ Series* A, No 1, 23.

[93] *Id*, 24.

circumstances, must be regarded as going beyond the intention of the parties'. More so, in their view, as the treaty stipulation in question affected the 'essential right' of Germany.[94] Thus, the two judges expressly contended that the factor of sovereignty and independence of States should influence the content of treaty obligations once these obligations are accepted through State consent. The Court could not adopt this approach as it would have undermined the stability of the treaty interpretation regime.

The WTO Appellate Body voiced an approach to the interaction between sovereignty and interpretation in its *Japan–Beverages* Report, similar to *Wimbledon*, emphasising that treaty obligations are derived from the exercise of sovereignty by States. This confirms that what matters for interpretation is the actual content of rules and obligations, not their origin of sovereignty.

State sovereignty possesses important residual significance that warns against presuming or inferring restrictions on sovereign rights and freedom of action of the State unless and to the extent that these follow from treaty provisions. This residual significance of sovereignty is also examined in jurisprudence. The *North Atlantic Fisheries* case discussed the presumptions to be adopted when it enquired into whether a treaty provision impacted on the ordinary sovereign prerogatives of the State. The principal approach of this case is that sovereignty need not be seen as more limited through treaty obligations than is necessary for unimpeded operation of these obligations. The Arbitral Tribunal addressed the issue of fishing rights in British waters to be exercised by American citizens 'in common' with British subjects, under the 1818 US-British Treaty. Under Article I of the Treaty, it was agreed that 'the Inhabitants of the said United States shall have forever, in common with the Subjects of His Britannic Majesty, the Liberty to take Fish of every kind'. The US contention was that the words 'in common' did not imply that the US nationals would be subject to coastal regulations as British subjects would.[95] Accepting the US submission would entail such construction of the 1818 Treaty as would imply that, in the absence of the words 'in common', British subjects would be precluded from fishing in British waters. The Tribunal disagreed, observing that 'It would have been the very opposite of the concept of territorial waters to suppose that, without a special treaty-provision, British subjects could be excluded from fishing in British waters.'[96]

In other words, the sovereign prerogatives of Britain were not restricted because the Treaty did not affect them. Not that sovereign rights are particularly special in impacting the meaning of treaty obligations; it was simply the case that the Treaty did not purport to affect those prerogatives of Great Britain. The approach that held

[94] Dissenting Opinion, *id*, 36.

[95] The US submission was that 'the words "in common with British subjects" used in the Treaty should not be held as importing a common subjection to regulation, but as intending to negative a possible pretention on the part of the inhabitants of the United States to liberties of fishery exclusive of the right of British subjects to fish'.

[96] JB Scott, *Hague Court Reports* 162–163.

the key to the solution was the textual approach. The silence of the text required presuming that the sovereign prerogatives in question were not limited.

In the same Award, the Arbitral Tribunal refused to deduce from the fact that US and British citizens were entitled to fish in common that the Treaty impliedly conferred on the US the right to cooperate and be consulted in whatever regulations Britain might design and exercise. As the Treaty was not about common fishing but fishing in common, no corresponding joint regulation could be implied. As the Tribunal put it:

> The exercise of such a right of consent by the United States would predicate an abandonment of its independence in this respect by Great Britain, and the recognition by the latter of a concurrent right of regulation in the United States. But the treaty conveys only a liberty to take fish in common, and neither directly nor indirectly conveys a joint right of regulation.[97]

As the Tribunal further observed, 'a line which would limit the exercise of sovereignty of a State within the limits of its own territory can be drawn only on the ground of express stipulation, and not by implication from stipulations concerning a different subject-matter'. The real question was 'whether the Treaty contains an abdication by Great Britain of the right which Great Britain, as the sovereign power, undoubtedly possessed when the Treaty was made, to regulate those fisheries'.[98] Here again, the textual approach held the key to the outcome.

The Tribunal concluded that the right of Great Britain to regulate fishing was inherent in its sovereignty.[99] This conclusion followed not from restrictive interpretation of the existing treaty regulation, but from the absence of treaty regulation covering the field within which Britain had the sovereign right to regulate fishing. This interpretative philosophy predates and anticipates both the *Lotus* and *Wimbledon* approaches to the interaction between sovereignty and international legal regulation.

In the *Lake Lanoux* Award, the Arbitral Tribunal rejected the thesis that a treaty-based derogation from territorial sovereignty had to be interpreted restrictively. As the Tribunal put it, sovereignty was the source of international obligations, but not more than that.[100]

The issue of restrictive interpretation arose in *Iron Rhine*, involving Article XII of the 1839 Separation Treaty between the Netherlands and Belgium, stipulating the possibility of construction of roads and canals on the Netherlands' territory, 'without prejudice to the exclusive rights of sovereignty over the territory which would be crossed by the road or canal in question'. In this case, the Arbitral Tribunal was dealing with the right to transit over the sovereign territory. The Netherlands contended that such a right could only arise on the basis of

[97] *Id*, 167–168.
[98] *Id*, 169.
[99] *Id*, 171.
[100] 12 *RIAA* 306.

specific agreement and as such must be construed restrictively, which assertion was challenged by Belgium.[101] The Tribunal referred to the jurisprudence of the Permanent Court which affirmed the intactness of sovereignty in the absence of specific treaty limitations and observed that 'beyond what rights of Belgium are provided for in Article XII of the 1839 Treaty of Separation, Netherlands sovereignty remains intact'.[102]

The Tribunal emphasised more generally on the thesis of restrictive interpretation that:

> The doctrine of restrictive interpretation never had a hierarchical supremacy, but was a technique to ensure a proper balance of the distribution of rights within a treaty system. The principle of restrictive interpretation, whereby treaties are to be interpreted in favour of state sovereignty in case of doubt, is not in fact mentioned in the provisions of the Vienna Convention. The object and purpose of a treaty, taken together with the intentions of the parties, are the prevailing elements for interpretation.[103]

The Tribunal further emphasised that restrictive interpretation had a particularly minor role in the case of human rights treaties, and noted the doctrinal assessment that 'the principle has not been relied upon in any recent jurisprudence of international courts and tribunals and that its contemporary relevance is to be doubted'.[104] In the light of *Lake Lanoux*, the Tribunal emphasised that the presumption of sovereignty must give way to the content of treaty obligations.[105] Consequently and crucially:

> the sovereignty reserved to the Netherlands under Article XII of the 1839 Treaty of Separation cannot be understood save by first determining Belgium's rights, and the Netherlands' obligations in relation thereto. This is to be done not by invocation of the principle of restrictive interpretation, but rather by examining—using the normal rules of interpretation identified in Articles 31 and 32 of the Vienna Convention—exactly what rights have been afforded to Belgium. All else falls within the Netherlands' sovereignty. Put differently, the Netherlands may exercise its rights of sovereignty in relation to the territory over which the Iron Rhine railway passes, unless this would conflict with the treaty rights granted to Belgium.[106]

Thus, the content and parameters of the sovereign rights of the State must be understood by reference to the scope and content of treaty obligations incumbent on that State. Sovereignty has no uniformly determined content applicable in all contexts of international legal relations. Sovereign prerogatives survive to the extent that the matter to which they relate is not regulated by treaty.

[101] *Arbitration Regarding Iron Rhine Railway (Belgium/Netherlands)*, Award of 24 May 2005, para 50.
[102] *Id*, para 51.
[103] *Id*, para 53.
[104] *Id*, para 53.
[105] *Id*, para 54.
[106] *Id*, paras 55–56.

Sovereign rights and prerogatives cannot affect the scope of established treaty rights and regulation.

At the same time, as the Tribunal's reasoning confirms, treaty obligations do not impair the residual sovereignty which is not their intendment to affect:

> The reservation of Netherlands' sovereignty ensures for it that, apart from the elements specified in terms in favour of Belgium, no further limitations of sovereignty are to be implied. But at the same time, the reservation of sovereignty cannot serve the converse purpose of detracting from the rights given to Belgium under Article XII.[107]

The Tribunal proceeds to further refine this point:

> The Netherlands has necessarily already derogated from its territorial sovereignty in allowing a railway to be built, at the request of another state, over its territory. The sovereignty reserved is over the territory over which the track runs. The Netherlands has forfeited no more sovereignty than that which is necessary for the track to be built and to operate to allow a commercial connection from Belgium to Germany across Limburg. It thus retains the police power throughout that area, the power to establish health and safety standards for work being done on the track, and the power to establish environmental standards in that area.[108]

The measure in question was the designation of Meinweg as a natural reserve area. The Netherlands had acknowledged Belgium's right to transit. This right was not affected by those environmental measures and, according to the Tribunal, 'the relationship between Belgium's right of transit and the Netherlands' rights of sovereignty remained in balance as intended under Article XII'.[109] On the one hand, restrictive interpretation does not apply and the sovereignty factor cannot diminish treaty obligations assumed. On the other hand, sovereignty remains intact beyond what has been undertaken under the Treaty. The philosophy underlying this interpretation seems to be that the construction of roads or canals on the Dutch territory entails only the rights linked to those arrangements and does not result in any extraterritorial jurisdiction of Belgium restricting Dutch sovereignty in a way similar to capitulations.

In general, the *Iron Rhine* case complements and further develops the parameters of the relationship between sovereignty and treaty obligation as specified in the *North Atlantic Fisheries* case. Both cases were decided in relation to territorial sovereignty and ensuing powers of the State. Both affirm that while sovereignty is not by itself a factor in the process of interpretation, it is not diminished more than is required under the specific clauses of the treaty.

Restrictive interpretation is normally rejected in the jurisprudence under the European Convention on Human Rights. In *Lawless*, the European Court of Human Rights disagreed with the Irish Government that the right of the

107 *Id*, para 67.
108 *Id*, para 87.
109 *Id*, para 95.

detainee to be brought before the Court was applicable if one was detained for the purposes of prosecution, but not for the purposes of crime prevention. The Court made it clear that the Irish position restricted the plain meaning of Article 5 obligations.[110] The contrast between restrictive interpretation and effective interpretation was evident in *Mathieu-Mohin and Clerfayt v Belgium*. The Court faced the plea that because the right to political participation in Article 3 Protocol 1 uses the phrase 'The High Contracting Parties undertake', 'It has sometimes been inferred from this that the Article does not give rise to individual rights and freedoms "directly secured to anyone" within the jurisdiction of these Parties.' This, according to the Court, would make applications regarding alleged breaches of Article 3 Protocol 1 inadmissible, because 'only a person claiming to be the victim of a violation of one of his own rights and freedoms has standing to petition the Commission' under what then was Article 25 of the Convention. The Court observed that 'Such a restrictive interpretation does not stand up to scrutiny,' and:

> the inter-State colouring of the wording of Article 3 [does] not reflect any difference of substance from the other substantive clauses in the Convention and Protocols. The reason for it would seem to lie rather in the desire to give greater solemnity to the commitment undertaken and in the fact that the primary obligation in the field concerned is not one of abstention or non-interference, as with the majority of the civil and political rights, but one of adoption by the State of positive measures to 'hold' democratic elections.[111]

The WTO jurisprudence has witnessed a reference to the presumption in favour of State sovereignty, but in a specific context. In *EC–Hormones* the Appellate Body considered that it could not 'lightly assume that sovereign states intended to impose upon themselves the more onerous, rather than the less burdensome, obligation by mandating *conformity* or *compliance with* such standards, guidelines and recommendations'. The Appellate Body treated this as an incidence of the *in dubio mitius* principle.[112] However, this cannot be soundly seen as an instance of restrictive interpretation, because the Appellate Body had just confirmed that the interpretative outcome it had arrived at was based on the plain meaning of the text of the treaty.[113] This is essentially different from making presumptions in the context of uncertainty, or narrowing down the meaning of clear text.

The real problem raised by the restrictive interpretation relates not to cases of its express use, which is not likely to occur frequently, due to the conceptual inconsistency of this notion, but to cases in which it is resorted to, as it were, on a *de facto* basis. In certain cases courts and tribunals end up by using restrictive interpretation without expressly professing their adherence to this approach. The

[110] *Lawless v Ireland*, Merits, No 332/57, Judgment of 1 July 1961, para 14.

[111] *Mathieu-Mohin and Clerfayt v Belgium*, Application No 9267/81, Judgment of 2 March 1987, paras 48–50.

[112] *EC–Hormones*, para 165 (emphasis original).

[113] See above Chapter 10; see further Chapter 3.

outcome is that in some cases the textual meaning of treaty provisions is misrepresented and perverted. This was the case in relation to interpretation of Article 6 of the European Convention on Human Rights in the *Al-Adsani* case, where the general international law argument, referring to rules assumed to exist but not proved with evidence, was used to cut down the actual meaning of Article 6 as construed in the *Golder* case.[114] A similar phenomenon was displayed in relation to Article 1 of the European Convention in the *Bankovic* case, where the European Court in principle accepted that States-parties can be liable under the Convention even if the relevant conduct is performed outside their national boundaries, yet qualified this by requiring the respondent State's 'effective control' over the relevant situation abroad. This requirement does not figure in the text of the Convention nor inherently follow from its object and purpose.[115]

3. Presumption against Redundancy

The essence of presumption against redundancy is that every single phrase or provision of a treaty has to be given effect as possessing its own independent meaning. This presumption is essentially based on the same conceptual ground as the principle of effectiveness. On its face, effectiveness requires giving full effect to the relevant clause of the treaty, and avoiding diminishing its ambit which follows from its text.

In jurisprudence, the presumption against redundancy has a long history of application, together with the affirmation of its close link with the principle of effectiveness. The Arbitral Tribunal in *North Atlantic Fisheries* faced the US plea that the expression 'coasts, bays, creeks or harbours' in Article I of the 1818 London Convention did not relate specifically to bays, in relation to which the US had renounced its fishing rights, but was 'intended to express and be equivalent to the word "coast" whereby the three marine miles would be measured from the sinuosities of the coast and the renunciation would apply only to the waters of bays within three miles'. The Tribunal's response was that:

> it is a principle of interpretation that words in a document ought not to be considered as being without any meaning if there is not specific evidence to that purpose and the interpretation referred to would lead to the consequence, practically, of reading the words 'bays, creeks and harbours' out of the Treaty; so that it would read 'within three miles of any of the coasts' including therein the coasts of the bays and harbours.[116]

This approach clearly demonstrates the inherent link between the textual approach and the presumption against redundancy.

[114] See above Chapter 10.
[115] See above Chapter 5; see further Orakhelashvili, *EJIL* (2003).
[116] Scott, 187–188.

Another early confirmation of the presumption against redundancy is provided by the *Cayuga Indians* Award, decided by the American-British Claims Arbitration Tribunal. In this litigation, Britain invoked Article IX of the Treaty of Ghent, by which the United States agreed to restore to the Indians with whom that government had been at war 'all the possessions, rights, and privileges which they may have enjoyed or been entitled to' in 1811 before the war.[117] The Tribunal was:

asked to hold that the article was only a 'nominal' provision, not intended to have any definite application. We can not agree to such an interpretation. Nothing is better settled, as a canon of interpretation in all systems of law, than that a clause must be so interpreted as to give it a meaning rather than so as to deprive it of meaning. We are not asked to choose between possible meanings. We are asked to reject the apparent meaning and to hold that the provision has no meaning. This we cannot do. We think the covenant in Article IX of the Treaty of Ghent must be construed as a promise to restore the Cayugas in Canada, who claimed to be a tribe or nation and had been in the war as such, to the position in which they were prior to the division of the nation at the outbreak of the war.[118]

In the *Namibia* case the International Court interpreted Article 80(1) of the United Nations Charter as stipulating that, despite the dissolution of the League of Nations, which formally meant the end of the Mandates system, the rights of all relevant States or peoples were not prejudiced.[119] Given that Article 80(1) referred to the possibility of a change in the status of mandated territories and peoples through the conclusion of specific agreements, the Court decided that in the absence of such agreements the ensuing obligations such as the reporting duty would continue unchanged. Article 80(1) kept rights and obligations arising out of the mandate intact against any claim of their possible lapse with the dissolution of the League of Nations. The demise of the League did not cause the termination of mandates.[120]

At the same time, the International Court confronted the argument of South Africa 'that Article 80, paragraph 1 [of the UN Charter], must be interpreted as a mere saving clause having a purely negative effect'. The Court responded that:

If Article 80, paragraph 1, were to be understood as a mere interpretative provision preventing the operation of Chapter XII from affecting any rights, then it would be deprived

[117] *Cayuga Indians*, Award rendered at Washington on 22 January 1926, 16 *AJIL* (1920), 574 at 576–577.

[118] *Id*, 587.

[119] Article 80 stipulates that, '1. Except as may be agreed upon in individual trusteeship agreements, made under Articles 77, 79, and 81, placing each territory under the trusteeship system, and until such agreements have been concluded, nothing in this Chapter shall be construed in or of itself to alter in any manner the rights whatsoever of any states or any peoples or the terms of existing international instruments to which Members of the United Nations may respectively be parties. 2. Paragraph 1 of this Article shall not be interpreted as giving grounds for delay or postponement of the negotiation and conclusion of agreements for placing mandated and other territories under the trusteeship system as provided for in Article 77.'

[120] Advisory Opinion, *ICJ Reports*, 1971, 34.

> of all practical effect. ... Likewise, if paragraph 1 of Article 80 were to be understood as a mere saving clause, paragraph 2 of the same Article would have no purpose. ... This provision was obviously intended to prevent a mandatory Power from invoking the preservation of its rights resulting from paragraph 1 as a ground for delaying or postponing what the Court described as 'the normal course indicated by the Charter, namely, conclude Trusteeship Agreements' (I.C.J. Reports 1950, p. 140). No method of interpretation would warrant the conclusion that Article 80 as a whole is meaningless.[121]

Therefore, the Court concluded that Article 80(1) had maintained the obligations of the Mandatory and the United Nations had become the appropriate forum for supervising the fulfilment of these obligations.[122]

The WTO Appellate Body examined the presumption against redundancy in *US–Gasoline*, in the context of the general rule of interpretation. In this case this issue arose in terms of construing the Article XX chapeau in relation to its specific derogation entitlements. As the Appellate Body observed:

> The provisions of the chapeau cannot logically refer to the same standard(s) by which a violation of a substantive rule has been determined to have occurred. To proceed down that path would be both to empty the chapeau of its contents and to deprive the exceptions in paragraphs (a) to (j) of meaning. Such recourse would also confuse the question of whether inconsistency with a substantive rule existed, with the further and separate question arising under the chapeau of Article XX as to whether that inconsistency was nevertheless justified. One of the corollaries of the 'general rule of interpretation' in the Vienna Convention is that interpretation must give meaning and effect to all the terms of a treaty. An interpreter is not free to adopt a reading that would result in reducing whole clauses or paragraphs of a treaty to redundancy or inutility.[123]

Similarly, in *Japan–Beverages*, the Appellate Body emphasised that the presumption against redundancy is an implication of the principle of effectiveness. This approach was applied to Article III:1 of the GATT, which was therefore viewed as providing the interpretative guide for other parts of this Article, and not affecting or diminishing their scope. Article III:1 provided the general principles and Article III:2 provided for specific obligations that were informed by those general principles. The opposite approach would render the words of Article III:1 meaningless.[124]

4. The Interpretation of Exceptions

Exception clauses are generally deemed as specific clauses deviating from, or limiting, the more general primary obligations under the relevant treaties. The issue

[121] *Id*, 35.
[122] *Id*, 37.
[123] *US–Gasoline*, AB Report, 21.
[124] *Japan–Beverages*, AB Report, 11, 16.

of interpretation of exceptions therefore arises, in conceptual and practical terms, as an allegedly individual, if not separate, aspect of treaty interpretation, mainly because it may give the impression of a shift in interpretative presumptions. Lauterpacht correctly emphasises that the principle of effectiveness provides no ready-made solution for cases where the principal provision and the exception from it are opposed. It is not a straightforward issue to assess which should be more effective: the primary provision or the exception.[125] The ultimate answer in specific cases depends not only on the wording of treaty provisions, but also on the object and purpose of the entire treaty.

Another related aspect of the problem is that exception clauses may be included in treaties to safeguard certain values that may or may not overlap with the primary object and purpose of the treaty.[126] The issue of balancing values arises only indirectly however, and in the framework in which the principles of interpretation are applied to discover what is the ultimate object and purpose of the treaty, that is the set of values which, by consent of the contracting parties, has obtained legal status.

It is not always a straightforward issue to determine what an exception clause is. As Qureshi specifies, 'the agencies for their determination are not specifically recognised as exceptions-creating ones, although they engage with exceptions in practice with their general remit'. Qureshi continues that '*de facto* exceptions are discerned through the judicial process. They are determined through the establishment both of the limits of a general rule and of the limits of the scope of an exception.'[127] In *EC–Hormones*, the WTO Appellate Body confronted the interpretation of the SPS Agreement, dealing in particular with the relevance of its Articles 3.1, 3.2, and 3.3. The Appellate Body rejected the assumption that Article 3.3 was an exception in relation to the first two paragraphs.[128] Articles 3.1 and 3.2 regulate the establishment of sanitary and phytosanitary standards on the basis of, or in conformity with, international standards. Article 3.3, on the other hand, entitles States to establish their own standards in this field, with a higher level of protection. As the Appellate Body put it, 'this right of a Member to establish its own level of sanitary protection under Article 3.3 of the SPS Agreement is an autonomous right and *not* an "exception" from a "general obligation" under Article 3.1'.[129]

The reasoning of the Appellate Body seems to imply substantive criteria of the importance of the relevant rights embodied in clauses that would respectively be classified as the primary rule and the exception. As soon as the context of the treaty allows the clause to be considered as an exception to primary obligations, such exception clauses will always be seen as limited in their scope and in their substantive or temporal effects. This seems to be dictated by the requirement not to

[125] Lauterpacht (1958), 229–230.
[126] See above Chapters 7 and 10.
[127] A Qureshi, *Interpreting WTO Agreements* (2006), 102.
[128] *EC–Hormones*, para 169 (emphasis original).
[129] *Id*, para 172 (emphasis original).

impede the operation of the primary obligations that form the core of the object and purpose of the treaty. There is some sort of interpretative presumption stated in the Appellate Body report in *US–Shrimp*:

> the language of the chapeau makes clear that each of the exceptions in paragraphs (a) to (j) of Article XX is a *limited and conditional* exception from the substantive obligations contained in the other provisions of the GATT 1994, that is to say, the ultimate availability of the exception is subject to the compliance by the invoking Member with the requirements of the chapeau.[130]

Obviously this should not be seen as a qualification of the textual approach, because exceptions as well as primary provisions must be interpreted in terms of their plain meaning. This prompts the emphasis on the limited ambit of such exceptions, because the lack of their determinacy could otherwise endanger the integrity of the primary obligations under the relevant treaty.

In *US–Gasoline*, the WTO Appellate Body had to interpret the ambit of the exception under Article XX(g) GATT entitling States-parties to take measures 'relating to the conservation of exhaustible natural resources'. The Appellate Body stated that this exception must be read in accordance with the object and purpose of the General Agreement. As for the interpretative policy:

> the phrase 'relating to the conservation of exhaustible natural resources' may not be read so expansively as seriously to subvert the purpose and object of Article III:4. Nor may Article III:4 be given so broad a reach as effectively to emasculate Article XX(g) and the policies and interests it embodies. The relationship between the affirmative commitments set out in, *e.g.*, Articles I, III and XI, and the policies and interests embodied in the 'General Exceptions' listed in Article XX, can be given meaning within the framework of the General Agreement and its object and purpose by a treaty interpreter only on a case-to-case basis, by careful scrutiny of the factual and legal context in a given dispute, without disregarding the words actually used by the WTO Members themselves to express their intent and purpose.[131]

It must be noted that the Appellate Body does not stipulate any sort of general interpretative presumption, for instance by stating that exceptions must be interpreted restrictively. This can further be seen in the example of the Appellate Body's treatment of the argument that in order to constitute a valid Article XX(g) measure, it must be 'primarily aimed at' the conservation of natural resources. As the Appellate Body puts it, 'the phrase "primarily aimed at" is not itself treaty language and was not designed as a simple litmus test for inclusion or exclusion from Article XX(g)'. Thus, the crucial issue is the interpretation of the text of the treaty which holds the key to the meaning of the exception clause. The test of 'primarily aimed at' can in a way be relevant for the characterisation of the nature of the measure, but not as the ultimate criterion of its legality.[132]

130 *US–Shrimp*, AB Report, para 157 (emphasis original).
131 *US–Gasoline*, 16ff.
132 *Id*, 17.

The reason for this interpretative policy is that:

> while the exceptions of Article XX may be invoked as a matter of legal right, they should not be so applied as to frustrate or defeat the legal obligations of the holder of the right under the substantive rules of the General Agreement. If those exceptions are not to be abused or misused, in other words, the measures falling within the particular exceptions must be applied reasonably, with due regard both to the legal duties of the party claiming the exception and the legal rights of the other parties concerned.[133]

As the Appellate Body observed in terms of general interpretative policy, 'The fundamental theme is to be found in the purpose and object of avoiding abuse or illegitimate use of the exceptions to substantive rules available in Article XX.'[134] In other words, the interpretation of clauses to determine the extent of the margin of appreciation available to States-parties to a treaty must be guided by the need to avoid abuses of this margin of appreciation. This constitutes the object and purpose of exception clauses. For this purpose, the identification of the objective scope of the relevant clauses is indispensable for precluding the subjective and abusive invocation of exception clauses.

This approach is further reinforced by the Appellate Body's approach that 'The burden of demonstrating that a measure provisionally justified as being within one of the exceptions set out in the individual paragraphs of Article XX does not, in its application, constitute abuse of such exception under the chapeau, rests on the party invoking the exception. That is, of necessity, a heavier task than that involved in showing that an exception, such as Article XX(g), encompasses the measure at issue.' At the same time, the Appellate Body emphasises that the exceptions are meant to cover and justify actions that are otherwise not compatible with the 'primary' obligations under the same treaty:

> The provisions of the chapeau cannot logically refer to the same standard(s) by which a violation of a substantive rule has been determined to have occurred. To proceed down that path would be both to empty the chapeau of its contents and to deprive the exceptions in paragraphs (a) to (j) of meaning. Such recourse would also confuse the question of whether inconsistency with a substantive rule existed, with the further and separate question arising under the chapeau of Article XX as to whether that inconsistency was nevertheless justified. One of the corollaries of the 'general rule of interpretation' in the Vienna Convention is that interpretation must give meaning and effect to all the terms of a treaty. An interpreter is not free to adopt a reading that would result in reducing whole clauses or paragraphs of a treaty to redundancy or inutility.[135]

It therefore seems that the principle of effectiveness as an interpretative principle applies to exception clauses as well. There seems to be no specific presumption

[133] *Id*, 20.
[134] *Id*, 23.
[135] *Id*, 20–21.

with regard to these clauses which in the end are treaty clauses on the same footing as any other clause. In other words, exception clauses must be construed as effective, but as exceptions. The principle of effectiveness cannot enable exception clauses to exceed their profile as exceptions and encroach on what is regulated under the 'primary' provisions under the treaty.

In *US–Shrimp*, the Appellate Body observed that 'because the GATT 1994 itself makes available the exceptions of Article XX, in recognition of the legitimate nature of the policies and interests there embodied, the right to invoke one of those exceptions is not to be rendered illusory'.[136] In the same case, the Appellate Body stated that:

> It is not necessary to assume that requiring from exporting countries compliance with, or adoption of, certain policies (although covered in principle by one or another of the exceptions) prescribed by the importing country, renders a measure *a priori* incapable of justification under Article XX. Such an interpretation renders most, if not all, of the specific exceptions of Article XX inutile, a result abhorrent to the principles of interpretation we are bound to apply.[137]

The Appellate Body again applied the principle of effectiveness to the interpretation of exceptions. Having found in this case that the definition of exhaustible natural resources did not exclude renewable natural resources, the Appellate Body consequently affirmed that the relevant exception under Article XX GATT must be viewed as including a reference to renewable resources. Living resources were as exhaustible as non-living ones and hence 'in line with the principle of effectiveness in treaty interpretation, measures to conserve exhaustible natural resources, whether living or non-living, may fall within Article XX(g)'.[138]

The approach supporting arguably restrictive interpretation of exceptions can be found in the jurisprudence of the European Court of Human Rights. In human rights treaties too, exceptions are, in empirical terms, those which qualify the provisions that are closer to the treaty's object and purpose. In the context of the margin of appreciation, and arguably in a way different from the developments in the WTO jurisprudence, the European Court upholds the thesis for the restrictive interpretation of exceptions. Under this view, it seems that the restrictive interpretation of exceptions is a corollary of the effective interpretation of the primary human rights clauses. But the difference in practice may not be as great. In fact, the Appellate Body also emphasises that exceptions operate in a limited and conditional way. The principle of effectiveness is applied to them in relation to the very basic right to invoke these exceptions, and then in terms of the chapeau which by itself puts further limitations on the operability of specific exceptions under Article XX GATT. Thus, the Appellate Body acts in a context where the exceptions are already of limited and conditional ambit. Effective

[136] *US–Shrimp*, para 156.
[137] *Id*, para 120.
[138] *US–Shrimp*, para 131.

interpretation has to ensure that they can be invoked if the State-party so decides, but this cannot guarantee that the relevant measure will be seen as compatible with the relevant covered agreement.

In fact, the European Court's restrictive interpretation of exceptions is never meant to restrain the invocation of exceptions in terms of legitimate aim, but merely relates to the analysis of specific measures allegedly covered by the relevant invocation. Thus, in the end the ECHR and WTO contexts are not very radically different. As the Court stated in the *Klass* case dealing with alleged infringement of privacy through telephone surveillance, Article 8(2) of the Convention:

> since it provides for an exception to a right guaranteed by the Convention, is to be narrowly interpreted. Powers of secret surveillance of citizens, characterising as they do the police state, are tolerable under the Convention only in so far as strictly necessary for safeguarding the democratic institutions.[139]

Then the Court proceeded to examine this problem in terms of the margin of appreciation. It may be asked whether this is really a question of restrictive interpretation rather than the rigorous application of the conditions of the margin of appreciation. However, in *United Communist Party*, the European Court links the issue of strict construction to that of the margin of appreciation:

> the exceptions set out in Article 11 are, where political parties are concerned, to be construed strictly; only convincing and compelling reasons can justify restrictions on such parties' freedom of association. In determining whether a necessity within the meaning of Article 11 § 2 exists, the Contracting States have only a limited margin of appreciation, which goes hand in hand with rigorous European supervision embracing both the law and the decisions applying it, including those given by independent courts.[140]

It is arguable that the restrictive, or strict, construction of exception clauses in the context of the European Convention may follow from the object and purpose of this instrument.

In the *Silver* case, the European Court addressed the interpretation of exceptions with reference to Article 8(2) of the Convention and emphasised that 'those paragraphs of Articles of the Convention which provide for an exception to a right guaranteed are to be narrowly interpreted'. The Court applied this approach to its use of the margin of appreciation.[141] In *Vogt*, the European Court emphasised that the exceptions under Article 10(2) must be 'narrowly interpreted and the necessity for any restrictions must be convincingly established'. This entailed that the necessity of the relevant governmental measure had to serve 'pressing social need'.[142]

In the *McCann* case, the European Court emphasised that Article 2 safeguarding the right to life enshrines one of the basic values of democratic societies. It not only safeguards the right to life but sets out the circumstances in which the

[139] *Klass v FRG*, Application No 5029/71, 6 September 1978, para 42.
[140] *United Communist Party*, para 46.
[141] *Silver v UK*, Nos 5947/72, 6205/73, 7052/75, Judgment of 25 March 1983, para 97.
[142] *Vogt v Germany*, Application No 17851/91, 26 September 1995, para 52.

deprivation of life may be justified. The text of Article 2, read as a whole, demonstrated that paragraph 2 did not primarily define instances where it is permitted intentionally to kill an individual, but described the situations where it is permitted to 'use force' which may result, as an unintended outcome, in the deprivation of life. The use of force, however, must be no more than 'absolutely necessary' for the achievement of one of the purposes. This followed from the principle that the exceptions admitted under Article 2 were to be strictly construed. In particular, the force used must be strictly proportionate to the achievement of the aims set out in Article 2.[143] Therefore, the Court stated that its task was to 'subject deprivations of life to the most careful scrutiny, particularly where deliberate lethal force is used, taking into consideration not only the actions of the agents of the State who actually administer the force but also all the surrounding circumstances including such matters as the planning and control of the actions under examination'.[144]

In *Council of Civil Service Unions v UK*, the European Commission on Human Rights also tackled the issue of interpretation of exceptions, in this case with reference to Article 11 of the Convention. This case is significant for its peculiar treatment of the claim that exceptions should be 'narrowly construed' since, as the applicant had put it, 'a broad interpretation would remove millions of public sector employees throughout Europe from the protection of Article 11'. This would be disproportionate and would fail in terms of the requirement that the relevant restriction must be necessary in a democratic society. Furthermore, the restriction on the right to association could not have meant the destruction of this right.

The Commission relied on the fact that the 'democratic society' requirement under Article 11(2) did not necessarily apply to members of the State administration, because their position was regulated by a separate saving clause in the same paragraph. The Commission further refused to accept that the restriction of the right under Article 11(2) could not mean the complete prohibition on the exercise of this right. This clause was sufficiently broad to cover these measures.[145] Under this approach, the textual approach is predominant and interpretative presumptions have no specific value.

In some cases, the autonomous meaning of treaty clauses can justify their narrow construction. For instance, in the *Vogt* case, the Court in principle upheld the narrow construal of the notion of 'administration of the State' under Article 11(2) of the Convention which is about restricting freedom of assembly for members of the State administration. The Court in principle approved the reading according to which teachers could not be part of the State administration and subjected to Article 11(2) restrictions even if they were considered as part of the State administration under the German legal system.[146]

143 *McCann v UK*, Application No 18984/91, 25 September 1995, paras 147–149.
144 *Id*, para 150.
145 *Council of Civil Service Unions v UK*, 50 *DR* (1987), 228.
146 *Vogt*, paras 67–68.

5. Institutional Implications of Effective Interpretation

Originally, Hersch Lauterpacht related the effective operation of treaties to the effective construction of powers of institutions established on the basis of these treaties.[147] More specifically, this involves considering the implied powers of international organisations and the inherent powers of international tribunals.

(a) Implied Powers of International Organisations

The criteria of the object and purpose of the treaty, including the principle of effectiveness, have some relevance and implications in construing the scope of institutional powers which derive from treaty instruments. Normally States possess all the powers emanating from their sovereignty unless they have agreed to their restriction through the rule of international law. International organisations only possess the powers delegated to them.

The concept of implied rights or powers operates as a concept of treaty interpretation in general, which means that certain rights and powers necessary for the operation of those expressly stated can be implied in the relevant treaty.[148] International organisations are enterprises that need to exercise their functions and this may require implying some powers which are not expressly stipulated. Judicial practice witnesses the use of principles and logic of treaty interpretation for understanding the scope of powers of international organs, which confirms that the issue of implied powers is, in the final analysis, that of interpretation of constituent instruments.

More specifically, implied powers of international organisations are the incidence of effective interpretation of their constituent instruments. The principle of effectiveness requires implying those 'extensions' of treaty provisions and obligations which follow from the expressly stated ones. Thus, implied powers as an aspect of effectiveness refer to those extensions of expressly delegated powers which are necessary for their effective implementation. The doctrine of implied powers cannot be understood to imply the presence of certain powers simply for the sake of increasing the overall effectiveness of international institutions.

In the *Reparations* Advisory Opinion, the International Court affirmed that the United Nations enjoyed international legal personality. The Court did not deduce this legal personality from some sort of general desirability or utility of international organisations possessing it. The Court rather proceeded from the analysis of those powers, among others, which the Organisation actually had and exercised. The existence and exercise of those specific powers implied

[147] Lauterpacht (1958), 274.
[148] See above Chapter 10.

that the Organisation shall thus be seen as an international legal person.[149] The Court emphasised that implied powers are those which are implied in the constituent instrument of the Organisation,[150] as opposed to powers allegedly implied in the character of the Organisation or required for its general efficiency or successful involvement, or any related abstract considerations.

Haraszti correctly urges caution in this field, suggesting that:

> only such rights may be regarded as implied in the sphere of rights expressly guaranteed by a treaty, without which the rights thus granted cannot be exercised at all, or can only be exercised at the expense of sacrifices wholly disproportionate to the end to be achieved.[151]

Bernhardt formulates the following parameters for measuring the scope of implied powers. In the first place, the issue of which powers have to be implied should be addressed not at the outset of the analysis, but only after the textual interpretation of the constituent instrument has been completed. The purpose of the treaty is of particular importance. Secondly, the issue of which powers can be implied depends on the particular treaty, not on any general formula. Thirdly, Bernhardt formulates the principle of reciprocal interaction between the dogma of sovereignty and implied powers. The stronger the former is, the less room there is for the latter. However, Bernhardt complements this analysis with a criterion based on subjectivity, suggesting that this issue depends on the interpreter's perception of the state of international order.[152]

It seems that Bernhardt's third criterion is in contradiction with the first two. If the interpreter has to be guided by methods of interpretation, it is unclear how the interpreter's own perception as to the state of international order could be relevant in this process. This is even more problematic given that the problem of implied powers affects the sensitive field of the delegation of powers to international organisations. Member States cannot be told that the organisation they have established possesses more powers than they have stipulated, because this follows from the interpreter's perception. They can only be told so on the basis that the very constitutive instrument of delegation requires these implied powers to be exercised. In other words, the delegated nature of institutional powers should never be forgotten.

Thus, the implied powers of an international organisation are ascertained just as the principle of effectiveness operates in the case of treaty interpretation in general. Thus, the discourse on implied powers of international organisations is in reality discourse on the relevance of the methods of treaty interpretation as applied

[149] *Reparations for Injuries in the Service of the United Nations*, Advisory Opinion, *ICJ Reports*, 1949, 174 at 178.

[150] *Id*, 180; see also G Haraszti, *Some Fundamental Problems of the Law of Treaties* (1973), 171.

[151] Haraszti (1973), 172.

[152] Bernhardt (1963), 98–99 ('Seine Auffassung über den Stand der internationaler Ordnung wird nicht unerheblich den Umfang der zu implizierender Rechte und Pflichten bestimmen.')

to constituent instruments of the relevant organisations and powers expressly specified under them. The methods of interpretation relevant in this context are the textual, or plain meaning, method, the object and purpose of the treaty, and the principle of effectiveness. As Sir Elihu Lauterpacht observes, 'the principle which plays the largest role in the interpretation of international constitutions is effectiveness'. The doctrine of effectiveness has also acquired the shape of implied powers.[153]

The extension of institutional powers can take place on the basis of subsequent practice under the constituent instrument of the relevant organisation. The power grown into the organisation on the basis of subsequent practice is not strictly an implied power. It is a power additionally conferred upon it by the parties on the basis of their agreement. The general international law factor or the analogy between the positions of different organisations cannot be of direct relevance either, as the merit of implied powers has to be assessed in terms of the position of the individual international organisation.

The *Certain Expenses* Advisory Opinion is a significant illustration of how textual interpretation, in conjunction with the teleological method, can justify implying powers that have not been stipulated. In this case the Court dealt with the question of whether the expenses incurred by the United Nations for peace operations, the establishment of which was not provided for in the Charter, constituted expenses of the United Nations. In its initial adherence to the effective interpretation, the Court emphasised that 'the term "expenses of the Organization" means all the expenses and not just certain types of expenses which might be referred to as "regular expenses" '.[154] There was no reason for restrictive interpretation of the term 'expenses' on account of the fact that the maintenance of peace and security was the primary responsibility of the Security Council. As the Court stressed, primary responsibility is not an exclusive one. The General Assembly was not excluded from activities in this field and its actions could likewise incur expenses on behalf of the United Nations.[155]

The relevant peace operations in the Middle East and the Congo, the cost of which was at issue in this case, were considered by the Court as directed at achieving the purposes of the United Nations under Article 1 of the Charter. Thus, even though the relevant activity was not based on an expressly delegated power, the Court treated these matters as implied powers. As for the expenses incurred in the exercise of the implied powers, the Court observed that:

> In determining whether the actual expenditures authorized constitute 'expenses of the Organization within the meaning of Article 17, paragraph 2, of the Charter', the Court agrees that such expenditures must be tested by their relationship to the purposes of the United Nations in the sense that if an expenditure were made for a purpose which is not

[153] E Lauterpacht, The Development of the Law of International Organisation by the Decisions of International Tribunals, 151 *Recueil des Cours* (III-1976), 420, 423.

[154] *Certain Expenses of the United Nations (Article 17, paragraph 2, of the Charter)*, Advisory Opinion of 20 July 1962, *ICJ Reports*, 1962, 151 at 161–162.

[155] *Id*, 163–165.

one of the purposes of the United Nations, it could not be considered an 'expense of the Organization'.[156]

The specific purpose of the Organisation in this case related to the maintenance of international peace and security. As the Court put it:

> These purposes are broad indeed, but neither they nor the powers conferred to effectuate them are unlimited. Save as they have entrusted the Organization with the attainment of these common ends, the Member States retain their freedom of action. But when the Organization takes action which warrants the assertion that it was appropriate for the fulfilment of one of the stated purposes of the United Nations, the presumption is that such action is not *ultra vires* the Organization.[157]

This often-quoted passage from the Court's Opinion includes some essential observations regarding the interpretation of treaties. The Court affirmed that member States cannot plead their residual sovereignty to prevent the Organisation from exercising its implied powers in pursuance of its Charter-based purposes. This, in turn, illustrates the link between the effective interpretation and its primacy over the pleas of residual sovereignty. These were the factors that caused 'expenses' under Article 17 to be defined in the broadest possible terms, such that they included expenses for activities not even mentioned in the Charter.

In another case, textual interpretation was employed to support the operation of broad institutional powers. In the *Namibia* Advisory Opinion, the International Court adopted the effective interpretation of several provisions of the UN Charter, with the aim of construing the implied powers of the relevant UN principal organs. It was argued in this case that the UN Security Council could not enact binding decisions outside the framework of Chapter VII coercive measures. The Court responded that the plain meaning of Article 25, which confers binding force on the Council's decisions, did not limit this binding force to Chapter VII decisions. In addition, the Court applied the presumption against redundancy method by specifying that:

> If Article 25 had reference solely to decisions of the Security Council concerning enforcement action under Articles 41 and 42 of the Charter, that is to say, if it were only such decisions which had binding effect, then Article 25 would be superfluous, since this effect is secured by Articles 48 and 49 of the Charter [which specify the duty of member States to cooperate with the Council in relation to its enforcement measures].[158]

By way of effective interpretation, the Court observed that the decisions thus adopted bind all members of the UN, including those who are not members of the Council and who have voted against the decision. As the Court put it, 'To hold otherwise would be to deprive this principal organ of its essential functions and powers under the Charter.'[159]

[156] *Id*, 167.
[157] *Id*, 168.
[158] *ICJ Reports*, 1971, 53.
[159] *Id*, 54.

Also in the *Namibia* case, and following its earlier pronouncements in *International Status of South-West Africa*, the Court examined Article 10 of the Charter, which authorises the General Assembly to discuss any questions or any matters within the scope of the Charter and to make recommendations on these questions or matters to the members of the Organisation. The Court affirmed that this power of discussion included the right to receive reports originally received by the League of Nations Council regarding the administration of mandated territories. The Court affirmed that this was the corollary of the broader power under Article 10.[160]

Further effective interpretation of the Charter provisions with the result of construing implied powers is evident from the Court's treatment of Article 24. The issue was whether the Security Council could validly demand that South Africa withdraw from Namibia. The Court noted that Articles 24(1) and 24(2) specifically defined the Council's powers, which did not directly include the power to adopt decisions such as this. Nevertheless, the Court emphasised that 'The reference in paragraph 2 of this Article to specific powers of the Security Council under certain chapters of the Charter does not exclude the existence of general powers to discharge the responsibilities conferred in paragraph 1.'[161] In this case, the effective interpretation of Article 24 'added up' to the Council's expressly stated powers, which were motivated by the object and purpose of the Charter as an interpretative factor. The relevant purpose of the Charter was the achievement of self-determination and the end of colonialism. The Council was presumed to possess the powers required for this and the Charter was deemed to impliedly include the entitlement to exercise such powers.

To recapitulate, the textual and teleological interpretation of constituent instruments of international organisations constitutes the driving force behind the doctrine of implied powers. The purposes of international organisations are the same as the object and purpose of their constitutive treaties. Effective construction of the text and purposes of constituent instruments provides the basis both for the broad construction of expressly stipulated powers, and the implying of some such powers that are not stipulated in the treaty.

(b) Inherent Powers of International Tribunals

The concept of inherent powers is conceptually similar to implied powers, in that both refer to powers that have not expressly been stipulated in the treaty. There is also a conceptual difference between implied powers of international organisations and inherent powers of international tribunals. International organisations are diverse. Some are meant to be a forum for discussion, others are meant to be involved in operational activities, some have general scope of powers while others are restricted to a particular area of international life. International tribunals, on

[160] *Id*, 37. [161] *Id*, 52.

the other hand, have one cardinally important common feature: they are meant to resolve the disputes submitted to them in a complete, final and binding manner. This is the basic essence of the international judicial function.

Consequently, this general formula is relevant in terms of determining what powers can be exercised by the relevant tribunal. In this way, the relevant powers can be inherent. To illustrate, every single international tribunal inevitably needs the power to determine its own jurisdiction, known as *competence de la competence* or *Kompetenz-Kompetenz*, in order to exercise its judicial function meaningfully.

The issue can also be perceived as one of implied powers. In such a case the argument can point to the intention of States-parties to the constituent instrument of the tribunal and the interpretation of that instrument in accordance with the principle of effectiveness. The argument would be that the parties intended that the relevant tribunal should operate effectively and exercise its judicial function meaningfully, for which the relevant judicial powers have to be implied to be possessed by the tribunal. These two options do not contradict each other. Instead they can provide alternative explanations for the single institutional phenomenon of certain powers being exercised by a judicial organ without those powers being mentioned in its constituent instrument.

International judicial jurisdiction, as is known, derives from the consent of States, there being no jurisdiction until and unless consent has been given in the first place.[162] Nevertheless, the concept of international jurisdiction as absolutely dependent upon and limited by the will and consent of States[163] fails to reflect properly the essence of the problem. Such an approach seems to ignore the fact

[162] On the implications of and limits on the consensual principle, see A Orakhelashvili, The Concept of International Judicial Jurisdiction: A Reappraisal, 3 *The Law and Practice of International Courts and Tribunals* (2003), 501–550.

[163] Thirlway, The Law and Procedure of the International Court of Justice, *BYIL* (1998), 4, 6. 'When Jurisdiction is referred to, it must always be asked, "jurisdiction to do what?" Jurisdiction or competence is not, in the sense in which those terms are used in relation to a dispute, a general property vested in the court or tribunal contemplated: it is the power, conferred by the consent of the parties, to make a determination on specified disputed issues which will be binding on the parties because that is what they have consented to.' See also, for a particular scepticism about the inherent powers of the Court, *id*, 21. Thirlway construes the Court's incidental jurisdiction as one based on the inherent powers of the Court to reach conclusions as to its unwillingness to exercise the jurisdiction. Briggs, on the other hand, sees the incidental jurisdiction of the Court in the light of inherent powers which the Court may resort to in order to support the exercise of its principal jurisdiction. The Court may compulsorily exercise these incidental powers regardless of consent by the respondent. Briggs, The Incidental Jurisdiction of the International Court of Justice as Compulsory Jurisdiction, in VD Heydte, Seidl-Hohenveldern, Verosta & Zemanek (ed), *Völkerrecht und Rechtliches Weltbild. Festschrift für Alfred Verdross* (1960), 92–93, 95. For discussion of conceptual issues related to inherent powers see Gaeta, Inherent Powers of International Courts and Tribunals in LC Vorhah *et al* (eds), *Man's Inhumanity to Man, Essays on International Law in Honour of Antonio Cassese* (2003), 353–372. On the nature and scope of inherent powers see generally Orakhelashvili, Concept of International Judicial Jurisdiction: (2003), 501 at 534–538. See also A Orakhelashvili, The World Bank Inspection Panel in Context: Institutional Aspects of the Accountability of International Organisations, 2 *International Organisations Law Review* (2005), 57–102. For the most recent analysis of this problem see C Brown, *A Common Law of International Adjudication* (2007), and The Inherent Powers of International Courts and Tribunals, 76 *BYIL* (2005), 195.

of the existence of certain elements of inherent jurisdiction of international tribunals. Such inherent elements of judicial jurisdiction are present even in cases where there is no clear evidence that the parties have explicitly consented to them by having conferred such powers upon the Court.

In certain cases, tribunals adhere to a broad view on their jurisdiction. In the *Tadic* case, the International Criminal Tribunal for the Former Yugoslavia confronted the question of the notion and extent of its jurisdiction. The Tribunal concluded that its jurisdiction was not identical with its competence *ratione materiae, personae* and *temporis*[164] as enshrined in articles 2 to 5 of its Statute. Rather, the Tribunal took a broad view of its jurisdiction which it considered as encompassing the consideration of all aspects connected with its functioning:

> Jurisdiction is not merely an ambit or sphere (better described in this case as 'competence'); it is basically—as is visible from the Latin origin of the word itself, *jurisdictio*—a legal power, hence necessarily a legitimate power, 'to state the law' *(dire de droit)* within this ambit, in an authoritative and final manner.[165]

Although the jurisdiction of the International Court is said to be based exclusively on the will and consent of States, in cases when such consent is expressed, the Court must understand this consent not narrowly, but in accordance with the need to preserve its judicial function and to exercise its functions as the principal judicial organ of the United Nations. Once there is evidence that a State agrees to the Court's jurisdiction, its consent must be considered as an agreement to the power of the Court to preserve the integrity of its judicial function. Such jurisdiction is not limited to the aspects *ratione materiae, personae* and *temporis* in declarations of acceptance, in a compromise or in treaties containing a jurisdictional clause, but covers each and every issue the clarification of which is related to the exercise of the Court's judicial function. Even though the Court's jurisdiction is limited by the Statute and by various jurisdictional titles which may exist under Article 36, such limitations may not be invoked in order to hinder the Court in acting when this is required by the very essence of its judicial function:

> The constitutive instrument of an international tribunal can limit some of its jurisdictional powers, but only to the extent to which such limitation does not jeopardise 'its judicial character'... Such limitations cannot, however, be presumed and, in any case, they cannot be deduced from the concept of jurisdiction itself.[166]

In *Tadic*, the review of decisions of the United Nations Security Council was an issue which the Tribunal asserted as an issue of its own jurisdiction, the clarification of which was essential for exercising its so-called ordinary jurisdiction.[167] The jurisdiction of the International Court therefore involves the clarification

[164] Contrary to Fitzmaurice, (1986), 434–435.
[165] *Tadic*, Decision by the Appellate Chamber, IT-94-1-AR72, 2 October 1995, para. 10.
[166] *Id*, para. 11.
[167] *Id*, para. 12.

and review of any legal situation or circumstance which may be a precondition for the exercise by the Court of jurisdiction *ratione materiae*, *personae* and *temporis* which is conferred on it under jurisdictional instruments in accordance with its Statute. This power pertains to the inherent jurisdiction of the Court[168] and therefore exists irrespective of whether the Court's Statute explicitly empowers it to make such a determination or review.

The inherent elements of jurisdiction must be presumed to exist to the extent that they are necessary for the proper administration of the judicial function as such. It is well established that international tribunals possess the inherent jurisdiction to award remedies in disputes they adjudicate.[169] In *Chorzów Factory*, the Permanent Court accepted the view that the power to award reparation, as a natural consequence of every internationally wrongful act, was within the Court's jurisdiction and no additional consent of the parties was necessary.[170] In *Corfu Channel*, the International Court considered that it possessed the inherent jurisdiction to calculate compensation, as this issue was a precondition for the finality of the settlement of a dispute.[171] In *Fisheries Jurisdiction*, the Court, despite objections by the respondent, construed the issue of compensation for wrongful acts as an inherent part of the dispute and thus affirmed its inherent jurisdiction to decide on this issue.[172] In *Nicaragua*, the Court expressly affirmed that 'jurisdiction to determine the merits of a dispute entails jurisdiction to determine reparation'.[173] These instances confirm, in particular, that the inherent elements of the Court's jurisdiction are necessary to ensure 'the effectiveness of the undertaking contained in the jurisdictional clause' and the Court should be considered as possessing the relevant jurisdictional powers.[174]

In the material sense, the principle of consent serves not as the basis of the entire judicial jurisdiction, but of one of its elements only, namely the so-called 'primary' or 'substantive' jurisdiction. Only this type of jurisdiction requires a consensual acceptance by States. The existence and operation of other elements of judicial jurisdiction, designated as its inherent or incidental aspects, depends not on the consent of States, but on the mere fact of existence of a given tribunal and its constituent instrument. This may hold true for *competence de la competence*, indication of provisional measures, interpretation of judgments, admissibility of third-party intervention, award of remedies and other issues. The non-consensual nature of those powers is further demonstrated by the fact that tribunals possess and exercise some of these powers even in the absence of corresponding provisions in their constituent instruments. This was very clear in *LaGrand*, where the consensual principle

168 *Id*, para. 14.

169 Brownlie, Remedies in the International Court of Justice in V Lowe & G Fitzmaurice (eds), *Fifty Years of the International Court of Justice* (1996), 557–558.

170 *Chorzów Factory*, *PCIJ Series* A, No 7 (1926), 23.

171 *Corfu Channel*, Merits, *ICJ Reports*, 1949, 26.

172 *Fisheries Jurisdiction*, *ICJ Reports*, 1974, 203.

173 *Nicaragua*, Merits, *ICJ Reports*, 1986, 142.

174 Lauterpacht, (1958), 246, 248.

was pleaded with regard to powers to issue binding provisional measures and to award certain remedies, such as guarantees of non-repetition. The Court was not explicitly empowered under its Statute to exercise any of these powers, but it spoke in the language of inherent powers, and dismissed the objections.[175] A similar approach prevailed in the *Avena* case where the International Court overruled consent-related objections of the United States and affirmed its inherent power to award remedies in general and guarantees of repetition in particular.[176]

To conclude, the inherent power to award compensation is based on effective interpretation of the relevant constituent instrument of the tribunal. Tribunals must be assumed to have certain inherent powers, in the absence of their express conferral, in order to effectively exercise their judicial function. Furthermore, through exercise of their inherent powers, tribunals are in a position to determine the scope of substantive jurisdiction. The very question 'To what extent is the principle of consent relevant?' has thus to be determined through the exercise of non-consensual judicial powers.

[175] On this issue, see A. Orakhelashvili, Questions of International Judicial Jurisdiction in the *LaGrand* case, *Leiden Journal of International Law*, No 1, 2002, at 105–130.

[176] See on both these cases below, Chapter 12.

12

Interpretation of Jurisdictional Instruments

1. Doctrinal Argument

The consensual basis of international judicial jurisdiction is often perceived as relevant in determining the principles applicable to the interpretation of jurisdictional instruments. The key question is whether the consensual nature of jurisdiction warrants the adoption of any specific method of interpretation of such instruments. As Fitzmaurice points out, 'neither a deliberately liberal nor a deliberately restrictive interpretation of such clauses can be justified'.[1] He suggests that the only thing which is required is strict proof of consent.[2] But he also maintains that 'there is a need for caution and restraint in construing *all* jurisdictional clauses [because they are jurisdictional ones]. ... To say this, is quite a different thing from advocating any deliberately "restrictive" interpretation of such clauses.'[3] But in essence, this is a repetition of the same proposition in different terms. If there is a need for restraint in construction of a jurisdictional clause because it is a jurisdictional clause, then it is difficult to imagine how they should not be interpreted restrictively. On the other hand, as Lauterpacht suggests, an intention to confer jurisdiction on a tribunal 'must, and can, be proved in the same way as any other obligation undertaken in a treaty or an instrument equivalent thereto'.[4] There seems thus to be no requirement under international law to adopt a restrictive interpretation of *any* instrument;[5] for the only purpose interpretation serves is the clarification of the meaning of a text.

[1] G Fitzmaurice, *The Law and Procedure of the International Court of Justice* (1986), 513.

[2] *Id*, 514.

[3] *Id*, 505 (emphasis original); it is noteworthy that here Fitzmaurice explains the need for restraint and caution in construing jurisdictional clauses not because they are different from treaties, but because they are jurisdictional. In the policy perspective, Fitzmaurice favours interpretation in favour of the respondent (and this confirms that his distinction between the notions of restrictive interpretation and caution and restraint is rather half-hearted). For a similar view see E Lauterpacht, *Aspects of Administration of International Justice* (1991), 23.

[4] H Lauterpacht, *The Development of International Law by the International Court* (1958), 338–339.

[5] According to Shihata, 'the concept of restrictive interpretation proved to have no significance in the work of the Court related to the interpretation of jurisdictional instruments', *The Power of the International Court to Determine its Own Jurisdiction* (1965), 190. See also in support of this view Bin Cheng, *General Principles of Law* (1953), 277–278, for the judicial practice regarding jurisdictional clauses.

The Court pointed out, by reference to its previous jurisprudence that:

> the establishment or otherwise of jurisdiction is not a matter for the parties but for the Court itself. Although a party seeking to assert a fact must bear the burden of proving it, this has no relevance for the establishment of the Court's jurisdiction, which is a question of law to be resolved in the light of the relevant facts. That being so, there is no burden of proof to be discharged in the matter of jurisdiction. Rather, it is for the Court to determine from all the facts and taking into account all the arguments advanced by the Parties, whether the force of the arguments militating in favour of jurisdiction is preponderant, and to ascertain whether an intention on the part of the Parties exists to confer jurisdiction upon it.[6]

The Court's reference to intention in this context, and in such a way, confirms that the fact of the intention of the State is not connected with presumptions for or against the existence of jurisdiction in the given case. In other words, intention is not something that impacts the standards of interpretation but something that is ascertained after the use of interpretative methods as they stand. International obligations relating to judicial settlement of international disputes are fully fledged obligations like any other obligation in which States can place confidence. Therefore, jurisdictional clauses must be interpreted just like any other conventional obligation, in accordance with their genuine meaning.

2. Interpretation of Special Agreements and Compromissory Clauses

As the Permanent Court observed in the *Lotus* case regarding the interpretation of Special Agreements, 'It is rather to the terms of this agreement than to the submissions of the Parties that the Court must have recourse in establishing the precise points which it has to decide.'[7] In another case, Judge Hudson formulated the essence of the judicial task of interpreting Special Agreements that submit disputes to the Court:

> It is the task of the Court to interpret this special agreement. In the performance of this task, the Court is not bound by the interpretations given to the instrument by the parties. Nor is it bound to confine itself to dealing with the instrument in the light of the arguments advanced by the parties. The questions to be decided are those contained in the special agreement as the Court itself construes that agreement; they may or may not be the same as those to which the parties have addressed themselves. Whatever may be the position when obligatory jurisdiction is being exercised, in answering a question placed before it by a special agreement the Court must have full freedom to construe the terms of

[6] *Fisheries Jurisdiction* (Spain v Canada), Judgment of 4 December 1998, paras 37–38 (references deleted).

[7] *Lotus*, *PCIJ Series* A, 10, at 13.

the agreement, to say what is the question which the agreement requires it to answer, and to frame its answer in accordance with the applicable law.[8]

The interpretative policy thus formulated emphasises that any relevance of auto-interpretation is excluded and a judicial organ has to decide on the basis of applicable law. The long-standing jurisprudence elaborates upon the principles of interpretation that are applicable in this field.

In the *Lighthouses* case, the Permanent Court of International Justice had to interpret a Special Agreement concluded between France and Greece in order to establish the precise import of the question it contained. The question was whether the contract involved in the case 'was duly entered into and was accordingly operative as regards the Greek Government in so far as it concerned lighthouses situated in the territories assigned to it after the Balkan wars or subsequently'.[9] The parties disagreed on the scope of this question. France argued that while the question asked whether the contract was validly concluded under Ottoman law before World War I, it did not include the issue of 'what binding effect, if any, the contract possesses as regards Greece in the territories in which certain lighthouses are situated'. The Special Agreement referred, according to France, to the validity of the contract under Ottoman law and then asked whether that contract '*is accordingly* operative as regards the Greek Government,' thus treating the opposability of the contract towards Greece as a mere emanation of its validity under Ottoman law and as an issue that should not be examined on its merits as an independent issue. France similarly argued that the issue of the intention of the parties to the contract was also excluded from the ambit of the question.[10]

The Court pointed out that the words 'duly entered into' did not have a technical meaning. Where the text and context of the Special Agreement was insufficient for discovering what the parties had meant thereby, the Court had 'to consult the documents preparatory to the Special Agreement, in order to satisfy itself as to the true intention of the Parties'. The Preamble referred to the representations France had made to Greece for the recognition of the validity of the contract that had proved fruitless, and therefore found that the dispute between the two parties turned on this point. While the Agreement used the words 'validity of the contract' and did not specifically refer to the validity as against Greece, the Court found that the precise import of the question the Agreement put was unclear, because the notion of validity could be understood either as including the validity of the contract as against Greece or not including that issue.[11] From the preceding events, the Court was unable to conclude that the issue of the contract being 'duly entered into' necessarily referred to its validity as regards the

[8] *Lighthouses in Crete and Samos*, 17 March 1934, *PCIJ Series* A/B, No 71, at 120.

[9] *Lighthouses Case* (France v Greece), 8 October 1934, *PCIJ Series* A/B, No 62, 4 at 13.

[10] *Id*, 13, 14–15 (emphasis added).

[11] *Id*, 13–14.

successor Government.[12] However, the history of the Special Agreement did not exclude the possibility that the words 'duly entered into' included compatibility both with Ottoman and international law.[13] Therefore, the Court rejected the restrictive interpretation of the Special Agreement and upheld the outcome which required that it look at multiple aspects of the dispute. This the Court achieved by reference, among other things, to the preparatory work as the text of the Agreement had not been very clear.

The issue of how a Special Agreement should be interpreted in order to include or exclude submissions by parties to the proceedings also was addressed in the *Borchgrave* case.[14] The Spanish preliminary objection asked the Court 'to decide that the Spanish Government is responsible for its failure to exercise sufficient diligence in the apprehension and prosecution of the persons guilty of the crime on the person of Baron Jacques de Borchgrave', a Belgian national resident in Madrid. Spain requested the Court to declare that it lacked jurisdiction on that point. Spain alleged that the case involved two different areas of responsibility: that of killing the Belgian national and that of failing to apprehend the murderers. Therefore, Spain argued that the Special Agreement was to be interpreted 'strictly' and if so interpreted it would include only the first issue and not the second one. Spain submitted in particular that 'it would be unreasonable to suppose that, sixty days after the disappearance of Baron Jacques de Borchgrave, while its investigation of the matter was still in progress, the Spanish Government would have agreed to submit the question of responsibility for lack of diligence to the Court'. In addition, the diplomatic correspondence showed that the Belgian Government had no intention of including the question of this responsibility in the Special Agreement.[15] Article 1 of the Special Agreement requested the Court, in general terms, to 'to say whether, having regard to the circumstances of fact and of law concerning the case, the responsibility of the Spanish Government is involved'.[16] Drawing on this clause of general character, Spain in effect proposed to use the circumstances of conclusion of the Agreement as the factor that required excluding the issue of due diligence from the scope of the Agreement.

The Court started its analysis by observing that while the Special Agreement was about the death of Baron de Borchgrave, it did not specify the points at issue in this controversy. At the same time, there was 'no limiting reference to the subject-matter of the dispute,' and the Court added that 'Such is the whole of the substance of the Special Agreement. So unlimited are its terms, so free is the text from qualifying expressions, that the Agreement may be said to be characterized by its generality.' Although the Agreement was meant to submit to the Court the dispute '*à propos* the death of Baron Jacques de Borchgrave,' the Court stated

[12] *Id*, 15.
[13] *Id*, 16.
[14] *Borchgrave* (Preliminary Objections), 6 November 1937, *PCIJ Series* A/B, No 72, 158.
[15] *Id*, 162–163.
[16] *Id*, 159.

that 'The term *à propos* is in no sense limitative, and in itself it sets no restriction on the jurisdiction of the Court.'[17]

In order to ascertain the scope of that dispute or controversy, the Court decided to examine the diplomatic correspondence between the two States after the death of Borchgrave, and it discovered that Belgium had duly raised the issue of investigation of the murder in this case, and the apprehension and punishment of the perpetrators. The attitude of Belgium subsequent to the conclusion of the Agreement similarly confirmed that the narrow understanding of the scope of dispute as limited to the fact of murder only was unfounded. Therefore, the Court overruled the preliminary objection of Spain and asserted its jurisdiction over the entire controversy.[18] This case is illustrative of the application of the principle of effectiveness and of the rejection of restrictive interpretation. The text of the jurisdictional clause, even if broadly drafted, should be deemed to include all aspects of the dispute that is before the Court. This case also confirms, albeit indirectly, that jurisdictional clauses must be deemed to cover all the legal aspects of the dispute that can be so characterised in terms of the substantive law applicable to the dispute, unless a contrary intention of the parties can be unambiguously established by reference to clear interpretative data.

In *Corfu Channel*, the International Court of Justice had to interpret a Special Agreement between the UK and Albania to determine whether it imposed on Albania the duty to compensate for its lack of vigilance which ultimately caused mine incidents with British ships near the Albanian coast. The second question in the Agreement requested the Court to determine whether there was 'any duty to pay compensation'. During the oral proceedings Albania, 'for the first time' as the Court put it, argued that the Court did not have to assess the amount of compensation.[19]

The Court observed that the text gave rise to certain doubts. But the Court also noted that a positive answer to the first question in the Agreement would automatically mean that compensation was due, and that the second question would be superfluous unless the parties meant something other than the mere statement that compensation was due,[20] which was not at all certain because it would be completely understandable if the parties just wanted the Court to answer the question whether Albania was responsible for the mining, and to answer the second question in accordance with its literal meaning.

The Court's crucial argument was, however, that 'it would indeed be incompatible with the generally accepted rules of interpretation to admit that a provision of this sort occurring in a special agreement should be devoid of its purport and effect'.[21] Therefore the Special Agreement was deemed to request the Court

[17] *Id*, 164.
[18] *Id*, 167–168.
[19] *Corfu Channel*, Merits (UK v Albania), *ICJ Reports*, 1949, 4 at 23.
[20] *Id*, 23–24.
[21] *Id*, 24.

to assess the amount of compensation, which the Court did at a later stage, in accordance with the interpretative principle of effectiveness. The Court's reference to 'the generally accepted rules of interpretation' as the basis of its approach certifies that it considered the principle of effectiveness as the governing canon of jurisdictional instruments, and more broadly as the governing principle of the interpretation of treaties and international acts in general.

In accordance with the principles of treaty interpretation, the Court also referred to subsequent practice of the parties to establish that 'it was not their intention, by entering into the Special Agreement, to preclude the Court from fixing the amount of compensation'.[22] The Court could not possibly have meant that subsequent practice itself proved intention that was previous to it and embodied in the Special Agreement. The Court in fact based its approach on the text of the Agreement and its understanding by the parties. The Agreement, apart from asking whether compensation was due from Albania for the damage caused to British warships, also asked the Court to decide whether satisfaction was due from the UK to Albania for its unauthorised naval operations in Albanian waters. Albania had not disputed that the Court was competent under the Special Agreement to determine what kind of satisfaction was due. As a general attitude, the Court concluded that 'it cannot be supposed that the Parties, while drafting these clauses in the same form, intended to give them opposite meanings—the one as giving the Court jurisdiction, the other as denying such jurisdiction'.[23] In the end, as we can see, textual interpretation of jurisdictional instruments proved crucial.

In *Ambatielos* (Preliminary Objections), the Court rejected a plea for restrictive interpretation of jurisdictional clauses. The Court had to clarify whether its jurisdiction could be established on the basis of the 1926 Declaration adopted together with the 1926 Anglo-Greek Treaty of Commerce and Navigation that replaced the similar 1886 Treaty. The 1926 Declaration provided that the 1926 Treaty did not prejudice private claims under the 1886 Treaty and provided recourse to arbitration under it.[24] The Court observed that the Declaration, which embodied the understanding of both parties, covered all possible claims under the 1886 Treaty. The Court emphasised that to introduce differences in terms of which cases were and which cases were not subject to arbitral jurisdiction 'introduces a distinction for which the Court sees no justification in the plain language of the Declaration'.[25] That the Court applied the principle of effectiveness to jurisdictional clauses and was unwilling to interpret the relevant clause restrictively is clear from President McNair's objections that Article 36(1) of the Court's Statute did not envisage 'so slender a consensual foundation as is afforded

[22] *Id*, 25.

[23] *Id*, 25–26.

[24] *Ambatielos* (Greece v UK), Preliminary Objections, Judgment of 1 July 1952, *ICJ Reports*, 1952, 28 at 36.

[25] *Id*, 41; see further at 45.

by the use of one of these venerable and routine formulas'.[26] While McNair was vigorously arguing for the relevance of the principle of consent as the basis of judicial jurisdiction, the Court's treatment of the issue makes it clear that the sole relevance the consensual principle can have is based on the interpretation of the relevant instruments through the normal interpretative principles. Should jurisdiction be established through such process, the principle of consent can do precious little to upset this outcome.

In *Fisheries Jurisdiction* (UK v Iceland) the Court had to interpret the compromissory clause included in the Exchange of Notes of 11 March 1961 between the two parties pursuant to Article 36(1) of the Court's Statute. The resulting treaty provided that the Icelandic Government would give the UK six months' notice of the extension of its fisheries jurisdiction and any disputes on such extension should be submitted to the Court. The dispute related to 'the extension by Iceland of its fisheries jurisdiction beyond the 12-mile limit in the waters above its continental shelf'. The Court had to determine 'whether the resulting dispute falls within the compromissory clause of the 1961 Exchange of Notes as being one for determination by the Court'. As a matter of interpretative policy of jurisdictional clauses, the Court reiterated that it would normally apply the principle 'according to which there is no occasion to resort to preparatory work if the text of a convention is sufficiently clear in itself. However, having regard to the peculiar circumstances or the present proceedings, as set forth in paragraph 12 above [which related to the non-appearance of Iceland before the Court], and in order fully to ascertain the scope and purpose of the 1961 Exchange of Notes, the Court will undertake a brief review of the negotiations that led up to that exchange.'[27] The Court found that it had jurisdiction on the basis of the Exchange of Notes, and this conclusion was reinforced by the drafting history, which demonstrated that proposals providing for conditionality for recourse to the International Court were replaced by those providing for the unconditional right of the UK to seise the Court.[28] As the Court put it:

This history reinforces the view that the Court has jurisdiction in this case, and adds emphasis to the point that the real intention of the parties was to give the United Kingdom Government an effective assurance which constituted a *sine qua non* and not merely a severable condition of the whole agreement: namely, the right to challenge before the Court the validity of any further extension of Icelandic fisheries jurisdiction in the waters above its continental shelf beyond the 12-mile limit. In consequence, the exercise of jurisdiction by the Court to entertain the present Application would fall within the terms of the compromissory clause and correspond exactly to the intentions and expectations of both

[26] *Id*, 62 (Dissenting Opinion); for a similar attitude see the Joint Dissenting Opinion of Judges McNair, Basdevant, Klaestad and Read at the merits stage of the same case, *ICJ Reports*, 1953, 28–29.

[27] *Fisheries Jurisdiction* (UK v Iceland), Jurisdiction of the Court, Judgment of 2 February 1973, *ICJ Reports*, 1973, 3 at 8–10.

[28] *Id*, 11–12.

Parties when they discussed and consented to that clause. It thus appears from the text of the compromissory clause, read in the context of the 1961 Exchange of Notes and in the light of the history of the negotiations, that the Court has jurisdiction.[29]

Therefore, judicial jurisdiction was an essential part of the deal, part of the object and purpose of the Exchange of Notes, and the Court interpreted this treaty so as to make the jurisdictional clause effective and free of any conditionality.

Judge Waldock took the matter further, declaring at the merits stage that while the object and purpose of the 1961 Agreement was to give the UK an assurance of judicial settlement, that object and purpose would also require the Court to declare the Icelandic expansion of fisheries zones to 50 miles void, so as not to allow Iceland to benefit from its own wrong by leaving the issue of invalidity open.[30] While on the one hand Judge Waldock had a point that possibly linked invalidity with the object and purpose of the 1961 Treaty, it is also true that this Treaty was meant to regulate bilateral relations between the two parties and hence the Court's task was to settle the dispute on a bilateral basis, for which the finding of non-opposability was presumably quite sufficient.

At the merits stage of this case, the Court had to interpret the interim agreement on the fisheries dispute between the UK and Iceland, pending the final settlement. The Court acknowledged that originally, 'the United Kingdom insisted upon receiving an assurance concerning the future extension of Iceland's fishery jurisdiction and a compromissory clause was then included in the Exchange of Notes which was agreed by the Parties on 11 March 1961'. After a decade of disagreements, the Interim Agreement, which was set out in the Icelandic note, was concluded in 1973 and was supposed to run for two years without affecting the position of any party with respect to the substantive dispute.[31] As the Court described it, the 1973 arrangement was, unlike the 1961 Exchange of Notes, an interim arrangement not designed to settle the dispute. Therefore, the Court was not supposed to decline to exercise jurisdiction on the grounds of the dispute having been settled.[32] As for construing the scope of the 1961 compromissory clause, the Court observed that:

this gives the Court jurisdiction with respect to 'a dispute in relation to such extension', i.e., 'the extension of fisheries jurisdiction around Iceland'. The present dispute was occasioned by Iceland's unilateral extension of its fisheries jurisdiction. However, it would be too narrow an interpretation of the compromissory clause to conclude that the Court's jurisdiction is limited to giving an affirmative or a negative answer to the question of whether the extension of fisheries jurisdiction, as enacted by Iceland on 14 July 1972, is in conformity with international law. In the light of the negotiations between the Parties,...in which the questions of fishery conservation measures in the area and

[29] *Id*, 12–13.

[30] Separate Opinion, *Fisheries Jurisdiction*, Merits (UK v Iceland), Judgment of 25 July 1974, *ICJ Reports* 1974, 117–118.

[31] *Id*, 3 at 12–13, 17–18.

[32] *Id*, 19–20.

Iceland's preferential fishing rights were raised and discussed, and in the light of the proceedings before the Court, it seems evident that the dispute between the Parties includes disagreements as to the extent and scope of their respective rights in the fishery resources and the adequacy of measures to conserve them. It must therefore be concluded that those disagreements are an element of the 'dispute in relation to the extension of fisheries jurisdiction around Iceland'.[33]

Furthermore, as the Court observed:

> the dispute before the Court must be considered in all its aspects. Even if the Court's competence were understood to be confined to the question of the conformity of Iceland's extension with the rules of international law, it would still be necessary for the Court to determine in that context the role and function which those rules reserve to the concept of preferential rights and that of conservation of fish stocks. Thus, whatever conclusion the Court may reach in regard to preferential rights and conservation measures, it is bound to examine these questions with respect to this case. Consequently, the suggested restriction on the Court's competence not only cannot be read into the terms of the compromissory clause, but would unduly encroach upon the power of the Court to take into consideration all relevant elements in administering justice between the Parties.[34]

Judge Waldock also argued that due to the Court's 1973 pronouncement on the scope of the compromissory clause under the Exchange of Notes, this clause should be construed as encompassing the issue of preferential fishery rights along with the limits of the fishery zones of Iceland.[35] Given all that, this case offers yet more evidence of the vigorous affirmation of the principle of effectiveness and the rejection of restrictive interpretation. The need to effectively resolve the dispute arising under the jurisdictional clause caused the construction of the scope of that clause so as to make it as effective as possible.

Judge Nagendra Singh upheld the Court's approach in considering all aspects of the dispute. Consequently, the principle of consent could not operate to restrict the jurisdiction of the Court which needed to be exercised effectively:

> it was in the overall interests of settlement of the dispute that certain parts of it which were inseparably linked to the core of the conflict were not separated in this case to be left unpronounced upon. The Court has, of course, to be mindful of the limitations that result from the principle of consent as the basis of international obligations, which also governs its own competence to entertain a dispute. However, this could hardly be taken to mean that a tribunal constituted as a regular court of law when entrusted with the determination of a dispute by the willing consent of the parties should in any way fall short of fully and effectively discharging its obligations. It would be somewhat disquieting if the Court were itself to adopt either too narrow an approach or too restricted an interpretation of

33 *Id*, 21.

34 *Id*, 21–22.

35 *Id*, 122–123, 125 (Separate Opinion).

those very words which confer jurisdiction on the Court such as in this case 'the extension of fisheries jurisdiction around Iceland' occurring in the compromissory clause of the Exchange of Notes of 1961. Those words could not be held to confine the competence conferred on the Court to the sole question of the conformity or otherwise of Iceland's extension of its fishery limits with existing legal rules.[36]

This proves again that the textual method of interpretation is always more relevant than the presumptive relevance of the consensual basis of jurisdiction.

Judge Gros took a more restrictive view, asserting that the Court could not extend the jurisdiction recognised by States and had only to decide on the Icelandic extension of the fishery zone.[37] The Court had also exceeded its jurisdiction by requiring the parties to reach an equitable settlement.[38] The conservation issue was, according to Judge Gros, not an element of dispute under the 1961 Exchange of Notes.[39] Judge Onyeama followed a similar line of reasoning.[40]

In the *Tunisia–Libya Continental Shelf Case* the Court dealt with the interpretation of the Special Agreement by which the case was submitted to it. Under Article 1 of that Agreement, the parties asked the Court to determine the principles and rules applicable to the delimitation of their continental shelves, and specifically to take into account, among other things, 'equitable principles' and 'new accepted trends' of the law of the sea, especially in terms of the Third UN Conference on the subject.[41]

Generally, the determination of applicable law can be crucial in deciding the case. The Court pointed out that the work of the UN Conference had not come to an end and hence its 'trends' could not by themselves constitute *lex specialis* between the parties which could have given them such status had they so wished and stipulated in the Special Agreement. But they had not been so specific. Hence, the Court shared Tunisia's approach that those 'trends' could serve as 'factors of interpretation of the existing rules'. Nevertheless, the Court concluded that it could not ignore the provisions of the draft UN convention on the law of the sea 'if it came to the conclusion that the content of such provision is binding upon all members of the international community because it embodies or crystallizes a pre-existing or emergent rule of customary law'.[42] The Court's approach confirmed its willingness to give fullest possible effect to the Special Agreement. Even if it were based on consent, it must be interpreted

[36] Declaration of Judge Nagendra Singh, *id*, 42.
[37] Dissenting Opinion of Judge Gros, *id*, 126, 129.
[38] *Id*, 136.
[39] *Id*, 148.
[40] Dissenting Opinion of Judge Onyeama, *id*, 1974, 173.
[41] *Case concerning Continental Shelf* (Tunisia/Libyan Arab Jamahiriya), Judgment of 24 February 1982, *ICJ Reports*, 1982, 18 at 37.
[42] *Id*, 38.

so as to enable the Court to resolve the dispute taking into consideration all relevant legal factors.

The Court confronted another disagreement of the parties as to the interpretation of Article 1:

> From one aspect, the dispute is whether Article 1 submits to the Court two distinct questions, namely, first, what are the applicable rules and principles of international law, and secondly, what is the practical method for their application; or whether these are simply two facets of a single question. From another aspect, and expressed in more practical form, the dispute relates to the degree of precision of the judgment of the Court, and the corresponding extent or absence of freedom of the Parties and their experts in defining the line of delimitation.[43]

According to Tunisia, the Court's task was to specify practical ways of applying legal principles and itself to decide on both legal and practical points, after which the parties would be left with the task of technical application of what had been determined by the Court and thus the dispute would be resolved in such a way as to leave no substantial disagreements between the parties. According to Libya, however, the Court was not authorised to carry the matter right up to the ultimate point before the purely technical work. As the Court rightly stated, Libya had thus argued in favour of restrictive interpretation of the Special Agreement.[44] In fact, the submissions of the two parties clearly illustrate the tension between restrictive interpretation and the principle of effectiveness. The arguments of Tunisia constituted a plea for such interpretation of the Special Agreement as would ensure the effective resolution of the dispute between the two States.

The Court refused to see any cardinal distinction between the method of delimitation and the practical method of application of rules and principles governing delimitation. Therefore, the whole controversy was 'of minor importance'. The essence of judicial function required precision from the Court as to what it decided. This upheld the interpretation of the Special Agreement exactly as requiring the precise delimitation of the relevant continental shelves.[45] Therefore, the essence of judicial function brought about the upholding of the principle of effectiveness as the principle governing jurisdictional clauses, and rejection of the relevance of restrictive interpretation.

The Separate Opinion of Judge Jimenez de Arechaga confirms that the issue of the interpretation of the Special Agreement was interlinked with the degree of precision of the Court's judgment. Had the Court gone along with the broad terms of Libya's submissions, this would have left further room for negotiations and substantial disagreement between the parties after the judgment had been rendered. The text of the Agreement required such indication of the delimitation principles as would have enabled the parties and their experts

43 *Id*, 39.
44 *Id*, 39.
45 *Id*, 39–40.

to delimit the maritime boundaries 'without any difficulties', as opposed to the situation where the implementation of the Court's judgment would depend upon the subsequent agreement of the parties. The Court must prefer such construction of the Agreement as would enable it to exercise its judicial function of deciding the dispute efficiently, finally and precisely. Consequently:

> It would certainly be incompatible with the Statute and with the Court's position as a Court of Justice to accept the interpretation of the Special Agreement which would not advance the settlement of the dispute and which would be dependent for its application on the subsequent agreement of the Parties.[46]

In the *Libya–Malta Continental Shelf Case*, the parties requested the Court, by the Special Agreement, to determine what principles and rules of international law were applicable to the determination of the boundary of their continental shelves, and 'how in practice such principles and rules can be applied by the two Parties in this particular case in order that they may without difficulty delimit such areas by an agreement'.[47] While Malta argued that the Court should delimit the boundary, Libya argued that its task was limited to stating the applicable principles. While Libya preferred that the boundary line were drawn not by the Court but by the parties through an agreement, Malta disagreed, suggesting that in such case 'the reference of the dispute to the Court would then fail to achieve its main purpose'. Malta submitted that the purpose of the Special Agreement was to enable the parties to delimit their shelf boundaries without difficulty, which could not be achieved unless the Court stated in the clearest possible terms how this exercise was to be carried out. Thus, while Malta submitted that the Court should suggest a specific line, Libya argued that the Court should not particularise any method of delimitation.[48] Therefore, in this case too, the interpretation of a jurisdictional clause was to take place in the context of conflict between restrictive interpretation and the principle of effectiveness.

The Court began by observing that its jurisdiction derived from the Special Agreement and the definition of the relevant boundaries was a matter of interpretation of the Special Agreement through ascertainment of the intention of the parties. The Court observed in this jurisdictional context and, in a way most noteworthy from the interpretation perspective, that 'The Court must not exceed the jurisdiction conferred upon it by the Parties, but it must also exercise that jurisdiction to its full extent.'[49] Therefore, if the Court were to decide how the relevant principles were to be implemented in practice 'without difficulty', it had to indicate the methods resulting from applicable principles. Whether the Court should indicate an actual delimitation line would depend upon the

[46] Separate Opinion, *id*, 1982, 100–102.

[47] *Case concerning Continental Shelf* (Libyan Arab Jamahiriya/Malta), Judgment of 3 June 1985, *ICJ Reports*, 1985, 13 at 22.

[48] *Id*, 23.

[49] *Id*, 23–24.

applicable methods. Some methods, such as that of median line, could have only one outcome, while other more indirect methods would require the Court to back them by more detailed indications of criteria. The Court did not consider itself debarred by the Special Agreement from indicating the specific line.[50]

The *Libya–Malta* case again illustrates that the field of interpretation of jurisdictional instruments does not admit of restrictive interpretation. When acting on the basis of the principle of consent on which jurisdiction is based, tribunals are nevertheless bound to give full effect to jurisdictional instruments so as to make them workable and effective.

In the *Tehran Hostages* case, the Court addressed the jurisdictional clause under Article XXI of the 1955 Iran–US Treaty, according to which 'Any dispute between the High Contracting Parties as to the interpretation or application of the present Treaty, not satisfactorily adjusted by diplomacy, shall be submitted to the International Court of Justice, unless the High Contracting Parties agree to settlement by some other pacific means.' The Court specified that:

> While that Article does not provide in express terms that either party may bring a case to the Court by unilateral application... the intention of the parties in accepting such clauses is clearly to provide for such a right of unilateral recourse to the Court, in the absence of agreement to employ some other pacific means of settlement.[51]

In terms of underlying approach, the Court stressed that interpretation was required:

> The very purpose of a treaty of amity, and indeed of a treaty... to promote friendly relations between the two countries concerned. It is precisely when difficulties arise that the treaty assumes its greatest importance, and the whole object of Article XXI, paragraph 2, of the 1955 Treaty was to establish the means for arriving at a friendly settlement of such difficulties by the Court or by other peaceful means. It would, therefore, be incompatible with the whole purpose of the 1955 Treaty if recourse to the Court under Article XXI, paragraph 2, were now to be found not to be open to the parties precisely at the moment when such recourse was most needed.[52]

Thus, the need to follow the object and purpose of the 1955 Treaty induced the Court to interpret it as implying what was not expressly provided. It is also important that this case reaffirms the Court's policy of not interpreting compromissory clauses restrictively even in the face of political contingencies.[53]

In *Armed Actions*, the International Court had to interpret Article XXXI of the 1948 American Treaty on Pacific Settlement of Disputes (Bogota Pact) whereby States-parties had agreed to 'recognize, in relation to any other American State, the jurisdiction of the [International] Court as compulsory *ipso facto*, without the

[50] *Id*, 24.

[51] *United States Diplomatic and Consular Staff in Tehran* (US/Iran), Judgment, *ICJ Reports*, 1980, 3 at 27.

[52] *Id*, 28.

[53] See above Chapter 2.

necessity of any special agreement so long as the present Treaty is in force, in all disputes of a juridical nature'.[54] The Honduran interpretation of this clause was that it incorporated 'into the Pact ... the system of recognition of the Court's jurisdiction under the regime of the "optional clause", i.e., Article 36, paragraph 2, of the [Court's] Statute'. Thus, Honduras argued that Article XXXI required the additional acceptance of to the Court's jurisdiction through a unilateral declaration.[55]

The Court observed that the 'interpretation advanced by Honduras—that Article XXXI must be supplemented by a declaration—is incompatible with the actual terms of the Article. In that text, the parties "declare that they recognize" the Court's jurisdiction "as compulsory *ipso facto*" in the cases there enumerated.'[56] The Court observed that the Article XXXI commitment is an autonomous commitment, independent of any other comparable or parallel commitment. Not only did it not require making a separate declaration recognising the Court's jurisdiction, but also it was not impacted upon by declarations that were made externally to it, that is under Article 36(2).[57]

The Court proceeded to confirm this result of textual interpretation by resorting to the preparatory work. The attitudes of States in the process of ratification and entry into force of the Bogota Pact, together with their subsequent attitudes, confirmed viewing Article XXXI as separate from the operation of Article 36 of the Court's Statute.[58]

Honduras advanced yet another restrictive interpretation of Article XXXI, by arguing that jurisdiction under it operated only after resort to the conciliation procedures under Article XXXII of the Bogota Pact. Nicaragua responded that Article XXXI was an autonomous provision and established jurisdiction independently, whatever the requirement under other Articles of the Pact. The Court emphasised that the Honduran interpretation ran counter to the terms of Article XXXI, which made no reference to Article XXXII.[59] The Court explained that the Honduran interpretation would empty Article XXXI of all content if it were to be admitted that prior conciliation was to be resorted to before jurisdiction of the Court could be established.[60] In order not to presume Article XXXI as redundant, the Court held that the two Articles provided two distinct ways of establishing the Court's jurisdiction. One of them established direct access to the Court and the other required prior resort to conciliation. As Nicaragua had relied on Article XXXI, prior resort to conciliation was irrelevant.[61a]

[54] *Border and Transborder Armed Actions* (Nicaragua v Honduras), Jurisdiction of the Court and Admissibility of the Application, Judgment of 20 December 1988, *ICJ Reports*, 1988, 69 at 78.
[55] *Id*, 82–83.
[56] *Id*, 84.
[57] *Id*, 85.
[58] *Id*, 85–88.
[59] *Id*, 88–89.
[60] *Id*, 89.
[61a] *Id*, 89–90.

It is significant that despite the options of contextual interpretation of the Bogota Pact in this case, namely by viewing Articles XXXI and XXXII as interconnected, which could be a defensible outcome in terms of the textual reading, the Court opted for the effective interpretation of jurisdictional clauses, and affirmed the autonomous operation of jurisdiction under Article XXXI. This approach clearly follows the principle of effectiveness which requires choosing from the two possible readings of the text the one which is more conducive to the general object and purpose of the treaty.

The *Armed Actions* case is also significant for judging the merit of doctrinal contentions that the words have no inherent meaning and the latter must be clarified by reference to context. Context certainly cannot be used to narrow down the meaning of the text, or make the relevant treaty rule less effective. It was sufficient for the Court that Article XXXI made no reference to Article XXXII, even though the latter arguably formed part of the former's context.

In the *Arbitral Award* (Guinea-Bissau v Senegal) case the Court had to interpret the Arbitration Agreement between the two States, to establish whether the Arbitral Award delivered on the basis of that Agreement had properly applied it and consequently was valid. The Court specified, pursuant to the *King of Spain* case, that its function was not to act as a court of appeal in relation to the award but merely to decide on its validity.[61b] Invalidity could result from a decision in excess of, or through failure to exercise, jurisdiction:

> Such manifest breach might result from, for example, the failure of the Tribunal properly to apply the relevant rules of interpretation to the provision of the Arbitration Agreement which govern its competence. An arbitration agreement (*compromis d'arbitrage*) is an agreement between States which must be interpreted in accordance with the general rules of international law governing the interpretation of treaties.

The Court further referred to its earlier jurisprudence on the interpretation of treaties, especially the textual and teleological methods, reflected in the Vienna Convention.[62] Furthermore, as the Court specified, 'when States sign an arbitration agreement, they are concluding an agreement with a very specific object and purpose: to entrust an arbitration tribunal with the task of settling a dispute in accordance with the terms agreed by the parties, who define in the agreement the jurisdiction of the tribunal and determine its limits'.[63] The Court decided the issue by textual analysis of the Arbitration Agreement, namely the fact that the questions put were conditional on each other and the Tribunal was bound to follow this. The preparatory work did not refer to any agreement on the case should the Court answer the first question but not the second one, and hence confirmed the ordinary meaning of Article 2 of the Agreement. The object

[61b] *Arbitral Award* made by the king of Spain, merits, Judgment of 18 November 1960, *ICJ Reports*, 1960, 192.

[62] *Arbitral Award* (Guinea-Bissau v Senegal), *ICJ Reports*, 1989, 54 at 68–70.

[63] *Id*, 70.

and purpose of the Agreement was the settlement of their maritime dispute, but the text was quite clear in its requirements and scope. On this basis, the Court affirmed that the parties' consent had only been given to answer the questions in such a way as presented in the Agreement.[64]

The Separate Opinion of Judge Shahabuddeen also examines aspects of interpretation, and admits that narrow textual meaning can defeat the true object and purpose of the treaty and that the text of the Agreement indicates the general desire for the comprehensive settlement of the dispute. However, 'operative provisions of the Agreement demonstrate a specific intention not fully congruent with that general desire, in the sense that the intention, as so demonstrated, was indeed to realise that desire, and to realise it through the arbitration provided for, but only subject to a condition precedent which, as it turned out, was not satisfied'. The Agreement was simply not meant to produce comprehensive delimitation.[65] The principle of effectiveness enabling the Tribunal to decide the dispute in its entirety was irrelevant because this was not admitted by the text of the Agreement. The Tribunal was not permitted to perfect the legal instrument but merely to interpret it.[66]

In *Qatar–Bahrain* the International Court addressed the interpretation of the jurisdictional clause embodied in the compromissory clauses under the 1987 and 1990 agreements between the parties. The Court emphasised that the parties differed 'as to the meaning to be given to those texts when read together and, hence, as to the scope of that commitment'. Qatar maintained that jurisdiction was clearly and unconditionally conferred upon the Court. Bahrain, on the other hand, asserted that the consent given in respect of jurisdiction was subject to conclusion of a Special Agreement. The agreements referred to the Tripartite Committee, whose role was conceived of by Qatar as solely procedural in the process of the exercise of judicial jurisdiction, and by Bahrain as essential in bringing the case before the Court.[67]

The Court disagreed with Bahrain, and refused to read into the agreement a condition that was not there, namely the essential role of the Tripartite Committee in establishing jurisdiction. As the Court put it, assessing subsequent conduct of the parties, 'the two States had nonetheless agreed to submit to the Court all the disputed matters between them, and the Committee's only function was to ensure that this commitment was given effect, by assisting the parties to approach the Court and to seise it in the manner laid down by its Rules'. The parties had acknowledged the role of the Committee, but they did not take the view that proceeding through the Committee was the only possible way of establishing jurisdiction.[68] Therefore

[64] *Id*, 70–71.
[65] *Id*, 113–114 (Separate Opinion).
[66] *Id*, 117.
[67] *Case concerning Maritime Delimitation and Territorial Questions between Qatar and Bahrain* (Qatar v Bahrain), Jurisdiction and Admissibility, Judgment of 15 February 1995, *ICJ Reports*, 1995, 6 at 15–16.
[68] *Id*, 16.

the Court emphasised that subsequent attitudes and practice of the parties could be relevant only as far as it established an agreement between them, in the way required under Article 31 of the Vienna Convention.

The textual aspect of interpretation was involved in terms of Article 2 of the Doha Minutes, the relevant clause of the Arabic text of which was presented by Qatar as enabling resort to the Court by 'the parties' and by Bahrain as referring to 'the two parties'. The Court specified that 'in the first case, the text would leave each of the Parties with the option of acting unilaterally, and, in the second, it would imply that the question be submitted to the Court by both Parties acting in concert, either jointly or separately'.[69] The Court referred to the use of the word 'may' in the relevant provision, which envisaged the legal right. Thus, the Court concluded that the ordinary meaning of this expression implied that the right could be the subject of unilateral exercise. Any other interpretation 'would deprive the phrase of its effect and could well, moreover, lead to an unreasonable result'.[70]

The Court thus adopted the approach which interprets jurisdictional clauses in terms of their object and purpose and the principle of effectiveness. As a further manifestation of this approach, the Court had:

> difficulty in seeing why the 1990 Minutes, the object and purpose of which were to advance the settlement of the dispute by giving effect to the formal commitment of the Parties to refer it to the Court, would have been confined to opening up for them a possibility of joint action which not only had always existed but, moreover, had proved to be ineffective. On the contrary, the text assumes its full meaning if it is taken to be aimed, for the purpose of accelerating the dispute settlement process, at opening the way to a possible unilateral seisin of the Court.[71]

Thus, the whole analysis of the Court proceeds from the approach of effectiveness of treaty obligations, including jurisdictional clauses. The attitude that jurisdictional instruments should be interpreted strictly or with caution is noticeably absent in the Court's reasoning.

The Court also addressed the relevance of preparatory work, and held that the *travaux* of the Doha Minutes had to be used with caution, because of their fragmentary nature.[72] The Court noted that the initial draft authorised resort to the Court by a party unilaterally, and this formulation was not accepted. But the final text did not provide that the seisin had to be performed by the two parties together. The Court was 'unable to see why the abandonment of a form of words corresponding to the interpretation given by Qatar to the Doha Minutes should imply that they must be interpreted in accordance with Bahrain's thesis'. Whatever the motives of each of the parties, the Court could only 'confine itself to the actual terms of the Minutes as the expression of their common intention

69 *Id*, 18. 70 *Id*, 18–19.
71 *Id*, 19. 72 *Id*, 21.

and to the interpretation of them which it has already given'.[73] This approach strikingly illustrates the Court's limited and functional view of the *travaux*—they are relevant only in so far as they explain what is actually said in the finally adopted text; not if they can be used to undermine the ultimately adopted agreement.

A further restrictive view was advocated by Bahrain in terms of distinguishing between jurisdiction and seisin, claiming that even if judicial jurisdiction existed, it could only be exercised on the basis of joint seisin. The Court refused to treat this issue as a separate and distinct one, and reiterated that unilateral seisin was allowed because it followed from its interpretation of the Doha Minutes.[74]

The Court's approach was opposed by Judge Schwebel, who argued that jurisdiction had to be denied on the basis of the primary importance of the *travaux* in this case. Judge Schwebel proceeded from the assumption, unsupported by the agreed authority (as distinguished from quoting the passages by Rapporteurs and individual members of the International Law Commission), that the use of *travaux* could undermine the text of the treaty,[75] which arguably was unclear.[76] The *travaux* were 'no less evidence of the intention of the parties when they contradict as when they confirm the allegedly clear meaning of the text or context of treaty provisions'.[77] Judge Schwebel further argued that predominant importance should be accorded to the change of phrases in the preparatory process, which in his view established that the unilateral seising of the Court was excluded. The meaning of the final text was, according to Judge Schwebel, not crucially relevant.[78] Curiously enough, Judge Schwebel went so far as to infer the object and purpose of the Doha Minutes from their *travaux* (while normally the text has to be the primary guidance for this). Using the dubious interpretation he had put upon the *travaux*, he proclaimed that the object and purpose of the Doha Minutes was to exclude unilateral recourse to the Court.[79]

Judge Schwebel further emphasised that far from confirming the textual meaning of the Doha Minutes, the preparatory work vitiated it. The contradiction between the two rendered the text, in his view, manifestly unreasonable.[80] Judge Schwebel referred to the word 'may' used in the pertinent clause, but argued that while this word could imply a unilateral right, it did not require a unilateral seisin, or disallow a joint seisin.[81]

The merit of Judge Schwebel's argument is unclear, because not excluding the joint seisin or not requiring a certain action does not imply excluding the relevant right. The contrary view advocated by Judge Schwebel clearly results in a severely

[73] *Id*, 22.
[74] *Id*, 23–24.
[75] Dissenting Opinion of Vice-President Schwebel, *id*, 27 at 31.
[76] *Id*, 37–38.
[77] *Id*, 39.
[78] *Id*, 34–36.
[79] *Id*, 36.
[80] *Id*, 36.
[81] *Id*, 37.

restrictive interpretation of jurisdictional instruments that is not accepted in practice. The Court adopted the view that different methods of seisin can coexist under the Doha Minutes, and each of them can be exercised. The Court thus refused to admit the restrictive interpretation and subscribed to the principle of effectiveness. Judge Schwebel's reasoning effectively admitted that the text of the Doha Minutes permitted the unilateral seising of the Court, and established judicial jurisdiction. That said, the application of Vienna Convention principles could not possibly overturn jurisdiction thus established. In international judicial practice, upsetting the methodology of the Vienna Convention by putting a supplementary rule before the General Rule of Interpretation is practically unthinkable. Consequently, what Judge Schwebel opposed was not the particular outcome the Court reached, but the entire regime of treaty interpretation under the Vienna Convention on the Law of Treaties.

In *LaGrand*, which concerned the sentencing to death and execution of two German nationals in the United States without affording them the opportunity to contact the consul of the State of their nationality, Germany invoked, as the jurisdictional basis, Article I of the Optional Protocol Concerning Compulsory Settlement of Disputes to the 1963 Vienna Convention on Consular Relations, which provides that 'disputes arising out of the interpretation or application of the Convention shall lie within the compulsory jurisdiction of the International Court of Justice and may accordingly be brought before the Court by an application made by any party to the dispute being a Party to the present Protocol'. On the basis of this jurisdictional clause, Germany asked the Court to rule that the provisional measures order by which the Court demanded that the United States stay the execution of the death sentence was binding and that the United States was responsible for breaching it; and that the Court was competent to impose on the United States a duty to provide guarantees of non-repetition in favour of Germany and its nationals.[82] With regard to both these submissions, the United States argued that under a jurisdictional clause such as Article I of the Optional Clause, the Court had no jurisdiction to do any of those things. Judicial actions like those would overstep the limits of the consent that the United States had given to the Court's jurisdiction, and it had never consented to the Court doing anything like that. The Court was considered incompetent 'to impose any obligations that are additional to or that differ in character from those to which the United States consented when it ratified the Vienna Convention'.[83]

The Court's treatment of the scope of Article I was motivated by considerations underlying the principle of effectiveness, namely enabling the Court to decide the dispute submitted to it with finality and efficiency. Therefore, in relation to its competence to judge the non-compliance with its earlier order of provisional measures, the Court observed that 'Where the Court has jurisdiction

[82] *LaGrand* (Germany v USA), Merits, *ICJ Reports*, 2001, paras 43–44, 46–48.
[83] *Id*, para 46.

to decide a case, it also has jurisdiction to deal with submissions requesting it to determine that an order indicating measures which seeks to preserve the rights of the Parties to this dispute has not been complied with.'[84] In terms of its competence to order the guarantees of non-repetition, the Court observed that 'where jurisdiction exists over a dispute on a particular matter, no separate basis for jurisdiction is required by the Court to consider the remedies a party has requested for the breach of the obligation'.[85] Thus, the Court dismissed the objections based on the alleged relevance of the principle of consent, compliance with which would cause it to decide the dispute without finality and efficiency. The effectiveness of the jurisdictional clause was treated as the prevailing consideration.

In *Avena*, which involved the sentencing to death of several Mexican nationals in the United States without affording them the opportunity to see the Mexican consular agent as required under the 1963 Vienna Convention on Consular Relations, Mexico asked the Court to affirm that a dispute regarding remedies for violations of the Convention was a dispute as to interpretation and application of the Convention and was thus within the Court's jurisdiction under Article I of the Optional Protocol. The United States contended that the Court lacked jurisdiction as Mexico's submissions 'asked the Court to decide questions which do not arise out of the interpretation or application of the Vienna Convention, and which the United States never agreed to submit to the Court'.[86] The third US objection to the jurisdiction of the Court related to the Mexican claim that it was entitled to *restitutio in integrum* and the US was under an obligation to re-establish the situation that existed prior to the convictions and sentencing of the Mexican nationals in violation of international law. The US submitted that by subsuming remedial powers into the scope of the Court's jurisdiction under the Optional Protocol, the Court would assert its power to review the appropriateness of the sentences passed within the US legal system.[87] Mexico referred to the Court's power to interpret the Vienna Convention and to determine the appropriate forms of reparation for the breaches.[88]

The Court approved Mexico's approach, as it was 'unable to uphold the contention of the United States that, even if the Court were to find that the breaches of the Vienna Convention were committed by the United States of the kind alleged by Mexico, it would still be without jurisdiction to order *restitutio in integrum* as requested by Mexico'.[89] This once again bore witness to the irrelevance of the principle of consent in cases where the scope of adjudication is determined by the need for effective construction of jurisdictional clauses.

[84] *Id*, para 45.
[85] *Id*, para 48.
[86] *Avena* (Mexico v USA), Merits, *ICJ Reports*, 2004, para 26.
[87] *Id*, paras 31–32.
[88] *Id*, para 33.
[89] *Id*, para 34.

The Court's approach on the basis of its long-standing practice confirms that the interpretation of jurisdictional instruments is not exempt from the regime of the law of treaties just because they are jurisdictional, nor is the applicability of the principles of treaty interpretation modified in any serious way. The judicial treatment of the principle of consent depends entirely on the interpretative outcome. This principle has no independent essence and scope of its own: jurisdiction will be exercised or declined depending on the textual interpretation of the jurisdictional instrument as required under the law of treaties. In addition, the object and purpose of jurisdictional clauses must also be considered, namely the need to enable the Court to decide disputes with finality, completeness and efficiency.

3. Interpretation of Declarations under the Optional Clause of the International Court's Statute

Once it is clarified that the specifically jurisdictional character of an instrument does not require restrictive interpretation, nor any deviation from the regime of interpretation applicable to treaties, it must also be examined whether the same can be restated for the Declarations under Article 36(2) of the International Court's Statute. Although it has been established above that the relations under Optional Clause declarations are in fact treaty relations,[90] the following analysis will concentrate on the use of interpretative principles as opposed to the nature of the acts interpreted. The outcome of the present section is however relevant for the interpretation of both treaties and unilateral acts.

At least one State before the UN International Law Commission has suggested that in interpreting Optional Clause declarations the subjective factor of intention attaches 'much higher interpretative significance to unilateral acts', and this approach has been shared by the Special Rapporteur Rodriguez-Cedeno[91] This observation contradicts the inherent nature of Optional Clause declarations, and also the practice of the International Court on this issue. Following the Permanent Court's practice, the intention of the declarant State is ascertained from the text of its declaration, and restrictive interpretation is irrelevant.[92]

In *Anglo-Iranian Oil Company*, the International Court dealt with the Iranian Declaration under the Optional Clause recognising the Court's jurisdiction in relation to the treaties and conventions to which Iran was a party. The Court observed that the Declaration was drafted in such a way that a literal reading of it could convey two different meanings. Therefore, the Court could not 'base itself on a purely grammatical interpretation of the text. It must seek

[90] See above Chapter 9.
[91] Fourth Report of ILC Special Rapporteur Rodriguez-Cedeno, A/CN.4/519, 23 (Austria).
[92] C Amerasinghe, *Jurisdiction of International Tribunals* (2003), 107–108.

the interpretation which is in harmony with a natural and reasonable way of reading the text, having regard to the intention of the Government of Iran at the time when it accepted the compulsory jurisdiction of the Court.' The Court stayed mainly within the bounds of the textual approach, observing that the 'Declaration must be interpreted as it stands, having regard to the words actually used'.[93]

The reasons why the Court considers it necessary in certain cases to examine the intention of a declarant State are not substantially different from the same phenomenon in the law of treaties. As Judge McNair noted, the Court's examination of the intention of the respondent was caused by textual ambiguity in the declaration. As he remarked on the different interpretations suggested by the applicant and the respondent, 'both interpretations are grammatically possible... Moreover, both are possible as a matter of substance; both make sense, though the effects of the two interpretations are quite different. In short, there is a real ambiguity in the text, and, for that reason, it is justifiable and necessary to go outside the text and see whether any light is shed by the surrounding circumstances.'[94]

It is thus clear that had the text of the declaration been sufficiently clear, the Court would not have needed to examine the intention of the respondent or any other factor. This method is identical to the normal methods of interpretation of treaties under the Vienna Convention. The very basis of the principles applicable to the interpretation of declarations has its roots in the law of treaties and the alleged distinction between the rules governing the interpretation of the various instruments concerned is artificially invented rather than real.

The Court in *Anglo-Iranian Oil Company* rejected the submission of the United Kingdom that no provision in the Iranian Declaration could be viewed as superfluous, observing that the text of the Iranian Declaration was not a treaty text resulting from negotiations but the result of unilateral drafting and Iran could have inserted certain words *ex abundanti cautela*, even though they might seem superfluous, strictly speaking.[95] Nevertheless, the Court adhered to the textual method throughout its entire interpretative exercise. It referred to Iran's apparent desire to exclude capitulatory treaties from the Court's jurisdiction, but in doing so it followed the textual meaning of the Iranian Declaration.

The most recent statement of the International Court was made in the *Fisheries Jurisdiction* (Spain v Canada) case, where the Court emphasised that the

[93] *Anglo-Iranian Oil Co.* (UK v Iran), Preliminary Objection, Judgment of 22 July 1952, *ICJ Reports*, 1952, 93 at 104–105.

[94] Individual Opinion of President McNair, *id*, 117–118; see also Dissenting Opinion of Judge Read, *id*, 142, confirming the relevance of the same method analogous to treaty interpretation by reference to earlier jurisprudence of the Court on this issue. Judge Read emphasised that a declaration should be 'construed in such a manner as to give effect to the intention of the State, as indicated by the words used; and not by a restrictive interpretation, designed to frustrate the intention of the State in exercising this sovereign power', *id*, 143.

[95] Id, 105.

Optional Clause declarations should be interpreted 'in a natural and reasonable way, having due regard to the intention of the State concerned at the time when it accepted the compulsory jurisdiction of the Court'.[96] Most importantly, the Court held that:

> The regime relating to interpretation of declarations made under Article 36 of the Statute is not identical with that established for the interpretation of treaties by the Vienna Convention on the Law of Treaties. ... The Court observes that the provisions of that Convention may only apply analogously to the extent compatible with the *sui generis* character of the unilateral acceptance of the Court's jurisdiction.[97]

In terms of the *sui generis* character of the Optional Clause declarations, the Court did not specify any implication of such a character that would subject them to interpretation principles different from those applicable to treaties, apart from stating in paragraph 51 of the Judgment that the *contra proferentem* rule was not applicable to the unilaterally drafted instrument. This issue was in any event specific and without prejudice to the principal interpretative approach of the Court.

As for the actual methods of interpretation, the Court specified that 'it will thus interpret the relevant words of a declaration, including a reservation contained therein, in a natural and reasonable way, having due regard to the intention of the State concerned at the time when it accepted the compulsory jurisdiction of the Court. The intention of a reserving State may be deduced not only from the text of the relevant clause, but also from the context in which the clause is to be read, and an examination of evidence regarding the circumstances of its preparation and the purposes intended to be served.'[98] A further preference for the textual approach is evidenced by the Court's statement that 'an existing declaration has been replaced by a new declaration which contains a reservation, as in this case, the intentions of the Government may also be ascertained by comparing the terms of the two instruments'.[99] So, although the Declaration 'should be interpreted in a manner compatible with the effect sought by the reserving State',[100] it is presumed that this effect was sought through the appropriate drafting of the text.

The intention of the reserving State as such cannot be the decisive factor in construing the meaning of the Declaration and the reservations it contains. Optional clause declarations are made in a legal environment that also includes the addressee States. The relevance of their understanding of what the Declaration

[96] *Fisheries Jurisdiction* (Spain v Canada), Judgment of 4 December 1998, *ICJ Reports*, 1998, para 49.

[97] *Id*, para 46.

[98] *Id*, para 49.

[99] *Id*, para 50.

[100] *Id*, para 52.

says evidences that the outcome depends on more than just the intention of the reserving State. The only way addressees can understand the Declarations is to resort to their texts, and this introduces a reciprocal element into allegedly unilateral concept of intention. The fact that the Court always bases its analysis on the text is incompatible with understanding intention as the predominant factor and proves that in reality the decisive factor is inherently reciprocal and contractual—the intention embodied in the text of the Declaration as it can be reasonably understood by the addressee States.

The empirical perspective confirms the above conclusions. Although the Court emphasised the *sui generis* character of the Optional Clause declarations, the relevant parts of the judgment devoted to the interpretation of the respondent's declaration do not involve any method of interpretation which would be divergent from, or unjustified in the light of, the provisions of the Vienna Convention. Paragraphs 62–84 interpret the words used in the Canadian declaration according to their textual meaning and context. The Court notes on each and every occasion the priority of text in interpreting a declaration.[101] The real dispute between the parties was merely as to the interpretation of particular clauses, which each party was willing to construe in a manner most favourable to itself, and not a difference on general rules which may govern the interpretation of those clauses in particular cases.[102] The judgment does not support any view that an abstract, or even empirical, intention of a declarant State prevails over or determines the actual provisions of a declaration. On the contrary, it is the very text of a declaration which is taken as an indicator of intention of a reserving State. All this justifies doubting that the Court resorted to any method of interpretation unwarranted by the Vienna Convention on the Law of Treaties. The issue in both *Anglo-Iranian Oil Company* and *Fisheries Jurisdiction* was not that a declaration was not to be interpreted as a treaty, but rather which of the suggested interpretations of the declaration was correct. It is therefore important not to perceive these decisions as illustrating an approach that they do not uphold.

It must be understood that there is no uniform system of rules on interpretation except those applicable to treaties,[103] and the rules of interpretation applicable to Optional Clause declarations cannot be essentially different from the rules of treaty interpretation.[104] One is bound to be unsuccessful in searching for the *lex specialis* on interpretation of any particular type of international instruments. Tribunals may not invent a new method of interpretation, for they simply apply the methods which are established in the law.

[101] *Id*, paras 48, 50, 66, 76.
[102] *Id*, para 61.
[103] Cf Bernhardt, Interpretation in International Law, 2 *EPIL* (1995), 1416 at 1423.
[104] C Tomuschat, Article 36 in Zimmerman *et al* (eds), *The Statute of the International Court of Justice. A Commentary* (2006), 589, at 627.

4. Evaluation

The practice of international tribunals confirms that jurisdictional instruments, whether embodied in a treaty in the narrow sense, or in the exchange of unilateral declarations, operate as treaty clauses and are regularly interpreted as such. The rules of interpretation laid down in the 1969 Vienna Convention on the Law of Treaties guide the interpretation of such jurisdictional clauses. The fact that judicial jurisdiction is based on consent does not have any more relevance than the assertion that international obligations in general are assumed through the expression of consent. The factor of consent is essential in bringing about jurisdictional obligations. But the further operation of those obligations cannot be prejudged by the fact that they are consensual. This further process is instead guided by principles of interpretation which are designed so as to ensure adherence to the agreement between States in good faith and in accordance with its text and the object and purpose. The specific relevance of the object and purpose of treaty obligations in the field of judicial jurisdiction necessarily involves such interpretation of jurisdictional clauses as ensures final, complete and effective resolution of the relevant disputes.

13

Interpretation of Unilateral Acts and Statements

1. General Aspects

In general, the need to interpret unilateral acts, actions and statements of States serves the purpose of ascertaining the intention of the author State, just as in relation to any other legal act. This is done for one of the following purposes: to prove the existence and scope of the obligation undertaken; to prove the intention of acting in a certain way or performing a certain act; to find evidence of the commission of an internationally wrongful act; to ascertain an element of valid State practice; or to prove the acknowledgment of a rival claim. Like agreements, unilateral acts and statements also need interpretation for clarifying their meaning and scope. For legal stability and certainty, it is natural that such acts and statements should be interpreted according to consistent and established methods.

Failure to interpret unilateral acts and statements properly can lead to curious results. In the *Armed Activities* (DRC v Uganda) case, the International Court dealt with the statement of Rwanda's Justice Minister that the Rwandan reservations about humanitarian treaties including the Genocide Convention would be withdrawn 'shortly'. This statement was made a few months before the Court delivered its decision, yet the Court refused to see this factor as impacting the legality and effects of the Rwandan reservation to Article IX of the Genocide Convention, stating merely that the Minister's statement did not indicate any time-frame.[1] It can be conceded that the period between the statement and the delivery of the Judgment was not long enough to justify the Court's interference by clarifying the impact on the reservation. But if so, the Court ought to have stated this expressly, instead of leaving the issue uncertain as it did, and in any case the Court ought to have clarified the meaning of the Minister's statement by interpreting it in accordance with its ordinary meaning and possibly by construing it as effective as it could be given its textual content.

[1] *Armed Activities* (DRC v Rwanda), Judgment of 3 February 2006, General List No 126, paras 49–53.

The relevance of interpretation for unilateral acts is affirmed in the *Nuclear Tests* case among others and in the International Law Commission's work on unilateral acts. In *Nuclear Tests*, the International Court emphasised that 'not all unilateral acts imply obligation; but a State may choose to take up a certain position in relation to a particular matter with the intention of being bound—the intention is to be ascertained by interpretation of the act'.[2]

2. Principles of Interpretation of Unilateral Acts and Statements

In an attempt to elaborate upon the applicable rules of interpretation, the ILC Special Rapporteur asks whether the rules of the Vienna Convention can be transposed to the law of unilateral acts, and points to the fundamental difference that 'a unilateral act is the manifestation of the will of one or more States in individual, collective or concerted form, in which other States, and in particular the addressee State, do not participate'.[3] This approach neglects the fact that even if the addressee does not participate in the technical process of drafting and announcing unilateral declarations, it still participates in the broader process in which the respective effects follow from that unilateral act: through its silence or protest, the recipient State impacts the effects of the unilateral act and demonstrates its expectations as to the content and scope of that act. The author State expresses its intention not in a vacuum but in a manner communicated to the recipient States which draw appropriate conclusions and offers appropriate reactions.

Rodriguez-Cedeno argues that 'the aim of interpretation [of unilateral acts] is to determine the intention of the parties to an act or of the State or States which formulate an act, giving priority to the terms of the agreement or declaration'. Interpretation is based 'first and foremost on the terms and their meaning'.[4] Nevertheless, in the draft article suggested by Rodriguez-Cedeno, the factor of intention is expressed separately from the factors of text and terms,[5] which contradicts the earlier attitude. This draft article in fact introduces intention as a free-standing interpretative factor and admits that this factor can potentially modify the outcome arrived at through the interpretation of the text. The Special Rapporteur's approach fails to reflect the link between the intention and the text of the act, as particularly seen above in the example of jurisdictional instruments.

As the International Court stated in *Nuclear Tests*, the intention to be bound by an act 'confers on the declaration the character of the legal undertaking'.[6] At the same time, making intention clear follows from the content of the relevant act or instrument as it is to be understood by the addressees. In other words, intention is inferred from objective, or objectively verifiable, factors, such as the

[2] *Nuclear Tests* (Australia v France), Judgment, *ICJ Reports*, 1974, 267.
[3] Fourth Report, A/CN.4/519, 24–25, paras 108–109.
[4] *Id*, 26, para 116.
[5] *Id*, 35.
[6] *Nuclear Tests*, 267, 269.

content of the statement and its communication to the addressees, in terms of the literal meaning of the words used. As Bernhardt emphasises, the factor of understanding by the addressee or the international community at large of the intention expressed is equally as important as the original factor of intention.[7]

Rodriguez-Cedeno argues against the relevance of the object and purpose of unilateral acts as an interpretative factor for unilateral acts, because object and purpose is specifically a treaty concept,[8] and has a fundamentally treaty-based connotation.[9] But this ignores the fact that, like any other act or transaction, unilateral acts are performed for a reason and with calculation, and hence they do have an object and purpose.

In his Fourth Report, Rodriguez-Cedeno expressly subscribes to restrictive interpretation of unilateral acts, including jurisdictional declarations. As he states, 'in accordance with the case law and the doctrine, there is no doubt whatever that the restrictive criterion predominates in this context'.[10] This sweeping statement is however not supported in practice, as already seen in the example of Optional Clause declarations and as will be seen below as well. True, the International Court in *Nuclear Tests* pointed out that 'When States make statements by which their freedom of action is to be limited, a restrictive interpretation is called for',[11] but the Court did not apply this principle to the French declaration in question. In fact, the Court emphasised that unilateral statements cannot be subjected to an arbitrary power of reconsideration by the author State, and that a legal relationship is created when the relevant unilateral act is taken cognisance of and confidence is placed in it by other States.[12] This is essentially a process of bilateral agreement. This obviously impacts the applicable standards of interpretation, and the Court was explicit in identifying the interpretative relevance of 'the actual substance of these statements',[13] which is not far from adopting a textual view. Practice instead shows that unilateral acts and statements are interpreted in a similar if not the same way as other international acts.

The International Law Commission has formulated the following approach on interpreting unilateral declarations:

> A unilateral declaration entails obligations for the formulating State only if it is stated in clear and specific terms. In the case of doubt as to the scope of the obligations resulting from such a declaration, such obligations must be interpreted in a restrictive manner. In interpreting the content of such obligations, weight shall be given first and foremost to the text of the declaration, together with the context and the circumstances in which it was formulated.[14]

[7] R Bernhardt, Interpretation in International Law, 2 *EPIL* (1995), 1416 at 1423.
[8] Fourth Report, A/CN.4/519, 30–31, para 137.
[9] Fifth Report, A/CN.4/525/Add.1, 13, para 133.
[10] Fourth Report, A/CN.4/519, 27–28, paras 126–127.
[11] *Nuclear Tests*, 267.
[12] *Id*, 268, 270.
[13] *Id*, 269.
[14] Draft Articles on Unilateral Acts and Commentary thereto, *ILC Report* 2006, 377.

Thus, the Commission expressly subscribes to the restrictive interpretation of unilateral acts. At the same time, the Commission emphasises the 'first and foremost' importance of the text of the declaration. In the Commentary the Commission further observes that 'priority consideration must be given to the text of the unilateral declaration, which best reflects its author's intentions'.[15] This makes the Commission's approach internally inconsistent, because the clarity of the text by itself removes the relevance of any restrictive interpretation.

In *Eastern Greenland*, the Permanent Court refused to view the Norwegian Declaration made by Foreign Minister Ihlen as a recognition of Danish sovereignty over Eastern Greenland. The Foreign Minister had promised Denmark that Norway would not create any problem for Norway's efforts to obtain sovereignty over that part of Greenland. After 'a careful examination of the words used', the Court was unable to establish that such a statement could imply the definitive recognition of Danish sovereignty.[16] Such was the outcome of textual interpretation.

Along with that, the Court used the principle of effectiveness to establish that the same statement constituted definitive renunciation by Norway of any claim over Eastern Greenland. The Foreign Minister's statement was binding upon Norway, and it was unconditional and definitive.[17] The principles used in both cases are the same as apply to the interpretation of treaties.

In *Minority Schools in Albania*, the Court interpreted the 1921 Albanian Declaration addressed to the League of Nations Council, in which Albania undertook to guarantee equality to minorities in fact and in law. The Court stated that it would construe this Declaration in terms of its text and also consider the fact that it was intended that the general principles of the minorities' treaties should be accepted.[18] In other words, the Declaration would be construed in terms of its object and purpose. At the same time, the Court applied to the Declaration the same principle of effectiveness as it applied to the treaty text in the *Polish Nationality* case.[19] Therefore, the cases of *Eastern Greenland* and *Albanian Minority Schools* confirm that the regime of treaty interpretation in principle applies to unilateral acts as well. This is so because both types of instruments are expressions of will and intention, and both of them create legitimate expectation.

The question of interpretation of statements arose in *Burkina-Faso/Mali* which involved the issue of the effects of decisions of the Mediation Commission set up by a decision of Heads of State of Upper Volta, Mali and Togo. In this case,

[15] *Id*, 378.

[16] *Legal Status of Eastern Greenland*, Judgment of 5 April 1933, *PCIJ Series* A/B, No 53, 22 at 69.

[17] *Id*, 71–72.

[18] *Minority Schools in Albania*, Advisory Opinion of 6 April 1935, *PCIJ Series* A/B, No 64, 4 at 16–17.

[19] *Id*, 20; the placing of the Albanian Declaration within the context of the law of treaties in this case is also confirmed in doctrine, see M Jokl, *De l'interprétation des traités normatifs d'après de la doctrine et la jurisprudence internationales* (1936), 78.

the statement of the President of Mali of 11 April 1975 was quoted, according to which Mali would not dispute the decision of the Commission regarding the frontier between Burkina Faso and Mali.[20] At the same time, both parties agreed in this case that the Commission lacked the power to issue binding decisions.[21]

Burkina Faso contended that Mali was bound by the Legal Sub-Commission of the Mediation Commission, because this followed from the statement of the President of Mali. Mali responded that these factors could not bring about the effect which Burkina Faso attributed to them because the Commission had no power to bind the States and moreover the Presidential statement was merely 'a witticism of the kind regularly uttered at press conferences'. In addition, the Commission's recommendations were not final as a further stage of making recommendations was envisaged after reconnoitring the relevant frontier areas, and the Commission was instructed accordingly.[22]

The Court observed, with regard to the *Nuclear Tests* case, that statements like that of the President of Mali 'concerning legal or factual situations' can have the effect of creating legal obligations. But this can happen only where the State makes clear its intention to be bound according to the terms of the act.[23] However, the statement in *Burkina-Faso/Mali* was made in the institutional context of the competence of the Mediation Commission. As the parties did not accept the binding character of the Commission's decisions by normal means as they would have done had they so chosen, for instance through the agreement based on reciprocity, the unilateral statement of the President of Mali had no legal implications in this case.[24]

The Court's attitude that the issue of the binding power of the Commission is crucial leaves open a range of issues. The Court's approach does not clarify whether the Presidential statement involved in this case could have the effect of estoppel by way of accepting the non-binding decision as binding. It is clear that too much was at stake and by holding that the Presidential statement had bound Mali to the boundary settlement the Court would have decided the major issue. However, the Court circumvented the issue of the inherent effect of unilateral acts that can be brought about if interpreted by reference to their terms. In addition the Court could still have referred to the unfinalised status of the Commission conclusions and thus neutralised, in this specific case, the effect that the statement of the Mali President would otherwise produce.

In *Nicaragua*, the Court took the textual view of interpretation of statements and refused to see any legal obligation in the declaration of the Nicaraguan Junta which stated the objective of installing a new regime by democratic means. The

[20] *Case Concerning Frontier Dispute* (Burkina-Faso/Republic of Mali), Judgment of 22 December 1986, 554 at 571.

[21] *Id*, 572.

[22] *Id*, 573.

[23] *Id*, 573.

[24] *Id*, 574.

Court could not see in this declaration any legal commitment by Nicaragua as to the principle or method of holding democratic elections. The relevant passage of the declaration fell short of stating strict obligations, speaking instead of 'dedicat[ing] every effort'.[25]

While in many cases the outcome of the act is the assumption of an international obligation, in other cases this involves some factual situation and can also be interpreted as an admission of that situation, which will in its turn be followed by legal consequences, among which the assumption of legal obligations can also be found.

If an act itself is legal, a wrong motive behind it cannot deprive it of its legality. As the Court pointed out in *Nicaragua*, if it was duly established that Nicaragua had perpetrated an armed attack on El Salvador, the United States could legally invoke collective self-defence, 'even though there may be the possibility of an additional motive, other than that officially proclaimed by the United States. . . . The existence of an additional motive, other than that officially proclaimed by the United States, could not deprive the latter of its right to collective self-defence.'[26]

The valid exercise of the right to collective self-defence is just an exercise of rights and does not, unless specifically so required by the content of the relevant rule, depend on the existence of specific intentions or motives. When an act is just an exercise of a right, it is not interpreted as an independent act, but only in the context of and in terms of compliance with the rule on the basis of which it is performed. If it fits within the norm it is legal; if not then it is not. In other words, such acts are independent as acts, but have no independent legal basis.

But acts that do not specifically fall within the authorisation conferred by a legal norm need an alternative legal basis for validity and lawfulness; unless such is found and identified, these acts are illegal. Therefore, the stated intention, the actual intention proved in context, and correspondence with the legal framework are crucial factors for identifying the legality, scope and effects of the relevant legal acts, actions or statements.

In *Nicaragua*, the International Court dealt with the issue of transboundary arms movement and pointed out that the facts were unclear and disputed. The secrecy of some facts and the non-appearance of the respondent had made it more difficult to prove what had really happened and to whom the relevant conduct was to be attributed.[27] The material before the Court included various documents, but also:

> statements by representatives of States, sometimes at the highest political level. Some of these statements were made before official organs of the State or of an international or regional organisation, and appear in the official records of those bodies. Others, made

[25] *Nicaragua* (Merits), Judgment, *ICJ Reports*, 1986, 14 at 131–132.
[26] *Id*, 71.
[27] *Id*, 38–39.

during press conferences or interviews, were reported by the local or international press. The Court takes the view that statements of this kind, emanating from high-ranking official political figures, sometimes indeed of the highest rank, are of particular probative value when they acknowledge facts or conduct unfavourable to the State represented by the person who made them. They may then be construed as a form of admission.[28]

The Court suggested that the statements must be interpreted to find out what they admit. The Court's reasoning implies that there are interpretative principles applicable to the process of evidencing the occurrence of certain facts or conduct.

The Court, according to *Nicaragua*, will obviously treat such statements in accordance with the requirements of the law of evidence so that equality between parties is guaranteed.[29] At the same time, the Court has to 'attach considerable significance to the declarations made by the responsible authorities of the States concerned in view of the difficulties which it had to face in determining the facts'.[30]

Such declarations, apart from their probative value, can involve legal effects, and *Nicaragua* refers to *Nuclear Tests* to support this statement, which implies that the Court has, at least for some purposes, placed declarations having probative value as admissions within the same category as declarations whereby States unilaterally assume obligations.

Declarations can be regarded as evidence of truth of facts or that these facts are attributable to the States which are the authors of the declaration, and to a lesser degree, of the legal qualification of these acts.[31] Within the context of *jus ad bellum* with which the Court was dealing, the Court observed that Nicaragua:

has drawn attention to the invocation of collective self-defence by the United States, and contended that 'the use of such justification of collective self-defence constitutes a major admission of direct and substantial United States involvement in the military and paramilitary operations' directed against Nicaragua. The Court would observe that the normal purpose of an invocation of self-defence is to justify conduct which would otherwise be wrongful. If advanced as a justification in itself, not coupled with a denial of the conduct alleged, it may well imply both an admission of the conduct in the absence of the justification of self-defence. This reasoning would do away with any difficulty in establishing the facts, which would have been the subject of an implicit overall admission by the United States, simply through its attempt to justify them by the right of self-defence.[32]

Under this view, the operative side of the statement is crucial: even if the specific conduct is not admitted, the effect of the content of the statement is to imply that conduct of this kind did take place. This, coupled with the reference to *Nuclear Tests*, confirms that the Court has viewed all unilateral acts similarly at

[28] *Id*, 41.
[29] *Id*, 41.
[30] *Id*, 42.
[31] *Id*, 43.
[32] *Id*, 44–45.

least for certain interpretative purposes. After all, all unilateral acts or statements express intention and are meant to make a difference; while individual acts can have different effects depending on their designation, they can be subjected to similar interpretative exercises to find out whether they are meant to produce these effects. This is not far away from the normal pattern of the principle of effectiveness.

The statement of the US President on the mining of Nicaraguan ports by Nicaraguan vessels was deemed by the Court as proving US involvement in laying those mines.[33] In addition, general statements of foreign policy in relation to covert action in the Central American region were also interpreted by the Court as an admission by the United States of its participation in planning, funding and overseeing the *contras* operations, which resulted in serious violations of international humanitarian law.[34]

The Court also dealt with the statements of the President of Nicaragua regarding the alleged arms flow from Nicaragua to El Salvador. One statement was quoted in which the President referred to the effort to stop that flow and referred to the desire to cooperate with the Salvadorian people.[35] In another statement, the President expressed a readiness to stop the arms flow but demanded in return that the United States stop attacking Nicaragua through 'arming the gangs that kill our people, burn our crops and force us to divert enormous human and economic resources into war'.[36]

In order to understand whether this was an admission of the conduct, the Court engaged in textual interpretation of the statement. The statement raised 'questions as to its meaning, namely as to what exactly the Nicaraguan Government was offering to stop'. In an earlier statement the President asked the United States to provide the information necessary for tracking down the alleged arms flow. Judging from a contextual perspective, the Court could not 'regard remarks of this kind as an admission that that Government was in fact doing what it had already officially denied and continued to deny publicly'.[37]

In determining the significance of these statements, the Court pointed to some background factors such as the ideological similarity between the Nicaraguan Government and the rebels in neighbouring countries, and the consequent political interest of Nicaragua in weakening the Government of El Salvador, including the President's express statement of desire that the guerrillas triumph in El Salvador. But this statement, together with the desire to collaborate with the Salvadorian people, could not amount to an admission that assistance was given to the rebels.[38] Consequently this was not proved.

33 *Id*, 47–48.
34 *Id*, 49, 61.
35 *Id*, 76.
36 *Id*, 79.
37 *Id*, 79–80; further on denial see *id*, 80–81.
38 *Id*, 82.

The difference between the Nicaraguan and US statements is that the US admitted its covert action and also invoked the right to collective self-defence—the action that generically belongs to the category of military activities. Nicaragua, on the other hand, merely expressed its aspirations as to certain political outcomes and did not admit to having been engaged in any kind of military activity. The Court seems to have required a clear and unequivocal statement which, in its terms, amount to an admission, in order to qualify as an admission. This may be a requirement of the evidentiary standard of strict evidence which is needed to prove breaches of *jus ad bellum*, but to qualify as proper evidence for such purposes, it is necessary for the statement to be interpreted in terms of its ordinary meaning to clarify whether it can count as evidence.

In the *Genocide* case (*Bosnia–Serbia*), the claim was made that the Serbian Government had, through the statement of its Council of Ministers of 15 June 2005, admitted that the massacres in Serbia had constituted genocide and accepted legal responsibility for it. The statement affirmed the criminal responsibility of all who committed war crimes, organised them or ordered them. The Court affirmed in general terms its ability to find admissions in the statements of the Government and accord to them such legal effect as may be appropriate. The Court found that 'the declaration of 15 June 2005 was of a political nature; it was clearly not intended as an admission, which would have had a legal effect in complete contradiction to the submissions made by the Respondent before this Court, both at the time of the declaration and subsequently'.[39]

The Court did not directly elaborate upon the applicable methods of interpretation. Yet the absence of any admission in the text of the statement of the Council of Ministers of legal responsibility for the events in Srebrenica seems to have been the crucial factor in inducing the Court not to see any legal implications arising out of it.

In *Minquiers and Ecrehos*, the International Court referred to the 1819 letter of the French foreign minister, in which the Minquiers were stated to be '*possédés par L'Angleterre*', and in one of the charts enclosed the Minquiers group was indicated as being British. The Court applied a fairly textual interpretation to this statement. France argued that this admission could not be invoked against it, as it was made in the course of negotiations which did not result in agreement. But the Court observed that this statement 'was not a proposal or a concession made during negotiations, but a statement of facts transmitted to the Foreign Office by the French Ambassador, who did not express any reservation in respect thereof. This statement must therefore be considered as evidence of the French official view at that time.'[40] Similarly, the *Minquiers and Ecrehos* case demonstrates that pure fact can be interpreted in such a way as to constitute admission. This related to the British protest against France regarding house construction by a French national

[39] Judgment of 26 February 2007, General List No 91, paras 377–378.
[40] *ICJ Reports*, 1953, 71.

on the relevant island through the French lease. The French Government did not reply but the construction was stopped.[41]

The issue of admission by unilateral act was dealt with by the Ethiopia–Eritrea Boundary Commission. This related to the admission by Ethiopia that the towns of Fort Cadorna and Tserona, which were situated on the Ethiopian side of the boundary under the 1900 Treaty, were undisputed Eritrean places. This statement was included in written submissions by Ethiopia to the Commission. The Commission considered that it had to take this admission into account and ensure that these towns were placed in Eritrean territory.[42]

There is also the judicial practice of interpreting acts of States that constitute primarily an expression of will through their domestic legislation. The *Fisheries Jurisdiction* case confirms that the interpretation of unilateral acts and declarations of States is based on the textual method. The Court had to ascertain the meaning and effect of Icelandic Regulations issued on 14 July 1972 and their impact on the claims of Iceland's preferential rights to certain maritime areas. According to these regulations, all fishing activities by foreign vessels were prohibited in the relevant areas. The Court approached this issue on the basis of the primacy of the text, and stated that:

> The language of the relevant government regulations indicates that their object is to establish an exclusive fishery zone, in which all fishing by vessels registered in other States, including the United Kingdom, would be prohibited. The mode of implementation of the regulations, carried out by Icelandic governmental authorities vis-à-vis United Kingdom fishing vessels, before the 1973 interim agreement, and despite the Court's interim measures, confirms this interpretation.[43]

This finding enabled the Court to see the contradiction between Icelandic regulations and high sea freedoms determining the outer limits of validity of preferential fishing rights. The Court had to conclude that these regulations conflicted with international law. This was the basis of further findings as to the lack of opposability of Icelandic claims.

The International Court seems to have adhered to the effectiveness of interpretation of unilateral acts, as particularly emphasised by its treatment in the *Cameroon–Nigeria* case of the 1946 Order in Council:

> The Court considers, however, that a reading of the text of the Order in Council permits it to determine which tributary should be used in order to fix the boundary. The Court observes in this connection that, just as with the Thomson-Marchand Declaration, the Order in Council describes the course of the boundary by reference to the area's physical characteristics. Here again, the text of this description must have been drafted in such a way as to render the course of the boundary as readily identifiable as possible. The description of the boundary in the Order in Council starts from the north, and provides

[41] *Id*, 71–72.
[42] Award of the Commission, paras 4.69–4.71.
[43] *Fisheries Jurisdiction*, Merits, *ICJ Reports*, 1974, 27.

for it to run 'up the River Sama to the point where it divides into two'. Thus the inference is that the drafters of the Order in Council intended that the boundary should pass through the first confluence reached coming from the north.[44]

The authors of a unilateral act are supposed to be intend to bring about legal positions that are straightforward, workable and readily identifiable, just as is the presumption in relation to the parties to a treaty. Therefore, unilateral acts and statements should be interpreted in accordance with their terms and the ordinary meaning of the words and phrases used to ascertain what their meaning is. The ascertainment of the legality and legal effects of the action or attitude expressed can either follow the ascertainment of the meaning of the statement, or be logically anterior to that task. Simply put, there is an admission if the words and phrases used result in admitting something.

In some cases, acts performed by States and accompanying attitudes are to be interpreted in terms of their real meaning and impact, as opposed to stated intentions. For instance, as the Iran–US Claims Tribunal observed, in order to clarify whether a governmental act amounts to expropriation, 'the intent of the government is less important than the effects of the measures on the owner, and the form of the measures of control or interference is less important than the reality of the impact'.[45] The International Court adopted the same approach in the case concerning the *Wall in the Occupied Palestinian Territory*, concerning the real effect of the Wall that Israel constructed in Palestine.[46] In this case, Israel had disclaimed any intention to annex the relevant territories, submitting that the Barrier was a temporary measure, did not annex territories to the State of Israel, and that Israel was 'ready and able, at tremendous cost, to adjust or dismantle a fence if so required as part of a political settlement'. The Wall would not change the legal status of the territory in any way.[47] The Court was not convinced by these submissions. It stated that it could not remain indifferent to certain fears expressed to it that the route of the Wall would prejudge a future frontier between Israel and Palestine, and the fear that Israel may integrate the settlements. The Court considered that the construction of the Wall and its associated regime created a '*fait accompli*' on the ground that could well become permanent, in which case, and notwithstanding the formal characterisation of the Wall by Israel, it would be tantamount to *de facto* annexation. More so, as the planned route of the Wall would separate 16 per cent of Palestinian territory from the rest of it.[48] Therefore, in such cases, the real meaning of the act

[44] *Cameroon–Nigeria*, Merits, *ICJ Reports*, 2002, 398; for similar interpretation of domestic legal instruments, namely colonial orders, see *Benin–Niger*, *ICJ Reports*, 2005, 122, 127, where the Chamber of the Court interpreted these colonial orders to see if their meaning and the intention behind them confirmed that these orders were part of the relevant *effectivités*.

[45] *Tippets*, 6 IUSCT Reports 1984, 219; see also *Phelps*, 10 IUSCT Reports 1986, 121.

[46] Advisory Opinion of 9 July 2004, General List No 131.

[47] Opinion, para 116.

[48] Opinion, para 121.

in its context will prevail over the stated intention of the author State. Had the Court refused to adopt such reasoning, the construction of the Wall would have escaped falling into the scope of the principle of non-recognition of illegal territorial acquisitions.

The ascertainment of the source of intention behind unilateral act or statement similarly arises in other situations. In *Ambatielos* (Preliminary Objections) the Court interpreted the British Declaration of Ratification of the 1926 Anglo-Greek Treaty as the simultaneous ratification of the appended Declaration. The inference from the text was that the Government conceived the process of ratification as a unity.[49] This conclusion was contradicted by President McNair, who contended that the Court could not reach such a conclusion without proving adequate intention of the parties.[50] Judge Basdevant asserted a similar attitude, mainly by suggesting that the process of drafting the British Ratification did not express the will of the State, because the physical operations of writing, recording and transmitting such declarations 'do not contribute to the formation of the will' of the State. Such operations are derived from tradition which is followed 'scrupulously, and therefore blindly, by the officials entrusted with this material task'. The Judge goes so far as to suggest that when the Head of State signed the ratification instrument he did not direct his mind to details such as the relevance of the Declaration.[51]

But Judge Basdevant's approach misunderstands the legal effect of unilateral acts and statements. What matters, and entails the expression of the intention, is the valid making of the acts and its communication to the recipient State. Whether this is done as an extraordinary event or routinely cannot be a crucial factor.

The Court's practice also confirms that unilateral acts must be interpreted in context, wherever such context can be indicative of the intention of the author States. Even if an act *prima facie* looks like a proper assumption of obligation, acceptance of legal position, or waiver, its context may dispel such assumptions. In *US Nationals in Morocco*, the Court examined US-French correspondence to ascertain whether there was an acceptance of US capitulatory jurisdiction. The Court observed that individual statements, taken in isolation and detached from their context, could amount to such acceptance. But the Court could not ignore the 'general tenor of correspondence', which indicated that the consular jurisdiction should be viewed as temporary in the context of broader solutions sought by France and the US.[52] The treatment of the Nicaraguan attitude in *Nicaragua* raises the further issue of the relationship between a single act or declaration and the continuous expression of attitude. Nicaragua could have 'admitted' arms flow through its territory but that was allegedly not an admission because its

[49] *ICJ Reports*, 1952, 43–44.
[50] *Id*, 60–61 (Dissenting Opinion).
[51] *Id*, 69–70 (Dissenting Opinion).
[52] *ICJ Reports*, 1952, 200–201.

continuous attitude was precisely a denial of what was 'admitted'. This looks similar to the custom-generation process whereby continuous practice overrides the relevance of single acts and expressions: they are regarded as deviations from more general State practice.

The context in which State actions are performed is also relevant for defining the relevant standard of presumption. It seems that the assumption of an obligation will not be presumed unless the respective actions clearly evidence this, the whole outcome not being upset by the context. In *Ligitan/Sipadan*, the Court refused to accept that adherence to the boundary line fixed in the 1891 Anglo-Dutch Convention was the factor motivating Indonesia and Malaysia to fix that line as the limit of their respective national jurisdictions while granting oil concessions. 'These limits may have been simply the manifestation of the caution exercised by the Parties in granting their concessions. That caution was all the more natural in the present case because negotiations were to commence soon afterwards between Indonesia and Malaysia with a view to delimiting the continental shelf.'[53]

3. Interpretation of Schedules of Commitments in WTO Law

The WTO Panel in *US–Sections 301–310* applied a high threshold for clarifying whether a unilateral statement by a State should be seen as an assumption of legal obligation:

> Attributing international legal significance to unilateral statements made by a State should not be done lightly and should be subject to strict conditions. Although the legal effects we are ascribing to the US statements made to the DSB through this Panel are of a more narrow and limited nature and reach compared to other internationally relevant instances in which legal effect was given to unilateral declarations, we have conditioned even these limited effects on the fulfilment of the most stringent criteria. A sovereign State should normally not find itself legally affected on the international plane by the casual statement of any of the numerous representatives speaking on its behalf in today's highly interactive and inter-dependant world nor by a representation made in the heat of legal argument on a State's behalf.[54]

The WTO jurisprudence offers sufficient material for confirming the above conclusions, especially reinforcing the approach that the distinction between treaties and unilateral acts does not necessarily relate to their nature. Most pertinently, the relevant issues arise with regard to the interpretation of Schedules of Commitments. This relates to the interpretation of originally unilateral acts that eventually form part of the treaty framework. The Appellate Body in

[53] *Sovereignty over Pulau Ligitan and Pulau Sipadan* (Indonesia/Malaysia), Judgment of 17 December 2002, General List No 102 para 79.

[54] *US–Sections 301–310*, para 7.118.

EC–Computer Equipment examined the relevance of the object and purpose of the WTO Agreement for interpreting the schedules of concessions, agreeing:

with the Panel that the security and predictability of 'the reciprocal and mutually advantageous arrangements directed to the substantial reduction of tariffs and other barriers to trade' is an object and purpose of the WTO Agreement, generally, as well as of the GATT 1994. However, we disagree with the Panel that the maintenance of the security and predictability of tariff concessions allows the interpretation of a concession in the light of the 'legitimate expectations' of exporting Members, i.e., their *subjective* views as to what the agreement reached during tariff negotiations was. The security and predictability of tariff concessions would be seriously undermined if the concessions in Members' Schedules were to be interpreted on the basis of the subjective views of certain exporting Members alone. Article II:1 of the GATT 1994 ensures the maintenance of the security and predictability of tariff concessions by requiring that Members not accord treatment less favourable to the commerce of *other* Members than that provided for in their Schedules.[55]

Thus, the object and purpose of the WTO Agreement had no immediate impact on the interpretative outcome and could not be viewed as a factor that promoted subjectivism in the interpretative process. The Appellate Body further elaborated upon the relevance of the author State's intention in relation to Schedules of Commitment:

The purpose of treaty interpretation is to establish the common intention of the parties to the treaty. To establish this intention, the prior practice of only one of the parties may be relevant, but it is clearly of more limited value than the practice of all parties. In the specific case of the interpretation of a tariff concession in a Schedule, the classification practice of the importing Member, in fact, may be of great importance. However, the Panel was mistaken in finding that the classification practice of the United States was not relevant.[56]

In more general terms, the WTO Appellate Body emphasised that:

The purpose of treaty interpretation under Article 31 of the Vienna Convention is to ascertain the common intentions of the parties. These common intentions cannot be ascertained on the basis of the subjective and unilaterally determined 'expectations' of one of the parties to a treaty. Tariff concessions provided for in a Member's Schedule—the interpretation of which is at issue here—are reciprocal and result from a mutually-advantageous negotiation between importing and exporting Members. A Schedule is made an integral part of the GATT 1994 by Article II:7 of the GATT 1994. Therefore, the concessions provided for in that Schedule are part of the terms of the treaty. As such, the only rules which may be applied in interpreting the meaning of a concession are the general rules of treaty interpretation set out in the Vienna Convention.[57]

[55] *European Communities–Customs Classification of Certain Computer Equipment*, AB-1998-2, Report of the Appellate Body, WTDS62/AB/R, 5 June 1998, para 81 (emphasis original).

[56] *Id*, para 93.

[57] *Id*, para 84.

In *US–Gambling*, the issue on which the US appealed against the Panel's decision was whether subsector 10.D of the US Schedule to the GATS, allowing 'other recreational services (except sporting)', included specific commitments regarding gambling and betting. The United States maintained that it expressly excluded 'sporting', the ordinary meaning of which includes gambling, from its commitment for recreational services. The US further argued that the Panel in this case had misinterpreted the ordinary meaning of 'sporting' and improperly elevated certain preparatory work for the GATS to the status of context for the interpretation of the relevant United States' commitment. Furthermore, according to the United States, in concluding that the ordinary meaning of 'sporting' does not cover gambling, the Panel misapplied the customary rules of treaty interpretation and disregarded relevant WTO decisions. The US further reinforced its argument by reference to the applicability of the plain meaning method under the 1969 Vienna Convention. According to the US, preparatory work is merely a supplementary means of interpretation: a WTO panel may look to preparatory work only to confirm an interpretation made in accordance with Article 31 of the Vienna Convention, or if such interpretation leaves the meaning ambiguous or unclear or leads to a result that is manifestly absurd or unreasonable. In this case, the Panel had misapplied the Vienna Convention principles to support a meaning that was at odds with the ordinary meaning of the 'sporting' exclusion in the United States' Schedule. The way schedules must be interpreted is in accordance with their plain meaning. The Panel had misapplied the Vienna Convention and in fact elevated the relevance of preparatory work as the principal method of interpretation. Thus the Panel ignored the plain meaning of the schedule. The Panel was wrong in construing any purported ambiguity against the United States and failing to acknowledge that there was no mutual understanding between the parties to the services negotiations as to the coverage of gambling in the United States' Schedule. In the United States' submission, such an approach, if upheld, would allow Members to expand negotiated commitments through dispute settlement.[58]

Antigua, on the other hand, argued that the plain meaning rule under Article 31 was merely a general rule of interpretation rather than being at the top of the hierarchy of interpretative methods. Therefore, the meaning of 'sporting' had to be examined in the light of the preparatory work, which suggested that 'sporting' did not include gambling.[59]

The US argument in this case is most significant in its perception that the textual method of interpretation requires upholding the presumption of clarity of the commitments included in the text. In fact, what the US objected to was the use of perceived or constructed ambiguity with a view to replacing the interpretative

[58] United States–Measures Affecting the Cross-border Supply of Gambling and Betting Services, AB-2005-1, Report of the Appellate Body, WT/DS285, ABR, 7 April 2005 paras 14–19.

[59] *Id*, paras 46–50.

method, which enjoys a privileged position, with one which only has secondary importance. The Antiguan argument, on the other hand, was directly opposed to the primary relevance of the text.

The Appellate Body, in terms of specifying interpretative approach applicable to seemingly unilateral acts, specified that:

> although each Member's Schedule represents the tariff commitments that bind one Member, Schedules also represent a common agreement among all Members. Accordingly, the task of ascertaining the meaning of a concession in a Schedule, like the task of interpreting any other treaty text, involves identifying the common intention of Members, and is to be achieved by following the customary rules of interpretation of public international law, codified in Articles 31 and 32 of the Vienna Convention.

As GATS specifies that schedules are inherent parts of Agreements, their interpretation likewise involves clarification of the common intention. Therefore, Articles 31 and 32 of the Vienna Convention applied to the interpretative process.[60] The Appellate Body considered that the issue whether 'sporting' includes gambling must be resolved by literal interpretation of the former by reference to dictionary data. The Appellate Body in this respect criticised the Panel for not stopping its interpretative exercise after having clarified that the literal meaning of 'sporting' does not include gambling and betting. The Panel's approach was to consult what it understood as part of 'context'—the negotiation documents of the Uruguay Round. The Appellate Body eventually upheld the Panel's finding that subsection 10.D of the United States' Schedule to the GATS includes specific commitments on gambling and betting services, but for reasons different from those advanced by the Panel.

4. Interpretation of Interpretative Declarations

A particular type of unilateral act is constituted by interpretative declarations whereby States-parties to a treaty express their view as to the meaning of one or another of their provisions. The interpretative declaration should be interpreted in a way similar to other instruments. The European Court of Human Rights emphasised in the *Belilos* case that the content and scope of an interpretative declaration by Switzerland was to be determined by reference to its text and terms. The Court referred to the fact that interpretative declarations, though different from reservations to treaties and not mentioned under the European Convention on Human Rights, were indeed made by States on several occasions. The clarification of their nature was therefore important. The Court emphasised that:

[60] *Id*, paras 158–160.

In order to establish the legal character of such a declaration, one must look behind the title given to it and seek to determine the substantive content. In the present case, it appears that Switzerland meant to remove certain categories of proceedings from the ambit of Article 6(1) and to secure itself against an interpretation of that Article which it considered to be too broad.[61]

The Government argued that the preparatory work of the declaration had to be addressed in understanding whether it was a declaration or reservation. The Court emphasised in response that:

the Court recognises that it is necessary to ascertain the original intention of those who drafted the declaration. In its view, the documents show that Switzerland originally contemplated making a formal reservation but subsequently opted for the term 'declaration'.[62]

But the Court ultimately examined this declaration in terms of its textual wording and severed it, having qualified it as a reservation.

The interpretation of interpretative declarations has formed part of the International Law Commission's work on reservations to treaties. As the ILC's draft guidelines on reservations suggest:

To determine whether a unilateral statement formulated by a State or an international organization in respect of a treaty is a reservation or an interpretative declaration, it is appropriate to interpret the statement in good faith in accordance with the ordinary meaning to be given to its terms, in light of the treaty to which it refers. Due regard shall be given to the intention of the State or the international organization concerned at the time the statement was formulated.[63]

The Commission also emphasised that:

for the purpose of determining the legal nature of a statement formulated in respect of a treaty, it shall be interpreted 'in the light of the treaty to which it refers'. This constitutes, in the circumstances, the principal element of the 'context' mentioned in the general rule of interpretation set out in article 31 of the 1969 and 1986 Vienna Conventions. Whereas a reservation or an interpretative declaration constitutes a unilateral instrument, separate from the treaty to which it relates, it is still closely tied to it and cannot be interpreted in isolation.[64]

The Commission also commented on the relevance of preparatory work in this context, in a way relevant for all unilateral acts:

In the everyday life of the law it would appear difficult to recommend that the preparatory work be consulted regularly in order to determine the nature of a unilateral declar-

[61] *Belilos v Switzerland, No 10328/83*, Judgment of 29 April 1988 para 49.

[62] *Id*, para 48.

[63] *Draft guidelines on reservations to treaties provisionally adopted by the Commission on first reading*, II *YbILC* 1999, 91 at 92; the relevance of the factor of intention is examined in the analysis regarding the Optional Clause declarations, see above Chapter 12.

[64] *Id*, 109.

ation relating to a treaty: it is not always made public, and in any case it would be difficult to require foreign Governments to consult it. This is the reason why draft guideline 1.3.1 does not reproduce the text of article 32 of the 1969 and 1986 Vienna Conventions and, without alluding directly to the preparatory work, merely calls for account to be taken of 'the intention of the State or the international organization concerned at the time the statement was formulated.[65]

This statement presumably clarifies the relevance of the factor of intention in this context. If the Commission's reasoning is followed in this field, then intention of the State is placed at a secondary level, on the same level at which the preparatory work would be placed in the case of treaties. This factor is both important and helpful to avoid promoting auto-interpretation by States. It has also to be emphasised that such ranking of the intention factor essentially differs from the ILC's approach taken with regard to unilateral acts, in the case of which intention of the State can be seen as the factor promoting subjectivism.

5. Interpretation of Submissions to International Tribunals

Yet another category of unilateral statements consists in the submissions of States made to international tribunals. There is a certain degree of similarity between interpreting submissions to tribunals and unilateral statements in general. Judicial submissions are in essence unilateral acts, and their interpretation can be of crucial importance for what the outcome of the case will be. As the International Court put it, 'It has never been contested that the Court is entitled to interpret the submissions of the parties, and in fact is bound to do so; this is one of the attributes of its judicial functions.'[66] At the same time, judicial submissions are made in the context of proceedings and must be construed in terms of the requirements of the proper conduct of judicial decision-making. This may impact the standards of interpretation as well. As the Court emphasised in *Fisheries Jurisdiction*:

In order to identify its task in any proceedings instituted by one State against another, the Court must begin by examining the Application. However, it may happen that uncertainties or disagreements arise with regard to the real subject of the dispute with which the Court has been seised, or to the exact nature of the claims submitted to it. In such cases the Court cannot be restricted to a consideration of the terms of the Application alone nor, more generally, can it regard itself as bound by the claims of the Applicant.[67]

Furthermore, 'The Court will itself determine the real dispute that has been submitted to it. It will base itself not only on the Application and final submissions, but on diplomatic exchanges, public statements and other pertinent evidence.'[68]

[65] *Id*, 109.
[66] *Nuclear Tests* (New Zealand v France), 466.
[67] *Fisheries Jurisdiction* (Spain v Canada), Judgment of 4 December 1998, para 29.
[68] *Id*, para 31.

Depending on their subject matter, submissions must be interpreted by reference to the governing legal framework and their historical background can also be of use. In *Interpretation of Judgments Nos. 7 and 8*, the Court dealt with German submissions requesting it to interpret its previous judgments, and the Court had to examine whether the German submissions referred to the dispute as was required by Article 60 of the Court's Statute dealing with disputes regarding the interpretation of the Court's previous decisions. For this reason, the Court examined the preceding facts in the relations between Germany and Poland and established that the German request was related to the dispute between the two States and was therefore admissible.[69] Most notably, the Court stated that it should interpret German submissions as simply constituting an indication of the points of interpretation in dispute: 'construed in any other way, the Application in question would not satisfy the express conditions' under Article 60.[70] Such submissions would have been inadmissible.

In *Admissibility of Hearings*, the question whether the hearings before the Committee on South-West Africa were admissible was interpreted as the question whether the General Assembly had the right to authorise the Committee to conduct such hearings. This was done because the General Assembly had been involved in the process of clarification of this issue.[71] It seems that the Court identified the true object of the claim: it would make little sense to indicate that there was a right to conduct hearings, without indicating who can perform this right.

In the *WHO–Egypt* case, the Court stated its task to clarify 'the full meaning and implications of the hypothetical question on which it is asked to advise. . . . if [the Court] is to remain faithful to the requirements of its judicial character in the exercise of its advisory jurisdiction, it must ascertain what are the legal questions formulated in the request'.[72] Therefore, even though the question asked referred only to Article 37 of the Agreement between WHO and Egypt, the Court concluded that the real question was about the principles and rules applicable to the transfer of the WHO Regional Office from Egypt. The reply to the questions as they are literally understood may be not only ineffectual but also 'actually misleading as to the legal rules applicable to the matter under consideration'. The Court would not discharge its obligation if it 'did not take into consideration all the pertinent legal issues involved in the matter to which the questions are addressed'.[73] Following this case in *Mortished*, the Court stated that 'it might be

69 *Interpretation of Judgments Nos. 7 and 8*, Judgment No 13 of 16 December 1927, *PCIJ Series* A, No 13, 4 at 12–15.

70 *Id*, 16–17.

71 *Admissibility of Hearings of Petitioners by the Committee on South-West Africa*, Advisory Opinion, 1 June 1956, *ICJ Reports*, 1956, 23 at 25–26.

72 *Interpretation of the Agreement of 25 March 1951 between the WHO and Egypt*, Advisory Opinion, 20 December 1980, *ICJ Reports*, 1980, 73 at 87–88.

73 *Id*, 88–89.

possible to reply to the question on its own terms, but the reply would not appear to resolve the questions really in issue'.[74]

Given all that, it can be stated that the Court interprets judicial submissions in accordance with their plain meaning, but also in a way enabling them to have their proper effect in the context of judicial proceedings, which is quite similar to interpretation in accordance with the object and purpose.

6. Interpretation of Waivers

Lastly, the interpretation of unilateral acts amounting to a waiver must be considered. It is conventional wisdom that waiver cannot be presumed, and there is doctrinal agreement on this point.[75] Interpretation of acts that may involve waiver is quite strict. As the NAFTA Tribunal emphasised in *Waste Management* regarding the issue of waiver under NAFTA Article 1121, 'any waiver must be clear, explicit and categorical, it being improper to deduce same from expressions the meaning of which is at all dubious'.[76] As Visscher states, waiver shall be interpreted as covering only what indisputably follows from the manifestation of will under it.[77]

The basic issue of interpretative presumptions applicable to waivers is whether (final) waiver can be implied in a certain statement; and what the scope of the waiver thus established is. Once the waiver is established, it must be interpreted in accordance with its plain meaning, without any element of restriction of its scope. In *US Nationals in Morocco*, the United States argued that the renunciation by Great Britain of its consular jurisdiction was geographically limited. This argument did not succeed. In the same case, the Court examined whether the declarations of France and Spain on the renunciation of their rights and privileges were meant as the renunciation of all their privileges arising out of the capitulatory regime, or whether this was considered as a temporary undertaking. The Court, having examined the text and wording of declarations, rejected the argument that such waivers were meant to be temporary; instead, such renunciation must be regarded as a complete renunciation of rights and privileges.[78] This approach favours the interpretation of unilateral statements that include waiver on the basis of the principle of effectiveness.

[74] *Application for Review of Judgment No. 273 of the UN Administrative Tribunal*, Advisory Opinion, 20 July 1982, *ICJ Reports*, 1982, 326.

[75] E Suy, *Les actes juridiques unilateraux* (1962), 159ff; FA Mann, Reflection on the Prosecution of Persons Abducted in Breach of International Law in Y Dinstein & M Tabory (eds), *International Law at a Time of Perplexity. Essays in Honour of Shabtai Rosenne* (1989), 410.

[76] *Waste Management Inc v United Mexican States* (Award of 2 June 2000), ARB(AF)/98/2 para 18.

[77] Visscher (1963), 196.

[78] *ICJ Reports*, 1952, 192, 194–195, 205.

The interpretation of waivers of right by a State is addressed in the *Barcelona Traction* case. In this case Spain as the respondent argued that Belgium's discontinuance of the case it had earlier instituted, recorded in the Court's Order of 10 April 1961, precluded it from bringing any further proceedings in the matter of the Barcelona Traction company.[79] The Respondent's main arguments with the relevance of the interpretation process were that the fact that the instrument of discontinuance did not contain an express renunciation of any further right of action was not conclusive; a discontinuance must be taken to involve such a renunciation unless the contrary is stated, or the right to take further action is expressly reserved; and in this case there was an understanding between the parties that the discontinuance did involve such a renunciation and would be final, not only as regards the proceedings in question but also for the future.[80] The Court refused to infer that discontinuance *a priori* includes an inherent element of final renunciation, and held that this question must be resolved by reference to the circumstances of the case. Thus, 'each case of discontinuance must be approached individually in order to determine its real character'.[81]

In terms of the nature of judicial proceedings, the Court stated that the aim of the legal framework is:

to facilitate as much as possible the settlement of disputes—or at any rate their non-prosecution in cases where—the claimant party was for any reason indisposed to discontinue. This aim would scarcely be furthered however, if litigants felt that solely by reason of a discontinuance on their part they would be precluded from returning to the judicial process before the Court, even if they should otherwise be fully in a position to do so.[82]

In terms of interpretative presumptions, the Court stated that it would not:

accept the Respondent's second principal contention, namely that a discontinuance must always and in principle be taken as signifying a renunciation, unless the contrary is indicated or unless the right to start new proceedings is expressly reserved. The two conceptions are mutually contradictory: a notice of discontinuance of proceedings cannot both be in itself a purely procedural and 'neutral' act, and at the same time be, *prima facie* and in principle, a renunciation of the claim. There is no need to discuss this contention any further, except to say that, in view of the reasonable and legitimate circumstances which, as has already been seen, may motivate a discontinuance, without it being possible to question the right of further action, the Court would, if any presumption governed the matter, be obliged to conclude that it was in the opposite sense to that contended for by the Respondent; and that a discontinuance must be taken to be no bar to further action, unless the contrary clearly appeared or could be established.

[79] *Barcelona Traction* (Belgium v Spain), Preliminary Objections, Judgment of 24 July 1964, *ICJ Reports,* 1964, 6 at 17.
[80] *Id*, 17–18.
[81] *Id*, 18–19.
[82] *Id*, 20.

Although, according to the Court, the effect of discontinuance is the end of judicial proceedings in the case, the real question in this case was what the discontinuance implied. This had to be independently established.[83] This separate and independent evidence was not shown.

In terms of the circumstances of the case, the Court referred to the situation in which the Belgian Government was conducting negotiations with Spain on this matter. The initial discontinuance met the Spanish desire not to negotiate about the claims alleging injurious conduct of its officials while judicial proceedings were in progress. The Belgian side would not in this context forego its advantage to re-institute proceedings should negotiations not yield the desired result. This, together with the absence in the text of the discontinuance instrument of an intention to renounce the right to institute further proceedings, confirmed the absence of the required 'very clear proof' that the Belgian discontinuance of litigation on the matter of Barcelona Traction was final and conclusive.[84]

The Court's approach confirms the principle that limitations on the freedom of action of the State, in this case to institute further proceedings, cannot be established in the absence of the required evidence. In interpretative terms, this must be established through analysis of the text, and the meaning of rights and obligations inferable from it provides guidance. The interpretation of waivers is subject to the primacy of the text.

[83] *Id*, 21.
[84] *Id*, 23.

14

Interpretation of Institutional Decisions

1. Decisions of International Organisations

The interpretation of institutional decisions is reinforced both by their contractual elements and the considerations on the basis of which which the respective institutional powers are exercised. Therefore, the principle of effective interpretation respecting the rationale of the given decision is fully applicable in this field. In *Jaworzina*, the Permanent Court interpreted the 1920 Decision of the Conference of Ambassadors in accordance with its terms, and concluded that 'not only a final solution [of the border issues] was intended, but one which would have immediate effect'.[1] It was contended that the 1920 Conference Decision determined only part of the frontier and the delimitation of the rest was still open. The Court rejected this plea and upheld the view based on the principle of effectiveness.[2]

The most problematic field in this context is the regime of interpretation of UN Security Council resolutions. These instruments combine in themselves elements of an agreement between States and elements of 'statutory' or regulatory administrative acts. As international norms on interpretation are not related to the requisite standards of national legal systems, it seems that the latter element cannot be predominant and purely international legal standards must be ascertained.

There are, as Frowein elaborates, various ways in which this issue can be approached. While Frowein rejects the relevance of restrictive interpretation of treaties, he considers that where resolutions include coercive measures against States—'most severe encroachment upon the sovereignty'—the interpretation favourable to the sovereignty is fully justified.[3] But it seems that there could not be legitimate justification for construing restrictively what the Security Council has expressly enacted in the exercise of its mandate to maintain international peace

[1] *Question of Jaworzina (Polish-Czechoslovakian Frontier)*, Advisory Opinion of 6 December 1923, *PCIJ Series* B, No 8, 6 at 29.

[2] Id, 31–38.

[3] J Frowein, Unilateral Interpretation of Security Council Resolutions—A Threat to Collective Security? V Götz, D Selmer & R Wolfrum (eds), *Liber Amicorum Günther Jaenicke—Zum 85. Geburtstag* (Springer 1999), 97 at 112.

and security under the Charter. Restrictive interpretation of resolutions may in some circumstances obstruct the operation of the collective security mechanism.

The effective interpretation of Security Council resolutions was upheld by the International Court in the *Namibia* case. The Court emphasised that the Council's decision adopted under Article 25 was to be treated as producing a specific and definitive legal obligation. The Court emphasised that 'Once the Court is faced with such a situation, it would be failing in the discharge of its judicial functions if it did not declare that there is an obligation, especially upon Members of the United Nations, to bring that situation to an end.'[4]

The effective interpretation of Security Council resolutions follows from the need to give proper effect to the will of and agreement within the Security Council. The words and phrases included in the resolution are the ones on which the Council as a whole has agreed. The Council may decide to qualify its demands in terms of time, space or kind but unless it expresses its intention to do so, its demands and prescriptions have to be given full and proper effect. If a Council resolution requires the cessation of hostilities, then it requires the cessation of entire hostilities at once. If a Council resolution requires a withdrawal from occupied territory, then it requires such withdrawal from the entire occupied territory. Even if at the preparatory stage doubts are expressed as to the completeness of ambit of the provisions in the relevant resolution, it is the actual text that defines the obligations of the relevant States.

As Wood suggests, the judicial authority on the interpretation of Security Council resolutions in the *Namibia* advisory opinion refers to the ascertainment of the binding character of a resolution as opposed to ascertainment of its content.[5] At the same time, the ascertainment of whether the resolution is intended to be binding clarifies the meaning of the resolution, and is thus interpretation, in the same way as any other interpretative exercise. The *Namibia* criteria of reference to the resolution's language (plain meaning), context and preparatory work[6] are quite similar to the principles adopted for interpretation of other categories of acts.

The ICTY dealt with the interpretation of Security Council resolutions in the example of its Statute as part of Resolution 827(1993). The Appeals Chamber stated in *Tadic* that the Statute shall be construed literally and logically.[7] For a better understanding of the scope and meaning of the provisions, the Appeals Chamber in *Tadic* considered their object and purpose, which in that case was identified as the need to enable the Tribunal to prosecute war crimes both in international and internal conflicts,[8] and this outcome was reaffirmed in *Seselj*.[9]

[4] *ICJ Reports*, 1971, 54.

[5] M Wood, The Interpretation of Security Council Resolutions, 2 *Max-Plank YBUNL* (1998), 73 at 75.

[6] *ICJ Reports*, 1971, 53.

[7] *Tadic*, IT-94-1-72, 2 October 1995, paras 83, 87.

[8] *Id*, paras 71, 77.

[9] *Seselj*, IT-03–67-AR72.1, 31 August 2004, para 12.

The preparatory work as represented by the Secretary-General's Report on the establishment of the Tribunal was also used in *Tadic.*[10] Judge Abi-Saab in *Tadic* also upheld the Tribunal's approach, and observed that the provisions of the Statute must be interpreted in a way which preserves their autonomous field of application, that is in accordance with the *effet utile* principle.[11]

It seems that Frowein's abovementioned concerns can be accommodated by the use of the standard principle of interpretation of the plain and ordinary meaning of terms, which means that nothing that is expressed can be disregarded and nothing that is not expressed can be implied. The need for such interpretation becomes clear given the attempts to imply authorisation or approval of the use of force where nothing similar has been expressed in the resolution.

If this approach is applicable to Security Council Resolutions, the implication is that the text and plain meaning of the relevant resolution must be taken as the basis for determining what has been agreed upon. Security Council resolutions are, to an important extent, agreements between States-members of the Council. It follows that the text of the relevant Resolution has primacy over what is said during the deliberations, or after the adoption of the resolution. After all, it is the text that embodies the agreement and joint attitude of the Council's membership—all other statements express the view of individual member-States only. If the view of the member-State expressed individually at whichever stage differs from the view it voted for in the resolution, then the view expressed in the resolution prevails in relation to all relevant States.

In the law of treaties, respect for the written word as the dominant interpretative principle is the prerequisite for legal stability and predictability. If these factors are to be present in the decision-making of the Security Council and not be replaced by mutual distrust and legal chaos, the textual approach has to be adhered to in interpreting the resolutions of the Council. It must, again, be borne in mind that the Vienna Convention rules on interpretation are the only set of rules on this subject. There is no other set of rules applicable to interpretation of other instruments, such as unilateral acts, or decisions of international organisations. No set of rules of interpretation formulated by academics, legal advisers or diplomats can have the same authority as the codified set of authoritative rules.

Consequently, the outcome is that whether the Vienna Convention formally applies to Security Council resolutions, or whether such application takes place by analogy, the textual principle is still the dominant principle in interpreting these resolutions. Obviously resolutions of the Security Council are not identical, though they are similar, to treaties. But it is not enough to say that Security Council resolutions are different from treaties; it is also necessary to emphasise in what way they are different, and what factors cause such difference. On their face, and in terms of the process of their adoption, resolutions, just like treaties, express

[10] *Tadic*, para 82.

[11] Separate Opinion, Section IV.

agreement between States-members of the Security Council and embody their expressed intention for the attention of all.

Therefore, as far as the process of identification of the original content of a Security Council resolution is concerned, the difference between treaties and Security Council resolutions is not the most crucial question. The meaning following from clearly written text can be identified in Security Council resolutions in just the same way as in treaties.

Consequently, even though the Vienna Convention does not formally apply to Security Council resolutions, its principles of interpretation embody more than those pertinent in the case of agreements covered by the scope of the Vienna Convention. In particular, given the essence of Security Council resolutions as agreements expressed in the written word on which reliance can be placed, the distinction drawn between the general rule of interpretation and secondary methods of interpretation becomes particularly important. As with treaties, the general rule of interpretation putting emphasis on the ordinary meaning of the written word is the inevitable precondition for ensuring legal certainty in the process of adoption and implementation of Security Council resolutions.

Obviously, there are situations where there are no direct contradictions between what the text of a Security Council resolution says and how the member-State interprets it. These are cases where the relevant members may claim that the relevant resolution provides for *more* or *less* than what it actually says, among other things, because the resolution does not say anything about that *more* or *less*, and it does not expressly contradict the assumption that *more* or *less* is permissible and allowed.

The NATO air campaign which had not been authorised by the Security Council nor otherwise justified under the UN Charter, ended with the adoption of Security Council Resolution 1244 (1999), whereby the Council approved the international security presence in Kosovo. This has been interpreted by some as retrospective approval of the armed attack on Yugoslavia, although nothing in the text of the Resolution confirms this and a resolution approving the war against the FRY would not have been supported by the required majority in the Council.

Institutional justification for the war against Iraq was sought in the two Security Council resolutions: Resolution 678 (1990) and Resolution 1441 (2003). Resolution 678 (1990) was adopted after the Iraqi invasion of Kuwait in 1990 and provided for authorisation of the member-States cooperating with the Government of Kuwait to use 'all necessary means' to ensure Iraqi withdrawal and the restoration of peace and security in the area. The ensuing campaign against Iraq ended with the liberation of Kuwait and the adoption of Security Council resolution 687 (1991) which laid down the parameters of the settlement in terms of compensation, border demarcation and arms inspections.

In 2003, the US invoked Resolution 678 as one of the bases that justified its invasion of Iraq. This was based on the construction of Resolution 678 as authorising repeated use of force against Iraq, instead of being restricted in its effect to the situation pertaining to the war in 1990–1991.[12] However, nothing in Resolution 678 shows that it was meant as an indefinite, repeatedly invocable authorisation. As Lowe observes, it cannot be argued 'that Resolution 678 gave each one of the States in the 1991 coalition, acting either alone or jointly with some or all of the others, the right to take any action, anytime, anywhere, that it considers it necessary or desirable in pursuit of the aim of restoring peace and security in the area'.[13]

The reference to Council Resolution 1441 (2003) was intended to demonstrate that the Security Council had authorised the use of force against Iraq by threatening it with 'serious consequences' of failure to cooperate with UN inspectors to demonstrate that it did not possess weapons of mass destruction. The reference to 'serious consequences' was interpreted as a reference to authorisation of the use of force.[14] But 'serious consequences' can be a much broader notion not necessarily including the use of force. It is the collective will of the Security Council that matters and the proceedings of the adoption of Resolution 1441 do not demonstrate any collective support for the authorisation of the use of force. As Corten observes, if the Security Council had wished to authorise the use of force, it could have done so expressly.[15] As Lowe further suggests:

> It is simply unacceptable that a step as serious and important as a massive military attack upon a State should be launched on the basis of a legal argument dependent upon dubious inferences drawn from the silences in Resolution 1441 and the muffled echoes of earlier resolutions, unsupported by any contemporary authorisation to use force.[16]

In general, the arguments of implicit previous or subsequent approval of the use of force in the institutional context are arguments of desperation, raised where no other justification of the relevant use of force can be found. These arguments also undermine the factor of reliability in international dealings, because they force States not to consent to any document, whether a treaty or a Security Council Resolution, which does not expressly exclude an outcome they are unwilling to see happen. This can make reaching agreement on many issues impossible because States would be constantly afraid of having their word interpreted as consent to something to which they have never consented. It therefore seems that strict standards of textual interpretation that take the written word for what it literally means and exclude what could have been said but was never said is the only option for promoting an atmosphere in which States will be ready to give their agreement to certain deals, and thus promote international cooperation, without being concerned about their words being twisted afterwards.

[12] J Yoo, International Law and the War in Iraq, 97 *AJIL* (2003), 569–571; M Sapiro, The Fall of Saddam Hussein: Security Council Mandates and Pre-emptive Self-Defense, 97 *AJIL* (2003), 578–582.

[13] V Lowe, The Iraq Crisis: What Now? 52 *ICLQ* (2003), 866.

[14] J Stromseth, Law and Force After Iraq: A Transitional Moment, 97 *AJIL* (2003), 630–631.

[15] O Corten, Opération *Iraqi Freedom*: Peut-on admettre l'argument de l' 'authorisation implicite' du Conseil de Securité? *Revue Belge de Droit International* (2003/1), 213.

[16] Lowe (2003), 866.

That such concerns have become real following the discourse as to the meaning of resolutions 1244, 678 and 1441 was clear in the process of adoption of Security Council resolution 1696 (2006) demanding the termination of Iran's uranium enrichment programme. In the process of adoption, some members of the Council supported a resolution that would provide for sanctions against Iran should it refuse to comply. The propensity among some members of the Council to read implied authorisations for enforcement measures into resolutions which do not even mention them led to the insistence of other members that there should be included, *ex abundanti cautela*, a specific provision in paragraph 8 of the resolution stating that a separate decision would need to be taken on any enforcement measures.

The entire discourse on the construction of these two Security Council resolutions is reminiscent of Vattel's assessment of the methods of drafting that promote the ambiguity and uncertainty. That such ambiguity can obtain from collective decision-making is a fact of life. This requires precisely the adherence to Vattel's priority for the use of such interpretative methods which frustrates the design of those who introduce ambiguity. The textual method respecting the plain and ordinary meaning of terms is the most appropriate method for achieving this task.

The interpretation of institutional or collective decisions arises in WTO law as well. This relates above all to collective decisions that grant to certain contracting parties a waiver from complying with the obligations under the covered agreements. One such waiver was granted in relation to the Lomé Agreement between the EC and the ACP States in relation to the import of agricultural production. This took place on 9 December 1994. The aim was to permit the European Communities to give preferential treatment to products originating from ACP States as required by the relevant provisions of the Lomé Agreement.

In *EC–Bananas*, the WTO Appellate Body had to clarify and determine what was covered by the Lomé Waiver. It was asked whether the Lomé Waiver applied not only to breaches of Article I:1 of the GATT 1994, but also to breaches of Article XIII of the GATT 1994, with respect to the EC's country-specific tariff quota allocations for traditional ACP States.[17] The Panel had concluded that the Lomé Waiver should be interpreted so as to waive not only compliance with the obligations of Article I:1, but also compliance with the obligations under Article XIII. This conclusion allegedly followed from the need to give 'real effect' to the Lomé Waiver and from the 'close relationship' between Articles I and XIII:1.[18]

The Appellate Body disagreed with the Panel's approach. It stated that in order to ascertain what was required by the Lomé Waiver, its text must be examined. Furthermore, it stated that:

> The wording of the Lomé Waiver is clear and unambiguous. By its precise terms, it waives only 'the provisions of paragraph 1 of Article I of the General Agreement ... to the extent

[17] *European Communities–Regime for the Importation, Sale and Distribution of Bananas*, AB-1997–3, Report of the Appellate Body, WT/DS27/AB/R, 9 September 1997, paras 179ff.

[18] *Id*, paras 181–182.

necessary' to do what is 'required' by the relevant provisions of the Lomé Convention. The Lomé Waiver does not refer to, or mention in any way, any other provision of the GATT 1994 or of any other covered agreement. Neither the circumstances surrounding the negotiation of the Lomé Waiver, nor the need to interpret it so as to permit it to achieve its objectives, allow us to disregard the clear and plain wording of the Lomé Waiver by extending its scope to include a waiver from the obligations under Article XIII.[19]

In terms of the interpretative policy, the Appellate Body stated that:

Although the WTO Agreement does not provide any specific rules on the interpretation of waivers, Article IX of the WTO Agreement and the Understanding in Respect of Waivers of Obligations under the General Agreement on Tariffs and Trade 1994, which provide requirements for granting and renewing waivers, stress the exceptional nature of waivers and subject waivers to strict disciplines. Thus, waivers should be interpreted with great care.[20]

Given that, and 'In view of the truly exceptional nature of waivers from the non-discrimination obligations under Article XIII, it is all the more difficult to accept the proposition that a waiver that does not explicitly refer to Article XIII would nevertheless waive the obligations of that Article.'[21] Thus, the interpretation 'with great care' amounted in this case to textual interpretation.

2. Decisions of International Tribunals

Judicial decisions constitute the only kind of acts, among those considered in this contribution, that do not embody a consensual element, but are delivered in a way binding upon the parties. In addition, this issue is different from other issues of interpretation because it is always subject to the statutory framework laying down the preconditions and parameters in which the interpretative task can be exercised. These are embodied in Article 60 of the International Court's Statute, which provides that, 'in the event of dispute as to the meaning or scope of the Judgment, the Court shall construe it upon the request of any party'. As the Court put it, its jurisdiction under Article 60 is a 'special jurisdiction' independent of the consent-based jurisdiction under Article 36 of the Statute. As this is statutory jurisdiction, the Court refused to admit that the parties could derogate from such jurisdiction through their Special Agreement.[22]

[19] *Id*, para 183.
[20] *Id*, para 185.
[21] *Id*, para 187.
[22] *Application for Revision and Interpretation of the Judgment of 24 February 1982 in the Case concerning the Continental Shelf* (Tunisia v Libyan Arab Jamahiriya), 10 December 1985, *ICJ Reports*, 1985, 192 at 216.

In the case concerning *Interpretation of Judgments Nos. 7 and 8*, the Permanent Court was asked by the German Government to pronounce that certain actions of the Polish Government were not in accordance with the two above-mentioned Judgments of the Court. The Court observed that the request was subject to Article 60 of its Statute. Based on this provision, the Court laid down, for the first time, the requirements for admissibility of requests for interpretation: the dispute as to the meaning and scope of the judgment had to exist and the object of the request must be interpretation.[23] The scope of the interpretation includes the clarification of the points that have been settled with binding force in the Judgment, and also the differences as to whether the relevant point has been decided with binding force.[24] For interpretation of its judgments, the Court cannot be bound by the formulae adopted by the parties, but must be able to take an unhampered decision.[25] The Court observed that the finding in the previous Judgment that Germany was entitled to alienate the Chorzow Factory was decided with binding force and that Judgment, as a declaratory judgment, was intended to ensure that the legal situation thus recognised would have binding force once and for all.[26]

In *Asylum*, the International Court practically reiterated the Permanent Court's findings as to the required characteristics of requests to interpret judgments. The Court in particular observed that 'the real purpose of the request must be to obtain an interpretation of the judgment. This signifies that its object must be solely to obtain clarification of what the Court has decided with binding force, and not to obtain the answer to questions not so decided. Any other construction of Article 60 would nullify the provision of the article that the judgment is final and without appeal.'[27] The Court found that the questions asked of it were in reality 'new questions, which cannot be decided by means of interpretation. Interpretation can in no way go beyond the limits of the Judgment.' There was in this case no dispute as to the definite points of the Judgment, but one party argued that certain points in it were ambiguous and the other party considered that they were clear. This, according to the Court could not form the subject of a dispute under Article 60, because Article 79 of the Rules of the Court required specifying 'the precise point or points in dispute'.[28] Therefore, the Court refused to accede to the request for interpretation. On the one hand, the Rules may have been a restriction on what otherwise would have been a normal interpretative task. On the other hand, one may ask why the clarification of ambiguous points cannot be an interpretative task; this can very well be a 'point in dispute'.

[23] *Interpretation of Judgments Nos. 7 and 8*, Judgment No 13 of 16 December 1927, *PCIJ Series* A, No 13, 4 at 5, 9–10.

[24] *Id*, 10–11.

[25] *Id*, 16.

[26] *Id*, 20.

[27] *Asylum* (Interpretation), Judgment of 27 November 1950, 395 at 402.

[28] *Id*, 403.

In *Request for Interpretation*, Nigeria asked the Court to construe the 1998 Preliminary Objections Judgment on *Land and Maritime Boundary* as limiting Nigeria's responsibility in this case which could only be established in relation to the facts and incidents that were mentioned in Cameroon's application.[29] The Court decided not to consider these requests because otherwise it would impair Cameroon's right to present certain issues of fact and law as authorised in the previous judgment on Preliminary Objections.[30]

Subject to these statutory requirements, it must be observed that what the Court does in relation to interpretation of its judgments is quite akin to the normal interpretative process, even though it is not absolutely clear whether there are crystallised principles. However, at the second stage of *Ambatielos* the Court noted that the words 'in so far as this claims is based on the Treaty of 1886' used in the Judgment on Preliminary Objections must be understood in the sense in which they were used.[31]

In the *Voting Procedure* Opinion, the Court had to interpret its earlier Advisory Opinion of 11 July 1950 to clarify what was meant by the 'degree of supervision' to be exercised by the General Assembly over the Mandatory. The Court concluded, by reference to the ordinary and natural meaning of the relevant words, that the degree of supervision related to substantive and not procedural issues. This interpretation was further confirmed 'by an examination of the circumstances which led' to the use of these words.[32]

In another case, the Court interpreted its Advisory Opinion of 11 July 1950 in terms of its overall rationale, that is object and purpose. This purpose was to safeguard the 'sacred trust of civilisation' in South-West Africa. Therefore, the Court pointed out in its Advisory Opinion on *Admissibility of Hearings*, that 'in interpreting the particular sentences in the Opinion of 11 July 1950, it is not permissible, in the absence of express words to the contrary, to attribute to them a meaning which would not be in conformity with this paramount purpose'.[33]

All this is very similar to normal interpretative processes. Whatever the precise legal nature of judicial decisions, they are meant to express attitudes and convey messages, just like any other legal act. The means of their interpretation cannot therefore be too distanced from the principles applicable to other acts and instruments.

[29] *Request for Interpretation*, Judgment (Nigeria v Cameroon), 25 March 1999, para 7.

[30] *Id*, para 16.

[31] *Ambatielos* (Greece v UK), Merits: Obligation to Arbitrate, Judgment of 19 May 1953, 10 at 16.

[32] *Voting Procedure on Questions Relating to Reports and Petitions Concerning the Territory of South-West Africa*, Advisory Opinion of 7 June 1955, *ICJ Reports*, 1955, 67 at 72–74.

[33] *Admissibility of Hearings of Petitioners by the Committee on South-West Africa*, Advisory Opinion, 1 June 1956, *ICJ Reports*, 1956, 23 at 28.

15

Interpretation of Customary Rules

It was concluded above that the process of the emergence of customary rules is in principle dependent on processes that can only be explained by consensual positivism.[1] The factor which allegedly limits the relevance of positivism is that once rules are established, they are deemed to acquire their own existence and pursue their own rationale.

The interpretation of customary rules relates to a peculiar field which does not address any written document or oral statement *per se*. The issue addressed here is not about the process of custom-formation and the interpretation of State action and practice to establish whether it is accompanied by the *opinio juris* required to form customary law. It rather relates to the construction of the scope of established customary rules, as is the case with interpretation of treaties and other acts.

Another necessary caveat is that the interpretation of custom is not the same as deriving legal regulation by analogy. Analogy involves the generalisation of a specific legal regulation applicable to a particular context so that it can, given the nature of other context, apply to it as well. The field of custom interpretation relates, on the other hand, to clarifying the modes and details of applicability of general customary rules to specific situations to which they are designed to apply due to their general scope.

As customary rules in principle constitute agreements, States have expectations as to their content and scope, that is the scope of the consensus reached. The issue of interpretative methods is thus a pressing one. In order to clarify the meaning and scope of customary rules some criteria are necessary which are coherent and generally acceptable in terms of the consensual character of international law and the rationale of relevant rules.

Before we proceed to clarify the applicable methods of interpretation, two preliminary issues must be addressed. These issues derive from the fact that customary rules are unwritten and there is no authoritative text from which the content of such rules *per se* can be derived.

The first issue is the object of interpretation, and whether the interpretative process relates to the customary rule itself or the acts and declarations that

[1] See above Chapter 4.

provide for it in the course of State practice. The interpretation of such statements can indeed be useful in comprehending the general rule.[2] However, this can only be used as evidence of the customary rule, and the methods of interpretation must be those that relate to the essence of that rule, not to the pieces of evidence.

The second issue is the relationship between the interpretation of custom and that of other instruments that may embody the counterparts of the relevant customary rule. There is much less direct evidence regarding the principles of interpretation of custom than interpretation of treaties. Yet, there is sufficient evidence to demonstrate the applicable legal framework, and the link between the interpretative methods and the factor of the essence and rationale of customary rules.

As the International Court observed in *Nicaragua*, 'rules which are identical in treaty law and in customary international law are also distinguishable by reference to the methods of interpretation and application. A State may accept a rule contained in a treaty not simply because it favours the application of the rule itself, but also because the treaty establishes what that State regards as desirable institutions or mechanisms to ensure implementation of the rule.'[3] This passage merely refers to the motivation of States in acceding to treaties, such as the existence of the body that will interpret and apply the treaty, without prejudice to the methods of interpretation. In terms of subject matter, the treaty rule is part of the agreed treaty framework and its content may not always be the same as that of its customary counterpart. Also, the interpretation of the treaty rule makes sense only with respect to the parties to the treaty, and cannot prejudice the content of customary rule commanding a more general consensus than a treaty *lex specialis*.

Customary rule should be interpreted independently from its conventional counterpart, according to the rationale it independently possesses. The applicable methods of interpretation have to do with the nature of customary rules.

The methods of interpretation of treaties are codified in Articles 31 and 32 of the 1969 Vienna Convention on the Law of Treaties, and constitute the only set of authoritative rules of interpretation. The Vienna Convention provisions accord priority to those interpretative methods which refer to the plain meaning of the treaty provision and the object and purpose of the treaty.

This leads to the relevance of the principle of effectiveness.[4] The rationale underlying the interpretation of a treaty and of custom is the same—the preservation of the integrity of the legal rule. The factor of the completeness of the rule as an element of its rationale can also be a criterion for interpreting customary rules. Customary rules, just like treaty rules, have their own rationale and intendment.

[2] A Bleckmann, Zur Feststellung und Auslegung von Völkergewohnheitsrecht, *ZaöRV* (1977), 505 at 525.

[3] *ICJ Reports*, 1986, 95.

[4] See above Chapter 11.

Bleckmann suggests several methods for interpreting customary rules. First of all, there is grammatical interpretation, which refers to the literal and usual meaning of the rule as it is commonly accepted. Despite some difficulties, literal interpretation can clarify the core of the rule and the definitions of the concepts referred to in the rule.[5] Systemic interpretation relates to placing the rule in the context of other relevant rules, and to eliminating controversies.[6] The logical connection between customary rules is lower than between rules embodied in the same treaty instrument,[7] and consequently conflicts between customary rules are more likely. The systemic approach is, consequently, useful in this area, for reconciling rules that are not in any *lex specialis* relationship to each other.

The teleological interpretation of customary rules refers to the aim of the relevant rule. As Bleckmann puts it, this rule can be transferred to the field of interpretation of custom even more easily than other principles. The real challenge to the decision-maker in such cases is the proper identification of the aim and rationale of the relevant customary rule.[8]

The reference to the rationale of customary rules can be seen as an aspect of natural law. It can, on the other hand, be explained by reference to the limits of positivism and the ensuing need to consider the rationale of rules in existence, which is independent from their allegedly consensual origin.

The Court referred to certain basic considerations 'inherent in the nature of the territorial sea' as a factor in judging the legality of a delimitation on the basis of the 1935 Decree of Norway, and thus applying the customary rule on territorial sea delimitation. This inherent nature related to the close relation of the relevant sea area to the soil and the ensuing practical needs and local requirements of the coastal State.[9] This is similar to the *North Sea* case, in terms of the criteria of interpretation of rules (though not necessarily in terms of the interpretative outcome).

As Judge Tanaka emphasised in *North Sea*, 'the method of logical and teleological interpretation can be applied in the case of customary law as in the case of written law'.[10] As the Court's judgment in *North Sea* confirms, the Court was not against the principle that customary rules can and should be interpreted in terms of their rationale and purpose. But such interpretation cannot expand the meaning of the relevant rule and include in it requirements not covered by its scope. In this context, this meant that the delimitation of the continental shelf by reference to equidistance could not be seen as the outcome of interpretation of the rule regarding entitlement to the continental shelf.

[5] Bleckmann (1977), 526.
[6] *Id*, 526–528.
[7] *Id*, 527.
[8] *Id*, 528.
[9] *ICJ Reports*, 1951, 133.
[10] *ICJ Reports*, 1969, 181.

In developing an interpretative approach, Judge Tanaka proceeded from the argument of the inherent nature of the institution of the continental shelf, and argued that:

> the rule with regard to delimitation by means of the equidistance principle constitutes an integral part of the continental shelf as a legal institution of teleological construction. For the existence of the continental shelf as a legal institution presupposes delimitation between the adjacent continental shelves of coastal States. . . . Delimitation itself and delimitation by the equidistance principle serve to realize the aims and purposes of the continental shelf as a legal institution.

Consequently, according to Judge Tanaka, equidistance is inherent in the concept of the continental shelf, in the sense that without this provision the institution as a whole cannot attain its own end. The equidistance principle was seen as the logical conclusion following from the fundamental rules on the continental shelf. The recognition of the latter by Germany logically implied its recognition of the former.[11]

Judge Morelli in the same case, also upholding the rule of equidistance, develops a consistent view of the interpretation of custom, independently of the correctness of the outcome of the interpretation of that specific rule. Judge Morelli begins by pointing out that: 'Once the existence of a rule of general international law which confers certain rights over the continental shelf on various States considered individually is admitted, the necessity must be recognized for such a rule to determine the subject-matter of the rights which it confers.' If the rule on the continental shelf:

> did not indicate the criterion for apportionment, it would be an incomplete rule. But, unlike other incomplete rules which no doubt exist in the international legal system, this rule is one the incomplete nature of which would have a most particular importance, because it is the determination of the very subject-matter of the rights conferred by the rule that would be omitted. Such an omission would totally destroy the rule.[12]

This statement also confirms the relevance of the rationale of the rule in interpreting its scope. From here Judge Morelli proceeds to argue that the criterion of apportionment is an inherent part of the fundamental rule on the continental shelf. Therefore, Judge Morelli suggests that:

> The rule, or, more correctly, the criterion for apportionment, can only be a rule or criterion which operates automatically, so as to make it possible to determine, upon the basis of such criterion, the legal situation existing at any given moment. This requirement could not be satisfied by the rule which the Court declares as the only rule governing the matter, a rule that would oblige the States concerned to negotiate an agreement in order to delimit the continental shelf between themselves. Such a rule, for so long as the

[11] *Id.*
[12] Dissenting Opinion, *id*, 200.

agreement which it contemplates has not been concluded, would allow a situation of uncertainty to persist with regard to the apportionment of the continental shelf.[13]

The statement captures the essence of the process of custom interpretation. According to Judge Morelli, equidistance is the logical emanation of the concept of the continental shelf, there being no need to ascertain from State practice whether a specific custom has been established on this matter.[14]

This suggests that the rationale for the continental shelf rule cannot be one which requires a negotiated equitable solution, instead of providing a ready-made regulation. As the Court's view in *North Sea* and other subsequent delimitation cases confirm, the fundamental rule on the continental shelf does not provide a specific ready-made delimitation rule for the very reason that States cannot agree on it. The existing rule, under this approach, cannot by implication include legal regulation on which it does not expressly pronounce and on which moreover there is no consensus in the community of nations.

As the International Court similarly emphasised in *Gulf of Maine*, in the matter of maritime delimitation customary law can 'only provide a few basic legal principles, which lay down guidelines to be followed with a view to an essential objective'.[15] The rest had to be ascertained by reference to equitable criteria to which these principles referred.

Fundamental rules are linked to the indeterminacy of what is supposed to provide specific guidance on delimitation of maritime spaces, in the absence of specific applicable delimitation rules. As the Court specified in *Gulf of Maine*:

It is therefore unrewarding, especially in a new and still unconsolidated field like that involving the quite recent extension of the claims of States to areas which were until yesterday zones of the high seas, to look to general international law to provide a ready-made set of rules that can be sued for solving any delimitation problems that arise. A more useful course is to seek a better formulation of the fundamental rule, on which the Parties were fortunate enough to agree.[16]

Nevertheless, the defect in the interpretative outcome of Judge Morelli's reasoning does not affect the correctness and inherent utility of the *principles of interpretation* developed in his Dissenting Opinion. These principles are indispensable for the interpretative exercise in the field of customary law.

The *Fisheries* case regarding the delimitation of territorial sea raises the issue of whether and how a properly established customary rule can apply to circumstances which fall within its ambit, yet are of such an exceptional nature as to make its application difficult if not impossible. In this case, the Court accepted that it could not determine the inner boundary of Norway's territorial sea by simply following the coastal configuration, and that this boundary should begin

13 *Id*, 200–201.
14 *Id*, 202.
15 *ICJ Reports*, 1984, 290.
16 *Id*, 299.

with the straight baselines connecting the designated points of coast with each other. The Court specified that the relevant part of the Norwegian coast 'call[ed] for the application of the different method'.[17]

The treatment of the territorial sea delimitation in the *Fisheries* case can in principle be considered as falling within one of the following categories: admitting the derogation from the otherwise applicable rule of the configuration of coast; reading an inherent exception into the existing general customary rule, dictated by the special configuration of the coast; or interpreting the general rule with a view to clarifying its applicability to the special circumstances such as on the Norwegian coast.

As Fitzmaurice admits, the Court's treatment of the 'normal' low-water mark rule on the limit of territorial sea in *Fisheries* does not result in admitting the departure from that rule because of the exceptional circumstances of the configuration of the coast. Such circumstances rather made the uniform applicability of the general rule impossible. Therefore, the Court, without rejecting the relevance of the general low-water mark rule, accepted its special application in this case.[18] Thus, Fitzmaurice advocates the solution 'within' the rule, that is the solution based on interpretation. The reasoning seems to be that the 'normal' rule itself and by its rationale allowed for the specific circumstances Norway had advanced.

This seems to be a defensible argument. This process still resembled derogation, because of the other States' acquiescence in what Norway was doing—it could also be seen as acquiescence in the specific interpretation of the rule.[19]

Whether or not this approach is right, Fitzmaurice's reasoning affirms the point of interpretation that the application of customary rules should be guided by the interpretation based on their rationale. In this context, Fitzmaurice seems to advance an approach similar to the margin of appreciation: the essential conditions of exceptional circumstances justifying separate regulation would be '(i) that the circumstances should be truly exceptional, and not merely unusual; and (ii) that no other method of meeting them would be possible except by a deviation from the normal rule'.[20]

The Court itself applied some sort of margin of appreciation in evaluating the relationship between the general direction of the coast and Norwegian baselines:

> The Norwegian Government admits that the base-lines must be drawn in such a way as to respect the general direction of the coast and that they must be drawn in a reasonable manner. The United Kingdom Government contends that certain lines do not follow the general direction of the coast, or do not follow it sufficiently closely, or that they do not

[17] *ICJ Reports*, 1951, 129.

[18] Fitzmaurice (1986), 148–149, 154.

[19] The correct view seems to be that the legality of the Norwegian method of delimitation was based on the consideration by the UK and other interested States of this practice and exceptional geography that motivated it, and acquiescence in all this specific regulation.

[20] Fitzmaurice (1986), 150.

respect the natural connection existing between certain sea areas and the land formations separating or surrounding them. For these reasons, it is alleged [by the UK] that the line drawn is contrary to the principles which govern the delimitation of the maritime domain. . . .

The base-line has been challenged on the ground that it does not respect the general direction of the coast. It should be observed that, however justified the rule in question may be, it is devoid of any mathematical precision. In order properly to apply the rules, regard must be had for the relation between the deviation complained of and what, according to the terms of the rule, must be regarded as the *general* direction of the coast. Therefore, one cannot confine oneself to examining one sector of the coast alone, except in a case of manifest abuse; nor can one rely on the impression that may be gathered from a large scale chart of this sector alone. In the case in point, the divergence between the base-line and the land formations is not such that this is a distortion of the general direction of the Norwegian coast.[21]

Fitzmaurice claims that the concepts of 'manifest abuse' and 'distortion' constitute another element of uncertainty,[22] though these are in fact the criteria for judging whether the margin of appreciation has been properly used. It would seem that abuse would be present in the case of distortion.

Further elaboration of the criteria for applying this customary rule in accordance with its rationale can be found in the Separate Opinion of Judge Hsu Mo:

The expression 'to conform to the general direction of the coast', being one of Norway's own adoption and constituting one of the elements of a system established by herself, should not be given a too liberal interpretation, so liberal that the coast line is almost completely ignored. It cannot be interpreted to mean that Norway is at liberty to draw straight lines in any way she pleases provided they do not amount to a deliberate distortion of the general outline of the coast when viewed as a whole. It must be interpreted in the light of the local conditions in each sector with the aid of a relatively large scale chart. If the words 'to conform to the general direction of the coast' have any meaning in law at all, they must mean that the base-lines, straight as they are, should follow the configuration of the coast as far as possible and should not unnecessarily and unreasonably traverse great expanses of water, taking no account of land or islands situated within them.[23]

Thus, Judge Hsu Mo interprets the customary rule, emphasising its object and purpose and requiring compliance with it of any admissible exception to that rule.

The problem of uniformity of rules thus arises. In this respect, Visscher develops the view of custom as generalised guidance only. Although not strictly correct, this perspective still offers some guidance on interpreting customary rules. The differentiated application of customary rules, adapted to the diversity of factual situations, does not impair their existence or unity.[24] 'It is only in its essential

[21] *ICJ Reports*, 1951, 141–142.
[22] Fitzmaurice (1986), 235.
[23] *ICJ Reports*, 1951, 154–155.
[24] Ch de Visscher, *Theory and Reality in Public International Law* (1968), 160.

components that an international custom escapes these individualising inferences and remains the expression of the common and general law.'[25] Visscher further argues that 'if there are basic elements in the customary rule which, owing to their exact correspondence with the common needs of the great majority of States, call for general application, there are others, of a secondary character, which can only be applied with differentiations adapting them to particular situations'.[26]

To discern how far this approach can be applied usefully, the difference must be specified, on a general scale, between regulatory rules and reference rules. Regulatory rules are those that regulate the conduct of States and prescribe specific outcomes in relation to them; reference rules are those which do not by themselves apply to the required outcomes, but prescribe the circumstances with reference to which the legality of the outcomes must be determined. From this perspective, regulatory customary rules are those whose specific and detailed content, or general content that can be applied without the further stage of normative or quasi-normative analysis, commands sufficient general consensus. Therefore, the issue raised by Visscher cannot be clarified except on the basis of the analysis of the content of individual customary rules, and there can be no preconceived approach dividing customary rules into different categories.

Another cognate issue arising is that of the precision of a customary rule. Absolute precision is allegedly not necessary for the rule to have ascertainable content and govern the given situation. In the *Fisheries* case the Court found that 'the absence of rules having the technically precise character' did not prevent the delimitation undertaken by the Norwegian Government from being subject to certain principles which governed the validity of this delimitation.[27] As Fitzmaurice observes, the absence of the precision of the relevant rule still leaves the matter to be judged by the 'general and preponderant trend' of the law on the subject. Otherwise, much of international law would be incapable of practical application. In terms of the *Fisheries* case, Fitzmaurice identifies from the Court's judgment the criteria that the Court used in terms of such general rationale of rules: the inherent nature of the territorial sea to be adapted to the diverse facts, and the requirement that the general direction of the coast must be followed in so far as this is possible.[28]

Some useful points on the precision of rules are contained in Judge De Castro's Opinion in *Fisheries Jurisdiction*. In this case, Judge De Castro came to the conclusion that 'there is in international law no binding and uniform rule fixing the maximum extent of the jurisdiction of States with regard to fisheries'. However, by reference to Fitzmaurice, Judge De Castro asserted that 'so soon as it is admitted that international law governs the question of the breadth of the territorial sea, it follows automatically that international law must also prescribe *a* standard

[25] Visscher (1968), 160.
[26] *Id*, 159.
[27] *ICJ Reports*, 1951, 132.
[28] Fitzmaurice (1986), 151–152, referring to *ICJ Reports*, 1951, 129, 133.

maximum breadth, universally valid and obligatory in principle... If this is not so, then international law would *not* govern the question of the extent of the territorial sea.'[29] Therefore, the flexibility of the rule was not a reason for denying its existence, and some criteria had to be elaborated upon. Arguably, following from the teleological perspective, Judge De Castro further submitted that 'To leave to the unfettered will of each State the uncontrolled power to lay down the limits of exclusive fishing zones is contrary to the spirit of international law.'[30] The completeness of the rule was required, because 'The appropriation of an exclusive fisheries zone in an area hitherto considered as part of the free seas is equivalent to deprivation of other peoples of their rights.'[31] And only the presence of definable limits could avoid such legal uncertainty.

The point of precision confirms the relevance of interpretation methods. Imprecision and generality cannot prevent the rule from having its effect and from applying to specific situations covered by its content. Interpretation methods assume their relevance in ensuring that customary rule properly applies within the field it covers.

There is a further case demonstrating that in the case of unwritten rules their rationale shall assume an important role in construing their scope, and that customary rules have their object and purpose in the same way as other rules or instruments. In *Burkina-Faso/Mali*, the International Court examined the emergence of the *uti possidetis* rule as customary rule and observed that 'its obvious purpose is to prevent the independence and stability of new States being endangered by fratricidal struggles provoked by the challenging of frontiers following the withdrawal of the administering power'. Furthermore, 'the essence of the principle lies in its primary aim of securing respect for the territorial boundaries at the moment when independence is achieved'.[32] This reference to the object and purpose of the customary rule (denoted by the Court as 'obvious purpose', 'essence' and 'aim'), and the overarching policy goal that underlined this object and purpose, enabled it to consider that the applicability of this principle was not limited to the South American region in which it was originated, but also extended to situations in Africa. As the Court put it, this is 'a principle of a general kind which is logically connected with... decolonisation wherever it occurs'.[33] The same rationale of the rule explained that the *uti possidetis* rule does not conflict with the principle of self-determination, because, by guaranteeing the stability of the frontiers of the entities that emerged through the exercise of their right to self-determination, and thus enabling them to survive, the *uti possidetis* rule served exactly the same

[29] *ICJ Reports*, 1974, 95–96 (emphasis original).

[30] *Id*, 96.

[31] *Id*, 97; Judge De Castro's analysis further proceeded to identify the normative content by reference to the concepts with which the Court's judgment decided the case, that is the scope of relevance of special interests, historic rights, and equity.

[32] *Case Concerning Frontier Dispute* (Burkina-Faso/Republic of Mali), 22 December 1986, 554 at 565–566.

[33] *Id*, 565–566.

goal as the principle of self-determination and, instead of conflicting with this principle, impacted its interpretation as well.[34]

In NAFTA arbitration, it is not *per se* necessary to argue the point of customary law, but with the 2001 FTC Interpretation on the scope of the 'fair and equitable treatment' standard under Article 1105 NAFTA,[35] it became necessary for tribunals to base their decisions on customary law. The principal point in a number of arbitrations has been whether the traditional customary international law standard embodied in the *Neer* decision delivered in 1926 was still a governing standard for the treatment of investors, and thus whether the violation of investors' rights under Article 1105 NAFTA required crossing the threshold of 'egregious' conduct or was liberalised due to the different state of customary law at the time when decisions were delivered.

However, while interpreting the Article 1105 reference to customary law, the Tribunal in *Mondev* referred not to the need 'to show *opinio juris* or to amass sufficient evidence demonstrating it. The question rather is: what is the content of customary international law providing for fair and equitable treatment and full protection and security in investment treaties?'[36] This is the statement of an interpretative mission to ascertain the meaning and scope of the established customary rule.

At the final stage of *Pope & Talbot*, the Arbitral Tribunal considered Canada's suggestion that the state of customary law had been frozen in amber since the *Neer* decision and that the Tribunal could only condemn such conduct as had acquired an 'egregious' character.[37] The Tribunal rejected this static conception of international law and held that this body of law had since evolved.[38] The same principle was followed by the Tribunal in *Thunderbird*, though it stated that despite the evolution of customary law the threshold still remained high. In order to find a breach of Article 1105 NAFTA and customary law, the relevant conduct had to 'amount to a gross denial of justice or manifest arbitrariness falling below acceptable international standards'.[39] The Tribunal did not find that Article 1105 was violated.

A violation of Article 1105 was not found in *Waste Management* either, even though this decision also considered the *Neer* standard as modified through subsequent evolution. Even if the *Neer* standard of outrage, bad faith, wilful neglect of the duty, or insufficiency of governmental authority did not exclusively apply,

[34] *Id*, 567.

[35] See below Chapter 16.

[36] *Mondev International Ltd. and USA* (Award), Case No ARB(AF)/99/2, 11 October 2002 para 113.

[37] *Pope & Talbot Inc and the Government of Canada* (Award on Damages, NAFTA Chapter 11 Arbitration), 21 May 2002 para 57.

[38] The same was in principle stated in *ADF* (Award), para 179.

[39] *International Thunderbird Gaming Corporation and the United Mexican States* (Partial Award on Merits), 26 January 2006, para 194.

it was still necessary to find that the Government's conduct was 'grossly unfair or unreasonable'.[40]

Furthermore, the *Waste Management* Tribunal specified, by referring to the concept of denial of justice, that the minimum standard of fair and equitable treatment:

> is infringed by conduct attributable to the State and harmful to the claimant if the conduct is arbitrary, grossly unfair, unjust or idiosyncratic, is discriminatory and exposes the claimant to sectional or racial prejudice, or involves a lack of due process leading to an outcome which offends judicial propriety—as might be the case with a manifest failure of natural justice in judicial proceedings or a complete lack of transparency and candour in an administrative process.

This was the standard that the Tribunal applied to the determination of whether a breach of Article 1105(1) had taken place.[41] Given that these terms and concepts are unclear, there seems to be no great difference between the *Neer* standard and the allegedly evolved standard.

The Tribunal in *Mondev* rejected the argument that the relevant standard was limited to *Neer*, because *Neer* itself was about the failure of the police to investigate the killing of a foreign national, so that it was concerned with State responsibility for the actions of private persons, not about the treatment of foreign investment. Therefore, it could not be assumed that the BIT and NAFTA standards of customary law could be limited to the *Neer* principle.[42]

Interpretation of the nationality rule of customary law has been repeatedly undertaken by international tribunals. The early practice regarding the scope of the nationality rule, including the PCIJ jurisprudence, dealt with the 'first limb' of the continuous nationality rule—the moment when the injury is suffered.[43] Subsequent ICJ cases did not really discuss the continuity issue: *Nottebohm* was about effective nationality while *Barcelona Traction* dealt with the nationality of corporations as opposed to that of individuals. Each of these cases somehow interpreted the nationality rule with the purpose of construing it as something meaningful: people should not be allowed to rely on the protection of a State to which they do not actually belong (*Nottebohm*) and respondent States will not be burdened by double actions by corporations and shareholders (*Barcelona Traction*). These clarifications and constructions of the rule have presented the nationality rule as the rule that serves the need to enable States to protect those private persons and entities who are really their nationals, thereby emphasising the relevance of diplomatic protection as an incidence of the traditional bilateralism construct

[40] *Waste Management Inc. v United Mexican States* (Award), 30 April 2004, paras 93–96.

[41] *Waste Management*, para 98.

[42] *Mondev* (Award), para 115.

[43] M Mendelson, Runaway Train: The 'Continuous Nationality' Rule from *Panevezys-Saldutiskis Railway* case to *Loewen*, Weiler (ed), *International Investment Law Arbitration: Leading Cases from the ICSID, NAFTA, Bilateral and Customary International Law* (2005), at 9, referring especially to *Panevezys-Saldutiskis* judgment of the PCIJ.

of international law. This has confirmed the object and purpose of the nationality rule—to secure the protection of State rights in bilateral contexts.

The general rationale behind the disposal of the nationality issue was dealt with by the Arbitral Tribunal in *Loewen*. The Tribunal pointed out that Chapter 11 NAFTA represents a progressive development in international law whereby an individual investor can resort to arbitration. At the same time, 'the format of NAFTA was clearly intended to protect the investors of one Contracting Party against unfair practices occurring in one of the other Contracting Parties. It was not intended to and could not affect the rights of American investors in relation to practices of the United States that adversely affect such American investors. Claims of that nature can only be pursued under domestic law.'[44] The Claimant argued that it had the requisite nationality at the time the claim arose and thus it was immaterial that the beneficiary of the claim was an American citizen. The Tribunal responded that 'in international law parlance, there must be continuous national identity from the date of events giving rise to the claim, which date is known as *dies a quo*, through the date of the resolution of the claim, which date is known as *dies ad quem*'.[45]

The issue that the investor pressed as relevant was that of *lex specialis*, arguing that NAFTA Articles 1116 and 1117 dealt with the nationality requirement. The Tribunal replied that these clauses were concerned with nationality only *dies a quo* and did not specify whether the nationality must continue up to the time of resolution of the claim. Therefore, the silence of the Treaty required the application of customary international law to resolve the question of continuous nationality.[46] This coincided with the Tribunal's power under Article 1131 to decide the dispute in accordance with 'applicable rules of international law'.[47]

The Tribunal noted that several BITs and also the Iran-US Agreement modified the customary law requirement of continuous nationality but NAFTA had no such requirement incorporated in it. Continuous nationality was justified under general international law with the requirement for a link between the State and the individual; 'if that tie were ended, so was the justification' of the nationality rule.[48] The NAFTA claims were conceived in terms of public international law disputes and dealt with rights belonging not to investors *per se* but to States-parties.[49]

The Tribunal's reasoning evidences that the body specifically designed to protect private investors' rights is conscious of the legal framework of public international law within which it is set up and confirms that the protection of

[44] *The Loewen Group, Inc. and Raymond L. Loewen and United States of America* (Award, Case No ARB(AF)/98/3), 26 June 2003, para 223, 42 *ILM* (2003), 811 at 846.

[45] *Id*, 847, para 225.

[46] *Id*, 847, para 226.

[47] *Id*, 847, para 228.

[48] *Id*, 847, para 230.

[49] *Id*, 847–848, paras 231–233.

investors' rights must be exercised bearing in mind the character of the NAFTA Treaty which is specifically designed to operate on the basis of traditional inter-State bilateralism. The *Loewen* Tribunal did not examine evidence to prove the existence of the relevant customary rule in one or another guise. Instead, the Tribunal considered the existing nationality rule from the viewpoint of its rationale and consequently interpreted it in terms of whether it encompassed the continuity requirement. As the nationality rule is intended to serve the interests of States in bilateral disputes, its object and purpose requires that States should be able to vindicate the rights of an individual or a corporation only if the latter continue to be their nationals. Standing before the institutionalised arbitration system is restricted accordingly.

Criticising the *Loewen* Tribunal's decision, Mendelson notes that a change of nationality after the making of claim but before the commencement of litigation should not make a difference to the cause of action,[50] and that the continuous nationality requirement involves extensive interpretation through prolonging *dies ad quem* to the date of the award.[51] Mendelson suggests that the Tribunal would have done better if it had established that the extended continuity rule it upheld was itself established as customary law and had positively demonstrated that such specific rule applied not just to diplomatic protection but to investor claims as well.[52] But the distinction between diplomatic protection and investor claims is not that straightforward. The investor claims field is just an institutionalised area of the bilateral diplomatic protection process and is subject to the same customary rules unless the relevant treaties expressly exclude them.

An attempt to interpret the nationality rule in terms of diplomatic protection is made in the *Ahmadou Sadio Diallo* case, in the submissions of the Democratic Republic of the Congo, in the context of the link between the national State and the rights of a company. The DRC argued that under positive international law a distinction exists between the rights of the company and those of shareholders. Therefore, the only acts capable of violating the direct rights of shareholders would be 'acts of interference in relations between the company and its shareholders'. The arrest and expulsion of the relevant individual did not constitute such interference.[53] The Court responded with acceptance, stating that the diplomatic protection rule relates to the violation of the rights of the legal person that has the nationality of the protecting State. Therefore, customary international law did not admit of an exception to the rule that the protection of individual shareholders cannot involve the vindication of the rights of the company itself.[54]

[50] M Mendelson, Runaway Train: The 'Continuous Nationality' Rule from *Panevezys-Saldutiskis Railway* case to *Loewen* in T Weiler (ed), *International Investment Law Arbitration: Leading Cases from the ICSID, NAFTA, Bilateral Treaties and Customary International Law* (2005), 11.

[51] *Id*, 45.

[52] *Id*.

[53] *Ahmadou Sadio Diallo*, Preliminary Objections, General List No 103, Judgment of 24 May 2007, paras 51ff.

[54] *Id*, para 64.

The Court further affirmed that the rationale of the diplomatic protection rule is the nationality link between the State and the entity that has legal personality under domestic law.[55] Consequently, the rights of the relevant entity can be vindicated only insofar as there is such a nationality link, and to the extent of the injury to that specific entity as such. Any other interpretation would contradict the rationale of customary rule on diplomatic protection.

NAFTA practice has also dealt with interpreting the customary rule on expropriation. In *Pole & Talbot*, the investor claimed that there existed a 'well-recognised international legal principle that expropriation refers to an act by which governmental authority is used to deny *some* benefits of property'. Under general international law, limitations on a State's right to expropriate private property included so-called 'creeping' expropriation, a process that has the effect of taking property through staged measures.[56] Canada responded that 'mere interference is not expropriation; rather, a significant degree of deprivation of fundamental rights of ownership is required'.[57] The investor accepted that the customary international law definition of expropriation did not include measures such as export control.[58] Therefore, if there is a rule against expropriation it has to cover anything that will effectively amount to expropriation.

In *CME v the Czech Republic*,[59] the Arbitral Tribunal dealt with the scope of actions that are subsumable within the deprivation of investors of their investments by host States. As the Tribunal pointed out, regulatory measures are common to all economic and legal systems and are different from the deprivation of property. However, the Czech Government's action in relation to the broadcasting company went beyond the normal broadcasting regulation.

The expropriation claim was sustained even if no express expropriation took place. *De facto* expropriations are also expropriations; they do not involve an express taking but they 'effectively neutralise the benefit of the property of the foreign owner' and thus are subject to expropriation claims. The Tribunal emphasised that 'this is undisputed under international law',[60] which is supposedly a reference to the customary rule. Although acting within the BIT field, the Tribunal did not deal, with regard to this specific issue, with treaty terms but examined the customary rule in terms of its interpretation, even though it did so in a less straightforward manner in terms of interpretation of the rules, and also paid attention to the evidentiary side.

Another interesting area of the interpretation of custom involves the treatment of the rule on the denial of justice. The *Thunderbird* Award states that 'acts that

[55] *Id*, paras 88–90.

[56] *Pope & Talbot* (Interim Award), para 84 (emphasis original).

[57] *Pope & Talbot* (Interim Award), para 88.

[58] *Pope & Talbot* (Interim Award), para 103.

[59] *CME Czech Republic BV (Netherlands) v The Czech Republic*, UNCITRAL Arbitration, 13 September 2001, paras 591ff, 602–603.

[60] *Id*, para 604.

would give rise to a breach of the minimum standard of treatment prescribed by NAFTA and customary international law are those that, weighed against the given factual context, amount to a gross denial of justice or manifest arbitrariness falling below acceptable international standards'.[61]

In *Loewen*, the Arbitral Tribunal construed the scope of the rule on denial of justice in order to find whether there was a breach of Article 1105 NAFTA. The parties were in agreement that there is a customary rule against denial of justice, requiring States to maintain a fair and effective system of justice, and to make it available to individuals. However, the respondent argued that the customary rule required that the applicant establish that the decisions of Mississippi courts constituted a manifest injustice towards the applicants. The respondent invoked a range of doctrinal authorities to suggest that the claimant had to prove the occurrence of 'manifest injustice', 'gross unfairness' or 'flagrant and inexcusable violation' committed in bad faith as opposed to judicial error.[62]

The Tribunal responded that 'neither State practice, nor the decisions of international tribunals nor the opinion of commentators support the view that bad faith or malicious intention is an essential element of unfair and inequitable treatment or denial of justice. Manifest injustice in the sense of a lack of due process leading to an outcome which offends a sense of judicial propriety is enough.'[63] The rationale impliedly accepted seems to be the need not to construe the rule on denial of justice in too limited a way so as not to deprive it of its effective applicability.

[61] *Thunderbird* (Award), para 194.
[62] *Loewen*, paras 129–130, 42 *ILM* (2003), 832.
[63] *Id*, 832, para 132.

16

The Agencies of Interpretation

The role of interpretative agencies involves the institutional question of the propriety of action by the relevant actor in interpreting the relevant instrument. Interpretative competence can belong, as the case may be, to different international actors. Such competence can (a) rest with individual States-parties; (b) be conferred to treaty-based organs expressly, by way of delegation; (c) be part of regular adjudicatory powers of international judicial and quasi-judicial organs. The ultimate merit of each option, as well as the allocation of interpretative competence between different actors, must be guided by the need to guarantee the integrity of the relevant international rules, obligations and instruments.

Another crucial aspect of the designation of interpretative agency is the type of its interpretative competence. Is such competence exclusive, or concurrent with other residual and subsidiary competences? The implication of the delegated nature of interpretative powers of international organs is that this competence is never unlimited. The issue of the excess of powers (*ultra vires*) can arise if the relevant body goes beyond what has been delegated to it. An inherent aspect of this problem is the distinction between interpretation and amendment of legal rules and instruments.

As Sir Elihu Lauterpacht observes, the correct solution of the problem of the agency of interpretation can hardly be found in a single rule. It is possible that, in addition to their obligations under the principal instrument, for States-parties to establish additional or different obligations by means of a collateral instrument.[1]

While States-parties possess the competence to interpret a treaty, the problem of auto-interpretation involves subjectivism and is inimical to the applicable legal framework. In some instances, auto-interpretation is perceived as a problem linked with the (non)existence of an adjudication mechanism to perform the interpretation.[2] Subjective interpretation is constrained not by what Johnstone calls 'external rules of interpretation' but 'by the existence of a relatively unified interpretive community'.[3] Against this background, Johnstone locates

[1] E Lauterpacht, The Development of the Law of International Organisation by the Decisions of International Tribunals, 151 *Recueil des Cours* (III-1976), 446.

[2] I Johnstone, Treaty Interpretation: The Authority of Interpretive Communities, 12 *Michigan JIL* (1990–91), 371–372.

[3] *Id*, 387.

compliance with the Anti-Ballistic Missile (ABM) Treaty within the political process within, and partly outside, the United States which allegedly was responsible for preventing the process from being reinterpreted. In more general terms, Johnstone argues that disputes between interpreters are resolvable not according to rules of interpretation but by prescription, argument, judgment and persuasion.[4]

The basic problem with Johnstone's analysis from the perspective of legal science is that it perceives the interpretative process as some process of socialising, thereby making the interpretative outcome dependent on the reactions in that social context which may or may not overlap with the community of States-parties to the relevant treaty. In legal reality, if such overlap is lacking and the correlation of wills of States-parties is not identified, the interpretative outcomes cannot be influenced. If, however, one speaks of interpretative communities but in essence identifies the relevance of the will and agreement of the relevant States-parties, then one effectively discusses the factors that are already recognised under Articles 31 and 32 of the Vienna Convention.

In *Asylum*, the Court addressed the issue of whether, under the 1928 Havana Convention on Political Asylum, a State-party could unilaterally define the offence for which asylum may or may not be granted. This Convention laid down certain rules relating to diplomatic asylum, but did not contain any provision conferring on the State granting asylum a unilateral competence to define the offence with binding force for the territorial State. The Colombian Government still submitted that 'such a competence is implied in that Convention and is inherent in the institution of asylum'.[5] Thus, Colombia asserted that the State-party could unilaterally determine the meaning and scope of its treaty obligations.

The Court responded that the alleged right of unilateral qualification was not implied under the Havana Convention. This was even clearer from the Convention's preamble which was aimed at 'fixing rules'.[6] Similarly, the Court examined the content of Article 2 of the Havana Convention and rejected such interpretation as would entitle Colombia 'to decide alone whether the conditions provided by Articles I and 2 of the Convention for the regularity of asylum are fulfilled'.[7]

In practice, interpretation is often attempted through a unilateral interpretative declaration of States.[8] The purpose of an interpretative declaration, according to Voïcu, is not to modify the effect of the treaty, but to make it more precise.[9]

[4] *Id*, 378.
[5] *Asylum Case* (Colombia/Peru), Judgment of 20 November 1950, *ICJ Reports*, 1950, 266 at 274.
[6] *Id*, 275.
[7] *Id*, 279.
[8] On interpretation of interpretative declarations see Chapter 13 above.
[9] I Voïcu, *De l'interprétation authentique des traités internationaux* (1968), 185.

As Special Rapporteur Waldock formulated, 'An explanatory statement or statement of intention or of understanding as to the meaning of the treaty... does not amount to a variation in the legal effect of the treaty.'[10] Similarly, the International Law Commission in its draft guidelines on reservations to treaties defined interpretative declaration as 'a unilateral statement, however phrased or named, made by a State or by an international organization whereby that State or that organization purports to specify or clarify the meaning or scope attributed by the declarant to a treaty or to certain of its provisions'.[11] At the same time, as demonstrated above, interpretative declarations are by no means conclusive. They can be reviewed by tribunals in terms of their genuine content and ambit.

Binding interpretations can only emanate from such organs that are competent to apply the law.[12] In this respect one has to specify the categories of authentic interpretation and authoritative interpretation.

In some cases the relevant treaties expressly designate specific organs as agencies of interpretation. Article 119 of the ICC Statute envisages the role of the Assembly of States-parties in relation to the interpretation of the Statute. The Assembly may itself resolve the issue or refer it to another dispute settlement body such as the International Court. Article 279 of the 1982 Law of the Sea Convention provides that disputes regarding the interpretation of the Convention must be resolved peacefully. Articles 280 to 296 provide for a number of other means whereby such disputes must be resolved, including arbitration and judicial settlement through the Law of the Sea Tribunal. Human rights treaties also provide for the role of one or another organ to deal with the questions of interpretation of the relevant treaty. For instance, Article IX of the Genocide Convention refers relevant disputes to the International Court, and Article 22 of the Torture Convention refers to arbitration as well as the International Court.

It seems that if the relevant agency (group of States, court or another organ) is invested with interpretative power, this may displace the otherwise applicable interpretative principles and outcome. For instance, Kelsen seems to subordinate principles to agency, stating that the agency endowed by States-parties by the power to interpret can choose which methods of interpretation to adopt.[13]

The real question that arises is whether the delegation of interpretative authority implies complete absolution from subjection to the principles that (would

[10] H Waldock, First Report on the Law of Treaties, II *YbILC* 1962, 27 at 31–32.

[11] II *YbILC* 1999, 92.

[12] I Tammelo, *Treaty Interpretation and Practical Reason—Towards a General Theory of Legal Interpretation* (1967), 6.

[13] H Kelsen, *Principles of International Law* (1967), 459; the relevance of subsequent practice in interpretation also provides the context where States are in charge of the treaty, see above Chapter 10.

otherwise) govern the interpretative process. Any treaty-based designation of interpretative competence of the relevant organ is a delegation of powers. Therefore, the existence of limits on such interpretative power is inherent in such a delegation. In the first place, the delegated power to interpret cannot go beyond the normal task of interpretation, that is the clarification of what has been agreed in the relevant treaty.

In some cases the applicable principle predetermines the identity of the agency. For instance, the autonomous character of concepts and meanings in the treaty clause by itself excludes the role of the State as an interpreting agency. Another crucial question is whether the treaty-based designation of the interpretative agency excludes, overrules or diminishes the impact of the normal rules and principles of interpretation. It has to be accepted that interpretation, performed by whichever agency, must be limited to the task of clarification of meaning, as opposed to modification of the legal position. Therefore, the designated agencies should still be seen as subject to the substantive principles of interpretation.

The issue of authentic interpretation attracted doctrinal attention at earlier stages of doctrinal thinking. Phillimore elaborated on the essence of this process in the following way:

> Authentic Interpretation, in its strict sense, means the exposition given by the Lawgiver himself;... but this kind of interpretation generally takes the form of a new law, reciting and removing the doubts of the old one; and this mode of interpretation may, of course, be adopted in the case of Treaties. The contracting powers may promulgate a subsidiary and explanatory Treaty, the preamble of which, like the preamble of a Statute, may be declaratory with respect to existing doubts upon the construction of a former convention. But this is, in fact, not so much a particular mode of Interpretation, as the enactment of a new law, or the conclusion of a new Treaty, as the case may be.[14]

Authentic interpretation comprises only such interpretation under which the interpretative outcome as to the content of the rule enjoys the same level of binding force as the pertinent interpreted provision. Authentic interpretation is present only in those narrow circumstances in which the parties to a treaty additionally agree, in whatever form, on the content and ambit of the relevant provision.[15] Authentic interpretation, adopted in whatever form, prevails over any other interpretation.[16] Ehrlich also emphasises that authentic interpretation is not bound to have any particular form.[17] Authentic interpretation emanates from the same entities which have adopted the relevant rule. The parties could even derogate from the interpretation rendered by judicial and arbitral organs.[18]

[14] R Phillimore, *Commentaries upon International Law* (1855), 72.
[15] R Bernhardt, *Die Auslegung der völkerrechlicher Verträge* (1963), 44–45; Kelsen (1967), 459.
[16] P Reuter, *Introduction to the Law of Treaties* (1985), 73.
[17] L Ehrlich, L'interprétation des traités, 24 *Recueil des cours* (1928-IV), 1 at 36.
[18] Voïcu (1968), 117–118, 121.

Authentic interpretations 'come from the law-makers themselves'. Thus, they 'are not interpretations but rather new legal enactments'.[19] It is also stated that authentic interpretation removes the distinction between interpretation and amendment of treaties, because it has the same binding effect as the formal amendment of treaties.[20]

In an extensive and so far the only study of authentic interpretation in international law, Voïcu refers to a case in which the authentic interpretation performed by the parties practically resulted in the amendment of the treaty. The US-Libyan Military Agreement of 9 September of 1954, under which a US Air Force base was established on Libyan territory, provided for concurrent jurisdiction of the two States over US personnel. Through the interpretative agreement of 24 February 1955, which was made retroactively applicable as of 30 October 1954, the concurrent jurisdiction over the personnel was replaced by the exclusive jurisdiction of the United States, and consequently all prosecutions in Libya were discontinued.[21]

Voïcu affirms that subsequent practice in the sense of what is now the Vienna Convention can constitute authentic interpretation of the treaty, because it constitutes the agreement between the parties.[22] At the same time, Voïcu takes a rather limited view of interpretation agreements. Under this perspective, the rights and obligations of the parties are governed by the original treaty, while the interpretative agreement merely provides the necessary precision.[23] Similarly, Yasseen suggests that the agreement as to interpretation of the treaty is only declaratory in its effect. In any case, whether or not the interpretation agreement aspires to modifying the treaty, it has (bilateral) effect only as between its parties. If more is attempted, such agreement would be subject to the effects of Article 41 of the 1969 Vienna Convention dealing with *inter partes* modification of the treaty.[24]

Authoritative interpretation is that performed by the treaty-based organ that is empowered with such competence. It differs from authentic interpretation which the parties perform jointly.[25] In some cases, the terms 'authoritative' and 'authentic' are used more or less interchangeably. As Schwarzenberger observes, any judicial interpretation of a treaty is authoritative. The narrower meaning of authoritative interpretation refers to that performed by States-parties.[26]

[19] Tammelo (1967), 6.

[20] W Karl, *Vertrag und spätere Praxis in Völkerrecht—Zum Einfluß der Praxis auf Inhalt und Bestand völkerrechlicher Verträge* (1983), 46.

[21] Voïcu (1968), 88–89.

[22] *Id*, 105.

[23] *Id*, 93.

[24] MK Yasseen, L'interprétation des traités d'après la Convention de Vienne sur le Droit des Traités, 151 *Recueil des Cours* (1976-III), 1 at 45–46.

[25] M Heymann, *Einseitige Interpretationserklärungen zu multilateralen Veträgen* (2005), 51–52.

[26] G Schwarzenberger, *International Law* (1957), vol. 1, 537.

The phenomenon of authoritative interpretation is present in the WTO legal system. Article IX:2 of the WTO Agreement provides that 'The Ministerial Conference and the General Council shall have the exclusive authority to adopt interpretations of this Agreement and of the Multilateral Trade Agreements.' This Article further provides that such decisions 'shall be taken by a three-fourths majority of the Members'. The Appellate Body in *Japan–Beverages* concluded that 'the fact that such an "exclusive authority" in interpreting the treaty has been established so specifically in the WTO Agreement is reason enough to conclude that such authority does not exist by implication or by inadvertence elsewhere'.[27]

Article IX:2 WTO Agreement vests certain organs with the authoritative interpretation power, but does not define the notion of authoritative interpretation, nor specify whether such interpretative competence is exclusive or whether it can be reviewed.

One limitation stated in doctrine is that an authoritative interpretation must by definition relate to and interpret the pre-existing rules of the relevant treaty. It cannot create new rules. A related question, however, is whether the authoritative interpretation can establish an autonomous rule of interpretation and whether the conduct of the State in contravention of the interpretation means that it is in violation of the relevant treaty rules.[28]

In WTO practice the term authoritative interpretation is referred to mainly to specify that the relevant explanation, such as that provided by the Appellate Body Secretariat, is not an authoritative interpretation. The Appellate Body has on some occasions referred to the exclusive power of the Ministerial Conference to adopt authoritative interpretations under Article IX:2.[29]

Although initially there were some doubts, the competence of WTO Panels and the Appellate Body to interpret WTO Agreements is recognised.[30] In *US–Shrimp*, the Appellate Body held that the findings of the Panel regarding the interpretation of the Article XX chapeau, and its interpretative analysis constituted an error in legal interpretation and accordingly reversed them.[31]

It is suggested that in order to be effective, authoritative interpretation has to be binding, otherwise the WTO Panels and Appellate Body would not be able to rely on such interpretations. Non-binding 'authoritative' interpretation would come close to, but still not constitute, subsequent agreement or practice under Article 31(2) of the Vienna Convention. Thus, the WTO organs would not

[27] *Japan—Taxes on Alcoholic Beverages*, AB-1996-2, WT/DS8/AB/R, 4 October 1996, at 12.

[28] C-D Ehlermann & L Ehring, The Authoritative Interpretation under Article IX:2 of the Agreement Establishing the World Trade Organisation: Current Law, Practice and Possible Improvements, 8 *JIEL* (2005), 803 at 812.

[29] *Id*, 804.

[30] *Id*, 813.

[31] *US—Import Prohibition of certain shrimp and shrimp products*, AB-1998-4 Report of the Appellate Body, WT/DS58/AB/R, 12 October 1998, para 122.

be able to use these interpretations to impact the rights and duties of member-States.[32]

The Appellate Body in the *US–FSC* dealt with the claim that the 1981 Council action related to the adoption of four panel reports regarding Japan's export subsidies and constituted authoritative interpretation. The GATT Council adopted this resolution, stating that 'with respect to these cases, and in general' the economic processes located outside the territorial boundaries of the exporting State do not have to be taxed and should not be regarded as export activities under Article XVI:4 GATT. These words 'in general' served as the basis of the assertion that the Council action constituted the authoritative interpretation.[33] The Report emphasised that the authoritative interpretation cannot be presumed to be performed unless the rigorous standard of proof as to this having taken place has been discharged. That includes the expression of intention to impact the rights and duties of member-States. As the Appellate Body put it:

> If the contracting parties had intended to make an *authoritative* interpretation of Article XVI:4 of the GATT 1947, binding on all contracting parties, they would have said so in reasonably recognizable terms. We think it most unlikely that the Chairman would have stated that the action did '*not affect the rights and obligations of contracting parties*', if it represented an authoritative interpretation of Article XVI:4 of the GATT 1947.[34]

The Appellate Body further clarifies the essence of authoritative interpretation:

> Under the *WTO Agreement*, an authoritative interpretation by the Members of the WTO, under Article IX:2 of that Agreement, is to be distinguished from the rulings and recommendations of the DSB, made on the basis of panel and Appellate Body Reports. In terms of Article 3.2 of the DSU, the rulings and recommendations of the DSB serve only 'to clarify the existing provisions of those agreements' and 'cannot add to or diminish the rights and obligations provided in the covered agreements'.

The Appellate Body further clarifies that 'an authoritative, and generally binding, interpretation of Article XVI:4 would, in all probability, have been perceived by the contracting parties as affecting their rights and obligations and would not, therefore, have been accompanied by such a statement'. Thus, the 1981 Council action was an integral part of the resolution regarding the adoption of relevant panel reports, and hence was binding on the parties to that case only.

This approach raises the question to what extent such authoritative interpretation could constitute the interpretation proper, as opposed to the modification of the treaty. The clarification on these questions depends on two factors, one of which is the relevance of normal interpretation principles in the process of

[32] Ehlermann & Ehring (2005), 807–808.

[33] *US-Tax Treatment of 'Foreign Sales Corporations'*, AB-1999-9, Report of the Appellate Body, WT/DS108/AB/R, 24 February 2000, paras 105–110 (emphasis original).

[34] *Id*, para 112 (emphasis original).

authoritative interpretation, and the second of which is the type of competence of the organ in charge with authoritative interpretation, especially the relationship of that competence to that of other organs in charge with the application of WTO law.

In terms of the relevance of institutional allocation of powers for the nature of authoritative interpretation, it has been pointed out that:

> the proposition that an authoritative interpretation may not modify the law would arguably mean that the Appellate Body could review any such interpretation as regards whether it constitutes a 'permissible' interpretation of the relevant provisions under the customary rules of interpretation. If the (authoritative) interpretation is inconsistent with the Vienna rules on interpretation, it would be legally incorrect. This would mean that the General Council or the Ministerial Conference would have exercised its authority *ultra-vires*. As a consequence, the incorrect authoritative interpretation would be invalid and not bind the Members. If one were to disagree with this legal consequence and submit that the *ultra-vires* nature would leave untouched the validity and binding nature of the authoritative interpretation at issue, one would hardly have to discuss this whole question of how far an authoritative interpretation may go.[35]

Another option is also contemplated, namely that even if the authoritative interpretation went beyond the delegated institutional powers and the legal framework of interpretation, it would still enjoy *de facto* validity because there would be no regular procedure for overturning it. However, it still remains possible for the panels and the Appellate Body to review the authoritative interpretation in the sense that it genuinely constitutes interpretation. The outcome could be that the authoritative interpretation may be declared as being without legal effect.[36]

It is also suggested that the preceding options indicate on balance that the General Council and the Ministerial Conference do not need to apply treaty interpretation rules, and they may thus develop the existing WTO law, rather than simply clarifying it. The attribute of 'authoritativeness' arguably supports this outcome. In a way moderating this arguably blanket outcome, it is submitted that 'possible candidates for a "development" of WTO law through an authoritative interpretation could be situations where the existing rules are ambiguous or contain gaps, or rules that have proven in practice to be very difficult or even impossible to apply'.[37]

But this approach does not clarify the dilemma. If the General Council and the Ministerial Conference have the treaty-based right to develop WTO law, it is hardly sensible to suggest that this right extends to some fields but not others, let alone that the question of ambiguity and gaps can be a matter of disagreement in individual situations. The text of Article IX:2 does not indicate a subject-matter limitation on the competence that it vests in the WTO organs.

[35] Ehlermann & Ehring (2005), 809.
[36] *Id*, 809–810.
[37] *Id*, 810.

The key to the essence of the problem lies with the fact that the notion of 'authoritative' is merely an adjective to relate to the process of interpretation. Even if authoritative, the process under Article IX:2 is still one of interpretation. This is even clearer from the wording of this article precluding the WTO organs from undermining the regime of amendment of WTO-covered agreements.

The issue inherent in and attendant upon any assertion of the existence of authoritative interpretation power is the clarification of whether such power is exclusive in relation to any other comparable institutional power that could be exercised in relation to the same interpretation context. The affirmation of exclusivity naturally involves assuming, or proving, that the relevant treaty instrument embodies the intention to vest the particular organ with the task of interpretation to the exclusion of the similar competence of other organs.

As emphasised in the Harvard Draft on the Law of Treaties, interpretation of treaties is essentially a judicial task. The neutral judge or arbitrator is more likely to arrive at a fair and unbiased interpretation.[38] The problem in this field is the same as that with the enforcement of international law in general in the absence of the centralised authority. But in this specific field the presence of the methods of interpretation, arranged as they are under the Vienna Convention, can indicate which interpretation is right.

The absence, in the charters of international organisations, of express provisions allocating interpretative competence does not imply absence of the interpretative competence itself. Institutional organs are competent to interpret the relevant provisions of their charters, and they regularly perform this task, expressly or implicitly.[39]

The source of the interpretative competence of judicial and arbitral organs lies with their constitutive instruments. In this case the interpretative competence operates strictly within the limits of contractual designation. At the same time, this interpretation cannot be authentic because tribunals cannot modify or overrule the content of established rules and instruments.[40] International organisations do not possess sovereignty and hence they have no primary and binding interpretative competence in relation to their constitutive instruments. States cannot transfer their entire competence of interpretation to the organisations that are their creatures.[41]

It seems that in the end it matters which interpretation is correct, not by which entity it is performed. This former question is addressed by reference to normal principles of interpretation that are aimed at discovering the parameters of the original expression of will by the relevant actor. Consequently, in the absence of the designated agency with exclusive competence to interpret, the question of agency reverts to that of principles.

[38] Harvard Draft on the Law of Treaties and its Commentary, 29 *AJIL Supplement* (1935), 973.
[39] Voïcu (1968), 123.
[40] *Id*, 114–115.
[41] *Id*, 128.

Unless there is some statutory or other designation of an organ as the interpretative agency, caution must be exercised with regard to the attitudes of organs claiming such a role. In *Danube Commission*, the Permanent Court faced the plea that the Definitive Statute for Danube was authoritatively interpreted by the Interpretative Protocol, which was the Annex of the Danube Conference records, and the parties were in dispute as to its value and meaning. If the Romanian construction were accepted, the Protocol would go beyond the Statute. In such a case it would have been binding only if it were its authoritative interpretation. The Court held that this was not the case. The Protocol was not an agreement and was not even mentioned in the Statute. It was not the decision of the Danube Commission either and even if it were, 'the Commission had no power to decide to abandon the functions with which it was entrusted under existing international treaties'. The Court could only consider the Protocol as part of the *travaux* and whatever its implications, it was 'certain that it cannot prevail against the Definitive Statute'.[42]

The considerations of legal stability demand that it be known who is in charge of interpretation of treaties, in order to ensure their consistent application. In the *Second Admissions* case, Judge Azevedo pointed out that had the International Court resorted to the *travaux* to interpret the UN Charter, it would have become clear that these materials envisaged the possibility of conflict between possible interpretations of the same text by more than one principal organ of the United Nations. Unless such conflicts are resolved, 'chaos would result in the interpretation'.[43] In the case at hand, the Court refused to resort to the *travaux* due to the clarity of the text. But if other scenarios develop, there must be guidance in place for ascertaining which institution should ultimately be responsible for an interpretation that would be final and conclusive for other organs.

The International Court's recognition, through the construction of the preparatory work of the UN Charter, that each principal organ is competent, in the first place at least, to interpret its own competence,[44] is in fact a pronouncement on the power of these organs to interpret the Charter, and the rejection of the exclusivity of the interpretative competence of any of them. But the requirements of consistency dictate that there must be limits on such distribution of interpretative competence. Otherwise, conflicting interpretations would not be avoided. As interpretation is a legal task, also affirmed by the Court in the *First Admissions* case, it is logical that the organ which is in ultimate charge of interpretation is the organ whose mandate requires application of, and is constrained by, international law, to the exclusion of other considerations, that is the International Court. Its task to interpret that United Nations Charter and draw conclusions on the interpretative outcomes arrived

[42] *Jurisdiction of the European Commission of the Danube*, Advisory Opinion of 8 December 1927, *PCIJ Series* B, No 14, 5 at 32–35.

[43] Dissenting Opinion, *Second Admissions* case, *ICJ Reports*, 1950, 26.

[44] *Certain Expenses of the United Nations* (Advisory Opinion), *ICJ Reports*, 1962.

at by other principal organs is quite an ordinary task from the perspective of interpretation as such, but from the institutional perspective it could acquire a dimension that has a quite revolutionary reputation in some quarters—that of judicial review.

Judicial review of the acts of international organisations is practised by international tribunals and encompasses some politically sensitive situations.[45] The link between consistent interpretation and judicial review of the attitude of the organs of international organisations is illustrated in the International Court's practice. In *IMCO*, the Dissenting Opinion of Judge Klaestad perceives the Court's adherence to the plain meaning method in interpreting Article 28(a) of the IMCO Convention as the Court's review of the interpretation performed by the IMCO Assembly. Judge Klaestad did not believe that the Assembly 'exercised its discretionary power in an improper or arbitrary way'.[46] Interpretation of Article 28(a) was certainly implied in the Assembly's application of this provision. The Court's interpretation inherently constitutes a review of that exercised by the Assembly.

The attitude that the International Court is bound to follow the interpretation made by other principal organs, for instance in the interests of international peace and security, need be mentioned only to be dismissed. Such approach has no statutory basis—the Court's Statute expressly allocates the task of interpretation as one of the inherent tasks of the Court, and there is no provision in the UN Charter that would contradict this position. Therefore, judicial review is optimal, possible, and even necessary to ensure that the Charter is ultimately interpreted as a legal instrument.

In relation to disputes duly submitted to it, the International Court enjoys a comprehensive interpretative competence, and is competent to interpret all relevant legal instruments and norms. As the Court has maintained repeatedly, interpretative function falls within its normal judicial powers.[47] The Court has also asserted its role as the exclusive interpretative agency. In *Ambatielos*, the Court observed that it would itself decide whether there was a duty to resort to arbitration under the 1926 Declaration, that is interpret this Declaration to establish whether there was jurisdiction.[48] As the Court emphasised in *Fisheries Jurisdiction*, the establishment or otherwise of its jurisdiction, and consequently the interpretation of jurisdictional instruments, 'is not a matter for the parties but for the Court itself'. This was stated in the context of interpretation of jurisdictional instruments.[49]

In relation to unilateral acts too, the Court has confirmed the same position. The *Nuclear Tests* case affirmed that it was for the Court 'to form its own view of

[45] See above Chapter 2; see further Chapter 17 below.
[46] Dissenting Opinion, *ICJ Reports*, 1960, 175.
[47] *ICJ Reports*, 1947–48, 61; *ICJ Reports*, 1950, 6.
[48] *ICJ Reports*, 1952, 44.
[49] *Fisheries Jurisdiction* (Spain v Canada), Judgment of 4 December 1998, para 37.

the meaning and scope intended by the author of a unilateral declaration which may create a legal obligation'.[50] The European Court of Human Rights also asserts a similar role for itself. In *Belilos*, the European Court emphasised in relation to the construction of the interpretative declaration by Switzerland that this competence lay with the Court, and was not affected by (the lack of expression of attitudes) by States-parties. As the Court put it, 'The silence of the depositary and the Contracting States does not deprive the Convention institutions of the power to make their own assessment.'[51] More generally, the finding of the autonomous meaning of certain terms of the European Convention on Human Rights in the *Engel* case inherently implies the Court's assertion of its primary if not exclusive competence to interpret the Convention.

In *EC–Bananas*, the EC and ACP States argued before the Panel that the latter was not entitled to interpret the Lomé Waiver because it derived from the Lomé Agreement and only its parties were entitled to interpret it. The Panel reasoned on the basis of interpretative necessity and observed that in order to find out whether the EC's obligations under Article XIII GATT were waived, it had to interpret the Waiver.

This implies that the parties to the Lomé Agreement, appearing as parties before the Panel, asserted the power of auto-interpretation. The Panel responded that the GATT Contracting Parties had 'incorporated a reference to the Lomé Convention into the Lomé waiver, the meaning of the Lomé Convention became a GATT/WTO issue, at least to that extent. Thus, we have no alternative but to examine the provisions of the Lomé Convention ourselves in so far as it is necessary to interpret the Lomé waiver. Moreover, we note that in their submissions to us, it appears that the EC and the ACP countries are not in accord on some aspects of what is required by the Lomé Convention.'[52]

In terms of Security Council resolutions, there is a practice whereby the Security Council exercises the role of authentic interpreter of resolutions.[53] But when the political consensus for adopting the relevant interpretative decision is not forthcoming, the risk of unilateral interpretation increases. The ICTY stated in *Tadic* and confirmed in *Seselj* that the interpretation of a resolution by some Council members and not challenged by the rest of the membership can be regarded as authoritative interpretation,[54] but it is also happens that members assert mutually exclusive interpretations, as was the case with regard to resolutions 678 and 1441 on Iraq. There are no institutional safeguards against this, apart from possible incidental judicial review by the International Court. The most reliable

[50] *Nuclear Tests* (Australia v France), Judgment, *ICJ Reports*, 1974, 267, 269.

[51] *Belilos v Switzerland*, No 10328/83, Judgment of 29 April 1988 para 47.

[52] *EC-Regime for the Importation, Sale and Distribution of Bananas*, Panel Report, WT/DS27/R/MEX, 22 September 1997, paras 7.97–98.

[53] See M Wood, The Interpretation of Security Council Resolutions, 2 *Max-Planck YBUNL* (1998), 83–84.

[54] *Tadic*, IT-94-1-72, 2 October 1992, para 88; *Seselj*, IT-03-67-AR72.1, 31 August 2004, para 6.

safeguard remains the adherence to the textual approach that significantly reduces the members' margin of interpretative freedom.

The issue of interpretative competence is raised in the context of the UN Commission on the Limits of Continental Shelf, which was established under the 1982 Law of the Sea Convention. The competence of the Commission relates to receiving applications from States-parties regarding extension of the outer limit of their continental shelves. The 2004 ILA Report on the Legal Issues of the Outer Continental Shelf states, in terms of implied powers, that 'In order to make recommendations to coastal States, it has to make an independent evaluation of the submissions of coastal States in respect of the outer limits of the continental shelf. The CLCS has to be presumed to have the competence that is required to carry out these tasks.'[55] It follows that while:

> the Convention does not charge the Commission to consider and make recommendations on legal matters, ... the Commission has to be presumed to be competent to deal with issues concerning the interpretation or application of Article 76 or other relevant articles of the Convention to the extent this is required to carry out the functions which are explicitly assigned to it.

This may include the interpretation of specific provisions of Article 76.[56] In general, the competence to interpret and apply the Convention rests with States-parties. Still, given the above, the Commission is 'only competent to deal with the interpretation of the provisions of Article 76 and other provisions of the Convention to the extent this is necessary to carry out the functions which have been assigned to it under the Convention. As a consequence, this competence has to be interpreted restrictively.'[57] In other words, the interpretative competence of the Commission is functional. The need for interpreting this competence restrictively has to be understood as restricting this competence to matters that fall within the Commission's powers. It does not justify a restrictive view of the interpretation power that serves the valid exercise of the Commission's powers.

The 2004 ILA Report on Outer Continental Shelf describes the implications of the Commission's interpretative power:

> The CLCS should not interpret these provisions in such a way that they place additional obligations on coastal States. On the other hand, neither should the Commission reduce the obligations resting on coastal States under the Convention.
>
> Secondly, the CLCS in general should accept the interpretations of relevant provisions of the Convention provided by the coastal State making a submission. Only if the Commission considers that the interpretation of the coastal State cannot reasonably be

[55] D Ong & AG Oude Elferink, *ILA Report on Legal Issues of the Outer Continental Shelf* (2004), 4.
[56] *Id*, 5.
[57] *Id*, 5–6.

considered to be in accordance with the Convention, the Commission should reject that interpretation.[58]

It seems that this is not really a restrictive version of interpretation power. It is instead a power meant to ensure the textual interpretation of the relevant Convention provisions.

National jurisprudence also raises the issue of the relationship between interpretations made by the designated agency and the individual State-party. As seen above, the House of Lords in *Jones* upheld the interpretation of Article 14 of the Torture Convention as a provision requiring remedies to be granted for torture only if the act or torture is committed within the forum State. This provision had also been interpreted by the UN Torture Committee as requiring provision of remedies for torture wherever committed.[59] Confronting the conclusion of the UN Committee, the House of Lords held that the Committee had no legislative powers and its decisions had no binding authority and legal value.[60]

This case presents a conflict between interpretation made by the individual State-party to the Convention, and that produced by the Committee that has been designated under the Convention as the body responsible for interpreting and implementing the Convention. The real question is not whether the Committee can issue binding decisions but whether, being an organ authoritatively entrusted with the task of interpretation and application of the Convention, it can interpret the Convention better than States. If the interpretation made by the supervisory organ can be rejected just because it is not binding, then there can be more than one 'permissible' interpretation, and this undermines the interpretation regime under the Vienna Convention. Interpretation is about the meaning of the treaty clause, not about the binding nature of institutional powers, and in this case the Committee's interpretation of Article 14 was perfectly in accordance with its textual meaning, as well as the Convention's object and purpose to improve the position of individual victims, instead of depriving them of legal venues for claiming remedies. The approach of the House of Lords in essence asserts the power of auto-interpretation of treaties and undermines not only the effectiveness of human rights treaties but the stability of treaty obligations in general.

[58] *Id*, 6; the same is reiterated in D Ong & AG Oude Elferink, *ILA Report on Legal Issues of the Outer Continental Shelf* (2006), 11.

[59] CAT/C/CO/34/CAN, paras 4(g) and 5(f).

[60] *Jones v Saudi Arabia* [2006] UKHL 26, Decision of 14 June 2006, paras 23 (*per* Lord Bingham), 57 (*per* Lord Hoffman).

PART V

TREATY INTERPRETATION AND INDETERMINATE PROVISIONS OF NON-LAW

17

The Essence of and Response to the Indeterminacy of Treaty Provisions

1. Conceptual Aspects

This part of the study deals with the process of treaty interpretation in cases where treaty provisions refer to the indeterminate notions of non-law. The key issue in this process is the use of treaty interpretation methods to clarify the meaning of these indeterminate provisions in the face of the factors or pleas of indeterminacy, residual sovereign freedom and the issues of interaction between law and politics.

It is doctrinally acknowledged that the degree of determinacy of the treaty text may vary.[1] Johnstone proposes tackling indeterminacy by resorting to the concept of interpretative community, suggesting that 'the meaning of a word or set of words is always clear or capable of being clarified because communication occurs within situations'.[2] While the exchange of views and communication between States can provide useful evidence, this factor cannot replace the need for resort to normal methods of treaty interpretation. In general, the inclusion in treaties of indeterminate notions of non-law raises serious issues in terms of transparency of legal regulation and predictability of interpretative outcomes. Therefore, the use of methods of interpretation for clarifying the content of indeterminate notions is indispensable for locating the scope and content of these notions.

In practice there are, on the whole, several permissible options for locating the meaning and scope of indeterminate notions in treaty clauses. The utility and permissibility of each option depends on the context of the relevant treaty framework. One way is to perceive the relevant indeterminate notion as mirroring the legal position under the pertinent rules of general international law. Another way is to search for its autonomous meaning. Yet another way is to 'leave it alone' where it has no crucial impact on legal outcome. This concerns the cases where it is possible, and required, to reach a legal outcome in the case by reference to factors independent of, and additional to, the relevant indeterminate notion. This

[1] I Johnstone, Treaty Interpretation: The Authority of Interpretive Communities, 12 *Michigan JIL* (1990–91), 371.

[2] Johnstone (1990–91), 378.

process involves initial deference to the State claiming that the relevant situation is covered by the given indeterminate concept, and a subsequent review of that situation through other established criteria, such as necessity or proportionality. It would not be right to assume that this process should be performed by deferring to the presumption in favour of State sovereignty. The problem really faced is not that of sovereignty but of interpretation which has to clarify the actual meaning of treaty provisions. Indeterminate notions are part of treaty arrangements and their meaning must be located through ordinary methods of interpretation.

In addition, the indeterminacy of treaty clauses is a phenomenon that may increase room for subjectivism in a way that does not promote legal certainty. A treaty, being an enterprise designed to achieve its object and purpose, requires that the indeterminacy of its clauses be kept within limits. It naturally follows that where the treaty text can be straightforwardly applied to facts, there is no room for indeterminacy.

2. Presumption against Indeterminacy of Treaty Provisions in Jurisprudence

In its practice, the International Court has adopted an approach that requires not adding to treaty rights and obligations such indeterminate conditions as may complicate their content, make it less intelligible, and thus promote the prospect of auto-interpretation by States of their treaty obligations. The *Admissions* case tackles the possible indeterminacy of treaty regulation following from the alleged relevance of political factors. The International Court's Advisory Opinion clearly specifies that the superimposition of political factors on treaty text is impermissible and likely to lead to uncertainty of rights and obligations. The Court's approach especially confirms that the context in which indeterminacy appears in the treaty text may require viewing the relevance of that indeterminacy as limited. After having identified the conditions for admission to the UN with those exclusively stipulated in Article 4 of the Charter, the Court observed that:

> Nor can it be argued that the conditions enumerated represent only an indispensable minimum, in the sense that political considerations could be superimposed upon them, and prevent the admission of an applicant which fulfils them. Such an interpretation would be inconsistent with the terms of paragraph 2 of Article 4, which provide for the admission of '*tout Etat remplissant ces conditions*'—'any *such* State'. It would lead to conferring upon Members an indefinite and practically unlimited power of discretion in the imposition of new conditions. Such a power would be inconsistent with the very character of paragraph 1 of Article 4 which, by reason of the close connexion which it establishes between membership and the observance of the principles and obligations of the Charter,

clearly constitutes a legal regulation of the question of the admission of new States. To warrant an interpretation other than that which ensues from the natural meaning of the words, a decisive reason would be required which has not been established.[3]

But this was only one side of the coin. Its other side still demonstrated that political considerations could still play a role in the process of admission of new States to the United Nations. As the Court put it:

Article 4 does not forbid the taking into account of any factor which it is possible reasonably and in good faith to connect with the conditions laid down in that Article. The taking into account of such factors is implied in the very wide and very elastic nature of the prescribed conditions; no relevant political factor, that is to say, none connected with the conditions of admission is excluded.[4]

Yet this was not the end of the matter. The elasticity of Article 4 requirements and the discretionary appreciation of the fulfilment of the membership conditions had to be understood in the context of the principle that:

The political character of an organ cannot release it from the observance of the treaty provisions established by the Charter when they constitute limitations on its powers or criteria for its judgment. To ascertain whether an organ has freedom of choice for its decisions, reference must be made to the terms of its constitution. In this case, the limits of this freedom are fixed by Article 4 and allow for a wide liberty of appreciation. There is therefore no conflict between the functions of the political organs, on the one hand, and the exhaustive character of the prescribed conditions, on the other.[5]

Thus, while on the one hand the textual interpretation contributed to the exclusive understanding of the membership conditions, 'the very wide and very elastic nature' of the prescribed conditions still allowed some room for political discretion. While this allegedly followed from the text of Article 4 as opposed to the general relevance of political factors in treaty interpretation, the Court's only specified limitation against abusing political discretion is the principle of good faith, as opposed to specific substantive obligations or limitations.

In the later Advisory Opinion on *IMCO*, the Court specified more straightforward legal limitations on exercising (political) discretion by States within the framework of international organisations. Reflecting the approach that where the treaty text can be straightforwardly applied to facts, there is no room for indeterminacy, the *IMCO* case serves as an example of applying a presumption against indeterminacy of treaty clauses. The question before the International Court was whether the treaty clause regulating the criteria of the election of IMCO member-States to the Consultative Committee implied any other criteria than those expressly mentioned in this clause. The Court rejected this assumption on the

[3] *ICJ Reports*, 1947–48, 62–63.
[4] *Id*, 63.
[5] *Id*, 64.

basis that implying such conditions would introduce uncertainty to the manner of their application. The Court stated that:

> This reliance upon registered tonnage in giving effect to different provisions of the Convention and the comparison which has been made of the texts of Articles 60 and 28(a), persuade the Court to the view that it is unlikely that when the latter Article was drafted and incorporated into the Convention it was contemplated that any criterion other than registered tonnage should determine which were the largest ship-owning nations. In particular it is unlikely that it was contemplated that the test should be the nationality of stock-holders and of others having beneficial interests in every merchant ship; facts which would be difficult to catalogue, to ascertain and to measure. To take into account the names and nationalities of the owners or shareholders of shipping companies would, to adopt the words of the representative of the United Kingdom during the debate which preceded the election, 'introduce an unnecessarily complicated criterion'. Such a method of evaluating the ship-owning rank of a country is neither practical nor certain. Moreover, it finds no basis in international practice, the language of international jurisprudence, in maritime terminology, in international conventions dealing with safety at sea or in the practice followed by the Organization itself in carrying out the Convention. On the other hand, the criterion of registered tonnage is practical, certain and capable of easy application.[6]

In other words, the States-parties to the IMCO Treaty were presumed to have agreed to something that has straightforward meaning capable of practical application to facts. Similarly, the Court refused to introduce the factual criteria for clarifying the meaning of Article 28(a):

> The Court having reached the conclusion that the determination of the largest ship-owning nations depends solely upon the tonnage registered in the countries in question, any further examination of the contention based on a genuine link is irrelevant for the purpose of answering the question which has been submitted to the Court for an advisory opinion.[7]

The Court's approach also reflects the textual interpretation of treaty clauses, namely the inadmissibility of reading into them conditions that are not stipulated in the text, as was affirmed by the Permanent Court in *Polish Nationality* and later by the WTO Appellate Body.[8] In other words, the textual approach promotes the presumption against the indeterminacy of treaty provisions. The outcome allegedly is that each and every treaty provision should be interpreted in accordance with its plain and ordinary meaning, as far as this is possible in linguistic terms.

While the *IMCO* Opinion refused to imply in the treaty provision the fact-related indeterminate condition, the International Court's judgment in *Oil*

[6] *Constitution of the Maritime Safety Committee of the Inter-Governmental Maritime Consultative Organisation*, Advisory Opinion of 8 June 1960, *ICJ Reports,* 1960, 150 at 169.

[7] *Id*, 171.

[8] See above Chapter 10.

Platforms has gone the opposite way. In *Oil Platforms*, which addressed the US bombing of Iranian oil installations, the Court examined Article X(1) of the 1955 Iran-US Treaty, which requires that there must be freedom of commerce 'between the territories of High Contracting Parties'. The Court affirmed that this provision would be breached if the destruction of Iranian oil platforms, in this case by US, had an effect upon the export trade in Iranian oil.[9] Iran argued that the attacks had prevented the production of oil that was to be imported into the US, while the US denied this.[10]

The Court noted that such attacks could, in principle, constitute an interference with the freedom of commerce in oil. However, for the purposes of Article X there had to be commerce in oil between the territories of the contracting parties. Although the Reshadat platforms had in the past produced oil that was imported into the US, at the time of the US attack they were inactive due to an earlier Iraqi attack. The Court held that whilst the US attack on these platforms could have affected the potential for future commerce, they did not have an effect on the freedom of commerce between the states as such. Hence there was no breach of Article X(1). The Court also referred to the US Executive Order 12613 of 29 October 1988, which prohibited the import of Iranian oil into the US with immediate effect. Although the attacks on the Reshadat platforms had taken place before that date, production could not have resumed before its issuance, after which further imports of oil from Iran were impossible. With regard to the Salman and Nasr platforms, the Court noted that the Executive Order was already in force at the time of the attack. Hence there could have been no commerce between the US and Iran in oil produced on these platforms.[11] Thus the Court concluded that the US attacks on the Iranian oil platforms did not violate Article X(1) since they did not hamper the export of the oil produced at those platforms to the US.[12]

Judge Simma strongly dissented with the view that injuring the potential for commerce in oil was not an injury to the freedom of commerce. He also thought that the fact that the Reshadat platforms had been destroyed in an earlier attack did not exclude them from the protection of Article X(1), arguing that even if it would have taken Iran longer to render the installations attacked in 1987 operational again, reducing them to ruins was as obvious a violation of Iran's freedom of commerce as there could possibly be.[13] In addition, Judges Simma and Al-Khasawneh subscribed to an even more expansive interpretation

[9] *Oil Platforms* (Islamic Republic of Iran v United States of America), Merits, Judgment of 6 November 2003, para 83.

[10] *Id*, paras 84, 86–87.

[11] *Id*, paras 90–93.

[12] *Id*, paras 95–99.

[13] Judge Simma, Separate Opinion, *id*, para 26.

of Article X(1), believing that commerce between Iran and the US included commerce through a third country.[14]

The Court thus adopted a factually oriented approach when determining whether the US attacks on the oil platforms had actually obstructed commerce in oil between Iran and the US. It took into account the factual state of the oil platforms at the time of the attacks and of the prevailing state of Iran–US trade relations. This, it is submitted, falls short of effective interpretation and should be contrasted with Judge Simma's approach, which is consistent with the principle of effective interpretation of treaties.

The striking general feature of the Court's reasoning in this case is that in effect Article X of the 1955 Treaty is presented not as a free-standing treaty provision capable of independently producing legal effect, but as a provision whose content depends on the factual situation prevailing at the relevant point of time. The most controversial issue relating to the interpretation and application of Article X(1) was the manner in which the Court recognised and treated the US Executive Order 12613 as a relevant factor. Curiously and anomalously, the unilateral conduct of the State-party was deemed enough to define the scope of treaty obligations. By saying that the Iranian oil platforms ceased to be protected by Article X(1) once trade in oil was halted by Executive Order 12613, the Court effectively suggests that a State can unilaterally determine the content of its treaty obligations and whether action taken amounts to a breach. Executive Order 12613 does not form part of the 1955 Treaty. It should not prejudice the issue of whether the Iranian oil platforms were protected by Article X(1). Moreover, if Executive Order 12613 were subsequently suspended or abolished, commerce in oil between Iran and the US could again occur. Under international law, every instrument of national law, such as Executive Order 12613, is merely a fact. It is indisputable that municipal laws are merely facts, and their legality is to be judged in terms of international law.[15] Facts can be important but, especially if based on the unilateral conduct of a party, they cannot influence the content of treaty clauses such as Article X(1). The Court was not justified in resorting to factual instead of normative analysis at this point and it should have concluded that the attacks on the oil platforms did indeed violate Article X(1) of the 1955 Treaty.

The presumption against indeterminacy and the reluctance to add to treaty provisions extra conditions not reflected in their text is familiar in the jurisprudence of the European Court of Human Rights as well. In *Brogan v UK*, the European Court of Human Rights dealt with the detention of individuals on the ground of an alleged terrorist threat, and found that the requirements

[14] Judge Simma, Separate Opinion, *id,* para 32; Judge Al-Khasawneh, Dissenting Opinion, paras 3–6.

[15] *Certain German Interests in Polish Upper Silesia*, Judgment of 25 May 1926, *PCIJ Series* A, No 7, 19. In *Free Zones*, the Permanent Court noted that a State cannot refer to its domestic legislation in order to limit the scope of its international obligations, Judgment of 7 June 1934, *PCIJ Series* A/B, No 46, 167.

of Article 5(3) on the prompt release of detained individuals were not fulfilled. The Court observed that none of the applicants was either brought 'promptly' before a judicial authority or released 'promptly' following their arrest. The failure to fulfil these conditions was sufficient to find a violation of Article 5(3). The Court refused to read additional conditions into the treaty text—in this case the need to combat terrorism—as influencing the scope of the treaty clause and the legality of the action contradicting it. The Court observed in this regard that 'The undoubted fact that the arrest and detention of the applicants were inspired by the legitimate aim of protecting the community as a whole from terrorism is not on its own sufficient to ensure compliance with the specific requirements of Article 5(3).'[16]

The Court's finding confirms that if treaty provisions are to be interpreted in terms of their plain meaning and in accordance with the principle of effectiveness, they have to be interpreted on their face, without any, still less undefined, conditions being read into their text. The considerations of legitimate aim are relevant in terms of Articles 8 to 11 of the Convention in relation to the specific aims mentioned in their relevant clauses, but not in provisions that contain no reference to it.

This approach is further required because the parties to a treaty must be presumed to have agreed to what they intelligibly understood. Only where the relevant terms cannot be defined in an objectively intelligible way, but inherently imply a need for appreciation on which the parties may reasonably differ, can it be justified to hold that the treaty clause is indeterminate.

Specified exceptions to treaty clauses, such as the exception clauses in Article 5 of the European Convention on Human Rights, which determine the conditions under which the State is allowed to detain individuals, are different from the exception clauses in Articles 8 to 11 of the Convention, which refer to policy considerations. The words included in 'normal' exception clauses can be clarified through interpretation. The policy grounds referred to in the margin of appreciation clauses are not definable in an objective and straightforward way, and their relevance has to be determined by a more systemic interpretation which consists in focusing, through the methods of interpretation, on the rationale and principal constituents of the relevant treaty framework.

The WTO Appellate Body Report in *US-Shrimp* confirms that the assessment of the criteria of non-law included in treaty provisions and their applicability to facts is essentially a task of treaty interpretation. As the Report states, in the process of determining the legality of State recourse to policy reasons in the case of conservation of exhaustible natural resources:

> Article XX(g) requires that the measure sought to be justified be one which 'relat[es] to' the conservation of exhaustible natural resources. In making this determination, the

[16] *Brogan v UK*, Nos 11209/84, 11234/84, 11266/84 & 11386/85, Judgment of 29 November 1988, para 62.

treaty interpreter essentially looks into the relationship between the measure at stake and the legitimate policy of conserving exhaustible natural resources.[17]

Thus, the assessment of the policy purpose as such is a matter of treaty interpretation. Even if policy analysis is not part of judicial function, it becomes so if the relevant policy is part of the treaty regime. This is so if only because the relevance of the policy factor in the treaty framework rests on the agreement between States-parties to confer such relevance to it. It is the interpreter's duty to ascertain the parameters of that agreement which inherently includes the ambit of and limits on the relevance of the relevant policy factor. The interpreter has at his disposal only the methods provided for under the Vienna Convention on the Law of Treaties. The review of policy goals serves the same goal as treaty interpretation in general—preserving the integrity of treaty obligations.

3. Emergency and Security Interest Exceptions

Arguably, the interpretation of indeterminate clauses in exception or derogation clauses cannot be conducted by reference to the treaty's object and purpose. The policy factors referred to in these clauses do not by themselves follow from the relevant treaty's object and purpose but in reality impose some limitations on it. Therefore, the object and purpose has no primary importance for locating the meaning of these policy factors. The organ that performs the interpretative task is presumably not going to verify each and every policy factor invoked by the State in terms of their consistency with the treaty's object and purpose.

On the other hand, the treaty's object and purpose can be useful in identifying the outer limits of the scope of these exception and derogation clauses. More specifically this concerns the interaction of these clauses with more substantive obligations within the relevant treaty framework. An alternative way of testing the limitations can be the adoption of the necessity and proportionality test which moreover forms part of the relevant exception and derogation clauses.

In the context of the European Convention on Human Rights, the interpretation of indeterminate concepts related to 'legitimate aim' embodied in Articles 8 to 11, or Article 1 of Protocol I, such as protection of public order, health or morals, public safety, economic well-being, prevention of crime and disorder or national security, sometimes depends on the evolutionary meaning and scope of these concepts. As the relevant legal rule has no fixed scope, the European Court examines attitudes across Europe to find the standards of morality applicable throughout the Convention membership.

[17] *US–Import Prohibition of Certain Shrimp and Shrimp Products*, AB-1998-4, Report of the Appellate Body, WT/DS 58/AB/R, 12 October 1998.

Therefore, in this field the assumption of law, being a matter of appreciation, plays a certain role. Nevertheless, this is due to the lack of generally accepted definitions of the relevant concepts. The element of subjectivity inherent in policy notions that are part of exception clauses in Articles 8 to 11 of the European Convention is evident from the fact that the European Court of Human Rights will not itself examine the justification of the action of the State-party under these exceptions, unless the State-party expressly invokes the relevant exception clause. The European Court hardly ever defines the headings of legitimate aim in general terms. It only identifies the conduct as justified or unjustified under the particular heading. Normally when the State invokes one of these policy factors, the appropriate allowance is given to this invocation. While they are the starting point for the Court's consideration of margin of appreciation issues, they themselves offer no solution. They do not by themselves cause or prevent the finding of violation of the European Convention. The solution instead depends on the analysis of necessity and proportionality which, as affirmed on multiple occasions, has to be ascertained on an objective basis.[18]

This phenomenon is illustrated particularly in the case of *United Communist Party*, which dealt with the dissolution of a political party by the Turkish authorities. The European Court of Human Rights accepted that at the material time a situation existed that threatened the national security of Turkey. The implication is that in principle Turkey would have been able to take measures under Article 11(2) of the European Convention to restrict the exercise of the freedom of association if such would be required by the need to preserve its national security. But this factor entailed only that much, and did not prejudge the legality of specific measures the Turkish Government would be taking in countering this emergency. In line with this, the existence of a threat to national security did not in this case provide a legal justification for the Turkish prohibition of the relevant political party, which was found by the Court as contrary to Article 11.

It must be observed that nowhere in this judgment did the Court try to define 'national security' in a straightforward manner. It sufficed that the matter *prima facie* fell within this indeterminate notion, which merely provided the starting-point for the Court's analysis, as opposed to its eventual finding on the legality of State conduct.

In the *Broniowski* case, the European Court accepted that the aims pursued by the State in relation to the enactment of the statutes that impeded the realisation of the applicant's entitlement were subsumable within the 'legitimate aim'. The Court accepted 'that during the political, economic and social transition undergone by Poland in recent years, it was necessary for

[18] See above Chapter 8.

the authorities to resolve such issues' as the reform of local government and agriculture.[19]

Similar criteria apply to the interpretation of the emergency clause under Article 15 of the European Convention. In some cases the pronouncement on the existence of a state of emergency of this kind is quite brief. In the *Aksoy* case, for instance, the Court observed that 'the particular extent and impact of PKK terrorist activity in South-East Turkey has undoubtedly created, in the region concerned, a "public emergency threatening the life of the nation" '.[20] In *Lawless*, the emergency under Article 15 was identified in a more rigorous manner pointing to the evidence on the ground:

> the existence at the time of a 'public emergency threatening the life of the nation', was reasonably deduced by the Irish Government from a combination of several factors, namely: in the first place, the existence in the territory of the Republic of Ireland of a secret army engaged in unconstitutional activities and using violence to attain its purposes; secondly, the fact that this army was also operating outside the territory of the State, thus seriously jeopardising the relations of the Republic of Ireland with its neighbour; thirdly, the steady and alarming increase in terrorist activities from the autumn of 1956 and throughout the first half of 1957.[21]

In *Brannigan*, the European Court of Human Rights applied a similar rigorous test and emphasised that:

> it falls to each Contracting State, with its responsibility for 'the life of [its] nation', to determine whether that life is threatened by a 'public emergency' and, if so, how far it is necessary to go in attempting to overcome the emergency. By reason of their direct and continuous contact with the pressing needs of the moment, the national authorities are in principle in a better position than the international judge to decide both on the presence of such an emergency and on the nature and scope of derogations necessary to avert it. Accordingly, in this matter a wide margin of appreciation should be left to the national authorities.

But the Court further observed that 'It is [still] for the Court to rule on whether inter alia the States have gone beyond the "extent strictly required by the exigencies" of the crisis. . . . in exercising its supervision the Court must give appropriate weight to such relevant factors as the nature of the rights affected by the derogation, the circumstances leading to, and the duration of, the emergency situation.'[22] Thus, the Court elaborated upon the criteria for dealing with the application of this indeterminate concept.

The need to examine the genuineness of the claimed state of emergency stated in *Brannigan* points in the same direction as the Court's policy to interpreting the notion of an emergency threatening the life of the nation. In *Lawless*, the

[19] *Broniowski v Poland*, 31443/96, Judgment of 22 June 2004, para 158.

[20] *Aksoy v Turkey*, 21987/93, Judgment of 18 December 1996, paras 69–70.

[21] *Lawless v Ireland*, No 332/57, Judgment of 1 July 1961, para 28.

[22] *Brannigan v UK*, Nos 14553/89 & 14554/89, Judgment of 25 May 1989, para 43.

European Court emphasised that 'in the general context of Article 15 of the Convention, the natural and customary meaning of the words "other public emergency threatening the life of the nation" is sufficiently clear'. The meaning of such an emergency referred to an exceptional situation of crisis or emergency which affects the whole population and constitutes a threat to the organised life of the community of which the State is composed. This was the natural and customary meaning of this conception.[23]

Thus, it may be observed that attempts to conceive of the content of the indeterminate notion of the emergency as threatening the life of the nation may be based on the use of literal and textual interpretative methods, or on a reference to the particular constituents of the relevant situation to assess its character. In other words, the method may be categorical, and interpret the concept of threat literally; or empirical, and refer to its constituents on the ground. In any of these cases, the result is essentially the same, being based on the two mutually complementary criteria.

In fact, the textual meaning of the threat refers above all to the *real*, *genuine* and *existing* threat: in order to qualify under the relevant treaty clause, the emergency situation must refer to an established and genuinely existing situation of sufficient scale. Such requirement of genuineness severely limits the ambit within which such judicial or political appreciation could be validly made. The European supervision that, according to the European Court, accompanies the use of the margin of appreciation by the State, is a tool whereby the Court is in a position to test the use of the policy discretion by the State. In individual cases the affirmation of the State's respective judgment as to its policy measures implies the review of those invocations of policy. The principal test seems to be that of reality and genuineness.

The requirement of genuineness and reality applies to emergency derogations under Article 4 of the International Covenant on Civil and Political Rights, which specifies in the relevant part that 'In time of public emergency which threatens the life of the nation and the existence of which is officially proclaimed, the States Parties to the present Covenant may take measures derogating from their obligations under the present Covenant to the extent strictly required by the exigencies of the situation.' As the UN Human Rights Committee emphasised in its General Comment No 29:

> The issues of when rights can be derogated from, and to what extent, cannot be separated from the provision in article 4, paragraph 1, of the Covenant according to which any measures derogating from a State party's obligations under the Covenant must be limited 'to the extent strictly required by the exigencies of the situation'. This condition requires that States parties provide careful justification not only for their decision to proclaim a state of emergency but also for any specific measures based on such a proclamation. If States purport to invoke the right to derogate from the Covenant during, for instance,

[23] *Lawless*, para 28.

a natural catastrophe, a mass demonstration including instances of violence, or a major industrial accident, they must be able to justify not only that such a situation constitutes a threat to the life of the nation, but also that all their measures derogating from the Covenant are strictly required by the exigencies of the situation.[24]

Thus, the derogating State is obliged to describe the relevant situations it invokes under Article 4 and to confirm that they are indeed of a gravity and magnitude to justify the derogation from the Covenant rights under Article 4. At the same time, the Committee emphasises that the State-party likewise has to demonstrate that the measures it takes to meet the relevant emergency are adequate and proportional to this aim.

This obligation to justify emergency measures as those addressing the *real* emergency is reinforced by the procedural obligation under Article 4(3) to notify the UN Secretary-General regarding these measures. The duty of notification is the duty to describe the parameters of the emergency situation and demonstrate its reality and genuineness. As the General Comment specifies:

A State party availing itself of the right of derogation must immediately inform the other States parties, through the United Nations Secretary-General, of the provisions it has derogated from and of the reasons for such measures. Such notification is essential not only for the discharge of the Committee's functions, in particular in assessing whether the measures taken by the State party were strictly required by the exigencies of the situation, but also to permit other States parties to monitor compliance with the provisions of the Covenant. In view of the summary character of many of the notifications received in the past, the Committee emphasizes that the notification by States parties should include full information about the measures taken and a clear explanation of the reasons for them, with full documentation attached regarding their law.[25]

Given these requirements, further assessment of the legality of State action under human rights treaty emergency clauses would be conducted on the basis of the criteria of necessity and proportionality. This provides a clear yardstick against which the legality of derogation can be tested. Consequently, the test of reality and genuineness resolves the problem of indeterminacy in the case of human rights treaty emergency clauses.

The reality test follows from the relevance of the plain and ordinary meaning method of interpretation. The very interpretation of indeterminate provisions in treaties entails the requirement that the situations they refer to must exist in reality and on the ground. The plain meaning method cannot clarify what specific kinds of situations are subsumable within these indeterminate provisions, not least because these specific situations are not mentioned in the treaty text. But what the plain meaning method certainly justifies and requires is application to the underlying facts of the relevant indeterminate treaty clause that requires the real and genuine existence of the situation it covers on the ground. If the

24 General Comment No 29, para 5.
25 General Comment No 29, para 17.

States-parties to the treaty are agreed on the relevance of the indeterminate notion in question and have conferred normative significance to it, they must be presumed to have envisaged that the relevant situation would exist on the ground, even though it may be difficult to define the relevant indeterminate notion on its face.

The WTO jurisprudence has duly expanded on the interpretation of indeterminate notions encompassed by the covered agreements. In *US–Shrimp*, the Appellate Body emphasised that in this case the legitimacy of the policy goal of conservation of sea turtles invoked by the United States was not objectionable in terms of being a legitimate policy goal under Article XX GATT.[26] But, as the Appellate Body further observed:

> conditioning access to a Member's domestic market on whether exporting Members comply with, or adopt, a policy or policies unilaterally prescribed by the importing Member may, to some degree, be a common aspect of measures falling within the scope of one or another of the exceptions (a) to (j) of Article XX. Paragraphs (a) to (j) comprise measures that are recognized as *exceptions to substantive obligations* established in the GATT 1994, because the domestic policies embodied in such measures have been recognized as important and legitimate in character. It is not necessary to assume that requiring from exporting countries compliance with, or adoption of, certain policies (although covered in principle by one or another of the exceptions) prescribed by the importing country, renders a measure *a priori* incapable of justification under Article XX.[27]

Thus, the Appellate Body emphasises that the existence of a policy purpose of the State-party can be legitimate as such. The Appellate Body also emphasises that the mere presence of a policy goal was not sufficient to ensure the legality of the relevant measure:

> The policy goal of a measure at issue cannot provide its rationale or justification under the standards of the chapeau of Article XX. The legitimacy of the declared policy objective of the measure, and the relationship of that objective with the measure itself and its general design and structure, are examined under Article XX(g), and the treaty interpreter may then and there declare the measure inconsistent with Article XX(g). If the measure is not held provisionally justified under Article XX(g), it cannot be ultimately justified under the chapeau of Article XX. On the other hand, it does not follow from the fact that a measure falls within the terms of Article XX(g) that that measure also will necessarily comply with the requirements of the chapeau. To accept the argument of the United States would be to disregard the standards established by the chapeau.[28]

A straightforward *a priori* definition of the ambit of the policy goal was not necessary, and presumably not even feasible within the confines of one single case. It sufficed that the relevance of that policy goal was identified for the purposes of judging the US measures involved in this specific case. The policy goal of environmental protection in this case was only initially relevant, the

[26] *US–Shrimp*, para 135.
[27] *Id*, Appellate Body Report, para 121.
[28] *Id*, para 149.

rest of the legal analysis depending on the application of the Article XX chapeau criteria, as well as the necessity and proportionality of the measures.[29]

This analysis demonstrated that while international tribunals allow States-parties to the relevant treaty to invoke their policy goals to justify their conduct under the relevant exception and derogation clauses, they do not allow States-parties to engage in auto-interpretation. The original invocation of policy goals by the State is subjected to rigorous application to it of objective criteria of necessity, proportionality, arbitrariness and non-discrimination, which hold the ultimate key to the determination of legality of State conduct. Consequently, non-law as part of treaty provisions has only a limited impact on the rights and obligations of States or non-State actors.

4. Determination of the 'Threat to the Peace' under Article 39 of the United Nations Charter

Under Article 39 of the United Nations Charter, 'The Security Council shall determine the existence of any threat to the peace, breach of the peace, or act of aggression and shall make recommendations, or decide what measures shall be taken in accordance with Articles 41 and 42 [of the Charter], to maintain or restore international peace and security.' The finding by the Security Council that a 'threat to the peace' exists entails certain legal consequences both within the realm of the Charter as well as of general international law:

(a) Upon finding a 'threat to the peace', the Security Council is empowered, by virtue of Articles 41 and 42 of the Charter, to initiate coercive non-military or military measures against a State or non-State actor, such as the severance of communications, trade, economic and/or diplomatic relations. In the event that they are or would be ineffective, the Council may decide on the use of armed force.
(b) By virtue of the operation of Articles 2(5), 25, 48 and 103 of the Charter, all member-States of the United Nations are obliged to support and implement coercive measures initiated by the Security Council.
(c) The Security Council, acting pursuant to its enforcement powers under Chapter VII, may disregard the domestic jurisdiction of States, which the United Nations is otherwise obliged to respect (Article 2 (7) of the Charter).

It is thus clear that by determining that a situation is a 'threat to the peace', the Council is empowered to bring about wide-reaching legal consequences with significant impact on sovereign rights, interests and obligations of the target State and third States, and drastic changes in existing legal relations. The enforcement

[29] It also mattered that the Appellate Body had to clarify whether the US measure was 'primarily aimed at' the preservation of exhaustible natural resources; see above Chapter 11.

function, as well as the discretion afforded to the Council, are very wide indeed. The outer limit of this enforcement function, especially under Article 39, which is initially based on political consensus, has to be seen in terms of the general framework determining the relationship between the powers of the Security Council and international law. Thus, the legal constraints on the political process under Article 39 follow both from the text of this Article which requires the factual existence of a 'threat to the peace', and from the relevant standards of the Charter.

The concept of peace, a term of the foremost importance in Article 39, is not positively defined in the Charter. In its ordinary meaning, peace denotes the absence of war. But peace as understood by the Security Council has a much broader meaning: peace under the Charter includes not only the absence of inter-State wars but also other factors pertaining to the economic, ecological and humanitarian dimensions of international relations.[30] As suggested, 'the concept of the threat to the peace can be understood in an extraordinarily broad manner when there is unanimity within the Security Council'.[31] The Council has made its Article 39 determinations, and consequently applied its Chapter VII powers, in situations both involving and not involving inter-State armed conflict. In the case of Southern Rhodesia, the establishment of minority rule and racist policies was characterised by the Council as a 'threat to the peace', and enforcement measures comprising arms and oil embargoes were applied. Resolution 688 (1991) declared the mass flow of refugees from Iraq as a 'threat to the peace'. In Resolution 940 (1994), the removal of the legitimate government of Haiti was also considered a threat to the peace, notwithstanding the purely domestic character of the situation. In Resolution 794 (1993), the Council addressed the failure of statehood and 'magnitude of human tragedy' in Somalia as a threat to the peace. The non-extradition by Libya of the two individuals suspected of having organised the explosion of Pan-Am 103 over UK territory was also deemed a 'threat to the peace' under resolutions 748 (1992) and 843 (1993). In all these cases the Council imposed extensive enforcement measures including, in some cases, the authorisation of member-States to use armed force.

The practice shows that the Council considers it appropriate to make Article 39 determinations in a wide variety of situations. At the same time, the repertoire of such determinations does not help to clarify the content of a 'threat to the peace'. An analysis based on past determinations under Article 39 would be simply retrospective and descriptive. The necessity to find some objective or objectivised criteria

[30] Statement of the Heads of States and Governments of Members of the Security Council, 31 January 1992: 'The absence of wars and military conflicts among States does not in itself ensure international peace and security. The non-military sources of instability in the economic, social, humanitarian and ecological fields have become threats to peace and security. The United Nations membership as a whole, working through the appropriate bodies, needs to give the highest priority to the solution of these matters.' UN doc S/PV.3046.

[31] J Frowein, On article 39 in B Simma (ed), *The Charter of the United Nations. A Commentary* (1994), 612.

for defining the scope of peace, and threats to the peace, and thus clarifying the legal limits on the Council's political discretion, is obvious.

It is often suggested that determinations under Article 39 are conclusive and within the absolute discretion of the Security Council.[32] A formalistic definition of a 'threat to the peace' is often used; it is defined as 'a situation which the organ, competent to impose sanctions, declares to be an actual threat to the peace'.[33] This definition places the emphasis on the discretionary power of the Security Council and not upon the content of the concept. On this view, the Council was designed to adopt purely political decisions, and the determination of a 'threat to the peace' is viewed from this angle.[34] This argument is widely shared in doctrine. According to Reisman, the UN collective security mechanism was intended to operate according to the will and discretion of the permanent members of the Security Council.[35] Kooijmans refers in this regard to 'the complete discretion the Security Council has with regard to the interpretation of the three concepts "threat to the peace", "breach of the peace" and "act of aggression"'.[36] A 'threat to the peace' under the Charter is therefore supposed to be equivalent to what the Council determines it to be. Nevertheless, the relevant Charter provisions as well as the imperative of legal certainty require rejecting the view that the power of the Council under Article 39 is based exclusively on political discretion, free of all visible limitation.

The clause in Article 39 that the Council 'shall determine the existence of any threat to the peace' inherently requires the application of the pre-existing concept to the facts, albeit with the use of discretion. It does not result in authorisation to legislate and to view it as doing so would contradict the basic nature of international law which knows of no legislative power over States. Under this framework, the Council possesses political discretion as to the initial determination of the substance of 'threats to the peace', but the legal limitation on this discretion following from the text of Article 39 is that such determination must relate to something that exists and threatens the peace. The discretion provided enables the Council to cover a range of situations not specified in the Charter; it does not empower the Council to extend its determination to anything it likes.

[32] R Lapidoth, Some Reflections on the Law and Practice Concerning the Imposition of Sanctions by the Security Council, 30 *Archiv des Völkerrechts* (1992), 115.

[33] Definition by J Combacau, quoted in P Kooijmans, The Enlargement of the Concept 'Threat to the Peace' in P-M Dupuy (ed), *The Development of the Role of the Security Council* (1993), 111.

[34] P Kooijmans, The ICJ: Where Does It Stand? in S Muller, D Raic & H Thuranzsky (eds), *The International Court of Justice. Its Future Role after Fifty Years* (1997), 416.

[35] M Reisman, Peacemaking, 18 *Yale Journal of International Law* (1993), 418.

[36] P Kooijmans, The Enlargement of the Concept, 'Threat to the Peace' in P-M Dupuy (ed), *The Development of the Role of the Security Council* (1993), 111. But Kooijmans adds: 'Although the Security Council is completely free to decide whether a situation constitutes a threat to the peace, one may ask whether it is fully in conformity with the spirit of the Charter to impose sanctions if the threat is not actual and efforts to resolve the dispute have not been completely exhausted', *id*, 117.

While the determination of a 'threat to the peace' involves a political judgment of the Council members, Article 39 is a treaty provision subject to normal rules of treaty interpretation.[37] The practice of the Council is definitely helpful and important, but the primary importance in determining what may or may not be encompassed within that concept of a 'threat to the peace' depends on textual, contextual and systematic interpretation of Article 39 as a treaty provision. The Council's practice can be useful as subsequent practice in terms of treaty interpretation.[38]

The textual meaning of a 'threat to the peace' does not by itself divulge its potential legal and political connotations. The notion of a 'threat to the peace' under Article 39 presumably has an autonomous meaning. It is not identical to the literal and casual meaning the word 'peace' may possess. The context of Article 39 indicates that it is not primarily about how the relevant situation threatens the peace, but about the situations singled out and determined as a 'threat to the peace' by the Security Council.

Resorting to context, however, one can easily discover that no provision of the Charter envisages the role of the Council as entitled to adopt decisions on the basis of its unfettered discretion. The general stipulation under Articles 24 and 25 is that the Council shall act in accordance with the purposes and principles of the Charter and that its decisions must correspond to the Charter. Even if these provisions do not expressly mention the power under Article 39, they cannot be without relevance for it. The ICTY also resorts to the subsequent practice argument in specifying that the conduct or situation can 'constitute a "threat to the peace" according to the settled practice of the Security Council and the common understanding of the United Nations membership in general'.[39] There is however very little to be inferred from the common understanding of the UN membership, apart from the silence of members which is in most cases inconclusive.

Thus, interpretative principles, in falling short of providing affirmative guidance for understanding what facts and situations 'threats to the peace' can cover, can only provide general criteria dictated by the factors of good faith and legal certainty, for ascertaining the area within which the Council can make its Article 39 determinations, and for judging the propriety and legality of these determinations in individual cases.

The Security Council's determination may, as part of political action, relate to a situation that is not of sufficient gravity and scale. The UN Secretary-General's High-level Panel has emphasised that 'The Council's decisions have often been

[37] The UN Charter is subject to the normal rules of treaty interpretation as embodied in the 1969 Vienna Convention on the Law of Treaties, Article 5.

[38] According to Article 31 of the 1969 Vienna Convention, a treaty must be interpreted in accordance with the ordinary meaning of its terms and in the light of its object and purpose. Subsequent practice establishing an agreement as to the meaning of the treaty shall also be taken into account.

[39] *Tadic*, Appeal Chamber, 2 October 1995, para 30.

less than consistent, less than persuasive and less than fully responsive to very real State and human security needs.'[40] The Panel thereby implies that the enforcement powers of the Security Council necessarily have to be used for combating real threats and serving real needs. The Council's political discretion is meant to be used for these purposes.

The Council's real task consists in determining *what* the threat is, *how* it is identified, *what* means are justified to be used in addressing it, and *how* the use of those means will contribute to the removal of the threat. The very fact that this process involves the application of the treaty framework requires that some degree of legal certainty is guaranteed. The exemplary way of achieving this level of transparency is demonstrated in the Council's Resolution 1676 (2006) on the situation in Somalia, addressing the aftermath of the imposition of the arms embargo on this country. In this Resolution, the Council:

Condemning the significant increase in the flow of weapons and ammunition supplies to and through Somalia, which constitutes a violation of the arms embargo and a serious threat to the Somali peace process,

Concerned about the increasing incidents of piracy and armed robbery against ships in waters off the coast of Somalia, and its impact on security in Somalia, *Reiterating* its insistence that all Member States, in particular those in the region, should refrain from any action in contravention of the arms embargo and should take all necessary steps to hold violators accountable,

Reiterating and *underscoring* the importance of enhancing the monitoring of the arms embargo in Somalia through persistent and vigilant investigation into the violations, bearing in mind that strict enforcement of the arms embargo will improve the overall security situation in Somalia,

Determin[ed] that the situation in Somalia constitutes a threat to international peace and security in the region.

Another similar instance is provided by Resolution 1735 (2006), in which the Council ordered States to take a range of antiterrorist measures against Al-Qaeda. The Council:

Reaffirming the need to combat by all means, in accordance with the Charter of the United Nations and international law, threats to international peace and security caused by terrorist acts, stressing in this regard the important role the United Nations plays in leading and coordinating this effort,

Stressing that terrorism can only be defeated by a sustained and comprehensive approach involving the active participation and collaboration of all States, and international and regional organizations to impede, impair, isolate, and incapacitate the terrorist threat...

Noting the need for robust implementation of the measures in paragraph 1 of this resolution as a significant tool in combating terrorist activity...

[40] *Report of the Secretary-General's High-level Panel on Threats, Challenges and Change*, 2 December 2004, A/59/565, 56.

Expressing its deep concern about criminal misuse of the internet by Al-Qaida, Usama bin Laden, and the Taliban, and other individuals, groups, undertakings, and entities associated with them, in furtherance of terrorist acts,

Noting with concern the changing nature of the threat presented by Al-Qaida, Usama bin Laden and the Taliban, and other individuals, groups, undertakings and entities associated with them, in particular the ways in which terrorist ideologies are promoted,

Stress[ed] the importance of meeting all aspects of the threat that Al-Qaida, Usama bin Laden and the Taliban, and other individuals, groups, undertakings and entities associated with them represent to international peace and security,

and went on to order a range of Chapter VII antiterrorist measures.

The reality of the problem of the lack of transparency in Article 39 determinations is illustrated by other examples, such as Resolution 1737 (2006), which imposed certain sanctions on Iran to address its non-compliance with international demands to freeze its uranium enrichment programme. The Council refers, in the preambular paragraphs of the Resolution, to the concerns expressed by the International Atomic Energy Agency regarding Iran's nuclear programmes. The Council's entire reasoning is based on a concern not that Iran had actually been doing something problematic, but that it had not proved to the Council's satisfaction that it had done nothing like that. The problems identified were that certain Iranian nuclear programmes '*could* have a military nuclear dimension' and that 'Iran has not established full and sustained suspension' of its presumed activities.

That said, Resolution 1737 does not specify what is actually in the Iranian conduct that constitutes a 'threat to the peace', which is not the best exercise from the viewpoint of legal certainty. The later Resolution 1747 (2007), which follows the cause of Resolution 1737 and expands the sanctions imposed on Iran under it, does not make any proper factual finding of a 'threat to the peace' either. Nor can the imposition of sanctions for presumed or expected conduct of the State amount to a proper discharge of Chapter VII responsibilities. One only needs to recall Resolution 1441 (2003), whereby the Council vigorously demanded the cooperation of Iraq in the matter of the weapons of mass destruction which, it transpired subsequently, Iraq had never owned. For its part, resolution 1441 does not link the Article 39 determination to Iraq's actual conduct either, although it states in paragraph 1 that Iraq is in material breach of Resolution 687 (1991) requiring full disclosure of its programmes for weapons of mass destruction and ballistic missiles. The lack of monitoring of non-existent weapons programmes was effectively pronounced as a 'threat to the peace' under Article 39. These cases also illustrate the above-mentioned phenomenon of achieving consensus among the Council members on taking the Chapter VII action without properly and transparently identifying the actual threat, as opposed to presumed or possible threats.

Resolution 1718 (2006) was adopted in the process of six-party talks regarding the policies and conduct of the Democratic Peoples' Republic of Korea (DRPK) in terms of the development of nuclear weapons. North Korea had earlier announced its withdrawal from the 1968 Non-Proliferation Treaty, Article X of which gives States-parties such right.

Resolution 1718 proceeds with identifying the 'threat to the peace' in the combined circumstances of North Korea's withdrawal from the Treaty and its claim of having performed a nuclear test. The Council responded by '*Expressing the gravest concern* at the claim by the Democratic People's Republic of Korea (DPRK) that it has conducted a test of a nuclear weapon on 9 October 2006, and at the challenge such a test constitutes to the Treaty on the Non-Proliferation of Nuclear Weapons and to international efforts aimed at strengthening the global regime of non-proliferation of nuclear weapons, and the danger it poses to peace and stability in the region and beyond.' And further:

> *Expressing* its firm conviction that the international regime on the non-proliferation of nuclear weapons should be maintained and recalling that the DPRK cannot have the status of a nuclear-weapon state in accordance with the Treaty on the Non-Proliferation of Nuclear Weapons, *Deploring* the DPRK's announcement of withdrawal from the Treaty on the Non-Proliferation of Nuclear Weapons and its pursuit of nuclear weapons, *Deploring further* that the DPRK has refused to return to the Six-Party talks without precondition...
>
> *Expressing* profound concern that the test claimed by the DPRK has generated increased tension in the region and beyond, and *determining* therefore that there is a clear threat to international peace and security.

Therefore, in the relevant parts of the operative paragraphs of the resolution, the Council:

> 1. *Condemns* the nuclear test proclaimed by the DPRK on 9 October 2006 in flagrant disregard of its relevant resolutions... including that such a test would bring universal condemnation of the international community and would represent a clear threat to international peace and security;
> 2. *Demands* that the DPRK not conduct any further nuclear test or launch of a ballistic missile;
> 3. *Demands* that the DPRK immediately retract its announcement of withdrawal from the Treaty on the Non-Proliferation of Nuclear Weapons;
> 4. *Demands* further that the DPRK return to the Treaty on the Non-Proliferation of Nuclear Weapons and International Atomic Energy Agency (IAEA) safeguards...
> 5. *Decides* that the DPRK shall suspend all activities related to its ballistic missile programme and in this context re-establish its pre-existing commitments to a moratorium on missile launching;
> 6. *Decides* that the DPRK shall abandon all nuclear weapons and existing nuclear programmes in a complete, verifiable and irreversible manner... and shall provide the IAEA transparency measures extending beyond these requirements, including such access to individuals, documentation, equipments and facilities as may be required and deemed necessary by the IAEA.

But most unusually, paragraph 8 imposes on the DPRK sanctions that do not really address the threat to the peace identified in the Resolution. Apart from the prohibition on supplying North Korea items of nuclear technology, the Resolution also bans supplying a number of items that have no relation whatsoever to its nuclear programmes, such as tanks, military aircraft, helicopters, artillery systems, warships and even luxury goods. The Council does not explain why the application of such measures is necessary for halting the North Korean nuclear programme and in what way it will contribute to this goal. Such disproportionate response is even more unjustified as two of the principal facts addressed by the Council were not straightforward threats to peace. One of them was the merely *claimed* nuclear test, and the second one related to the legal right of North Korea to quit the Nuclear Non-Proliferation Treaty.

All this militates in favour of assuming that the legality of determinations under Article 39 is guided by the test of reality and genuineness. The Security Council's determination must relate to real facts of the kind and scale that justify the measures adopted under Chapter VII. The requirement of good faith is relevant only after the substantive issues regarding the type and kind of situation and ensuing measures have been addressed. Any examination of the Council's observance of the good faith principle must relate to an examination of the situation on the ground, which is covered by the relevant Article 39 determination.

Regarding the agency competent to pronounce on the interpretation of Article 39, the International Court initially emphasised that each principal organ of the United Nations could interpret its competence in the first place.[41] At the same time, the decision of the Appeals Chamber of the International Criminal Tribunal for the Former Yugoslavia in the *Tadic* case may provide useful guidance. Having concluded that 'neither the text nor the spirit of the Charter conceives of the Security Council as *legibus solutus* (unbound by law)', the Tribunal went on to examine the issue which falls directly within the ambit of the Council's powers under Article 39. The Tribunal examined the determination of a 'threat to the peace' by the Council, questioned whether the concrete situation dealt with by the Council indeed was a 'threat to the peace', and passed its own judgment on all of these issues.[42] The judgement of the tribunal is unambiguous on these issues and this makes it unclear how one could be serious in suggesting that the International Court of Justice which is the principal judicial organ of the United Nations does not possess the powers which have been exercised by a tribunal established as a subsidiary organ of the Security Council.

5. 'Self-Judging' Clauses

Several bilateral or multilateral treaties include derogation, withdrawal, denunciation or termination clauses conditional upon circumstances referring to the

[41] *Certain Expenses*, *ICJ Reports*, 1962, 167.

[42] *Tadic*, Decision by Appellate Chamber (1995) IT-94-1-AR72, paras 28–30.

essential security interests of contracting parties. This notion of 'essential security interests' is conceptually cognate to the doctrine of important issues or essential interests that were, according to early doctrinal opinion, excluded from international adjudication, the unsustainability of which theory was exposed by Hersch Lauterpacht.[43] The difference between the two doctrines is that 'essential security interests' are now part of treaty arrangements. Thus, the range of relevant issues includes not merely the inherent merit of the policy notions embodied in the relevant clauses, but also their standing within the broader context of the treaty. Compulsory jurisdiction is not always provided for under the terms of treaties here under consideration, which increases the need for substantive legal criteria for judging the action of the relevant States-parties. Yet there still may be the possibility of the interpretation of such 'self-judging' clauses being adjudicated upon by the International Court. In terms of substance, what we surely know is that the involvement of political factors cannot make these clauses non-justiciable or exempt them from the normal regime of treaty interpretation.[44]

In *CMS*, the ICSID Tribunal examined Article XI BIT, according to which 'This Treaty shall not preclude the application by either Party of measures necessary for the maintenance of public order, the fulfillment of its obligations with respect to the maintenance or restoration of international peace or security, or the protection of its own essential security interests.' It should be noted that this clause, unlike human rights treaty emergency clauses, does not refer to a *concrete* situation that would justify emergency measures to protect essential interests. It merely allows the invocation of this exception by reference to the protection of essential interests. There is no guidance as to the required type of situation in which this clause must be invoked.

The claimant argued that the clause was not self-judging and therefore required the Tribunal and not the Respondent to decide when or to what extent essential security interests were at stake. The claimant also argued that 'economic crises do not fall within the concept of "essential security interests," which is limited to war, natural disaster and other situations threatening the existence of the State'.[45] The Respondent argued that Article XI was to be interpreted broadly and this was the intention of the parties. 'The self-judging character of these provisions…should not be understood as precluding their submission to arbitration as the Tribunal must determine whether Article XI applies and whether measures taken thereunder comply with the requirements of good faith.' Security interests included economic security, particularly in the context of a crisis as severe as that of Argentina, and this was sufficient for releasing Argentina from its treaty obligations.[46]

[43] See above Chapter 1.

[44] See above Chapters 2 and 9.

[45] *CMS*, paras 339–340.

[46] On the process and modalities of judicial review see A Orakhelashvili, The Acts of the Security Council: Meaning and Standards of Review, 11 *Max-Planck Yearbook of United Nations Law* (2007), 143.

The Tribunal had to determine 'whether Article XI of the Treaty can be interpreted in such a way as to provide that it includes economic emergency as an essential security interest'. Thus, it emphasised that 'While the text of the Article does not refer to economic crises or difficulties of that particular kind, as concluded above, there is nothing in the context of customary international law or the object and purpose of the Treaty that could on its own exclude major economic crises from the scope of Article XI.'[47] The Tribunal further observes that a bilateral investment treaty shall be interpreted as attending the concerns of both parties. If the concept of essential security interests were limited to immediate political and national security concerns, particularly of international character, and were to exclude economic emergencies, it would result in an unbalanced understanding of Article XI. This approach would not accord with the rules of treaty interpretation.[48] This may be an implicit reference to the treaty's object and purpose.

The Respondent insisted on the self-judging nature of this clause. It believed it was 'free to determine when and to what extent necessity, emergency or the threat to its security interests need the adoption of extraordinary measures'. The Tribunal's task would be to determine whether Article XI would be invoked in good faith.[49] This approach is conceivably correct in regarding good faith as the criterion for the exercise of treaty rights. However, if the right is seen as having self-judging content, then good faith can do very little in restraining the discretion of the State.

The Tribunal concluded that the Article XI clause was not self-judging.[50] Furthermore, and most importantly, the Tribunal's 'judicial review is not limited to an examination of whether the plea has been invoked or the measures have been taken in good faith. It is a substantive review that must examine whether the state of necessity or emergency meets the conditions laid down by customary international law and the treaty provisions and whether it thus is or is not able to preclude wrongfulness.'[51]

The issue of the self-judging character of the emergency clause has been raised in relation to Article XXI GATT, which may be used to justify certain GATT-inconsistent measures.[52] There has been no conclusive third-party pronouncement on the ambit of this provision and the ensuing claims of its self-judging character. With a view to predicting what this clause could cover in terms of real life, it is

[47] *Id*, para 359.
[48] *Id*, para 360.
[49] *Id*, para 367.
[50] *Id*, para 373.
[51] *Id*, para 374.
[52] According to Article XXI(b) GATT, nothing in this Agreement can be interpreted 'to prevent any contracting party from taking any action which it considers necessary for the protection of its essential security interests (i) relating to fissionable materials or the materials from which they are derived; (ii) relating to the traffic in arms, ammunition and implements of war and to such traffic in other goods and materials as is carried on directly or indirectly for the purpose of supplying a military establishment; (iii) taken in time of war or other emergency in international relations'.

suggested that Article XX may be resorted to protect strategic domestic production capability, to adopt trade sanctions on political grounds, or restrict arms exports.[53]

In *US—Trade Measures Affecting Nicaragua*, the GATT Panel examined the invocation of Article XXI GATT by the United States. The US argued that 'no recommendation could be proposed to remove the embargo since to do so would imply a judgement on the validity of the national security justification which Article XXI, by its terms, left to the exclusive judgement of the contracting party taking the action'.[54] Nicaragua, on the other hand, characterised the US embargo in the light of Article XXI as follows:

> This provision could be invoked only if two conditions were met: first, the measure adopted had to be necessary for the protection of essential security interest and, second, the measure had to be taken in time of war or other emergency in international relations. Neither of these conditions were fulfilled in this present case. Obviously, a small developing country such as Nicaragua could not constitute a threat to the security of the United States. The embargo was therefore not necessary to protect any essential security interest of that country. Nor was there any 'emergency' in the sense of Article XXI. Nicaragua and the United States were not at war and maintained full diplomatic relations. If there was tension between the two countries, it was due entirely to actions by the United States in violation of international law. A country could not be allowed to base itself on the existence of an 'emergency' which it had itself created.[55]

The US response was related both to substantive and procedural points:

> This provision, by its clear terms, left the validity of the security justification to the exclusive judgement of the contracting party taking the action. The United States could therefore not be found to act in violation of Article XXI. In any case, the Panel's terms of reference made it clear that it could examine neither the validity of, nor the motivation for, the United States' invocation of Article XXI:(b)(iii). The United States' compliance with its obligations under the General Agreement was therefore not an issue before the Panel. The United States added that it disagreed with Nicaragua's assessment of the security situation but it did not wish to be drawn into a debate on a matter that fell outside the competence of the GATT in general and the Panel in particular.[56]

Because of the limits imposed on the Panel's terms of reference, it could not pursue this matter any further.[57] The Panel further noted the contrast between the interpretative approaches advanced by Nicaragua and the US, that is between interpreting Article XXI in accordance with international law, and interpreting it in accordance with the judgment of the party that invoked the Article XII exception.[58]

[53] P Van den Bossche, *The Law and Policy of the World Trade Organization* (2005), 629.

[54] *United States—Trade Measures Affecting Nicaragua*, Report by the Panel, L/6053, 13 October 1986, para 4.1.

[55] *Id*, para. 4.5

[56] *Id*, para 4.6.

[57] *Id*, para 5.3.

[58] *Id*, para 5.2.

The United States expressly submitted that the examination of the invocation of Article XXI was a political question that was outside the judicial or quasi-judicial function, stating that 'the Panel would be drawn into a consideration of the political situation motivating the United States to invoke Article XXI'.[59]

The GATT Panel Report also raises the issue of interpreting indeterminate concepts in treaties in accordance with international law. This can be seen from Nicaragua's argument that emergency situations under Article XXI must be equated to situations in which self-defence can be invoked under international law. Nicaragua argued that:

> Article XXI was analogous to the right of self-defence in international law. This provision could be invoked only by a party subjected to direct aggression or armed attack and not by the aggressor or by parties indirectly at risk. Nicaragua added that it must be borne in mind that GATT did not exist in a vacuum but was an integral part of the wider structure of international law, and that the General Agreement must not be interpreted in a way inconsistent with international law.[60]

This point, again, could not be tested in this litigation, because of the latter's structural limits.

The principal issue that Article XXI GATT raises is its justiciability. It is emphasised that in principle the members should be able to seek judicial review of national determinations under Article XXI. It is acknowledged that Article XXI refers to the measures considered necessary by the Member State. Nevertheless, the total absence of judicial review would render this clause lable to abuse without redress. Thus, the Panels should be able to check the reasonableness of the Member State's determination of necessity in such cases, and verify this process in terms of compliance with the good faith principle to avoid abuse.[61]

While these points are all correct and valid, the missing principal point here is that in order for reasonableness and abuse issues to be assessed, some assessment of the actual measures undertaken in invocation of Article XXI must be performed. Otherwise it could be impossible to pronounce on the points of reasonableness and abuse. Therefore, resort to the test of reality and genuineness may acquire some relevance in this field as well.

If, as undoubtedly is the case, other States-parties must be informed of the details of the measures, and the reasonableness of and good faith behind these measures can and must be assessed, it is difficult to escape the conclusion that this process would necessarily involve a judgment regarding the type and scale of the measures as such.

In 1947, Czechoslovakia brought before the GATT Council an issue regarding an export restriction imposed by the United States under Article XII. In the

[59] *Id*, para 4.9.

[60] *United States—Trade Measures Affecting Nicaragua*, Report by the Panel, L/6053, 13 October 1986, para 4.5.

[61] Bossche (2005), 630.

debate, the United Kingdom representative supported rejecting this complaint because the entire matter was guided by the subjective determination by the United States:

> the United States action would seem to be justified because every country must be the judge in the last resort on questions relating to its own security. On the other hand, every Contracting Party should be cautious not to take any step which might have the effect of undermining the General Agreement. Particular cases involved should be examined in detail by the two governments concerned; no purpose would be served by a general inquest by the contracting parties.[62]

This British statement, supportive as it is of the US position, still postulates some limits on the propriety of subjective determinations of States under Article XXI. On the other hand, the 1982 Decision of the GATT Contracting Parties specifies the procedural requirements of action under Article XXI, namely to inform other Member States to the 'fullest extent possible' regarding these measures.[63] If such obligation exists, then the self-judging nature of Article XXI rights relates merely to the initial assessment of the relevant measures, while other States retain the right to make a judgment regarding the ultimate effect and legality of these measures, in terms of the existence of a security threat, necessity and proportionality. It is hardly thinkable that the duty to notify would have been stipulated unless it referred to genuine events as the object of notification.

6. Indeterminate Provisions in Arms Control and Disarmament Treaties

A number of treaties concluded on the matters of arms control and disarmament, and dealing with what constitute very sensitive issues of international politics, contain withdrawal clauses that arguably vest the contracting parties with the power of auto-interpretation. According to Article X of the 1968 Non-Proliferation Treaty:

> Each Party shall in exercising its national sovereignty have the right to withdraw from the Treaty if it decides that extraordinary events, related to the subject matter of this Treaty, have jeopardized the supreme interests of its country. It shall give notice of such withdrawal to all other Parties to the Treaty and to the United Nations Security Council three months in advance. Such notice shall include a statement of the extraordinary events it regards as having jeopardized its supreme interests.

There is thus a requirement that the State-party shall at least notify and explain to other States-parties what 'supreme interests' are endangered and by which

[62] *Corrigendum to the Summary Record of the Twenty-second Meeting*, GATT/CP.3/SR.22, Corr.1.

[63] L/5426, quoted in Bossche (2005), 630.

'extraordinary events'. This presumably makes it possible to assume that the mere judgment and decision of the withdrawing State-party is not a sufficient criterion.

According to Article XV(2) of the (now defunct) 1972 ABM Treaty:

> Each Party shall, in exercising its national sovereignty, have the right to withdraw from this Treaty if it decides that extraordinary events related to the subject matter of this Treaty have jeopardized its supreme interests. It shall give notice of its decision to the other Party six months prior to withdrawal from the Treaty. Such notice shall include a statement of the extraordinary events the notifying Party regards as having jeopardized its supreme interests.

A similar clause is included in Article XIX(3) of the 1979 Strategic Armament Limitation Treaty (SALT). In contrast Article IX CTBT Treaty states merely that 'Each State Party shall, in exercising its national sovereignty, have the right to withdraw from this Treaty if it decides that extraordinary events related to the subject matter of this Treaty have jeopardized its supreme interests.' There is no duty of notification and explanation stipulated in this case.

When announcing its withdrawal from the ABM Treaty in 2001, the US Government notified the relevant governments in the following way:

> Since the Treaty entered into force in 1972, a number of state and non-state entities have acquired or are actively seeking to acquire weapons of mass destruction. It is clear, and has recently been demonstrated, that some of these entities are prepared to employ these weapons against the United States. Moreover, a number of states are developing ballistic missiles, including long-range ballistic missiles, as a means of delivering weapons of mass destruction. These events pose a direct threat to the territory and security of the United States and jeopardize its supreme interests. As a result, the United States has concluded that it must develop, test, and deploy anti-ballistic missile systems for the defense of its national territory, of its forces outside the United States, and of its friends and allies.
>
> Pursuant to Article XV, paragraph 2, the United States has decided that extraordinary events related to the subject matter of the Treaty have jeopardized its supreme interests. Therefore, in the exercise of the right to withdraw from the Treaty provided in Article XV, paragraph 2, the United States hereby gives notice of its withdrawal from the Treaty. In accordance with the terms of the Treaty, withdrawal will be effective six months from the date of this notice.[64]

What is striking in this statement is that it fails to refer to specific factual events that objectively and observably endanger the United States to an extent justifying such drastic measures. The entire reasoning is based on certain events that are expected to occur. What is missing here is the specification of whether the relevant entities are able to reach the territory of the United States with their missiles, and whether the United States would be unable to defend itself from such threats through using its current arrangements and capabilities.

[64] US Note of 13 December 2001, addressed to the Russian Federation, Belarus, Kazakhstan and Ukraine.

In doctrinal terms, few scholars examine the legal aspects of this problem.[65] Some commentators write on the ABM Treaty and other treaties having comparable withdrawal clauses but do not enquire into the possible international legal limits and criteria governing a State-party's decision to withdraw from treaties.[66]

Müllerson observes that recourse to Article XV(2) requires the presence of concrete threats to supreme interests of the State-party. These threats ought to have materialised after the Treaty entered into force.[67] This may be one of the starting points in assessing the 'margin of appreciation' of the State-party. This could also perhaps raise to some extent the relevance of the principle of good faith. The more observable the rule becomes, the more obvious the role of the good faith principle. As Müllerson perceives it, the reference to extraordinary events in Article XV(2) of the AMB Treaty means that it is up to each party to assess these extraordinary events in the light of its supreme interests. At the same time, 'the withdrawing party has the obligation *vis-à-vis* its treaty partner to justify in good faith the necessity of withdrawal from the Treaty'.[68] It must be emphasised though that the requirement of good faith is not mentioned in the Treaty in this regard. In general terms, good faith does not independently generate obligations. It may only attach to existing obligations.[69] In this case, the obligation is indeterminate and good faith cannot assist us unless we know what the content of the obligation is in the first place.

At the same time, the principle of good faith is not a legal principle of free-standing operability, but depends on the content and operation of substantive rules of international law. The reality test is indispensable for the principle of good faith to have any meaningful application in this field. This test is not merely a product of academic thinking, but an indispensable requirement if the operation of indeterminate treaty provisions is not to be equated with unlimited self-judging discretion of individual States-parties or their groups.

7. The Evaluation of General Characteristics of 'Self-Judging' Clauses

In general, it may be asked what self-judging means. There is no authoritative or otherwise generally accepted definition of this notion. Nor have such clauses ever been conclusively denoted as self-judging by any adjudicating body. What the

[65] See eg, R Müllerson, The ABM Treaty: Changed Circumstances, Extraordinary Events, Supreme Interests and International Law, 50 *ICLQ* (2001), 508.

[66] See eg, J Rhinelander, The ABM Treaty—Past, Present and Future, 6 *JCSL* (2001), 91 at 103–104.

[67] Müllerson (2001), 531.

[68] Müllerson (2001), 531.

[69] *Border and Transborder Armed Actions* (Nicaragua v Honduras), *ICJ Reports*, 1988, 69.

treaty interpreter has to confront in these 'self-judging' clauses is their wording to be understood in their context and the treaty's object and purpose, as opposed to the abstract and, as it were, unofficial characterisation of these clauses as 'self-judging'.

On the other hand, it is possible to understand 'self-judging' clauses as referring to the initial determination made by the relevant State, without excluding a judgment by other States or adjudicators. In other words, the relevant State may invoke the emergency withdrawal clause by characterising the relevant situation as falling within the ambit of that clause. But that invocation will not be lawful merely because the State has so characterised it. The crucial factor still relates to the assessment of the genuine correlation between the content of the 'self-judging' clause, the attitude expressed by the invoking State, the state of things on the ground, and its legality. Such correlation of different factors enables the initial determination to be reviewed, leading to the invocation of the self-judging clause.

In fact, whether or not the relevant treaty emergency clause is denoted as 'self-judging', its legal implications are the same. Whether or not the relevant treaty provision mentions the discretion of the State-party to 'consider' the relevant events as threats to its essential interests, the constituent elements of legal relations it gives rise to are the same as those under treaty emergency clauses that do not refer to the 'self-judging' discretion of the State-party, such as human rights treaty emergency clauses. In any of these cases, what happens is that the relevant State-party makes an initial determination under the relevant clause and its obligation is to notify the other parties or the relevant agency about the merit of these measures. Whether or not the relevant treaty emergency clause looks to be 'self-judging', it is hardly sustainable to argue that it does not refer to a genuine emergency. Once this requirement of genuineness is acknowledged, in all cases the requirements of necessity and proportionality come into play, as these are implied in the wording of all relevant emergency clauses. Consequently, a reference to the 'self-judging' character of certain treaty emergency clauses is not of crucial importance for the assessment of their legal implications.

In general, a duty to inform other States-parties regarding the events that require resort to emergency clauses is included in human rights treaties, arms control and disarmament treaties and other agreements. Is such notification intended to be conclusive in terms of communicating the State's judgment? Or does the requirement of communication mean that from that communication some objectively identifiable yardstick would be provided on the basis of which further judgments on the legality of emergency measures could be assessed?

Obviously, one should be careful not to infer from a mere procedural obligation of notification a substantive limitation on the powers of the State. On the other hand, the data included in the instrument of notification will allow the interpreter to see whether the claimed emergency situation refers to real and genuine facts or to a non-existent emergency. The very reason behind the duty of communication is to provide other States and agencies with information about what the relevant

State claims under the treaty exception clause. If the intendment behind the relevant treaty clauses was that the State-party should be absolutely free to determine the legality of its derogation, then there would be no reason to impose on it a duty to notify. If the judgment rests exclusively with the relevant State-party, it would suffice for it to state that the emergency exists and it would by no means be obliged to describe it for the very simple reason that the emergency could be anything it might so denote. The very existence of the duty to notify inherently implies that there is a limit separating what can validly be claimed under emergency clauses from what cannot. The judgment on this is not the exclusive property of the State that invokes the emergency. Therefore, the reporting clauses cannot be seen as having no independent content. They relate to something that is material and substantial. Denying this conclusion would contradict the accepted principle that treaty provisions cannot be considered as redundant and inutile. Effective construction of the duty to report or notify necessarily requires that the subject matter of the relevant notification is genuine and really existent on the ground. At the same time, if under the treaty the relevance of the reporting clause refers not to a genuine threat and emergency, but to any situation subsumable within the subjective discretionary judgment of one State-party, including situations that do not genuinely constitute such threats, then that treaty ends up mandating the action in bad faith.

It must be concluded that the GATT Security Exceptions, or similar exceptions in disarmament and arms control treaties are related to the most sensitive fields of national security. Article XXI GATT, for instance, clearly delineates its field of operation by these measures. The sensitivity of these security questions may resemble the old doctrine of political issues and disputes allegedly left out of international legal regulations. Moreover, in this case, States-parties reciprocally reserve to themselves and each other the right to interpret these exceptions. The approach of subjectivism and discretion may thus be defended in this field by appealing to the high sensitivity of these issues and suggesting that States should perhaps be left alone to make their independent judgment in this limited area, with the respective legal implications for treaty relations.

At the same time, the existence of the notification requirement in those emergency withdrawal clauses cannot be without implications. It would hardly be justified to assume that a treaty stipulates the obligation of a State-party to notify other States-parties regarding a certain factual state of events, but does not require that those events have some real connotation, as opposed to merely being the product of the notifying State's subjective and discretionary determination. Consequently, it must be assumed that there are certain substantive standards to determine the legality of withdrawal under the emergency withdrawal clauses, which is possible through the assessment of the actual situation in the specific case, its scale and type, and correlation with it of the relevant measures undertaken by the State-party.

18

Equity and Equitable Considerations in Treaties

The specificity of problems raised by equitable notions embodied in treaty provisions differs importantly from the above-examined notions relating to emergency and security interests. On their face, these equitable notions, once they are applicable, can potentially claim to have a free-standing impact on the resolution of the relevant controversies. There are no arrangements similar to the margin of appreciation that could restrain their effect. While equitable notions sometimes imply the balancing of the relevant equitable factors, as is the case with equity in the law of maritime delimitation, this is not always the case, as confirmed by the application in practice of the notion of 'fair and equitable treatment'. While equity in the law of the sea considers what is equitable to all States involved in the dispute, 'fair and equitable treatment' in the law of foreign investment only focuses on what is equitable in relation to the investor. The indeterminacy of these equitable notions raises serious questions as to how their content should be identified in a way that preserves the predictability of the legal framework from the perspective of all actors involved in the litigation. With this in mind, the following analysis will expand on equity in maritime delimitation and 'fair and equitable treatment' in the law of foreign investment.

1. Equity in the Law of Maritime Delimitation

In some cases, a treaty provision requiring delimitation through the 'equidistance–special circumstances' rule was applied as the basis for adjudicating delimitation.[1] The identity of 'special circumstances' as the treaty rule with the 'relevant circumstances' of delimitation as an aspect of equity under general international law follows from the common context of maritime delimitation to which both concepts relate. This strengthens the presumption of the identity between the two notions.

In the *Anglo-French Continental Shelf* Arbitration, the Arbitral Tribunal addressed the relationship of the 'equidistance–special circumstances' rule of the

[1] On the identity of 'relevant circumstances' and 'special circumstances' see above, Chapter 8.

continental shelf delimitation under Article 6 of the 1958 Geneva Convention with the legal position under general international law. The UK insisted that the burden of showing that special circumstances displaced the equidistance rule rested with France. France for its part contested the applicability of Article 6 and insisted that equitable principles under customary law applied to this delimitation process.[2] The Tribunal stressed that the 'equidistance–special circumstances' rule under Article 6 was a single rule. The very reference to 'special circumstances' in Article 6 made it possible for a number of circumstances to be invoked. This, consequently, 'further underline[d] the full liberty of the Court in appreciating the geographical and other circumstances relevant to the delimitation of the continental shelf boundary, and at the same time reduce[d] the possibility of any difference in the appreciation of these circumstances under Article 6 and customary law'.[3]

Thus, the Tribunal acted in the context of open-ended and indeterminate prescription under the treaty clause which, as a matter of fact, coincided with the response to this problem under customary law. Therefore, the Tribunal was able to conclude that there was no visible contradiction between Article 6 and customary law. But this followed from the nature of the rule under Article 6 itself, and not from any perceived general principle that treaties shall be interpreted so as to correspond to general international law. The Tribunal emphasised that it:

> does not overlook that under Article 6 the equidistance principle ultimately possesses an obligatory force which it does not have in the same measure under the rules of customary law; for Article 6 makes the application of the equidistance principle a matter of treaty obligation for Parties to the Convention.

But equidistance was still qualified by 'special circumstances' which ultimately referred to equitable considerations. They gave 'particular expression to a general rule that, failing agreement, the boundary between States abutting on the same continental shelf is to be determined on equitable principles'. The appropriateness of equidistance as one of the equitable options depended on the appreciation of all relevant geographical and other circumstances. Equidistance had no inherent value.[4] Given that the treaty clause referring to 'special circumstances' was by itself indeterminate, these circumstances having no identifiable content of their own, the Tribunal had to conceive of it as linked to equity under general international law. Otherwise the Tribunal would have no independent means to assess what these 'special circumstances' were.

The Tribunal's approach was further shared by the International Court in the *Jan Mayen* case, where the Court stated the following:

[2] *UK-French Continental Shelf* case (1977), 54 *ILR* 303, para 67.
[3] *Id*, para 69.
[4] *Id*, para 70.

If the equidistance-special circumstances rule of the 1958 Convention is . . . to be regarded as expressing a general rule based on equitable principles, it must be difficult to find any material difference—at any rate in regard to delimitation between opposite coasts—between the effect of Article 6 and the effect of the customary rule which also requires a delimitation based on equitable principles.[5]

In other words, the crucial factor was the substantive identity between the relevant treaty and customary rules, rather than any requirement to interpret treaties in accordance with customary international law. Similarly, the:

statement [under Articles 73 and 84 of the 1982 Law of the Sea Convention] of an 'equitable solution' as the aim of any delimitation process reflects the requirements of customary law as regards the delimitation both of continental shelf and of exclusive economic zones.[6]

The 'special circumstances' under Article 6 and 'relevant circumstances' under customary law were essentially the same. Therefore, 'It cannot be surprising if an equidistance-special circumstances rule [embodied in a treaty] produces much the same result as an equitable principles-relevant circumstances rule [of customary law] in the case of opposite coasts, whether in the case of a delimitation of continental shelf, of fishery zone, or of an all-purpose single boundary.'[7] Likewise, Judge Weeramantry saw equity as a tool to interpret the meaning of 'special circumstances' under Article 6 of the 1958 Geneva Convention.[8] From this perspective, 'special circumstances' are clarified by reference to equity under general international law, having no identifiable content and meaning of their own.

This problem also raises the issue of the interpretation of exception clauses that include conditions of non-law. The scope of such exceptions cannot be straightforwardly defined and depends on the relevant circumstances under the given heading of non-law. This issue was raised in the *North Sea* case in relation to Article 6 of the 1958 Continental Shelf Convention, under which the delimitation of bordering continental shelf areas has to be based on equidistance and such specific circumstances as were present in the relevant case. Judge Tanaka suggested that the 'special circumstances' clause:

does not constitute an independent principle which can replace equidistance, but it means the adaptation of this principle to concrete circumstances. If for the foregoing reasons the exceptional nature of this clause is admitted, the logical consequence would be its strict interpretation. *Exceptiones sunt strictissimae interpretationis.*[9]

Similarly, Judge Lachs argued that this 'special circumstances' clause 'should not be interpreted otherwise than in a restrictive manner.' One piece of evidence

[5] *ICJ Reports* 1993, 58.
[6] *Id*, 59.
[7] *Id*, 62.
[8] Separate Opinion, *id*, 249.
[9] Dissenting Opinion, *ICJ Reports,* 1969, 186.

Judge Lachs invoked to support this position was the position of the International Law Commission on the factor of exceptional configuration of the coast as the justification for departure from equidistance.[10] Thus, the gist of the judges' argument was to uphold the applicability of the equidistance method which they understood to be the primary provision as opposed to the exception based on special circumstances.

On the other hand, the real question is reduced to whether there are or are not such special circumstances as may require deviation from the equidistance principle. As soon as there are such special circumstances, their relevance cannot be eliminated by arguments of restrictive or strict construction of exceptions generally. This process is not about restrictive interpretation, but about the analysis of the situation on the ground to determine whether the relevant special circumstances actually exist. This approach seems to have guided the International Court's decision in this case, in which it refused to apply the equidistance method.[11]

In the *Anglo-French* case, the Arbitral Tribunal also addressed the reference in Article 6 to 'special circumstances' justifying deviation from the otherwise applicable equidistance rule. The Tribunal stressed that in this case 'special circumstances' referred to an equitable solution. The use of any method thus depended on the appreciation of geographical and other circumstances rather than on a fixed rule.[12]

2. 'Fair and Equitable Treatment' in Investment Treaties

(a) General Aspects of Interpretation

The practice of international investment arbitration witnesses the use of certain interpretative methods under the Vienna Convention on the Law of Treaties to determine the meaning of the 'fair and equitable treatment' standard for the treatment of foreign investors.[13] These methods relate mainly to the plain meaning and object and purpose of the treaty. As the PCA Tribunal Award in *Saluka* emphasises, 'fair and equitable treatment' is not a concept to be applied *ex aequo et bono*, but by reference to law.[14] Hence the Tribunal accepts that there are some limits on indeterminacy and the criteria for clarifying the meaning of this indeterminate notion.

In *Saluka Investments*, the Arbitral Tribunal acting under the UNCITRAL Rules addressed the 'fair and equitable treatment' standard under Article 3

[10] Dissenting Opinion, *id*, 1969, 216.
[11] See above Chapter 8.
[12] *Anglo-French*, para 70.
[13] See above Chapter 8.
[14] *Saluka Investments BV v the Czech Republic*, Partial Award, 17 March 2006, para 284.

of the BIT between the Netherlands and the Czech Republic. According to Article 3, 'Each Contracting Party shall ensure fair and equitable treatment to the investments of investors of the other Contracting Party and shall not impair, by unreasonable or discriminatory measures, the operation, management, maintenance, use, enjoyment or disposal thereof by those investors.'[15] The *Saluka* Award expressly illustrates the difference between the judicial task in the case of NAFTA, which requires that the interpretative process shall be conducted in accordance with general international law, and a BIT which contains no such requirement:

> Whichever the difference between the customary and the treaty standards may be, this Tribunal has to limit itself to the interpretation of the 'fair and equitable treatment' standard as embodied in Article 3.1 of the Treaty. That Article omits any express reference to the customary minimum standard. The interpretation of Article 3.1 does not therefore share the difficulties that may arise under treaties (such as the NAFTA) which expressly tie the 'fair and equitable treatment' standard to the customary minimum standard. Avoidance of these difficulties may even be regarded as the very purpose of the lack of a reference to an international standard in the Treaty. This clearly points to the autonomous character of a 'fair and equitable treatment' standard such as the one laid down in Article 3.1 of the Treaty.[16]

The issue of how the notion of 'fair and equitable treatment' must be conceived as part of the treaty framework of which it is part has also been raised in the light of this. As Brower remarks, 'it seems evident that the phrase 'fair and equitable treatment' is intentionally vague, designed to give adjudicators the power to articulate the range of principles necessary to achieve the treaty's purpose in particular disputes'.[17]

This statement implies, on the one hand, that 'fair and equitable treatment' is exclusively a treaty-derived and treaty-specific standard. On the other hand, it implies that 'fair and equitable treatment' has no established meaning that can be generalised across the board. It can only be located as part of the treaty arrangement and as serving the purpose of this arrangement. Consequently, it could in principle mean whatever the relevant treaty framework designates it to mean and this must be established on the basis of interpretation of that treaty through the use of normal interpretative methods. But what the relevant treaties normally do is to refer to 'fair and equitable treatment' in relation to the context of treatment of foreign investors that is also regulated under general international law.

[15] *Id*, paras 280, 285.

[16] *Id*, para 294.

[17] C Brower, Remarks on 'Fair and Equitable Treatment under NAFTA's Investment Chapter', 96 *ASIL Proceedings* (2002), 11.

(b) Object and Purpose of the Treaty

Brower suggests that the notion of 'fair and equitable treatment' under NAFTA must be interpreted by reference to NAFTA's object and purpose, which above all requires ensuring a predictable commercial framework for investors. 'Those rules cannot reasonably sustain an interpretation that collapses "fair and equitable treatment" into everything short of the most unimaginable forms of government misconduct.'[18] Similarly, the *Metalclad* Award emphasises that 'An underlying objective of NAFTA is to promote and increase cross-border investment opportunities and ensure the successful implementation of investment initiatives.'[19] The Tribunal further refers to the requirement of transparency and understands it:

> to include the idea that all relevant legal requirements for the purpose of initiating, completing and successfully operating investments made, or intended to be made, under the Agreement should be capable of being readily known to all affected investors of another Party. There should be no room for doubt or uncertainty on such matters. Once the authorities of the central government of any Party (whose international responsibility in such matters has been identified in the preceding section) become aware of any scope for misunderstanding or confusion in this connection, it is their duty to ensure that the correct position is promptly determined and clearly stated so that investors can proceed with all appropriate expedition in the confident belief that they are acting in accordance with all relevant laws.[20]

In *Pope & Talbot*, the NAFTA Tribunal observed that Article 102(2) NAFTA requires interpreting the Treaty in accordance with the objectives set out in Article 102(1), among which the substantial increase of investment opportunities is to be found. Therefore, the Tribunal supported the reading of Article 1105 NAFTA as including standards going beyond customary international law, because if NAFTA served the purposes stated in Article 1102, which includes the ban on discrimination, it could not be interpreted as allowing the parties to afford to each others' nationals less favourable treatment than they would afford to their own nationals and to nationals of a number of other countries as required by the relevant Bilateral Investment Treaties. Furthermore, according to the Tribunals:

> it is doubtful that the NAFTA parties would want to present to potential investors and investments from other NAFTA countries the possibility that they would have no recourse to protection against anything but egregiously unfair conduct. The aim of NAFTA seems to be quite the opposite.[21]

[18] Brower (2002), 11.
[19] *Metalclad*, para 75.
[20] *Id*, para 76.
[21] *Pope & Talbot Inc and the Government of Canada* (Award on Merits, NAFTA Chapter 11 Arbitration), 12 April 2001 paras 115–116.

In *Azurix*, the issue before the ICSID Tribunal was to clarify the ambit of 'fair and equitable treatment' under the US-Argentine Bilateral Investment Treaty. The Arbitral Tribunal began by observing that 'the BIT is an international treaty that should be interpreted in accordance with the rules of interpretation established by the Vienna Convention'. This Convention required consideration of the Treaty's context and its object and purpose.[22] The Tribunal continued that:

> As regards the purpose and object of the BIT, in its Preamble, the parties state their desire to promote greater cooperation with respect to investment, recognize that 'agreement upon the treatment to be accorded such investment will stimulate the flow of private capital and the economic development of the Parties', and agree that 'fair and equitable treatment of investment is desirable in order to maintain a stable framework for investment and maximum effective use of economic resources.' It follows from the ordinary meaning of the terms fair and equitable and the purpose and object of the BIT that fair and equitable should be understood to be treatment in an even-handed and just manner, conducive to fostering the promotion of foreign investment. The text of the BIT reflects a positive attitude towards investment with words such as 'promote' and 'stimulate'. Furthermore, the parties to the BIT recognize the role that fair and equitable treatment plays in maintaining 'a stable framework for investment and maximum effective use of economic resources'.[23]

Similarly, the *CMS* Award asserts that 'one principal objective of the protection envisaged is that fair and equitable treatment is desirable "to maintain a stable framework for investments and maximum effective use of economic resources." There can be no doubt, therefore, that a stable legal and business environment is an essential element of fair and equitable treatment.'[24]

The *Saluka* Award also emphasises the relevance of the Treaty's purposes for understanding the scope of 'fair and equitable treatment'. The Tribunal refers to the purpose of the Netherlands-Czech BIT, which encourages such treatment of investors as will 'stimulate the flow of capital and technology and the economic development of the Contracting Parties' and consequently 'fair and equitable treatment is desirable'.[25] The object and purpose of the Dutch-Czech BIT was seen by the Tribunal as impacting the meaning of 'fair and equitable treatment':

> The protection of foreign investments is not the sole aim of the Treaty, but rather a necessary element alongside the overall aim of encouraging foreign investment and extending and intensifying the parties' economic relations. That in turn calls for a balanced approach to the interpretation of the Treaty's substantive provisions for the protection of investments, since an interpretation which exaggerates the protection to be accorded to foreign investments may serve to dissuade host States from admitting foreign investments

[22] *Azurix Corp. and the Argentine Republic*, ICSID Case No ARB/01/12, Award of 14 July 2006 para 359.

[23] *Id*, para 360.

[24] *CMS*, para 274.

[25] *Saluka*, para 298.

and so undermine the overall aim of extending and intensifying the parties' mutual economic relations.

Seen in this light, the 'fair and equitable treatment' standard prescribed in the Treaty should therefore be understood to be treatment which, if not proactively stimulating the inflow of foreign investment capital, does at least not deter foreign capital by providing disincentives to foreign investors. An investor's decision to make an investment is based on an assessment of the state of the law and the totality of the business environment at the time of the investment as well as on the investor's expectation that the conduct of the host State subsequent to the investment will be fair and equitable.[26]

Therefore, a foreign investor could expect that:

the Czech Republic implements its policies *bona fide* by conduct that is, as far as it affects the investors' investment, reasonably justifiable by public policies and that such conduct does not manifestly violate the requirements of consistency, transparency, even-handedness and non-discrimination. In particular, any differential treatment of a foreign investor must not be based on unreasonable distinctions and demands, and must be justified by showing that it bears a reasonable relationship to rational policies not motivated by a preference for other investments over the foreign-owned investment.[27]

In all these three cases tribunals further used the treaty interpretation reasoning to hold that 'fair and equitable treatment' does require that States afford to investors guarantees higher than required under general international law. This has somehow ended up imposing on States certain obligations which they could hardly foresee while concluding the relevant investment treaties. Under this scheme, the indeterminate notion of 'fair and equitable treatment' potentially imposes on States-parties any possible obligation that is conducive to the interests of the investor, without these obligations being known to States in an *a priori* and straightforward way.

In reality all this reasoning of tribunals does is to describe the link between 'fair and equitable treatment' and general treaty purposes of economic development. But it does not itself clarify what the treaty standard of 'fair and equitable treatment' means and how far it goes. It is one thing to say that 'fair and equitable treatment' promotes investment opportunity and economic development. It is quite another thing to argue that these purposes vest 'fair and equitable treatment' with any particular content. Object and purpose can potentially influence the choice between two equally defensible meanings of the text.[28] But it cannot fill an indeterminate notion with specific content.

Soundly enough, the *Saluka* Tribunal recognises that the promotion of investment is not the only purpose of the BIT. Therefore, the Tribunal accepts that 'an interpretation which exaggerates the protection to be accorded to foreign investments may serve to dissuade host States from admitting foreign investments and

[26] *Id*, paras 300–301.
[27] *Id*, para 307.
[28] See above Chapter 10.

so undermine the overall aim of extending and intensifying the parties' mutual economic relations'.[29] Therefore, the Tribunal conceives of the impact of the object and purpose on interpreting 'fair and equitable treatment' thus:

> The 'fair and equitable treatment' standard prescribed in the Treaty should therefore be understood to be treatment which, if not proactively stimulating the inflow of foreign investment capital, does at least not deter foreign capital by providing disincentives to foreign investors. An investor's decision to make an investment is based on an assessment of the state of the law and the totality of the business environment at the time of the investment as well as on the investor's expectation that the conduct of the host State subsequent to the investment will be fair and equitable.[30]

This argument, although purportedly aimed at further clarifying the 'fair and equitable treatment' standard under the Treaty, does not do so. It only explains that investment should not be deterred. But this is a very broad approach and under different circumstances different investors will evaluate differently whether or not, and by which factors, they are deterred from investing. Relatively high taxes or trade union regulation may well be factors that deter foreign investors. Yet it is not seriously arguable that investment treaties will censure tax and trade union policies of the State if these policies do not suit the investor's climate. On the other hand, the Tribunal refers to 'the investor's expectation that the conduct of the host State subsequent to the investment will be fair and equitable'. This is yet another circular approach, suggesting that 'fair and equitable treatment' under a Treaty applies where the investor expects to be treated fairly and equitably.

The emphasis on the expectations of the investor as such further corroborates the circularity problem as one of subjectivity. It is highly debatable whether the subjective assessment of expectations by an entity which is not even a party to the relevant investment treaty will be the guiding factor in locating the meaning of the clause in that treaty. As the analysis on treaty interpretation has demonstrated beyond doubt, the subjective expectation of the relevant entity cannot be a material factor in determining the meaning of the treaty provision.

The Tribunal does not feel deterred by the circularity of its approach, and in order to give some impression of objectivity, it deduces, from its own understanding of the Treaty's object and purpose, another standard of the treatment of investors:

> By virtue of the 'fair and equitable treatment' standard included in Article 3.1 the Czech Republic must therefore be regarded as having assumed an obligation to treat foreign investors so as to avoid the frustration of investors' legitimate and reasonable expectations.[31]

[29] *Saluka*, para 300.
[30] *Id*, para 301.
[31] *Id*, para 302.

The Tribunal arguably tries to minimise the destructive effect of this approach, and states that:

> while it subscribes to the general thrust of these and similar statements, it may be that, if their terms were to be taken too literally, they would impose upon host States' obligations which would be inappropriate and unrealistic. Moreover, the scope of the Treaty's protection of foreign investment against unfair and inequitable treatment cannot exclusively be determined by foreign investors' subjective motivations and considerations. Their expectations, in order for them to be protected, must rise to the level of legitimacy and reasonableness *in light of the circumstances*.[32]

But the Tribunal seems to reserve for its own discretion the clarification of what these 'circumstances' are. The Tribunal's allegedly subtle but still observable approach is to pay lip-service to the need of States for legal security yet assert the standard according to which its subjective discretion will be able to bring about any result it deems appropriate.

The Tribunal's interpretative conclusion runs thus:

> The 'fair and equitable treatment' standard in Article 3.1 of the Treaty is an autonomous Treaty standard and must be interpreted, in light of the object and purpose of the Treaty, so as to avoid conduct of the Czech Republic that clearly provides disincentives to foreign investors. The Czech Republic, without undermining its legitimate right to take measures for the protection of the public interest, has therefore assumed an obligation to treat a foreign investor's investment in a way that does not frustrate the investor's underlying legitimate and reasonable expectations. A foreign investor whose interests are protected under the Treaty is entitled to expect that the Czech Republic will not act in a way that is manifestly inconsistent, non-transparent, unreasonable (*i.e.* unrelated to some rational policy), or discriminatory (*i.e.* based on unjustifiable distinctions). In applying this standard, the Tribunal will have due regard to all relevant circumstances.[33]

This observation reaffirms the Tribunal's adherence to the subjectivity and uncertainty of criteria to determine what 'fair and equitable treatment' is. The principal question is what the required 'rational policies' are and through which means arbitral tribunals can determine them. Judicial organs are not designed to pronounce on issues of policy of a respective State.[34] They can only apply established rules of law.

While some of these requirements mentioned in *Saluka* are clear and anyway present in the general international law standard on the treatment of foreign investment, others are merely the product of the Tribunal's policy of replacing one ambiguity with another. This concerns in the first place the requirement that the Government's conduct be 'reasonable' and related to 'rational' policy. Thus, the Tribunal assumes the role of assessing the policies of the Government which is not part of its judicial activities. This is not about policy grounds expressly placed within the context of adjudication and subjected to further conditions,

[32] *Id*, para 304 (emphasis original).
[33] *Id*, para 309.
[34] See above Chapter 2.

such as those applicable under the margin of appreciation clauses of ECHR and WTO Agreements.[35] In this case the Tribunal declared on its own that it could judge the policy of the State, without adducing any evidence that its treaty-based mandate warranted this approach. Likewise, it is not easy to see how the 'manifestly inconsistent' conduct should be defined. Overall, this mirrors the tendency in other cases in which tribunals try to assert an approach based on their subjective appreciation of the Government's conduct.

The outcome in *Saluka* contradicts the outcome achieved in some other cases. As the NAFTA Tribunal emphasised in *SD Myers*, the 'fair and equitable treatment' standard does not create an 'open-ended mandate to second-guess government decision-making'.[36]

The *Azurix* Award also tries to present 'fair and equitable treatment' as the higher standard by reference to the purposes it pursues. The Award specifies that:

> The standards of conduct agreed by the parties to a BIT presuppose a favorable disposition towards foreign investment, in fact, a pro-active behavior of the State to encourage and protect it. To encourage and protect investment is the purpose of the BIT. It would be incoherent with such purpose and the expectations created by such a document to consider that a party to the BIT has breached the obligation of fair and equitable treatment only when it has acted in bad faith or its conduct can be qualified as outrageous or egregious.[37]

In fact, if 'fair and equitable treatment' were limited to egregious conduct, it still could and would be serving those goals that the *Saluka* Tribunal mentions. The object and purpose of the treaty does not by itself generate specific treaty obligations. It can only provide guidance in understanding the scope of otherwise existing treaty obligations. In the case of indeterminate concepts with no independent and identifiable content, the approach of a judicial decision-maker can present these two tasks as converging. This results, again, in the danger of imposing on the host State obligations it had no chance of knowing of in advance.

The ICSID Tribunal in *Tecmed* goes even further, arguing 'that this provision of the Agreement, in light of the good faith principle established by international law, requires the Contracting Parties to provide to international investments treatment that does not affect the basic expectations that were taken into account by the foreign investor to make the investment'. Furthermore:

> The foreign investor expects the host State to act in a consistent manner, free from ambiguity and totally transparently in its relations with the foreign investor, so that it may know beforehand any and all rules and regulations that will govern its investments, as well as the goals of the relevant policies and administrative practices or directives, to be able to plan its investment and comply with such regulations. Any and all State actions

[35] See above Chapter 8.

[36] *S.D. Myers and Government of Canada* (Partial Award, NAFTA Arbitration under the UNCITRAL Rules), 13 November 2000 para 261.

[37] *Azurix*, para 372.

> conforming to such criteria should relate not only to the guidelines, directives or requirements issued, or the resolutions approved thereunder, but also to the goals underlying such regulations. The foreign investor also expects the host State to act consistently, i.e. without arbitrarily revoking any pre-existing decisions or permits issued by the State that were relied upon by the investor to assume its commitments as well as to plan and launch its commercial and business activities.[38]

This is arguably a clear requirement. But in practice it could entail ramifications that encompass the entire or a large part of the economic policy of a State. There is no indication either in investment treaties, or in their object and purpose as declared in their preambles, that such treaties are concluded with this intendment.

More generally, it seems that conceiving of 'fair and equitable treatment' as part of the treaty's object and purpose does not inherently require viewing this standard as detached from, or going beyond, the state of general international law. In general, it has to be asked in what sense a treaty would, as a legal instrument, refer to the notion of 'fair and equitable treatment'. Would it require that the investor be treated fairly and equitably in relation to its legal rights, or would it require the same in terms of common-sense fairness and equity which will always generate disagreements depending on one's subjective perception of justice and fairness? On balance it appears sounder to accept that treaty instrument dealing with legal safeguards for investors uses the notion of 'fair and equitable treatment' as referring to the legal rights of investors in international or national law.

It seems moreover that a standard of treatment of foreign investors purportedly forming part of general international law and focusing on the prohibition of abuse of power, discrimination, arbitrariness, and denial of justice,[39] would make perfect sense as an element of a predictable and favourable investment framework under investment treaties. When predictable and favourable framework is referred to, it must be asked: predictable and favourable in relation to what? It would be perfectly sound to suggest that the investor must have predictability and certainty that it will not be unlawfully deprived of its possessions, will not be subjected to violence or discrimination and will not be precluded from access to fair judicial process including the award of remedies. But it is quite another matter to claim that the investor can legally expect that nothing disagreeable will ever happen to it and that the host government will refrain from doing anything that, falling short of abuse, deprivation or violent harassment, could have an indirect or remote effect on investment.

To recapitulate, it is one thing to argue that a treaty provision must be conceived in the light of the treaty's object and purpose and this is a basic interpretative rule. It goes further than that, however, to argue that the treaty's object and

[38] *Tecnicas Medioambientales Tecmed S.A v The United Mexican States*, Case No ARB(AF)/00/2, Award of 29 May 2003 para 154.

[39] See above Chapter 8.

purpose can give to a notion included in the treaty, but not defined, a meaning that would purportedly correspond to that object and purpose but would still not be clear as to its scope and ambit.

(c) Autonomous Meaning of 'Fair and Equitable Treatment'

It is often argued in doctrine and jurisprudence that 'fair and equitable treatment' possesses autonomous meaning, and the protection standard it offers is independent of the standard(s) available under general international law. FA Mann advances a view of interpretation of treaty clauses based on 'fair and equitable treatment' which is related to the principle of plain meaning as well as that of autonomous meaning. Tribunals, according to Mann, 'will have to decide whether in all the circumstances the conduct in issue is fair and equitable or unfair and inequitable. No standard defined by other words is likely to be material. The terms are to be understood and applied independently and autonomously.'[40]

Although both the principles of plain and autonomous meaning are valid interpretative principles, it is not clear how they can help in interpreting a notion which has no established, objectively ascertainable meaning. What Mann denotes as 'independent' or 'autonomous' can in practice be only the meaning that has no other legitimacy behind it apart from the subjective judgment of the decision-maker. As arbitral practice demonstrates, this judgment mainly consists in making a choice between the assertion of one party that the relevant treatment is 'fair and equitable' and that of the other party that it is not. Mann's approach does not go further than suggesting that the treatment is unfair and inequitable if tribunals view it so.

The *Saluka* Award attempts a textual interpretation of 'fair and equitable treatment'. Under this approach, the ordinary meaning of this standard is just, even-handed, unbiased, legitimate.[41] The Tribunal noted the claimant's assertion that 'fair and equitable treatment' is a specific and autonomous treaty standard.[42] The Tribunal shared this view. The Netherlands-Czech BIT omitted any reference to customary international law, and the interpretative problem arising from other treaties referring to customary law was not present in this case. This arguably pointed to the autonomous character of 'fair and equitable treatment' under the Treaty.[43] Although Article 4(1) of the BIT dealt with in *Tecmed* conceives of 'fair and equitable treatment' as part of international law, the Tribunal still asserts that this is an autonomous concept:

> The Arbitral Tribunal understands that the scope of the undertaking of fair and equitable treatment under Article 4(1) of the Agreement described above is that resulting from an

[40] FA Mann, British Treaties for the Promotion and Protection of Investments, 5 *BYIL* (1982), 244.
[41] *Saluka*, para 297.
[42] *Id*, para 285.
[43] *Id*, paras 294, 309.

autonomous interpretation, taking into account the text of Article 4(1) of the Agreement according to its ordinary meaning (Article 31(1) of the Vienna Convention).[44]

Thus, the Tribunal asserts the autonomous interpretation of the concept whose meaning in the Treaty is clearly linked to international law. Proceeding from its initial false premise, the Tribunal further develops its approach:

If the above were not its intended scope, Article 4(1) of the Agreement would be deprived of any semantic content or practical utility of its own, which would surely be against the intention of the Contracting Parties upon executing and ratifying the Agreement since, by including this provision in the Agreement, the parties intended to strengthen and increase the security and trust of foreign investors that invest in the member States, thus maximizing the use of the economic resources of each Contracting Party by facilitating the economic contributions of their economic operators.[45]

Thus, after knowingly misreading the text of the relevant treaty clause, the Tribunal asserts that if the autonomous interpretation is not accepted, this clause would lose its utility. In other words, this is an attempt to use the principle of effectiveness for enlarging or changing the textual scope of the Treaty, and to do so without depicting any outer limit of the obligation thus construed. The use of the presumption against redundancy in this case is not justified in such a way. Such a treaty clause could perfectly well maintain its utility by being construed as referring to general international law. The Tribunal's guessing as to what the parties' intention is ignores the basic principle that such intention is to be inferred from the text of the Treaty itself.

To illustrate, on the basis of its broad interpretation of 'fair and equitable treatment', the *Azurix* Tribunal specifies as breaches of 'fair and equitable treatment' the insistence of the Government on terminating the concession itself, on the alleged basis of abandonment by the company, as opposed to acknowledging the company's notice of termination, and on what the Tribunal denotes as 'politicisation' of the Concession.[46] In *CMS* the Tribunal stated that the Government's measures had transformed and altered the business and legal environment.[47] Does this mean that the Government has no right to impact the business environment? Will every such impact be seen as breach of an international treaty? Does the investor's ability to plan and implement its investment require the Government to desist from any action that impacts the situation in the investment field?

This state of great uncertainty and the lack of any consistent method to resolve it objectively and intelligibly to the satisfaction of all actors involved requires an acceptance that the 'autonomous' or 'purposive' interpretation of 'fair and equitable treatment' cannot produce any transparent, predictable and generally accepted result.

[44] *Tecmed*, para 155.
[45] *Id*, para 156.
[46] *Azurix*, paras 374, 378.
[47] *CMS*, para 275.

(d) The Proper Approach: Identity of 'Fair and Equitable Treatment' with the (Minimum) Standard of General International Law

While normally treaties are *lex specialis,* in some cases they can expressly incorporate general international law standards. Article 102(2) NAFTA provides that the NAFTA Agreement shall be interpreted among other things in accordance with applicable rules of international law. This may be seen as a special regulation in relation to Article 31 of the 1969 Vienna Convention on the Law of Treaties, according to general international law a more important place.[48] The interpretative relevance for the construction of treaties of general international law is provided for in Article 1131(1) NAFTA according to which the Chapter 11 Tribunal must decide the cases on the basis of the Agreement and applicable rules of international law. The Arbitral Tribunal in *Thunderbird* acknowledged this, for instance.[49] Once the Agreement itself provides for the role of general international law, its use by Tribunals as an interpretative factor is less problematic and cannot be seen as circumvention of the will and intention of the States-parties to the Agreement.

The interpretative role of general international law is especially important in cases where the relevant treaty provisions have no definite and determinate meaning. This is the case with regard to investment treaties that stipulate the 'fair and equitable treatment' of investors. Treaties constitute *lex specialis* in relation to general international law only in so far as they suggest a determinate legal outcome, independent of the subjective judgment of the decision-maker. There can be no autonomous meaning of 'fair and equitable treatment' if its content depends on subjective appreciation. The authors of the treaty could not provide a higher degree of protection than that under general international law without even defining the content and scope of the relevant protection standard. This is a further reason why 'fair and equitable treatment' must be seen as linked to the legal position under general international law as closely as possible.

The NAFTA Tribunal in *Mondev* emphasised that the scope of 'fair and equitable treatment' has to be identified 'by reference to international law, ie, by reference to the normal sources of international law determining the minimum standard of treatment of foreign investors'.[50] With the 2001 FTC

[48] Article 31(3)(c) of the Vienna Convention requires that the relevant rules of international law are taken into account when the treaty is interpreted. The NAFTA Treaty, on the other hand, requires interpretation in accordance with the relevant rules of international law.

[49] *International Thunderbird Gaming Corporation and the United Mexican States* (Award), 26 January 2006, para 89.

[50] *Mondev International Ltd and United States of America,* Case No. ARB(AF)/99/2, Award of 11 October 2002, paras 119–120.

Interpretation,[51] it became necessary for NAFTA tribunals to base their decisions on customary law, along with the NAFTA Agreement itself. The principal point in a number of arbitrations has been whether the traditional customary international law standard embodied in the *Neer* decision delivered in 1927 was still a governing standard for the treatment of investors, and thus whether the violation of investors' rights under Article 1105 NAFTA required crossing the threshold of 'egregious' conduct or was liberalised due to the different state of customary law at the time when decisions of NAFTA Tribunals were delivered.

The Arbitral Tribunal in *SD Myers* considered that the words 'fair and equitable treatment and full protection and security' in Article 1105 cannot be seen in isolation, but, as the text suggests, in conjunction with the introductory phrase, 'treatment in accordance with international law'.[52] The Arbitral Tribunal in *Mondev* considered that the terms 'fair and equitable treatment' and 'full protection and security' under Article 1105(1) are, in the view of the NAFTA parties, references to existing elements of customary international law.[53]

In *Pope & Talbot*, the investor argued that the requirements of Article 1105(1) referred to all sources of international law, such as customary law or the parties' other treaty obligations. Canada, on the other hand, suggested that before a violation of international law could be found under Article 1105(1), it had to be established that the conduct in question was 'egregious'. As the investor referred to the broad range of sources or evidence of law, it argued that these developments had liberalised the 'egregious' conduct threshold that would otherwise be applicable.[54]

The Tribunal also addressed another possibility—that of the requirement of fair and equitable treatment being additional to the requirements of international law, although the text of Article 1105(1) considers these standards to be 'included' in the international law requirements. Thus, investors under NAFTA were 'entitled to the international law minimum, *plus* the fairness elements'. The Tribunal adopted this reading, mainly because this followed allegedly from the regime of bilateral investment treaties, and concluded that 'compliance with the fairness elements must be ascertained free of any threshold that might be applicable to the evaluation of measures under the minimum standards of international law'. The *Pope & Talbot* Tribunal disagreed with the *SD Myers* Tribunal on the issue of interpretation.[55] But the approach that Article 1105(1) provides for the international law standard plus the fairness elements is not free of problems in terms of the text of that provision, which expressly contains the word 'including'. Nevertheless, at the

[51] See, for details, the next section.

[52] *SD Myers* (Partial Award), 13 November 2000, paras 262–263.

[53] *Mondev*, para 122.

[54] *Pope & Talbot and the Government of Canada* (Award on the Merits of Phase 2), paras 105–109.

[55] *Pope & Talbot* (Merits), paras 110–111.

merits stage in *Pope & Talbot*, the NAFTA Tribunal determined that the Article 1105 requirement to accord investors fair and equitable treatment 'was independent of, not subsumed by the requirement to accord them treatment required by international law'.[56]

This discourse relates to two independent but interrelated questions: the scope of the relevant customary international law in terms of fair treatment; and whether, whatever the scope of customary law, the NAFTA standard of treatment is limited to it or extends also to other rules of international law. In principle, the parties could either have added new requirements to the existing state of customary international law, or expressed through treaty clauses their legal conviction that the relevant international law standards include the fairness requirements.

In terms of the NAFTA Free Trade Commission's Interpretation of July 31, 2001, of Article 1105(1) NAFTA, this provision incorporates and refers to the customary international law standard regarding the treatment of aliens. As the Commission suggests, 'the concepts of "fair and equitable treatment" and "full protection and security" do not require treatment in addition to or beyond what is required by the customary international law minimum standard of treatment of aliens'. The reaction of arbitral tribunals to this interpretation was diverse.

One reaction consisted in affirming the relevance of customary international law, but asserting that it was evolving or had evolved regulation regarding the treatment of foreign investors. The *Pope & Talbot* Tribunal at the damages stage considered that the Commission's Interpretation led to an absurd result because the relief denied under Article 1105 would be restored by reference to Article 1103 on most favoured nation treatment.[57] The Arbitral Tribunal in *Thunderbird* stated, by reference to the Free Trade Commission's Interpretative Declaration, that 'The content of the minimum standard should not be rigidly interpreted and it should reflect evolving international customary law.'[58]

Mondev develops the view of the evolutionary approach to customary law in order to accommodate the concept of 'fair and equitable treatment' in this context. According to the Award:

> there can be no doubt that, by interpreting Article 1105(1) to prescribe the customary international law minimum standard of treatment of aliens as the minimum standard of treatment to be afforded to investments of investors of another Party under NAFTA, the term 'customary international law' refers to customary international law as it stood no earlier than the time at which NAFTA came into force. It is not limited to the international law of the 19th century or even of the first half of the 20th century, although decisions

[56] *Pope & Talbot and the Government of Canada* (Award in Respect of Damages, NAFTA Chapter 11 Arbitration), 31 May 2002, para 8.

[57] *Pope & Talbot* (Damages), para 12.

[58] *International Thunderbird Gaming Corporation and the United Mexican States* (Partial Award on Merits), 26 January 2006 para 194.

from that period remain relevant. In holding that Article 1105(1) refers to customary international law, the FTC interpretations incorporate current international law, whose content is shaped by the conclusion of more than two thousand bilateral investment treaties and many treaties of friendship and commerce. Those treaties largely and concordantly provide for 'fair and equitable' treatment of, and for 'full protection and security' for, the foreign investor and his investments. Correspondingly the investments of investors under NAFTA are entitled, under the customary international law which NAFTA Parties interpret Article 1105(1) to comprehend, to fair and equitable treatment and to full protection and security.[59]

The NAFTA Tribunal in *ADF* also confirmed that the standard of 'fair and equitable treatment' does not have any autonomous and free-standing content. As the Tribunal noted, 'any general requirement to accord "fair and equitable treatment" and "full protection and security" must be disciplined by being based upon State practice and judicial or arbitral caselaw or other sources of customary or general international law'.[60]

Strikingly enough, the *Pope & Talbot*, *Mondev* and *ADF* arbitral tribunals do not substantially examine the ultimate merit and intrinsic content of the 'fair and equitable treatment' standard, but take a highly empirical view of referring to previous arbitral decisions. The principal line of reasoning of arbitral decisions is that the traditional standard of the treatment of aliens—requiring the involvement of egregious, outrageous, shocking or otherwise extraordinary conduct in the treatment of investors—as enshrined in the Arbitral Award in *Neer* delivered in 1927 relates to the law as it stood in the 1920s. The standard has evolved since then and now encompasses more than conduct which is arbitrary or egregious. In asserting this, the ICSID and NAFTA tribunals refer to prior ICSID and NAFTA decisions. They invoke no evidence that could prove that their understanding of 'fair and inequitable treatment' is accepted in the way of formation of international legal rules.

One problematic issue in the process is the reference to case law along with the sources of international law. If judicial practice is invoked merely as evidence of the otherwise developed standards in general international law, this seems quite acceptable. But if the reference to case law implies according it free-standing relevance in generating the normative regime of treatment of foreign investment, this approach regards a certain standard as established without there being sufficient agreement and acceptance by the community of States.

According to *Azinian*, 'The only conceivably relevant substantive principle of Article 1105 is that a NAFTA investor should not be dealt with in a manner

[59] *Mondev*, para 125.

[60] *ADF Group and USA*, Case No ARB(AF)/00/1, 9 January 2003 para 184.

that contravenes international law.'[61] According to *Genin*, the essence of the 'fair and equitable treatment' standard is to provide a standard detached and different from the national law standard, but requiring an 'international minimum standard... but that is, indeed, a *minimum* standard'. The Tribunal further emphasises that 'Acts that would violate this minimum standard would include acts showing a wilful neglect of duty, an insufficiency of action falling far below international standards, or even subjective bad faith.'[62] Thus, *Genin* does not unconditionally require the presence of bad faith, but only lists it as one of the constituents of a breach of the 'fair and equitable treatment' standard. Similarly, the *Loewen* Award puts an emphasis on the presence in State conduct of discrimination and denial of justice. It excludes the requirement of bad faith and malicious intention.[63]

In *CMS/Argentina*, the Respondent argued that the standard of 'fair and equitable treatment' is 'too vague to allow for any clear identification of its meaning' that it only provides a general and basic principle equated to an international minimum standard.[64] The Award specifies that unlike the context of some other disputes involving 'the choice between requiring a higher treaty standard and that of equating it with the international minimum standard', in this case:

> the Treaty standard of fair and equitable treatment and its connection with the required stability and predictability of the business environment, founded on solemn legal and contractual commitments, is not different from the international law minimum standard and its evolution under customary law.[65]

Thus, the Tribunal proceeds from the assumption that the broad BIT standard of 'fair and equitable treatment' is, as it stands, part of general international law.

The *Azurix* Award addresses the notion of 'fair and equitable treatment' as embodied in Article II(2)(a) of the 1991 US-Argentine Bilateral Investment Treaty. According to this provision, 'investment shall at all times be accorded fair and equitable treatment,... and shall in no case be accorded treatment less than required by international law'.[66] The claimant argued that the separate reference to the two standards of treatment meant that these were two different standards. Another part of the Argentine argument was that the 'fair and equitable treatment' standard should not be applied to allegations of breach of property rights, which is a matter of expropriation as opposed to unfair and inequitable treatment.

[61] *Robert Azinian, Kenneth Davitian, & Ellen Baca v The United Mexican States*, Case No. ARB(AF)/97/2, Award of 1 November 1999, para 92.

[62] *Alex Genin, Eastern Credit Limited, Inc. and A.S. Baltoil and the Republic of Estonia*, Case No ARB/99/2 para 367 (emphasis original).

[63] *The Loewen Group, Inc. and Raymond L. Loewen and United States of America* (Award, Case No ARB(AF)/98/3), 26 June 2003, para 309, 42 *ILM* (2003), 811.

[64] *CMS*, para 270.

[65] *CMS/Argentina*, para 284.

[66] *Azurix Corp. and the Argentine Republic*, ICSID Case No ARB/01/12, Award of 14 July 2006, para 324.

The 'confusion between expropriatory acts and acts constituting unfair treatment [would render] render one of the two claims invalid'. The claimant argued that the 'legitimate and reasonable expectations' of parties, so-called 'investment backed-expectations', provided a touchstone for the 'fair and equitable treatment' standard. The claimant added that 'What are independent are the rights under the BIT not necessarily the measures that have breached those rights.'[67]

Argentina argued, by reference to *SD Myers*, *Genin* and *Azinian*, that the 'fair and equitable treatment standard is inextricably linked to the general international law standard and has no autonomous significance, and requires treatment in addition to that latter standard'.[68] In this context, *Azurix* tries to distinguish between the regulation under Article 1105(1) NAFTA, which requires 'treatment in accordance with international law, including fair and equitable treatment and full protection and security', and thus treats them as a single standard, and the US-Argentine BIT which allegedly treats these requirements as separate from each other.[69] The Award proceeds to suggest that in the BIT:

> Fair and equitable treatment is listed separately. The last sentence ensures that, whichever content is attributed to the other two standards, the treatment accorded to investment will be no less than required by international law. The clause, as drafted, permits to interpret fair and equitable treatment and full protection and security as higher standards than required by international law. The purpose of the third sentence is to set a floor, not a ceiling, in order to avoid a possible interpretation of these standards below what is required by international law.[70]

Thus, the treatment must be 'fair and equitable' 'at all times', and in addition 'in no case' should it be 'less than required by international law'. If these standards are different, then the treaty clause seems to treat the 'fair and equitable treatment' standard as the desirable and optional standard. Thus, should the State fail to accord 'fair and equitable treatment', it must nevertheless guarantee the international law treatment.

However, the Treaty cannot be seen as mandatorily prescribing, using the words 'at all times' and 'in no case', the concurrent and cumulative application of the two divergent standards. This would be the inescapable conclusion if it were accepted that the Treaty conceives of the two standards as different from each other. There can be no treaty obligation requiring two different things to be done at the same time. Therefore, the conclusion should be that the Treaty conceives of the two standards as identical. The 'fair and equitable treatment' standard is the description of the international law standard.

The *Azurix* reference to the meaning of 'fair and equitable treatment' as just, even-handed, unbiased and legitimate[71] overlooks that this can make perfect

67 *Id*, paras 336ff, 346.
68 *Id*, paras 325ff.
69 *Id*, para 343.
70 *Id*, para 361.
71 *Id*, para 360.

sense if the 'fair and equitable treatment' standard is seen as identical to the international law standard focusing on arbitrariness and denial of justice, as explained in a number of arbitral awards.

The Investor in *Saluka* argued that the 'fair and equitable treatment' standard is 'a specific and autonomous Treaty standard,' while the Czech Republic suggested that this was in fact the same as the minimum standard under international law.[72] According to *Saluka*, the customary standard of 'fair and equitable treatment' is different from, and lower than, the same standard under the Treaty whose content is influenced by its object and purpose. The *Saluka* Award acknowledges that the customary standard of 'fair and equitable treatment' is limited to the international minimum standard. As the Tribunal puts it:

> the customary minimum standard is in any case binding upon a State and provides a minimum guarantee to foreign investors, even where the State follows a policy that is in principle opposed to foreign investment; in that context, the minimum standard of 'fair and equitable treatment' may in fact provide no more than 'minimal' protection. Consequently, in order to violate that standard, States' conduct may have to display a relatively higher degree of inappropriateness.[73]

However, the Tribunal proceeds on the basis that the context of this standard being embodied in a BIT influences its level of protection:

> Bilateral investment treaties, however, are designed to promote foreign direct investment as between the Contracting Parties; in this context, investors' protection by the 'fair and equitable treatment' standard is meant to be a guarantee providing a positive incentive for foreign investors. Consequently, in order to violate the standard, it may be sufficient that States' conduct displays a relatively lower degree of inappropriateness.[74]

The Tribunal's reasoning makes the content of the relevant standard conditional upon the kind of policy the State pursues. It is obviously true that concluding the investment agreement implies an investment-friendly policy. However, the impact on the rights of the State and investor is due not to the policy *per se* but to the operation of the investment treaty clauses. However the Award contains another significant statement:

> Whatever the merits of this controversy between the parties may be, it appears that the difference between the Treaty standard laid down in Article 3.1 and the customary minimum standard, when applied to the specific facts of a case, may well be more apparent than real. To the extent that the case law reveals different formulations of the relevant thresholds, an indepth analysis may well demonstrate that they could be explained by the contextual and factual differences of the cases to which the standards have been applied. ... in that context, the minimum standard of 'fair and equitable treatment' may in fact provide no more than 'minimal' protection. Consequently, in order

[72] *Saluka*, para 286.
[73] *Id*, para 292.
[74] *Id*, para 293.

to violate that standard, States' conduct may have to display a relatively higher degree of inappropriateness.[75]

At the same time, *Saluka* emphasises that Article 3 of the BIT did not refer to the international law standard.[76] The Tribunal concludes that the 'fair and equitable treatment' standard requires the Czech Republic not to act in a way frustrating the investor's 'underlying legitimate and reasonable expectations'.[77] What the *Saluka* Award suggests is that the 'fair and equitable treatment' standard can have one type of content on its own and different content as part of the Treaty and construed in the context of its objectives. This approach is deficient because, as the previous section has demonstrated, object and purpose cannot independently give specific meaning to a treaty provision on 'fair and equitable treatment'.

The *Azurix* Tribunal emphasised that the BIT required that 'the treatment accorded to investment will be no less than required by international law'. Consequently, 'fair and equitable treatment' set a higher standard than international law. But while the Tribunal considered this as an outcome of textual interpretation, it nevertheless refused to:

consider that it is of material significance for its application of the standard of fair and equitable treatment to the facts of the case. ... the minimum requirement to satisfy this standard has evolved and the Tribunal considers that its content is substantially similar whether the terms are interpreted in their ordinary meaning, as required by the Vienna Convention, or in accordance with customary international law.[78]

Therefore, the Tribunal equates the outcomes under the two interpretative methods. The Tribunal does not attempt to adduce sufficient evidence to support its thesis that the legal position under general international law has evolved accordingly. The *CMS* Award similarly asserts that:

While the choice between requiring a higher treaty standard and that of equating it with the international minimum standard might have relevance in the context of some disputes, the Tribunal is not persuaded that it is relevant in this case. In fact, the Treaty standard of fair and equitable treatment and its connection with the required stability and predictability of the business environment, founded on solemn legal and contractual commitments, is not different from the international law minimum standard and its evolution under customary law.[79]

The *Tecmed* Tribunal likewise asserts that 'the commitment of fair and equitable treatment included in Article 4(1) of the Agreement is an expression and part of the bona fide principle recognized in international law'.[80] This approach

[75] *Id*, paras 291–292.
[76] *Id*, para 294.
[77] *Id*, para 309.
[78] *Azurix*, para 361.
[79] *CMS*, para 285.
[80] *Tecmed*, para 153.

seems to be exaggerated because the principle of good faith cannot by itself constitute a rule or obligation; it merely complements otherwise existing rules and obligations. The treaty provision that purportedly expresses a substantive obligation cannot be seen as a crystallisation of the principle of good faith alone, still less a stipulation to practice good faith in relation to anything under the sun. The *Tecmed* Tribunal makes the situation even less predictable when it asserts the role of good faith in relation to an indeterminate treaty obligation, without first attempting to clarify its substantive content.

To recapitulate the assessment of the arbitral practice, there must be some yardstick, some point of reference relying on which tribunals will be able to identify its meaning, without engaging in subjective speculation and manipulation. While in the law of maritime delimitation treaty provisions referring to equity have always been considered as actually referring to equity under general international law, in international investment arbitration the practice is divided as to the proper role of customary law in assessing what conduct breaches the 'fair and equitable treatment' standard. Such ambivalence of practice is not conducive to legal certainty, transparency and predictability of legal relations in relation to a notion which has no independent meaning or scope. According autonomous and treaty-derived meaning to 'fair and equitable treatment' results in promoting the indeterminacy manipulated by subjective appreciation by decision-makers and thus, most problematically, in imposing on States-parties to the relevant investment treaty more wide-reaching obligations than they can be reasonably understood to have consented to. The only proper approach for tribunals is to enquire, in the first place, what the actual state of customary law regarding the treatment of foreign investment is, and apply the 'fair and equitable treatment' provisions by reference to that.

(e) The Construction of 'Fair and Equitable Treatment' by the NAFTA Free Trade Commission

The issue of interpretative agency arises in terms of the status of the 2001 NAFTA Free Trade Commission's interpretation of Article 1105(1) NAFTA, and it must be asked whether and to what extent this organ can take decisions that identify the parties' intentions. The FTC consists of cabinet-level representatives of the parties and its mandate includes the resolution of disputes regarding the interpretation of the NAFTA Agreement. Its interpretation of the Agreement is binding on Arbitral Tribunals under Article 1131(2).

As seen above, the FTC Interpretation of Article 1105(1) affirmed that the international law standards on the treatment of foreign investment under that Article were in fact limited to standards under customary international law. It is pertinent to examine whether such exercise was legitimate and how far it can go.

It could be asserted that the NAFTA Free Trade Commission's interpretation is in essence an *ultra vires* amendment of the investment protection standard under Article 1105. Brower points out that the case for the existence of an *ultra vires* amendment can be made in this context by reference to the FTC's reference to customary international law as opposed to 'applicable rules of international law', in the light of which Article 1131 requires the NAFTA Treaty to be interpreted.[81]

On the other hand, every treaty is a *lex specialis*, and the reference to 'applicable' international law in Article 1131 inherently means the law that is in force as between the parties to NAFTA. The rest of international law is simply not the applicable law in this context. This concerns above all the bilateral investment treaties which, although elaborating upon the notion of 'fair and equitable treatment', constitute applicable law either between the NAFTA parties and third States, or as between third States exclusively. Such law cannot be the 'applicable' law for the purposes of NAFTA interpretation. On the other hand, customary international law is presumed to be general and applicable to all States and thus constitute the applicable law for the NAFTA parties too. Therefore, the FTC interpretation could be seen as an *ultra vires* amendment if it could be proved that it disregards such rules as derive from the conventional law applicable to the *inter se* relations of the NAFTA parties. This can hardly be proved. On the other hand, the FTC interpretation in fact corresponds to the textual meaning of Article 1105 which conceives 'fair and equitable treatment' as part of international law.

In *Loewen*, the Claimant argued that the Commission's Interpretation of Article 1105(1) went beyond interpretation and amounted to an unauthorised amendment of the NAFTA Treaty, but did not further press this claim in proceedings.[82] The Tribunal in *Pope & Talbot* went on to examine whether the Commission's Interpretation was a valid interpretative exercise. As Article 1105(1) referred to 'international law', the investor argued that the Commission's reference to customary international law did violence to the text. Canada, on the other hand, argued that the Tribunal could not challenge the Interpretation which was binding on it. The Tribunal found this argument unpersuasive and stated that:

> If a question is raised whether, in issuing an interpretation, the Commission has acted in accordance with Article 1105, an arbitral tribunal has a duty to consider and decide that question and not simply to accept that whatever the Commission has stated to be an interpretation is one for the purposes of Article 1131(2).
>
> The Tribunal must therefore consider for itself whether the Commission's action can properly be qualified as an 'interpretation.' That question will, of course, depend on what a proper interpretation of Article 1105 might be.[83]

Therefore, the Tribunal subscribed to the approach that the institutional powers of the Free Trade Commission are constrained by the substantive

[81] Brower, (2002), 11.
[82] *Loewen*, 831–832.
[83] *Pope & Talbot* (Damages), paras 20–24.

outcome of treaty interpretation principles as applied to NAFTA. In institutional terms, the process of examining this issue can be denoted as judicial review.

The Tribunal examined the text of the FTC interpretation, which did not refer to customary international law as a limiting factor, as well as *travaux preparatoires* to confirm this result, and concluded that it was not interpretation but revision of the NAFTA text.[84] In the final analysis, the Tribunal held that the application of the Commission's Interpretation to the facts of the case would lead to the same result which the Tribunal achieved at the merits stage—the stage at which the decision was motivated by reasons directly opposed to the FTC reasoning. The Tribunal achieved this result by construing the state of customary law.[85]

After *Pope & Talbot*, Arbitral Tribunals recognised the binding force of the Commission's Interpretation. In *Mondev*, the United States maintained that the FTC Interpretation constituted the definitive statement of what the parties intended in Article 1105(1); the scope of that clause was restricted to the pre-existing customary law and was intended to prevent the 'misinterpretations' of Article 1105(1) by NAFTA Tribunals. The Commission's Interpretation clearly manifested the parties' will not to subject themselves, in terms of the arbitral procedure, to obligations other than pre-established customary law.[86] The Claimant did not suggest disregarding the Commission's Interpretation either.[87]

The *Mondev* Tribunal justified the FTC's reference to customary international law, even though Article 1105 refers to international law, because the concept of the 'minimum standard of treatment' has historically been understood as a reference to the minimum standard under customary law.[88]

In *ADF*, the investor argued that the Tribunal had to examine whether the Commission's interpretation was permissible, which was a question of the governing law and fell within the Tribunal's powers.[89] Canada maintained that the FTC Interpretation was binding on the Tribunal and constituted the proper basis for interpreting Article 1105(1) NAFTA. The FTC was vested with 'the prime and final authority as the interpreter of the NAFTA' and its interpretation was 'the full expression of what the NAFTA Parties intended'.[90] Mexico also accepted that the Arbitration Tribunal had no power to 'second-guess the FTC'.[91]

[84] *Pope & Talbot* (Damages), paras 46–47.
[85] *Pope & Talbot* (Damages), para 52.
[86] *Mondev*, para 103.
[87] *Id*, para 107.
[88] *Id*, para 121.
[89] *ADF Group and USA*, Case No ARB(AF)/00/1, 9 January 2003, para 120.
[90] *Id*, para 117.
[91] *Id*, para 125.

As the Tribunal observed, there was no need to embark upon an enquiry into the distinction between interpretation and revision:

> whether a document submitted to a Chapter 11 Tribunal purports to be an amendatory agreement in respect of which the Parties' respective internal constitutional procedures necessary for the entry into force of the amending agreement have been taken, or an interpretation rendered by the FTC under Article 1131(2), we have the Parties themselves—all the Parties—speaking to the Tribunal. No more authentic and authoritative source of instruction on what the Parties intended to convey in a particular provision of NAFTA, is possible.[92]

Further references to the Commission's binding interpretative powers and the primacy of that binding force over the Tribunal's implied power to determine the governing law have been made, and must be understood, in the context of the Tribunal's reference to the will of all parties. This is a reference to bilateralism: the Tribunal referred to the unique circumstances of the case, where the interpretative agency represented all the parties to the Treaty which protected no other interests than those of the States-parties themselves. Therefore, they could treat the text of the NAFTA Agreement at their will.

92 *Id*, para 177.

Conclusion

The concluding of the complex and multi-level argument developed throughout this monograph has to be initiated by reverting to the original fundamental thesis that the consensual character of international law requires adopting the approach of the effectiveness of legal regulation for the sake of construing the original consent and agreement as effective and meaningful. This approach is inevitable if the independent existence and profile of international law are considered. The approach favouring the preserving of indeterminacy and ambiguity is essentially an approach opposing the consensual foundation of international law.

Seen from this perspective, it does not appear surprising that those versions of natural law which were aimed at undermining positivist premises of international law, the interest-based approach of Scelle, or the New Haven policy-oriented school, go hand in hand in their opposition to the positivist understanding of international legal regulation, and its consequent effectiveness. This is further complemented by developments in recent years which, by reference to the 'war on terror', assert some approaches regarding change and modification of the relevant international legal regulation, without adducing evidence that such change is feasible or material.[1]

The specific problems examined in this study demonstrate and follow through the tension between these doctrinal perceptions. This is visible in terms of the general debate on how legal regulation emerges, whether it is based on State consent, or other factors such as power and values; more specifically, whether factors of non-law, such as fact or interest, can generate legal regulation, or play a crucial role in this process, in replacing, or diminishing the relevance of, the consent and agreement of States. This doctrinal tension is also evident in the argument as to whether indeterminacy involving political factors can enable manipulation of the content and scope of legal rules, which more specifically is expressed through the debate on which factors do and which do not count in the process of interpretation.

This study has been developed to demonstrate the deficiency and shortcomings of an approach that justifies indeterminacy being used for political interests. There may be different degrees of contestability, uncertainty and indeterminacy of words and phrases included in international legal instruments. The ways of dealing with them are also diverse, depending on the type of uncertainty and indeterminacy. With regard to situations where contestability relates to textual

[1] On these phenomena see A Orakhelashvili, Legal Stability and Claims of Change: The International Court's Treatment of *Jus ad Bellum* and *Jus in Bello*, *Nordic Journal of International Law* (2006), 371–407.

meaning, including relativity and degree, treaty interpretation methods have to be deployed to clarify them. In terms of indeterminacy referring to non-law, treaty interpretation methods are likewise useful, even if they cannot provide a straightforward definition of the relevant terms. What, however, interpretation methods can do is to tackle non-law concepts constructively and clarify, through the application of the reality test, the good faith principle and the principle of effectiveness, and their implication in relation to each particular case.

This analysis has demonstrated that the methods of interpretation are similar in terms of all categories of acts and serve the inherent rationale of interpretation—to clarify the meaning of legal norms and instruments on the basis of their rationale. In determining the applicable methods of interpretation, it matters not whether and how the rules of interpretation relevant for different categories of acts and rules are codified in the relevant instruments. It rather matters what exigencies follow from the inherent consensual and contractual character of the relevant rules and instruments. As seen in the example of the different categories of acts, the principles of interpretation tend to consider the fact that legal instruments do not just embody the intention of the entity that adopts them, but also they are understood by addressees in terms of their face value and plain meaning. Therefore, the whole interpretative process tends to reject the reference to the factor of subjectivity in interpretation. Whatever the form of the legal instrument, it has to be interpreted in accordance with pre-determined legal rules—some of which are codified, as is the case with the law of treaties, and others that are developed in practice—that uphold the interpretation of instruments in accordance with their plain meaning and in a way to give them the effect that follows from their object and purpose. The ultimate purpose of this is to ensure the effectiveness of legal regulation.

Effectiveness in interpretation serves the more general principle of completeness, determinacy and effectiveness of legal regulation. The methods of interpretation are aimed at preserving the original consent, will and intention behind the relevant legal instruments and thus at ensuring the determinacy of the relevant provision by enabling its application to facts. These methods are consistently aimed at confronting claims as to the indeterminacy of treaty provisions.

Bibliography

Abi-Saab, G, The Proper Role of International Law in Combating Terrorism, A Bianchi (ed), *Enforcing International Law Norms against Terrorism* (2004), xiii

Ago, R, Positive Law and International Law, 51 *AJIL* (1957), 691

Akehurst, M, Custom as a Source of International Law, 47 *BYIL* (1975–76), 1

——, Equity and General Principles of Law, 25 *ICLQ* (1976), 801

Alexandrov, S, The 'Baby Boom' of Treaty-Based Arbitrations and The Jurisdiction of ICSID Tribunals: Shareholders as 'Investors' and Jurisdiction *Ratione Temporis*, 4 *LPICT* (2005), 19

Austin, J, *The Province of Jurisprudence Determined* (1954)

Bernhardt, R, *Die Auslegung völkerrechlicher Verträge* (1963)

——, Interpretation in International Law, 2 *EPIL* (1995), 1416

——, Evolutive Treaty Interpretation, Especially of the European Convention of Human Rights, 42 *GYIL* (1999)

Birnie, P, & Boyle, A, *International Law and the Environment* (2002), 84ff

Bleckmann, A, Völkergewohnheitsrecht trotz widersprüchlicher Praxis? *ZaöRV* (1976), 374

——, Zur Feststellung und Auslegung von Völkergewohnheitsrecht, *ZaöRV* (1977), 505

Brierly, JL, *The Law of Nations* (1949)

——, *The Basis of Obligation in International Law* (1958)

Briggs, H, The Incidental Jurisdiction of the International Court of Justice as Compulsory Jurisdiction, in VD Heydte, Seidl-Hohenveldern, Verosta & Zemanek (eds), *Völkerrecht und Rechtliches Weltbild. Festschrift für Alfred Verdross* (1960)

Brower, C, Remarks on 'Fair and Equitable Treatment under NAFTA's Investment Chapter', 96 *ASIL Proceedings* (2002), 9

Brown, C, The Inherent Powers of International Courts and Tribunals, 76 *BYIL* (2005), 195

Brown, C, *A Common Law of International Adjudication* (2007)

Brown, ED, *The International Law of the Sea* (1994), vol I

Brownlie, I, *International Law and the Use of Force by States* (1963)

——, Remedies in the International Court of Justice, V Lowe & M Fitzmaurice (eds), *Fifty Years of the International Court of Justice* (1996)

——, *Principles of Public International Law* (2003)

Cassese, A, *International Law* (2005)

Cavanaugh, K, Policing the Margins: Rights Protection and the European Court of Human Rights, *EHRLR* (2006), 422

Chang, YT, *The Interpretation of Treaties by Judicial Tribunals* (1933)

Charney, J, The Persistent Objector Rule and the Development of Customary International Law, 56 *BYIL* (1985), 1

Cheng, B, *General Principles of Law* (1953)

Churchill, R, & Lowe, AV, *The Law of the Sea* (1999)

Cohen, M, The Notion of 'State Survival' in International Law, L Boisson de Chazournes & P Sands (eds), *International Law, the International Court of Justice and Nuclear Weapons* (1999), 293

Condorelli, L, Custom, in M Bedjaoui (Gen ed), *International Law: Achievements and Prospects* (1991), 179

Crnic-Grotic, V, Object and Purpose of Treaties in the Vienna Convention on the Law of Treaties, 7 *Asian Yearbook of International Law* (1997), 141

Dinstein, Y, *The Conduct of Hostilities under the Law of International Armed Conflict* (2004)

——, *War, Aggression and Self-Defence* (2005)

Ehlermann CD, & Ehring, L, The Authoritative Interpretation under Article IX:2 of the Agreement Establishing the World Trade Organisation: Current Law, Practice and Possible Improvements, 8 *JIEL* (2005), 803

Ehrlich, L, L'interprétation des traités, 24 *Recueil des cours*, (1928-IV), 1

Evans, M, *Relevant Circumstances and Maritime Delimitation* (1989)

——, Maritime Delimitation and Expanding Categories of Relevant Circumstances, 40 *ICLQ* (1991), 1

Falk, R, On Treaty Interpretation and the New Haven Approach: Achievements and Prospects, 8 *Virginia JIL* (1967–1968), 323

Fitzmaurice, G, The Law and Procedure of the International Court of Justice: Treaty Interpretation and Certain other Treaty Points, *BYIL* (1951), 1

——, The Law and Procedure of the International Court of Justice, 30 *BYIL* (1953), 1

——, The Law and Procedure of the International Court of Justice 1951–1954, 34 *BYIL* (1957), 203

——, The General Principles of International Law Considered from the Standpoint of the Rule of Law, 92 *RdC* (II-1957), 1

——, Vae Victis *or Woe to the Negotiators! Your Treaty or Our Interpretation of It* (Review Article), 65 *AJIL* (1971), 358

——, *The Law and Procedure of the International Court of Justice* (1986)

Franck, T, *Fairness in International Law and Institutions* (1995)

Franck, T, Legitimacy and Democratic Entitlement, in G Fox & B Roth (ed), *Democratic Governance and International Law* (2001), 25

French, D, Treaty Interpretation and the Incorporation of Extraneous Legal Rules, 55 *ICLQ* (2006), 281

Friedmann, W, The Uses of 'General Principles of Law' in the Development of International Law, 57 *AJIL* (1963), 279

Frowein, J, Unilateral Interpretation of Security Council Resolutions—A Threat to Collective Security? V Götz, P Selmer & R Wolfrum (eds), *Liber Amicorum Günther Jaenicke—Zum 85. Geburtstag* (Springer 1999), 97

Gaeta, P, Inherent Powers of International Courts and Tribunals, in LC Vorhah *et al* (eds), *Man's Inhumanity to Man*, Essays on International Law in Honour of Antonio Cassese (2003), 353

Hall, WE, *A Treatise on International Law* (1895)

Haraszti, G, *Some Fundamental Problems of the Law of Treaties* (1973)

Harris, D, O'Boyle, M, & Warbrick, C, *The Law of the European Convention on Human Rights* (1995)

Helfer, L, Consensus, Coherence and the European Convention on Human Rights, 26 *Cornell International Law Journal* (1993), 133
Heymann, M, *Einseitige Interpretationserklärungen zu multilateralen Veträgen* (2005)
Higgins, R, *The Development of International Law through the Political Organs of the United Nations* (1963)
——, Policy Considerations and the International Judicial Process, 17 *ICLQ* (1968), 58
——, *Problems and Process: International Law and How We Use It* (1995)
Hyde, CC, *Concerning the Interpretation of Treaties*, 3 *AJIL* (1909), 46
——, *International Law, Chiefly as Interpreted and Applied by the United States* (1922), vol II
——, Judge Anzilotti on the Interpretation of Treaties, 27 *AJIL* (1933), 502
Jacobs, F, Varieties of Approach to Treaty Interpretation: With Special Reference to the Draft Convention on the Law of Treaties before the Vienna Diplomatic Conference, 18 *ICLQ* (1969), 318
Jennings, RY, Equity and Equitable Principles, 42 *Annuaire Suisse De Droit International* (1986), 27
——, The Principles Governing Maritime Boundaries, in Hailbronner, Ress & Stein (eds), *Staat und Völkerrechtsordnung, Festschrift für Karl Doehring* (1989), 397
Johnson, D, Acquisitive Prescription in International Law, 27 *BYIL* (1950), 332
Johnstone, I, Treaty Interpretation: The Authority of Interpretive Communities, 12 *Michigan JIL* (1990–91), 371
Jokl, M, *De l'interprétation des traités normatifs d'après de la doctrine et la jurisprudence internationales* (1936)
Karagiannakis, M, State Immunity and Fundamental Human Rights, 11 *Leiden Journal of International Law* (1998), 9
Karl, W, *Vertrag und spätere Praxis in Völkerrecht—Zum Einfluß der Praxis auf Inhalt und Bestand völkerrechlicher Verträge* (1983)
Kelsen, H, *Law and Peace in International Relations* (Harvard 1947)
——, *General Theory of Law and State* (1961)
Kelsen, H, *Principles of International Law* (R Tucker ed, 1967)
Klabbers, J, International Legal Histories: Declining Importance of *Travaux Préparatoires* in Treaty Interpretation? *NILR* 2003, 267
Köck, H, *Vertragsinterpretation und Vertragsrechtskonvention. Zur Bedeutung der Artikel 31 und 32 der Wiener Vertragsrechtskonvention 1969* (1976)
Kooijmans, P, The Enlargement of the Concept "Threat to the Peace", in P-M Dupuy (ed), *The Development of the Role of the Security Council* (1993)
——, The ICJ: Where Does It Stand? in S Muller, D Raic & H Thuranzsky (eds), *The International Court of Justice. Its Future Role after Fifty Years* (1997)
Koskenniemi, M, *From Apology to Utopia* (2004)
Kreindler, R, 'Fair and Equitable Treatment'—A Comparative International Law Approach, 3 *Transnational Dispute Management* (2006), Issue 3
Kunz, J, Roberto Ago's Theory of Spontaneous International Law, 52 *AJIL* (1958), 85
Lapidoth, R, Equity in International Law, 22 *Israel Law Review* (1987), 161
Lauterpacht, E, The Development of the Law of International Organisation by the Decisions of International Tribunals, 151 *Recueil des Cours* (III-1976), 377
Lauterpacht, H, *The Function of Law in the International Community* (1933)

Lauterpacht, H, Some Observations on Preparatory Work in the Interpretation of Treaties, 48 *Harvard Law Review* (1934–1935), 549

——, Restrictive Interpretation and Effectiveness in the Interpretation of Treaties, *BYIL* (1949), 47

——, Sovereignty Over Submarine Areas, 27 *BYIL* (1950), 375

——, *The Development of International Law by the International Court* (1958)

——, I *Collected Papers* (1970)

Leach, P, *Taking the Case before the European Court of Human Rights* (2005)

Lennard, M, Navigating by the Stars: Interpreting the WTO Agreements, 5 *JIEL* (2002), 19

Lewis, T, What Not To Wear: Religious Rights, The European Court, and the Margin of Appreciation, 56 *ICLQ* (2007), 395

Lowe, AV, The Role of Equity in International Law, 12 *Australian Yearbook of International Law* (1992), 54

——, Sustainable Development and Unsustainable Arguments, in Boyle & Freestone (ed), *International Law and Sustainable Development* (1999), 19

——, The Iraq Crisis: What Now? 52 *ICLQ* (2003), 859

Mann, FA, British Treaties for the Promotion and Protection of Investments, 5 *BYIL* (1982), 241

——, Reflection on the Prosecution of Persons Abducted in Breach of International Law, in Y Dinstein & M Tabory (eds), *International Law at a Time of Perplexity. Essays in Honour of Shabtai Rosenne* (1989), 407

Martens, G-F, *Précis du droit des gens moderne de l'Europe* (1831)

Matsushita, M, Schoenbaum T, & Mavroidis, P, *The World Trade Organisation: Law, Practice and Policy* (2006)

Mbaye, K, L'intérêt pour agir devant la Cour Internationale de Justice, 209 *RdC* (1988-II), 223

McDougal, M, International Law, Power and Policy: A Contemporary Conception, 82 *Recueil des cours* (I-1953), 133

——, The International Law Commission's Draft Articles Upon Interpretation: Textuality *Revidivus*, 61 *AJIL* (1967), 992

McDougal, MS, Lasswell, HD, & Miller, JC, *The Interpretation of International Agreements and World Public Order* (1967)

McGibbon, I, The Scope of Acquiescence in International Law, 31 *BYIL* (1954), 143

McHarg, A, Reconciling Human Rights and the Public Interest: Conceptual Problems and Doctrinal Uncertainty in the Jurisprudence of the European Court of Human Rights, 62 *Modern Law Review* (1999), 671

McNair, AD, *The Law of Treaties* (1961)

Mendelson, M, The Subjective Element in Customary International Law, 76 *BYIL* (1995), 177

——, The Formation of Customary International Law, 272 *RdC* (1998-II), 165

——, On the Quasi-Normative Effect of Maritime Boundary Agreements, in N Ando, E McWhinney & R Wolfrun (eds), *Liber Amicorum for Judge Shigeru Oda* (2002), 1069

——, Runaway Train: The 'Continuous Nationality' Rule from *Panevezys-Saldutiskis Railway* case to *Loewen*, in Weiler (ed), *International Investment Law Arbitration: Leading Cases from the ICSID, NAFTA, Bilateral Treaties and Customary International Law* (2005), 97

Morgenthau, H, Positivism, Functionalism, and International Law, 34 *AJIL* (1940), 260

Müllerson, R, The ABM Treaty: Changed Circumstances, Extraordinary Events, Supreme Interests and International Law, 50 *ICLQ* (2001), 509

Nelson, LDM, The Roles of Equity in the Delimitation of Maritime Boundaries, 84 *AJIL* (1990), 837

O'Connell, DP, *The International Law of the Sea* (1982), vol I

Orakhelashvili, A, Questions of International Judicial Jurisdiction in the *LaGrand* case, 1 *Leiden Journal of International Law*(2002), 105

——, State Immunity and International Public Order, 45 *German YIL* (2002), 227

——, *Restrictive Interpretation of Human Rights Treaties in the Recent Jurisprudence of the European Court of Human Rights*, 14 *EJIL* (2003), 529

——, The Concept of International Judicial Jurisdiction: A Reappraisal, 3 *LPICT* (2003), 501

——, The World Bank Inspection Panel in Context: Institutional Aspects of the Accountability of International Organisations, 2 *International Organisations Law Review* (2005), 57

——, Legal Stability and Claims of Change: the International Court's Treatment of *Jus ad Bellum* and *Jus in Bello*, 75 *Nordic JIL* (2006), 371

——, *Peremptory Norms in International Law* (2006)

——, State Immunity and International Public Order Revisited, 49 *German YIL* (2006), 327

——, The Idea of European International Law, 17 *EJIL* (2006), 315

——, Interpretation of Jurisdictional Instruments in International Dispute Settlement, *Law and Practice of International Courts and Tribunals*, volume 6(1), 2007, 159

——, The Acts of the Security Council: Meaning and Standards of Review, 11 *Max-Planck Yearbook of United Nations Law* (2007), 143

Ovey, C & White, R, *The European Convention on Human Rights* (2006)

Pannizon, M., *Good Faith in the Jurisprudence of the WTO* (2006)

Pauwelyn, J, *Conflict of Norms in Public International Law* (2003)

——, How to Win a WTO Dispute Based on Non-WTO Law? 37 *Journal of World Trade* (2003), 997

Pellet, A, The Normative Dilemma: Will and Consent in International Law-making, 12 *Australian YIL* (1988–89), 22

Pfluger, F, *Die Einseitigen Rechtsgeschäfte im Völkerrecht* (1936)

Phillimore, R, *Commentaries upon International Law*, Volume II (Philadelphia, 1855), vol II

Quenedec, JP, La notion d'Etat Intèressè en droit international, 255 *RdC* (1995-V), 339

Qureshi, A, *Interpreting WTO Agreements* (2006)

Reisman, M, Peacemaking, 18 *Yale Journal of International Law* (1993)

Reuter, P, *Introduction to the Law of Treaties* (1985)

Rhinelander, J, The ABM Treaty—Past, Present and Future, 6 *JCSL* (2001), 91

Rosenne, S, *Breach of Treaty* (1985)

Rothpfeffer, T, Equity in the North Sea Continental Shelf Cases, 42 *Nordic Journal of International Law* (1972), 81

Rozakis, C, Compromises of State Interests and their Repercussions upon the Rules of Delimitation of the Continental Shelf: From the Truman Proclamation to the 1982 Convention on the Law of the Sea, in CS Rozakis & CA Stephanou (eds), *The New Law of the Sea* (1983), 155

Sands, P, International Courts and the Application of the Concept of 'Sustainable Development', 3 *Max Planck YBUN* (1999), 389
Sands, P, *Principles of International Environmental Law* (2003)
Scelle, G, *Précis de droit des gens* (1923)
Schachter, O, *International Law in Theory and Practice* (1991)
Schwarzenberger, G, Jus Pacis ac Belli? Prolegomena to a Sociology of International Law, 37 *AJIL* (1943), 460
——, *International Law*(1957), vol I
——, *International Law and Order* (1971)
Schwebel, S, May Preparatory Work be Used to Correct Rather than Confirm the 'Clear' Meaning of a Treaty Provision? in J Makarczyk (ed), *Theory of International Law at the Threshold of the 21st Century: Essays in Honour of Krzysztof Skubiszewski* (1996), 541
——, The Influence of Bilateral Investment Treaties on Customary International Law, Investor-State Disputes and The Development of International Law, *ASIL Proceedings* (2004), 27
Shanker, D, The Vienna Convention on the Law of Treaties, the Dispute Settlement System of the WTO and the Doha Declaration on the TRIPs Agreement, 36 *Journal of World Trade* (2002), 721
Shany, Y, Toward a General Margin of Appreciation Doctrine in International Law? 16 *EJIL* (2005), 907
Shihata, I, *The Power of the International Court to Determine its Own Jurisdiction* (1965)
Simma, B, The Contribution of Alfred Verdross to the Theory of International Law, 6 *EJIL* (1995), 1
Skubiszewski, K, Elements of Custom and the Hague Court, *ZaöRV* (1971), 810
Slaughter, A-M, International Law in a World of Liberal States, 6 *EJIL* (1995), 503
Spencer, JH, *L'interprétation des traités par les travaux préparatoires* (1934)
Stone, J, Fictitional Elements in Treaty Interpretation—A Study in the International Judicial Process, 1 *Sydney Law Review* (1953–1955), 344
Sur, S, *L'interprétation en droit international public* (1974)
Suy, E, *Les actes juridiques unilateraux* (1962)
Sweeney, J, Margins of Appreciation: Cultural Relativity and the European Court of Human Rights, 54 *ILCQ* (2005), 459
Tammelo, I, *Treaty Interpretation and Practical Reason—Towards a General Theory of Legal Interpretation* (1967)
Thirlway, H, The Law and Procedure of the International Court of Justice, *BYIL* (1989), 1
——, The Law and Procedure of the International Court of Justice, *BYIL* (1990), 1
——, The Law and Procedure of the International Court of Justice 1960–1989, *BYIL* (1994), 1
——, The Law and Procedure of the International Court of Justice 1960–1989: Supplement, 2005, *BYIL* 2005, 1
Tomuschat, C, Article 36, in A Zimmerman *et al* (eds), *The Statute of the International Court of Justice. A Commentary* (2006), 589
Van den Bossche, P, *The Law and Policy of the World Trade Organisation* (2005)
Van Dijk & Van Hoof, *Theory and Practice of the European Convention on Human Rights* (2006)

Vascianne, S, The Fair and Equitable Treatment Standard in International Investment Law and Practice, *BYIL* (1999), 99

Vattel, E, *The Law of Nations or the Principles of Natural Law applied to the Conduct and to the Affairs of Nations and of Sovereigns* in Scott (ed), *Classics of International Law* (1916)

Verdross, A, Entstehungsweisen und Geltungsgrund des universellen völkerrechtlichen Gewohnheitsrechts, 29 *ZaöRV* (1969), 635

Verdross, A, & Köck, H, Natural Law: The Tradition of Universal Reason and Authority, in R MacDonald & D Johnson (eds), *The Structure and Process of International Law* (1983), 42

Visscher, Ch de, *Problèmes d interprétation judiciaire en droit international public* (1963)

——, *Theory and Reality in Public International Law* (1968)

Voïcu, *De l'interprétation authentique des traités internationaux* (1968)

Weil, P, 'The Court Cannot Conclude Definitively ...' *Non Liquet* Revisited, 38 *Columbia JTL* (1998), 109

Waldock, H, The Anglo-Norwegian Fisheries Case, 28 *BYIL* (1951), 113

Westlake, J, *International Law*(1910), vol I

——, *Collected Papers on International Law* (1914)

Wheaton, H, *Elements of International Law* (1866)

Wolff, Ch, *The Law of Nations Treated According to a Scientific Method* (1934)

Wood, M, The Interpretation of Security Council Resolutions, 2 *Max-Plank YBUNL* (1998), 73

Yasseen, M, L'interprétation des traités d'après la Convention de Vienne sur le Droit des Traités, 151 *Recueil des Cours* (1976-III), 1

Yourow, HC, The Margin of Appreciation Doctrine in the Dynamics of European Human Rights Jurisprudence, 3 *Connecticut Journal of International Law* (1987–1988), 111

Yü, TC, *The Interpretation of Treaties* (1927)

Index

The manufacturer's authorised representative in the EU for product safety is Oxford University Press España S.A. of el Parque Empresarial San Fernando de Henares, Avenida de Castilla, 2 – 28830 Madrid (www.oup.es/en or product.safety@oup.com). OUP España S.A. also acts as importer into Spain of products made by the manufacturer.

www.ingramcontent.com/pod-product-compliance
Ingram Content Group UK Ltd.
Pitfield, Milton Keynes, MK11 3LW, UK
UKHW020851150926
475595UK00003B/116
9780199546220